Java 9 Revealed

For Early Adoption and Migration

Kishori Sharan

Apress®

Java 9 Revealed: For Early Adoption and Migration

Kishori Sharan
Montgomery, Alabama, USA

ISBN-13 (pbk): 978-1-4842-2591-2   ISBN-13 (electronic): 978-1-4842-2592-9
DOI 10.1007/978-1-4842-2592-9

Library of Congress Control Number: 2017939348

Managing Director: Welmoed Spahr
Editorial Director: Todd Green
Acquisitions Editor: Steve Anglin
Development Editor: Matthew Moodie
Technical Reviewer: Manuel Jordan Elera
Coordinating Editor: Mark Powers
Copy Editor: Kezia Endsley
Compositor: SPi Global
Indexer: SPi Global
Artist: SPi Global
Cover image designed by Freepik.

Distributed to the book trade worldwide by Springer Science+Business Media New York, 233 Spring Street, 6th Floor, New York, NY 10013. Phone 1-800-SPRINGER, fax (201) 348-4505, e-mail orders-ny@springer-sbm.com, or visit www.springeronline.com. Apress Media, LLC is a California LLC and the sole member (owner) is Springer Science + Business Media Finance Inc (SSBM Finance Inc). SSBM Finance Inc is a **Delaware** corporation.

For information on translations, please e-mail rights@apress.com, or visit http://www.apress.com/rights-permissions.

Apress titles may be purchased in bulk for academic, corporate, or promotional use. eBook versions and licenses are also available for most titles. For more information, reference our Print and eBook Bulk Sales web page at http://www.apress.com/bulk-sales.

Any source code or other supplementary material referenced by the author in this book is available to readers on GitHub via the book's product page, located at www.apress.com/9781484225912. For more detailed information, please visit http://www.apress.com/source-code.

Contents at a Glance

Contents

About the Author

Kishori Sharan works as a senior software engineer lead at IndraSoft, Inc. He earned a master's of science degree in computer information systems from Troy State University, Alabama. He is a Sun-certified Java 2 programmer and has over 20 years of experience in developing enterprise applications and providing training to professional developers using the Java platform.

About the Technical Reviewer

Manuel Jordan Elera is an autodidactic developer and researcher who enjoys learning new technologies for his own experiments and creating new integrations.

Manuel won the 2010 Springy Award–Community Champion and Spring Champion 2013. In his little free time, he reads the Bible and composes music on his guitar. Manuel is known as dr_pompeii. He has tech reviewed numerous books for Apress, including *Pro Spring, 4th Edition* (2014), *Practical Spring LDAP* (2013), *Pro JPA 2, Second Edition* (2013), and *Pro Spring Security* (2013).

Read his 13 detailed tutorials about many Spring technologies and contact him through his blog at http://www.manueljordanelera.blogspot.com. You can also follow him on Twitter @dr_pompeii.

Acknowledgments

My wife Ellen was patient when I spent long hours at my computer working on this book. I want to thank her for all of her support in writing this book.

I want to thank my family members and friends for their encouragement and support: my mom Pratima Devi; my elder brothers, Janki Sharan and Dr. Sita Sharan; my nephews, Gaurav and Saurav; my sister Ratna; my friends, Karthikeya Venkatesan, Preethi Vasudev, Rahul Nagpal, Ravi Datla; and many more friends not mentioned here.

I would like to thank my coworkers, Forrest "Corky" Butts, Antonio Mathews, and Yolanda Robinson, for their support.

My sincere thanks are due to the wonderful team at Apress for their support during the publication of this book. Thanks to Mark Powers, the Editorial Operations Manager, for providing excellent support and for being exceptionally patient with me when I was slow in producing manuscript. My special thanks to Manuel Jordan Elera, the technical reviewer, whose thorough approach reviewing the book helped weed out many technical errors.

Last but not least, my sincere thanks to Steve Anglin, the Lead Editor at Apress, for taking the initiative for the publication of this book.

Introduction

How This Book Came About

The Java community is excited to see the module system and Java shell finally added to the Java platform in JDK 9, and so am I. After all, we had to wait over 10 years to see this module system in action. Several previous JDK releases saw prototypes of the module system, which were later dropped. The introduction of the module system in JDK 9 has also been a bumpy ride. It went through several iterations of proposals and prototypes. I started writing this book in early 2016. I have to admit that this was a difficult book to write. I had to race against the JDK release date and the changes the Java team was making to the module system. I would write about a topic to find a few months later that the final release date for JDK 9 had moved and whatever I had written was no longer valid. Today is the last day of February 2016 and it seems that the dust has finally settled—the Java team and the Java community are happy with the module system—and you are going to get this book as it exists today. JDK 9 is scheduled to be released in late July 2017. JDK 9 is feature complete at the time of this writing. It is very unlikely that you will see many instances where something covered in this book does not work. However, five months is a long time in terms of software releases, so don't be surprised if a piece of code does not work and you have to tweak it a bit to make it work when you read this book.

In the beginning, this book was supposed to be 140 pages. As my writing progressed, I thought it would be a disservice to readers to write a book so short covering one of the biggest additions to the Java platform. I thank my publisher who never complained about me adding hundreds of pages to the book. I devoted nine chapters (Chapter 2 to Chapter 10) solely to describing the new module system. Chapter 11 covers the Java shell (JShell) with unmatched details.

I spent countless hours researching this topic. I was writing on topics that were under development. There were no materials on the Internet or in books that I could find to learn about these topics. One of the biggest challenges was the fast-changing JDK implementation during the development phase. My main sources of research were the Java source code, Java Enhancement Processes (JEPs), and Java Specification Requests (JSRs). I also spent quite a bit of time reading the Java source code to learn more about some of the new topics in JDK 9. It was always fun to play with Java programs, sometimes for hours, and then add them to the book. Sometimes, it was frustrating to see that the code worked a week ago and then did not work anymore. Subscribing to the mailing lists for all JDK 9 projects helped me to stay in sync with the JDK development team. A few times I had to go through all the bugs on a JDK topic to verify that there was a bug that had not been fixed yet.

All's well that ends well. Finally, I am happy that I was able to include everything that matters to readers interested in learning Java SE 9. I hope you enjoy reading the book and benefit from it.

The Structure of the Book

This book contains 20 chapters. Chapter 1 is an introduction to JDK 9 and how to work with the book and its source code. Chapters 2 through 10 cover the module system. These chapters are designed to be read sequentially.

Chapter 11 covers the Java Shell (JShell) in detail. For the most part, you can read Chapter 11 without reading the first 10 chapters. However, I recommend you read them sequentially for a complete understanding.

You can read Chapters 12 through Chapter 20 in any order. They cover independent topics. The last chapter is a catch-all chapter. If a topic was small enough not to require a chapter of its own, I stuffed it into this final chapter.

The Audience

This book is designed for experienced Java developers who are familiar with Java SE 8. Parts of the book use Streams API, Time API, and Lambdas introduced in Java SE 8. If you know Java SE 7 or earlier versions, you can certainly benefit reading Chapters 1 through 11 of this book. These chapters teach you the module system and the Java shell.

Readers are advised to use the API documentation for the Java programming language as much as possible while using this book. The Java API documentation is where you will find a complete list of everything available in the Java class library. You can download (or view) the Java API documentation from Oracle's official web site at www.oracle.com. While you read this book, you need to practice writing Java programs yourself. You can also practice by tweaking the programs provided in the book. It does not help much in your learning process if you just read this book and do not practice writing your own programs. Remember that "practice makes perfect," which is also true in learning how to program using JDK 9.

Source Code and Errata

Source code and errata for this book can be accessed via http://www.apress.com/us/book/9781484225912.

Questions and Comments

Please direct all your questions and comments to the author at ksharan@jdojo.com.

CHAPTER 1

■ ■ ■

Introduction

In this chapter, you will learn:

- What's included in JDK 9
- How to read this book
- System requirements to use the examples in this book
- How to install NetBeans
- How to download and use the supplied source code for the examples in this book

Introduction to JDK 9

JDK is the ninth major release of the Java Development Kit and is scheduled to be released in late July 2017. It comes with several exciting new features. This book covers the features that are useful to Java application developers in their daily programing life. You can find a complete list of all the features at http://openjdk.java.net/projects/jdk9/.

One of the most important and most exciting features of JDK 9 is the *module system*, which was developed under a project with the code name *Jigsaw*. JDK designers had been trying to introduce the module system to the Java platform for over 10 years. It was planned to be part of a few previous JDK releases and was later dropped. Jigsaw also delayed the JDK 9 release several times. Jigsaw is being released now and you will be able to see it in action.

What was so difficult about Jigsaw that it took so many years to complete? The main goal of Jigsaw was to provide Java developers a way to develop applications in terms of software components called *modules*. A module can export its API for public use and encapsulate its internals. A module can also declare dependency on other modules and these dependencies can be verified at startup, thus avoiding runtime surprises related to missing types. The JDK itself is broken into a set of interacting modules. This provides a scalable runtime. If your application uses a subset of the JDK, you now can create a runtime image that contains JDK modules used in your application and your application modules. All these features of the module system seem normal. The main issue that had been haunting JDK designers was the backward compatibility and migration and adaptation path for the module system. Java has been around for over 20 years. Any big feature, including the module system, must be easily adoptable. After several iterations of redesigns and refinements based on feedback from the Java community, finally it is here! I devote nine chapters (Chapters 2 through 10), which is over 40% of the book, to describing the module system.

Another significant addition to JDK 9 is JShell, which is a REPL (Read-Eval-Print Loop) for Java. JShell is a command-line tool and an API, and it allows you to execute a snippet of code and get immediate feedback. Before JShell, you had to write a complete program, compile it, and run it to get feedback. JShell is a tool that you will use in your daily development and you might wonder how you programmed in Java for so many years without it. JShell is vital for beginners and can help them quickly learn the Java language without understanding the details of the program structure such as modules and packages. I devote Chapter 11 to discussing JShell.

© Kishori Sharan 2017
K. Sharan, *Java 9 Revealed*, DOI 10.1007/978-1-4842-2592-9_1

There are several other additions to JDK 9 that will make your life easier as a developer. To name a few, they are the Reactive Streams API, collection factory methods, the incubating HTTP/2 Client API, the Stack-Walking API, the Platform Logging API, and unified JVM logging. I cover these topics extensively in this book.

How to Read This Book

This book consists of 20 chapters. Chapters 2 through 10 cover only one topic, which is the module system. They are designed to be read sequentially. It is true that you may be able to migrate your existing application to JDK 9 without knowing anything about the module system. However, if you want to take advantage of the benefits provided by JDK 9, you must learn the module system and start using it to develop new Java applications and migrate legacy ones to JDK 9. Chapters 11 through 20 can be read in any order.

Chapter 2, "The Module System," includes a brief history of the issues faced by Java developers using JDK version 8 and earlier. It introduces the module system and explains how it solves the problems of API encapsulation, configuration, and scalability. The chapter introduces many new terms related to the module system. If you do not understand all of them, keep reading. Subsequent chapters and examples will make them clear with more explanation.

Chapter 3, "Creating Your First Module," gives you a glimpse of modules in action. It shows you step-by-step how to declare a module, write code in a module, compile a module, and run a class, which is part of a module. This chapter does not go into details of a module declaration.

Chapter 4, "Module Dependency," is an intensive hands-on chapter on the module system. It builds on the previous two chapters and dives deeper into declaring a module's dependencies and exporting packages of a module. It shows you how to declare different types of modules, how to mix modular and non-modular code into a Java application, and several other options that are available with the module system. It is a must-understand chapter for any serious Java developer planning to use JDK 9.

Chapter 5, "Implementing Services," shows you how to take advantage of the simple directives of the module system to implement services in JDK 9. The chapter also explains how services were implemented before JDK 9.

Chapter 6, "Packaging Modules," explains different formats you can use to package your modules and when one format should be used over others. Up to JDK 8, you had only one way to package your Java applications, which was using JAR files. This chapter shows you how to package your modules using the JMOD format.

Chapter 7, "Creating Custom Runtime Images," explains how to create custom runtime images using the jlink tool in an internal format called JIMAGE.

Chapter 8, "Breaking Changes in JDK 9," explains changes in JDK 9 that may break your existing applications if you migrate to JDK 9. The chapter also suggests how to fix the broken code and mentions alternatives, if any, offered by JDK 9.

Chapter 9, "Breaking Module Encapsulation," explains how it is possible to break the main premise of the module system, which is encapsulation. JDK 9 provides several non-standard command-line options that will let you break into the otherwise encapsulated non-accessible module code. You may need to do this if you are migrating legacy applications, which used to have access to JDK internal APIs or third-party libraries, but in JDK 9, those internal APIs have been encapsulated in modules.

Chapter 10, "The Module API," explains how you can access the module system programmatically using the Module API. Whatever can be done using module declarations and command-line options can also be done using the Module API.

Chapter 11, "The Java Shell," covers the JShell tool and the JShell API in detail. It covers printing a message, declaring classes, and using existing modules inside the jshell tool. It describes how to configure the jshell tool and how to use the JShell API to execute snippets of code.

Chapter 12, "Process API Updates," covers additions to the Process API in JDK 9. The chapter does not cover the Process API in its entirety since JDK 1.0.

Chapter 13, "Collection API Updates," covers additions to the Collection API in JDK 9, such as static factory methods to create lists, sets, and maps.

Chapter 14, "The HTTP/2 Client API," explains the new incubating HTTP/2 Client API in JDK 9. It is part of the incubator module, which means it is not standardized yet. In JDK 10, it will be standardized and become part of Java SE platform or will be removed.

Chapter 15, "Enhanced Deprecation," explains the modifications to the Deprecation annotation type, how to use the @SuppressWarnings annotation in JDK 9, and how to use the jdeprscan tool to scan your code to find the use of the deprecated JDK APIs.

Chapter 16, "Stack Walking," covers the Stack-Walking API introduced in JDK 9. You can use this new API to traverse the call stack and find caller class references.

Chapter 17, "Reactive Streams," covers the Reactive Streams API, which is a Java implementation of the reactive specification.

Chapter 18, "Streams API Updates," explains the new methods added to the Streams API. It also explains new collectors added to the Streams API.

Chapter 19, "Platform and JVM Logging," explains the new Platform Logging API that you can use to log messages from platform classes to a custom logger. It shows you how to use Log4j to log platform messages. The chapter shows you how to access JVM logs using the command-line option and how to customize the JVM messages before logging.

Chapter 20, "Other Changes in JDK 9," covers all the other changes in JDK 9 that are of interest to application developers and were not covered in previous chapters. Each section in this chapter covers an independent topic. You can jump to a section of your interest and skip the rest. The chapter covers a range of topics, including an underscore being a keyword in JDK 9, improved try-with-resources bocks, private methods in interfaces, how to use streams of Optional, how to use filters during object deserialization, new methods in the I/O API, and more.

System Requirements

You need to install JDK 9 on your computer to use the programs in this book and to write your own programs.

At the time of this writing, JDK 9 is still in development. It is expected to be released for production use in late July 2017. Its current version is *Early Access* Build 157. You can download and install the latest version of JDK 9 from https://jdk9.java.net/download/. Follow the instructions on this page to download and install JDK 9 specific to your operating system.

It is important that you verify your JDK 9 installation. You can use the java command with the -version option to print the version of the JDK installed on your computer:

```
c:\> java -version
```

```
java version "9-ea"
Java(TM) SE Runtime Environment (build 9-ea+157)
Java HotSpot(TM) 64-Bit Server VM (build 9-ea+157, mixed mode)
```

Notice the version 9-ea in the output. That indicates that I have JDK version 9 Early Access installed on my computer. If you are using the final release, you may see only 9 as the version information.

When you run this command, you may get an error like the one shown here:

```
c:\> java -version
```

```
'java' is not recognized as an internal or external command,
operable program or batch file.
```

The error indicates that the directory containing the java command has not been added to the PATH environment variable on your computer. The java command is in the JDK_HOME\bin directory, where JDK_HOME is the directory in which you have installed JDK 9. I installed JDK 9 on Windows in the C:\java9 directory, so on my computer, the java command is in the C:\java9\bin directory. You can add the JDK_HOME\bin directory to the PATH environment variable using the method specific to your operating system. Or you can refer to the command using its full path, for example, C:\java9\bin\java on Windows. The following command uses the full path of the java command on Windows to print the version information:

```
c:\> C:\java9\bin\java -version
```

```
java version "9-ea"
Java(TM) SE Runtime Environment (build 9-ea+157)
Java HotSpot(TM) 64-Bit Server VM (build 9-ea+157, mixed mode)
```

Installing the NetBeans IDE

If you want to compile and run all programs in this book, you need to have an integrated development environment (IDE) such as NetBeans or Eclipse installed on your computer. At the time of this writing, no IDE fully supports the module system in JDK 9. I used the daily latest builds of NetBeans to write all the programs for this book. Currently, NetBeans supports creating one module per NetBeans project. That is, if you want to create three Java modules in NetBeans, you need to create three NetBeans Java project. One Java module can refer to other Java modules using project dependencies in NetBeans. Currently, NetBeans does not support multi-module Java projects. You can find the latest information on support for the module system in NetBeans at the wiki page: http://wiki.netbeans.org/JDK9Support.

You can download the latest daily build of NetBeans supporting JDK 9 from the following link: http://bits.netbeans.org/download/trunk/nightly/latest/.

There are many types of downloads on this page. The smallest one is less than 100MB and it is for Java SE. This download will work for you, except for Chapter 14, which uses a web application. You need the Java EE version of NetBeans to run all the examples in Chapter 14.

NetBeans will run on top of JDK 8 as well as JDK 9. I suggest installing JDK 9 before installing NetBeans. If you have multiple JDKs, currently NetBeans picks up JDK 8 by default. You need to point the NetBeans installation to the JDK 9 installation directory for it to use JDK 9 by default. If you have installed NetBeans on top of JDK 8, in Chapter 3, I describe a step-by-step process for using JDK 9 as the Java platform for your projects inside the NetBeans IDE. Throughout the book, I included screenshots of the NetBeans windows and images to assist you in using it to write your programs and configure the IDE to compile and run Java 9 programs.

Before you start playing with the Java 9 code, make sure you install NetBeans or any other IDE that supports the module system in JDK 9.

Downloading the Source Code

You can download the source for the book's examples from http://www.apress.com/us/book/9781484225912. The source is a ZIP file. The root directory in the ZIP file is Java9Revealed. If you are using Windows, it is recommended that you unzip the source code in C:\ directory. This will create a C:\Java9Revealed directory and all source code will be copied underneath.

All the examples in this book assume that the supplied source code is in the C:\Java9Revealed directory. If you are using an operating system other than Windows and/or you have copied the source code in a directory other than C:\, you need to substitute the directory in the examples with yours.

On non-Windows platforms, you need to use the platform-specific path syntax. For example, on Linux, you need to replace C:\Java9Revealed with a path like /usr/ks/Java9Revealed.

Each module in the source is in a separate NetBeans project and is stored in a separate directory. Sometimes, the chapter examples use several modules. You will find a directory for each such module. For example, Chapter 5 creates five modules named com.jdojo.prime, com.jdojo.prime.generic, com.jdojo.prime.faster, com.jdojo.prime.probable, and com.jdojo.prime.client. You will find the following five directories in the downloadable source code:

- Java9Revealed/com.jdojo.prime

- Java9Revealed/com.jdojo.prime.generic

- Java9Revealed/com.jdojo.prime.faster

- Java9Revealed/com.jdojo.prime.probable

- Java9Revealed/com.jdojo.prime.client

Each directory that contains a NetBeans project contains the following sub-directories that are of interest: build, dist, and src. For example, for the com.jdojo.prime module, you will find the following directories:

- Java9Revealed/com.jdojo.prime/build

- Java9Revealed/com.jdojo.prime/dist

- Java9Revealed/com.jdojo.prime/src

The src sub-directory contains the source code for the module. The build sub-directory contains the compiled code for the module. The dist sub-directory contains the modular JAR. Examples in this book refer to the build and dist sub-directories. If the examples do not run as expected, you may need to open the project in NetBeans and run the Clean and Build feature, which will remove the contents of the build and dist sub-directories, recompile the code for that project in the build sub-directory, and recreate the modular JAR in the dist sub-directory. Consider the following command:

```
C:\Java9Revealed> java --module-path com.jdojo.intro\build\classes
--module com.jdojo.intro/com.jdojo.intro.Welcome
```

The command assumes that C:\Java9Revealed is your current directory. It uses the relative path com.jdojo.intro\build\classes, which corresponds to C:\Java9Revealed\com.jdojo.intro\build\classes. If run across such commands in this book, you can replace the relative path with yours according to your current directory and where you copied the source code.

You can also run classes from inside NetBeans, which is much easier than using command prompts. A few of the examples in this book are built step-by-step and I show you output for more than one step. For those examples, the source code for this book contains a copy of the program in the final step. You need to edit the source code if you want to see the outputs at every step.

It is likely that the class file format will change a bit in the book's compiled examples by the time you use them. I strongly recommend you open all the NetBeans projects in the NetBeans IDE and run Clean and Build on all of them before trying to use them.

CHAPTER 2

▦ ▦ ▦

The Module System

In this chapter, you will learn:

- How the Java source code used to be written, packaged, and deployed prior to JDK 9 and the underlying issues with that approach

- What a module is in JDK 9

- How to declare modules and their dependencies

- How to package modules

- What a module path is

- What observable modules are

- How to print the list of observable modules

- How to print the description of a module

This chapter is meant to give you a brief conceptual overview of the module system introduced in JDK 9. Subsequent chapters cover all these concepts in detail, with examples. Don't worry if you do not understand all module-related concepts the first time. Once you gain experience developing modular code, you can come back and re-read this chapter.

Life Before Java 9

Prior to JDK 9, developing a Java application involved the following steps:

- The Java source code was written in the form of Java types such as classes, interfaces, enums, and annotations.

- Types were arranged into packages. A type always belonged to a package—explicitly or implicitly. A package was a logical collection of types, essentially providing a namespace for the types contained in it. A package may have public types, private types, and some types that are internal implementations even though declared public.

- The compiled code for types was packaged into one or more JAR files, also known as application JARs because they contained application code. The code in one package might span multiple JARs.

© Kishori Sharan 2017
K. Sharan, *Java 9 Revealed*, DOI 10.1007/978-1-4842-2592-9_2

- The application might use libraries. Libraries were also supplied as one or more JAR files, also known as library JARs.

- The application was deployed by placing all JAR files, application JARs, and library JARs on the class path.

Figure 2-1 shows a typical arrangement of code packaged in a JAR file. The figure shows only the packages and types, excluding other contents such as the manifest.mf file and resource files.

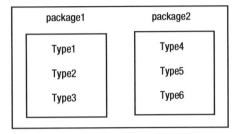

Figure 2-1. *The code arrangement in a JAR file*

For over 20 years, the Java community lived with this way of writing, compiling, packaging, and deploying Java code. However, the 20-year long journey has not been as smooth as you would hope! There were inherent problems in arranging and running Java code this way:

- A package was simply a container for types without enforcing any accessibility boundary. A public type in a package is accessible in all other packages; there was no way to prevent this global visibility of public types in a package.

- Packages were open for extension, except packages starting with java and javax. If you had types in a JAR with package-level access, they could be accessed inside other JARs that defined types in a package named the same as yours.

- The Java runtime saw a flat set of packages loaded from a list of JARs. There was no way to know whether you had multiple copies of the same type in different JARs. The runtime would load the type found in a JAR that was encountered first on the class path.

- You could have cases of missing types at runtime caused by not including one of the JARs required by your application in the class path. Missing types raise their ugly heads as runtime errors when the code tries to use them.

- There was no way to know at startup that some types used in the application were missing. You could also include a wrong version of a JAR file and receive an error at runtime.

These problems were so frequent and infamous in the Java community that they got a name—*JAR-hell.* I have been through JAR-hell several times during my job as a Java developer! The term JAR-hell even has its own Wikipedia entry at https://en.wikipedia.org/wiki/Java_Classloader#JAR_hell.

Packaging the JDK and JRE was also a problem. They were available as a huge monolithic artifacts, thus increasing the download time, startup time, and the memory footprint. The monolithic JRE made it impossible to use Java on devices with little memory. If you deploy your Java applications to the cloud, you pay for the memory you use. Most often, the monolithic JRE uses more memory than is required, which means you pay more for the cloud service. The Compact profiles introduced in Java 8 took a step forward in reducing JRE size—and hence the runtime memory footprint—by allowing you to package a subset of the JRE in a custom runtime image called a *compact profile.*

▨ **Tip**   In early access releases, JDK 9 contained three modules named `java.compact1`, `java.compact2`, and `java.compact3` that corresponded to the three compact profiles in JDK 8. Later, they were dropped because the modules in JDK give you full control over the list of modules you can include in your custom JRE.

You can put these problems in the JDK/JRE before JDK 9 into three categories:

- Unreliable configuration
- Weak encapsulation
- Monolithic structure of the JDK/JRE

Figure 2-2 shows the how the Java runtime sees all JARs on the class path and how code in one JAR can be accessed from other JARs without any restrictions, except for the ones specified by the type declarations in terms of access controls.

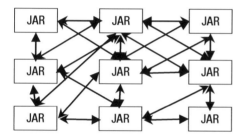

Figure 2-2. *JARs on the class path as loaded and accessed by the Java runtime*

Java 9 addresses these problems by introducing a new way of developing, packaging, and deploying Java applications. In Java 9, a Java application consists of small interacting components called *modules*. Java 9 has organized the JDK/JRE as a set of modules as well. The focus of this chapter is an overview of modules. Subsequent chapters explain modules in detail.

The New Module System

Java 9 introduced a new program component called a *module*. You can think of a Java application as a collection of interacting modules with a well-defined boundaries and dependencies between those modules. The module system was developed with the following goals:

- Reliable configuration
- Strong encapsulation
- Modular JDK/JRE

These goals were to solve the problems faced in developing and deploying Java applications prior to Java 9. *Reliable configuration* solves the problem of the error-prone class path mechanism used to look up types. A module must declare explicit dependencies on other modules. The module system verifies the dependencies in all phases of the application development—compile-time, link time, and runtime. Suppose a module declares a dependency on another module and the second module is missing at startup. The JVM detects that a dependency is missing and fails at startup. Prior to Java 9, such an application would generate a runtime error (not at startup) when the missing types were used.

Strong encapsulation solves the problem of accessibility-at-will of public types across JARs on the class path. A module must explicitly declare which of its public types are accessible to other modules. A module cannot access public types in another module unless those modules explicitly make their public types accessible. A public type in Java 9 does not mean that it is accessible to all parts of the program. The module system has added more refined accessibility control. I explain the accessibility controls in another chapter.

▓ **Tip** Java 9 provides reliable configuration by allowing a module to declare explicit dependency and verifying those dependencies in all phases of development. It provides strong encapsulation by allowing a module to declare packages whose public types are accessible to other modules.

JDK 9 was rewritten by breaking down its predecessor's monolithic structure into a set of modules called *platform modules*. JDK 9 also introduced an optional phase called *link time*, which may occur between compile-time and runtime. During link time, you use a linker, which is a tool called `jlink` that ships with the JDK 9, to create a custom runtime image of your application that includes only the modules used in your application. This shrinks the size of the runtime to its optimum size.

What Is a Module?

A *module* is a named collection of code and data. It can contain Java code and native code. Java code is organized as a set of packages containing types such as classes, interfaces, enums, and annotations. The data may include resources such as image files and configuration files.

For Java code, a module acts as a collection of zero or more packages. Figure 2-3 shows three modules named `policy`, `claim`, and `utility` in which the `policy` module contains two packages, the `claim` module contains one package, and the `utility` module contains no packages.

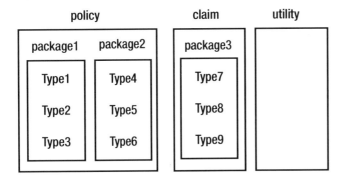

Figure 2-3. *Arrangement of types, packages, and modules*

A module is much more than just a container of packages. Apart from its name, a module definition contains the following:

- A list of other modules it *requires* (or depends on)
- A list of packages it *exports* (its public APIs) that other modules can use
- A list of packages that it *opens* (its entire API, public and private) to other modules for reflective access

- A list of services it *uses* (or discovers and loads using the `java.util.ServiceLoader` class)

- A list of implementations for services that it *provides*

When you work with a module, you work with one or more of these aspects. I cover a few more theoretical aspects of modules before I show you how to define your own modules.

The Java SE 9 Platform Specification divides the platform into a set of modules known as *platform modules*. An implementation of the Java SE 9 platform may contain some or all of the platform modules, thus providing a scalable Java runtime. Standard modules have names prefixed with `java`. Examples of Java SE standard modules are `java.base`, `java.sql`, `java.xml`, and `java.logging`. APIs in standard platform modules are supported and are intended for use by developers.

Non-standard platform modules are part of the JDK, but not specified in the Java SE Platform Specification. These JDK-specific modules have names prefixed with `jdk`. Examples of JDK-specific modules are `jdk.charsets`, `jdk.compiler`, `jdk.jlink`, `jdk.policytool`, and `jdk.zipfs`. APIs in the JDK-specific modules are not intended for use by developers. These APIs are typically used in the JDK itself and by library developers who cannot easily get the desired functionality using the Java SE APIs. If you use APIs from these modules, they might not be supported or could change in the future without notice.

JavaFX is not part of the Java SE 9 Platform Specification. However, JavaFX-related modules are installed when you install JDK/JRE. JavaFX modules names are prefixed with `javafx`. Examples of JavaFX modules are `javafx.base`, `javafx.controls`, `javafx.fxml`, `javafx.graphics`, and `javafx.web`.

The `java.base` module, which is part of the Java SE 9 platform, is the primordial module. It does not depend on any other modules. The module system knows only about the `java.base` module. It discovers all other modules through the dependencies specified in the modules. The `java.base` module exports core Java SE packages such as `java.lang`, `java.io`, `java.math`, `java.text`, `java.time`, `java.util`, etc.

Module Dependencies

Up to JDK 8, a public type in one package could be accessed by other packages without any restrictions. In other words, packages did not control the accessibility of the types they contained. The module system in JDK 9 provides fine-grained control over the accessibility of types.

Accessibility across modules is a two-way agreement between the used module and the using module: A module explicitly makes its public types available for use by other modules and the modules using those public types explicitly declare dependency on the first module. All non-exported packages in a module are private to the module and they cannot be used outside the module.

Making public APIs in a package available to other modules is known as *exporting* that package. If a module named `policy` makes the public types in a package named pkg1 available to other modules, it is said that the `policy` module *exports* the package pkg1. If a module named `claim` declares a dependency on the `policy` module, it is said that the `claim` module *reads* the `policy` module. If the `claim` module reads the `policy` module, it means that all public types in the exported packages of the `policy` module can be accessed inside the `claim` module. A module can also export a package selectively only to one or more named modules. Such exports are called *qualified exports* or *module-friendly exports*. The public types in a package in a qualified export are accessible only to the specified named modules.

In the context of the module system, three terms—*requires, reads,* and *depends on*—are used interchangeably. Java documentation promotes the usage of the term *reads* in such contexts. The following three statements mean the same: P reads Q, P requires Q, and P depends on Q, where P and Q are two modules.

Figure 2-4 depicts the dependency between two modules named `policy` and `claim`. The `policy` module contains two packages named pkg1 and pkg2 and it exports the package pkg1, which I have shown using the dashed boundary to distinguish it from package pkg2, which is not exported. The `claim` module contains two packages, pkg3 and pkg4, it does not export any package. It declares a dependency on the `policy` module.

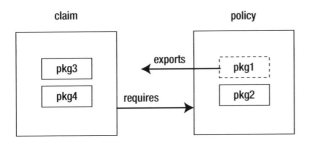

Figure 2-4. *Declaring dependency between modules*

In JDK 9, you can declare these two modules as follows:

```
module policy {
    exports pkg1;
}

module claim {
    requires policy;
}
```

■ **Tip**   The syntax for indicating dependency in a module is asymmetric—you export a *package*, but require a *module*.

This module declaration requires you to know the module name if your module depends on another module. Several Java frameworks and tools rely heavily on reflection to access your non-exported module's code at runtime. They provide great features such as dependency injection, serialization, implementation for the Java Persistence API, code-automation, and debugging. Spring, Hibernate, and XStream are examples of such frameworks and libraries. These frameworks and libraries do not know about your application modules. However, they need access to the types in your modules to do their job. They also need access to private members of your modules, which breaks the premise of strong encapsulation in JDK 9. When a module exports a package, other modules that depend on the first module can access only the public API in the exported package. To grant deep reflective access (accessing public as well as private APIs) on all packages of a module at runtime, you can declare an *open* module.

Figure 2-5 shows an open module named policy.model. I show the module and its packages in dashed boundaries to indicate that the module is open and the packages are accessible to any other module. The jdojo.jpa module accesses the types in the policy.model module at runtime using reflection. The jdojo.jpa module provides implementation for JPA and the policy.model module explicitly depends on the jdojo.jpa module.

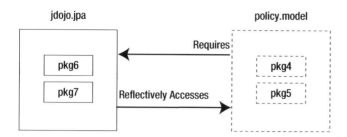

Figure 2-5. *An open module that allows reflective access to all its members*

In JDK 9, you can declare these two modules as follows:

```
open module policy.model {
    requires jdojo.jpa;
}

module jdojo.jpa {
    // The module exports its packages here
}
```

Module Graph

The module system knows about only one module: java.base. The java.base module does not depend on any other modules. All other modules implicitly depend on the java.base module.

The modular structure of an application can be visualized as a graph called a *module graph*. In a module graph, each module is represented as a node. A directed edge from a module to another module exists if the first module depends on the second module. A module graph is constructed by resolving the dependencies of a set of initial modules called *root modules* against a set of modules known to the module system called *observable modules*.

░ **Tip** Module resolution or resolving a module means that modules on which this module depends are available. Suppose a module named P depends on two modules named Q and R. Resolving module P means you locate modules Q and R and recursively resolve module Q and R.

A module graph is constructed by resolving the module dependencies at compile-time, link time, and runtime. The module resolution starts at root modules and follows the dependency links until the java.base module is reached. Sometimes, you may have a module on the module path, but you might get an error that the module is not found. This can happen if the module was not resolved and was not included in the module graph. For a module to be resolved, it needs to be in the dependency chain starting from the root modules. A default set of root modules is selected based on the way the compiler or the Java launcher is invoked. You can also add modules to the default set of root modules. It is important to understand how default root modules are selected in different situations:

- If the application code is compiled from the class path or the main class is run from the class path, the default set of root modules consists of the java.se module and all the non-java.* system modules such as jdk.* and javafx.*. If the java.se module is not present, the default set of root modules consists of all java.* and non-java.* modules.

- If your application consists of modules, the default set of root modules depends on the phase:

    - At compile-time, it consists of all modules being compiled.

    - At link time, it is empty.

    - At runtime, it contains the module that contains the main class. You use the --module or -m option with the java command to specify the module and its main class to be run.

Continuing with the example of two modules named policy and claim, suppose pkg3.Main is the main class in claim and both modules are packaged as modular JARs in the C:\Java9Revealed\lib directory. Figure 2-6 shows the module graph that is constructed at runtime when the following command is used to run the application:

```
C:\Java9Revealed>java -p lib -m claim/pkg3.Main
```

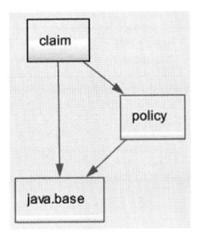

Figure 2-6. *An example of a module graph*

The claim module contains the main class of the application. Therefore, claim is the only root module when the module graph is created. The policy module is resolved because the claim module depends on the policy module. The java.base module is resolved because all other modules depend on it and so do these two modules.

The complexity of a module graph depends on the number of the root modules and the level of dependencies among the modules. Suppose, apart from depending on the policy module, the claim module also depends on the platform module named java.sql. The new declaration of the claim module looks like this:

```
module policy {
    requires policy;
    requires java.sql;
}
```

Figure 2-7 shows the module graph that will be constructed when you run the pkg3.Main class in the claim module. Notice that the java.xml and java.logging modules are also present in the graph because the java.sql module depends on them. In the graph, the claim module is the only root module.

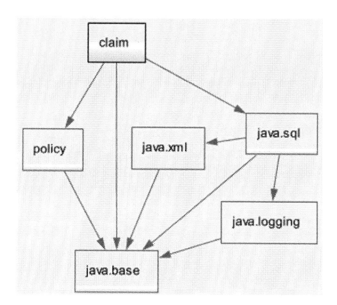

Figure 2-7. *A module graph showing a dependency on the java.sql module*

Figure 2-8 shows one of the most complex module graphs for the platform module named java.se. The module declaration for the java.se module is as follows:

```
module java.se {
    requires transitive java.sql;
    requires transitive java.rmi;
    requires transitive java.desktop;
    requires transitive java.security.jgss;
    requires transitive java.security.sasl;
    requires transitive java.management;
    requires transitive java.logging;
    requires transitive java.xml;
    requires transitive java.scripting;
    requires transitive java.compiler;
    requires transitive java.naming;
    requires transitive java.instrument;
    requires transitive java.xml.crypto;
    requires transitive java.prefs;
    requires transitive java.sql.rowset;
    requires java.base;
    requires transitive java.datatransfer;
}
```

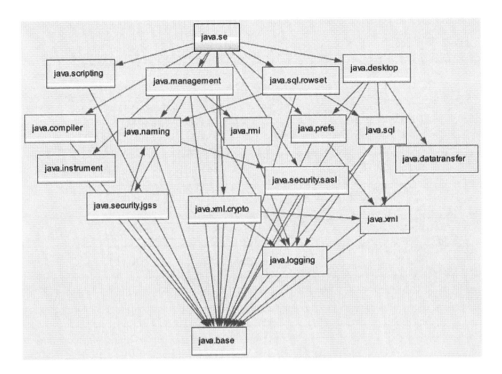

Figure 2-8. *A module graph with the java.se module as the root module*

Sometimes, you need to add modules to the default set of root modules so the added modules are resolved. You can specify the additional root modules using the --add-modules command-line option during compile-time, link time, and runtime:

```
--add-modules <module-list>
```

Here, <module-list> is a comma-separated list of module names.

You can use the following special values as a module list with the --add-modules option that have special meaning:

- ALL-DEFAULT
- ALL-SYSTEM
- ALL-MODULE-PATH

All three special values are valid at runtime. You can use the ALL-MODULE-PATH value only at compile-time.

If ALL-DEFAULT is used as the module list, the default set of root modules used when the application is run from the class path is added to the root set. This is useful for an application that is a container and hosts other applications that may need other modules not required by the container application itself. This is a way to make all Java SE modules available to the container, so any of the hosted applications may use them.

If ALL-SYSTEM is the used as the module list, all system modules are added to the root set. This is useful for running test harnesses.

If ALL-MODULE-PATH is the used as the module list, all modules found on module paths are added to the root set. This is useful for tools such as Maven, which ensures that all modules on the module path are needed by the application.

▓ **Tip** You may receive an error that a module is not found even when the module is present on the module path. In such cases, you need to add the missing module to the default set of root modules using the --add-modules command-line option.

JDK 9 supports a useful non-standard command-line option that prints the diagnostic messages describing the steps used to resolve modules while the module graph is constructed. The option is -Xdiag:resolver. The following command runs the pkg3.Main class in the claim module. A partial output is shown. At the end of the diagnostic messages, you will find a Result: section that lists the resolved modules.

```
C:\Java9Revealed>java -Xdiag:resolver -p lib -m claim/pkg3.Main
```

```
[Resolver] Root module claim located
[Resolver]    (file:///C:/Java9Revealed/lib/claim.jar)
[Resolver] Module java.base located, required by claim
[Resolver]    (jrt:/java.base)
[Resolver] Module policy located, required by claim
[Resolver]    (file:///C:/Java9Revealed/lib/policy.jar)
...
[Resolver] Result:
[Resolver]    claim
[Resolver]    java.base
...
[Resolver]    policy
```

Aggregator Modules

You can create a module that contains no code of its own. It collects and re-exports the contents of other modules. Such a module is called an *aggregator module*. Suppose there are several modules that depend on five modules. You can create an aggregator module for those five modules, and now, your modules can depend on only one module—the aggregator module.

Aggregator modules exist for convenience. Java 9 contains several aggregator modules such as java.se and java.se.ee. The java.se module gathers parts of the Java SE that do not overlap with Java EE. The java.se.ee module gathers all of the modules that comprise the Java SE, including modules that overlap with the Java EE.

Declaring Modules

This section contains a quick overview of the syntax used to declare modules. I explain each part in greater detail in subsequent chapters. If you do not understand everything mentioned about modules in this section, keep reading. I will cover them again with examples in later chapters.

A module is defined using a module declaration, which is a new construct in the Java programming language. The syntax is as follows:

```
[open] module <module> {
      <module-statement>;
      <module-statement>;
      ...
}
```

The presence of the open modifier, which is optional, declares an *open module*. An open module exports all its packages to be accessed by other modules using reflection. <module> is the name of the module being defined. <module-statement> is a module statement. You can have zero or more module statements in a module declaration. If it is present, it can be one of five types of statements:

- An exports statement

- An opens statement

- A requires statement

- A uses statement

- A provides statement

The exports and opens statements are used to control access to the module's code. The requires statement is used to declare dependency of a module to another module. The uses and provides statements are used to express service consumption and service provision, respectively. The following is an example of a module declaration of a module named myModule:

```
module myModule {
      // Exports the packages - com.jdojo.util and
      // com.jdojo.util.parser
      exports com.jdojo.util;
      exports com.jdojo.util.parser;

      // Reads the java.sql module
      requires java.sql;

      // Opens com.jdojo.legacy package for reflective access
      opens com.jdojo.legacy;

      // Uses the service interface java.sql.Driver
      uses java.sql.Driver;

      // Provides the com.jdojo.util.parser.FasterCsvParser
      // class as an implementation for the service interface
      // named com.jdojo.util.CsvParser
      provides com.jdojo.util.CsvParser
            with com.jdojo.util.parser.FasterCsvParser;
}
```

You can create an open module by using the open modifier in the module declaration. An open module grants reflective access to all its packages to other modules. You cannot use opens statements inside an open module because all packages are implicitly open in an open module. The following snippet of code declares an open module named myLegacyModule:

```
open module myLegacyModule {
    exports com.jdojo.legacy;
    requires java.sql;
}
```

Module Names

A module name can be a Java-*qualified* identifier. A qualified identifier is one or more identifiers separated by a dot, for example, policy, com.jdojo.common, and com.jdojo.util. If any part in a module name is not a valid Java identifier, a compile-time error occurs. For example, com.jdojo.common.1.0 is not valid module name because two parts, 1 and 0, in the name are not valid Java identifiers.

Similar to the package-naming convention, use the reverse-domain name pattern to give your modules unique names. Using this convention, the simplest module, which is named com.jdojo.common, may be declared as follows:

```
module com.jdojo.common {
    // No module statements
}
```

A module name does not hide variables, types, and packages with the same name. Therefore, you can have a module as well as a variable, a type, or a package with the same name. The context of their use will differentiate which name is referring to what kind of entity.

In JDK 9, open, module, requires, transitive, exports, opens, to, uses, provides, and with are restricted keywords. They are explained briefly later in this chapter and in detail in subsequent chapters. They have special meaning only when they appear in module declarations at specific positions. You can use them as identifiers everywhere else in programs. For example, the following module declaration is valid, even though it does not use an intuitive module name:

```
// Declare a module named module
module module {
    // Module statements go here
}
```

The first module word is interpreted as a keyword and the second one is a module name.

You can declare a variable named module anywhere in your program:

```
String module = "myModule";
```

Controlling Access to Modules

An exports statement exports the specified package of the module to all modules or a list of named modules at compile-time and runtime. It takes the following two forms:

- exports <package>;

- exports <package> to <module1>, <module2>...;

Examples of using the exports statement are as follows:

```
module M {
    exports com.jdojo.util;
    exports com.jdojo.policy
        to com.jdojo.claim, com.jdojo.billing;
}
```

An opens statement grants reflective access to the specified package to all modules or a list of specified modules at runtime. Other modules can access all types in the specified package and all members (private and public) of those types using reflection. The opens statement takes the following forms:

- opens <package>;

- opens <package> to <module1>, <module2>...;

Examples of using the opens statement are as follows:

```
module M {
    opens com.jdojo.claim.model;
    opens com.jdojo.policy.model to core.hibernate;
    opens com.jdojo.services to core.spring;
}
```

▓ **Tip** Compare the effects of the exports and opens statements. The exports statement lets you access only *the public API* of the specified package at *compile-time* and *runtime,* whereas the opens statement lets you access *public* and *private* members of all types in the specified package using *reflection* at *runtime.*

If a module needs to access public types from another module at compile-time and private members of types in the same at runtime using reflection, the second module can export and open the same package as shown:

```
module N {
    exports com.jdojo.claim.model;
    opens com.jdojo.claim.model;
}
```

You will come across three phrases when reading about modules:

- A module M exports a package P

- A module M opens a package Q

- A module M contains a package R

The first two phrases correspond to the exports and opens statements in a module. The third phrase means that the module contains a package named R that is neither exported nor opened. In the early design of the module system, the third situation was phrased as "A module M *conceals* a package R".

Declaring Dependency

A requires statement declares dependence of the current module to another module. A "requires N" statement in a module named M means that the module M depends on (or reads) the module N. The statement takes the following forms:

- requires <module>;

- requires transitive <module>;

- requires static <module>;

- requires transitive static <module>;

The static modifier in a requires statement makes the dependence mandatory at compile-time, but is optional at runtime. A "requires static N" statement in a module named M means that the module M depends on the module N and the module N must be present at compile-time in order to compile the module M; however, the presence of module N at runtime in order to use module M is optional. The transitive modifier in a requires statement causes any module, which depends on the current module to have implicit dependence on the module specified in the requires statement. Suppose there are three modules P, Q, and R. Suppose the module Q contains a "requires transitive R" statement. If the module P contains a "requires Q" statement, it means that the module P implicitly depends on the module R.

Configuring Services

Java allows using a service provider mechanism in which service providers and service consumers are decoupled. JDK 9 allows you to implement services using the uses and provides module statements.

A uses statement specifies the name of a *service interface* that the current module may discover and load using the java.util.ServiceLoader class. It takes the following form:

```
uses <service-interface>;
```

An example of using a uses statement is as follows:

```
module M {
    uses com.jdojo.prime.PrimeChecker;
}
```

Here, com.jdojo.PrimeChecker is a service interface whose implementation classes will be provided by other modules. The module M will discover and load the implementations of this interface using the java.util.ServiceLoader class.

A provides statement specifies one or more service provider implementation classes for a service interface. It takes the following form:

```
provides <service-interface>
    with <service-impl-class1>, <service-impl-class2>...;
```

An example of using the `provides` statement is as follows:

```
module N {
    provides com.jdojo.prime.PrimeChecker
        with com.jdojo.prime.generic.GenericPrimeChecker;
}
```

It is possible for the same module to provide service implementations and discover and load the service. A module can also discover and load one kind of service and provide implementation for another kind of service. The following are a few examples:

```
module P {
    uses com.jdojo.CsvParser;

    provides com.jdojo.CsvParser
        with com.jdojo.CsvParserImpl;

    provides com.jdojo.prime.PrimeChecker
        with com.jdojo.prime.generic.FasterPrimeChecker;
}
```

Module Descriptors

After learning about how to declare modules in the previous section, you may have several questions about the source code for a module declaration:

- Where do you save a module declaration's source code? Is it saved in a file? If so, what is the filename?

- Where do you place the module declaration source code file?

- How is the source code for a module's declaration compiled?

I will answer these questions before I show you the first modular program in action.

Compiling Module Declarations

A module declaration is stored in a file named `module-info.java`, which is stored at the root of the source file hierarchy for that module. The Java compiler compiles a module declaration to a file named `module-info.class`. The `module-info.class` file is known as a *module descriptor* and it is placed at the root of the compiled code hierarchy for the module. If you package the compiled code for a module in a JAR file, the `module-info.class` file is stored at the root of the JAR file.

A module declaration does not contain executable code. In essence, it contains configurations for a module. Why don't we keep a module declaration in a text file in XML or JSON format instead of in a class file? The class file was chosen as a module descriptor because a class file has an extensible, well-defined format. A module descriptor contains the compiled form of a source-level module declaration. It can be augmented by tools, e.g. the `jar` tool, to include additional information in class file attributes after the module declaration is initially compiled. The class file format also allows developers to use imports and annotations in a module declaration.

Module Version

In the initial prototype of the module system, a module declaration also included a module version. Including the module version in the declaration made the implementation of the module system complex, so the module version was dropped from the declaration.

The extensible format of the module descriptor (class file format) is exploited to add a version to a module. When you package a module's compiled code into a JAR, the jar tool provides an option to add the module's version, which is finally added to the module-info.class file. I explain how to add information to a module descriptor in Chapter 3.

Module Source Files Structure

Let's walk through an example of organizing the source code and the compiled code for a module named com.jdojo.contact. The module contains packages for working with contact information, such as addresses and phone numbers. It contains two packages:

- com.jdojo.contact.info

- com.jdojo.contact.validator

The com.jdojo.contact.info package contains two classes—Address and Phone. The com.jdojo.contact.validator package contains one interface named Validator and two classes called AddressValidator and PhoneValidator. Figure 2-9 shows the contents of the com.jdojo.contact module.

com.jdojo.contact

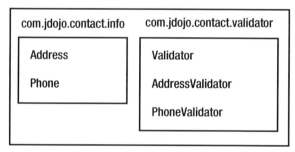

Figure 2-9. *Contents of a module named com.jdojo.contact*

In Java 9, several options have been added to the Java compiler tool, javac. It allows you to compile one module at a time or multiple modules at a time. If you want to compile multiple modules at a time, you *must* store the source code for each module under a directory, which has the same name as the name of the module. You can follow this source directory naming convention even if you have only one module.

Suppose you want to compile the source code for the com.jdojo.contact module. You can store its source code in a directory named C:\j9r\src, which contains the following files:

```
module-info.java
com\jdojo\contact\info\Address.java
com\jdojo\contact\info\Phone.java
com\jdojo\contact\validator\Validator.java
com\jdojo\contact\validator\AddressValidator.java
com\jdojo\contact\validator\PhoneValidator.java
```

Note that you need to follow the package hierarchy to store the source files for interfaces and classes as you have been doing since Java 1.0.

If you want to compile multiple modules at once, you must name the source code directory `com.jdojo.contact`, which is the same as the module's name. In this case, you might store the module's source code in a directory called `C:\j9r\src`, whose contents are as follows:

```
com.jdojo.contact\module-info.java
com.jdojo.contact\com\jdojo\contact\info\Address.java
com.jdojo.contact\com\jdojo\contact\info\Phone.java
com.jdojo.contact\com\jdojo\contact\validator\Validator.java
com.jdojo.contact\com\jdojo\contact\validator\AddressValidator.java
com.jdojo.contact\com\jdojo\contact\validator\PhoneValidator.java
```

The compiled code for the module will follow the same directory hierarchy as you saw previously.

Packaging Modules

A module's artifacts can be stored in:

- A directory
- A modular JAR file
- A JMOD file, which is a new module-packaging format introduced in JDK 9

A Module in a Directory

When the compiled code for a module is stored in a directory, the root of the directory contains the module descriptor (the `module-info.class` file) and the sub-directories mirror the package hierarchy. Continuing from the example in the previous section, suppose you store the compiled code for the `com.jdojo.contact` module in the `C:\j9r\mods\com.jdojo.contact` directory. The directory's contents would be as follows:

```
module-info.class
com\jdojo\contact\info\Address.class
com\jdojo\contact\info\Phone.class
com\jdojo\contact\validator\Validator.class
com\jdojo\contact\validator\AddressValidator.class
com\jdojo\contact\validator\PhoneValidator.class
```

A Module in a Modular JAR

The JDK ships with a `jar` tool to package Java code in a JAR (**J**ava **Ar**chive) file format. The JAR format is based on the ZIP file format. JDK 9 has enhanced the `jar` tool to package a module's code in a JAR. When a JAR contains the compiled code for a module, the JAR is called a *modular JAR*. A modular JAR contains a `module-info.class` file at the root.

Wherever you were using JARs before JDK 9, you can use modular JARs now. For example, modular JARs can be placed on the class path and, in that case, the `module-info.class` file in the modular JAR is ignored because `module-info` is not a valid class name in Java.

While packaging a modular JAR, you can use various options available in the `jar` tool, which were added in JDK 9, to add pieces of information to the module descriptor such as a module version and the main class name.

■ **Tip** A modular JAR is a JAR in all respects, except it contains a module descriptor at the root.

Typically, a non-trivial Java application consists of multiple modules. A modular JAR can contain the compiled code for only *one* module. There is a need to package all modules of an application into a single JAR to simplify shipping an application in one artifact. At the time of this writing, this is an open issue, and it's described at `http://openjdk.java.net/projects/jigsaw/spec/issues/#MultiModuleExecutableJARs`.

Continuing the example from the previous section, the modular JAR's contents for the `com.jdojo.contact` module is as follows. Note that a JAR always contains a `MANIFEST.MF` in the `META-INF` directory.

```
module-info.class
com/jdojo/contact/info/Address.class
com/jdojo/contact/info/Phone.class
com/jdojo/contact/validator/Validator.class
com/jdojo/contact/validator/AddressValidator.class
com/jdojo/contact/validator/PhoneValidator.class
META-INF/MANIFEST.MF
```

A Module in a JMOD File

JDK 9 introduced a new format, called *JMOD*, to package modules. A JMOD file uses a `.jmod` extension. JDK modules are compiled into JMOD formats and are placed in the `JDK_HOME\jmods` directory; for example, you will find a `java.base.jmod` file that contains the contents of the `java.base` module. JMOD files are supported only at compile-time and link time. They are not supported at runtime. I will explain the JMOD format in detail in Chapter 6.

Module Path

The class path mechanism to look up types has existed since the beginning of the JDK. A class path is a series of directories, JAR files, and ZIP files. When Java needs to look up a type at various phases (compile-time, runtime, during usage of tools, etc.), it uses the entries from the class path to find the type.

Java 9 types exist as part of modules. Java needs to look up modules during different phases, not types as it did prior to Java 9. Java 9 introduced a new mechanism to look up modules and it is called *module path*.

A *module path* is a sequence of path names containing modules, where a path name may be a path to a modular JAR, a JMOD file, or a directory. The path names are separated by a platform-specific path-separator character, which is a colon (:) on the UNIX-like platforms and a semicolon (;) on the Windows platform.

It is easy to understand when a path name is a modular JAR or a JMOD file. In this case, if the module descriptor in the JAR or JMOD file contains the module definition for the module being looked up, the module is found. If a path name is a directory, the following two cases exist:

- If a class file exists at the root of the directory, the directory is considered to have a module definition. The class file at the root will be interpreted as the module descriptor. All other files and sub-directories will be interpreted as part of this one module. If multiple class files exist at the root, the first found file is interpreted as the module descriptor. After a few experiments, the JDK 9 build 126 seems to pick up the first class file in alphabetically sorted order. This way of storing a module compiled code is sure to give you a headache. Therefore, avoid adding a directory to the module path if the directory contains multiple class files at root.

- If a class file does not exist at the root of the directory, the contents of the directory are interpreted differently. Each modular JAR or a JMOD file in the directory is considered a module definition. Each sub-directory, if it contains a `module-info.class` file at its root, is considered to have a module definition in exploded directory tree format. If a sub-directory does not contain a `module-info.class` file at its root, it is not interpreted as containing a module definition. Note that if a sub-directory contains a module definition, its name does not have to be the same as the module name. The module name is read from the `module-info.class` file.

The following are valid module paths on Windows:

- `C:\mods`

- `C:\mods\com.jdojo.contact.jar;C:\mods\com.jdojo.person.jar`

- `C:\lib;C:\mods\com.jdojo.contact.jar;C:\mods\com.jdojo.person.jar`

The first module path contains the path to a directory named `C:\mods`. The second module path contains paths to two modular JARs—`com.jdojo.contact.jar` and `com.jdojo.person.jar`. The third module path contains three elements—the path to a directory `C:\lib` and the paths to two modular JARs—`com.jdojo.contact.jar` and `com.jdojo.person.jar`. The equivalent of these paths on a UNIX-like platform are shown:

- `/usr/ksharan/mods`

- `/usr/ksharan/mods/com.jdojo.contact.jar:/usr/ksharan/com.jdojo.person.jar`

- `/usr/ksharan/lib:/usr/ksharan/mods/com.jdojo.contact.jar:/usr/ksharan/mods/com.jdojo.person.jar`

The best way to avoid module path problems is not to use an exploded directory as a module definition. Have two directories as the module path—one directory containing all application modular JARs and another containing all modular JARs for external libraries. For example, you can use `C:\applib;C:\extlib` as a module path on Windows where the `C:\applib` directory contains all application modular JARs and the `C:\extlib` directory contains all external libraries' modular JARs.

JDK 9 has updated all its tools to use a module path to look up modules. Those tools provide new options to specify a module path. Until JDK 9, you have seen UNIX-style options that start with a hyphen (-), for example, -cp and -classpath. With so many additional options in JDK 9, JDK designers were running out of short names for options that were also meaningful to developers. Therefore, JDK 9 started using GNU-style options where an option starts with two consecutive hyphens and the words are separated by hyphens. Here are a few examples of GNU-style command-line options:

- --class-path

- --module-path

- --module-version

- --main-class

- --print-module-descriptor

■ **Tip**   To print a list of all standard options supported by a tool, run the tool with the --help or -h option and, for all non-standard options, run the tool with the -X option. For example, the java -h and java -X commands will print a list of standard and non-standard options for the java command, respectively.

Most of the tools in JDK 9, such as javac, java, and jar, support two options to specify a module path on the command line. They are -p and --module-path. The existing UNIX-style options will continue to be supported for backward compatibility. The following two commands show you how to use the two options for specifying the module path for the java tool:

```
// Using the GNU-style option
C:\>java --module-path C:\applib;C:\lib other-args-go-here

// Using the UNIX-style option
C:\>java -p C:\applib;C:\extlib other-args-go-here
```

I use the GNU-style option, --module-path, to specify the module path in all the examples in this book. When you use the GNU-style option, you can specify the value for the option in one of two forms:

- --<name> <value>

- --<name>=<value

The previous command can also be written as follows:

```
// Using the GNU-style option
C:\>java --module-path=C:\applib;C:\lib other-args-go-here
```

When using spaces as name-value separators, you need to use at least one space. When you are using a = as a separator, you must not include any spaces around it. The option --module-path=C:\applib is valid. The option --module-path =C:\applib is invalid because =C:\applib will be interpreted as a module path, which is an invalid path.

Observable Modules

During the module lookup process, the module system uses different types of module paths to locate modules. The set of modules found on the module paths together with system modules are known as *observable modules*. You can think of observable modules as a set of all the modules available to the module system in a specific phase, for example, compile-time, link time, and runtime, or available to a tool.

JDK 9 added a new option named `--list-modules` for the java command. The option can be used to print two types of information: the list of observable modules and a description of one or more modules. The option can be used in two forms:

- `--list-modules`

- `--list-modules <module1>,<module2>...`

In the first form, the option is not followed with any module names. It prints the list of observable modules. In the second form, the option is followed with a comma-separated list of module names, which prints the module descriptors for the specified modules.

The following command prints the list of observable modules, which includes only the system modules:

```
c:\Java9Revealed> java --list-modules
```

```
java.base@9-ea
java.se.ee@9-ea
java.sql@9-ea
javafx.base@9-ea
javafx.controls@9-ea
jdk.jshell@9-ea
jdk.unsupported@9-ea
...
```

The output shown is partial. Each entry in the output contains two parts—a module name and a version string separated by an @ sign. The first part is the module name and the second part is the version string of the module. For example, in `java.base@9-ea`, `java.base` is the module name and `9-ea` is the version string. In the version string, the number 9 stands for JDK 9 and ea stands for *early access*. You may get a different output for version strings when you run the command.

I placed three modular JARs in my `C:\Java9Revealed\lib` directory. If I provide `C:\Java9Revealed\lib` as the module path to the java command, those modules will be included in the list of observable modules. The following command shows how the list of observable modules changes when you specify a module path. Here, `lib` is a relative path and `C:\Java9Revealed` is the current directory.

```
C:\Java9Revealed>java --module-path lib --list-modules
```

```
claim (file:///C:/Java9Revealed/lib/claim.jar)
policy (file:///C:/Java9Revealed/lib/policy.jar)
java.base@9-ea
java.xml@9-ea
javafx.base@9-ea
jdk.unsupported@9-ea
jdk.zipfs@9-ea
...
```

Note that, for application modules, the `--list-modules` option also prints their location. This information is helpful in troubleshooting when you are getting unexpected results and you do not know which modules are being used and from which locations.

The following command specifies the `com.jdojo.intro` module as an argument to the `--list-modules` option to print the module's description:

```
C:\Java9Revealed>java --module-path lib --list-modules claim
```

```
module claim (file:///C:/Java9Revealed/lib/claim.jar)
  exports com.jdojo.claim
  requires java.sql (@9-ea)
  requires mandated java.base (@9-ea)
  contains pkg3
```

The first line of the output contains the module name and the modular JAR location containing the module. The second line indicates that the module exports the `com.jdojo.claim` module. The third line indicates that the module requires the `java.sql` module. The fourth line indicates that the module depends on the mandated `java.base` module. Recall that every module, except the `java.base` module, depends on the `java.base` module. You will see the `requires mandated java.base` line in every module's description, except for the `java.base` module. The fifth line states that the module contains a package named pkg3, which is neither exported nor opened.

You can also print the description of system modules, for example, `java.base` and `java.sql`, using the `--list-modules`. The following command prints the description of the `java.sql` module.

```
C:\Java9Revealed>java --list-modules java.sql
```

```
module java.sql@9-ea
  exports java.sql
  exports javax.sql
  exports javax.transaction.xa
  requires transitive java.xml
  requires mandated java.base
  requires transitive java.logging
  uses java.sql.Driver
```

Summary

Packages in Java have been used as containers for types. An application consisted of several JARs placed on the class path. Packages acted as containers for types without enforcing any accessibility boundaries. Accessibility of a type was embedded in the type declaration using modifiers. If a package contained internal implementations, there was no way to prevent other parts of the program from accessing the internal implementations. The class path mechanism searched for a type linearly when the type was used. This lead to another issues of receiving errors at runtime when types are missing from the deployed JARs—sometimes long after the application was deployed. These problems can be categorized into two types: encapsulation and configuration.

JDK 9 introduced the module system. It provides a way to arrange Java programs. It has two main goals: *strong encapsulation* and *reliable configuration*. Using the module system, an application consists of modules, which are named collections of code and data. A module controls—through its declaration— the parts of the module that can be accessed by other modules. A module that accesses parts of another module must declare dependence to the second module. The two aspects—controlling access and declaring dependence—are the basis of achieving the goal of strong encapsulation. A module's dependency is resolved at startup. In JDK 9, if a module depends on another module and the second module is missing when you run your application, you will receive an error at startup rather than sometime after the application is running. This is the basis for reliable configuration.

A module is defined using a module declaration. The source code for a module is typically stored in a file named `module-info.java`. A module is compiled into a class file, which is typically named `module-info.class`. The compiled module declaration is called a *module descriptor*. A module declaration does not allow you to specify a module version. Tools such as the `jar` tool that packages a module into a JAR can add the module version to the module descriptor.

A module is declared using the `module` keyword, which is followed by the module name. A module declaration can use five types of module statements: `exports`, `opens`, `requires`, `uses`, and `provides`. An `exports` statement exports the specified package of the module to all modules or a list of named modules at compile-time and runtime. An `opens` statement grants reflective access to the specified package to all modules or a list of specified modules at runtime. Other modules can access all types in the specified package and all members (private and public) of those types using reflection. The `uses` and `provides` module statements are used to configure a module to discover service implementations and provide service implementations of a specific service interface.

As of JDK 9, `open`, `module`, `requires`, `transitive`, `exports`, `opens`, `to`, `uses`, `provides`, and `with` are restricted keywords. They have special meaning only when they appear in module declarations at specific positions.

A module's source code and compiled code are arranged in a directory, a JAR file, or a JMOD file. In a directory and a JAR file, the `module-info.class` file is located at the root.

Similar to the class path, JDK 9 introduced the module path. However, they differ in the way they are used. The class path is used to search a type's definition whereas the module path is used to locate modules, not a specific type in the module. Java tools such as `java` and `javac` have been updated to use module paths as well as class paths. You can specify the module path to these tools using the `--module-path` or `-p` option.

JDK 9 introduced GNU-style options to be used with tools. The options start with two dashes and each word is separated by a dash, for example, `--module-path`, `--class-path`, `--list-modules`, etc. If an option accepts a value, the value can follow the option after a space or a =. The following two options are the same:

- `--module-path C:\lib`
- `--module-path=C:\lib`

The list of modules available to the module system in a phase (compile-time, runtime, tools, etc.) is known as observable modules. You can use the `--list-modules` options with the `java` command to list the observable modules available at runtime. You can also use this option to print the description of a module.

CHAPTER 3

▨ ▨ ▨

Creating Your First Module

In this chapter, you will learn:

- How to write modular Java programs

- How to compile modular programs

- How to package the artifacts of a module into a modular JAR file

- How to run a modular program

In this chapter, I explain how to work with a module—from writing the source code to compiling, packaging, and running the program. This chapter is divided into two parts. The first part shows you all the steps to write and run a module program using the command line. The second part repeats the same steps using the NetBeans IDE.

At the time of this writing, the NetBeans IDE is still under development and it does not support all JDK 9 features. For example, currently you need to create a new Java project in NetBeans for every module you create. In its final release, NetBeans will allow you to have multiple modules in one Java project. I cover more specific JDK 9 options when I use the command prompt than when using the NetBeans IDE.

The program explained in this chapter is very simple. When the program is run, it prints a message and the name of the module to which the main class belongs.

Using the Command Prompt

The following sub-sections describe the steps to create and run your first module using the command prompt.

Setting Up the Directories

You will use the following directory hierarchy to write, compile, package, and run the source code:

- `C:\Java9Revealed`

- `C:\Java9Revealed\lib`

- `C:\Java9Revealed\mods`

- `C:\Java9Revealed\src`

- `C:\Java9Revealed\src\com.jdojo.intro`

© Kishori Sharan 2017
K. Sharan, *Java 9 Revealed*, DOI 10.1007/978-1-4842-2592-9_3

These directories are set up on Windows. On a non-Windows operating system, you can set up a similar directory hierarchy. C:\Java9Revealed is the top-level directory and it contains three sub-directories: lib, mods, and src.

The src directory is used to store the source code, which contains a sub-directory named com.jdojo.intro. I have named the sub-directory com.jdojo.intro because I want to create a module named com.jdojo.intro and store its source code under this sub-directory. Is it necessary, in this case, to name the sub-directory as com.jdojo.intro? The answer is no. I could have named the sub-directory differently or I could have stored the source directly in the src directory without having the com.jdojo.intro sub-directory. However, it is good practice to name the directory to store a module's source code the same as the module name. The Java compiler has options that will help you compile the source code for multiple modules in one shot if you follow this naming convention.

You will use the mods directory to store the compiled code in an exploded directory hierarchy. If you want, you will be able to run the program using the code in this directory.

After compiling the source code, you will package it into a modular JAR and store it in the lib directory. You can use the modular JAR to run the program or you can ship the module JAR to other developers who can run the program.

In the remaining part of this section, I use a relative path to a directory such as src or src\com.jdojo. intro. Those relative paths are relative to the C:\Java9Revealed directory. For example, src means C:\Java9Revealed\src. If you are using a non-Windows operating system or following another directory hierarchy, please make the appropriate adjustments.

Writing the Source Code

You can use a text editor of your choice, e.g., Notepad on Windows, to write the source code. Let's start by creating a module named com.jdojo.intro. Listing 3-1 contains the module declaration.

Listing 3-1. The Declaration of a Module Named com.jdojo.intro

```
// module-info.java
module com.jdojo.intro {
    // No module statements
}
```

The module declaration is simple. It contains no module statements. Save it in a file named module-info.java in the src\com.jdojo.intro directory.

You will create a class named Welcome, which will be stored in the com.jdojo.intro package. Note that you are giving the package the same name as the module. Do you have to keep the module and package names the same? The answer is no. You can choose any other package name you want. The class will have a method whose signature will be public status void main(String[]). This method will serve as the entry point for the application. You will print the message inside this method.

You want to print the name of the module of which the Welcome class is a member. JDK 9 added a class called Module in the java.lang package. An instance of the Module class represents a module. Every Java type in JDK 9 is a member of a module, even the primitive types such as int, long, and char. All primitive types are members of the java.base module. The Class class in JDK 9 has a new method named getModule() that returns the module reference that the class is a member of. The following snippet of code prints the module name of the Welcome class.

```
Class<Welcome> cls = Welcome.class;
Module mod = cls.getModule();
String moduleName = mod.getName();
System.out.format("Module Name: %s%n", moduleName);
```

You can replace the four statements with one statement:

```
System.out.format("Module Name: %s%n",
                  Welcome.class.getModule().getName());
```

■ **Tip** All primitive data types are members of the `java.base` module. You can use `int.class.getModule()` to get the reference of the module of the `int` primitive data type.

Listing 3-2 contains the complete source code for the `Welcome` class. Save the source code in a file named `Welcome.java` in a directory `com\jdojo\intro`, which would be a sub-directory of the `src\com.jdojo.intro` directory. At this point, the paths for your source code files will look like this:

- `C:\Java9Revealed\src\com.jdojo.intro\module-info.java`

- `C:\Java9Revealed\src\com.jdojo.intro\com\jdojo\intro\Welcome.java`

Listing 3-2. The Source Code for the Welcome Class

```
// Welcome.java
package com.jdojo.intro;

public class Welcome {
    public static void main(String[] args) {
        System.out.println("Welcome to the Module System.");

        // Print the module name of the Welcome class
        Class<Welcome> cls = Welcome.class;
        Module mod = cls.getModule();
        String moduleName = mod.getName();
        System.out.format("Module Name: %s%n", moduleName);
    }
}
```

Compiling the Source Code

You will use the Java compiler, the `javac` command, to compile the source code and save the compiled code in the `C:\java9Revealed\mods` directory. The `javac` command is in the `JDK_HOME\bin` directory. The following command compiles the source code. The command is entered in one line, not three:

```
C:\Java9Revealed>javac -d mods --module-source-path src
 src\com.jdojo.intro\module-info.java
 src\com.jdojo.intro\com\jdojo\intro\Welcome.java
```

Notice that `C:\Java9Revealed` is the current directory when this command is run. The `-d mods` option tells the Java compiler to store all compiled class files into the `mods` directory. Note that you are running the command from the `C:\java9revealed` directory, so the `mods` directory in the command means the `C:\Java9Revealed\mods` directory. If you want, you can replace this option with `-d C:\Java9Revealed\mods`.

The second option, `--module-source-path src`, specifies that the sub-directories of the `src` directory contain the source code for multiple modules, where each sub-directory name is the same as the module name for which the sub-directory contains the source files. This option has a few implications:

- Under the `src` directory, you must store a module's source file under a sub-directory, which must be named the same as the module.

- The Java compiler will mirror the directory structure under the `src` directory while storing the generated class files in the `mods` directory. That is, all generated class files for the `com.jdojo.intro` module will be stored in the `mods\com.jdojo.intro` directory mirroring the package hierarchy.

- If you do not specify this option, the generated class files will be placed directly under the `mods` directory.

The last two arguments of the `javac` command are the source files—one for the module declaration and one for the `Welcome` class declaration. If the `javac` command runs successfully, the following two class files are generated under the `C:\Java9Revealed\mods\com.jdojo.intro` directory:

- `module-info.class`

- `com\jdojo\intro\Welcome.class`

You are done compiling the source code.

The following command compiles the source for the `com.jdojo.intro` module using the old style that existed before JDK 9. It uses only the `-d` option, which specifies where to place the compiled class files.

```
C:\Java9Revealed>javac -d mods\com.jdojo.intro
    src\com.jdojo.intro\module-info.java
    src\com.jdojo.intro\com\jdojo\intro\Welcome.java
```

The output of the following command is the same as the previous command. However, it will not work if you want to compile multiple modules' source code in one command and place the compiled code in module-specific directories.

Using the `--module-version` option for `javac`, you can specify a version of the module being compiled. The module version is stored in the `module-info.class` file. The following command produces the same set of compiled files as the previous command, except it stores 1.0 as the module version in the `module-info.class` file:

```
C:\Java9Revealed>javac -d mods\com.jdojo.intro
  --module-version 1.0
  src\com.jdojo.intro\module-info.java
  src\com.jdojo.intro\com\jdojo\intro\Welcome.java
```

How do you confirm that the `javac` command stored the module version in the `module-info.class` file? You can use the `javap` command to dissemble Java class files. If you specify the path to a `module-info.class` file, the `javap` command prints the module's definition, which contains the module's version, if present, after the module name. The printed module name is in the form moduleName@moduleVersion, if the module version is present. Run the following command to verify the recorded module name by the previous command:

```
C:\Java9Revealed>javap mods\com.jdojo.intro\module-info.class
```

```
Compiled from "module-info.java"
module com.jdojo.intro@1.0 {
  requires java.base;
}
```

The jar tool has been enhanced in JDK 9. It lets you specify the module version when you create a modular JAR. In the next section, I show you how to specify a module version using the jar tool.

If you want to compile multiple modules, you will need to specify each source file as an argument to the javac command. This is a lot of typing. I will give you a shortcut command for Windows and UNIX to compile all the modules in one go. Use the following command on one line in Windows:

```
C:\Java9Revealed>FOR /F "tokens=1 delims=" %A in ('dir src\*.java /S /B') do javac -d mods
--module-source-path src %A
```

The command loops through all .java files under the src directory and compiles them one at a time. I could not find a command in Windows that can pass all source files to the javac command in one go. You may need to adjust the directory names in the command according to your directory structure. If you are following this example's directory structure, this command will work for you. If you save the command in a batch file and run the batch file to compile all source files, you need to replace a %A with a %%A.

The UNIX equivalent of this command is:

```
$ javac -d mods --module-source-path src $(find src -name "*.java")
```

Packaging the Module Code

Let's package the module's compiled code into a modular JAR. You will need to use the jar tool, which is located in the JDK_HOME\bin directory. The following command will do the job. The command is entered in one line, not in multiple lines. I broke the command into several lines for clarity. Note that the last part of the command is a dot, which means the current directory.

```
C:\Java9Revealed>jar --create
 --file lib/com.jdojo.intro-1.0.jar
 --main-class com.jdojo.intro.Welcome
 --module-version 1.0
 -C mods/com.jdojo.intro .
```

This command uses several options:

- The --create option indicates that you want to create a new modular JAR.

- The --file option is used to specify the location and the name of the new modular JAR. You are storing the new modular JAR in the lib directory and its name would be com.jdojo.intro-1.0.jar. I included the version number as 1.0 in the name of the modular JAR.

- The --main-class option specifies the fully qualified name of the class having the public static void main(String[]) method as the entry point for the application. When you specify this option, the jar tool will add an attribute in the module-info.class file whose value will be the name of the specified class. The jar tool also uses this option to add a Main-Class attribute to the MANIFEST.MF file.

35

- The --module-version option specifies the version of the module as 1.0. The jar tool will record this information in the attribute of the module-info.class file. Note that specifying the module version as 1.0 is not going to affect the name of the modular JAR. The 1.0 is included to indicate its version for the reader of the filename. The actual version of the module is specified by this option.

- The -C option is used to specify the directory that will be used as the current directory when the jar command is executed. The mods\com.jdojo.intro directory is specified as the current directory for the jar tool. This will make the jar tool read all the files to be included in the modular JAR from this directory.

- The last part of the command is a dot (.), which means that the jar tool needs to include all files and directories from the current directory mods\com.jdojo.intro. Note that this argument and the -C option work in tandem. If you do not provide the -C option, this dot is interpreted as the C:\Java9Revealed directory, which is the directory from which you are running the command.

When the command runs successfully, it creates the following file:

```
C:\Java9Revealed\lib\com.jdojo.intro-1.0.jar
```

To make sure that your modular JAR contains the definition of the com.jdojo.intro module, run the following command. The command is entered on one line.

```
C:\Java9Revealed>java --module-path lib --list-modules com.jdojo.intro
```

The command specifies the module path as the lib directory, which means that the lib directory will be used to search for application modules. You pass com.jdojo.intro as the module name to the --list-modules option, which will print the module description along with the module's location. If you get an output similar to the following, your modular JAR was created correctly:

```
module com.jdojo.intro@1.0 (file:///C:/Java9Revealed/lib/com.jdojo.intro-1.0.jar)
  requires mandated java.base (@9-ea)
  contains com.jdojo.intro
```

If you have trouble understanding this output, refer to Chapter 2, where I explain in detail how to list the observable modules and descriptions of a module using the --list-modules option of the java command.

Running the Program

You use the java command to run a Java program. The syntax is as follows:

```
java --module-path <module-path> --module <module>/<main-class>
```

Here, <module-path> is the module path used to locate modules. The --module option specifies the module to be run along with its main class. If your modular JAR contains the main-class attribute, you can specify only the <module> part and <main-class> will be read from the modular JAR.

░ **Tip** You can use the shorter versions -p and -m for the --module-path and --module options, respectively.

The following command will run the com.jdojo.intro.Welcome class in the com.jdojo.intro module. It is assumed that your current directory is C:\Java9Revealed and you have the modular JAR for the module located at C:\java9Revealed\lib\com.jdojo.intro-1.0.jar.

```
C:\Java9Revealed>java --module-path lib
 --module com.jdojo.intro/com.jdojo.intro.Welcome
```

```
Welcome to the Module System.
Module Name: com.jdojo.intro
```

The output indicates that the program was correctly executed. If you specify the main class while packaging the module code into a modular JAR, you can omit the main class name from the command. You had specified the com.jdojo.intro.Welcome class as the main class for this module, so the following command does the same job as the previous one:

```
C:\Java9Revealed>java --module-path lib --module com.jdojo.intro
```

```
Welcome to the Module System.
Module Name: com.jdojo.intro
```

You can also specify an exploded directory containing a module's code as the module path. Recall that you had compiled the module code into the mods directory. The following command works the same:

```
C:\Java9Revealed>java --module-path mods
 --module com.jdojo.intro/com.jdojo.intro.Welcome
```

```
Welcome to the Module System.
Module Name: com.jdojo.intro
```

Let's try running the module from the mods directory using only the module name:

```
C:\Java9Revealed>java --module-path mods --module com.jdojo.intro
```

```
module com.jdojo.intro does not have a MainClass attribute, use -m <module>/<main-class>
```

Oops! You received an error. The error message indicates that the module-info.class found in the mods\com.jdojo.intro directory does not contain the main class name. That is true. When you declare a module, you cannot specify a main method or a version in the module declaration. When you compile a module, you can specify only module version. You can specify the module's main class and its version when you package it using the jar tool. The module-info.class file in the lib\com.jdojo.intro-1.0.jar contains the main class name, whereas the module-info.class file in the mods\com.jdojo.intro directory does not. If you want to run a module whose compiled code is in an exploded directory, you must specify the main class name along with the module name.

The JDK also provides another option called -jar to run a main class from a JAR file. Let's use the following command to run this module:

```
C:\Java9Revealed>java -jar lib\com.jdojo.intro-1.0.jar
```

```
Welcome to the Module System.
Module Name: null
```

Oops! It seems that only the first line in the output is correct and the second line is incorrect. It found the main class and executed the code in its main() method. It printed the message correctly, but the module name is null. You know that you were able to run the module in previous commands, except the last one.

You need to understand the behavior of the java command in JDK 9. The -jar option existed before JDK 9. In JDK 9, a type can be loaded as part of a module via a module path or via a class path. If a type is loaded via a class path, the type becomes a member of a module called an *unnamed* module. The type loses its membership from its original module, even though the type is loaded from a modular JAR. In fact, if a modular JAR is placed on the class path, it is treated as a JAR (not a modular JAR), ignoring its module-info. class file. Every application class loader has an unnamed module. All types loaded by a class loader from the class path are members of that class loader's unnamed module. An unnamed module is also represented as an instance of the Module class whose getName() method returns null.

In the previous command, the modular JAR com.jdojo.intro-1.0.jar was treated as a JAR and all types defined in it—we have only one, the Welcome class—were loaded as part of the unnamed module of the class loader. This is the reason why you get the module name as null in the output. How did the java command find the main class name? Recall that when you specify the main class name to the jar tool, the tool stores the main class name at two places:

- In the module-info.class file

- In the META-INF/MANIFEST.MF file

This command reads the name of the main class from the META-INF/MANIFEST.MF file.

You can also use the java command with the --class-path option to run the Welcome class. You can place the lib\com.jdojo.intro-1.0.jar modular on the class path and in that case it will be treated as a JAR and the Welcome class will be loaded in the unnamed module of the application class loader. You were used to run a class this way before JDK 9. The following command does the job:

```
C:\Java9Revealed>java --class-path lib\com.jdojo.intro-1.0.jar
  com.jdojo.intro.Welcome
```

```
Welcome to the Module System.
Module Name: null
```

Using the NetBeans IDE

If you followed the previous sections on creating your first module using a command prompt, this section will be much easier to follow. In this section, I go through the steps to create your first module using the NetBeans IDE. Refer to Chapter 1 on how to install the NetBeans IDE that supports JDK 9 development. From now onward, I will use NetBeans to write, program, compile, package, and run all programs.

Configuring the IDE

Start the NetBeans IDE. If you open the IDE for the first time, it shows a pane titled Start Page, as shown in Figure 3-1. If you do not want this to show again, you can uncheck the checkbox labeled Show On Startup, which is on the upper-right corner of the pane. You can close the Start Page pane by clicking the X in the pane's header.

Figure 3-1. *The initial NetBeans IDE screen*

Select Tools ➤ Java Platforms to display the Java Platform Manager dialog box, as shown on in Figure 3-2. I am running the NetBeans IDE on JDK 1.8, which is shown in the Platforms list. If you are running it on JDK 9, the JDK 9 will be shown in the Platforms list and you do not need any further configuration; you can skip to the next section.

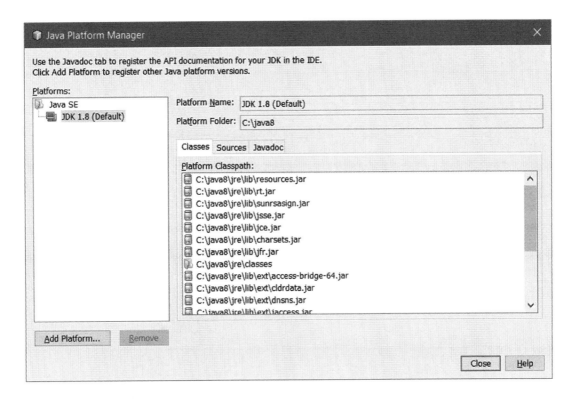

Figure 3-2. The Java Platform Manager dialog box

If you see JDK 9 in the Platforms list, your IDE has been configured to use JDK 9 and you can close the dialog box by clicking the Close button. If you do not see JDK 9 in the Platforms list, click the Add Platform button to open the Add Java Platform dialog box, as shown on in Figure 3-3. Make sure that the Java Standard Edition radio button is selected. Click the Next button to display the platform folders, as shown in Figure 3-4.

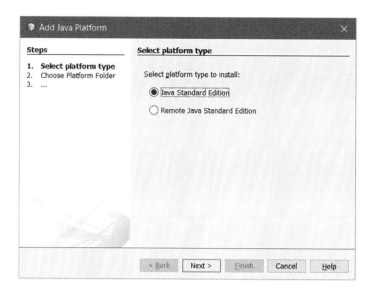

Figure 3-3. Select the platform type

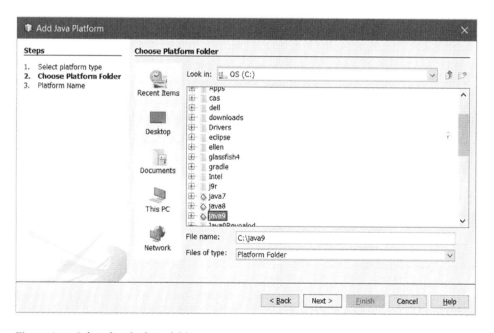

Figure 3-4. Select the platform folder

From the Add Java Platform dialog box, select the directory in which the JDK 9 is installed. I installed the JDK 9 in C:\java9, so I selected the C:\java9 directory. Click the Next button. The Add Java Platform dialog box, as shown in Figure 3-5, is displayed. The Platform Name and Platform Sources fields are prefilled.

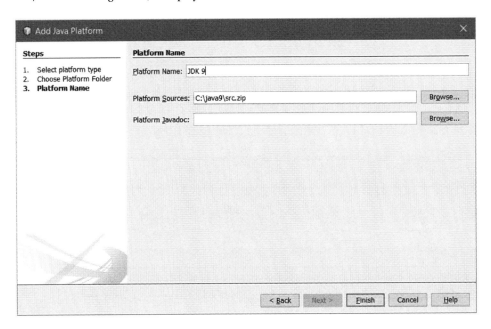

Figure 3-5. *The Add Java Platform dialog box*

Click the Finish button, which will bring you back to the Java Platform Manager dialog box showing JDK 9 as an item in the Platforms list as shown in Figure 3-6. Click the Close button to close the dialog box. You are done with configuring the NetBeans IDE to use JDK 9.

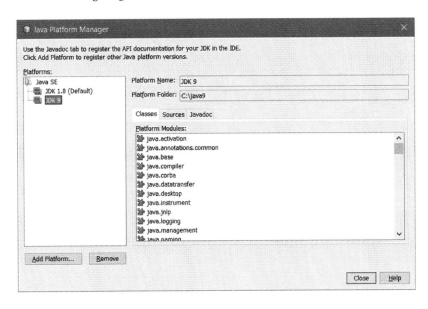

Figure 3-6. *The Java Platform Manager showing JDK 1.8 and JDK 9 as Java platforms*

Creating the Java Project

Select File ➤ New Project or press Ctrl+Shift+N to open a New Project dialog box, as shown in Figure 3-7. Make sure Java is selected in the Categories list and Java Application is selected in the Projects list. Click the Next button to open the New Java Application dialog box, as shown in Figure 3-8.

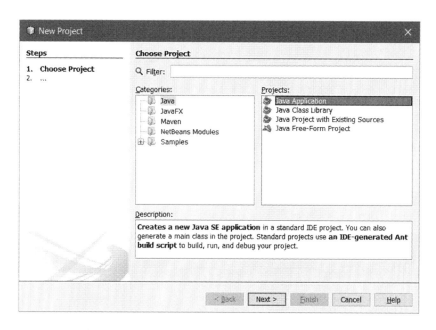

Figure 3-7. *The New Project dialog box*

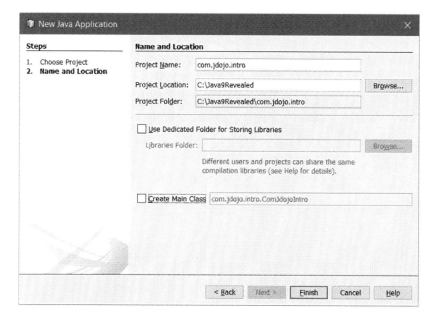

Figure 3-8. *The New Java Application dialog box*

Fill out the following pieces of information in the New Java Application dialog box:

- Enter com.jdojo.intro as the project name.

- Enter C:\Java9Revealed as the project location. You can enter any other location of your choice. This is the directory where the NetBeans project will be created.

- Leave the Use Dedicated Folder for Storing Libraries checkbox unchecked.

- Make sure the Create Main Class checkbox is unchecked.

Click the Finish button to finish creating the new Java project. Figure 3-9 shows the NetBeans IDE.

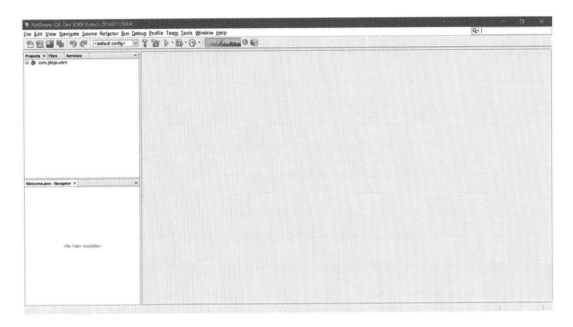

Figure 3-9. *The NetBeans IDE after creating the new Java project*

When you create a Java project, NetBeans creates a standard set of directories. You have created the com.jdojo.intro NetBeans project in the C:\Java9Revealed directory. NetBeans will create sub-directories to store the source files, compiled class files, and the modular JAR. It will also create setup directories and files for the project itself. The following sub-directories will be created to store source code, compiled code, and the modular JAR:

```
C:\Java9Revealed
    com.jdojo.intro
        build
            classes
        dist
        src
```

The com.jdojo.intro directory stores all types of files for this project. It is named after the NetBeans project name. The src directory is used to store all source code. The build directory stores all generated and compiled code. All compiled code for the project will be stored in the build\classes directory. The dist directory stores the modular JAR. Note that the build and dist directories are created by NetBeans when you add a class to the project, not at the time you create a project without adding a main class.

Setting the Project Properties

Your com.jdojo.intro project is still set to use the JDK 1.8. You need to change it to use the JDK 9. Select the project com.jdojo.intro in the Projects tab and right-click. Select the Properties menu item as shown in Figure 3-10. The Project Properties – com.jdojo.intro dialog box is displayed, as shown in Figure 3-11.

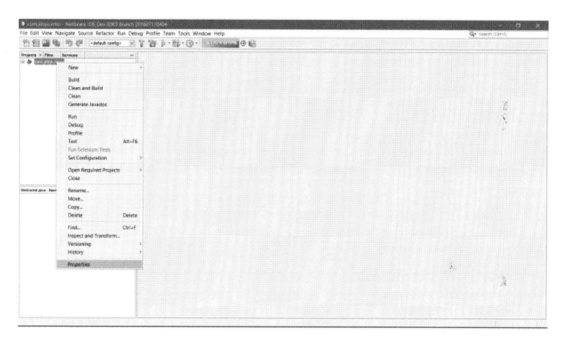

Figure 3-10. *Opening the Project Properties dialog box*

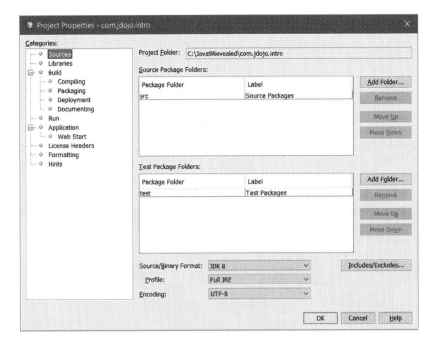

Figure 3-11. *The Project Properties – com.jdojo.intro dialog box*

Select the Libraries item from the Categories list. Select JDK 9 from the Java Platform drop-down list, as shown in Figure 3-12.

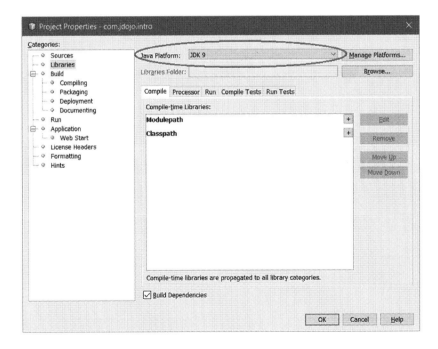

Figure 3-12. *Selecting JDK 9 as the Java platform for your project*

Select the Sources item from the Categories list. Select JDK 9 from the Source/Binary Format drop-down list, as shown in Figure 3-13.

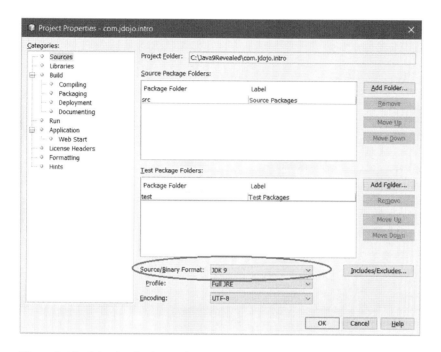

Figure 3-13. *Selecting the Source/Binary Format as JDK 9*

Click the OK button. You are done setting the JDK 9 as the Java platform and Source/Binary format for your com.jdojo.intro project.

Adding the Module Declaration

In this section, I show you how to define a module named com.jdojo.intro in your NetBeans project. To add a module definition, you need to add a file named module-info.java to the project. Right-click on the project node and select New from the menu, as shown in Figure 3-14. If you see a Java Module Info menu item, select that. Otherwise, select Other, which will display the New File dialog box, as shown in Figure 3-15.

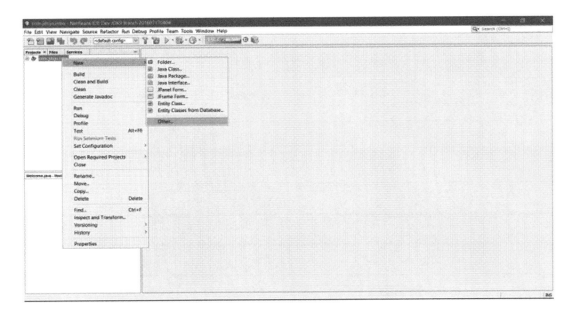

Figure 3-14. *Adding a module definition to a project*

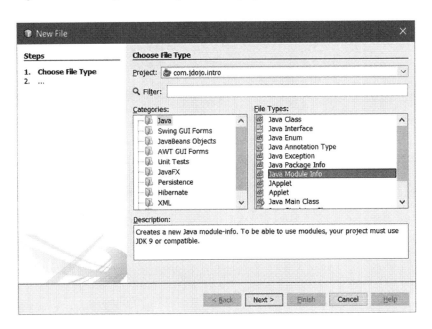

Figure 3-15. *The New File dialog box to add Java module info*

Select Java from the Categories list and Java Module Info from the File Types list. Click the Next button, which will display the New Java Module Info dialog box. Click the Finish button to finish creating the module's definition. A `module-info.java` file containing the module declaration is added to your project, as shown in Figure 3-16. The `module-info.java` file is added to the root of the source code directory and in the Projects file tree it is shown under the `<default-package>` item.

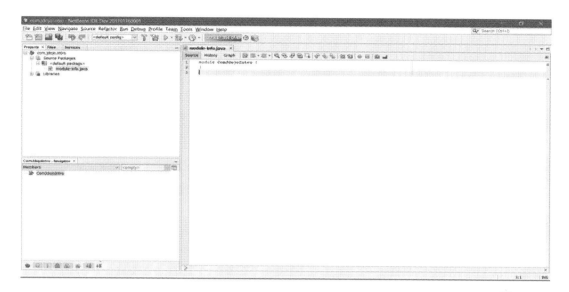

Figure 3-16. *The module-info.java file opened in the Editor*

The name of the module given by NetBeans is, by default, the same as the name of the project. The dots are removed and the initial letter of each part of the name is now in uppercase. Recall that you had given com.jdojo.intro as the project name and this is why the module name in the module-info.java file is ComJdojoIntro. Change the module name to com.jdojo.intro, as shown in Figure 3-17. Listing 3-1 contains the module declaration, which is practically the same when you used the command prompt in the previous section.

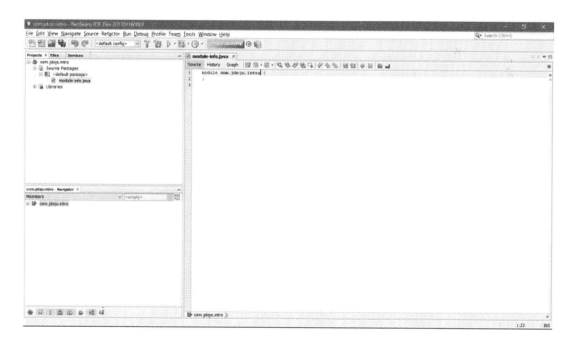

Figure 3-17. *The module-info.java file with com.jdojo.intro as the module name*

Viewing Module Graph

The NetBeans IDE lets you view a module graph. Open the module-info.java file for a module in the Editor and select the Graph tab in the Editor to view the module graph. The module graph for the com.jdojo.intro module is shown in Figure 3-18.

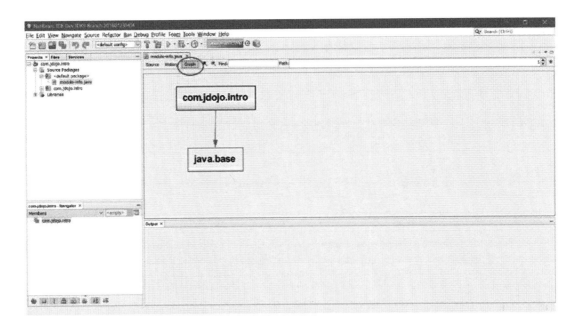

Figure 3-18. *The module graph for the com.jdojo.intro module*

You can zoom in and zoom out the module graph, change its layout, and save it as an image. Right-click in the graph area for these graph-related options. You can select a node in the graph to view only dependencies edges ending with or going from the node. You can also rearrange the module graph by moving the nodes around.

You can select the Source tab in the Editor when the module-info.java file is open to edit the source code of the module declaration.

Writing the Source Code

In this section, you will add a Welcome class to the com.jdojo.intro project. The class will reside in the com.jdojo.intro package. From the right-click menu of the project node, select New ➤ Java Class, which will open the New Java Class dialog box, as shown in Figure 3-19. Enter Welcome as the Class Name and com.jdojo.intro as the Package. Click the Finish button to close the dialog box.

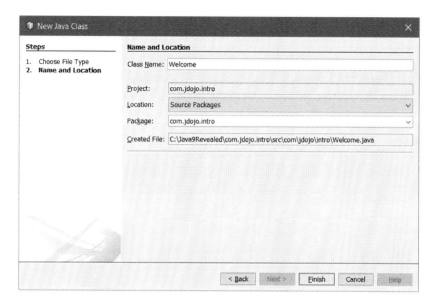

Figure 3-19. *Adding a Welcome class to the project*

Listing 3-2 contains the complete code for the Welcome class, which is the same when you were using a command prompt in the previous section. In NetBeans, replace the IDE-generated code of the Welcome class with the code in Listing 3-2. Figure 3-20 shows the source code for the Welcome class in the Editor.

Figure 3-20. *The source code for the Welcome class in the Editor*

Compiling the Source Code

When you are using the NetBeans IDE, your Java source files are compiled automatically when you save them. You can save source files by choosing File ➤ Save or by pressing Ctrl+S. You can turn off the Save on Compile feature for your project on the Project Properties page by unselecting the Compile on Save checkbox, as shown in Figure 3-21. By default, this checkbox is selected. You can access this dialog box by right-clicking on the project node and selecting Properties and then selecting Categories ➤ Build ➤ Compiling.

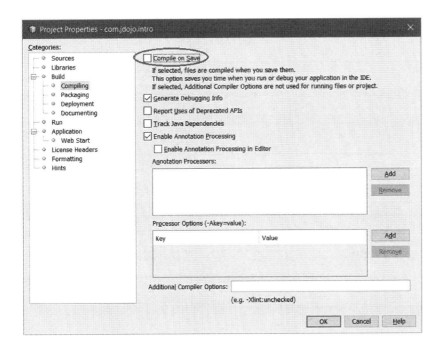

Figure 3-21. *Configuring the Compile on Save default option in NetBeans*

If you have turned off the Compile on Save feature for your project, you need to compile the source files manually by building your project. You can build a project choosing Run ➤ Build Project or by pressing F11. It is suggested that you keep the Compile On Save featured turned on.

Packaging the Module Code

You need to build your project to create a modular JAR for your module. Choose Run ➤ Build Project or press F11 to build your project. The modular JAR for your module is created in the `<project-directory>\`dist directory. The modular JAR is named after the NetBeans project name. The modular JAR for the `com.jdojo.intro` module will be at `C:\Java9Revealed\com.jdojo.intro\dist\com.jdojo.intro.jar`.

At the time of this writing, NetBeans does not provide support for adding the main class name and the module version name in the modular JAR. You can update the module's information in the modular JAR using the `jar` command-line tool. Use the `--update` option as shown. The command is entered in one line. It's shown here on multiple lines for clarity.

```
C:\Java9Revealed>jar --update
  --file com.jdojo.intro\dist\com.jdojo.intro.jar
  --module-version 1.0
  --main-class com.jdojo.intro.Welcome
```

You can verify that the modular JAR for com.jdojo.intro has been updated correctly using the
following command. You should get output similar to this:

```
C:\Java9Revealed>java --module-path com.jdojo.intro\dist
  --list-modules com.jdojo.intro
```

```
module com.jdojo.intro@1.0 (file:///C:/Java9Revealed/com.jdojo.intro/dist/com.jdojo.intro.jar)
  requires mandated java.base (@9-ea)
  contains com.jdojo.intro
```

Note that every time you build the project in the NetBeans IDE, the IDE will recreate the com.jdojo.
intro.jar file in the C:\Java9Revealed\com.jdojo.intro\dist directory. I showed you these command
to update the modular JAR file to include the main-class name and the module version as an example. The
final version of the NetBeans IDE, which will be released close to the same time as JDK 9, should let you add
these properties through the IDE.

Running the Program

Choose Run ➤ Run Project or press F6 to run your program. If you get the Run Project dialog box, as shown
in Figure 3-22, your project is not configured to run.

Figure 3-22. *The Run Project dialog box*

You have two options to run your program when your project is not configured to run:

- You can run a class that contains a main method. Note that when you are learning, several classes in your project may have a main method and you may want to use this option.

- You can configure your project to run. Use this option when you have only one class in your project that contains a main method.

To run a class, right-click the source file (the `.java` file) for the class that contains the `main()` method in the Projects tab inside the NetBeans IDE and select Run File or select the class file and press Shift+F6. To run the `Welcome` class, select the `Welcome.java` file and run it. The program output will be printed in the output pane, as shown in Figure 3-23.

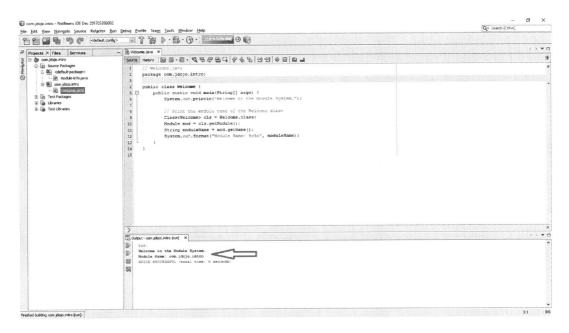

Figure 3-23. *Running the Welcome.java file*

To configure to run the project, right-click the project and select Properties. From the Project Properties dialog box, select the Run node in the Categories list. Enter `com.jdojo.intro.Welcome` as the value for the Main Class (see Figure 3-24). Click OK to close the dialog box.

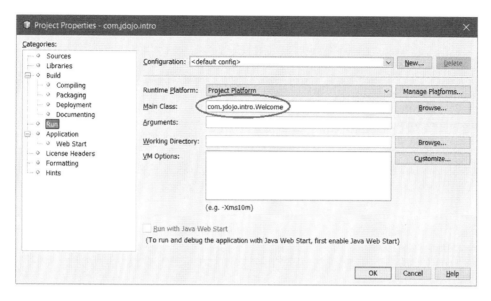

Figure 3-24. *Configuring your NetBeans project to run*

Once your project is configured to run, you can select Run ➤ Run Project or press F6 to run your project. Running your project will run the main class you have specified in the project's run configuration.

Summary

Developing a Java application using a module does not change the way Java types are arranged into packages. The source code for a module contains a `module-info.java` file at the root of the package hierarchy. That is, the `module-info.java` file is placed in the unnamed package. It contains the module declaration.

The `javac` compiler, the `jar` tool, and the `java` launcher have been enhanced in JDK 9 to work with modules. The `javac` compiler accepts new options such as `--module-path` used to locate application modules, `--module-source-path` to locate module's source code, and `--module-version` to specify the version of the module being compiled. The `jar` tool lets you specify the main class and module version for a modular JAR using the `--main-class` and `--module-version` options, respectively. The `java` launcher can be run in class path mode, module mode, or mixed mode. To run a class in a module, you need to specify the module path using the `--module-path` option. You need to specify the main class name using the `--module` option. The main class is specified in the form `<module>/<main-class>` where `<module>` is the module that contains the main class and `<main-class>` is the fully qualified name of the class containing the `main()` method serving as the entry point for the application.

In JDK 9, every type belongs to a module. If a type is loaded from the class path, it belongs to an unnamed module of the class loader that loads it. In JDK 9, every class loader maintains an unnamed module whose members are all types loaded by that class loader from the class path. A type loaded from the module path belongs to the module in which it was defined.

An instance of the `Module` class represents a module at runtime. The `Module` class is in the `java.lang` package. Use the `Module` class to know everything about a module at runtime. The `Class` class has been enhanced in JDK 9. Its `getModule()` method returns a `Module` instance representing the module this class is a member of. The `Module` class contains a `getName()` method that returns the name of the module as a `String`; for an unnamed module, the method returns `null`.

The NetBeans IDE is being updated to support JDK 9 and developing modular Java applications. At the time of this writing, NetBeans allows you to create modules, compile them, package them in modular JARs, and run them from within the IDE. You need to create a separate Java project for a module. Its final release will allow you to have multiple modules in one Java project. The IDE has support for adding the `module-info.java` file. The IDE has a very cool feature that allows you to view and save module graphs!

CHAPTER 4

■ ■ ■

Module Dependency

In this chapter, you will learn:

- How to declare module dependency
- What an implicit readability of a module means and how to declare it
- The difference between unqualified and qualified exports
- Declaring runtime optional dependency of a module
- How to open an entire module or its selected packages for deep reflection
- Accessibility types in JDK 9
- Splitting packages across modules
- Restrictions on module declarations
- Different types of modules: named, unnamed, explicit, automatic, normal, and open modules
- How to dissemble a module's definition using the javap tool

The example code in this chapter goes through several steps. The source code for this book contains the code used in the final step. If you want to see those examples in action at every step as you read through this chapter, you need to modify the source code a bit to keep it in sync with the step you are working on.

Declaring Module Dependency

If a module needs to use public types contained in another module, the second module needs to export the package containing the types and the first module needs to read the second module. Note that the dependency declarations in two modules are asymmetric—the type-provider module exports the *package* containing the types whereas the type-user module reads the *module*.

Suppose you have two modules named com.jdojo.address and com.jdojo.person. The com.jdojo. address module contains a package named com.jdojo.address, which contains a class named Address. The com.jdojo.person module wants to use the Address class from the com.jdojo.address module. Figure 4-1 shows the module graph for the com.jdojo.person module. Let's walk through the steps to develop these modules.

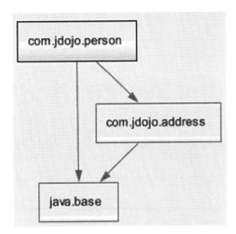

Figure 4-1. *The module graph for the com.jdojo.person module*

In NetBeans, you can create two Java projects named com.jdojo.address and com.jdojo.person. Each project will contain the code for a module with the same name as the project. Listing 4-1 and Listing 4-2 contain the module declaration and the code for the Address class. The Address class is a simple class with four fields and their getters and setters. I set the default values for these fields, so you don't have to type them in all examples.

Listing 4-1. The Module Declaration for the com.jdojo.address Module

```
// module-info.java
module com.jdojo.address {
    // Export the com.jdojo.address package
    exports com.jdojo.address;
}
```

Listing 4-2. The Address Class

```
// Address.java
package com.jdojo.address;

public class Address {
    private String line1 = "1111 Main Blvd.";
    private String city = "Jacksonville";
    private String state = "FL";
    private String zip = "32256";

    public Address() {
    }

    public Address(String line1, String line2, String city,
                   String state, String zip) {
        this.line1 = line1;
        this.city = city;
        this.state = state;
        this.zip = zip;
    }
```

```java
    public String getLine1() {
        return line1;
    }

    public void setLine1(String line1) {
        this.line1 = line1;
    }

    public String getCity() {
        return city;
    }

    public void setCity(String city) {
        this.city = city;
    }

    public String getState() {
        return state;
    }

    public void setState(String state) {
        this.state = state;
    }

    public String getZip() {
        return zip;
    }

    public void setZip(String zip) {
        this.zip = zip;
    }

    @Override
    public String toString() {
        return "[Line1:" + line1 + ", State:" + state +
                ", City:" + city + ", ZIP:" + zip + "]";
    }
}
```

An exports statement is used to export a package to all other modules or to some *named modules*. All public types in an exported package is accessible at compile-time and runtime. At runtime, you can use reflection to access only public members of public types. Non-public members of public types are inaccessible using reflection even if you use the setAccessible(true) method on those members. The general syntax for the exports statement is as follows:

```
exports <package>;
```

The statement exports all public types in <package> to all other modules. That is, any modules that read this module will be able to use all the public types in <package>.

The com.jdojo.address module exports the com.jdojo.address package, so the Address class, which is public and in the com.jdojo.address package, can be used by other modules. You will be using the Address class in the com.jdojo.person module in this example.

Listing 4-3 and Listing 4-4 contain the module declaration for the com.jdojo.person module and the code for the Person class.

Listing 4-3. The Module Declaration for the com.jdojo.person Module

```
// module-info.java
module com.jdojo.person {
    // Read the com.jdojo.address module
    requires com.jdojo.address;

    // Export the com.jdojo.person package
    exports com.jdojo.person;
}
```

Listing 4-4. A Person Class

```
// Person.java
package com.jdojo.person;

import com.jdojo.address.Address;

public class Person {
    private long personId;
    private String firstName;
    private String lastName;
    private Address address = new Address();

    public Person(long personId, String firstName, String lastName) {
        this.personId = personId;
        this.firstName = firstName;
        this.lastName = lastName;
    }

    public long getPersonId() {
        return personId;
    }

    public void setPersonId(long personId) {
        this.personId = personId;
    }

    public String getFirstName() {
        return firstName;
    }

    public void setFirstName(String firstName) {
        this.firstName = firstName;
    }

    public String getLastName() {
        return lastName;
    }
```

```
    public void setLastName(String lastName) {
        this.lastName = lastName;
    }

    public Address getAddress() {
        return address;
    }

    public void setAddress(Address address) {
        this.address = address;
    }

    @Override
    public String toString() {
        return "[Person Id:" + personId + ", First Name:" + firstName +
               ", Last Name:" + lastName + ", Address:" + address + "]";
    }
}
```

The Person class is in the com.jdojo.person module and it uses a field of the Address type, which is in the com.jdojo.address module. This means that the com.jdojo.person module reads the com.jdojo.address module. This is indicated by the requires statement in the com.jdojo.person module declaration:

```
// Read the com.jdojo.address module
requires com.jdojo.address;
```

A requires statement is used to specify a module's dependency to another module. If a module reads another module, the first module needs to have a requires statement in its declaration. The general syntax for the requires statement is as follows:

```
requires [transitive] [static] <module>;
```

Here, the <module> is the name of the module that the current module reads. Both transitive and static modifiers are optional. If the static modifier is present, the <module> module is mandatory at compile-time, but optional at runtime. The presence of the transitive modifier implies that a module that reads the current module implicitly reads the <module> module. I cover an example of using the transitive modifier in a requires statement shortly.

Every module implicitly reads the java.base module. The compiler adds a requires statement to reads the java.base module to a module declaration if the declaration does not already read the java.base module. The following two module declarations for a module named com.jdojo.common are the same:

```
// Declaration #1
module com.jdojo.common {
    // Compiler will add a read to the java.base module
}

// Declaration #2
module com.jdojo.common {
    // Add a read to the java.base module explicitly
    requires java.base;
}
```

The declaration of the com.jdojo.person module includes a requires statement implying that the com.jdojo.address module is required at compile-time as well as at runtime. When you compile the com.jdojo.person module, you must include the com.jdojo.address module in the module path. If you are using the NetBeans IDE, you can include a NetBeans project or a modular JAR in the module path. Right-click the com.jdojo.person project in NetBeans and select Properties. In the Categories list, select Libraries. Select the Compile tab and click the + sign on the Modulepath row and select Add Project from the menu, as shown in Figure 4-2. The Add Project dialog box is displayed, as shown in Figure 4-3.

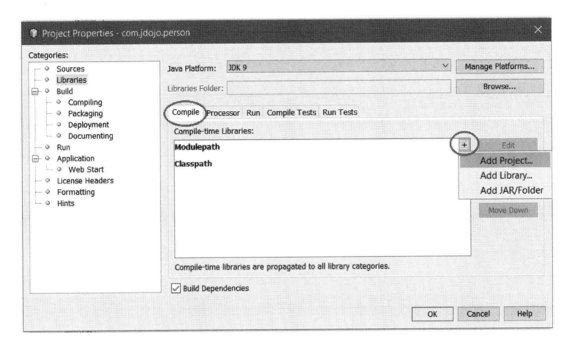

Figure 4-2. *Setting the module path for a project in NetBeans*

On the Add Project dialog box, navigate to the directory containing the com.jdojo.address module; select the module and click the Add Project JAR File button, which will bring you back to the Properties dialog box where you can see the added project to the module path, as shown in Figure 4-4. Click the OK button to finish this step.

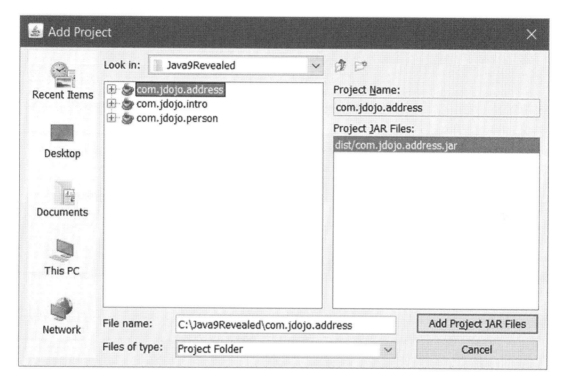

Figure 4-3. *Selecting a NetBeans project to add to the module path*

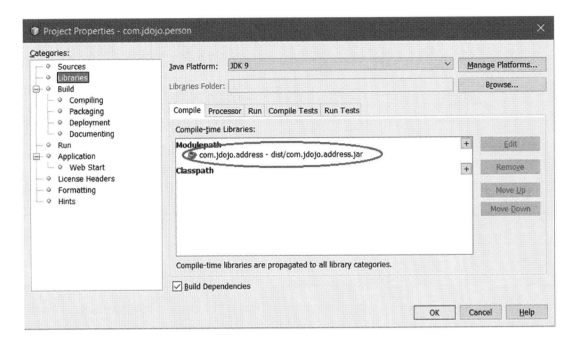

Figure 4-4. *A NetBeans project added to the module path*

The com.jdojo.person module also exports the com.jdojo.person package, so the public types in this package, for example, the Person class, may be used by other modules.

Listing 4-5 contains the code for a Main class, which is in the com.jdojo.person module. When you run this class, the output shows that you can use the Address class from the com.jdojo.address module. We are done with this example that shows how to use the exports and requires module statements. If you have any trouble running this example, refer to the next section that lists a few possible errors and their solutions.

Listing 4-5. A Main Class to Test the com.jdojo.person Module

```java
// Main.java
package com.jdojo.person;

import com.jdojo.address.Address;

public class Main {
    public static void main(String[] args) {
        Person john = new Person(1001, "John", "Jacobs");

        String fName = john.getFirstName();
        String lName = john.getLastName();
        Address addr = john.getAddress();

        System.out.printf("%s %s%n", fName, lName);
        System.out.printf("%s%n", addr.getLine1());
        System.out.printf("%s, %s %s%n", addr.getCity(),
                        addr.getState(), addr.getZip());
    }
}
```

64

John Jacobs
1111 Main Blvd.
Jacksonville, FL 32256

At this point, you can also run this example using a command prompt. You will need to include the compiled exploded directories or the modular JARs for the com.jdojo.person and com.jdojo.address modules to the module path. The following command uses the compiled classes from the build\classes directory under the two NetBeans projects:

```
C:\Java9Revealed>java --module-path
com.jdojo.person\build\classes;com.jdojo.address\build\classes
--module com.jdojo.person/com.jdojo.person.Main
```

When you build a NetBeans project containing a module, the modular JAR for the module is stored in a dist directory in the NetBeans project directory. When you build the com.jdojo.person project, it will create a com.jdojo.person.jar file in the C:\Java9Revealed\com.jdojo.person\dist directory. When you build a project in NetBeans, it also rebuilds all projects that the current project depends on. For this example, building the com.jdojo.person project will also rebuild the com.jdojo.address project. After building the com.jdojo.person module, you can run this example using the following command:

```
C:\Java9Revealed>java --module-path
com.jdojo.person\dist;com.jdojo.address\dist
--module com.jdojo.person/com.jdojo.person.Main
```

Troubleshooting the Example

If you are using the JDK 9 for the first time, a number of things can go wrong when you are working through this example. The following sections discuss a few scenarios with error messages and their corresponding solutions.

Empty Package Error

The error is as follows:

```
error: package is empty or does not exist: com.jdojo.address
    exports com.jdojo.address;
            ^
1 error
```

You will get this error when you compile the module declaration for the com.jdojo.address module without including the source code for the Address class. The module exports the com.jdojo.address package. You must have at least one type defined in the exported package.

Module Not Found Error

The error is as follows:

```
error: module not found: com.jdojo.address
    requires com.jdojo.address;
             ^

1 error
```

You will get this error when you compile the module declaration for the com.jdojo.person module without including the com.jdojo.address module in the module path. The com.jdojo.person module reads the com.jdojo.address module, so the former must be able to find the latter on the module path at compile-time as well as runtime. If you are using a command prompt, use the --module-path option to specify the module path for the com.jdojo.address module. If you are using NetBeans, refer to the previous section for how to configure the module path for the com.jdojo.person module.

Package Does Not Exist Error

The error is as follows:

```
error: package com.jdojo.address does not exist
import com.jdojo.address.Address;
                 ^
error: cannot find symbol
    private Address address = new Address();
            ^
  symbol:    class Address
  location: class Person
```

You will get this error when you compile the Person and Main classes in the com.jdojo.person module without adding a requires statement in the module declaration. The error message states that the compiler cannot find the com.jdojo.address.Address class. The solution is to add a requires com.jdojo.address statement to the module declaration for the com.jdojo.person module and add the com.jdojo.address module to the module path.

Module Resolution Exception

The partial error is as follows:

```
Error occurred during initialization of VM
java.lang.module.ResolutionException: Module com.jdojo.person not found
...
```

You may get this error for the following reasons when you attempt to run the example from the command prompt:

- The module path is not specified correctly.
- The module path is correct, but no compiled code in the specified directories or modular JARs is found on the module path.

Suppose you use the following command to run the example:

```
C:\Java9Revealed>java --module-path
com.jdojo.person\dist;com.jdojo.address\dist
--module com.jdojo.person/com.jdojo.person.Main
```

Make sure that the following modular JARs exist:

- C:\Java9Revealed\com.jdojo.person\dist\com.jdojo.person.jar

- C:\Java9Revealed\com.jdojo.address\dist\com.jdojo.address.jar

If these modular JARs do not exist, build the com.jdojo.person project in NetBeans.

If you are running the example using the modules' code from the exploded directories using the following command, make sure you compile the projects in NetBeans:

```
C:\Java9Revealed>java --module-path
com.jdojo.person\build\classes;com.jdojo.address\build\classes
--module com.jdojo.person/com.jdojo.person.Main
```

Implicit Readability

If a module can read another module without the first module including in its declaration a `requires` statement to read the second module, it is said that the first module *implicitly* reads the second module. Every module implicitly reads the java.base module. An implicit read is not limited to the java.base module. A module can also implicitly read another module, other than the java.base module. Before I show you how to add implicit readability to a module, I will build an example to see why we need this feature.

In the previous section, you created two modules called com.jdojo.address and com.jdojo.person where the second module reads the first module using the following declaration:

```
module com.jdojo.person {
    requires com.jdojo.address;
    ...
}
```

The Person class in the com.jdojo.person module refers to the Address class in com.jdojo.address module. Let's create another module named com.jdojo.person.test, which reads the com.jdojo.person module. The module declaration is shown in Listing 4-6.

Listing 4-6. The Module Declaration for the com.jdojo.person.test Module

```
// module-info.java
module com.jdojo.person.test {
    requires com.jdojo.person;
}
```

You need to add the com.jdojo.person project to the module path of the com.jdojo.person.test project. Otherwise, compiling the code in Listing 4-6 will generate the following error:

```
C:\Java9Revealed\com.jdojo.person.test\src\module-info.java:3: error: module not found:
com.jdojo.person
    requires com.jdojo.person;
1 error
```

Listing 4-7 contains the code for a Main class in the com.jdojo.person.test module.

Listing 4-7. A Main Class to Test the com.jdojo.person.test Module

```
// Main.java
package com.jdojo.person.test;

import com.jdojo.person.Person;

public class Main {
    public static void main(String[] args) {
        Person john = new Person(1001, "John", "Jacobs");

        // Get John's city and print it
        String city = john.getAddress().getCity();
        System.out.printf("John lives in %s%n", city);
    }
}
```

The code in the main() method is very simple—it creates a Person object and reads the value of the city in the person's address:

```
Person john = new Person(1001, "John", "Jacobs");
String city = john.getAddress().getCity();
```

Compiling the code for the com.jdojo.person.test module generates the following error:

```
com.jdojo.person.test\src\com\jdojo\person\test\Main.java:11: error: getCity() in Address is
defined in an inaccessible class or interface
        String city = john.getAddress().getCity();
                                        ^
1 error
```

The compiler message is not very clear. It is stating that the Address class is not accessible to the com.jdojo.person.test module. Recall that the Address class is in the com.jdojo.address module, which the com.jdojo.person.test module does not read. Looking at the code, it seems obvious that the code should compile. You have access to the Person class, which uses the Address class; so you should be able to use the Address class. Here, the john.getAddress() method returns an object of the Address type, which you do not have access to. The module system is simply doing its job in enforcing the encapsulation defined by the com.jdojo.address module. If a module wants to use the Address class, explicitly or implicitly, it must read the com.jdojo.address module. How do you fix it? The simple answer is for the com.jdojo.person.test module to read the com.jdojo.address module by changing its declaration to the one shown in Listing 4-8.

Listing 4-8. The Modified Module Declaration for the com.jdojo.person.test Module

```
// module-info.java
module com.jdojo.person.test {
    requires com.jdojo.person;
    requires com.jdojo.address;
}
```

When you added the `requires com.jdojo.address` statement in Listing 4-8, you will get another error that will state that the `com.jdojo.address` module is not found. Adding the `com.jdojo.address` project to the module path of the `com.jdojo.person.test` project will fix this error. The module path setting will look as shown in Figure 4-5.

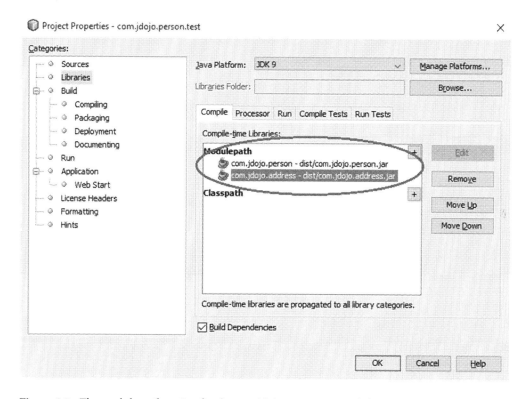

Figure 4-5. *The module path setting for the com.jdojo.person.test module*

Figure 4-6 shows the module graph for the com.jdojo.person.test module at this point.

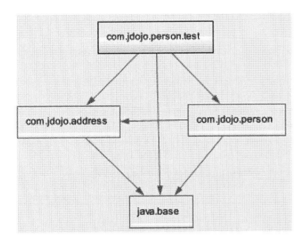

Figure 4-6. *The module graph for the com.jdojo.person.test module*

Compile and run the Main class in the com.jdojo.person.test module. It will print the following:

```
John lives in Jacksonville
```

You solved the problem by adding a requires statement. However, it is very likely that other modules that read the com.jdojo.person module will need to work with person's address and they will need to add a similar requires statement. If the com.jdojo.person module exposes types in its public API from more than one other module, modules reading the com.jdojo.person module will need to add a requires statement for each of those modules. It will be cumbersome for all those modules to add an extra requires statement. The JDK 9 designers realized this problem and provided a simple way to solve this. In this case, all you need to do is change the declaration for the com.jdojo.person module to add a transitive modifier in the requires statement to read the com.jdojo.address module. Listing 4-9 contains the modified declaration for the com.jdojo.person module.

Listing 4-9. The Modified Module Declaration for the com.jdojo.person Module

```
// module-info.java
module com.jdojo.person {
    // Read the com.jdojo.address module
    requires transitive com.jdojo.address;

    // Export the com.jdojo.person package
    exports com.jdojo.person;
}
```

Now, you can remove the requires statement that reads the com.jdojo.address module from the declaration of the com.jdojo.person.test module. You need to keep the com.jdojo.address project on the module path of the com.jdojo.person.test project because the com.jdojo.address module is still needed to use the Address type in this module. Recompile the com.jdojo.person module. Recompile and run the Main class in the com.jdojo.person.test module to get the desired output.

When a `requires` statement contains the `transitive` modifier, the module that depends on the current module implicitly reads the module specified in the `requires` statement. Referring to Listing 4-9, any module that reads the com.jdojo.person module implicitly reads the com.jdojo.address module. Essentially, an implicit read makes the module declaration simpler to read, but harder to reason about because, by just looking at a module declaration, you cannot see all its dependencies. Figure 4-7 shows the final module graph for the com.jdojo.person.test module.

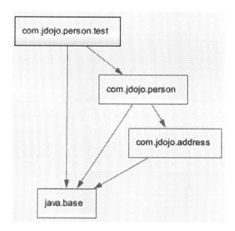

Figure 4-7. *The module graph for the com.jdojo.person.test module*

When modules are resolved, the module graph is augmented by adding a read edge for each transitive dependency. In this example, a read edge will be added from the com.jdojo.person.test module to the com.jdojo.address module, as shown by the dashed arrow in Figure 4-8.

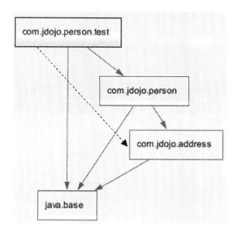

Figure 4-8. *The module graph for the com.jdojo.person.test module after augmenting it with implicit read edges*

Qualified Exports

Suppose you are developing a library or framework that consists of several modules. You have packages in a module that contains APIs only for internal use by some modules. That is, packages in that module need not be exported to all modules, rather its accessibility must be limited to a few named modules. This can be achieved using a qualified exports statement in the module declaration. The general syntax for using a qualified export is as follows:

```
exports <package> to <module1>, <module2>...;
```

Here, `<package>` is the name of the package to be exported by the current module and `<module1>`, `<module2>`, etc. are the names of modules that can read the current module. The following module declaration contains an unqualified export and a qualified export:

```
module com.jdojo.common {
    // An unqualified exports statement
    exports com.jdojo.zip;

    // A qualified exports statement
    exports com.jdojo.internal to com.jdojo.address;
}
```

The com.jdojo.common module exports the com.jdojo.zip package to all modules, whereas the com.jdojo.internal package belongs only to the com.jdojo.address module. All public types in the com.jdojo.zip module will be accessible in all modules that read the com.jdojo.common module. However, all public types in the com.jdojo.internal package will be accessible only to the com.jdojo.address module if the latter reads the former.

You can find many examples of qualified exports in the JDK 9. The java.base module contains sun.* and jdk.* packages that are exported to a few named modules. The following command prints the module declaration of java.base. The output shows a few of the qualified exports used in the java.base module.

```
c:\>javap jrt:/java.base/module-info.class
```

```
Compiled from "module-info.java"
module java.base {
  exports sun.net to jdk.plugin, jdk.incubator.httpclient;
  exports sun.nio.cs to java.desktop, jdk.charsets;
  exports sun.util.resources to jdk.localedata;
  exports jdk.internal.util.xml to jdk.jfr;
  exports jdk.internal to jdk.jfr;
  ...
}
```

Not all internal APIs in JDK 9 have been encapsulated. There are a few critical internal APIs in the sun.* packages, e.g., the class sun.misc.Unsafe, which were used by developers prior to JDK 9 and are still accessible in JDK 9. Those packages have been placed in the jdk.unsupported module. The following command prints the module declaration for the jdk.unsupported module:

```
C:\Java9Revealed>javap jrt:/jdk.unsupported/module-info.class
```

```
Compiled from "module-info.java"
module jdk.unsupported@9-ea {
  requires java.base;
  exports sun.misc;
  exports com.sun.nio.file;
  exports sun.reflect;
  opens sun.misc;
  opens sun.reflect;
}
```

Optional Dependency

The module system verifies the module dependencies at compile-time as well as at runtime. There are times when you want to make a module dependency mandatory at compile-time, but optional at runtime.

You may develop a library that performs better if a specific module is available at runtime. Otherwise, it falls back to another module that makes it perform less than optimal. However, the library is compiled against the optional module and it makes sure that the code dependent on the optional module is not executed if the optional module is not available.

Another example is a module that exports an annotation bundle. The Java runtime already ignores nonexistent annotation types. If an annotation used in a program is not present at runtime, the annotation is ignored. Module dependency is verified at startup and if a module is missing, the application won't start. Therefore, it is essential to declare such as module dependency on the module containing the annotation bundle as optional.

You can declare an optional dependency by using the static keyword in a requires statement:

```
requires static <optional-package>;
```

The following module declaration contains an optional dependency on the com.jdojo.annotation module:

```
module com.jdojo.claim {
    requires static com.jdojo.annotation;
}
```

It is allowed to have both transitive and static modifiers in a requires statement:

```
module com.jdojo.claim {
    requires transitive static com.jdojo.annotation;
}
```

The `transitive` and `static` modifiers can be used in any order if they're used together. The following declaration has the same semantics as the previous one:

```
module com.jdojo.claim {
    requires static transitive com.jdojo.annotation;
}
```

Accessing Modules Using Reflection

For over 20 years, Java has allowed access to all members—private, public, package, and protected—of a type using reflection. You were able to access a private member of a class or object. All you had to do was call the `setAccessible(true)` method on the member (`Field`, `Method`, etc.) object. I will refer to accessing non-public members of a type using reflection as *deep reflection* in the remainder of chapter.

When you export a package of a module, other modules can access only public types and public/protected members of those public types in the exported package—statically at compile-time or reflectively at runtime. This became a big issue during the design of the module system. There are several great frameworks such as Spring and Hibernate, which depend heavily on deep reflective access to members of types defined in application libraries.

Designers of the module system faced a big challenge in designing the deep reflective access to the modular code. Allowing deep reflection on the types of an exported package violated the *strong encapsulation* theme of the module system. It makes everything accessible to the outside code even if the module developer did not want to expose some part of the module. On the other hand, by not allowing deep reflection will devoid the Java community of some great widely used frameworks and it will also break many existing applications that rely on deep reflection. Many existing applications will simply not migrate to JDK 9 because of this limitation.

After a few iterations of design and experiments, the module system designers came up with a middle ground—you can have your cake and it eat too! The current design allows you have a module with strong encapsulation, deep reflective access, and partly both. Here are the rules:

- An exported package will allow access to only public types and their public members at compile-time and runtime. If you do not export a package, all types in that package are inaccessible to other modules. This provides strong encapsulation.

- You can open a module to allow deep reflection on all types in all packages in that module at runtime. Such a module is called an *open module*.

- You can have a normal module—a module that is not open for deep reflection—with specific packages opened for deep reflection at runtime. All other packages (not open packages) are strongly encapsulated. Packages in a module that allow for deep reflection are known as *open packages*.

- Sometimes, you may want to access types in a package at compile-time to write code in terms of the types in that package and, at the same time, you want deep reflective access to those types at runtime. You can export and open the same package to achieve this.

Open Modules

In the remainder of this section, I show you how to declare an open module and how to open a specific package for deep reflection. First, I give you the syntax. Use the open modifier before the module keyword to declare an open module:

```
open module com.jdojo.model {
    // Module statements go here
}
```

Here, the com.jdojo.model module is an open module. Other modules can use deep reflection on all types on all packages in this module. You can have exports, requires, uses, and provides statements in the declaration of an open module. You cannot have opens statements inside an open module. An opens statement is used to open a specific package for deep reflection. Because an open module opens all packages for deep reflection, an opens statement is not allowed inside an open module.

Opening Packages

Opening a package means allowing other modules to use deep reflection on the types in that package. You can open a package to all other modules or to a specific list of modules.

The syntax for the opens statement to open a package to all other modules is as follows:

```
opens <package>;
```

Here, <package> is available for deep reflection to all other modules. You can also open a package to specific modules using a qualified opens statement:

```
opens <package> to <module1>, <module2>...;
```

Here, <package> is opened for deep reflection only to <module1>, <module2>, etc. The following is an example of using the opens statement in a module declaration:

```
module com.jdojo.model {
    // Export the com.jdojo.util package to all modules
    exports com.jdojo.util;

    // Open the com.jdojo.util package to all modules
    opens com.jdojo.util;

    // Open the com.jdojo.model.policy package only to the
    // hibernate.core module
    opens com.jdojo.model.policy to hibernate.core;
}
```

The com.jdojo.model module exports the com.jdojo.util package, which means all public types and their public members are accessible at compile-time and for normal reflection at runtime. The second statement opens the same package for deep reflection at runtime. In summary, all public types and their public members of the com.jdojo.util package are accessible at compile-time and the package allows deep reflection at runtime. The third statement opens the com.jdojo.model.policy package only to the hibernate.core module for deep reflection, which means that no other modules can access any type of this package at compile-time and the hibernate.core module can access all types and their members using deep reflection at runtime.

> ▓ **Tip** A module that performs deep reflection on open packages of another module does not need to read the module containing the open packages. However, adding a dependence on a module with open packages is allowed and strongly encouraged—if you know the module name —so the module system can verify the dependency at compile-time and at runtime.

When a module M opens its package P for deep reflection to another module N, it is possible that the module N grants the deep reflective access that it has on package P to another module Q. The module N will need to do it programmatically using the addOpens() method of the Module class. Delegating reflective access to another module avoids opening the entire module to all other modules and, at the same time, it creates additional work on the part of the module that is granted the reflective access.

Using Deep Reflection

In this section, I explain how to open modules and packages for deep reflection. I start with a basic use case and build the example thereafter. In the example, I:

- Show you the code that attempts to do something using deep reflection. Typically, the code will generate errors.

- Explain the reasons behind the errors.

- Finally, I show you how to fix the errors.

I use a module named com.jdojo.reflect that contains a class named Item in the com.jdojo.reflect package. Listing 4-10 and Listing 4-11 contain the source code for the module and the class.

Listing 4-10. The Module Declaration for the com.jdojo.reflect Module

```
// module-info.java
module com.jdojo.reflect {
    // No module statements
}
```

Listing 4-11. A Class Named Item with Four Static Variables

```
// Item.java
package com.jdojo.reflect;

public class Item {
    static private int s = 10;
    static int t = 20;
    static protected int u = 30;
    static public int v = 40;
}
```

Notice that the module does not export any package and neither does it open any package. The Item class is very simple. It contains four static variables with each type of access modifiers—private, package, protected, and public. I have intentionally kept the class simple so you can focus on the module system rules, rather than understanding the code. You will be accessing these static variables using deep reflection throughout this example.

You will be using another module named com.jdojo.reflect.test. Listing 4-12 contains its declaration. It is a normal module with no module statement. That is, it has no dependency, except the default one that is on the java.base module.

Listing 4-12. The Module Declaration for the com.jdojo.reflect.test Module

```
// module-info.java
module com.jdojo.reflect.test {
    // No module statements
}
```

The com.jdojo.reflect.test module contains a class named ReflectTest, as shown in Listing 4-13.

Listing 4-13. A ReflectTest Class to Demonstrates Reflective Access to Types and Their Members in Other Modules

```
// ReflectTest.java
package com.jdojo.reflect.test;

import java.lang.reflect.Field;
import java.lang.reflect.InaccessibleObjectException;

public class ReflectTest {
    public static void main(String[] args) throws ClassNotFoundException {
        // Get the Class object for the com.jdojo.reflect.Item class
        // which is in the com.jdojo.reflect module
        Class<?> cls = Class.forName("com.jdojo.reflect.Item");

        Field[] fields = cls.getDeclaredFields();
        for (Field field : fields) {
            printFieldValue(field);
        }
    }

    public static void printFieldValue(Field field) {
        String fieldName = field.getName();

        try {
            // Make the field accessible, in case it is not accessible
            // based on its declaration such as a private field
            field.setAccessible(true);

            // Print the field's value
            System.out.println(fieldName + " = " + field.get(null));
        } catch (IllegalAccessException | IllegalArgumentException |
                InaccessibleObjectException e) {
            System.out.println("Accessing " + fieldName +
                            ". Error: " + e.getMessage());
        }
    }
}
```

The ReflectTest class is simple. In its main() method, it uses the Class.forName() method to load the com.jdojo.reflect.Item class and attempts to print the value of all four static fields of the class.

You can load a class from any module using the Class.forName() method if the class is available at runtime. The class does not have to be necessarily accessible using module dependency—exports and requires statements. You might question this rule. Doesn't it violate the strong encapsulation premise of the module system? How can you load a class from any module without the owning module exporting the package containing that class? It is allowed because you are loading the class descriptor (the Class object) of the class. Knowing the class descriptor does not mean that you can also create objects of that class and access members of the class. Strong encapsulation is about accessing only those types of a module that are exported or opened, not about loading a class descriptor.

Let's run the ReflectTest class. It will generate the following error:

```
Exception in thread "main" java.lang.ClassNotFoundException: com.jdojo.reflect.Item
        at java.base/jdk.internal.loader.BuiltinClassLoader.loadClass
        (BuiltinClassLoader.java:532)
        at java.base/jdk.internal.loader.ClassLoaders$AppClassLoader.loadClass
        (ClassLoaders.java:186)
        at java.base/java.lang.ClassLoader.loadClass(ClassLoader.java:473)
        at java.base/java.lang.Class.forName0(Native Method)
        at java.base/java.lang.Class.forName(Class.java:292)
        at com.jdojo.reflect.test/com.jdojo.reflect.test.ReflectTest.main
        (ReflectTest.java:12)
```

The error message is stating that a ClassNotFoundException was thrown when an attempt was made to load the com.jdojo.reflect.Item class. Didn't I say that you should be able load the class? My previous statement is still correct. This error stems from another problem.

When you attempt to load a class, the module containing the class must be known to the module system. If you received a ClassNotFoundException before JDK 9, it indicated that class is not in the class path. You would add the directory or the JAR that contains the class to the class path and the error will be resolved. In JDK 9, modules are found using the module path. So, let's add the com.jdojo.reflect module on the module path and then run the ReflectTest class. In NetBeans, you need to add the com.jdojo. reflect project into the module path of the com.jdojo.reflect.test module using the properties dialog box, as shown in Figure 4-9.

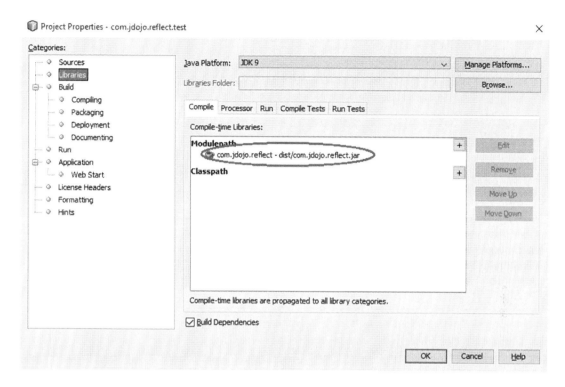

Figure 4-9. *Adding the com.jdojo.reflect project to the module path of the com.jdojo.reflect.test project in NetBeans*

You can also run the `ReflectTest` class using the following command, assuming that you have built both projects in NetBeans and the projects' `dist` directories contain modular JARs:

```
C:\Java9Revealed>java
--module-path com.jdojo.reflect\dist;com.jdojo.reflect.test\dist
--module com.jdojo.reflect.test/com.jdojo.reflect.test.ReflectTest
```

Running the `ReflectTest` class in NetBeans and on the command prompt returns the same `ClassNotFoundException` as before. So, it looks like adding the `com.jdojo.reflect` module to the module path did not help. But that is not entirely true. In fact, this step helped, but it solved only half of the problem. We need to understand and solve the other half, which is the module graph.

The module path in JDK 9 sounds similar to the class path, but they work differently. A module path is used to locate modules during module resolution—when the module graph is built and augmented. The class path is used to locate a class whenever a class needs to be loaded. To provide a reliable configuration, the module system makes sure all required dependencies for modules are present at startup. Once your application is started, all needed modules are resolved and adding more modules to the module path after the module resolution is over does not help. When you run the `ReflectTest` class—keeping both `com.jdojo.reflect` and `com.jdojo.reflect.test` modules on the module path—the module graph looks as shown in Figure 4-10.

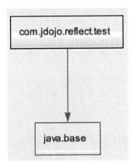

Figure 4-10. *The module graph when the ReflectTest class is run*

When you run a class from a module—as you are doing when you are running the `ReflectTest` class—the module that contains the main class is the only module used as the root. The module graph contains all modules that the main module depends on and their dependencies. In this case, the `com.jdojo.reflect.test` module is the only module in the default set of root modules and the module system has no clue about the existence of the `com.jdojo.reflect` module, even though the module is placed on the module path. What do you need to do so the `com.jdojo.reflect` module is included in the module graph? Add this module to the default set of root modules by using the `--add-modules` command-line VM option. The value to this option is a comma-separated list of modules to be added to the default set of root modules:

```
--add-modules <module1>,<module2>...
```

Figure 4-11 shows the Properties dialog box for the `com.jdojo.reflect.test` project in NetBeans with the VM option you need to use to add the `com.jdojo.reflect` module to the default set of root modules.

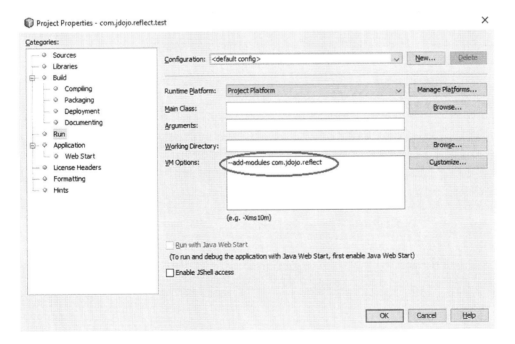

Figure 4-11. *Adding the com.jdojo.reflect module to the default set of root modules at runtime in NetBeans*

Figure 4-12 shows the module graph at runtime after you add the com.jdojo.reflect module to the default set of root modules.

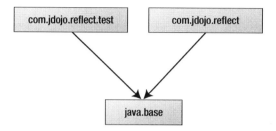

Figure 4-12. *The module graph after adding the com.jdojo.reflect module to the default set of root modules*

Another way of resolving the com.jdojo.reflect module is to add a requires com.jdojo.reflect; statement in the declaration of the com.jdojo.reflect.test module. This way, the com.jdojo.reflect module will be resolved as a dependency of the com.jdojo.reflect.test module. If you use this option, you do not need to use the --add-modules option.

Rerun the ReflectTest class in NetBeans. You can also use the following command to run it:

```
C:\Java9Revealed>java
--module-path com.jdojo.reflect\dist;com.jdojo.reflect.test\dist
--add-modules com.jdojo.reflect
--module com.jdojo.reflect.test/com.jdojo.reflect.test.ReflectTest
```

Accessing s. Error: Unable to make field private static int com.jdojo.reflect.Item.s accessible: module com.jdojo.reflect does not "opens com.jdojo.reflect" to module com. jdojo.reflect.test

Accessing t. Error: Unable to make field static int com.jdojo.reflect.Item.t accessible: module com.jdojo.reflect does not "opens com.jdojo.reflect" to module com.jdojo.reflect.test

Accessing u. Error: Unable to make field protected static int com.jdojo.reflect.Item.u accessible: module com.jdojo.reflect does not "opens com.jdojo.reflect" to module com.jdojo. reflect.test

Accessing v. Error: Unable to make field public static int com.jdojo.reflect.Item.v accessible: module com.jdojo.reflect does not "exports com.jdojo.reflect" to module com. jdojo.reflect.test

The output is much better. The com.jdojo.reflect.Item class was loaded successfully. When the program tried to call the setAccessible(true) on the fields, an InaccessibleObjectException was thrown for every field. Notice a difference in four error messages in the output. For the s, t, and u fields, the error messages state that you cannot access them because the com.jdojo.reflect module does not open the com.jdojo.reflect package. For the v field, the error message states that the module does not export the com.jdojo.reflect package. The reason behind different error messages is that the v field is public and the others are non-public. To access a public field, the package needs to be exported, which is the minimum allowable accessibility. For accessing non-public fields, the package must be opened, which is the maximum allowable accessibility.

Listing 4-14 contains a modified version of the module declaration for the com.jdojo.reflect module. It exports the com.jdojo.reflect package, so all public types and their public members are accessible to the outside code.

Listing 4-14. A Modified Version of the com.jdojo.reflect Module

```
// module-info.java
module com.jdojo.reflect {
    exports com.jdojo.reflect;
}
```

Recompile both modules and rerun the ReflectTest class the same way in NetBeans or using the following command:

```
C:\Java9Revealed>java
--module-path com.jdojo.reflect\dist;com.jdojo.reflect.test\dist
--add-modules com.jdojo.reflect
--module com.jdojo.reflect.test/com.jdojo.reflect.test.ReflectTest
```

```
Accessing s. Error: Unable to make field private static int com.jdojo.reflect.Item.s
accessible: module com.jdojo.reflect does not "opens com.jdojo.reflect" to module com.
jdojo.reflect.test

Accessing t. Error: Unable to make field static int com.jdojo.reflect.Item.t accessible:
module com.jdojo.reflect does not "opens com.jdojo.reflect" to module com.jdojo.reflect.test

Accessing u. Error: Unable to make field protected static int com.jdojo.reflect.Item.u
accessible: module com.jdojo.reflect does not "opens com.jdojo.reflect" to module com.jdojo.
reflect.test

v = 40
```

As expected, you were able to access the value of the v field, which is public. Exporting a package allows you to access only public types and their public members. You cannot access other non-public fields. To get deep reflective access to the Item class, the solution is to open the entire module or the package containing the Item class. Listing 4-15 contains a modified version of the com.jdojo.reflect module, which declares it as an open module. An open module exports all of its packages at runtime for deep reflection.

Listing 4-15. A Modified Version of the com.jdojo.reflect Module That Declares It as an Open Module

```
// module-info.java
open module com.jdojo.reflect {
    // No module statements
}
```

Recompile the modules and rerun the `ReflectTest` class in NetBeans using the following command:

```
C:\Java9Revealed>java
--module-path com.jdojo.reflect\dist;com.jdojo.reflect.test\dist
--add-modules com.jdojo.reflect
--module com.jdojo.reflect.test/com.jdojo.reflect.test.ReflectTest
```

```
s = 10
t = 20
u = 30
v = 40
```

The output shows that you were able to access all fields—public and non-public—of the `Item` class from the `com.jdojo.reflect.test` module. You can also get the same results by opening the `com.jdojo.reflect` package instead of opening the entire module. A modified version of the `com.jdojo.reflect` module declaration, as shown in Listing 4-16, achieves this. Recompile your modules and rerun the `ReflectTest` class as you did in the previous step and you will get the same results.

Listing 4-16. A Modified Version of the com.jdojo.reflect Module That Opens the com.jdojo.reflect Package for Deep Reflection

```
// module-info.java
module com.jdojo.reflect {
    opens com.jdojo.reflect;
}
```

This example is almost over! There are a few points to note:

- An open module or a module with open packages allows access to all types of members for deep reflection to other modules where other modules do not have to declare dependency on the first module. In this example, the `com.jdojo.reflect.test` module was able to access the `Item` class and its members without declaring a dependency on the `com.jdojo.reflect` module. This rule exists to make sure that the frameworks such as Hibernate and Spring that use deep reflection do not have to declare dependency on application modules to access them.

- If you want to access public APIs of a package at compile-time and want to access the same package using deep reflection at runtime, you can open as well as export the same package. In this example, we can export and open the `com.jdojo.reflect` package in the `com.jdojo.reflect` module.

- If a module is open or it opens packages, you can still declare dependency on them, but you don't have to. This rule helps migration to JDK 9. If your module uses deep reflection on other known modules, your module should declare dependency on those modules to get the benefit of reliable configuration.

Let's take a look at the final versions of these modules. Listing 4-17 and Listing 4-18 contain modified versions of these module declarations.

Listing 4-17. A Modified Version of the com.jdojo.reflect Module That Exports and Opens the com.jdojo. reflect Package

```
// module-info.java
module com.jdojo.reflect {
    exports com.jdojo.reflect;
    opens com.jdojo.reflect;
}
```

Listing 4-18. A Modified Version of the com.jdojo.reflect.test Module That Reads the com.jdojo.reflect Module

```
// module-info.java
module com.jdojo.reflect.test {
    requires com.jdojo.reflect;
}
```

Now, you do not need to use the --add-modules VM option when you run the ReflectTest class. The com.jdojo.reflect module will be resolved because of the requires com.jdojo.reflect; statement in the module declaration of the com.jdojo.reflect.test module. Figure 4-13 shows the module graph that is created when you run the ReflectTest class.

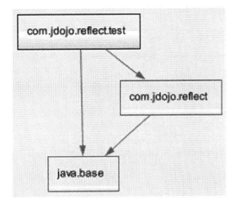

Figure 4-13. *The module graph for the final version of the com.jdojo.reflect and com.jdojo.reflect.test modules*

Rebuild both projects in NetBeans and run the ReflectTest class in NetBeans or using the following command. The output is the same as the previous output.

```
C:\Java9Revealed>java
--module-path com.jdojo.reflect\dist;com.jdojo.reflect.test\dist
--module com.jdojo.reflect.test/com.jdojo.reflect.test.ReflectTest
```

```
s = 10
t = 20
u = 30
v = 40
```

Have you thought about cases when your module needs to have deep reflective access to another module, which does not open any of its packages and you cannot modify its declaration? You can do this by using the --add-opens option. I discuss this option and many others in Chapter 9 when I describe different ways that JDK 9 lets you break module encapsulation.

Type Accessibility

Prior to JDK 9, there were four accessibility types:

- `public`
- `protected`
- `<package>`
- `private`

In JDK 8, a public type meant that it was accessible to all parts of the program. In JDK 9, this has changed. A public type may not be public to everyone. A public type defined in a module may fall into one of three categories:

- Public only within the defining module
- Public only to specific modules
- Public to everyone

If a type is defined public in a module, but the module does not export the package that contains the type, the type is public only within the module. No other modules can access the type.

If a type is defined public in a module, but the module uses a *qualified* exports to export the package that contains the type, the type will be accessible only to the modules specified in the to clause of the qualified export.

If a type is defined public in a module, but the module exports the package using an unqualified exports statement that contains the type, the type will be public to every module that reads the first module.

Splitting Packages Across Modules

Splitting packages into multiple modules is not *allowed*. That is, the same package cannot be defined in multiple modules. If types in the same package are in multiple modules, those modules should be combined into one module or you need to rename the packages. Sometimes, you can compile these modules successfully and receive a runtime error; other times, you receive a compile-time error. Splitting packages is not disallowed unconditionally as I mentioned in the beginning. You need to know the simple rule behind such errors.

If two modules named M and N define the same package named P, there must not exist a module Q such that the package P in both M and N modules is accessible to Q. In other words, the same package in multiple modules must not be readable to a module at the same time. Otherwise, an error occurs. If a module is using a type in a package that is found in two modules, the module system cannot make a decision for you, which may be wrong. It generates an error and wants you to fix the problem. Consider the following snippet of code:

```
// Test.java
package java.util;

public class Test {
}
```

If you compile the Test class in JDK 9 as part of a module or by itself, you will receive the following error:

```
error: package exists in another module: java.base
package java.util;
^
1 error
```

If you have this class in a module named M, the compile-time error is stating that the java.util package is readable by the module M in this module as well as in the java.base module. You must change the package for this class to something else that does not exist in any observable modules.

Restrictions in Module Declarations

There are several restrictions in declaring modules. If you violate them, you will get errors at compile-time or at startup:

- A module graph cannot contain circular dependencies. That is, two modules cannot read each other. If they do, they should be one module, not two. Note that it is possible to have circular dependencies at runtime by adding readability edges programmatically or using the command-line options.

- Module declarations do not support module versions. You will need to add module's version as the class file attribute using the jar tool or some other tools such as javac.

- The module system does not have a concept of sub-modules. That is, com.jdojo. person and com.jdojo.person.client are two separate modules; the second one is not a sub-module of the first one.

Types of Modules

Java has been around for over 20 years and applications, old as well as new, will keep using libraries that have not been modularized or will never be modularized. If JDK 9 forced everyone to modularize their applications, the JDK 9 would probably not be widely adopted. JDK 9 designers kept the backward compatibility in mind. You can adopt JDK 9 by modulating your application at your own pace or by deciding not to modularize at all—by just running your existing application in JDK 9. In most cases, your application that worked in JDK 8 or earlier will continue to work in JDK 9 without any changes. To ease migration, JDK 9 defines four types of modules:

- Normal modules

- Open modules

- Automatic modules

- Unnamed modules

In fact, you will come across six terms describing six different types of modules, which are, for a beginner to JDK 9, confusing at best. Other two types of modules are used to convey broader categories of these four types of modules. Figure 4-14 shows a pictorial view of all the module types.

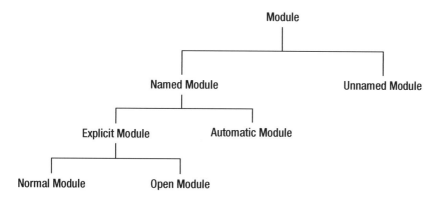

Figure 4-14. *Types of modules*

Before I describe main types of modules, I give brief definitions of the module types shown in Figure 4-14.

- A module is a collection of code and data.

- Based on whether a module has a name, a module can be a *named module* or an *unnamed module*.

- There are no further categories of unnamed modules.

- When a module has a name, the name can be given explicitly in a module declaration or the name can be generated automatically (or implicitly). If the name is given explicitly in a module declaration, it is called an *explicit module*. If the name is generated by the module system by reading the JAR filename on the module path, it is called an *automatic module*.

- If you declare a module without using the open modifier, it is called a *normal module*.

- If you declare a module using the open modifier, it is called an *open module*.

Based on these definitions, an open module is also an explicit module and a named module. An automatic module is a named module as it has a name, which is automatically generated, but it is not an explicit module because it is implicitly declared by the module system at compile-time and runtime. The following sub-sections describe these module types.

▓ **Tip**   If the Java platform was initially designed with the module system, you would have only one module type—the normal module! All other module types exist for backward compatibility and smooth migration and adoption of JDK 9.

Normal Modules

A module that is declared explicitly using a module declaration without using an open modifier is always given a name and it is called a *normal module* or simply a *module*. So far, you have been working with mostly normal modules. I have been referring to normal modules as modules and I will continue using this term in this sense unless I need to make a distinction between the four types of modules. By default, all types in a normal module are encapsulated. An example of a normal module is as follows:

```
module a.normal.module {
    // Module statements go here
}
```

Open Modules

If a module declaration contains the open modifier, the module is known as an open module. Refer to the previous section entitled "Open Modules" for more information on open modules. An example of an open module is as follows:

```
open module a.open.module {
    // Module statements go here
}
```

Automatic Modules

For backward compatibility, the class path mechanism to look up types still works in JDK 9. You have options to place your JARs on the class path, the module path, and a combination of both. Note that you can place modular JARs as well as JARs on both the module path and the class path.

When you place a JAR on the module path, the JAR is treated as a module, which is called an *automatic* module. The name *automatic* module is derived from the fact that the module is automatically defined out of a JAR—you do not explicitly declare the module by adding a `module-info.class` file. An automatic module has a name. What is the name of an automatic module? What modules does it read and what packages does it export? I will answer these questions shortly.

An automatic module is also a named module. Its name and version are derived from the name of the JAR file using the following rules:

- The `.jar` extension of the JAR file is removed. If the JAR filename is `com.jdojo.intro-1.0.jar`, this step removes the `.jar` extension and the following steps use `com.jdojo.intro-1.0` to derive the name of the module and its version.

- If the name ends with a hyphen followed by at least one digit, which is optionally followed by a dot, the module name is derived from the part of the name that precedes the last hyphen. The part that follows the hyphen is assigned as the version of the module if it can be parsed as a valid version. In this example, the module name will be derived from `com.jdojo.intro`. The version will be derived as 1.0.

- Every non-alphanumeric character in the name part is replaced with a dot and, in the resulting string, two consecutive dots are replaced with one dot. Also, all leading and trailing dots are removed. In this example, we do not have any non-alphanumeric characters in the name part, so the module name is com.jdojo.intro.

Applying these rules in sequence gives you a module name and a module version. At the end of this section, I show you how to determine the name of an automatic module using the JAR file. Table 4-1 lists a few JAR names, as well as the derived automatic module names and versions for them. Note that the table does not show the extension .jar in the JAR filenames.

Table 4-1. *Examples of Deriving Names and Versions of Automatic Modules*

JAR Name	Module Name	Module Version
com.jdojo.intro-1.0	com.jdojo.intro	1.0
junit-4.10.jar	junit	4.10
jdojo-logging1.5.0	(An error)	(No version)
spring-core-4.0.1.RELEASE	spring.core	4.0.1.RELEASE
jdojo-trans-api_1.5_spec-1.0.0	(An error)	1.0.0
_	(An error)	(No version)

Let's look at three odd cases in the table where you will receive an error if you place the JARs in the module path. The first JAR name that generates an error is jdojo-logging1.5.0. Let us apply the rules to derive the automatic module name for this JAR:

- There is no hyphen in the JAR name that is immediately followed by a digit, so there is no module version. The entire JAR name is used to derive the automatic module name.

- All non-alphanumeric characters are replaced with a dot. The resulting string is jdojo.logging1.5.0. Recall from Chapter 2 that every part of a module name must be a valid Java identifier. In this case, 5 and 0 are two parts in the module name, which are not valid Java identifiers. So, the derived module name is invalid. This is the reason you get an error when you add this JAR file to the module path.

Another JAR name that generates an error is jdojo-trans-api_1.5_spec-1.0.0. Let's apply the rules to derive the automatic module name for this JAR:

- It finds the last hyphen after which you have only digits and dots and splits the JAR name into two parts: jdojo-trans-api_1.5_spec and 1.0.0. The first part is used to derive the module name. The second part is the module version.

- All non-alphanumeric characters in the name part are replaced with a dot. The resulting string is jdojo.trans.api.1.5.spec, which is an invalid module name because 1 and 5 and are not valid Java identifiers. This is the reason you get an error when you add this JAR file to the module path.

The last entry in the table contains an underscore (_) as a JAR name. That is, the JAR file was named _.jar. If you apply the rules, the underscore will be replaced by a dot and that dot will be removed because it is the only character in the name. You end up with an empty string, which is not a valid module name.

A JAR placed on the module path will throw an exception if a valid automatic module name cannot be derived from its name. For example, the _.jar file on the module path will cause the following exception:

```
java.lang.module.ResolutionException: Unable to derive module descriptor for: _.jar
```

You can use the jar command with the --describe-module option to print the module descriptor for a modular JAR and to print the name of the derived automatic module name for a JAR. For a JAR, it also prints the list of packages the JAR contains. The general syntax to use the command is as follows:

```
jar --describe-module --file <path-to-JAR>
```

The following command prints the automatic module name for the JAR named cglib-2.2.2.jar:

```
C:\Java9Revealed>jar --describe-module --file lib\cglib-2.2.2.jar
```

```
No module descriptor found. Derived automatic module.

module cglib@2.2.2 (automatic)
  requires mandated java.base
  contains net.sf.cglib.beans
  contains net.sf.cglib.core
  contains net.sf.cglib.proxy
  contains net.sf.cglib.reflect
  contains net.sf.cglib.transform
  contains net.sf.cglib.transform.impl
  contains net.sf.cglib.util
```

The command prints a message that it did not find a module descriptor in the JAR file and it derived an automatic module from the JAR. If you use a JAR (e.g. cglib.1-2.2.2.jar) whose name cannot be converted to a valid automatic name, the jar command prints an error message and will tell you what is wrong with the JAR name, as shown:

```
C:\Java9Revealed>jar --describe-module --file lib\cglib.1-2.2.2.jar
```

```
Unable to derive module descriptor for: lib\cglib.1-2.2.2.jar
cglib.1: Invalid module name: '1' is not a Java identifier
```

Once you know the name of an automatic module, other explicit modules can read it using requires statements. The following module declaration reads the automatic module named cglib that comes from the cglib-2.2.2.jar on the module path:

```
module com.jdojo.lib {
    requires cglib;
    //...
}
```

An automatic module, to be used effectively, must export packages and read other modules. Let's look at the rules about this:

- An automatic module reads all other modules. It is important to note that readability from an automatic module to all other modules is added after the module graph is resolved.

- All packages in an automatic module are exported and opened.

The two rules are based on the fact that there is no practical way to tell which other modules an automatic module depends on and which packages of the automatic module other modules will need to compile for deep reflection.

An automatic module reading all other modules may create cyclic dependency, which is allowed after the module graph has been resolved. Recall that cyclic dependency between modules is not allowed during the module graph resolution. That is, you cannot have cyclic dependency in your module declarations.

Automatic modules do not have a module declaration, so they cannot declare dependencies on other modules. Explicit modules may declare dependencies on other automatic modules. Let's take a case where an explicit module M reads an automatic module P and the module P uses a type T in another automatic module Q. When you launch the application using the main class from module M, the module graph will consist of only M and P—excluding the java.base module in this discussion for brevity. The resolution process will start with the module M and will see that it reads another module P. The resolution process has no practical way to tell that the module P reads the module Q. You will be able to compile both modules P and Q by placing them on the class path. However, when you run this application, you will receive a ClassNotFoundException. The exception occurs when the module P tries to access a type from the module Q. To solve this problem, the module Q must be included in the module graph by adding it as a root module using the --add-modules command-line option and specifying Q as the value for this option.

The following command describes the automatic modules named cglib whose module declaration is derived from the cglib-2.2.2.jar file by placing the file on the module path. The output indicates that the automatic module named cglib exports and opens all of its packages.

```
C:\Java9Revealed>java --module-path lib\cglib-2.2.2.jar
--list-modules cglib
```

```
automatic module cglib@2.2.2 (file:///C:/Java9Revealed/lib/cglib-2.2.2.jar)
  exports net.sf.cglib.beans
  exports net.sf.cglib.core
  exports net.sf.cglib.proxy
  exports net.sf.cglib.reflect
  exports net.sf.cglib.transform
  exports net.sf.cglib.transform.impl
  exports net.sf.cglib.util
  requires mandated java.base
  opens net.sf.cglib.transform
  opens net.sf.cglib.transform.impl
  opens net.sf.cglib.beans
  opens net.sf.cglib.util
  opens net.sf.cglib.reflect
  opens net.sf.cglib.core
  opens net.sf.cglib.proxy
```

Unnamed Modules

You can place JARs and modular JARs on the class path. When a type is being loaded and its package is not found in any known modules, the module system attempts to load the type from the class path. If the type is found on the class path, it is loaded by a class loader and becomes a member of a module called *unnamed module* of that class loader. Every class loader defines an unnamed module whose members are all types it loads from the class path. An unnamed module does not have a name, so an explicit module cannot declare a dependency on it using a requires statement. If you have explicit module that needs to use the types in an unnamed module, you must use the JAR for the unnamed module as an automatic module by placing the JAR on the module path.

It is a common mistake to try to access types in an unnamed module from explicit modules at compile-time. This is simply not possible because an unnamed module does not have a name and an explicit module needs a module name to read another module at compile-time. Automatic modules act as bridges between explicit modules and unnamed modules, as shown in Figure 4-15. Explicit modules can access automatic modules using requires statements and the automatic modules can access unnamed modules.

Figure 4-15. *An automatic module acting as a bridge between an explicit module and an unnamed module*

An unnamed module does not have a name. This does not mean that an unnamed module's name is the empty string, "unnamed", or null. The following declaration for a module is invalid:

```
module some.module {
    requires "";        // A compile-time error
    requires "unnamed"; // A compile-time error
    requires unnamed;   // A compile-time error unless you have a named
                        // module whose name is unnamed
    requires null;      // A compile-time error
}
```

An unnamed module reads other modules and exports and opens all its packages to other modules using the following rules:

- An unnamed module reads every other module. Therefore, an unnamed module can access public types in all exported packages in all modules, including the platform modules. This rule makes it possible that applications using the class path that compiled and ran in Java SE 8 will continue to compile and run in Java SE 9, provided they use only standard, non-deprecated Java SE APIs.

- An unnamed module opens all its packages to all other modules. Therefore, it is possible that an explicit module can access types in unnamed modules using reflection at runtime.

- An unnamed module exports all its packages. An explicit module cannot read an unnamed module at compile-time. After the module graph is resolved, all automatic modules are made to read unnamed modules.

> **Tip** It is possible for an unnamed module to contain a package that is also exported by a named module. In such a case, the package in the unnamed module is ignored.

Let's look at two examples of using unnamed modules. In the first example, a normal module will access an unnamed module using reflection. Recall that a normal module cannot access an unnamed module at compile-time. In the second example, an unnamed module will access a normal module.

Normal Modules to Unnamed Modules

You do not declare an unnamed module. To have an unnamed module, you need to place a JAR or a modular JAR on the class path. You will reuse the com.jdojo.reflect module as an unnamed module by placing its modular JAR on the class path.

Listing 4-19 and Listing 4-20 contain the module declaration for a module named com.jdojo.unnamed. test and a Main class in the module, respectively. In the main() method, the class tries to load the com. jdojo.reflect.Item class and read its fields. To keep the code simple, I added a throws clause to the main method.

Listing 4-19. The Module Declaration for the com.jdojo.unnamed.test Module

```
// module-info.com
module com.jdojo.unnamed.test {
    // No module statements
}
```

Listing 4-20. A Main Class in the com.jdojo.unnamed.test Module

```
// Main.java
package com.jdojo.unnamed.test;

import java.lang.reflect.Field;

public class Main {
    public static void main(String[] args) throws Exception {
        Class<?> cls = Class.forName("com.jdojo.reflect.Item");

        Field[] fields = cls.getDeclaredFields();
        for (Field field : fields) {
            field.setAccessible(true);
            System.out.println(field.getName() + " = " +
                            field.get(null));
        }
    }
}
```

In NetBeans, add the com.jdojo.reflect project to the class path of the com.jdojo.unnamed.test project, as shown in Figure 4-16.

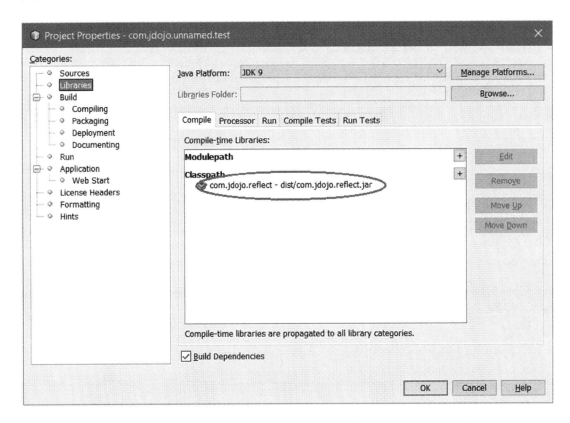

Figure 4-16. *Adding the com.jdojo.reflect project to the class path of the com.jdojo.unnamed.test project*

To run the Main class, use NetBeans or the following command. Make sure to build both projects—com.jdojo.reflect and com.jdojo.unnamed.test—before you run the command.

```
C:\Java9Revealed>java --module-path com.jdojo.unnamed.test\dist
--class-path com.jdojo.reflect\dist\com.jdojo.reflect.jar
--module com.jdojo.unnamed.test/com.jdojo.unnamed.test.Main
```

```
s = 10
t = 20
u = 30
v = 40
```

By putting the com.jdojo.reflect.jar on the class path, its Item class will be loaded into the unnamed module of the class loader. The output shows that you have successfully accessed the Item class in an unnamed module using deep reflection from the com.jdojo.unnamed.test module, which is a named module. If you try to access the Item class at compile-time, you will get a compile-time error because the com.jdojo.unnamed.test module cannot have a requires statement that can read an unnamed module.

Unnamed Modules to Normal Modules

In this section, I show you how to access types in a named module from an unnamed module. Create a Java project in NetBeans named com.jdojo.unnamed. This is not a modular project. It does not contain a module-info.java file containing a module declaration. It is a Java project that you used to create in JDK 8. Add a Main class to the project as shown in Listing 4-21. The class uses the Item class from the com.jdojo.reflect package, which is a member of an existing project named com.jdojo.reflect, which contains a module.

Listing 4-21. A Main Class in the com.jdojo.unnamed NetBeans Project

```
// Main.java
package com.jdojo.unnamed;

import com.jdojo.reflect.Item;

public class Main {
    public static void main(String[] args) {
        int v = Item.v;
        System.out.println("Item.v = " + v);
    }
}
```

The main class does not compile. It does not know where the Item class is. Let's add the com.jdojo.reflect project to the module path of the com.jdojo.unnamed project, as shown in Figure 4-17.

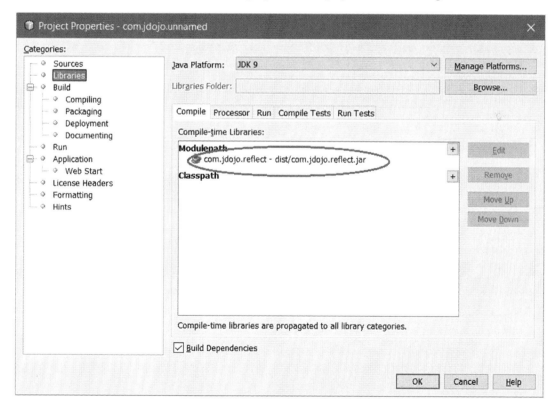

Figure 4-17. *Adding the com.jdojo.reflect project to the module path of the com.jdojo.unnamed project*

Trying to compile the com.jdojo.unnamed.Main class generates the following error:

```
C:\Java9Revealed\com.jdojo.unnamed\src\com\jdojo\unnamed\Main.java:4: error: package com.
jdojo.reflect is not visible
import com.jdojo.reflect.Item;
  (package com.jdojo.reflect is declared in module com.jdojo.reflect,
  which is not in the module graph)
1 error
```

The compile-time error is stating that the Main class cannot import the com.jdojo.reflect package because it is not visible. The message in parentheses gives you the actual reason and a hint to fix the error. You added the com.jdojo.reflect module to the module path. However, the module is not added to the module graph because there are no other modules that declare dependence on it. You can fix this error by adding the com.jdojo.reflect module to the default set of root modules using the --add-modules compiler option, as shown in Figure 4-18. Now, the com.jdojo.unnamed.Main class will compile fine.

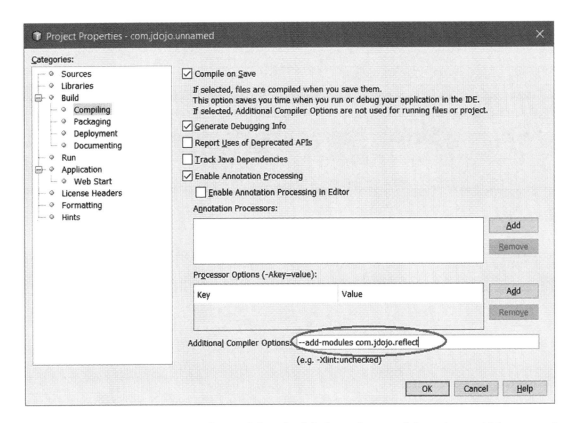

Figure 4-18. *Adding the com.jdojo.reflect module to the default set of root modules to the com.jdojo.unnamed project at compile-time*

Try to run the `com.jdojo.unnamed.Main` class in NetBeans or use the following command:

```
C:\Java9Revealed>java --module-path com.jdojo.reflect\dist
--class-path com.jdojo.unnamed\dist\com.jdojo.unnamed.jar
com.jdojo.unnamed.Main
```

```
Exception in thread "main" java.lang.NoClassDefFoundError: com/jdojo/reflect/Item
        at com.jdojo.unnamed.Main.main(Main.java:8)
Caused by: java.lang.ClassNotFoundException: com.jdojo.reflect.Item
        at java.base/jdk.internal.loader.BuiltinClassLoader.loadClass
        (BuiltinClassLoader.java:532)
        at java.base/jdk.internal.loader.ClassLoaders$AppClassLoader.loadClass
        (ClassLoaders.java:186)
        at java.base/java.lang.ClassLoader.loadClass(ClassLoader.java:473)
        ... 1 more
```

The runtime error states that the `com.jdojo.reflect.Item` class is not found. This time, the error is not as clear as it was when you tried to compile the class for the first time. However, the reason for this error is the same—the `com.jdojo.reflect` module is not included in the module graph at runtime. To fix it, you need to use the same `--add-modules` option, but this time for the VM. Figure 4-19 shows how to add this option in NetBeans.

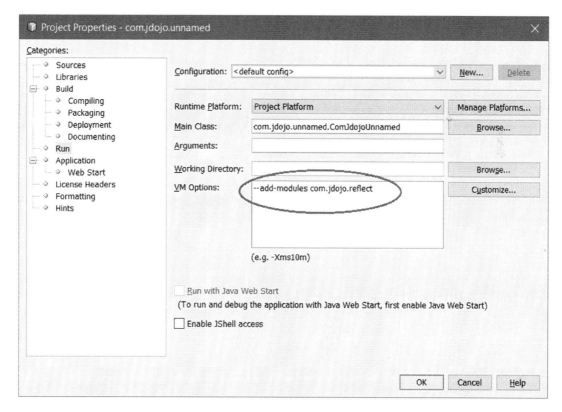

Figure 4-19. *Adding the com.jdojo.reflect module to the default set of root modules to the com.jdojo.unnamed project at runtime for the VM*

Rerun the `com.jdojo.unnamed.Main` class in NetBeans or use the following command:

```
C:\Java9Revealed>java --module-path com.jdojo.reflect\dist
--add-modules com.jdojo.reflect
--class-path com.jdojo.unnamed\dist\com.jdojo.unnamed.jar
com.jdojo.unnamed.Main
```

```
Item.v = 40
```

The output shows that an unnamed module was able to access the public types and their public members from an exported package of a named module. Note you will not be able to access other static variables (s, t, and u) of the `Item` class in the `com.jdojo.unnamed.Main` class because they are not public.

Migration Path to JDK 9

When you want to migrate your application to JDK 9, you should keep two benefits in mind that are provided by the module system: strong encapsulation and reliable configuration. You goal is to have an application that consists of normal modules with an exception of a few open modules. You might think that someone could give you a clear list of steps you need to perform to migrate your existing applications to JDK 9. However, that is not possible, keeping in mind the variety of applications, their inter-dependence of other code, and the different configuration needs. All I can do is lay out a few generic guidelines that may help you through the migration process.

Before JDK 9, a non-trivial Java application consisted of several JARs residing in three layers:

- Application JARs in the application layer—developed by application developers

- Library JARs in the library layer—provided by a third party

- Java runtime JARs in the JVM layer

JDK 9 has already modularized the Java runtime JARs by converting them to modules. That is, the Java runtime consists of modules and only modules.

The library layer consists of mainly third-party JARs placed on the class path. If you want to migrate your application to JDK 9, you may not get a modular version of the third-party JARs. You also do not have control on how the third-party JARs will be converted into modules by their vendors. You can place the library JARs onto the module path and treat them as automatic modules.

You have a choice to fully modularize your application code. The following are the choices you have for the module type selection—starting from the least desirable to the most desirable:

- Unnamed modules

- Automatic modules

- Open modules

- Normal module

The first step in migration is to check if your application runs in JDK 9 by placing all JARs—application JARs and libraries JARs—onto the class path, without any modification to your code. All types from the JARs on the class path will be part of unnamed modules. Your application in this state uses JDK 9 without any string encapsulation and reliable configuration.

Once your application runs as is in JDK 9, you can start converting the application code into automatic modules. All packages in an automatic module are both open for deep reflective access and exported for ordinary compile-time and runtime access to their public types. In this sense, it is no better than unnamed modules because it does not provide you with strong encapsulation. However, automatic modules provide you with reliable configuration because other explicit modules can declare dependence automatic modules.

You have another choice of converting your application code into open modules that offer a modest degree of stronger encapsulation: In open modules, all packages are open for deep reflective access, but you can specify which packages, if any, are exported for ordinary compile-time and runtime access. Explicit modules can also declare dependence on open modules – thus giving you a benefit of reliable configuration.

A normal module offers the strongest encapsulation, which lets you choose which packages, if any, are open, exported, or both. Explicit modules can also declare dependence on open modules, thus giving you the benefit of reliable configuration.

Table 4-2 contains the list of modules types with the degree of string encapsulation and reliable configuration they offer.

Table 4-2. *Module Types and the Varying Degrees of Strong Encapsulation and Reliable Configuration They Offer*

Module Type	Strong Encapsulation	Reliable Configuration
Unnamed	No	No
Automatic	No	Modest
Open	Modest	Yes
Normal	Strongest	Strongest

Dissembling Module Definitions

In this section, I explain the javap tool that ships with the JDK, which can be used to dissemble class files. This tool is very useful in learning the module system, especially in decompiling the module's descriptors.

At this point, you have two copies of the module-info.class file for the com.jdojo.intro module: one in the mods\com.jdojo.intro directory and another in the modular JAR in the lib\com.jdojo.intro-1.0.jar file. When you packaged the module's code into a JAR, you had specified a version and a main class for the module. Where did these pieces of information go? They were added to the module-info.class file as class attributes. Therefore, the contents of the two module-info.class files are not the same. How do you prove it? Start by printing the module declaration in both module-info.class files. You can use the javap tool, which is located in the JDK_HOME\bin directory, to dissemble code in any class file. You can specify a filename, an URL, or a class name to be dissembled. The following commands print the module declarations:

```
C:\Java9Revealed>javap mods\com.jdojo.intro\module-info.class
```

```
Compiled from "module-info.java"
module com.jdojo.intro {
  requires java.base;
}
```

```
C:\Java9Revealed>javap jar:file:lib/com.jdojo.intro-1.0.jar!/module-info.class
```

```
Compiled from "module-info.java"
module com.jdojo.intro {
  requires java.base;
}
```

The first command uses a filename and the second command uses an URL using the jar scheme. Both commands use relative paths. You can use absolute paths if you want.

The outputs indicate that both module-info.class files contain the same module declaration. You need to print the class information using the -verbose option (or the -v option) to see the class attributes. The following command prints the module-info.class file information from the mods directory and shows that the module version and main class name do not exist. A partial output is shown.

```
C:\Java9Revealed>javap -verbose mods\com.jdojo.intro\module-info.class
```

```
Classfile /C:/Java9Revealed/mods/com.jdojo.intro/module-info.class
  Last modified Jan 22, 2017; size 161 bytes
...
Constant pool:
    #1 = Class              #8                  // "module-info"
    #2 = Utf8               SourceFile
    #3 = Utf8               module-info.java
    #4 = Utf8               Module
    #5 = Module             #9                  // "com.jdojo.intro"
    #6 = Module             #10                 // "java.base"
    #7 = Utf8               9-ea
    #8 = Utf8               module-info
    #9 = Utf8               com.jdojo.intro
   #10 = Utf8               java.base
{
}
SourceFile: "module-info.java"
Module:
  #5,0                                          // "com.jdojo.intro"
  #0
  1                                             // requires
  #6,8000                                       // "java.base" ACC_MANDATED
  #7                                            // 9-ea
  0                                             // exports
  0                                             // opens
  0                                             // uses
  0                                             // provides
```

The following command prints the module-info.class file information from the lib\com.jdojo.intro-1.0.jar file and shows that the module version and main class name do exist. A partial output is shown. The relevant lines in the output have been shown in a boldface font.

```
C:\Java9Revealed>javap -verbose jar:file:lib/com.jdojo.intro-1.0.jar!/module-info.class
```

```
Classfile jar:file:lib/com.jdojo.intro-1.0.jar!/module-info.class
...
Constant pool:
  ...
  #6 = Utf8              com/jdojo/intro
  #7 = Package           #6                  // com/jdojo/intro
  #8 = Utf8              ModuleMainClass
  #9 = Utf8              com/jdojo/intro/Welcome
  #10 = Class        #9      // com/jdojo/intro/Welcome
  ...
  #14 = Utf8             1.0
  ...
{
}
SourceFile: "module-info.java"
ModulePackages:
  #7                                  // com.jdojo.intro
ModuleMainClass: #10                  // com.jdojo.intro.Welcome
Module:
 #13,0                                // "com.jdojo.intro"
 #14                                  // 1.0
 1                                    // requires
 #16,8000                             // "java.base" ACC_MANDATED
```

You can also dissemble the code for a class in a module. You need to specify the module path, the module name, and the fully qualified name of the class. The following command prints the code for the com. jdojo.intro.Welcome class from its modular JAR:

```
C:\Java9Revealed>javap --module-path lib
 --module com.jdojo.intro com.jdojo.intro.Welcome
```

```
Compiled from "Welcome.java"
public class com.jdojo.intro.Welcome {
  public com.jdojo.intro.Welcome();
  public static void main(java.lang.String[]);
}
```

You can also print the class information for system classes. The following command prints the class information for the java.lang.Object class from the java.base module. Note that you do not need to specify the module path when you print system class information.

```
C:\Java9Revealed>javap --module java.base java.lang.Object
```

```
Compiled from "Object.java"
public class java.lang.Object {
  public java.lang.Object();
  public final native java.lang.Class<?> getClass();
  public native int hashCode();
  public boolean equals(java.lang.Object);
  ...
}
```

How would you print the module declaration for a system module such as java.base or java.sql? Recall that system modules are packaged in special file format, not as modular JARs. JDK 9 has introduced a new URL scheme called jrt (jrt is short for Java runtime) to refer to the contents of the Java runtime image (or system modules). The syntax for using the jrt scheme is as follows:

```
jrt:/<module>/<path-to-a-file>
```

The following command prints the module declaration for the system module named java.sql:

```
C:\Java9Revealed>javap jrt:/java.sql/module-info.class
```

```
Compiled from "module-info.java"
module java.sql@9-ea {
  requires java.base;
  requires transitive java.logging;
  requires transitive java.xml;
  exports javax.transaction.xa;
  exports javax.sql;
  exports java.sql;
  uses java.sql.Driver;
}
```

The following command prints the module declaration for the java.se, which is an aggregator module:

```
C:\Java9Revealed>javap jrt:/java.se/module-info.class
```

```
Compiled from "module-info.java"
module java.se@9-ea {
  requires transitive java.sql;
  requires transitive java.rmi;
  requires transitive java.desktop;
  requires transitive java.security.jgss;
  requires transitive java.security.sasl;
  requires transitive java.management;
```

```
  requires transitive java.logging;
  requires transitive java.xml;
  requires transitive java.scripting;
  requires transitive java.compiler;
  requires transitive java.naming;
  requires transitive java.instrument;
  requires transitive java.xml.crypto;
  requires transitive java.prefs;
  requires transitive java.sql.rowset;
  requires java.base;
  requires transitive java.datatransfer;
}
```

You can also use the jrt scheme to refer to a system class. The following command prints the class information for the java.lang.Object class in the java.base module:

```
C:\Java9Revealed>javap jrt:/java.base/java/lang/Object.class
```

```
Compiled from "Object.java"
public class java.lang.Object {
  public java.lang.Object();
  public final native java.lang.Class<?> getClass();
  public native int hashCode();
  public boolean equals(java.lang.Object);
  ...
}
```

Summary

If a module needs to use public types contained in another module, the second module needs to export the package containing the types and the first module needs to read the second module.

A module exports its packages using the exports statement. A module can export its packages only to specific modules. Public types in exports packages are available to other modules at compile-time and runtime. An exported package does not allow deep reflection on non-public members of public types.

If a module wants to allow other modules to access all types of members—public and non-public—using reflection, the module must either be declared as an open module or the module can open packages selectively using an opens statement. A module accessing types from open packages does not need to read the module containing those open packages.

A module declares a dependence on another module using the requires statement. Such a dependence can be declared transitive using the transitive modifier. If module M declares a transitive dependence on module N, any module declaring a dependence on module M declares an implicit dependence on module N.

A dependence can be declared mandatory at compile-time, but optional at runtime using the static modifier in the requires statement. A dependency can be optional at runtime and transitive at the same time.

The module system in JDK 9 has changed the meaning of the public types. A public type defined in a module may fall into one of the three categories: public only within the defining module, public only to specific modules, or public to everyone.

Based on how a module is declared and whether it has a name, there are several types of modules. Based on whether a module has a name, a module can be a *named module* or an *unnamed module*. When a module has a name, the name can be given explicitly in a module declaration or the name can be generated automatically (or implicitly). If the name is given explicitly in a module declaration, it is called an *explicit module*. If the name is generated by the module system by reading the JAR filename on the module path, it is called an *automatic module*. If you declare a module without using the open modifier, it is called a *normal module*. If you declare a module using the open modifier, it is called an *open module*. Based on these definitions, an open module is also an explicit module and a named module. An automatic module is a named module as it has a name, which is automatically generated, but it is not an explicit module because it is implicitly declared by the module system at compile-time and runtime.

When you place a JAR (not a module JAR) on the module path, the JAR represents an automatic module whose name is derived from the JAR filename. An automatic module reads all the other modules and all its packages are exported and opened.

In JDK 9, a class loader can load a class from a module or from the class path. Every class loader maintains a module called unnamed module that contains all types that it loads from the class path. An unnamed module reads every other module. It exports and opens all its packages to all other modules. An unnamed module does not have a name, so an explicit module cannot declare a compile-time dependence on an unnamed module. If an explicit module needs to access types in an unnamed module, the former can use an automatic module as a bridge or use reflection.

You can use the `javap` tool to print the module declaration or attributes. Use the `-verbose` (or -v) option of the tool to print the class attributes of the module descriptor. JDK 9 stores the runtime image in a special format. JDK 9 introduced a new file scheme called `jrt` that you can use to access the contents of the runtime image. Its syntax is `jrt:/<module>/<path-to-a-file>`.

CHAPTER 5

▧ ▧ ▧

Implementing Services

In this chapter, you will learn:

- What services, service interfaces, and service providers are

- How to implement a service in JDK 9 and before JDK 9

- How to use a Java interface as a service implementation

- How to load service providers using the ServiceLoader class

- How to use the uses statement in a module declaration to specify the service interface that the current modules loads using the ServiceLoader class

- How to use the provides statement to specify a service provider provided by the current module for a service interface

- How to discover, filter, and select service providers based on their class without instantiating them

- How to package service providers before JDK 9

What Is a Service?

A specific functionality provided by an application (or a library) is known as a *service*. For example, you can have different libraries providing a *prime number service,* which can check if a number is a prime and generating the next prime after a given number. Applications and libraries providing implementations for a service are known as *service providers*. Applications using the service are called *service consumers* or *clients*. How does a client use the service? Does a client know all service providers? Does a client get a service without knowing any service providers? I answer these questions in this chapter.

Java SE 6 provided a mechanism to allow for loose coupling between service providers and service consumers. That is, a service consumer can use a service provided by a service provider without knowing the service provider.

In Java, a *service* is defined by a set of interfaces and classes. The service contains an interface or an abstract class that defines the functionality provided by the service and it is known as the *service provider interface* or simply *service interface*. Note that the term "interface" in "service provider interface" or "service interface" does not refer to an interface construct in Java. It can be a Java interface or an abstract class. It is possible, but not recommended, to use a concrete class as a service interface. Sometimes, a service interface is also called a *service type*—the type that is used to identify the service.

A specific implementation of a *service* is known as a *service provider*. There can be multiple service providers for a service provider interface. Typically, a service provider consists of several interfaces and classes to provide an implementation for the service interface.

© Kishori Sharan 2017
K. Sharan, *Java 9 Revealed*, DOI 10.1007/978-1-4842-2592-9_5

The JDK contains a java.util.ServiceLoader<S> class whose sole purpose is to discover and load service providers at runtime for a service interface of type S. The ServiceLoader class allows decoupling between the service consumers and the service providers. A service consumer knows only the service interface; the ServiceLoader class makes the instances of the service providers that are implementing the service interface available to consumers. Figure 5-1 shows a pictorial view of the arrangement of a service, service providers, and a service consumer.

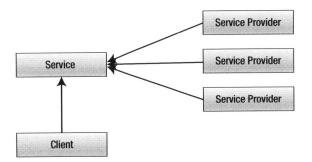

Figure 5-1. *The arrangement of a service, service providers, and a service consumer*

Typically, the service will use the ServiceLoader class to load all service providers and make them available to service consumers (or clients). This architecture allows for a plugin mechanism in which a service provider can be added or removed without affecting the service and service consumers. Service consumers know only about that service interface. They do not know about any specific implementations (service providers) of that service interface.

■ **Tip**   I suggest reading the documentation for the java.util.ServiceLoader class for a complete understanding of the service-loading facility provided by JDK 9.

In this chapter, I use a service interface and three service providers. Their modules, class/interface names, and brief descriptions are listed in Table 5-1. Figure 5-2 shows the classes/interfaces arranged as services, service providers, and service consumers, which can be compared with Table 5-1.

Table 5-1. *A List of Modules, Classes, and Interfaces Used in the Chapter Examples*

Module	Classes/Interfaces	Description
com.jdojo.prime	PrimeChecker	It acts as a service interface and a service
com.jdojo.prime.generic	GenericPrimeChecker	A service provider
com.jdojo.prime.faster	FasterPrimeChecker	A service provider
com.jdojo.prime.probable	ProbablePrimeChecker	A service provider
com.jdojo.prime.client	Main	A service consumer

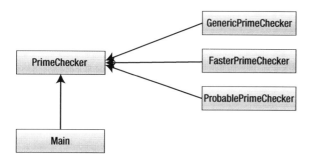

Figure 5-2. *The arrangement of a service, three service providers, and a service consumer used in the chapter's examples*

Discovering Services

In order for a service to be used, its providers need to be discovered and loaded. The java.util.ServiceLoader class does the work of discovering and loading the service providers. The module that discovers and loads service providers must contain a uses statement in its declaration, which has the following syntax:

```
uses <service-interface>;
```

Here, <service-interface> is the name of the service interface, which is a Java interface name, a class name, or an annotation type name. If a module uses the ServiceLoader<S> class to load the instances of service providers for a service interface named S, the module declaration must contain the following statement:

```
uses S;
```

▓ **Tip**   In my opinion, the statement name, uses, seems to be a misnomer. At first glance, it seems that the current module will use the specified service. However, that is not the case. A service is used by the clients, not by the module defining the service. A more intuitive statement name would have been discovers or loads. However, we have to live with the name we were given. You can understand its meaning correctly if you read its definition as: The module having the uses statement *uses* the ServiceLoader class to load the service providers for this service interface. You do not need to use the uses statement in client modules unless your client modules loads the service providers for the service. It is unusual for client modules to load services.

A module may discover and load more than one service interface. The following module declaration uses two uses statements indicating that it will discover and load service interfaces of type com.jdojo.PrimeChecker and com.jdojo.CsvParser:

```
module com.jdojo.loader {
    uses com.jdojo.PrimeChecker;
    uses com.jdojo.CsvParser:

    // Other module statements go here
}
```

A module declaration allows `import` statements. For better readability, you can rewrite this module declaration as follows:

```
// Import types from other packages
import com.jdojo.PrimeChecker;
import com.jdojo.CsvParser:

module com.jdojo.loader {
    uses PrimeChecker;
    uses CsvParser:

    // Other module statements go here
}
```

The service interface specified in a `uses` statement may be declared in the current module or another module. If it is declared in another module, the service interface must be accessible to the code in the current module. Otherwise, a compile-time error occurs. For example, the `com.jdojo.CsvParser` service interface used in the `uses` statement in the previous declaration may be declared in the `com.jdojo.loader` module or another module, say `com.jdojo.csvutil`. In the latter case, the `com.jdojo.CsvParser` interface must be accessible to the `com.jdojo.loader` module.

Service provider discovery occurs dynamically at runtime. Modules that discover service providers typically do not (and need not) declare compile-time dependency on the service provider modules because it is not possible to know all provider modules in advance. Another reason for service discoverer modules not declaring dependency on service provider modules is to keep the service provider and service consumer decoupled.

Providing Service Implementations

A module that provides implementations for a service interface must contain a `provides` statement. If a module contains a service provider, but does not contain a `provides` statements in its declaration, this service provider will not be loaded through the `ServiceLoader` class. That is, a `provides` statement in a module declaration is a way to tell the `ServiceLoader` class, "Hey! I provide an implementation for a service. You can use me as a provider whenever you need that service." The syntax for a `provides` statement is as follows:

```
provides <service-interface> with <service-implementation-name>;
```

Here, the `provides` clause specifies the name of the service interface and the `with` clause specifies the name of the class that implements the service provider interface. In JDK 9, a service provider may specify an interface as an implementation for a service interface. This may sound incorrect, but it is true. I provide an example where an interface serves as a service provider implementation type. The following module declaration contains two `provides` statements:

```
module com.jdojo.provider {
    provides com.jdojo.PrimeChecker with com.jdojo.impl.PrimeCheckerFactory;
    provides com.jdojo.CsvParser with com.jdojo.impl.CsvFastParser;

    // Other module statements go here
}
```

The first `provides` statement declares that `com.jdojo.impl.PrimeCheckerFactory` is one possible implementation for the service interface named `com.jdojo.PrimeChecker`. The second `provides` statement declares that `com.jdojo.impl.CsvFastParser` is one possible implementation for the service interface named `com.jdojo.CsvParser`. Before JDK 9, `PrimeCheckerFactory` and `CsvParser` had to be classes. In JDK 9, they can be classes or interfaces.

A module can contain any combination of `uses` and `provides` statements—the same module can provide implementation for a service and discover the same service; it can only provide implementation for one or more services, or it can provide implementation for one service and discover another type of service. The following module declaration discovers and provides the implementation for the same service:

```
module com.jdojo.parser {
    uses com.jdojo.XmlParser;

    provides com.jdojo.XmlParser with com.jdojo.xml.impl.XmlParserFactory;

    // Other module statements go here
}
```

For better readability, you can use `import` statements to rewrite the previous module declaration:

```
import com.jdojo.XmlParser;
import com.jdojo.xml.impl.XmlParserFactory

module com.jdojo.parser {
    uses XmlParser;

    provides XmlParser with XmlParserFactory;

    // Other module statements go here
}
```

▓ **Tip** The service implementation class/interface specified in the `with` clause of the `provides` statement must be declared in the current module. Otherwise, a compile-time error occurs.

The `ServiceLoader` class creates instances of the service implementation. When the service implementation is an interface, it simply loads and returns the interface reference. The service implementation (a class or an interface) must follow these rules:

- If the service implementation implicitly or explicitly declares a public constructor with no formal parameters, that constructor is called the *provider constructor*.

- If the service implementation contains a public static method named `provider` with no formal parameters, this method is called the *provider method*.

- The return type of the provider method must be the service interface type or its subtype.

- If the service implementation does not contain a provider method, the type of the service implementation must be a class with a provider constructor and the class must be of the service interface type or its subtype.

When the ServiceLoader class is requested to discover and load a service provider, it checks whether the service implementation contains a provider method. If a provider method is found, the returned value of the method is the service returned by the ServiceLoader class. If a provider method is not found, it instantiates the service implementation using the provider constructor. If the service implementation contains neither a provider method nor a provider constructor, a compile-time occur occurs.

With these rules, it is possible to use a Java interface as a service implementation. The interface should have a public static method named provider that returns an instance of the service interface type.

The following sub-sections walk you through the steps to implement a service in JDK 9. The last sub-section explains how to make the same service work in a non-modular environment.

Defining the Service Interface

In this section, you develop a service called *prime checker*. I am keeping the service simple, so you can focus on working with the service provider mechanism in JDK 9, rather than writing complex code to implement the service functionality. Requirements for this service are as follows:

- The service should provide an API to check if a number is a prime.

- Clients should be able to know the name of the service provider. That is, each service provider should be able to specify its name.

- Clients should be able to retrieve a service instance without specifying the name of the service provider. In this case, the first service provider found by the ServiceLoader class is returned. If no service provider is found, a RuntimeException is thrown.

- Clients should be able to retrieve a service instance by specifying a service provider name. If a service provider with the specified name does not exist, a RuntimeException is thrown.

Let's design the service. The functionality provided by the service will be represented by an interface named PrimeChecker. It will contain two methods:

```
public interface PrimeChecker {
    String getName();
    boolean isPrime(long n);
}
```

The getName() method returns the name of the service provider. The isPrime() method returns true if the specified argument is a prime, and it returns false otherwise. All service providers will implement the PrimeChecker interface. The PrimeChecker interface is our service interface (or service type).

The service needs to provide APIs to the clients to retrieve instances of the service providers. The service needs to discover and load all service providers before clients can retrieve them. The service providers are loaded using the ServiceLoader class. The class has no public constructor. You can use one of its load() methods to get its instance to load a specific type of service. You will need to pass the class of the service provider interface. The ServiceLoader class contains an iterator() method that returns an Iterator for all service providers of a specific service interface loaded by this ServiceLoader. The following snippet of code shows you how to load and iterate through all service provider instances for PrimeChecker:

```
// Load the service providers for PrimeChecker
ServiceLoader<PrimeChecker> loader = ServiceLoader.load(PrimeChecker.class);

// Iterate through all service provider instances
Iterator<PrimeChecker> iterator = loader.iterator();
```

```
if(iterator.hasNext()) {
    PrimeChecker checker = iterator.next();

    // Use the prime checker here...
}
```

Before JDK 8, you had to create a class to provide the discovering, loading, and retrieving features for your service. As of JDK 8, you can add `static` methods to interfaces. Let's add two static methods to our service interface for these purposes:

```
public interface PrimeChecker {
    String getName();
    boolean isPrime(long n);

    static PrimeChecker newInstance();
    static PrimeChecker newInstance(String providerName)
 }
```

The `newInstance()` method will return an instance of the `PrimeChecker` that is found first. Another version will return the instance of a service provider with the specified provider name.

Let's create a module named com.jdojo.prime. Listing 5-1 shows you the complete code for the `PrimeChecker` interface.

Listing 5-1. A Service Provider Interface Named PrimeChecker

```
// PrimeChecker.java
package com.jdojo.prime;

import java.util.ServiceLoader;

public interface PrimeChecker {
    /**
     * Returns the service provider name.
     *
     * @return The service provider name
     */
    String getName();

    /**
     * Returns true if the specified number is a prime, false otherwise.
     *
     * @param n The number to be check for being prime
     * @return true if the specified number is a prime, false otherwise.
     */
    boolean isPrime(long n);

    /**
     * Returns the first PrimeChecker service provider found.
     *
     * @return The first PrimeChecker service provider found.
     * @throws RuntimeException When no PrimeChecker service provider is found.
     */
```

```java
static PrimeChecker newInstance() throws RuntimeException {
    return ServiceLoader.load(PrimeChecker.class)
                        .findFirst()
                        .orElseThrow(() -> new RuntimeException(
                          "No PrimeChecker service provider found."));
}

/**
 * Returns a PrimeChecker service provider instance by name.
 *
 * @param providerName The prime checker service provider name
 * @return A PrimeChecker
 */
static PrimeChecker newInstance(String providerName) throws RuntimeException {
    ServiceLoader<PrimeChecker> loader = ServiceLoader.load(PrimeChecker.class);

    for (PrimeChecker checker : loader) {
        if (checker.getName().equals(providerName)) {
            return checker;
        }
    }

    throw new RuntimeException("A PrimeChecker service provider with the name '"
            + providerName + "' was not found.");
}
}
```

The declaration for the com.jdojo.prime module is shown in Listing 5-2. It exports the com.jdojo.prime package because the PrimeChecker interface will need to be used by the service provider modules and the client modules.

Listing 5-2. The Module Declaration for the com.jdojo.prime Module

```java
// module-info.java
module com.jdojo.prime {
    exports com.jdojo.prime;

    uses com.jdojo.prime.PrimeChecker;
}
```

You need to use a uses statement with the fully qualified name of the PrimeChecker interface because the code in this module (the newInstance() methods in this interface) will use the ServiceLoader class to load the service providers for this interface. If you want to use the simple name in the uses statement, add the appropriate import statement as shown in the previous sections.

That is all you have to do to define the prime checker service.

Defining Service Providers

In the next two sections, you will create two service providers for the `PrimeChecker` service interface. The first service provider will implement a generic prime checker whereas the second one will implement a faster prime checker. Later, you will create a client to test the service. You will have a choice to use one of these service providers or both.

These service providers will implement algorithms to check whether a given number is prime. It will be helpful for you to understand the definition of a prime number: A positive integer that is not divisible without remainder by 1 or itself is called a prime. 1 is not a prime. A few examples of primes are 2, 3, 5, 7, and 11.

Defining a Generic Prime Service Provider

In this section, you will define a generic service provider for the `PrimeChecker` service. Defining a service provider for a service is simply creating a class that implements the service interface or creating an interface that has a provider method. In this case, you will be creating a class named `GenericPrimeChecker` that implements the `PrimeChecker` interface and will contain a provider constructor.

This service provider will be defined in a separate module named `com.jdojo.prime.generic`. Listing 5-3 contains the module declaration. The module declaration will not compile at this time.

Listing 5-3. The Module Declaration for the com.jdojo.prime.generic Module

```
// module-info.java
module com.jdojo.prime.generic {
    requires com.jdojo.prime;

    provides com.jdojo.prime.PrimeChecker
        with com.jdojo.prime.generic.GenericPrimeChecker;
}
```

The `requires` statement is needed because this module will use the `PrimeChecker` interface from the `com.jdojo.prime` module. In NetBeans, add the `com.jdojo.prime` project to the module path of the `com.jdojo.prime.generic` project. This will get rid of the compile-time error in the module declaration, which is caused by the missing module `com.jdojo.prime` that is referenced in the `requires` statement.

The `provides` statement specifies that this module provides an implementation for the `PrimeChecker` interface and its `with` clause specifies the name of the implementation class. The implementation class must fulfill the following conditions:

- It must be a public concrete class. It can be a top-level or nested `static` class. It cannot be an inner class or an `abstract` class.

- It must have a pubic no-args constructor. This constructor is used by the `ServiceLoader` class to instantiate the service provider using reflection. Note that you are not providing a provider method in the `GenericPrimeChecker` class, which is an alternative to providing a no-args public constructor.

- An instance of the implementation class must be assignment-compatible with the service provider interface.

If any of these conditions are not met, a compile-time error occurs. Note that you do not need to export the `com.jdojo.prime.generic` package that contains the service implementation class because no client is supposed to directly depend on a service implementation. Clients need to know only the service interface, not any specific service implementation. The `ServiceLoader` class can access and instantiate the implementation class without the package containing the service implementation being exported by the module.

113

> ■ **Tip** If a module uses a `provides` statement, the specified service interface may be in the current module or another accessible module. The service implementation class/interface specified in the `with` clause must be defined in the current module.

Listing 5-4 contains the code for the GenericPrimeChecker class that is a service implementation for the PrimeChecker service interface. The isPrime() method returns the name of the service provider. I provided jdojo.generic.primechecker as its name. This is an arbitrary name. The isPrime() method returns true if the specified number is a prime; it returns false otherwise. The getName() method returns the provider name.

Listing 5-4. A GenericPrimeChecker Class: A Service Implementation Class for the PrimeChecker Service Interface

```java
// GenericPrimeChecker.java
package com.jdojo.prime.generic;

import com.jdojo.prime.PrimeChecker;

public class GenericPrimeChecker implements PrimeChecker {
    private static final String PROVIDER_NAME = "jdojo.generic.primechecker";

    @Override
    public boolean isPrime(long n) {
        if(n <= 1) {
            return false;
        }

        if (n == 2) {
            return true;
        }

        if(n%2 == 0) {
            return false;
        }

        for(long i = 3; i < n; i += 2) {
            if(n%i == 0) {
                return false;
            }
        }

        return true;
    }

    @Override
    public String getName() {
        return PROVIDER_NAME;
    }
}
```

That's all you have for this module. As mentioned earlier, to compile this module, you will need the com.jdojo.prime module in the module path. Compile and package this module as a modular JAR. At this point, there is nothing to test.

Defining a Faster Prime Service Provider

In this section, you will define another service provider for the PrimeChecker service interface. Let's call this a *faster* service provider because you will implement a faster algorithm to check for a prime. This service provider will be defined in a separate module named com.jdojo.prime.faster and the service implementation class is called FasterPrimeChecker.

Listing 5-5 contains the module declaration, which is similar to the one we had for the com.jdojo.prime.generic module. This time, only the class name in the with clause has changed.

Listing 5-5. The Module Declaration for the com.jdojo.prime.faster Module

```
// module-info.java
module com.jdojo.prime.faster {
    requires com.jdojo.prime;

    provides com.jdojo.prime.PrimeChecker
        with com.jdojo.prime.faster.FasterPrimeChecker;
}
```

The requires statement in the module declaration will require you to add the com.jdojo.prime project to the module path of the com.jdojo.prime.faster project in NetBeans, so the com.jdojo.prime module is found on the module path.

Listing 5-6 contains the code for the FasterPrimeChecker class whose isPrime() method executes faster than the isPrime() method of the GenericPrimeChecker class. This time, the method loops through all odd numbers starting at 3 and ending at the square root of the number being tested for a prime.

Listing 5-6. An Implementation Class Named FasterPrimeChecker for the PrimeChecker Interface Used as a Service Provider

```
// FasterPrimeChecker.java
package com.jdojo.prime.faster;

import com.jdojo.prime.PrimeChecker;

public class FasterPrimeChecker implements PrimeChecker {
    private static final String PROVIDER_NAME = "jdojo.faster.primechecker";

    // No provider constructor
    private FasterPrimeChecker() {
        // No code
    }

    // Define a provider method
    public static PrimeChecker provider() {
        return new FasterPrimeChecker();
    }
```

```
    @Override
    public boolean isPrime(long n) {
        if (n <= 1) {
            return false;
        }

        if (n == 2) {
            return true;
        }

        if (n % 2 == 0) {
            return false;
        }

        long limit = (long) Math.sqrt(n);
        for (long i = 3; i <= limit; i += 2) {
            if (n % i == 0) {
                return false;
            }
        }

        return true;
    }

    @Override
    public String getName() {
        return PROVIDER_NAME;
    }
}
```

Note the difference between the GenericPrimeChecker and FasterPrimeChecker classes, as shown in Listing 5-4 and Listing 5-6. The GenericPrimeChecker class contains a default constructor that serves as a provider constructor. It does not contain a provider method. The FasterPrimeChecker class makes the no-args constructor private, which does not qualify to be a provider constructor. Recall that a provider constructor is a public no-args constructor, which is used by the ServiceLoader class to instantiate the service implementation class. The FasterPrimeChecker class provides a provider method instead, which is declared as:

```
public static PrimeChecker provider() {/*...*/}
```

When the ServiceLoader class needs to instantiate the faster prime service, it will call this method. The method is very simple—it creates and returns an object of the FasterPrimeChecker class.

That's all you need for this module at this time. To compile this module, the com.jdojo.prime module needs to be in the module path. Compile and package this module as a modular JAR. At this point, there is nothing to test.

Defining a Fastest Prime Service Provider

In this section, I show you how to use a Java interface as a service implementation. You will define another service provider for the PrimeChecker service interface. Let's call this a *probable* prime service provider because it tells you that a number is probably a prime. This service provider will be defined in a separate module named com.jdojo.prime.probable and the service implementation interface is called ProbablePrimeChecker.

The service is about checking for a prime number. The BigInteger class in the java.math package contains a method called isProbablePrime(int certainty). If the method returns true, the number may be a prime. If the method returns false, the number is certainly not a prime. The certainty parameter determines the degree to which the method makes sure the number is prime before returning true. The higher the value of the certainty parameter, the higher the cost this method incurs and the higher the probability that the number is a prime when the method returns true.

Listing 5-7 contains the module declaration, which is similar to the ones we had before for the other two modules. This time, only the class/interface name in the with clause has changed.

Listing 5-7. The Module Declaration for the com.jdojo.prime.probable Module

```java
// module-info.java
module com.jdojo.prime.probable {
    requires com.jdojo.prime;

    provides com.jdojo.prime.PrimeChecker
        with com.jdojo.prime.probable.ProbablePrimeChecker;
}
```

The requires statement in the module declaration will require you to add the com.jdojo.prime project to the module path of the com.jdojo.prime.probable project in NetBeans, so the com.jdojo.prime module is found on the module path. Listing 5-8 contains the code for the ProbablePrimeChecker class.

Listing 5-8. An Implementation Interface Named ProbablePrimeChecker for the PrimeChecker Interface Used as a Service Provider

```java
// ProbablePrimeChecker.java
package com.jdojo.prime.probable;

import com.jdojo.prime.PrimeChecker;
import java.math.BigInteger;

public interface ProbablePrimeChecker {
    // A provider method
    public static PrimeChecker provider() {
        final String PROVIDER_NAME = "jdojo.probable.primechecker";

        return new PrimeChecker() {
            @Override
            public boolean isPrime(long n) {
                // Use 1000 for high certainty, which is an arbitrary big number I chose
                int certainty = 1000;
                return BigInteger.valueOf(n).isProbablePrime(certainty);
            }
```

```
        @Override
        public String getName() {
            return PROVIDER_NAME;
        }
    };
    }
}
```

The `ProbablePrimeChecker` interface consists of only one method, which is a provider method:

```
public static PrimeChecker provider() {/*...*/}
```

When the `ServiceLoader` class needs to instantiate the probable prime service, it will call this method. The method is very simple—it creates and returns an instance of the `PrimeChecker` interface. The `isPrime()` method uses the `BigInteger` class to check whether the number is a probable prime. The name of the provider is `jdojo.probable.primechecker`. Note that the interface does not extend the `PrimeChecker` interface. To be a service implementation, its provider method must return an instance of the service interface (the `PrimeChecker` interface) or its subtype. By declaring the return type of the provider method as `PrimeChecker`, you have fulfilled this requirement.

That's all you have for this module. To compile this module, you need to add the `com.jdojo.prime` module to the module path. Compile and package this module as a modular JAR. At this point, there is nothing to test.

Testing the Prime Service

In this section, you will test the service by creating a client application, which will be defined in a separate module named `com.jdojo.prime.client`. Listing 5-9 contains the module declaration.

Listing 5-9. The Module Declaration for the com.jdojo.prime.client Module

```
// module-info.java
module com.jdojo.prime.client {
    requires com.jdojo.prime;
}
```

The client module needs to know only about the service interface. In this case, the `com.jdojo.prime` module defines the service interface. Therefore, the client module reads the service interface module and nothing else. In a real world, the client module will be much more complex than this and it may read other modules as well. In NetBeans, for the `com.jdojo.prime.client` module for compile, you need to add the `com.jdojo.prime` project to its module path. Figure 5-3 shows the module graph for the `com.jdojo.prime.client` module.

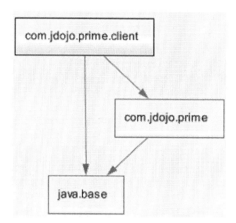

Figure 5-3. *The module graph for the com.jdojo.prime.client module*

■ **Tip** A client module is not aware of the service provider modules and it need not directly read them as such. It is the responsibility of the service to discover all service providers and make their instances available to clients. In this case, the `com.jdojo.prime` module defines the `com.jdojo.prime.PrimeChecker` interface, which is a service interface and also acts as a service.

Listing 5-10 contains the code for the client that uses the `PrimeChecker` service.

Listing 5-10. A Main Class to Test the PrimeChecker Service

```java
// Main.java
package com.jdojo.prime.client;

import com.jdojo.prime.PrimeChecker;

public class Main {
    public static void main(String[] args) {
        // Numbers to be checked for prime
        long[] numbers = {3, 4, 121, 977};

        // Try a default prime checker service provider
        try {
            PrimeChecker checker = PrimeChecker.newInstance();
            checkPrimes(checker, numbers);
        } catch (RuntimeException e) {
            System.out.println(e.getMessage());
        }
```

```
        // Try the faster prime checker
        try {
            PrimeChecker checker = PrimeChecker.newInstance("jdojo.faster.primechecker");
            checkPrimes(checker, numbers);
        } catch (RuntimeException e) {
            System.out.println(e.getMessage());
        }

        // Try the probable prime checker
        try {
            PrimeChecker checker = PrimeChecker.newInstance("jdojo.probable.primechecker");
            checkPrimes(checker, numbers);
        } catch (RuntimeException e) {
            System.out.println(e.getMessage());
        }
    }

    public static void checkPrimes(PrimeChecker primeChecker, long... numbers) {
        System.out.format("Using %s:%n",  primeChecker.getName());

        for (long n : numbers) {
            if (primeChecker.isPrime(n)) {
                System.out.printf("%d is a prime.%n", n);
            } else {
                System.out. printf("%d is not a prime.%n", n);
            }
        }
    }
}
```

The checkPrimes() method takes a PrimeChecker instance and var-args long numbers. It uses the PrimeChecker to check whether numbers are prime and prints corresponding messages. The main() method retrieves the default PrimeChecker service provider instance and the instances of the jdojo.faster.primechecker and jdojo.probable.primechecker service providers. It uses all three service providers instances to check the same set of numbers to be prime. Compile and package the module's code. If you run the Main class with only two modules, com.jdojo.prime and com.jdojo.prime.client, in the module path, you get the following output:

```
No PrimeChecker service provider found.
A PrimeChecker service provider with the name 'jdojo.faster.primechecker' was not found.
A PrimeChecker service provider with the name 'jdojo.probable.primechecker' was not found.
```

There was no service provider in the module path and, therefore, all three attempts to retrieve a service provider fail.

If you run the Main class with the com.jdojo.prime, com.jdojo.prime.generic, and com.jdojo.prime.client modules on the module path, you get the following output:

```
Using jdojo.generic.primechecker:
3 is a prime.
4 is not a prime.
121 is not a prime.
977 is a prime.
A PrimeChecker service provider with the name 'jdojo.faster.primechecker' was not found.
A PrimeChecker service provider with the name 'jdojo.probable.primechecker' was not found.
```

This time, you have one service provider, jdojo.generic.primechecker, in the module path. Therefore, an attempt to retrieve the default service provider will get you a PrimeChecker instance of this service provider. This is obvious in the first part of the output. An attempt to retrieve other service providers failed because they are not found on the module path.

If you run the Main class with the com.jdojo.prime, com.jdojo.prime.generic, com.jdojo.prime.faster, com.jdojo.prime.probable, and com.jdojo.prime.client modules on the module path, you get an output similar to the following output. The default provider is the one that is found first by the iterator. The output shows the generic service provider as the default, but you may get any other provider as the default provider when you run the program.

```
Using jdojo.generic.primechecker:
3 is a prime.
4 is not a prime.
121 is not a prime.
977 is a prime.
Using jdojo.faster.primechecker:
3 is a prime.
4 is not a prime.
121 is not a prime.
977 is a prime.
Using jdojo.probable.primechecker:
3 is a prime.
4 is not a prime.
121 is not a prime.
977 is a prime.
```

When the module system encounters a uses statement in a module declaration, it scans the module path to find all modules that contain provides statements that specify implementations for the service interface specified in the uses statement. In this sense, a uses statement in a module indicates an indirect optional dependency on other modules. That dependency is resolved at runtime.

Selecting and Filtering Providers

At times, you'll want to select providers based on their class names. For example, you may want to select only those prime service providers whose fully qualified class name starts with com.jdojo. A typical logic to achieve this would be to use the iterator returned by the iterator() method of the ServiceLoader class. However, this operator is costly. The iterator instantiates a provider before returning it to you even though the instantiation happens lazily—meaning a provider is instantiated when it is needed to be returned.

JDK 9 added a new method to the `ServiceLoader` class. The method's signature is as follows:

```
public Stream<ServiceLoader.Provider<S>> stream()
```

The `stream()` method returns a stream of instances of the `ServiceProvider.Provider` interface, which is declared as a nested interface in the `ServiceLoader` class as follows:

```
public static interface Provider<S> extends Supplier<S> {
    Class<? extends S> type();

    @Override
    S get();
}
```

An instance of the `ServiceLoader.Provider` interface represents a service provider. Its `type()` method returns the `Class` object of the service implementation. The `get()` method instantiates and returns the service provider. How does the `ServiceLoader.Provider` interface help? When you use the `stream()` method, each element in the stream is of the `ServiceLoader.Provider` type. You can filter the stream based on the class name or type of the provider, which will not instantiate the provider. You can use the `type()` method in your filters. When you find the desired provider, call the `get()` method to instantiate the provider. This way, you instantiate a provider when you know you need it, not when you are iterating through all providers.

The following is an example of using the `stream()` method of the `ServiceLoader` class. It gives you a list of all prime service providers whose class name starts with `com.jdojo`.

```
static List<PrimeChecker> startsWith(String prefix) {
    return ServiceLoader.load(PrimeChecker.class)
                        .stream()
                        .filter((Provider p) -> p.type().getName().startsWith(prefix))
                        .map(Provider::get)
                        .collect(Collectors.toList());
}
```

You can add this method to the `PrimeChecker` interface. You will need to add a few `import` statements when you add this method:

```
import java.util.List;
import java.util.ServiceLoader.Provider;
import java.util.stream.Collectors;
```

The following is an example of calling this method, for example, from the client class:

```
// Get the list of all prime services whose class names start with "com.jdojo"
List<PrimeChecker> jdojoService = PrimeChecker.startsWith("com.jdojo");
```

Testing Prime Service in Legacy Mode

Not all applications will be migrated to use modules. Your modular JARs for the prime service may be used along with other JARs on the class path. Suppose you placed all five modular JARs for the prime service in C:\Java9Revealed\lib directory. Run the com.jdojo.prime.client.Main class by placing the four modular JARs on the class path using the following command:

```
C:\Java9Revealed>java --class-path lib\com.jdojo.prime.jar;lib\com.jdojo.prime.client.
jar;lib\com.jdojo.prime.faster.jar;lib\com.jdojo.prime.generic.jar;lib\com.jdojo.prime.
probable.jar com.jdojo.prime.client.Main
```

```
No PrimeChecker service provider found.
A PrimeChecker service provider with the name 'jdojo.faster.primechecker' was not found.
A PrimeChecker service provider with the name 'jdojo.probable.primechecker' was not found.
```

The output indicates that using the legacy mode—the pre-JDK 9 mode by placing all modular JARs on the class path—did not find any of the service providers. In legacy mode, the service provider discovery mechanism is different. The ServiceLoader class scans all JARs on the class path looking for files in the META-INF/services directory. The filename is the fully qualified service interface name. The file path looks like this:

```
META-INF/services/<service-interface>
```

The contents of this file is the list of the fully qualified names of the service provider implementation classes/interfaces. Each class name needs to be on a separate line. You can use a single-line comment in the file. Text on a line starting from a # character is considered a comment.

The service interface name is com.jdojo.prime.PrimeChecker, so the modular JARs for the three service providers will have a file named com.jdojo.prime.PrimeChecker with the following path:

```
META-INF/services/com.jdojo.prime.PrimeChecker
```

You need to add the META-INF/services directory to the root of the source code directory. If you are using an IDE such as NetBeans, the IDE will take care of packaging the file for you. Listing 5-11, Listing 5-12, and Listing 5-13 contain the contents of this file for the modular JARs for the three prime service provider modules.

Listing 5-11. Contents of the META-INF/services/com.jdojo.prime.PrimeChecker File in the Modular JAR for the com.jdojo.prime.generic Module

```
# The generic service provider implementation class name
com.jdojo.prime.generic.GenericPrimeChecker
```

Listing 5-12. Contents of the META-INF/services/com.jdojo.prime.PrimeChecker File in the Modular JAR for the com.jdojo.prime.faster Module

```
# The faster service provider implementation class name
com.jdojo.prime.faster.FasterPrimeChecker
```

Listing 5-13. Contents of the META-INF/services/com.jdojo.prime.PrimeChecker File in the Modular JAR for the com.jdojo.prime.probable Module

```
# The probable service provider implementation interface name
com.jdojo.prime.probable.ProbablePrimeChecker
```

Recompile and repackage the modular JARs for the generic and faster prime checker service providers. Run the following command:

```
C:\Java9Revealed>java --class-path lib\com.jdojo.prime.jar;lib\com.jdojo.prime.client.
jar;lib\com.jdojo.prime.faster.jar;lib\com.jdojo.prime.generic.jar;lib\com.jdojo.prime.
probable.jar com.jdojo.prime.client.Main
```

```
Exception in thread "main" java.util.ServiceConfigurationError: com.jdojo.prime.
PrimeChecker: com.jdojo.prime.faster.FasterPrimeChecker Unable to get public no-arg
constructor
...

at com.jdojo.prime.client.Main.main(Main.java:13)
Caused by: java.lang.NoSuchMethodException: com.jdojo.prime.faster.
FasterPrimeChecker.<init>()
...
```

A partial output is shown. The output indicates a runtime exception when the ServiceLoader class tries to instantiate the faster prime service provider. You will get the same error when an attempt is made to instantiate the probable prime service provider. Adding information about a service in the META-INF/services directory is a legacy way of implementing services. For backward compatibility, the service implementation must be a class with a public no-args constructor. Recall that we provided a provider constructor only for the GenericPrimeChecker class. So, the other two prime services will not work in legacy mode. You can add a provider constructor to the FasterPrimeChecker class to make it work. However, it is not possible to add a provider constructor to an interface and the ProbablePrimeChecker will not work in the class path mode. You must load it from an explicit module to make it work.

▓ **Tip** Service providers deployed on the class path or as automatic modules on the module path must have a public no-args constructor.

The following command adds the modular JAR only for the generic prime service provider, which provides a public no-args constructor. The output shows that the provider was located, instantiated, and used successfully.

```
C:\Java9Revealed>java --class-path lib\com.jdojo.prime.jar;lib\com.jdojo.prime.client.
jar;lib\com.jdojo.prime.generic.jar com.jdojo.prime.client.Main
```

```
Using jdojo.generic.primechecker:
3 is a prime.
4 is not a prime.
121 is not a prime.
977 is a prime.
A PrimeChecker service provider with the name 'jdojo.faster.primechecker' was not found.
A PrimeChecker service provider with the name 'jdojo.probable.primechecker' was not found.
```

Summary

A specific functionality provided by an application (or a library) is known as a *service*. Applications and libraries providing implementations of a service are known as service providers. Applications using the service provided by those service providers are called *service consumers* or *clients*.

In Java, a *service* is defined by a set of interfaces and classes. The service contains an interface or an abstract class that defines the functionality provided by the service and it is known as the *service provider interface, service interface,* or *service type*. A specific implementation of a service interface is known as a *service provider*. There can be multiple service providers for a single service interface. In JDK 9, a service provider may be a class or an interface.

The JDK contains a java.util.ServiceLoader<S> class whose sole purpose is to discover and load service providers of type S at runtime for a specified service interface. If a JAR (modular or non-modular) containing a service provider is placed on the class path, the ServiceLoader class uses the META-INF/services directory to find the service providers. The name of the file in this directory should be the same as the fully qualified name of the service interface. The file contains the fully qualified name of the service provider implementation classes—one class name per line. The file can use a # character as the start of single-line comments. The ServiceLoader class scans all META-INF/services directories on the class path to discover service providers.

In JDK 9, the service provider discovery mechanism has changed. A module that uses the ServiceLoader class to discover and load the service providers needs to specify the service interface using a uses statement. The service interface specified in a uses statement may be declared in the current module or any module accessible to the current module. You can use the iterator() method of the ServiceLoader class to iterate over all service providers. The stream() method provides a stream of elements that are instances of the ServiceLoader.Provider interface. You can use the stream to filter and select a specific type of providers based on the provider's class names without having to instantiate all providers.

A module that contains a service provider needs to specify the service interface and its implementation class using a provides statement. The implementation class must be declared in the current module.

125

CHAPTER 6

■ ■ ■

Packaging Modules

In this chapter, you will learn:

- Different formats for packaging Java modules

- Enhancements to the JAR format

- What a multi-release JAR is

- How to create and use multi-release JARs

- What the JMOD format is

- How to use the jmod tool to work with JMOD files

- How to create, extract, and describe JMOD files

- How to list contents of JMOD files

- How to record hashes of modules in JMOD files for dependency validation

A module can be packaged in different formats to be used in three phases—compile-time, link time, and runtime. Not all formats are supported in all phases. JDK 9 supports the following formats to package modules:

- Exploded directory

- JAR format

- JMOD format

- JIMAGE format

Exploded directories and JAR format were supported before JDK 9. The JAR format has been enhanced in JDK 9 to support modular JARs and multi-release JARs. JDK 9 has introduced two new formats for packaging modules: JMOD format and JIMAGE format. I discuss the enhancements to the JAR format and the JMOD format in this section. Chapter 7 covers the JIMAGE format along with the jlink tool in detail.

The JAR Format

Chapter 3 covered how to use new options with the jar tool to create modular JARs. The jar tool is also used to list entries in a JAR file, and to extract and update the contents of a JAR file. The jar tool has supported these operations before JDK 9 and there is nothing new to these operations in JDK 9. In this chapter, I cover a new feature added to the JAR format, which is called a multi-release JAR.

© Kishori Sharan 2017
K. Sharan, *Java 9 Revealed*, DOI 10.1007/978-1-4842-2592-9_6

What Is a Multi-Release JAR?

As an experienced Java developer, you must have used a Java library/framework such as Spring framework, Hibernate, etc. You may be using Java 8, but those libraries may be still using Java 6 or Java 7. Why can't the library developers use the latest version to take advantage of the JDK's new features? One of the reasons is that not all library users use the latest JDK. Updating a library to use the newer version of the JDK means forcing all library users to migrate to that newer JDK, which is not possible in practice. Maintaining and releasing a library targeting different JDKs is another pain when packaging the code. Typically, you will find a separate library JAR for different JDKs. JDK 9 solves this problem by offering library developers a new way of packaging a library's code—using a single JAR containing the same release of a library for multiple JDKs. Such a JAR is called a *multi-release JAR*.

A multi-release JAR (MRJAR) contains the same release of a library (offering the same APIs) for multiple JDK versions. That is, you can have a library as a MRJAR that will work for JDK 8 and JDK 9. The code in the MRJAR will contain the class files compiled in JDK 8 and JDK 9. The classes compiled with JDK 9 may take advantage of the APIs offered by JDK 9, whereas the classes compiled with JDK 8 may offer the same library APIs written using JDK 8.

A MRJAR extends the already existing directory structure for a JAR. A JAR contains a root directory where all its contents reside. It contains a META-INF directory that is used to store metadata about the JAR. Typically, a JAR contains a META-INF/MANIFEST.MF file containing its attributes. Entries in a typical JAR look like this:

```
- jar-root
  - C1.class
  - C2.class
  - C3.class
  - C4.class
- META-INF
  - MANIFEST.MF
```

The JAR contains four class files and a MANIFEST.MF file. A MRJAR extends the META-INF directory to store classes that are specific to a JDK version. The META-INF directory contains a versions sub-directory, which may contain many sub-directories—each of them named the same as the JDK major version. For example, for classes specific to JDK 9, there may be the META-INF/versions/9 directory and, for classes specific to JDK 10, there may be a directory called META-INF/versions/10, etc. A typical MRJAR may have the following entries:

```
- jar-root
  - C1.class
  - C2.class
  - C3.class
  - C4.class
- META-INF
  - MANIFEST.MF
  - versions
    - 9
      - C2.class
      - C5.class
    - 10
      - C1.class
      - C2.class
      - C6.class
```

128

If this MRJAR is used in an environment that does not support MRJARs, it will be treated as a regular JAR—the contents in the root directory will be used and all other contents in META-INF/versions/9 and META-INF/versions/10 will be ignored. So, if this MRJAR is used with JDK 8, only four classes will be used: C1, C2, C3, and C4.

When this MRJAR is used in JDK 9, five classes are in play: C1, C2, C3, C4, and C5. The C2 class in the META-INF/versions/9 directory will be used instead of the C2 class from the root directory. In this case, the MRJAR is saying that it has a newer version of the C2 class for JDK 9 that overrides the version of C2 in the root directory that is for JDK 8 or earlier. The JDK 9 version also adds a new class named C5.

With a similar argument, the MRJAR overrides classes C1 and C2 and contains a new class named C6 for the JDK version 10.

Targeting multiple JDK versions in a single MRJAR, the search process in a MRJAR is different from a regular JAR. The search for a resource or class file in a MRJAR uses the following rules:

- The major version of the JDK is determined for the environment in which the MRJAR is being used. Suppose the major version of the JDK is N.

- To locate a resource or a class file named R, the platform-specific sub-directory under the META-INF/versions directory is searched starting at the directory for version N.

- If R is found in sub-directory N, it is returned. Otherwise, sub-directories for versions lower than N are searched. This process continues for all sub-directories under the META-INF/versions directory.

- When R is not found in the META-INF/versions/N sub-directories, the root directory of the MRJAR is searched for R.

Let's take an example using the previously shown structure of the MRJAR. Suppose the program is looking for C3.class and the current version of the JDK is 10. The search will start at META-INF/versions/10, where C3.class is not found. The search continues in META-INF/versions/9, where C3.class is not found. Now the search continues in the root directory, where C3.class is found.

As another example, suppose you want to find C2.class when the JDK version is 10. The search starts at META-INF/versions/10, where C2.class is found and returned.

As another example, suppose you want to find C2.class when the JDK version is 9. The search starts at META-INF/versions/9, where C2.class is found and returned.

As another example, suppose you want to find C2.class when the JDK version is 8. There is no JDK 8 specific directory named META-INF/versions/8. So, the search starts at the root directory, where C2.class is found and returned.

■ **Tip** In JDK 9, all tools that process JARs—such as java, javac, and javap—have been modified to work with multi-release JARs. APIs dealing with JARs have also been updated to deal with multi-release JARs.

Creating Multi-Release JARs

Once you know the search order of the directories in a MRJAR when a resource or class file is searched on a specific JDK version, it is easy to understand how classes and resources are found. There are some rules on the contents of JDK version-specific directories. I describe those rules in subsequent sections. In this section, I focus on creating MRJARs.

To run this example, you need JDK 8 and JDK 9 installed on your machine. If you do not have JDK 8, any other JDK in addition to JDK 9 will do. For the JDK other than version 8, you will need to change the code in the example, so the code will compile with your JDK.

I use a MRJAR to store the JDK 8 and JDK 9 versions of an application. The application consists of the following two classes:

- com.jdojo.mrjar.Main
- com.jdojo.mrjar.TimeUtil

The Main class creates an object of the TimeUtil class and calls a method in it. The Main class can be used as a main class to run the application. The TimeUtil class contains a getLocalDate(Instant now) method that takes an Instant as an argument and returns a LocalDate interpreting the instant in the current time zone. JDK 9 has added a new method to the LocalDate class, which is named ofInstant(Instant instant, ZoneId zone). We will update the application to use JDK 9 to take advantage of this new method in JDK 9 and will keep the old application that used the JDK 8 Time API for the same purpose.

The source code contains two NetBeans projects named com.jdojo.mrjar.jdk8 and com.jdojo.mrjar.jdk9, which are configured to use JDK 8 and JDK 9, respectively. Listing 6-1 and Listing 6-2 contain the code for the TimeUtil and Main class for JDK 8. In NetBeans, you need to change the Sources and Libraries properties for the com.jdojo.mrjar.jdk8 project to JDK 8 and for the com.jdojo.mrjar.jdk9 project to JDK 9. The source code for these projects is simple, so I will not provide any explanation. I could have made the getLocalDate() method in the TimeUtil class a static method. I kept it as an instance method, so you can see in the output (discussed later) which version of the class is instantiated. When you run the Main class, it prints the current local date, which may be different when you run this example.

Listing 6-1. A TimeUtil Class for JDK 8

```
// TimeUtil.java
package com.jdojo.mrjar;

import java.time.Instant;
import java.time.LocalDate;
import java.time.ZoneId;

public class TimeUtil {
    public TimeUtil() {
        System.out.println("Creating JDK 8 version of TimeUtil...");
    }

    public LocalDate getLocalDate(Instant now) {
        return now.atZone(ZoneId.systemDefault())
                .toLocalDate();
    }
}
```

Listing 6-2. A Main Class for JDK 8

```
// Main.java
package com.jdojo.mrjar;

import java.time.Instant;
import java.time.LocalDate;
```

```
public class Main {
    public static void main(String[] args) {
        System.out.println("Inside JDK 8 version of Main.main()...");

        TimeUtil t = new TimeUtil();
        LocalDate ld = t.getLocalDate(Instant.now());
        System.out.println("Local Date: " + ld);
    }
}
```

```
Inside JDK 8 version of Main.main()...
Creating JDK 8 version of TimeUtil...
Local Date: 2017-01-27
```

We will put all the JDK 9 classes in a module named com.jdojo.mrjar whose declaration is shown in Listing 6-3. Listing 6-4 and Listing 6-5 contain the code for the TimeUtil and Main classes for JDK 9.

Listing 6-3. A Module Declaration for a Module Named com.jdojo.mrjar

```
// module-info.java
module com.jdojo.mrjar {
    exports com.jdojo.mrjar;
}
```

Listing 6-4. A TimeUtil Class for JDK 9

```
// TimeUtil.java
package com.jdojo.mrjar;

import java.time.Instant;
import java.time.LocalDate;
import java.time.ZoneId;

public class TimeUtil {
    public TimeUtil() {
        System.out.println("Creating JDK 9 version of TimeUtil...");
    }

    public LocalDate getLocalDate(Instant now) {
        return LocalDate.ofInstant(now, ZoneId.systemDefault());
    }
}
```

Listing 6-5. A Main Class for JDK 9

```java
// Main.java
package com.jdojo.mrjar;

import java.time.Instant;
import java.time.LocalDate;

public class Main {
    public static void main(String[] args) {
        System.out.println("Inside JDK 9 version of Main.main()...");

        TimeUtil t = new TimeUtil();
        LocalDate ld = t.getLocalDate(Instant.now());
        System.out.println("Local Date: " + ld);
    }
}
```

```
Inside JDK 9 version of Main.main()...
Creating JDK 9 version of TimeUtil...
Local Date: 2017-01-27
```

I have shown the output that you will get when you run the `Main` class on JDK 8 and JDK 9. However, the purpose of this example is not to run those two classes individually, but rather to package them all in a MRJAR and run them from that MRJAR, which I am going to show you shortly.

The `jar` tool has been enhanced in JDK 9 to support creating MRJARs. In JDK 9, the `jar` tool accepts a new option, called `--release`. Its syntax is as follows:

```
jar <options> --release N <other-options>
```

Here, `N` is a JDK major version such as 9 for JDK 9. The value for `N` must be greater than or equal to 9. All files following the `--release  N` option are added to the `META-INF/versions/N` directory in the MRJAR.

The following command creates a MRJAR named `com.jdojo.mrjar.jar` and places it in the `C:\Java9Revealed\mrjars` directory, which is an existing directory:

```
C:\Java9Revealed>jar --create --file mrjars\com.jdojo.mrjar.jar
-C com.jdojo.mrjar.jdk8\build\classes .
--release 9 -C com.jdojo.mrjar.jdk9\build\classes .
```

Notice the use of the `--release  9` option in this command. All files from the `com.jdojo.mrjar.jdk9\build\classes` directory will be added to the `META-INF/versions/9` directory in the MRJAR. All files from the `com.jdojo.mrjar.jdk8\build\classes` directory will be added to the root of the MRJAR. The entries in the MRJAR will look like:

```
- jar-root
  - com
    - jdojo
      - mrjar
        - Main.class
        - TimeUtil.class
```

```
- META-INF
  - MANIFEST.MF
  - versions
    - 9
      - module-info.class
      - com
        - jdojo
          - mrjar
            - Main.class
            - TimeUtil.class
```

It is very helpful to use the --verbose option with the jar tool while creating MRJARs. The option prints out many useful pieces of information that help diagnose errors. The following is the same command as before, but with the --verbose option. The output shows what files were copied and their locations:

```
C:\Java9Revealed>jar --create --verbose --file mrjars\com.jdojo.mrjar.jar
-C com.jdojo.mrjar.jdk8\build\classes .
--release 9 -C com.jdojo.mrjar.jdk9\build\classes .
```

```
added manifest
added module-info: META-INF/versions/9/module-info.class
adding: com/(in = 0) (out= 0)(stored 0%)
adding: com/jdojo/(in = 0) (out= 0)(stored 0%)
adding: com/jdojo/mrjar/(in = 0) (out= 0)(stored 0%)
adding: com/jdojo/mrjar/Main.class(in = 1100) (out= 592)(deflated 46%)
adding: com/jdojo/mrjar/TimeUtil.class(in = 884) (out= 503)(deflated 43%)
adding: META-INF/versions/9/(in = 0) (out= 0)(stored 0%)
adding: META-INF/versions/9/.netbeans_automatic_build(in = 0) (out= 0)(stored 0%)
adding: META-INF/versions/9/.netbeans_update_resources(in = 0) (out= 0)(stored 0%)
adding: META-INF/versions/9/com/(in = 0) (out= 0)(stored 0%)
adding: META-INF/versions/9/com/jdojo/(in = 0) (out= 0)(stored 0%)
adding: META-INF/versions/9/com/jdojo/mrjar/(in = 0) (out= 0)(stored 0%)
adding: META-INF/versions/9/com/jdojo/mrjar/Main.class(in = 1328) (out= 689)(deflated 48%)
adding: META-INF/versions/9/com/jdojo/mrjar/TimeUtil.class(in = 814) (out= 470)(deflated 42%)
```

Suppose you want to create a MRJAR for JDK versions 8, 9, and 10. The following command will do the job, assuming that the com.jdojo.mrjar.jdk10\build\classes directory contains classes that are specific to JDK 10:

```
C:\Java9Revealed>jar --create --file mrjars\com.jdojo.mrjar.jar
-C com.jdojo.mrjar.jdk8\build\classes .
--release 9 -C com.jdojo.mrjar.jdk9\build\classes .
--release 10 -C com.jdojo.mrjar.jdk10\build\classes .
```

You can verify the entries in the MRJAR by using the `--list` option as follows:

```
C:\Java9Revealed>jar --list --file mrjars\com.jdojo.mrjar.jar
```

```
META-INF/
META-INF/MANIFEST.MF
com/
com/jdojo/
com/jdojo/mrjar/
com/jdojo/mrjar/Main.class
com/jdojo/mrjar/TimeUtil.class
META-INF/versions/9/
META-INF/versions/9/com/
META-INF/versions/9/com/jdojo/
META-INF/versions/9/com/jdojo/mrjar/
META-INF/versions/9/com/jdojo/mrjar/Main.class
META-INF/versions/9/com/jdojo/mrjar/TimeUtil.class
META-INF/versions/9/module-info.class
META-INF/versions/10/
META-INF/versions/10/com/
META-INF/versions/10/com/jdojo/
META-INF/versions/10/com/jdojo/mrjar/
META-INF/versions/10/com/jdojo/mrjar/TimeUtil.class
```

Suppose you have a JAR that contains resource and class files for JDK 8 and you want to update the JAR to make it a MRJAR by adding resource and class files for JDK 9. You can do so by updating the contents of the JAR using the `--update` option. The following command creates a JAR with only JDK 8 files:

```
C:\Java9Revealed>jar --create --file mrjars\com.jdojo.mrjar.jar
-C com.jdojo.mrjar.jdk8\build\classes .
```

The following command updates the JAR to make it a MRJAR:

```
C:\Java9Revealed>jar --update --file mrjars\com.jdojo.mrjar.jar
--release 9 -C com.jdojo.mrjar.jdk9\build\classes .
```

Take a look at this MRJAR in action. The following command runs the `Main` class in the `com.jdojo.mrjar` package, placing the MRJAR on the class path. JDK 8 is used to run the class.

```
C:\Java9Revealed> c:\java8\bin\java -classpath mrjars\com.jdojo.mrjar.jar com.jdojo.mrjar.
Main
```

```
Inside JDK 8 version of Main.main()...
Creating JDK 8 version of TimeUtil...
Local Date: 2017-01-27
```

The output shows that both classes, Main and TimeUtil, were used from the root directory of the MRJAR because JDK 8 does not support MRJAR. The following command runs the same class using the module path. JDK 9 was used to run the command:

```
C:\Java9Revealed> c:\java9\bin\java --module-path mrjars\com.jdojo.mrjar.jar --module com.
jdojo.mrjar/com.jdojo.mrjar.Main
```

```
Inside JDK 9 version of Main.main()...
Creating JDK 9 version of TimeUtil...
Local Date: 2017-01-27
```

The output shows that both classes, Main and TimeUtil, were used from the META-INF/versions/9 directory of the MRJAR because JDK 9 supports MRJAR and the MRJAR had versions of these classes specific to JDK 9.

Let's give this MRJAR a little twist. Create a MRJAR having the same contents, but without the Main. class file in the META-INF/versions/9 directory. In a real-world scenario, only the TimeUtil class has changed in the JDK 9 version of the application, so there is no need to package the Main class for JDK 9. The Main class for JDK 8 can also be used on JDK 9. The following command packages everything we did last time, except the Main class for JDK 9. The resulting MRJAR is named com.jdojo.mrjar2.jar.

```
C:\Java9Revealed>jar --create --verbose --file mrjars\com.jdojo.mrjar2.jar
-C com.jdojo.mrjar.jdk8\build\classes .
--release 9
-C com.jdojo.mrjar.jdk9\build\classes module-info.class
-C com.jdojo.mrjar.jdk9\build\classes com\jdojo\mrjar\TimeUtil.class
```

You can verify the contents of the new MRJAR using the following command:

```
C:\Java9Revealed>jar --list --file mrjars\com.jdojo.mrjar2.jar
```

```
META-INF/
META-INF/MANIFEST.MF
META-INF/versions/9/module-info.class
com/
com/jdojo/
com/jdojo/mrjar/
com/jdojo/mrjar/Main.class
com/jdojo/mrjar/TimeUtil.class
META-INF/versions/9/com/jdojo/mrjar/TimeUtil.class
```

If you run the Main class on JDK 8, you will get the same output as before. However, running it on JDK 9 will give you a different output:

```
C:\Java9Revealed>c:\java9\bin\java --module-path mrjars\com.jdojo.mrjar2.jar --module com.
jdojo.mrjar/com.jdojo.mrjar.Main
```

```
Inside JDK 8 version of Main.main()...
Creating JDK 9 version of TimeUtil...
Local Date: 2017-01-27
```

The output shows that the `Main` class was used from the JAR root directory whereas the `TimeUtil` class was used from the `META-INF/versions/9` directory. Note that you will get a different local date value. It prints the current date on your machine.

Rules for Multi-Release JARs

You need to follow a few rules while creating multi-release JARs. If you make a mistake, the `jar` tool will print errors. Sometimes, error messages are not intuitive. As I have suggested, it's best to run the `jar` tool with the `--verbose` option to get more details on errors.

Most of the rules are based on one fact: A MRJAR contains an API for one release of a library (or an application) for multiple JDK platforms. For example, you have a MRJAR named `jdojo-lib-1.0.jar` that may contain version 1.0 of the APIs for the library named `jdojo-lib`, and that library may use APIs from JDK 8 and JDK 9. That means that this MRJAR should provide the same API (in terms of public types and their public members) when it is used on JDK 8 on the class path, on JDK 9 on the class path, or on JDK 9 on the module path. If the MRJAR provides different APIs on JDK 8 and JDK 9, this is not a valid MRJAR. The following sections describe a few rules.

Modular Multi-Release JARs

A MRJAR can be a modular JAR and, in that case, it can contain a module descriptor, `module-info.class`, in the root directory, in one or more versioned directories, or a combination of both. The versioned descriptors must be identical to the root module descriptor, with a few exceptions:

- A versioned descriptor can have different non-transitive `requires` statements of `java.*` and `jdk.*` modules.

- Different module descriptors cannot have different non-transitive `requires` statements for non-JDK modules.

- A versioned descriptor can have different `uses` statements.

These rules are based on the fact that changes in implementation details are allowed, but not in the API itself. Allowing changes in the `requires` statement for non-JDK modules is considered a change in the API—it requires you to have different user-defined modules for different versions of the JDK. This is the reason why this is not allowed.

A modular MRJAR need not have a module descriptor in the root directory. This is what we had in our examples in the previous section. We had no module descriptor in the root directory, but had one in the `META-INF/versions/9` directory. This arrangement makes it possible to have non-modular code for JDK 8 and modular code for JDK 9 in one MRJAR.

Modular Multi-Release JARs and Encapsulation

If you add a new public type in a versioned directory, which is not present in the root directory, you will receive an error while creating a MRJAR. Suppose, in our example, you add a public class named `Test` for JDK 9. If the `Test` class is in the `com.jdojo.mrjar` package, it will be exported by the module and will be available to the code outside the MRJAR. Note that the root directory does not contain a `Test` class, so this MRJAR offers different public API for JDK 8 and JDK 9. In this case, adding a public `Test` class in the `com.jdojo.mrjar` package for JDK 9 will generate an error when you create a MRJAR.

Continuing with the same example, suppose you add the `Test` class to a `com.jdojo.test` package for JDK 9. Note that the module does not export this package. When you use this MRJAR on the module path, the `Test` class won't be accessible to the outside code. In this sense, this MRJAR offers the same public API for JDK 8 and JDK 9. However, there is a catch! You can also place this MRJAR on the class path in JDK 9 and, in that case, the Test class is accessible to the outside code—a violation of the modular encapsulation and a violation of the rule that a MRJAR should offer the same public API across JDK releases. Therefore, adding a public type to a non-exported package for a module in a MRJAR is also not allowed. If you attempt to do so, you will receive an error message similar to the following:

```
entry: META-INF/versions/9/com/jdojo/test/Test.class, contains a new public class not found
in base entries
invalid multi-release jar file mrjars\com.jdojo.mrjar.jar deleted
```

Sometimes, it is necessary to add more types for the same library to support a newer version of the JDK. These types must be added to support newer implementations. You can do it by adding package-private types to a versioned directory in a MRJAR. In this example, you can add the Test class for JDK 9 if you make the class non-public.

Multi-Release JARs and Boot Loader

The boot loader does not support multi-release JARs, for example, specifying MRJARs using the -Xbootclasspath/a option. Supporting this would have complicated the boot loader implementation for a rarely needed feature.

Same Versioned Files

A MRJAR is supposed to contain different versions of the same file in a versioned directory. If a resource or class file is the same across different platform releases, such a file should be added once to the root directory. Currently, the jar tool issues a warning if it sees the same entry in a multiple versioned directory with the same contents.

Let's see this rule in action. Copy the contents of the com.jdojo.mrjar.jdk9\build\classes directory to the com.jdojo.mrjar.jdk10\build\classes directory, so both directories have the same contents. Run the following command to create a MRJAR that will contain code for JDK versions 8, 9, and 10. Note that the files in versioned directories 9 and 10 will be the same. Warnings in the output are loud and clear.

```
C:\Java9Revealed>jar --create --file mrjars\com.jdojo.mrjar.jar
-C com.jdojo.mrjar.jdk8\build\classes .
--release 9 -C com.jdojo.mrjar.jdk9\build\classes .
--release 10 -C com.jdojo.mrjar.jdk10\build\classes .
```

```
Warning: entry META-INF/versions/9/com/jdojo/mrjar/Main.class contains a class that
is identical to an entry already in the jar
Warning: entry META-INF/versions/9/com/jdojo/mrjar/TimeUtil.class contains a class that
is identical to an entry already in the jar
```

Multi-Release JARs and JAR URL

Before MRJARs, all resources in a JAR lived in the root directory. When you requested a resource from a class loader (ClassLoader.getResource("com/jdojo/mrjar/TimeUtil.class")), the URL returned was similar to the following:

```
jar:file:/C:/Java9Revealed/mrjars/com.jdojo.mrjar.jar! com/jdojo/mrjar/TimeUtil.class
```

137

With MRJARs, a resource may be returned from the root directory or from a versioned directory. If you are looking for the `TimeUtil.class` file on JDK 9, the URL will be as follows:

```
jar:file:/C:/Java9Revealed/mrjars/com.jdojo.mrjar.jar!/META-INF/versions/9/com/jdojo/mrjar/
TimeUtil.class
```

If your existing code expected the `jar` URL of a resource in a specific format or you hand-coded a `jar` URL likewise, you may get surprising results with MRJARs. You need to look at your code again and change it to work with MRJARs, if you are repacking your JARs with MRJARs.

Multi-Release Manifest Attribute

A MRJAR contains a special attribute entry in its `MANIFEST.MF` file:

```
Multi-Release: true
```

The `Multi-Release` attribute is added by the `jar` tool for a MRJAR. If the value for this attribute is `true`, it means the JAR is a multi-release JAR. If its value is `false` or the attribute is missing, it is not a multi-release JAR. The attribute is added to the main section in the manifest file.

A new constant named `MULTI_RELEASE` has been added to the `Attributes.Name` class, which is in the `java.util.jar` package, to represent the new attribute `Multi-Release` in the manifest file. So, the `Attributes.Name.MULTI_RELEASE` constant represents the value for the `Multi-Release` attribute in Java code.

The JMOD Format

JDK 9 introduced a new format, called JMOD, to package modules. JMOD files are designed to handle more content types than JAR files can. JMOD files can package native code, configuration files, native commands, and other kinds of data. At the time of this writing, the JMOD format is based on the ZIP format, which is going to change in the future. The JDK 9 modules are packaged in JMOD format for you to use at compile-time and link time. JMOD format is not supported at runtime. You can find them in the `JDK_HOME\jmods` directory, where `JDK_HOME` is the directory in which you have installed the JDK 9. You can package your own modules in JMOD format. Files in the JMOD format have a `.jmod` extension. For example, the platform module named `java.base` has been packaged in the `java.base.jmod` file.

JMOD files can contain native code, which is a bit tricky to extract and link on-the-fly at runtime. This is the reason that JMOD files are supported at compile-time and link time, but not at runtime.

Using the jmod Tool

JDK 9 ships with a new tool called `jmod`. It is located in the `JDK_HOME\bin` directory. It can be used to create a JMOD file, list the contents of a JMOD file, print the description of a module, and record hashes of the modules used. The general syntax to use the jmod tool is as follows:

```
jmod <subcommand> <options> <jmod-file>
```

You must use one of the sub-commands with the `jmod` command:

- `create`
- `extract`
- `list`
- `describe`
- `hash`

The `list` and `describe` sub-commands do not accept any options. The `<jmod-file>` is the JMOD file you are creating or an existing JMOD file that you want to describe. Table 6-1 contains the list of options supported by the tool.

Table 6-1. *List of Options for the jmod Tool*

Option	Description
`--class-path <path>`	Specifies the class path where classes to be packaged can be found. `<path>` can be a list of paths to JAR files or directories containing application classes. Contents at `<path>` will be copied to the JMOD file.
`--cmds <path>`	Specifies a list of directories containing native commands, which need to be copied to the JMOD file.
`--config <path>`	Specifies a list of directories containing user-editable configuration files to be copied to the JMOD file.
`--dir <path>`	Specifies the target directory where the contents of the specified JMOD file will be extracted.
`--do-not-resolve-by-default`	If you create a JMOD file using this option, the module contained in the JMOD file will be excluded from the default set of root modules. To resolve such a module, you have to add it to the default set of root modules using the `--add-modules` command-line option.
`--dry-run`	Dry runs the hashing of modules. Using this option, computes and prints the hashes, but does not record them in the JMOD file.
`--exclude <pattern-list>`	Excludes file matching the supplied comma-separated pattern list, each element using one the following forms: `<glob-pattern>`, `glob:<glob-pattern>`, or `regex:<regex-pattern>`.
`--hash-modules <regex-pattern>`	Computes and records hashes to tie a packaged module with modules matching the given `<regex-pattern>` and depending on it directly or indirectly. The hashes are recorded in the JMOD file being created, or a JMOD file or modular JAR on the module path specified with the `jmod hash` command.
`--help, -h`	Prints the usage description and the list of all options for the jmod command.
`--header-files <path>`	Specifies a list of path as `<path>` where header files for native code to be copied to the JMOD file are located.
`--help-extra`	Prints help on additional options supported by the jmod tool.

(continued)

Table 6-1. (*continued*)

Option	Description
--legal-notices <path>	Specifies the location of the legal notices to be copied to the JMOD file.
--libs <path>	Specifies the list of directories containing native libraries to be copied to the JMOD file.
--main-class <class-name>	Specifies the main class name to be used to run the application.
--man-pages <path>	Specifies the location of the manual pages.
--module-version <version>	Specifies the module version to be recorded in the module-info.class file.
--module-path <path>, -p <path>	Specifies the module path to find the modules for hashing.
--os-arch <os-arch>	Specifies the operating-system architecture to be recorded in the module-info.class file.
--os-name <os-name>	Specifies the operating system name to be recorded in the module-info.class file.
--version	Prints the version of the jmod tool.
--warn-if-resolved <reason>	Specifies a hint to the jmod tool to issue a warning if a module is resolved, which has been deprecated, deprecated for removal, or incubating. The value for <reason> could be one of three: deprecated, deprecated-for-removal, or incubating.
@<filename>	Reads options from the specified file.

The following sections explain in detail how to use the jmod command. All commands used in this chapter are entered into one line. Sometimes, I show them on multiple lines for clarity in the book.

Creating JMOD Files

You can create a JMOD file using the create sub-command with the jmod tool. The contents of a JMOD file are the contents of a module. Assume the following directories and files exist:

```
C:\Java9Revealed\jmods
C:\Java9Revealed\lib\com.jdojo.prime.jar
```

The following command creates a com.jdojo.prime.jmod file in the C:\Java9Revealed\jmods directory. The contents of the JMOD file come from the com.jdojo.prime.jar file.

```
C:\Java9Revealed>jmod create --class-path lib\com.jdojo.prime.jar
jmods\com.jdojo.prime.jmod
```

Typically, the contents of the JMOD file come from a set of directories containing the compiled code for a module. The following command creates a com.jdojo.prime.jmod file. Its contents come from a directory mods\com.jdojo.prime. The command uses the --module-version option to set the module version that will be recorded in the `module-info.class` file found in the `com.jdojo.prime\build\classes` directory. Make sure to delete the JMOD file created in the previous step.

```
C:\Java9Revealed>jmod create --module-version 1.0
  --class-path com.jdojo.prime\build\classes jmods\com.jdojo.prime.jmod
```

What can you do with this JMOD file? You can place it on the module path to use it at compile-time. You can use it with the `jlink` tool to create a custom runtime image that you can use to run your application. Recall that you cannot use it at runtime. If you try to use a JMOD file at runtime by placing it on a module path, you will receive the following error:

```
Error occurred during initialization of VM
java.lang.module.ResolutionException: JMOD files not supported: jmods\com.jdojo.prime.jmod
...
```

Extracting JMOD File Contents

You can extract the contents of a JMOD file using the `extract` sub-command. The following command extracts the contents of the `jmods\com.jdojo.prime.jmod` file into a directory named `extracted`.

```
C:\Java9Revealed>jmod extract --dir extracted jmods\com.jdojo.prime.jmod
```

Without the `--dir` option, the JMOD file's contents are extracted into the current directory.

Listing JMOD File Contents

You can use the `list` sub-command with the `jmod` tool to print the names of all entries in a JMOD file. The following command lists the contents of the `com.jdojo.prime.jmod` file, which you created in the previous section:

```
C:\Java9Revealed>jmod list jmods\com.jdojo.prime.jmod
```

```
classes/module-info.class
classes/com/jdojo/prime/PrimeChecker.class
```

The following command lists the contents of the `java.base` module, which is shipped as a JMOD file named `java.base.jmod`. The command assumes that you have installed the JDK 9 in the `C:\java9` directory. The output is over 120 pages. A partial output is shown. Note that a JMOD file internally stores different types of content in different directories.

```
C:\Java9Revealed>jmod list C:\java9\jmods\java.base.jmod
```

```
classes/module-info.class
classes/java/nio/file/WatchEvent.class
classes/java/nio/file/WatchKey.class
bin/java.exe
bin/javaw.exe
native/amd64/jvm.cfg
```

```
native/java.dll
conf/net.properties
conf/security/java.policy
conf/security/java.security
...
```

Describing a JMOD File

You can use the describe sub-command with the jmod tool to describe the module contained in a JMOD file. The following command describes the module contained in the com.jdojo.prime.jmod file:

```
C:\Java9Revealed>jmod describe jmods\com.jdojo.prime.jmod
```

```
com.jdojo.prime@1.0
  requires mandated java.base
  uses com.jdojo.prime.PrimeChecker
  exports com.jdojo.prime
```

You can describe the platform modules using this command. The following command describes the module contained in the java.sql.jmod, assuming that you have installed the JDK 9 in the C:\java9 directory:

```
C:\Java9Revealed>jmod describe C:\java9\jmods\java.sql.jmod
```

```
java.sql@9-ea
  requires mandated java.base
  requires transitive java.logging
  requires transitive java.xml
  uses java.sql.Driver
  exports java.sql
  exports javax.sql
  exports javax.transaction.xa
  operating-system-name Windows
  operating-system-architecture amd64
```

Recording Modules Hashes

You can use the hash sub-command with the jmod tool to record hashes of other modules in the module-info.class file of a module contained in a JMOD file. The hashes will be used later for dependency validation. Suppose you have four modules in four JMOD files:

- com.jdojo.prime
- com.jdojo.prime.generic
- com.jdojo.prime.faster
- com.jdojo.prime.client

Suppose you want to ship these modules to your clients and ensure that the module code remains the same. You can achieve this by recording hashes for the com.jdojo.prime.generic, com.jdojo.prime.faster, and com.jdojo.prime.client modules in the com.jdojo.prime module. Let's see how to achieve this.

To compute the hashes for other modules, the jmod tool needs to find those modules. You will need to use the --module-path option to specify the module path where the other modules will be found. You also need to use the --hash-modules option to specify the list of patterns to be used for the modules whose hashes need to be recorded.

▨ **Tip** You can also use the --hash-modules and --module-path options with the jar tool to record hashes for dependent modules when you are packaging a module as a module JAR.

Use the following four commands to create the JMOD files for the four modules. Note that I used the --main-class option when creating the com.jdojo.prime.client.jmod file. I use it again in Chapter 7 when I discuss the jlink tool. If you get a "file already exists" error while running these commands, delete the existing JMOD file from the jmods directory and rerun the command.

```
C:\Java9Revealed>jmod create --module-version 1.0
--class-path com.jdojo.prime\build\classes jmods\com.jdojo.prime.jmod

C:\Java9Revealed>jmod create --module-version 1.0
--class-path com.jdojo.prime.generic\build\classes
jmods\com.jdojo.prime.generic.jmod

C:\Java9Revealed>jmod create --module-version 1.0
--class-path com.jdojo.prime.faster\build\classes
jmods\com.jdojo.prime.faster.jmod

C:\Java9Revealed>jmod create --main-class com.jdojo.prime.client.Main
--module-version 1.0
--class-path com.jdojo.prime.client\build\classes
jmods\com.jdojo.prime.client.jmod
```

Now you are ready to record hashes for all modules whose names start with com.jdojo.prime. in the com.jdojo.prime module using the following command:

```
C:\Java9Revealed>jmod hash --module-path jmods
  --hash-modules com.jdojo.prime.? jmods\com.jdojo.prime.jmod
```

```
Hashes are recorded in module com.jdojo.prime
```

Let's see the hashes that were recorded in the com.jdojo.prime module. The following command prints the module description along with the hashes recorded in the com.jdojo.prime module:

```
C:\Java9Revealed>jmod describe jmods\com.jdojo.prime.jmod
```

```
com.jdojo.prime@1.0
  requires mandated java.base
  uses com.jdojo.prime.PrimeChecker
  exports com.jdojo.prime
  hashes com.jdojo.prime.client SHA-256
2ffb0d4413501e389d6712450bd138bbe82ca8abeb4e8b5d29b0c307d90a2e91
  hashes com.jdojo.prime.faster SHA-256
687e07c429080c48bed89a649dca20fa26dc28fab88a4905f1b5070560622a0c
  hashes com.jdojo.prime.generic SHA-256
f24556ef69c4345ad7a8e5e59d31ea2d52c8749714ede0c0dedf128255450708
```

You can also record hashes for other modules when you create a new JMOD file using the create sub-command. Assuming that the three modules com.jdojo.prime.generic, com.jdojo.prime.faster, and com.jdojo.prime.client exist on the module path, you can use the following command to create the com.jdojo.prime.jmod file that will also record the hashes for the three modules:

```
C:\Java9Revealed>jmod create --module-version 1.0
--module-path jmods
--hash-modules com.jdojo.prime.?
--class-path com.jdojo.prime\build\classes jmods\com.jdojo.prime.jmod
```

You can dry run the hashing process for a JMOD file where the hashes will be printed, but not recorded. The dry run option is useful to make sure all the settings are correct without creating the JMOD file. The following sequence of commands steps you through the process. First, delete the jmods\com.jdojo.prime.jmod file, which you created in previous step.

The following command creates the jmods\com.jdojo.prime.jmod file without recording hashes for any other modules:

```
C:\Java9Revealed>jmod create --module-version 1.0
--module-path jmods
--class-path com.jdojo.prime\build\classes jmods\com.jdojo.prime.jmod
```

The following command dry runs the hash sub-command. It computes and prints the hashes for other modules, matching the regular expression specified in the --hash-modules option. No hashes will be recorded in the jmods\com.jdojo.prime.jmod file.

```
C:\Java9Revealed>jmod hash --dry-run --module-path jmods
 --hash-modules com.jdojo.prime.? jmods\com.jdojo.prime.jmod
```

```
Dry run:
com.jdojo.prime
  hashes com.jdojo.prime.client SHA-256
2ffb0d4413501e389d6712450bd138bbe82ca8abeb4e8b5d29b0c307d90a2e91
  hashes com.jdojo.prime.faster SHA-256
687e07c429080c48bed89a649dca20fa26dc28fab88a4905f1b5070560622a0c
  hashes com.jdojo.prime.generic SHA-256
f24556ef69c4345ad7a8e5e59d31ea2d52c8749714ede0c0dedf128255450708
```

The following command verifies that the previous command did not record any hashes in the JMOD file:

```
C:\Java9Revealed>jmod describe jmods\com.jdojo.prime.jmod
```

```
com.jdojo.prime@1.0
  requires mandated java.base
  uses com.jdojo.prime.PrimeChecker
  exports com.jdojo.prime
```

Summary

JDK 9 supports four formats to package modules: exploded directories, JAR files, JMOD files, and JIMAGE files. The JAR format has been enhanced in JDK 9 to support modular JARs and multi-release JARs. A multi-release JAR allows you to package the same version of a library or an application targeting different versions of the JDK. For example, a multi-release JAR may contain the code for a library version 1.2 that contains code for JDK 8 and JDK 9. When the multi-release JAR is used on JDK 8, the JDK 8 version of the library code will be used. When it is used on JDK 9, the JDK 9 version of the library code will be used. Files that are specific to a JDK version N are stored in the META-INF\versions\N directory of the multi-release JAR. Files that are common to all JDK versions are stored in the root directory. For environments not supporting multi-release JARs, such JARs are treated as regular JARs. The search order for a file is different in a multi-release JAR—all the versioned directories starting with the major version of the current platform are searched before the root directory is.

JMOD files are designed to handle more content types than JAR files can. They can package native code, configuration files, native commands, and other kinds of data. At the time of this writing, the JMOD format is based on the ZIP format, which is going to change in the future. The JDK 9 modules are packaged in JMOD format for you to use at compile-time and link time. The JMOD format is not supported at runtime. You can use the jmod tool to work with JMOD files.

CHAPTER 7

■ ■ ■

Creating Custom Runtime Images

In this chapter, you will learn:

- What a custom runtime image and the JIMAGE format are
- How to create a custom runtime image using the `jlink` tool
- How to specify the command name to run the application stored in a custom image
- How to use plugins with the `jlink` tool

What Is a Custom Runtime Image?

Before JDK 9, Java runtime image was available as a huge monolithic artifact—thus increasing the download time, startup time, and the memory footprint. The monolithic JRE made it impossible to use Java on devices with small memory. If you deploy your Java applications to a cloud, you pay for the memory you use; most often, the monolithic JRE uses more memory than required, thus making you pay more for the cloud service. The Compact profiles introduced in Java 8 took a step forward to reduce the JRE size—hence the runtime memory footprint—by allowing you to package a subset of the JRE in a custom runtime image called a *compact profile*.

Java 9 took a holistic approach to packaging runtime images. All platform code has been modularized. Your application code is also packaged as modules. In Java 9, you can create a custom runtime that will contain your application modules and only those platform modules used by your application. You can also package native commands in your runtime image. Another benefit of creating a runtime image is that you have to ship only one bundle—the runtime image—to your application users who are not needed to download and install a separate bundle of JRE to run your application.

The runtime image is stored in a special format called JIMAGE, which is optimized for space and speed. The JIMAGE format is supported only at runtime. It is a container format for storing and indexing modules, classes, and resources in the JDK. Searching and loading classes from a JIMAGE file is a lot faster than from JAR and JMOD files. The JIMAGE format is JDK-internal and developers will rarely need to interact with a JIMAGE file directly.

The JIMAGE format is expected to evolve significantly over time and, therefore, its internals are not exposed to developers. JDK 9 ships with a tool called `jimage`, which can be used to explore JIMAGE files. I explain the tool in detail in a separate section in this chapter.

■ **Tip** You use the `jlink` tool to create a runtime image, which uses a new file format called JIMAGE to store modules. JDK 9 ships with the `jimage` tool to let you explore the contents of a JIMAGE file.

A word of caution if your code is expecting the runtime image to be stored in a file named rt.jar file. The JDK runtime was stored in a rt.jar file before JDK 9, but that is no longer the case in JDK 9. This might break your code when you migrate your application to JDK 9.

Creating Custom Runtime Images

You can create a custom platform-specific runtime image using the jlink tool. The runtime image will contain specified application modules and only the needed platform modules, thus reducing the size of the runtime image. This is useful for applications running on embedded devices that have a small amount ot memory. The JDK 9 ships with the jlink tool. It is located in the JDK_HOME\bin directory. The general syntax for running the jlink tool is as follows:

```
jlink <options> --module-path <modulepath> --add-modules <mods> --output <path>
```

Here, <options> includes zero or more options for jlink, as listed in Table 7-1 and <modulepath> is the module path where the platform and application modules are located to be added to the image. Modules can be in modular JARs, exploded directories, and JMOD files. <mods> is a list of modules to be added to the image, which may cause additional modules to be added because of transitive dependencies on other modules. <path> is the output directory where the generated runtime image will be stored.

Table 7-1. *List of Options for the jlink Tool*

Option	Description
--add-modules <mod>,<mod>...	Specifies the list of root modules to resolve. All resolved modules will be added to the runtime image.
--bind-services	Performs full service binding during the linking process. If the added modules contain uses statements, jlink will scan all JMOD files on the module path to include all service provider modules in the runtime image for the service specified in the uses statement.
-c, --compress <0|1|2>[:filter=<pattern-list>]	Specifies the compression level of all resources in the output image. 0 means constant string sharing, 1 means ZIP, and 2 means both. An optional <pattern-list> filter can be specified to list the pattern of files to be included.
--disable-plugin <plugin-name>	Disables the specified plugin.
--endian <little|big>	Specifies the byte order of the generated runtime image. The default is the byte order of the native platform.
-h,--help	Prints the usage description and a list of all options for the jlink tool.
--ignore-signing-information	Suppress a fatal error when signed modular JARs are linked in the image. The signatures of related files of the signed modular JARs are not copied to the runtime image.

(*continued*)

Table 7-1. (*continued*)

Option	Description
`--launcher <command>=<module>`	Specifies the launcher command for the module. `<command>` is the name of the command you want to generate to launch your application, for example, `runmyapp`. The tool will create a scrip/batch file named `<command>` to run the main class in `<module>`.
`--launcher <command>=<module>` `/<main-class>`	Specifies the launcher command for the module and the main class. `<command>` is the name of the command you want to generate to launch your application, for example, `runmyapp`. The tool will create a script/batch file named `<command>` to run the `<main-class>` in `<module>`.
`--limit-modules <mod>,<mod>`	Limits the observable modules to those in the transitive closure of the named modules plus the main module, if specified, as well as any further modules specified with the `--add-modules` option.
`--list-plugins`	Lists the available plugins.
`-p, --module-path <modulepath>`	Specifies the module path where the platform and application modules will be found to be added to the runtime image.
`--no-header-files`	Excludes the include header files for the native code.
`--no-man-pages`	Excludes the manual pages.
`--output <path>`	Specifies the directory where the runtime image will be copied.
`--save-opts <filename>`	Saves the `jlink` options in the specified file.
`-G, --strip-debug`	Strips the debug information from the output image.
`--suggest-providers [<service-name>,...]`	If no service name is specified, it suggests the name of the providers of all services that would be linked for the added modules. If you specify one or more service names, it suggests providers of the specified service names. This option can be used before creating an image to know what services will be included when you use the `--bind-services` option.
`-v, --verbose`	Prints verbose output.
`--version`	Prints the version of the `jlink` tool.
`@<filename>`	Reads options from the specified file.

Let's create a runtime image that contains the four modules for the prime checker application and the required platform modules, which includes only the java.base module. Note that the following command includes only three modules from the prime checker application. The fourth one will be added because these three depend on that fourth module. The text following the command explains this in detail.

```
C:\Java9Revealed>jlink --module-path jmods;C:\java9\jmods
  --add-modules com.jdojo.prime.client,com.jdojo.prime.generic,com.jdojo.prime.faster
  --launcher runprimechecker=com.jdojo.prime.client
  --output primechecker
```

Before I explain all the options for this command, let's verify that the runtime image was created successfully. The command is supposed to copy the runtime image to the C:\Java9Revealed\primechecker folder. Run the following command to verify that the runtime image contains the five modules:

```
C:\Java9Revealed>primechecker\bin\java --list-modules
```

```
com.jdojo.prime@1.0
com.jdojo.prime.client@1.0
com.jdojo.prime.faster@1.0
com.jdojo.prime.generic@1.0
java.base@9-ea
```

If you get an output, which is similar to the shown here, the runtime image was created correctly. The module version number, which is shown after the @ sign in the output, may be different for you.

The --module-path option specifies two directories, jmods and C:\java9\jmods. I saved the four JMOD files for the prime checker application in the C:\Java9Revealed\jmods directory. The first element in the module path lets the jlink tool find all application modules. I installed the JDK 9 in the C:\java9 directory, so the second element in the module path lets the tool find the platform modules. If you do not specify the second part, you get an error:

```
Module java.base not found.
```

The --add-modules option specifies three modules of the prime checker application. You might wonder why we did not specify the fourth module com.jdojo.prime with this option. This list contains root modules, not just the modules to be included in the runtime image. The jlink tool will resolve all dependencies transitively for these root modules and include all the resolved dependent modules into the runtime image. The three modules depend on the com.jdojo.prime module, which will be resolved by locating it on the module path and, hence, will be included in the runtime image. The image will also contain the java.base module because all application modules implicitly depend on it.

The --output option specifies the directory where the runtime image will be copied. The command will copy the runtime image to the C:\Java9Revealed\primechecker directory. The output directory contains the following subdirectories and a file named release:

- bin
- conf
- include
- legal
- lib

The `bin` directory contains executable files. On Windows, it also contains dynamically-linked native libraries (`.dll` files).

The `conf` directory contains the editable configuration files such as `.properties` and `.policy` files.

The `include` directory contains C/C++ header files.

The `legal` directory contains legal notices.

The `lib` directory contains, among other files, the modules added to the runtime image. On Mac, Linux, and Solaris, it will also contain the system's dynamically-linked native libraries.

You used the `--launcher` option with the `jlink` command. You specified a command name, runprimechecker, and the module name was `com.jdojo.prime.client`. The `--launcher` option makes `jlink` create a platform-specific executable such as a `runprimechecker.bat` file on Windows in the `bin` directory. You can use this executable to run your application. The file contents are simply a wrapper for running the main class in this module. You can use this file to run the application:

```
C:\Java9Revealed> primechecker\bin\runprimechecker
```

```
Using jdojo.faster.primechecker:
3 is a prime.
4 is not a prime.
121 is not a prime.
977 is a prime.
Using jdojo.faster.primechecker:
3 is a prime.
4 is not a prime.
121 is not a prime.
977 is a prime.
A PrimeChecker service provider with the name 'jdojo.probable.primechecker' was not found.
```

You can also use the `java` command, which is copied to the `bin` directory by the `jlink` tool, to launch your application:

```
C:\Java9Revealed>primechecker\bin\java --module com.jdojo.prime.client
```

The output of this command will be the same as that of the previous command. Notice that you did not have to specify the module path. The linker, the `jlink` tool, took care of the module path when the runtime image was created. When you run the `java` command of the generated runtime image, it knows where to find the modules. Also notice that you did not have to specify the main class name to the command. You just specified the module name. You had already set the `main-class` attribute for the `com.jdojo.prime.client` module. When you run a module without specifying the main class, the `main-class` attribute set in the `module-info.class` file for that module is used as the main class.

Binding Services

In the previous section, you created a runtime image for the prime service client application. You had to specify the names of all service provider modules with the `--add-modules` option that you wanted to include in the image. In this section, I will show you how to bind services automatically while creating a runtime image using the `--bind-services` option with the `jlink` tool. This time, you need to add the module, which is the `com.jdojo.prime` module, to the module graph and the `jlink` tool will take care of the rest. The `com.jdojo.prime.client` module reads the `com.jdojo.prime` module, so adding the former into the module graph will also resolve the latter. The following command prints the list of suggested service providers for the runtime image. A partial output is shown.

```
C:\Java9Revealed>jlink --module-path jmods;C:\java9\jmods
--add-modules com.jdojo.prime.client
--suggest-providers
```

```
module com.jdojo.prime located (file:///C:/Java9Revealed/jmods/com.jdojo.prime.jmod)
    uses com.jdojo.prime.PrimeChecker
module com.jdojo.prime.client located (file:///C:/Java9Revealed/jmods/com.jdojo.prime.
client.jmod)
module java.base located (file:///C:/java9/jmods/java.base.jmod)
    uses java.lang.System$LoggerFinder
    uses java.net.ContentHandlerFactory
...

Suggested providers:
  module com.jdojo.prime.faster provides com.jdojo.prime.PrimeChecker, used by com.jdojo.prime
  module com.jdojo.prime.generic provides com.jdojo.prime.PrimeChecker, used by com.jdojo.prime
  module com.jdojo.prime.probable provides com.jdojo.prime.PrimeChecker, used by com.jdojo.prime
  module java.desktop provides java.net.ContentHandlerFactory, used by java.base
 ...
```

The command specifies only the com.jdojo.prime.client module to the --add-modules option. The com.jdojo.prime and java.base modules are resolved because the com.jdojo.prime.client module reads them. All resolved modules are scanned for the uses statement and, subsequently, all modules in the module path are scanned for service providers for the services specified in the uses statement. All service providers that are found are printed.

▓ **Tip**   You may specify arguments to the --suggest-providers option. If you are using it without arguments, make sure to specify it at the end of the command. Otherwise, the option after the --suggest-providers option will be interpreted as its arguments and you will receive an error.

The following command specifies com.jdojo.prime.PrimeChecker as the service name to the --suggest-providers option to print all service providers found for this service:

```
C:\Java9Revealed>jlink --module-path jmods;C:\java9\jmods
--add-modules com.jdojo.prime.client
--suggest-providers com.jdojo.prime.PrimeChecker
```

```
Suggested providers:
  module com.jdojo.prime.faster provides com.jdojo.prime.PrimeChecker, used by com.jdojo.prime
  module com.jdojo.prime.generic provides com.jdojo.prime.PrimeChecker, used by com.jdojo.prime
  module com.jdojo.prime.probable provides com.jdojo.prime.PrimeChecker, used by com.jdojo.prime
```

Using the same logic as described before, all three service providers were found. Let us create a new runtime image that includes all three service providers. The following command does the job:

```
C:\Java9Revealed>jlink --module-path jmods;C:\java9\jmods
--add-modules com.jdojo.prime.client
--launcher runprimechecker=com.jdojo.prime.client
--bind-services
--output primecheckerservice
```

Compare this command with the command used in the previous section. This time, you specified only one module with the --add-modules option. That is, you did not have to specify the names of service provider modules. You used the --bind-services option, so all service providers references in the added modules are added automatically to the runtime image. You have specified a new output directory named primecheckerservice. The following command runs the newly created runtime image:

```
C:\Java9Revealed>primecheckerservice\bin\runprimechecker
```

```
Using jdojo.generic.primechecker:
3 is a prime.
4 is not a prime.
121 is not a prime.
977 is a prime.
Using jdojo.faster.primechecker:
3 is a prime.
4 is not a prime.
121 is not a prime.
977 is a prime.
Using jdojo.probable.primechecker:
3 is a prime.
4 is not a prime.
121 is not a prime.
977 is a prime.
```

The output proves that all three prime checker service providers, which were in the module path, were added automatically to the runtime image.

Using Plugins with the jlink Tool

The jlink tool uses a plugin architecture to create runtime images. It collects all classes, native libraries, and configuration files into a set of resources. It builds a pipeline of transformers, which are plugins specified as command-line options. Resources are fed into the pipeline. Each transformer in the pipeline applies some kind of transformation to resources and the transformed resources are fed to the next transformer. At the end, jlink feeds the transformed resources to an image builder.

The JDK 9 ships the jlink tool with a few plugins. Those plugins define command-line options. To use a plugin, you need to use the command-line option for it. You can run the jlink tool with the --list-plugins options to print the list of all available plugins with their descriptions and command-line options:

C:\Java9Revealed>jlink --list-plugins

```
List of available plugins:

Plugin Name: class-for-name
Option: --class-for-name
Description: Class optimization: convert Class.forName calls to constant loads.

Plugin Name: compress
Option: --compress=<0|1|2>[:filter=<pattern-list>]
Description: Compress all resources in the output image.
Level 0: constant string sharing
Level 1: ZIP
Level 2: both.
An optional <pattern-list> filter can be specified to list the pattern of
files to be included.

Plugin Name: dedup-legal-notices
Option: --dedup-legal-notices=[error-if-not-same-content]
Description: De-duplicate all legal notices.  If error-if-not-same-content is
specified then it will be an error if two files of the same filename
are different.

Plugin Name: exclude-files
Option: --exclude-files=<pattern-list> of files to exclude
Description: Specify files to exclude. e.g.: **.java,glob:/java.base/native/client/**

Plugin Name: exclude-jmod-section
Option: --exclude-jmod-section=<section-name>
where <section-name> is "man" or "headers".
Description: Specify a JMOD section to exclude

Plugin Name: exclude-resources
Option: --exclude-resources=<pattern-list> resources to exclude
Description: Specify resources to exclude. e.g.: **.jcov,glob:**/META-INF/**

Plugin Name: generate-jli-classes
Option: --generate-jli-classes=@filename
Description: Takes a file hinting to jlink what java.lang.invoke classes to pre-generate. If
this flag is not specified a default set of classes will be generated.

Plugin Name: include-locales
Option: --include-locales=<langtag>[,<langtag>]*
Description: BCP 47 language tags separated by a comma, allowing locale matching
defined in RFC 4647. e.g.: en,ja,*-IN
```

```
Plugin Name: order-resources
Option: --order-resources=<pattern-list> of paths in priority order.  If a @file
is specified, then each line should be an exact match for the path to be ordered
Description: Order resources. e.g.: **/module-info.class,@classlist,/java.base/java/lang/**

Plugin Name: release-info
Option: --release-info=<file>|add:<key1>=<value1>:<key2>=<value2>:...|del:<key list>
Description: <file> option is to load release properties from the supplied file.
add: is to add properties to the release file.
Any number of <key>=<value> pairs can be passed.
del: is to delete the list of keys in release file.

Plugin Name: strip-debug
Option: --strip-debug
Description: Strip debug information from the output image

Plugin Name: strip-native-commands
Option: --strip-native-commands
Description: Exclude native commands (such as java/java.exe) from the image

Plugin Name: system-modules
Option: --system-modules
Description: Fast loading of module descriptors (always enabled)

Plugin Name: vm
Option: --vm=<client|server|minimal|all>
Description: Select the HotSpot VM in the output image.  Default is all

For options requiring a <pattern-list>, the value will be a comma separated
list of elements each using one the following forms:
  <glob-pattern>
  glob:<glob-pattern>
  regex:<regex-pattern>
  @<filename> where filename is the name of a file containing patterns to be
              used, one pattern per line
```

The following command uses the compress and strip-debug plugins. The compress plugin will compress the image, which will result in a smaller image size. I use the compression level 2 to have the maximum compression. The strip-debug plugin will remove the debugging information from the Java code, thus further reducing the size of the image. Make sure to delete the primechecker directory that was previously created before you run this command.

```
C:\Java9Revealed>jlink --module-path jmods;C:\java9\jmods
  --compress 2
  --strip-debug
  --add-modules com.jdojo.prime.client,com.jdojo.prime.generic,com.jdojo.prime.faster
  --launcher runprimechecker=com.jdojo.prime.client
  --output primechecker
```

■ **Tip** At the time of this writing, the plugin API is strictly experimental and the execution order of the plugins is not defined. In its early implementation, the `jlink` tool also supported custom plugins, which was later removed.

The jimage Tool

The Java runtime ships the modular runtime image in a JIMAGE file. The file is named `modules` and it is located in JAVA_HOME\lib, where JAVA_HOME could be your JDK_HOME or JRE_HOME. The `jimage` tool is used to explore the contents of JIMAGE files. It can:

- Extract entries from the JIMAGE file

- Print the summary of the contents stored in the JIMAGE

- Print the list of entries such as their name, size, offset, etc.

- Verify class files

The `jimage` tool is stored in the JDK_HOME\bin directory. The general format of the command is as follows:

jimage <subcommand> <options> <jimage-file-list>

Here, <subcommand> is one of the subcommands listed in Table 7-2. <options> is one or more options listed in Table 7-3; <jimage-file-list> is a space-separated list of JIMAGE files to be explored.

Table 7-2. *A List of Sub-Commands Used with the jimage Tool*

Sub-Command	Description
extract	Extracts all entries from the specified JIMAGE files to the current directory. Use the --dir option to specify another directory for extracted entries.
info	Prints the detailed information contained in the header of the specified JIMAGE file.
list	Prints the list of all modules and their entries in the specified JIMAGE file. Use the --verbose option to include the details of the entries such as its size, offset, and whether the entry is compressed.
verify	Prints a list of .class entries in the specified JIMAGE files that do not verify as classes.

Table 7-3. A List of Options Used with the jimage Tool

Option	Description
`--dir <dir-name>`	Specifies the target directory for the `extract` subcommand where the entries in the JIMAGE files will be extracted.
`-h, --help`	Prints a usage message for the `jimage` tool.
`--include <pattern-list>`	Specifies a list of patterns for filtering entries. The value for the pattern list is a comma-separated list of elements, each using one the following forms: • `<glob-pattern>` • `glob:<glob-pattern>` • `regex:<regex-pattern>`
`--full-version`	Prints full version information for the `jimage` tool.
`--verbose`	When used with the `list` sub-command, prints entry details such as size, offset, and compression level.
`--version`	Prints version information for the `jimage` tool.

I show a few examples of using the `jimage` command. Examples use the JDK 9 runtime image that is stored at `C:\java9\lib\modules` on my computer. You will need to replace this image location with yours when you run these examples. You can also use any custom runtime image created by the `jlink` tool in these examples.

The following command extracts all entries from the runtime image and copies them to the extracted_jdk directory. The command takes a few seconds to complete.

```
C:\Java9Revealed>jimage extract --dir extracted_jdk C:\java9\lib\modules
```

The following command extracts all image entries with the `.png` extension from the JDK runtime image into an extracted_images directory:

```
C:\Java9Revealed>jimage extract --include regex:.+\.png --dir extracted_images C:\java9\lib\
modules
```

The following command lists all entries in the runtime image. A partial output is shown:

```
C:\Java9Revealed>jimage list C:\java9\lib\modules
```

```
jimage: C:\java9\lib\modules

Module: java.activation
    META-INF/mailcap.default
    META-INF/mimetypes.default
...
Module: java.annotations.common
    javax/annotation/Generated.class
...
```

The following command lists all entries in the runtime image along with the entries' details. Notice the use of the --verbose option. A partial output is shown.

```
C:\Java9Revealed>jimage list --verbose C:\java9\lib\modules
```

```
jimage: C:\java9\lib\modules

Module: java.activation
Offset     Size   Compressed Entry
34214466   292             0 META-INF/mailcap.default
34214758   562             0 META-INF/mimetypes.default
...
Module: java.annotations.common
Offset     Size   Compressed Entry
34296622   678             0 javax/annotation/Generated.class
...
```

The following command prints the list of class files that are invalid. You may wonder how you make a class file invalid. Typically, you won't have an invalid class file—but hackers would! However, to run this example, I need to have an invalid class file. I used a simple idea—take a valid class file, open it in a text editor, and remove its contents partly and randomly to make it an invalid class file. I copied the contents of a compiled class file into the Main2.class file and removed some of its contents to make it an invalid class. I added the Main2.class file to the com.jdojo.prime.client module in the same directory as the Main.class. I recreated the runtime image using the previous command for the prime check application for this example. If you use the Java runtime image that comes with the JDK, you will not see any output because all class files in JDK runtime image are valid.

```
C:\Java9Revealed>jimage verify primechecker\lib\modules
```

```
jimage: primechecker\lib\modules
Error(s) in Class: /com.jdojo.prime.client/com/jdojo/prime/client/Main2.class
```

Summary

In JDK 9, the runtime image is stored in a special format called JIMAGE, which is optimized for space and speed. The JIMAGE format is supported only at runtime. It is a container format for storing and indexing modules, classes, and resources in the JDK. Searching and loading classes from a JIMAGE file is a lot faster than from JAR and JMOD files. The JIMAGE format is JDK-internal and developers will rarely need to interact with a JIMAGE file directly.

It ships with a tool called jlink that lets you create a runtime image in JIMAGE format for your application that will contain application modules and only those platform modules that are used by your application. The jlink tool can create runtime images from modules stored in module JARs, exploded directories, and JMOD files. JDK 9 ships with a tool called jimage that can be used to explore the contents of JIMAGE files.

CHAPTER 8

▓ ▓ ▓

Breaking Changes in JDK 9

In this chapter, you will learn:

- What the new JDK versioning scheme is

- How to parse a JDK version string using the `Runtime.Version` class

- What the new directory layout of the JDK/JRE 9 is

- How the Endorsed Standards Override Mechanism works in JDK 9

- Changes in using the extension mechanism in JDK 9

- How class loaders work in JDK 9 and how modules are loaded

- How resources are encapsulated in modules in JDK 9

- How to access resources in modules using the resource-finding methods in the `Module`, `Class`, and `ClassLoader` classes

- What the `jrt` URL scheme is and how to use it to access resources in the runtime image

- How to access JDK-internal APIs in JDK 9 and the list of removed JDK APIs in JDK 9

- How to replace classes and resources in a module using the `--patch-module` command-line option JDK 9

There are a few changes in JDK 9 that may break applications that ran fine in JDK 8. In this chapter, I describe those changes in detail.

The New JDK Versioning Scheme

Before JDK 9, the JDK versioning scheme was not intuitive to developers and was not easy for programs to parse. Looking at the two JDK versions, you could not tell the subtle differences between them. It was hard to answer a simple question: Which release contains the most recent security fixes, JDK 7 Update 55 or JDK 7 Update 60? The answer was not the obvious one, which you may have guessed—*JDK 7 Update 60*. Both releases contain the same security fixes. What is the difference between the JDK 8 Update 66, 1.8.0_66, and JDK 8u66 releases? They represent the same release. It was necessary to understand the versioning scheme in detail before you could understand the details contained in the version string. JDK 9 attempts to standardize the JDK versioning scheme, so it can be easily understood by humans, easily parsed by programs, and follows the industry-standard versioning scheme.

© Kishori Sharan 2017
K. Sharan, *Java 9 Revealed*, DOI 10.1007/978-1-4842-2592-9_8

JDK 9 contains a static nested class named `Runtime.Version`, which represents a version string for an implementation of the Java SE platform. It can be used to represent, parse, validate, and compare version strings.

A *version string* consists of the following four elements in order. Only the first one is mandatory:

- Version number
- Prerelease information
- Build information
- Additional information

The following regular expression defines the format for a version string:

`$vnum(-$pre)?(\+($build)?(-$opt)?)?`

A *short version string* consists of a version number optionally followed by prerelease information:

`$vnum(-$pre)?`

You can have a version string as short as `"9"`, which contains only the major version number, and as big as `"9.0.1-ea+154-20170130.07.36am"`, which contains all parts of a version string.

Version Number

A version number is a sequence of elements separated by periods. It can be an arbitrary length. Its format is as follows:

`^[1-9][0-9]*(((\.0)*\.[1-9][0-9]*)*)*$`

A version number may consist of one to four elements, as follows:

`$major.$minor.$security(.$addtionalInfo)`

The `$major` element represents the major version of a JDK release. It is incremented for a major release that that contains significant new features. For example, the major release for JDK 8 is 8 and for JDK 9 it's 9. When the major version number is incremented, all other parts in the version number are removed. For example, if you have a version number of 9.2.2.1, the new version number will be 10 when the major version number is incremented from 9 to 10.

The `$minor` element represents the minor version of a JDK release. It is incremented for a minor update release such as for bug fixes, new garbage collectors, new JDK-specific APIs, etc.

The `$security` element represents the security-level updates of a JDK release. It is incremented for a security update. This element is not reset when the minor version number is incremented. A higher value of `$security` for a given `$major` always indicates a more secure release. For example, a JDK release 9.1.7 is as secure as the JDK release 9.5.7 because the security level for both releases is the same, which is 7. As another example, the JDK release 9.2.2 is more secure than 9.2.1 because, for the same major version 9, the former's security level of 2 is greater than the latter's security level of 1.

The following rules apply to version numbers:

- All elements must be a non-negative integer.

- The first three elements are treated as major version, minor version, and security level, respectively; the rest, if present, are treated as additional information such as numbers indicating patch releases.

- Only the major version element is mandatory.

- Elements of a version number cannot contain leading zeros. For example, the major version of the JDK 9 is 9, not 09.

- Trailing elements cannot be zero. That is, you cannot have a version number as 9.0.0. It can be 9, 9.2, or 9.0.x, where x is a positive integer.

Prerelease Information

The $pre element in a version string is a prerelease identifier such as ea for an early-access release, snapshot for a prerelease snapshot, and internal for a developer internal build. It is optional. If it is present, it is prefixed with a hyphen (-) and must be an alphanumeric string matching the regular expression ([a-zA-Z0-9]+). The following version string contains 9 as a version number and ea as prerelease information.

9-ea

Build Information

The $build element in a version string is a build number incremented for each promoted build. It is optional. It is reset to 1 when any part of the version number is incremented. If it is present, it is prefixed with a plus sign (+) and must match the regular expression (0|[1-9][0-9]*). The following version string contains 154 as the build number.

9-ea+154

Additional Information

The $opt element in a version string contains additional build information such as the date and time of an internal build. It is optional. It is alphanumeric and can contain hyphens and periods. If it is present, it is prefixed with a hyphen (-) and must match the regular expression ([-a-zA-Z0-9\.]+). If $build is absent, you need to prefix the $opt value with a plus sign followed by a hyphen (+-) to specify the value for $opt. For example, in 9-ea+132-2016-08-23, $build is 132 and $opt is 2016-08-23; in 9+-123, $pre and $build are absent and $opt is 123. The following version string embeds a date and time for a release in its additional information element:

9-ea+154-20170130.07.36am

Parsing Old and New Version Strings

JDK releases have either been Limited Update releases that include new functionality and non-security fixes or Critical Patch Updates that only include fixes for security vulnerabilities. The version string included the version number, including the update number and the build number. Limited Update releases were numbered in multiples of 20. Critical Patch Updates used odd numbers, which were calculated by adding multiples of five to the prior Limited Update and, when needed, adding one to keep the resulting number odd. An example is 1.8.0_31-b13, which is update 31 of the major version 8 of the JDK. Its build number is 13. Note that prior to JDK 9, the version string always started with 1.

■ **Tip**   Your existing code that parses the version string to get the major version of a JDK release may fail in JDK 9 depending on the logic it uses. For example, if the logic looks for the major version at the second element by skipping the first, which used to be 1, the logic will fail. For example, if it returns 8 from 1.8.0, now it will return 0 from 9.0.1, where you would expect 9.

Version Changes to System Properties

In JDK 9, the values returned for the system properties that contain the JDK version string have changed. Table 8-1 contains the list of those system properties and their format. $vstr, $vnum, and $pre refer to version string, version number, and prerelease information, respectively.

Table 8-1.   *System Properties and Their Values in JDK 9*

System Property Name	Value
java.version	$vnum(\-$pre)?
java.runtime.version	$vstr
java.vm.version	$vstr
java.specification.version	$vnum
java.vm.specification.version	$vnum

Using the Runtime.Version Class

JDK 9 has added a static nested class called Runtime.Version whose instances represent version strings. The Version class does not have a public constructor. The only way to get its instance is to call its static method named parse(String vstr). The method may throw a runtime exception if the version string is null or invalid.

```
import java.lang.Runtime.Version;
...
// Parse a version string "9.0.1-ea+132"
Version version = Version.parse("9.0.1-ea+132");
```

The following methods in the `Runtime.Version` class return elements of a version string. The method names are intuitive enough to guess the type of element values they return.

- `int major()`

- `int minor()`

- `int security()`

- `Optional<String> pre()`

- `Optional<Integer> build()`

- `Optional<String> optional()`

Notice that for the optional elements, $pre, $build, and $opt, the return type is `Optional`. For the optional $minor and $security elements, the return type is `int`, not `Optional`, which will return zero if $minor and $security are absent in the version string.

Recall that the version number in a version string may contain additional information after the third element. The `Version` class does not contain a method to get the additional information directly. It contains a `version()` method that returns a `List<Integer>` where the list contains all elements of the version number. The first three elements in the list are $major, $minor, and $security. The remaining elements contain the additional version number information.

The `Runtime.Version` class contains methods to compare two version strings in terms of order and equality. You can compare them with or without the optional build information ($opt). Those comparison methods are as follows:

- `int compareTo(Version v)`

- `int compareToIgnoreOptional(Version v)`

- `boolean equals(Object v)`

- `boolean equalsIgnoreOptional(Object v)`

The expression `v1.compareTo(v2)` will return a negative integer, zero, or a positive integer if v1 is less than, equal to, or greater than v2. The `compareToIgnoreOptional()` method works the same way as the `compareTo()` method, except that it ignores the optional build information while comparing. The `equals()` and `equalsIgnoreOptional()` methods compare two version strings for equality with and without the optional build information.

Which version strings represent the latest build: `9.1.1` or `9.1.1-ea`? The first one does not contain the prerelease element whereas the second one does, so the first one is the latest build. Which version strings represents the latest build: `9.1.1` or `9.1.1.1-ea`? This time, the second one represents the latest build. The comparison occurs in sequence—$vnum, $pre, $build, and $opt. When the version number is greater, other elements in the version string are not compared.

The source code for this section is in a module named `com.jdojo.version.string` whose declaration is shown in Listing 8-1. Listing 8-2 contains a complete program that shows how to extract all parts of a version string using the `Runtime.Version` class.

Listing 8-1. A Module Declaration for a Module Named com.jdojo.version.string

```
// module-info.java
module com.jdojo.version.string {
    exports com.jdojo.version.string;
}
```

Listing 8-2. A VersionTest Class That Shows How to Use the Runtime.Version Class to Work with Version Strings

```java
// VersionTest.java
package com.jdojo.version.string;

import java.util.List;
import java.lang.Runtime.Version;

public class VersionTest {
    public static void main(String[] args) {
        String[] versionStrings = {
            "9", "9.1", "9.1.2", "9.1.2.3.4", "9.0.0",
            "9.1.2-ea+153", "9+132", "9-ea+132-2016-08-23", "9+-123",
            "9.0.1-ea+132-2016-08-22.10.56.45am"};

        for (String versonString : versionStrings) {
            try {
                Version version = Version.parse(versonString);

                // Get the additional version number elements
                // which start at 4th element
                String vnumAdditionalInfo = getAdditionalVersionInfo(version);

                System.out.printf("Version String=%s%n", versonString);
                System.out.printf("Major=%d, Minor=%d, Security=%d, Additional Version=%s,"
                        + " Pre=%s, Build=%s, Optional=%s %n%n",
                        version.major(),
                        version.minor(),
                        version.security(),
                        vnumAdditionalInfo,
                        version.pre().orElse(""),
                        version.build().isPresent() ? version.build().get().toString() : "",
                        version.optional().orElse(""));
            } catch (Exception e) {
                System.out.printf("%s%n%n", e.getMessage());
            }
        }
    }

    // Returns the version number elements from the 4th elements to the end
    public static String getAdditionalVersionInfo(Version v) {
        String str = "";

        List<Integer> vnum = v.version();
        int size = vnum.size();
        if (size >= 4) {
            str = str + String.valueOf(vnum.get(3));
        }
```

```
        for (int i = 4; i < size; i++) {
            str = str + "." + String.valueOf(vnum.get(i));
        }

        return str;
    }
}
```

```
Version String=9
Major=9, Minor=0, Security=0, Additional Version=, Pre=, Build=, Optional=

Version String=9.1
Major=9, Minor=1, Security=0, Additional Version=, Pre=, Build=, Optional=

Version String=9.1.2
Major=9, Minor=1, Security=2, Additional Version=, Pre=, Build=, Optional=

Version String=9.1.2.3.4
Major=9, Minor=1, Security=2, Additional Version=3.4, Pre=, Build=, Optional=

Invalid version string: '9.0.0'

Version String=9.1.2-ea+153
Major=9, Minor=1, Security=2, Additional Version=, Pre=ea, Build=153, Optional=

Version String=9+132
Major=9, Minor=0, Security=0, Additional Version=, Pre=, Build=132, Optional=

Version String=9-ea+132-2016-08-23
Major=9, Minor=0, Security=0, Additional Version=, Pre=ea, Build=132, Optional=2016-08-23

Version String=9+-123
Major=9, Minor=0, Security=0, Additional Version=, Pre=, Build=, Optional=123

Version String=9.0.1-ea+132-2016-08-22.10.56.45am
Major=9, Minor=0, Security=1, Additional Version=, Pre=ea, Build=132, Optional=2016-08-
22.10.56.45am
```

Changes to the JDK and JRE

The JDK and JRE have been modularized in Java SE 9. That warranted a few changes to their structures. A few other changes were made to improve performance, security, and maintainability. Most of these changes affect library developers and IDE developers rather than application developers. For the sake of discussing these changes, I put them into three broad categories:

- Layout changes

- Behavioral changes

- API changes

The following sections describe these changes in detail.

Layout Changes in JDK and JRE

Structural changes affect the way directories and files in runtime images are organized and affect their contents. Before Java SE 9, the JDK build system used to produce two types of runtime images—a Java Runtime Environment (JRE) and a Java Development Kit (JDK). The JRE was a complete implementation of the Java SE platform and the JDK had an embedded JRE and development tools and libraries. You could install only JRE or the JDK, which had an embedded JRE. Figure 8-1 shows the main directories in the JDK installation prior to Java SE 9. The JDK_HOME is the directory in which the JDK was installed. If you installed JRE only, you had directories only under the jre directory.

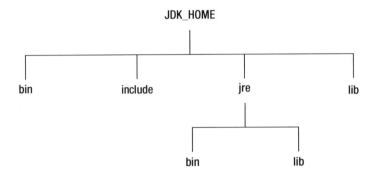

Figure 8-1. *JDK and JRE directory arrangements before Java SE 9*

In the JDK, prior to Java SE 9:

- The bin directory used to contain command-line development and debugging tools such as javac, jar, and javadoc. It also used to contain the java command to launch Java applications.

- The include directory contained C/C++ header files to be used while compiling native code.

- The lib directory contained several JARs and other types of files for the JDK's tools. It had a tools.jar file, which contained the Java classes for the javac compiler.

- The jre\bin directory contained essential commands such as the java command. On the Windows platform, it contained the system's runtime dynamically linked libraries (DLLs).

- The jre\lib directory contained user-editable configuration files such as .properties and .policy files.

- The jre\lib\endorsed directory contained JARs that allowed the Endorsed Standards Override Mechanism. This allowed the later versions of classes and interfaces that implement Endorsed Standards or Standalone Technology, which are created outside the Java Community Process, to be incorporated into the Java platform. These JARs were prepended to the JVM's bootstrap class path, thus overriding any definition of these classes and interfaces present in the Java runtime.

- The jre\lib\ext directory contained JARs that allowed the extension mechanism. This mechanism loaded all JARs in this directory by an extension class loader, which is the child of the bootstrap class loader and parent of the system class loader, which loads all application classes. By placing JARs in this directory, you can extend the Java SE platform. The contents of these JARs are visible to all applications that compile or run on this runtime image.

- The jre\lib directory contained several JARs. The rt.jar file contained the Java classes and resource files for the runtime. Many tools depended on the location of the rt.jar file.

- The jre\lib directory contained dynamically linked native libraries for non-Windows platforms.

- The jre\lib directory contained several other sub-directories, which contained runtime files such as fonts and images.

The root directory of the JDK and JRE, which is not embedded in a JDK, used to contain several files such as COPYRIGHT, LICENSE, and README.html. A release file in the root directory contained a key-value pair describing the runtime image such as the Java version, OS version, and architecture. The following code shows the partial contents of an example release file from JDK 8:

```
JAVA_VERSION="1.8.0_66"
OS_NAME="Windows"
OS_VERSION="5.2"
OS_ARCH="amd64"
BUILD_TYPE="commercial"
```

The Java SE 9 has flattened the directory hierarchy for the JDK and removed the distinction between a JDK and a JRE. Figure 8-2 shows the directories for a JDK installation in Java SE 9. The JRE installation in JDK 9 does not contain the include and jmods directories.

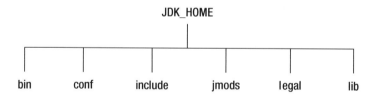

Figure 8-2. *JDK directory arrangements in Java SE 9*

In the JDK in Java SE 9:

- There is no sub-directory named jre.

- The bin directory contains all commands. On the Windows platform, it continues to contain the system's runtime dynamically linked libraries.

- The conf directory contains the user-editable configuration files such as .properties and .policy files that used to be in the jre\lib directory.

- The include directory contains C/C++ header files to be used while compiling the native code as before. It exists only in the JDK.

- The `jmods` directory contains the platform modules in JMOD format. You need it when creating a custom runtime image. It exists only in the JDK.

- The `legal` directory contains legal notices.

- The `lib` directory contains the dynamically linked native libraries on the non-Windows platform. Its sub-directories and files are not supposed to be directly edited or used by developers.

The root directory of the JDK 9 continues to have files such as COPYRIGHT and README. The `release` file in JDK 9 contains a new entry with a MODULES key whose value is a list of modules included in the image. Partial contents of a `release` file in a JDK 9 image are as follows:

```
MODULES=java.rmi,jdk.jdi,jdk.policytool
OS_VERSION="5.2"
OS_ARCH="amd64"
OS_NAME="Windows"
JAVA_VERSION="9"
JAVA_FULL_VERSION="9-ea+133"
```

I have shown only three modules in the list. In a full JDK install, this list will include all platform modules. In a custom runtime image, this list will contain only the modules that you include in the image.

▧ **Tip**   The `lib\tools.jar` in the JDK and the `lib\rt.jar` in the JRE have been removed from Java SE 9. Classes and resources that were available in these JARs are now stored in the `lib` directory in an internal format within a file named `modules`. A new scheme called `jrt` may be used to retrieve those classes and resources from the runtime image. Applications dependent on these JARs' locations will stop working.

Behavioral Changes

Behavioral changes will affect the runtime behavior of an application. The following sections explain those changes.

Endorsed Standards Override Mechanism

Prior to Java SE 9, you were able to use the Endorsed Standards Override Mechanism to use the newer versions of classes and interfaces that implement Endorsed Standards or Standalone APIs such as the `javax.rmi.CORBA` package and Java API for XML Processing (JAXP), which are created outside the Java Community Process. These JARs were prepended to the JVM's bootstrap class path, thus overriding any definition of these classes and interfaces present in the JRE. The locations of these JARs were specified by a system property named `java.endorsed.dirs` where directories were separated by platform-specific path-separator characters. If this property was not set, the runtime would look for the JARs in the `jre\lib\endorsed` directory.

Java SE 9 still supports the endorsed Standards and Standalone APIs Override mechanism. In Java SE 9, a runtime image consists of modules. To use this mechanism, you need to use the newer versions of the modules for the Endorsed Standards and Standalone APIs. You need to use the `--upgrade-module-path` command-line option. The value of this option is a list of directories containing modules for the Endorsed

Standards and Standalone APIs. The following command on Windows overrides the Endorsed Standards modules such as the `java.corba` module in JDK 9. The modules in the umod1 and umod2 directories will be used instead of the corresponding modules in the runtime image:

```
java --upgrade-module-path umod1;umod2 <other-options>
```

▓ **Tip** In Java SE 9, it is an error to create a `JAVA_HOME\lib\endorsed` directory and to set a system property named `java.endorsed.dirs`.

Extension Mechanism

Java SE prior to version 9 allowed an extension mechanism whereby you were able to extend the runtime image by placing JARs in directories specified by the system property `java.ext.dirs`. If this system property was not set, the `jre\lib\ext` directory was used as its default value. This mechanism loaded all JARs in this directory by an extension class loader, which is the child of the bootstrap class loader and the parent of the system class loader. It loads all application classes. The contents of these JARs were visible to all applications that compile or run on this runtime image.

Java SE 9 does not support the extension mechanism. If you need a similar functionality, you can place those JARs at the front of the class path. Having a directory named `JAVA_HOME\lib\ext` or setting a system property named `java.ext.dirs` causes an error in JDK 9.

Changes in Class Loaders

At runtime, every type is loaded by a class loader, which is represented by an instance of the `java.lang.ClassLoader` class. If you have an object reference `obj`, you can get its class loader reference by calling the `obj.getClass().getClassLoader()` method. You can get the parent of a class loader using its `getParent()` method.

Prior to version 9, the JDK used three class loaders to load classes, as shown in Figure 8-3. The direction of the arrow in the diagram indicates the delegation direction. You can add more class loaders, which would be a subclass of the `ClassLoader` class. The three class loaders in the JDK load classes from different locations and types.

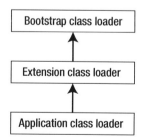

Figure 8-3. *Class loaders hierarchy in the JDK prior to version 9*

The JDK class loaders work in a hierarchical fashion—the bootstrap class loader being at the top of the hierarchy. A class loader delegates a class-loading request to the one above it. For example, if the application class loader needs to load a class, it delegates the request to the extension class loader, which in turn delegates the request to the bootstrap class loader. If the bootstrap class loader cannot load the class, the extension class loader attempts to load it. If the extension class loader cannot load the class, the application class loader attempts to load it. If the application class loader cannot load it, a ClassNotFoundException is thrown.

The bootstrap class loader is the parent of the extension class loader. The extension class loader is the parent of the application class loader. The bootstrap class loader has no parent. By default, the application class loader will be the parent of additional class loaders you create.

The bootstrap class loader loads bootstrap classes that consist of the Java platform, including the classes in JAVA_HOME\lib\rt.jar and several other runtime JARs. It is entirely implemented in the virtual machine. You can use the -Xbootclasspath/p and -Xbootclasspath/a command-line options to prepend and append additional bootstrap directories. You can specify a bootstrap class path using the -Xbootclasspath option, which will replace the default bootstrap class path. At runtime, the sun.boot.class.path system property contains the read-only value of the boot class path. The JDK represents this class loader by null. That is, you cannot get its reference. For example, the Object class is loaded by the bootstrap class loader and the expression Object.class.getClassLoader() will return null.

The extension class loader is used to load classes available through the extension mechanism located in JARs in the directories specified by the java.ext.dirs system property. To get the reference of the extension class loader, you need to get the reference of the application class loader and use the getParent() method on that reference.

The application class loader loads classes from the application class path specified by the CLASSPATH environment variable, or by the command-line option -cp or -classpath. The application class loader is also known as a *system class loader*, which is a kind of a misnomer that implies falsely that it loads system classes. You can get a reference to the application class loader using the static method named getSystemClassLoader() of the ClassLoader class.

JDK 9 keeps the three-level hierarchical class loader architecture for backward compatibility. However, there are a few changes in the way they load classes from the module system. Figure 8-4 shows the JDK 9 class loader hierarchy.

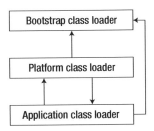

Figure 8-4. *Class loaders hierarchy in JDK 9*

Notice that in JDK 9, the application class loader can delegate to the platform class loader as well as the bootstrap class loader; the platform class loader can delegate to bootstrap class loader the application class loader. The following text describes the workings of the JDK 9 class loaders in detail.

In JDK 9, the bootstrap class loader is implemented in both library code and in the virtual machine. For backward compatibility, it is still represented by null in a program. For example, Object.class. getClassLoader() still returns null. However, not all Java SE platform and JDK modules are loaded by the bootstrap class loader. To name a few, modules loaded by the bootstrap class loader are java.base, java.logging, java.prefs, and java.desktop. Other Java SE platform and JDK modules are loaded by the platform class loader and the application class loader, which are described next. Options to specify the boot class path, -Xbootclasspath, and -Xbootclasspath/p, and the system property, sun.boot.class.path, are no longer supported in JDK 9. The -Xbootclasspath/a option is still supported and its value is stored in the system property called jdk.boot.class.path.append.

JDK 9 no longer supports the extension mechanism. However, it retains the extension class loader under a new name called the *platform class loader*. The ClassLoader class contains a new static method named getPlatformClassLoader() that returns the reference to the platform class loader. Table 8-2 contains the list of modules loaded by the platform class loader. The platform class loader serves another purpose. Classes loaded by the bootstrap class loader are granted all permissions by default. However, several classes do not need all permissions. Such classes have been de-privileged in JDK 9 and they are loaded by the platform class loader to improve security.

Table 8-2. *List of Modules Loaded by the Platform Class Loader in JDK 9*

java.activation	java.xml.ws.annotation	jdk.desktop
java.compiler	javafx.base	jdk.dynalink
java.corba	javafx.controls	jdk.javaws
java.jnlp	javafx.deploy	jdk.jsobject
java.scripting	javafx.fxml	jdk.localedata
java.se	javafx.graphics	jdk.naming.dns
java.se.ee	javafx.media	jdk.plugin
java.security.jgss	javafx.swing	jdk.plugin.dom
java.smartcardio	javafx.web	jdk.plugin.server
java.sql	jdk.accessibility	jdk.scripting.nashorn
java.sql.rowset	jdk.charsets	jdk.security.auth
java.transaction	jdk.crypto.cryptoki	jdk.security.jgss
java.xml.bind	jdk.crypto.ec	jdk.xml.dom
java.xml.crypto	jdk.crypto.mscapi	jdk.zipfs
java.xml.ws	jdk.deploy	

The application class loader loads the application modules found on the module path and a few JDK modules that provide tools or export tool APIs, as listed in Table 8-3. You can still use the static method named getSystemClassLoader() of the ClassLoader class to get the reference of the application class loader.

Table 8-3. *List of JDK Modules Loaded by the Application Class Loader in JDK 9*

jdk.attach	jdk.jartool	jdk.jstatd
jdk.compiler	jdk.javadoc	jdk.pack
jdk.deploy.controlpanel	jdk.jcmd	jdk.packager
jdk.editpad	jdk.jconsole	jdk.packager.services
jdk.hotspot.agent	jdk.jdeps	jdk.policytool
jdk.internal.ed	jdk.jdi	jdk.rmic
jdk.internal.jvmstat	jdk.jdwp.agent	jdk.scripting.nashorn.shell
jdk.internal.le	jdk.jlink	jdk.xml.bind
jdk.internal.opt	jdk.jshell	jdk.xml.ws

■ **Tip**   Before JDK 9, the extension class loader and the application class loader were an instance of the `java.net.URLClassLoader` class. In JDK 9, the platform class loader (the erstwhile extension class loader) and the application class loader are instances of an internal JDK class. If your code relied on the methods specific to the `URLClassLoader` class, your code may break in JDK 9.

The class loading mechanism in JDK 9 has changed a bit. The three built-in class loaders work in tandem to load classes. When the application class loader needs to load a class, it searches modules defined to all class loaders. If a suitable module is defined to one of these class loaders, that class loader loads the class—implying that the application class loader can now delegate to the bootstrap class loader and the platform class loader. If a class is not found in a named module defined to these class loaders, the application class loader delegates to its parent, which is the platform class loader. If class is still not loaded, the application class loader searches the class path. If it finds the class on the class path, it loads the class as a member of its unnamed module. If it does not find the class on the class path, a `ClassNotFoundException` is thrown.

When the platform class loader needs to load a class, it searches modules defined to all class loaders. If a suitable module is defined to one of these class loaders, that class loader loads the class. This implies that the platform class loader can delegate to the bootstrap class loader as well as to the application class loader. If a class is not found in a named module defined to these class loaders, the platform class loader delegates to its parent, which is the bootstrap class loader.

When the bootstrap class loader needs to load a class, it searches its own list of named modules. If a class is not found, it searches the list of files and directories specified through the command-line option -Xbootclasspath/a. If it finds a class on the bootstrap class path, it loads the class as a member of its unnamed module.

You can see the class loaders and the modules and classes they load in action. JDK 9 contains an option called -Xlog:modules that logs the debug or trace messages as they are loaded by the virtual machine. Its format is as follows:

```
-Xlog:modules=<debug|trace>
```

This option generates lots of output. I suggest you redirect the output to a file, so you can view it easily. The following command on Windows runs the client program for the prime checker and logs the module loading messages in a test.txt file. A partial output is shown. The output shows the class loaders that define modules.

```
C:\Java9Revealed>java -Xlog:modules=trace --module-path lib
 --module com.jdojo.prime.client/com.jdojo.prime.client.Main > test.txt
```

```
[0.022s][trace][modules] Setting package: class: java.lang.Object, package: java/lang,
loader: <bootloader>, module: java.base
[0.022s][trace][modules] Setting package: class: java.io.Serializable, package: java/io,
loader: <bootloader>, module: java.base
...
[0.855s][debug][modules] define_module(): creation of module: com.jdojo.prime.client,
version: NULL, location: file:///C:/Java9Revealed/lib/com.jdojo.prime.client.jar, class
loader 0x00000049ec86dd90 a 'jdk/internal/loader/ClassLoaders$AppClassLoader'{0x00000000895
d1c98}, package #: 1
[0.855s][trace][modules] define_module(): creation of package com/jdojo/prime/client for
module com.jdojo.prime.client
...
```

Accessing Resources

Resources are data that your application uses, such as images, audios, videos, text files, etc. Java provided a location-independent way to access resources by locating resources on the class path. You need to package resources the same way as you package your class files in JARs and add the JARs to the class path. Typically, class files and resources are packaged in the same JARs. Accessing resources is an important task that every Java developer performs. In next sections, I explain the APIs available in the JDK before release 9 and in JDK 9.

Accessing Resources Before JDK 9

In this section, I explain how resources were accessed in the JDK before release 9. If you already know how to access resources in the JDK before release 9, you can skip to the next section that describes how to access resources in JDK 9.

In Java code, a resource is identified by a resource name, which is a sequence of strings separated by a slash (/). For resources stored in JARs, a resource name is simply the path of the file stored in the JAR. For example, before JDK 9, the Object.class file in the java.lang package stored in rt.jar is a resource and its resource name is java/lang/Object.class.

Before JDK 9, you could use methods in the following two classes to access resources:

- java.lang.Class
- java.lang.ClassLoader

A resource is located by a ClassLoader. The resource-finding methods in a Class delegate to its ClassLoader. Therefore, once you understand the resource loading process used by a ClassLoader, you won't have problems in using the methods of the Class class. There are two differently named instance methods in both classes:

- URL getResource(String name)
- InputStream getResourceAsStream(String name)

Both methods find a resource the same way. They differ only in return type. The first method returns an URL whereas the second one returns an InputStream. The second method is equivalent to calling the first method and subsequently calling the openStream() on the returned URL object.

▒ **Tip**   All resource-finding methods return `null` if the specified resource is not found.

The `ClassLoader` class contains three additional static methods to find resources:

- `static URL getSystemResource(String name)`
- `static InputStream getSystemResourceAsStream(String name)`
- `static Enumeration<URL> getSystemResources(String name)`

These methods use the system class loader, which is also known as the application class loader, to find a resource. The first method returns the `URL` of the first resource found. The second method returns the `InputStream` for the first resource found. The third method returns an `Enumeration` of the URLs of all resources found with the specified resource name.

To find a resource, you have two types of methods to select from—getSystemResource* and getResource*. Before I discuss which method is best, it is important to understand that there are two types of resources:

- System resources
- Non-system resources

You must understand the difference between them to understand the resource finding mechanism. A system resource is a resource found on the class path—bootstrap class paths, JARs in the extension directories, and application class paths. A non-system resource may be stored in locations other than class path such as in specific directories, on the network, or in a database. The `getSystemResource()` method finds a resource using the application class loader delegating to its parent, which is the extension class loader, which in turn delegates to its parent, the bootstrap class loader. If your application is a standalone application, and it uses only the three built-in JDK class loaders, you will be fine using the static methods named getSystemResource*. It will find all resources on the class path, including the resources in the runtime image such as in the `rt.jar` file. If your application is an applet running in a browser, or an enterprise application running in an application server or a web server, you should use the instance methods named getResource*, which let you find a resource using a specific class loader. If you call the getResource* methods on a `Class` object, the current class loader, the class loader that loads the `Class` object, is used to find the resource.

Resource names passed to all methods in the `ClassLoader` class are absolute and they do not start with a slash (/). For example, when calling the `getSystemResource()` method of the `ClassLoader`, you would use `java/lang/Object.class` as the resource name.

The resource-finding methods in the `Class` class let you specify absolute and relative resource names. An absolute resource name starts with a slash whereas a relative resource name does not. When an absolute name is used, methods in the `Class` class remove the leading slash and delegate to the class loader that loaded the `Class` object to find the resource. The following call

```
Test.class.getResource("/resources/test.config");
```

is transformed into

```
Test.class.getClassLoader()
        .getResource("resources/test.config");
```

When a relative name is used, methods in the `Class` class prepend the package name, substituting dots in the package name with slashes followed with a slash, before delegating to the class loader that loaded the `Class` object to find the resource. Assuming that the `Test` class is in the `com.jdojo.test` package, the following call

```
Test.class.getResource("resources/test.config");
```

is transformed into

```
Test.class.getClassLoader()
        .getResource("com/jdojo/test/resources/test.config");
```

Let's look at an example of finding resources in a pre-JDK 9 release. I run the example using JDK 8. You can find its source code along with a NetBeans project in the downloadable source code for this book. The NetBeans project is named `com.jdojo.resource.preJDK9`. If you create your own project, make sure to change the Java platform and source for your project to JDK 8. The classes and resources are arranged as follows:

- `word_to_number.properties`

- `com/jdojo/resource/prejdk9/ResourceTest.class`

- `com/jdojo/resource/prejdk9/resources/number_to_word.properties`

The project contains two resource files: `word_to_number.properties` at the root and `number_to_word.properties` in the `com/jdojo/resource/prejdk9/resources` directory. The contents of these property files are shown in Listing 8-3 and Listing 8-4.

Listing 8-3. Contents of the word_to_number.properties File

```
One=1
Two=2
Three=3
Four=4
Five=5
```

Listing 8-4. Contents of the number_to_word.properties File

```
1=One
2=Two
3=Three
4=Four
5=Five
```

Listing 8-5 contains a complete program that shows how to find resources using different classes and their methods. The program demonstrates that you can use class files in your application as resources and you can find them using the same methods to find other types of resources.

Listing 8-5. A Test Class to Demonstrate How to Find Resources in Pre-JDK 9 Code

```java
// ResourceTest.java
package com.jdojo.resource.prejdk9;

import java.io.IOException;
import java.net.URL;
import java.util.Properties;

public class ResourceTest {
    public static void main(String[] args) {
        System.out.println("Finding resources using the system class loader:");
        findSystemResource("java/lang/Object.class");
        findSystemResource("com/jdojo/resource/prejdk9/ResourceTest.class");
        findSystemResource("com/jdojo/prime/PrimeChecker.class");
        findSystemResource("sun/print/resources/duplex.png");

        System.out.println("\nFinding resources using the Class class:");

        // A relative resource name - Will not find Object.class
        findClassResource("java/lang/Object.class");

        // An absolute resource name - Will find Object.class
        findClassResource("/java/lang/Object.class");

        // A relative resource name - will find the class
        findClassResource("ResourceTest.class");

        // Load the wordtonumber.properties file
        loadProperties("/wordtonumber.properties");

        // Will not find the properties because we are using
        // an absolute resource name
        loadProperties("/resources/numbertoword.properties");

        // Will find the properties
        loadProperties("resources/numbertoword.properties");
    }

    public static void findSystemResource(String resource) {
        URL url = ClassLoader.getSystemResource(resource);
        System.out.println(url);
    }

    public static URL findClassResource(String resource) {
        URL url = ResourceTest.class.getResource(resource);
        System.out.println(url);
        return url;
    }
```

```java
    public static Properties loadProperties(String resource) {
        Properties p1 = new Properties();
        URL url = ResourceTest.class.getResource(resource);
        if (url == null) {
            System.out.println("Properties not found: " + resource);
            return p1;
        }

        try {
            p1.load(url.openStream());
            System.out.println("Loaded properties from " + resource);
            System.out.println(p1);
        } catch (IOException e) {
            System.out.println(e.getMessage());
        }

        return p1;
    }
}
```

```
Finding resources using the system class loader:
jar:file:/C:/java8/jre/lib/rt.jar!/java/lang/Object.class
file:/C:/Java9Revealed/com.jdojo.resource.prejdk9/build/classes/com/jdojo/resource/prejdk9/
ResourceTest.class
null
jar:file:/C:/java8/jre/lib/resources.jar!/sun/print/resources/duplex.png

Finding resources using the Class class:
null
jar:file:/C:/java8/jre/lib/rt.jar!/java/lang/Object.class
file:/C:/Java9Revealed/com.jdojo.resource.prejdk9/build/classes/com/jdojo/resource/prejdk9/
ResourceTest.class
Loaded properties from /wordtonumber.properties
{One=1, Three=3, Four=4, Five=5, Two=2}
Properties not found: /resources/numbertoword.properties
Loaded properties from resources/numbertoword.properties
{5=Five, 4=Four, 3=Three, 2=Two, 1=One}
```

Accessing Resources in JDK 9

Before JDK 9, you were able to access resources from any JARs on the class path. In JDK 9, classes and resources are encapsulated in modules. In the first attempt, JDK 9 designers enforced the module encapsulation rules that resources in a module must be private to the module and, therefore, they should *only* be accessible to the code within that module. While this rule theoretically looked fine, it posed problems for frameworks that shared resources across modules and loaded class files as resources from other modules. A compromise was made to allow *limited* access to resources in modules and still enforce the module's encapsulation. JDK 9 contains resource-finding methods in three classes:

- `java.lang.Class`
- `java.lang.ClassLoader`
- `java.lang.Module`

The `Class` and `ClassLoader` classes have not received any new methods. The `Module` class contains a `getResourceAsStream(String name)` method that returns an `InputStream` if the resource is found; otherwise, it returns `null`.

Resource Naming Syntax

A resource is named using a sequence of strings separated by a slash, for example, `com/jdojo/states.png`, `/com/jdojo/words.png`, and `logo.png`. If a resource name starts with a slash, it is considered an absolute resource name.

A package name is computed from the resource name using the following rules:

- If the resource name starts with a slash, remove the leading slash. For example, for the resource name `/com/jdojo/words.png`, this step results in `com/jdojo/words.png`.

- Remove all characters from the resource name starting from the last slash. In this example, `com/jdojo/words.png` results in `com/jdojo`.

- Replace every remaining slash in the name with a period (`.`). So, `com/jdojo` is converted to `com.jdojo`. The resulting string is the package name.

There are situations when using these steps will result in an unnamed package or an invalid package name. Remember that a package name, if present, must consist of valid Java identifiers. If there is no package name, it is called an unnamed package. Consider `META-INF/resource/logo.png` as a resource name. Applying the previous set of rules, its package name will be computed as `META-INF.resources`, which is not a valid package name, but it is a valid path for a resource.

Rules to Find Resources

Because of backward compatibility and the module's system promise of strong encapsulation, new rules to find resources in JDK 9 are complicated and based on several factors:

- The type of the module that contains the resource: named, open, unnamed, or automatic module

- The module that is accessing the resource: Is it the same module or a different one?

- The package name of the resource being accessed: Is it a valid or invalid Java package? Is it an unnamed package?

- Encapsulation of the package that contains the resource: Is the package that contains the resource exported, opened, or encapsulated to the module accessing the resource?

- The file extension of the resource being accessed: Is the resource a `.class` file or some other type of file?

- Which class' method is being used to access the resource: `Class`, `ClassLoader`, or `Module`?

The following rules apply to a resource contained in a *named* module:

- If a resource name ends with `.class`, the resource can be accessed by code in any module. That is, any module can access class files in any named modules.

- If the package name computed from a resource name is not a valid Java package name, for example, `META-INF.resources`, the resource can be accessed by code in any module.

- If the package name computed from a resource name is an unnamed package, for example, for a resource name such as `words.png`, the resource can be accessed by code in any module.

- If the package containing the resource is opened to the module accessing the resource, the resource can be accessed by code in that module. A package can be opened to a module because the module defining the package is an open module, or the module opens the package to all other modules, or the module opens the package only to that specific module using a qualified `opens` statement. If a package is not opened in any of these ways, a resource in that package cannot be accessed by code outside that module.

- This rule is an offshoot of the previous rule. Every package in an unnamed, automatic, or open module is opened, so all resources in such modules can be accessed by code in all other modules.

▓ **Tip** A package in a named module must be opened, not exported, to access its resources. Exporting a package of a module allows other modules to access public types (not resources) in that package.

Various resource-finding methods in the `Module`, `Class`, and `ClassLoader` classes behave differently while accessing resources in named modules:

- You can use the `getResourceAsStream()` method of the `Module` class to access a resource in a module. This method is caller-sensitive. If the caller module is different, this method applies all the resource accessibility rules as described before.

- The `getResource*()` methods in the `Class` class for a class defined in a named module locate resources only in that named module. That is, you cannot use these methods to locate a class outside the named module that defines the class on which these methods are invoked.

- The `getResource*()` methods in the `ClassLoader` class locate resources in named modules based on the list of rules described earlier. These methods are not caller-sensitive. A class loader delegates a resource search to its parent before trying to locate the resource itself. These methods have two exceptions: 1) They locate resources only in unconditionally open packages. If a package is open to specific modules using a qualified `opens` statement, these methods will not locate resources in those packages. 2) They search modules defined in the class loader.

The Class object will find resources only in the module it is part of. It also supports absolute resource names that start with a slash and relative resource names that do not start with a slash. Here are a few examples of using the Class object:

```
// Will find the resource
URL url1 = Test.class.getResource("Test.class");

// Will not find the resource because the Test and Object classes are in different modules
URL url2 = Test.class.getResource("/java/lang/Object.class");

// Will find the resource because the Object and Class classes are in the same module,
java.base
URL url3 = Object.class.getResource("/java/lang/Class.class");

// Will not find the resource because the Object class is in the java.base module whereas
// the Driver class is in the java.sql module
URL url4 = Object.class.getResource("/java/sql/Driver.class");
```

Using the Module class to locate resources requires you to have the reference of the module. If you have access to a class in that module, using the getModule() method on that Class object gives you the module reference. This is the easiest way to get a module reference. Sometimes, you have the module name as a string, but not the reference of a class in that module. You can find the module reference from a module name. Modules are organized into layers that are represented by instances of the ModuleLayer class in the java.lang package. The JVM contains at least one layer called the boot layer. Modules in the boot layer are mapped to the built-in class loaders—bootstrap, platform, and application class loaders. You can get the reference of the boot layer using the boot() static method of the ModuleLayer class:

```
// Get the boot layer
ModuleLayer bootLayer = ModuleLayer.boot();
```

Once you get the reference of the boot layer, you can use its findModule(String moduleName) method to get the reference of a module:

```
// Find the module named com.jdojo.resource in the boot layer
Optional<Module> m = bootLayer.findModule("com.jdojo.resource");

// If the module was found, find a resource in the module
if(m.isPresent()) {
    Module testModule = m.get();
    String resource = "com/jdojo/resource/opened/opened.properties";
    InputStream input = module.getResourceAsStream(resource);
    if (input != null) {
        System.out.println(resource + " found.");
    } else {
        System.out.println(resource + " not found.");
    }
} else {
    System.out.println("Module com.jdojo.resource does not exist");
}
```

An Example of Accessing Resources in Named Modules

In this section, you'll see the resource-finding rules in action. You will package resources in a module named com.jdojo.resource whose declaration is shown in Listing 8-6.

Listing 8-6. A Module Declaration for a Module Named com.jdojo.resource

```
// module-info.java
module com.jdojo.resource {
    exports com.jdojo.exported;

    opens com.jdojo.opened;
}
```

The module exports the com.jdojo.exported package and opens the com.jdojo.opened package. The following is a list of all the files in the com.jdojo.resource module:

- module-info.class

- unnamed.properties

- META-INF\invalid_pkg.properties

- com\jdojo\encapsulated\encapsulated.properties

- com\jdojo\encapsulated\EncapsulatedTest.class

- com\jdojo\exported\AppResource.class

- com\jdojo\exported\exported.properties

- com\jdojo\opened\opened.properties

- com\jdojo\opened\OpenedTest.class

There are four class files. Only the module-info.class file is significant in this example. Other class files define a class with the same name without any details. All files with a .properties extension are resource files whose contents are not important in this example. The source code supplied with this book contains the contents of these files in the Java9Revealed\com.jdojo.resource directory. To save space, I will not show the contents of these files here.

The unnamed.properties file is in the unnamed package, so it can be located by code in any other module. The invalid_pkg.properties file is in the META-INF directory, which is not a valid Java package name, so this file can also be located by code in any other module. The com.jdojo.encapsulated package is not open, so the encapsulated.properties file cannot be located by code in other modules. The com.jdojo.exported package is not open, so the exported.properties file cannot be located by code in other modules. The com.jdojo.opened package is open, so the opened.properties file can be located by code in other modules. All class files in this module can be located by code in other modules.

Listing 8-7 contains the module declaration for a com.jdojo.resource.test module. The code in this module will try to access resources in the com.jdojo.resource module and the resources in this module itself. You will need to add the com.jdojo.resource module to this module path to compile it. Figure 8-5 shows the Properties dialog box for the com.jdojo.resource.test project in NetBeans. It adds the com.jdojo.resource module to its module path.

Listing 8-7. A Module Declaration for a Module Named com.jdojo.resource.test

```
// module-info.java
module com.jdojo.resource.test {
    requires com.jdojo.resource;

    exports com.jdojo.resource.test;
}
```

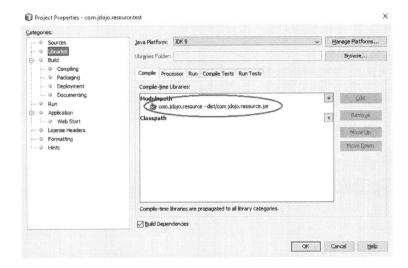

Figure 8-5. *Adding the com.jdojo.resource module to the module path of the com.jdojo.resource.test project in NetBeans*

The files in the com.jdojo.resource.test module are arranged as shown:

- module-info.class

- com\jdojo\resource\test\own.properties

- com\jdojo\resource\test\ResourceTest.class

The module contains a resource file named own.properties, which is in the com.jdojo.resource. test package. The own.properties file is empty. Listing 8-8 contains the code for the ResourceTest class. A detailed explanation of the code follows the output of this class.

Listing 8-8. A ResourceTest Class Demonstrating How to Access Resources in Named Modules

```
// ResourceTest
package com.jdojo.resource.test;

import com.jdojo.exported.AppResource;
import java.io.IOException;
import java.io.InputStream;
```

```java
public class ResourceTest {
    public static void main(String[] args) {
        // A list of resources
        String[] resources = {
            "java/lang/Object.class",
            "com/jdojo/resource/test/own.properties",
            "com/jdojo/resource/test/ResourceTest.class",
            "unnamed.properties",
            "META-INF/invalid_pkg.properties",
            "com/jdojo/opened/opened.properties",
            "com/jdojo/exported/AppResource.class",
            "com/jdojo/resource/exported.properties",
            "com/jdojo/encapsulated/EncapsulatedTest.class",
            "com/jdojo/encapsulated/encapsulated.properties"
        };

        System.out.println("Using a Module:");
        Module otherModule = AppResource.class.getModule();
        for (String resource : resources) {
            lookupResource(otherModule, resource);
        }

        System.out.println("\nUsing a Class:");
        Class cls = ResourceTest.class;
        for (String resource : resources) {
            // Prepend a / to all resource names to make them absolute names
            lookupResource(cls, "/" + resource);
        }

        System.out.println("\nUsing the System ClassLoader:");
        ClassLoader clSystem = ClassLoader.getSystemClassLoader();
        for (String resource : resources) {
            lookupResource(clSystem, resource);
        }

        System.out.println("\nUsing the Platform ClassLoader:");
        ClassLoader clPlatform = ClassLoader.getPlatformClassLoader();
        for (String resource : resources) {
            lookupResource(clPlatform, resource);
        }
    }

    public static void lookupResource(Module m, String resource) {
        try {
            InputStream in = m.getResourceAsStream(resource);
            print(resource, in);
        } catch (IOException e) {
            System.out.println(e.getMessage());
        }
    }
}
```

```
    public static void lookupResource(Class cls, String resource) {
        InputStream in = cls.getResourceAsStream(resource);
        print(resource, in);
    }

    public static void lookupResource(ClassLoader cl, String resource) {
        InputStream in = cl.getResourceAsStream(resource);
        print(resource, in);
    }

    private static void print(String resource, InputStream in) {
        if (in != null) {
            System.out.println("Found: " + resource);
        } else {
            System.out.println("Not Found: " + resource);
        }
    }
}
```

```
Using a Module:
Not Found: java/lang/Object.class
Not Found: com/jdojo/resource/test/own.properties
Not Found: com/jdojo/resource/test/ResourceTest.class
Found: unnamed.properties
Found: META-INF/invalid_pkg.properties
Found: com/jdojo/opened/opened.properties
Found: com/jdojo/exported/AppResource.class
Not Found: com/jdojo/resource/exported.properties
Found: com/jdojo/encapsulated/EncapsulatedTest.class
Not Found: com/jdojo/encapsulated/encapsulated.properties

Using a Class:
Not Found: /java/lang/Object.class
Found: /com/jdojo/resource/test/own.properties
Found: /com/jdojo/resource/test/ResourceTest.class
Not Found: /unnamed.properties
Not Found: /META-INF/invalid_pkg.properties
Not Found: /com/jdojo/opened/opened.properties
Not Found: /com/jdojo/exported/AppResource.class
Not Found: /com/jdojo/resource/exported.properties
Not Found: /com/jdojo/encapsulated/EncapsulatedTest.class
Not Found: /com/jdojo/encapsulated/encapsulated.properties

Using the System ClassLoader:
Found: java/lang/Object.class
Found: com/jdojo/resource/test/own.properties
Found: com/jdojo/resource/test/ResourceTest.class
Found: unnamed.properties
Found: META-INF/invalid_pkg.properties
Found: com/jdojo/opened/opened.properties
```

```
Found: com/jdojo/exported/AppResource.class
Not Found: com/jdojo/resource/exported.properties
Found: com/jdojo/encapsulated/EncapsulatedTest.class
Not Found: com/jdojo/encapsulated/encapsulated.properties

Using the Platform ClassLoader:
Found: java/lang/Object.class
Not Found: com/jdojo/resource/test/own.properties
Not Found: com/jdojo/resource/test/ResourceTest.class
Not Found: unnamed.properties
Not Found: META-INF/invalid_pkg.properties
Not Found: com/jdojo/opened/opened.properties
Not Found: com/jdojo/exported/AppResource.class
Not Found: com/jdojo/resource/exported.properties
Not Found: com/jdojo/encapsulated/EncapsulatedTest.class
Not Found: com/jdojo/encapsulated/encapsulated.properties
```

The lookupResource() methods are overloaded. They locate resources using the three classes: Module, Class, and ClassLoader. These methods pass the resource name and the resource reference to the print() method to print a message.

The main() method prepares a list of resources it wants to look up using different resource-finding methods. It stores the list in a String array:

```
// A list of resources
String[] resources = {/* List of resources */};
```

The main() method attempts to find all resources using the reference of the com.jdojo.resource module. Notice that the AppResource class is in the com.jdojo.resource module, so the AppResource.class.getModule() method returns the reference of the com.jdojo.resource module.

```
System.out.println("Using a Module:");
Module otherModule = AppResource.class.getModule();
for (String resource : resources) {
    lookupResource(otherModule, resource);
}
```

The code found all the class files and all resources in the unnamed, invalid, and open packages in the com.jdojo.resource module. Notice that java/lang/Object.class was not found because it is in the java.base module, not in the com.jdojo.resource module. Resources in the com.jdojo.resource.test module were not found for the same reason.

Now, the main() method locates the same resources using a Class object of the ResourceTest class, which is in the com.jdojo.resource.test module.

```
Class cls = ResourceTest.class;
for (String resource : resources) {
    // Prepend a / to all resource names to make them absolute names
    lookupResource(cls, "/" + resource);
}
```

185

This `Class` object will locate resources only in the `com.jdojo.resource.test` module, which is obvious in the output. In the code, I prepended the resource name with a slash, because the resource-finding methods in the `Class` class will treat a resource name, which does not start with a slash as a relative resource name and prepends the package name of the class to it.

In the end, the `main()` method uses the system and platform class loaders to locate the same set of resources:

```
ClassLoader clSystem = ClassLoader.getSystemClassLoader();
for (String resource : resources) {
    lookupResource(clSystem, resource);
}

ClassLoader clPlatform = ClassLoader.getPlatformClassLoader();
for (String resource : resources) {
    lookupResource(clPlatform, resource);
}
```

A class loader will locate resources in all modules known to the class loader itself or its ancestor class loaders. The system class loader loads the `com.jdojo.resource` and `com.jdojo.resource.test` modules, so it finds resources in these modules subject to the restrictions imposed by the resource-finding rules. Its parent's parent class loaders, which is the boot class loader, loads the `Object` class from the `java.base` module, so the system class loader can locate the `java/lang/Object.class` file.

The platform class loader does not load the `com.jdojo.resource` and `com.jdojo.resource.test` application modules. In the output, it is obvious that the platform class loader found only one resource, `java/lang/Object.class`, which was loaded by its parent, the boot class loader.

Accessing Resources in the Runtime Image

Let's walk through a few examples of accessing resources in the runtime image. Before JDK 9, you could use the `getSystemResource()` static method of the `ClassLoader` class. Here is the code that looked up the `Object.class` file in JDK 8:

```
import java.net.URL;
...
String resource = "java/lang/Object.class";
URL url = ClassLoader.getSystemResource(resource);
System.out.println(url);
```

```
jar:file:/C:/java8/jre/lib/rt.jar!/java/lang/Object.class
```

The output shows the returned URL using the `jar` scheme and pointing to the `rt.jar` file.

JDK 9 does not store a runtime image in JARs anymore. It is stored in an internal format that may be changed in the future. The JDK provides a way to access runtime resources in a format- and location-independent way using the `jrt` scheme. This code works in JDK 9 by returning an URL using the `jrt` scheme, not the `jar` scheme as shown:

```
jrt:/java.base/java/lang/Object.class
```

▓ **Tip** If your code accesses resources from the runtime image and expects an URL using the `jar` scheme, it needs to be changed in JDK 9 because you will get an URL using the `jrt` format.

The syntax for using the jrt scheme is as follows:

```
jrt:/<module-name>/<path>
```

Here, <module-name> is the name of a module and <path> is the path to a specific class or resource file in the module. Both <module-name> and <path> are optional. The URL, jrt:/, refers to all class and resource files stored in the current runtime image. The jrt:/<module-name> refers to all class and resource files stored in the <module-name> module. The jrt:/<module-name>/<path> refers to a specific class or resource file named <path> in the <module-name> module. The following are examples of two URLs using the jrt scheme to refer to a class file and a resource file:

- jrt:/java.sql/java/sql/Driver.class

- jrt:/java.desktop/sun/print/resources/duplex.png

The first URL names the class file for the java.sql.Driver class in the java.sql module. The second URL names the image file sun/print/resources/duplex.png in the java.desktop module.

▓ **Tip** You can access resources in the runtime image using the `jrt` scheme, which are rather inaccessible using the resource-fining methods in the `Module`, `Class`, and `ClassLoader` classes.

You can create an URL using the jrt scheme. The following snippet of code shows how to read an image file into an Image object and a class file into a byte array from the runtime image. Do not worry about the details such as modules and packages involved in this code:

```
// Load the duplex.png into an Image object
URL imageUrl = new URL("jrt:/java.desktop/sun/print/resources/duplex.png");
Image image = ImageIO.read(imageUrl);

// Use the image object here
System.out.println(image);

// Load the contents of the Object.class file
URL classUrl = new URL("jrt:/java.base/java/lang/Object.class");
InputStream input = classUrl.openStream();
byte[] bytes = input.readAllBytes();
System.out.println("Object.class file size: " + bytes.length);
```

```
BufferedImage@3e57cd70: type = 6 ColorModel: #pixelBits = 32 numComponents = 4 color space
= java.awt.color.ICC_ColorSpace@67b467e9 transparency = 3 has alpha = true isAlphaPre =
false ByteInterleavedRaster: width = 41 height = 24 #numDataElements 4 dataOff[0] = 3
Object.class file size: 1859
```

When can you use the jrt scheme in other forms, in order to represent all files in the runtime image and all files in a module? You can use the jrt scheme to refer to a module to grant permission in a Java policy file. The following entry in a Java policy file grants all permissions to the code in the java.activation module:

```
grant codeBase "jrt:/java.activation" {
    permission java.security.AllPermission;
}
```

Many tools and IDEs need to enumerate all modules, packages, and files in a runtime image. JDK 9 ships with a read-only NIO FileSystem provider for the jrt URL scheme. You can use this provider to list all class and resource files in the runtime image. There are tools and IDEs that will run on JDK 8, but will support the code development for JDK 9. Those tools also need to get the list of class and resource files in the JDK 9 runtime image. When you install JDK 9, it contains a jrt-fs.jar file in the lib directory. You can add this JAR file to the class path of the tools running on JDK 8 and use the jrt FileSystem as follows.

The jrt file system contains a root directory represented by a slash (/), which contains two sub-directories named packages and modules:

```
/
/packages
/modules
```

The following snippet of code creates a NIO FileSystem for the jrt URL scheme:

```
// Create a jrt FileSystem
FileSystem fs = FileSystems.getFileSystem(URI.create("jrt:/"));
```

The following snippet of code reads an image file and the contents of the Object.class file:

```
// Load an image from a module
Path imagePath = fs.getPath("modules/java.desktop", "sun/print/resources/duplex.png");
Image image = ImageIO.read(Files.newInputStream(imagePath));

// Use the image object here
System.out.println(image);

// Read the Object.class file contents
Path objectClassPath = fs.getPath("modules/java.base", "java/lang/Object.class");
byte[] bytes = Files.readAllBytes(objectClassPath);
System.out.println("Object.class file size: " + bytes.length);
```

```
BufferedImage@5f3a4b84: type = 6 ColorModel: #pixelBits = 32 numComponents = 4 color space
= java.awt.color.ICC_ColorSpace@5204062d transparency = 3 has alpha = true isAlphaPre =
false ByteInterleavedRaster: width = 41 height = 24 #numDataElements 4 dataOff[0] = 3
Object.class file size: 1859
```

CHAPTER 8 ▨ BREAKING CHANGES IN JDK 9

The following snippet of code prints all entries—class and resource files—in all modules in the runtime image. Similarly, you can create a Path for packages to enumerate all packages in the runtime image.

```
// List all modules in the runtime image
Path modules = fs.getPath("modules");
Files.walk(modules)
     .forEach(System.out::println);
```

```
/modules
/modules/java.base
/modules/java.base/java
/modules/java.base/java/lang
/modules/java.base/java/lang/Object.class
/modules/java.base/java/lang/AbstractMethodError.class
...
```

Let's look at a complete program that accesses resources from the runtime image. Listing 8-9 contains the module declaration for a module named com.jdojo.resource.jrt. Listing 8-10 contains the source code for a class named JrtFileSystem, which is in the com.jdojo.resource.jrt module.

Listing 8-9. A Module Declaration for a Module Named com.jdojo.resource.jrt

```
// module-info.java
module com.jdojo.resource.jrt {
    requires java.desktop;
}
```

Listing 8-10. A JrtFileSystem Class That Demonstrates the Use of the jrt URL Scheme to Access Resources from a Runtime Image

```
// JrtFileSystem.java
package com.jdojo.resource.jrt;

import java.awt.Image;
import java.io.IOException;
import java.net.URI;
import java.nio.file.FileSystem;
import java.nio.file.FileSystems;
import java.nio.file.Files;
import java.nio.file.Path;
import javax.imageio.ImageIO;

public class JrtFileSystem {
    public static void main(String[] args) throws IOException {
        // Create a jrt FileSystem
        FileSystem fs = FileSystems.getFileSystem(URI.create("jrt:/"));
```

189

```
        // Load an image from a module
        Path imagePath = fs.getPath("modules/java.desktop", "sun/print/resources/duplex.png");
        Image image = ImageIO.read(Files.newInputStream(imagePath));

        // Use the image object here
        System.out.println(image);

        // Read the Object.class file contents
        Path objectClassPath = fs.getPath("modules/java.base", "java/lang/Object.class");
        byte[] bytes = Files.readAllBytes(objectClassPath);
        System.out.println("Object.class file size: " + bytes.length);

        // List 5 packages in the runtime image
        Path packages = fs.getPath("packages");
        Files.walk(packages)
            .limit(5)
            .forEach(System.out::println);

        // List 5 modules' entries in the runtime image
        Path modules = fs.getPath("modules");
        Files.walk(modules)
            .limit(5)
            .forEach(System.out::println);
    }
}
```

```
BufferedImage@5bfbf16f: type = 6 ColorModel: #pixelBits = 32 numComponents = 4 color space =
java.awt.color.ICC_ColorSpace@27d415d9 transparency = 3 has alpha = true isAlphaPre =
false ByteInterleavedRaster: width = 41 height = 24 #numDataElements 4 dataOff[0] = 3
Object.class file size: 1859
packages
packages/com
packages/com/java.activation
packages/com/java.base
packages/com/java.corba
modules
modules/java.desktop
modules/java.desktop/sun
modules/java.desktop/sun/print
modules/java.desktop/sun/print/resources
```

Notice that the program prints only five entries from the packages and modules directories. Also notice that you were able to access sun/print/resources/duplex.png, which is in the java.desktop module. The java.desktop module does not open the sun.print.resources package. Using any of the resource-finding methods in the Module, Class, and ClassLoader classes to locate sun/print/resources/duplex.png will fail.

Using JDK Internal APIs

The JDK consists of public APIs and internal APIs. Public APIs are meant to be used to develop portable Java applications. The `java.*`, `javax.*`, and `org.*` packages in the JDK contain public APIs. If your application uses only public APIs, it is guaranteed to work on all operating systems supporting the Java platform. Another guarantee offered by such an application is that if it worked in the JDK version *n*, it will continue to work in the JDK version *n* + 1.

The `com.sun.*`, `sun.*`, and `jdk.*` packages are used to implement the JDK itself and they make up the internal APIs, which are not meant to be used by developers. Internal APIs are not guaranteed to work across all operating systems. Packages such as `com.sun.*` and `sun.*` are part of the Oracle JDK. These packages will not be available if you use a JDK from another vendor. Non-Oracle JDKs such as the JDK from IBM will use other package names to implement their internal APIs. Figure 8-6 shows the JDK APIs in different categories.

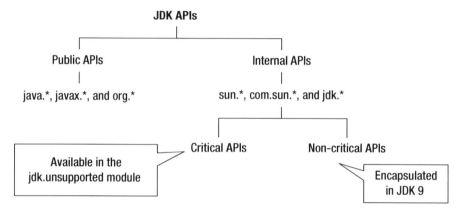

Figure 8-6. *Categories of JDK APIs based on their intended use*

Before modularization in JDK 9, it was possible to use any public classes from any JAR, even if those classes made up the JDK internal APIs. Developers and a few widely used libraries have been using JDK internal APIs for convenience or because the functionalities provided by those APIs were difficult to implement outside the JDK. Examples of such classes are `BASE64Encoder` and `BASE64Decoder`. They were used by developers for convenience because they were available as the JDK internal APIs in the `sun.misc` package, even though they were not difficult to develop. Another widely used class was the `Unsafe` class from the `sun.misc` package. It was difficult to develop a class outside the JDK to replace the `Unsafe` class because it accessed JDK internals.

Internal APIs that are used merely for convenience are not used outside the JDK or the supported replacements that exist for them have been categorized as non-critical internal APIs and they have been encapsulated in JDK 9. Examples are the `BASE64Encoder` and `BASE64Decoder` classes in the `sun.misc` package, which were added to JDK 8 in the `java.util` package as the `Base64.Encoder` and `Base64.Decoder` classes as part of the public APIs.

Internal APIs that were widely used but difficult to develop outside the JDK are categorized as critical internal APIs. They have been encapsulated in JDK 9 if their replacements exist. Critical internal APIs that are encapsulated in JDK 9 but can be used using a command-line option have been annotated with the @jdk.Exported annotation. JDK 9 does not provide replacements for the following classes, which are considered critical internal APIs. They are accessible through the jdk.unsupported module.

- com.sun.nio.file.ExtendedCopyOption
- com.sun.nio.file.ExtendedOpenOption
- com.sun.nio.file.ExtendedWatchEventModifier
- com.sun.nio.file.SensitivityWatchEventModifier
- sun.misc.Signal
- sun.misc.SignalHandler
- sun.misc.Unsafe
- sun.reflect.Reflection
- sun.reflect.ReflectionFactory

■ **Tip**   In JDK 9, most of the JDK internal APIs have been encapsulated in modules and are not accessible by default. You can still access them using the --add-reads non-standard command-line option.

The addPropertyChangeListener() and removePropertyChangeListener() methods in the following classes were deprecated in JDK 8 and have been removed from JDK 9:

- java.util.logging.LogManager
- java.util.jar.Pack200.Packer
- java.util.jar.Pack200.Unpacker

You can use the jdeps tool, which is located in the JAVA_HOME\bin directory, to find the class-level dependency of your code on the JDK internal APIs. You also need to use the --jdk-internals option as shown:

```
jdeps --jdk-internals --class-path <class-path> <input-path>
```

Here, <input-path> can be a path to a class file, a directory, or a JAR file. The command analyzes all classes on the <input-path> and <class-path>. The following command prints the usage of JDK internal APIs in the jersey-common.jar file, assuming that the JAR is in the C:\Java9Revealed\extlib directory. A partial output is shown:

```
C:\Java9Revealed>jdeps --jdk-internals extlib\jersey-common.jar
```

```
jersey-common.jar -> jdk.unsupported
   org.glassfish.jersey.internal.util.collection.ConcurrentHashMapV8 -> sun.misc.
Unsafe                                     JDK internal API (jdk.unsupported)

org.glassfish.jersey.internal.util.collection.ConcurrentHashMapV8$TreeBin -> sun.misc.
Unsafe                                     JDK internal API (jdk.unsupported)
...
```

Patching Module Contents

Sometimes, you may want to replace class files and resources of specific modules with another version for testing and debugging purposes. Before JDK 9, you were able to achieve this using the -Xbootclasspath/p option. This option has been removed in JDK 9. In JDK 9, you need to use the --patch-module non-standard command-line option. This option is available with javac and java commands. Its syntax is as follows:

```
--patch-module <module-name>=<path-list>
```

Here, <module-name> is the name of the module whose contents are being replaced. <path-list> is a list of JARs or directories containing the new module's contents; each element in the list is separated by a host-specific path-separator character, which is a semicolon on Windows and a colon on UNIX-like platforms.

You can use the --patch-module option multiple times for the same command, so you can patch multiple modules' contents. You can patch application modules, library modules, and platform modules.

▓ **Tip** When you're using the --patch-module option, you cannot replace the module-info.class files. Attempting to do so is silently ignored.

Now, we'll run through an example of patching the com.jdojo.intro module. You will replace the Welcome.class file in this module with a new Welcome.class file. Recall that we created the Welcome class in Chapter 3. The new class will print a different message. The new class declaration is shown in Listing 8-11. In the source code, this class is inside the com.jdojo.intro.patch NetBeans project.

Listing 8-11. Another Declaration of the Welcome Class

```
// Welcome.java
package com.jdojo.intro;

public class Welcome {
    public static void main(String[] args) {
        System.out.println("Hello Module System.");

        // Print the module name of the Welcome class
        Class<Welcome> cls = Welcome.class;
        Module mod = cls.getModule();
        String moduleName = mod.getName();
        System.out.format("Module Name: %s%n", moduleName);
    }
}
```

Now, you need to compile source code for the new `Welcome` class in Listing 8-11 using the following command:

```
C:\Java9Revealed>javac -Xmodule:com.jdojo.intro
  --module-path com.jdojo.intro\dist
  -d patches\com.jdojo.intro.patch com.jdojo.intro.patch\src\com\jdojo\intro\Welcome.java
```

This command will succeed even if you remove the first two options: `-Xmodule` and `--module-path`. However, these options will be needed when you compile a platform class such as `java.util.Arrays`. Otherwise, you will receive errors. The `-Xmodule` option specifies the module name to which the source code being compiled belongs. The `--module-path` option specifies where to find the module specified in the `-Xmodule` option. These options are used to locate other classes that are needed to compile the new class. In this case, the `Welcome` class does not depend on any other class in the `com.jdojo.intro` module. This is why removing these options won't affect the result in this case. The `-d` option specifies where the compiled `Welcome.class` file will be saved.

The following is the command used to run the original `Welcome` class from the `com.jdojo.intro` module:

```
C:\Java9Revealed>java --module-path com.jdojo.intro\dist
--module com.jdojo.intro/com.jdojo.intro.Welcome
```

```
Welcome to the Module System.
Module Name: com.jdojo.intro
```

It is time to run the `Welcome` class using the patched version. Here is the command that does this:

```
C:\Java9Revealed>java --module-path com.jdojo.intro\dist
  --patch-module com.jdojo.intro=patches\com.jdojo.intro.patch
  --module com.jdojo.intro/com.jdojo.intro.Welcome
```

```
Hello Module System.
Module Name: com.jdojo.intro
```

When the --patch-module option is used, the module system searches the paths specified in this option before searching the module path. Note that paths specified in this option contain contents of a module, but these paths are not module paths.

Summary

JDK 9 has made several breaking changes that you must be aware of if you are migrating your legacy applications to JDK 9.

The non-intuitive versioning scheme for the JDK has been revamped in JDK 9. A JDK version string consists of the following four elements in order: a version number, prerelease information, build information, and additional information. Only the first one is mandatory. The regular expression, $vnum(-$pre)?(\+($build)?(-$opt)?)?, defines the format for a version string. A short version string consists of only the first two elements: a version number optionally followed by prerelease information. You can have a version string as short as "9", which contains only the major version number and as big as "9.0.1-ea+154-20170130.07.36am", which contains all elements of a version string.

JDK 9 added a static nested class called Runtime.Version whose instances represent JDK version strings. The class does not have a public constructor. The only way to get its instance is to call its static method named parse(String vstr). The method may throw a runtime exception if the version string is null or invalid. The class contains several methods to get different parts of the version.

JDK 9 changed the directory layout of the JDK and JRE installation. Now, there is no distinction between a JDK and JRE installation, except that a JDK installation contains developer tools and a copy of platform modules in JMOD format that the JRE does not contain. You can build your own JRE (using the jlink tool) and it can contain any part of the JDK you need in the JRE.

Prior to Java SE 9, you could use the Endorsed Standards Override Mechanism to use the newer versions of classes and interfaces that implement Endorsed Standards or Standalone APIs. These include the javax.rmi.CORBA package and Java API for XML Processing (JAXP), which are created outside the Java Community Process. Java SE 9 still supports this mechanism. In Java SE 9, you need to use the --upgrade-module-path command-line option. The value for this option is a list of directories containing modules for the Endorsed Standards and Standalone APIs.

Java SE prior to version 9, allowed an extension mechanism whereby you were able to extend the runtime image by placing JARs in directories specified by the system property java.ext.dirs. If this system property was not set, the jre\lib\ext directory was used as its default value. Java SE 9 does not support the extension mechanism. If you need a similar functionality, you can place those JARs at the front of the class path.

Prior to version 9, the JDK used three class loaders to load classes. They were boot class loader, extension class loader and system class loader. They were arranged hierarchically—the boot class loader having no parent, the extension class loader having the boot class loader as its parent, and the system class loader having the extension class loader as its parent. Class loaders delegated the type loading requires to their parent, if any, before attempting to the load the type itself. JDK 9 kept the three class loaders arrangements for backward compatibility. JDK 9 does not support the extension mechanism, so the extension class loader has no meaning. JDK 9 has renamed the extension class loader as platform class loader whose reference can be obtained using the static getPlatformClassLoader() method of the ClassLoader class. In JDK 9, each class loader loads different types of modules.

In JDK 9, resources in a named module are encapsulated by default. A resource in a named module can be accessed by code in another module only if the resource is in an unnamed, invalid, or open package. All resources in a named module whose names end with .class (all class files) can be accessed by code in other modules. You can use an URL using the jrt scheme to access any resources in a runtime image.

Before JDK 9, it was possible to use JDK-internal APIs. Most JDK-internal APIs in JDK 9 have been encapsulated. Some have been made available through the `jdk.unsupported` module. You can use the `jdeps` tool with the `--jdk-internals` option to find the class-level dependency of your code on the JDK internal APIs.

Sometimes, you may want to replace class files and resources of specific modules with another version for testing and debugging purposes. Before JDK 9, you were able to achieve this using the `-Xbootclasspath/p` option, which has been removed in JDK 9. In JDK 9, you need to use the `--patch-module` non-standard command-line option. This option is available with the `javac` and `java` commands.

CHAPTER 9

Breaking Module Encapsulation

In this chapter, you will learn:

- What breaking a module's encapsulation is

- How to add dependency (add requires) to a module using the command-line option

- How to export non-exported packages of a module using the --add-exports command-line option and using the MANIFEST.MF file of an executable JAR

- How to open non-open packages of a module using the --add-opens command-line option and using the MANIFEST.MF file of an executable JAR

- How to increase readability of a module using the --add-reads command-line option

What Is Breaking Module Encapsulation?

One of the main goals of JDK 9 is to encapsulate types and resources in modules and export only those packages whose public types are intended to be accessed by other modules. Sometimes, you may need to break the encapsulation specified by a module to enable white-box testing or use unsupported JDK-internal APIs or libraries. This is possible by using non-standard command-line options at compile-time and runtime. Another reason for having these options is backward compatibility. Not all existing applications will be fully migrated to JDK 9 and will be modularized. If those applications need to use the JDK APIs or APIs provided by libraries that used to be public, but have been encapsulated in JDK 9, those applications have a way to keep working. A few of these options have corresponding attributes that can be added to the MANIFEST.MF file of the executable JARs to avoid using the command-line options.

Tip Every command-line option to break a module's encapsulation is also supported programmatically using the Module API, which is covered in detail in Chapter 10.

Although it may sound like that these options do the same things as before JDK 9, there is a word of caution when accessing JDK internal APIs without any restriction. If a package in a module is not exported or open, it means the module's designer did not intend for these packages to be used outside the module. Such packages may be modified or even removed from the module without any notice. If you still use these packages by exporting or opening them using command-line options, you do so at the risk of breaking your application!

Command-Line Options

Three module statements in a module declaration let a module encapsulate its types and resources and let other modules use the encapsulated types and resources from the first module. Those statements are exports, opens, and requires. There is a command-line option corresponding to each of these module statements. For the exports and opens statements, there are corresponding attributes that can be used in the manifest file of a JAR. Table 9-1 lists these statements and their corresponding command-line options and manifest attributes. I describe these options in detail in the following sections.

Table 9-1. *Module Statements with the Corresponding Command-Line Options and Manifest Attributes*

Module Statement	Command-Line Option	Manifest Attribute
exports	--add-exports	Add-Exports
opens	--add-opens	Add-Opens
requires	--add-reads	(no attribute is available)

■ **Tip**   You can use the --add-exports, --add-opens, and --add-reads command-line options more than once with the same command.

The --add-exports Option

The exports statement in a module declaration exports a package in the module to all or some other modules, so those modules can use the public APIs in that package. If a package is not exported by a module, you can export it using the command-line option named --add-exports. Its syntax is as follows:

```
--add-exports <source-module>/<package>=<target-module-list>
```

Here, <source-module> is the module that exports <package> to <target-module-list>, which is a comma-separated list of target module names. It is equivalent to adding a qualified exports statement to the declaration of <source-module>:

```
module <source-module> {
    exports <package> to <target-module-list>;

    // More statements go here
}
```

■ **Tip**   If the target module list is a special value, ALL-UNNAMED, for the --add-exports option, the module's package is exported to all unnamed modules. The --add-exports option is available for the javac and java commands.

The following option exports the sun.util.logging package in the java.base module to the com.jdojo.test and com.jdojo.prime modules:

```
--add-exports java.base/sun.util.logging=com.jdojo.test,com.jdojo.prime
```

The following option exports the sun.util.logging package in the java.base module to all unnamed modules:

```
--add-exports java.base/sun.util.logging=ALL-UNNAMED
```

The --add-opens Option

The opens statement in a module declaration opens a package in a module to all or some other modules, so those modules can use deep reflection to access all member types in that package at runtime. If a package of a module is not open, you can open it using the --add-opens command-line option. Its syntax is as follows:

```
--add-opens <source-module>/<package>=<target-module-list>
```

Here, <source-module> is the module that opens <package> to <target-module-list>, which is a comma-separated list of target module names. It is equivalent to adding a qualified opens statement to the declaration of <source-module>:

```
module <source-module> {
    opens <package> to <target-module-list>;

    // More statements go here
}
```

░ **Tip**   If the target module list is a special value, ALL-UNNAMED, for the --add-opens option, the module's package is open to all unnamed modules. The --add-opens option is available for the java commands. Using this option at compile-time with the javac command generates a warning and has no effect.

The following option opens the sun.util.logging package in the java.base module to the com.jdojo.test and com.jdojo.prime modules:

```
--add-opens java.base/sun.util.logging=com.jdojo.test,com.jdojo.prime
```

The following option opens the sun.util.logging package in the java.base module to all unnamed modules:

```
--add-opens java.base/sun.util.logging=ALL-UNNAMED
```

The --add-reads Option

The `--add-reads` option is not about breaking encapsulation. Rather, it is about increasing the readability of a module. During testing and debugging, it is sometimes necessary for a module to read another module even though the first module does not depend on the second module. The `requires` statement in a module declaration is used to declare dependency of the current module on another module. You can use the `--add-reads` command-line option to add a readability edge from a module to another module. This has the same effect of adding a `requires` statement to the first module. Its syntax is as follows:

```
--add-reads <source-module>=<target-module-list>
```

Here, `<source-module>` is the module whose definition is updated to read the list of modules specified in the `<target-module-list>`, which is a comma-separated list of target module names. It is equivalent to adding a `requires` statement to the source module for each module in the target module list:

```
module <source-module> {
    requires <target-module1>;
    requires <target-module2>;

    // More statements go here
}
```

▓ **Tip**   If the target module list is a special value, `ALL-UNNAMED`, for the `--add-reads` option, the source module reads all unnamed modules. This is the only way a named module can read unnamed modules. There is no equivalent module statement that you can use in a named module declaration to read an unnamed module. This option is available at compile-time and runtime.

The following option adds a read edge to the `com.jdojo.common` module to make it read the `jdk.accessibility` module:

```
--add-reads com.jdojo.common=jdk.accessibility
```

The --permit-illegal-access Option

The three previously mentioned command-line options to add exports, opens, and reads are solely for backwards compatibility. However, using these options is tedious when you need "illegal" access (reflective access to rather inaccessible members of types in modules) to several modules. The `--permit-illegal-access` option is available with the `java` command for such cases. As its name suggests, it permits illegal access by code in any unnamed module (code on the class path) to members of types in any named modules using deep reflection. Its syntax is as follows:

```
java --permit-illegal-access <other-options-and-arguments>
```

The `--permit-illegal-access` option does not permit illegal access by code in a named module to the members of types in other named modules. In such cases, you can combine this option with `--add-exports`, `--add-opens`, and `--add-reads` options.

▨ **Tip** The `--permit-illegal-access` option is available in JDK 9 and will be removed in JDK 10. Using this option prints warnings on the standard error stream. One warning prints a message stipulating this option will be removed in the future release. Other warnings report the details of the code that was granted the illegal access, the code to which the illegal access was granted, and the option that granted the access.

I will present an example of using all these options that allow breaking a module's encapsulation in the next section.

An Example

Let's walk through an example of breaking encapsulation. I use a trivial example. However, it serves the purpose of demonstrating all concepts and command-line options that can be used to break encapsulation.

You created the `com.jdojo.intro` module as your first module. It contains a `Welcome` class in the `com.jdojo.intro` package. The module does not export the package, so the `Welcome` class is encapsulated and cannot be accessed outside the module. In this example, you will call the `main()` method of the `Welcome` class from another module named `com.jdojo.intruder`, whose declaration is shown in Listing 9-1. Listing 9-2 shows the code for the `TestNonExported` class in this module.

Listing 9-1. The Declaration of a Module Named com.jdojo.intruder

```
// module-info.java
module com.jdojo.intruder {
    // No module statements
}
```

Listing 9-2. A Class Named TestNonExported

```
// TestNonExported.java
package com.jdojo.intruder;

import com.jdojo.intro.Welcome;

public class TestNonExported {
    public static void main(String[] args) {
        Welcome.main(new String[]{});
    }
}
```

The `TestNonExported` class contains only one line of code. It calls the static `main()` method of the `Welcome` class passing an empty `String` array. If this class is compiled and run, it will print the same message that was printed in Chapter 3 when the `Welcome` class was run:

```
Welcome to the Module System.
Module Name: com.jdojo.intro
```

If you try compiling the code for the com.jdojo.intruder module, you will get an error:

```
C:\Java9Revealed>javac --module-path com.jdojo.intro\dist
-d com.jdojo.intruder\build\classes
com.jdojo.intruder\src\module-info.java com.jdojo.intruder\src\com\jdojo\intruder\
TestNonExported.java
```

```
com.jdojo.intruder\src\com\jdojo\intruder\TestNonExported.java:4: error: package com.
jdojo.intro is not visible
import com.jdojo.intro.Welcome;
                  ^
  (package com.jdojo.intro is declared in module com.jdojo.intro, but module com.jdojo.
  intruder does not read it)
1 error
```

The command uses the --module-path option to include the com.jdojo.intro module on the module path. The compile-time error is pointing to the import statement that imports the com.jdojo.intro. Welcome class. It states that the package com.jdojo.intro is not visible to the com.jdojo.intruder module. That is, the com.jdojo.intro module does not export the com.jdojo.intro package that contains the Welcome class. To fix this error, you need to export the com.jdojo.intro package of the com.jdojo.intro module to the com.jdojo.intruder module using the --add-exports command-line option:

```
C:\Java9Revealed>javac --module-path com.jdojo.intro\dist
--add-exports com.jdojo.intro/com.jdojo.intro=com.jdojo.intruder
-d com.jdojo.intruder\build\classes
com.jdojo.intruder\src\module-info.java com.jdojo.intruder\src\com\jdojo\intruder\
TestNonExported.java
```

```
warning: [options] module name in --add-exports option not found: com.jdojo.intro
com.jdojo.intruder\src\com\jdojo\intruder\TestNonExported.java:4: error: package com.jdojo.
intro is not visible
import com.jdojo.intro.Welcome;
                  ^
  (package com.jdojo.intro is declared in module com.jdojo.intro, but module com.jdojo.
  intruder does not read it)
1 error
1 warning
```

This time, you get a warning and an error. The error is the same as before. The warning message is stating that the compiler could not find the com.jdojo.intro module. Because there is no dependency on this module, this module is not resolved even if it is in the module path. To resolve the warning, you need to add the com.jdojo.intro module to the default set of root module using the --add-modules option:

```
C:\Java9Revealed>javac --module-path com.jdojo.intro\dist
--add-modules com.jdojo.intro
--add-exports com.jdojo.intro/com.jdojo.intro=com.jdojo.intruder
-d com.jdojo.intruder\build\classes
com.jdojo.intruder\src\module-info.java
com.jdojo.intruder\src\com\jdojo\intruder\TestNonExported.java
```

This javac command succeeded even though the com.jdojo.intruder module does not read the com.jdojo.intro module. It seems to be a bug. If it is not a bug, there is no documentation that I could find to support this behavior. Later, you will see that the java command won't work for the same modules. If this command errors out with a message that the TestNonExported class cannot access the Welcome class, add the following option to it to fix it:

```
--add-reads com.jdojo.intruder=com.jdojo.intro
```

Let's try rerunning the TestNonExported class using the following command, which includes the com.jdojo.intruder module to the module path:

```
C:\Java9Revealed>java --module-path com.jdojo.intro\dist;com.jdojo.intruder\build\classes
--add-modules com.jdojo.intro
--add-exports com.jdojo.intro/com.jdojo.intro=com.jdojo.intruder
--module com.jdojo.intruder/com.jdojo.intruder.TestNonExported
```

```
Exception in thread "main" java.lang.IllegalAccessError: class com.jdojo.intruder.
TestNonExported (in module com.jdojo.intruder) cannot access class com.jdojo.intro.Welcome
(in module com.jdojo.intro) because module com.jdojo.intruder does not read module com.
jdojo.intro
        at com.jdojo.intruder/com.jdojo.intruder.TestNonExported.main(TestNonExported.java:8)
```

The error message is loud and clear. It states that the com.jdojo.intruder module must read the com.jdojo.intro module in order for the former to use the latter's Welcome class. You can fix the error by using the --add-reads option, which will add a read edge (an equivalent of a requires statement) in the com.jdojo.intruder module to read the com.jdojo.intro module. The following command does this:

```
C:\Java9Revealed>java --module-path com.jdojo.intro\dist;com.jdojo.intruder\build\classes
--add-modules com.jdojo.intro
--add-exports com.jdojo.intro/com.jdojo.intro=com.jdojo.intruder
--add-reads com.jdojo.intruder=com.jdojo.intro
--module com.jdojo.intruder/com.jdojo.intruder.TestNonExported
```

```
Welcome to the Module System.
Module Name: com.jdojo.intro
```

This time, you receive the desired output. Figure 9-1 shows the module graph that is created when this command is run.

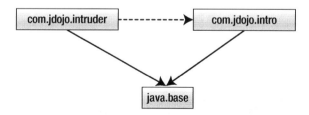

Figure 9-1. *The module graph after using the --add-modules and --add-reads options*

Both the com.jdojo.intruder and com.jdojo.intro modules are root modules. The com.jdojo.intruder module is added to the default set of root modules because the main class being run is in this module. The com.jdojo.intro module is added to the default set of root modules by the --add-modules option. A read edge is added from the com.jdojo.intruder module to the com.jdojo.intro module by the --add-reads option. I have shown the read edge from the former to the latter using a dashed line to make a point that it is added as a result of the --add-reads option, after the module graph is constructed. Use the -Xdiag:resolver option with this command to see how the modules are resolved.

Let's walk through another example that will show how to open a package to another module using the --add-opens command-line option. In Chapter 4, you had a com.jdojo.address module that contains an Address class in the com.jdojo.address package. The module exports the com.jdojo.address package. The class contains a private field named line1, which stores the first line of an address. There is a public getLine1() method that returns the value of the line1 field.

A TestNonOpen class, as shown in Listing 9-3, tries to load the Address class, creates an instance of the class, and accesses its public and private members. The TestNonOpen class is a member of the com.jdojo.intruder module. I added a bunch of exceptions in the throws clause of the main() method to keep the logic simple. In a real-world program, you would handle them in a try-catch block.

Listing 9-3. A Class Named TestNonOpen

```java
// TestNonOpen.java
package com.jdojo.intruder;

import java.lang.reflect.Constructor;
import java.lang.reflect.Field;
import java.lang.reflect.InvocationTargetException;
import java.lang.reflect.Method;

public class TestNonOpen {
    public static void main(String[] args)
            throws IllegalAccessException, IllegalArgumentException,
            NoSuchMethodException, ClassNotFoundException,
            InvocationTargetException, InstantiationException,
            NoSuchFieldException {

        String className = "com.jdojo.address.Address";

        // Get the class reference
        Class<?> cls = Class.forName(className);

        // Get the no-args constructor
        Constructor constructor = cls.getConstructor();

        // Create an Object of the Address class
        Object address = constructor.newInstance();

        // Call the getLine1() method to get the line1 value
        Method getLine1Ref = cls.getMethod("getLine1");
        String line1 = (String)getLine1Ref.invoke(address);
        System.out.println("Using method reference, Line1: " + line1);
```

```
        // Use the private line1 instance variable to read its value
        Field line1Field = cls.getDeclaredField("line1");
        line1Field.setAccessible(true);
        String line11 = (String)line1Field.get(address);
        System.out.println("Using private field reference, Line1: " + line11);
    }
}
```

Try compiling the TestNonOpen class:

```
C:Java9revealed> javac -d com.jdojo.intruder\build\classes
com.jdojo.intruder\src\com\jdojo\intruder\TestNonOpen.java
```

The TestNonOpen class compiles fine. Note that it accesses the Address class using deep reflection and the compiler has no knowledge of the fact that this class is not allowed to read the Address class and its private fields. Now try running the TestNonOpen class:

```
C:Java9revealed> java --module-path com.jdojo.address\dist;com.jdojo.intruder\build\classes
--add-modules com.jdojo.address
--module com.jdojo.intruder/com.jdojo.intruder.TestNonOpen
```

```
Using method reference, Line 1: 1111 Main Blvd.
Exception in thread "main" java.lang.reflect.InaccessibleObjectException: Unable to make
field private java.lang.String com.jdojo.address.Address.line1 accessible: module com.jdojo.
address does not "opens com.jdojo.address" to module com.jdojo.intruder
        at java.base/java.lang.reflect.AccessibleObject.checkCanSetAccessible(Accessible
        Object.java:207)
        at java.base/java.lang.reflect.Field.checkCanSetAccessible(Field.java:171)
        at java.base/java.lang.reflect.Field.setAccessible(Field.java:165)
        at com.jdojo.intruder/com.jdojo.intruder.TestNonOpen.main(TestNonOpen.java:35)
```

I added the com.jdojo.address module to the default set of root modules using the --add-modules option. You were able to instantiate the Address class even if the com.jdojo.intruder module does not read the com.jdojo.address module. There two reasons for this:

- The com.jdojo.address module exports the com.jdojo.address package, which contains the Address class. Therefore, the Address class is accessible to other modules, provided other modules read the com.jdojo.address module.

- The Java Reflection API assumes readability for all reflective operations. This rule assumes that the com.jdojo.intruder module reads the com.jdojo.address module, even if in its module declaration the com.jdojo.intruder module does not read the com.jdojo.address module. If you were to use types from the com.jdojo. address package at compile-time, for example, declaring a variable of the Address class type, the com.jdojo.intruder module must read the com.jdojo.address module either in its declaration or at command-line.

The output shows that the TestNonOpen class was able to call the public getLine1() method of the Address class. However, it threw an exception when it tried to access the private line1 field. Recall that if a type is exported by a module, other modules can use reflection to access the public members of that type. For other modules to access the private members of the type, the package containing the type must be open. The com.jdojo.address package is not open. Therefore, the com.jdojo.intruder module cannot access the private line1 field of the Address class. To do so, you can use the --add-opens option to open the com.jdojo.address package to the com.jdojo.intruder module:

```
C:Java9revealed> java --module-path com.jdojo.address\dist;com.jdojo.intruder\build\classes
--add-modules com.jdojo.address
--add-opens com.jdojo.address/com.jdojo.address=com.jdojo.intruder
--module com.jdojo.intruder/com.jdojo.intruder.TestNonOpen
```

```
Using method reference, Line1: 1111 Main Blvd.
Using private field reference, Line1: 1111 Main Blvd.
```

It is time to see the --permit-illegal-access option in action. Let's try running the TestNonOpen class from the class path as shown:

```
C:\Java9Revealed>java --module-path com.jdojo.address\dist
--class-path com.jdojo.intruder\build\classes
--add-modules com.jdojo.address com.jdojo.intruder.TestNonOpen
```

```
Using method reference, Line1: 1111 Main Blvd.
Exception in thread "main" java.lang.reflect.InaccessibleObjectException: Unable to make
field private java.lang.String com.jdojo.address.Address.line1 accessible: module com.jdojo.
address does not "opens com.jdojo.address" to unnamed module @9f70c54
        at java.base/java.lang.reflect.AccessibleObject.checkCanSetAccessible(Accessible
        Object.java:337)
        at java.base/java.lang.reflect.AccessibleObject.checkCanSetAccessible(Accessible
        Object.java:281)
        at java.base/java.lang.reflect.Field.checkCanSetAccessible(Field.java:175)
        at java.base/java.lang.reflect.Field.setAccessible(Field.java:169)
        at com.jdojo.intruder.TestNonOpen.main(TestNonOpen.java:34)
```

As it is evident from the output, the TestNonOpen class, which is loaded into an unnamed module because it is on the class path, was able to read the exported type and its public methods in the com.jdojo. address module. However, it could not access the private instance variable. You can fix this by using the --permit-illegal-access option as shown:

```
C:\Java9Revealed>java --module-path com.jdojo.address\dist
--class-path com.jdojo.intruder\build\classes
--add-modules com.jdojo.address
--permit-illegal-access com.jdojo.intruder.TestNonOpen
```

```
WARNING: --permit-illegal-access will be removed in the next major release
Using method reference, Line1: 1111 Main Blvd.
WARNING: Illegal access by com.jdojo.intruder.TestNonOpen (file:/C:/Java9Revealed/com.jdojo.
intruder/build/classes/) to field com.jdojo.address.Address.line1 (permitted by --permit-
illegal-access)
Using private field reference, Line1: 1111 Main Blvd.
```

Notice that the warnings because of the `--permit-illegal-access` option and messages from the
`TestNonOpen` class are mingled in the output.

Using Manifest Attributes of a JAR

An executable JAR is a JAR file that can be used to directly run a Java application using the `-jar` option like so:

```
java -jar myapp.jar
```

Here, `myapp.jar` is called an executable JAR. An executable JAR in its `MANIFEST.MF` file contains
an attribute named `Main-Class` whose value is the fully qualified name of the main class that the `java`
command is supposed to run. Recall that there are other kinds of JARs such as modular JARs and multi-
release JARs. It does not matter which kind of JAR a JAR is based on; an executable JAR is defined only in the
context of the way it is used to launch an application using the `-jar` option.

Consider an existing application that is shipped as an executable JAR. Suppose the application uses deep
reflection to access JDK internal APIs. It worked fine in JDK 8. You want to run the executable JAR on JDK 9.
JDK internal APIs in JDK 9 have been encapsulated, Now, you must use the `--add-exports` and `--add-opens`
command-line options along with the `-jar` option to run the same executable JAR. Using new command-
line options in JDK 9 provides a solution. However, it is little inconvenient for the end users of the executable
JAR. To use JDK 9, they need to know the new command-line options that they need to use. To ease such
migrations, two new attributes for the `MANIFEST.MF` file of executable JARs have been added to JDK 9:

- `Add-Exports`
- `Add-Opens`

These attributes are added to the main section of the manifest file. They are counterparts of the two
command-line options: `--add-exports` and `--add-opens`. There is one difference in using these attributes.
They export and open packages of modules to all unnamed modules. So, you specify a list of source modules
and their packages without specifying target modules as values for these attributes. In other words, in
a manifest file, you can export or open a package to all unnamed modules or none, but not to selected
modules. Values of these attributes are space-separated lists of slash-separated module-name/package-
name pairs. Here is an example:

```
Add-Exports: m1/p1 m2/p2 m3/p3 m1/p1
```

This entry will export the package `p1` in module `m1`, package `p2` in module `m2`, and package `p3` in module
`m2` to all unnamed modules. Rules for parsing manifest files are lenient and allow for duplicates because
historically it was allowed. Notice a duplicate entry `m1/p1` in the value. At runtime, these packages will be
exported to all unnamed modules.

Let's walk through an example. I keep the example simple so you can focus on the use of these new attributes. The java.lang.Long class contains a private static field named serialVersionUID, which is declared as follows:

```
private static final long serialVersionUID = 4290774380558885855L;
```

Listing 9-4 contains the code for a TestManifestAttributes class that uses deep reflection to access the Long.serialVersionUID field. The class is in the com.jdojo.intruder module. An existing application does not use modules and they will be developed using JDK version 8 or lower. However, for this example, it does not make any difference.

Listing 9-4. A Class Named TestManifestAttributes

```java
// TestManifestAttributes.java
package com.jdojo.intruder;

import java.lang.reflect.Field;

public class TestManifestAttributes {
    public static void main(String[] args) throws NoSuchFieldException,
                    IllegalArgumentException, IllegalAccessException {

        Class<Long> cls = Long.class;
        Field svUid = cls.getDeclaredField("serialVersionUID");
        svUid.setAccessible(true);
        long svUidValue = (long)svUid.get(null);
        System.out.println("Long.serialVersionUID=" + svUidValue);
    }
}
```

The TestManifestAttributes class compiles without any errors. Let's package it in an executable JAR. Listing 9-5 shows the contents of the MANIFEST.MF file in the executable JAR that you would have before JDK 9. Remember that the MANIFEST.MF file is stored in the META-INF directory under the root of the JAR file. So, we will keep the same contents for the time being.

Listing 9-5. The MANIFEST.MF File Contents

```
Manifest-Version: 1.0
Main-Class: com.jdojo.intruder.TestManifestAttributes
```

The following command will create an executable JAR named com.jdojo.intruder.jar: The executable JAR will be placed in the com.jdojo.intruder\dist directory. Alternatively, you can *clean* and *build* the com.jdojo.intruder projects from within the NetBeans IDE to create this JAR.

```
C:\Java9Revealed>jar --create --file com.jdojo.intruder\dist\com.jdojo.intruder.jar
--manifest=com.jdojo.intruder\src\META-INF\MANIFEST.MF
-C com.jdojo.intruder\build\classes.
```

Now run the executable JAR:

```
C:\Java9Revealed>java -jar com.jdojo.intruder\dist\com.jdojo.intruder.jar
```

```
Exception in thread "main" java.lang.reflect.InaccessibleObjectException: Unable to make
field private static final long java.lang.Long.serialVersionUID accessible: module java.
base does not "opens java.lang" to unnamed module @224aed64
        at java.base/java.lang.reflect.AccessibleObject.checkCanSetAccessible(Accessible
        Object.java:207)
        at java.base/java.lang.reflect.Field.checkCanSetAccessible(Field.java:171)
        at java.base/java.lang.reflect.Field.setAccessible(Field.java:165)
        at com.jdojo.intruder.TestManifestAttributes.main(TestManifestAttributes.java:10)
```

The runtime error is stating that the application cannot access the private static serialVersionUID because the java.lang package in the java.base module is not open. You learned how to use the --add-opens command-line option to open a package in a module to other modules in the previous section. Let's try that option first:

```
C:\Java9Revealed>java --add-opens java.base/java.lang=ALL-UNNAMED
-jar com.jdojo.intruder\dist\com.jdojo.intruder.jar
```

```
Long.serialVersionUID=4290774380558885855
```

This command works fine and it verifies that the command-line option is a solution in this case. Let's fix this error using the Add-Opens attribute in the MANIFEST.MF file, as shown in Listing 9-6.

Listing 9-6. The Final Version of the MANIFEST.MF File

```
Manifest-Version: 1.0
Main-Class: com.jdojo.intruder.TestManifestAttributes
Add-Opens: java.base/java.lang
```

Recreate the executable JAR using the same command and run it:

```
C:\Java9Revealed>java -jar com.jdojo.intruder\dist\com.jdojo.intruder.jar
```

```
Long.serialVersionUID=4290774380558885855
```

The application runs fine. Let's verify that the Add-Opens attribute is ignored if the JAR is not used as an executable JAR. How can you verify this? It is simple. Run the application by placing the executable JAR on the class path or on the module path and you should expect a runtime error. Note that you will be able to run this application on the module path because you are using JDK 9 and had a module descriptor in the JAR. For older applications, you have only one option—run it from the class path. The following command runs the application from the class path:

```
C:\Java9Revealed>java --class-path com.jdojo.intruder\dist\com.jdojo.intruder.jar com.jdojo.
intruder.TestManifestAttributes
```

```
Exception in thread "main" java.lang.reflect.InaccessibleObjectException: Unable to make
field private static final long java.lang.Long.serialVersionUID accessible: module java.
base does not "opens java.lang" to unnamed module @17ed40e0
        at java.base/java.lang.reflect.AccessibleObject.checkCanSetAccessible(Accessible
        Object.java:207)
        at java.base/java.lang.reflect.Field.checkCanSetAccessible(Field.java:171)
        at java.base/java.lang.reflect.Field.setAccessible(Field.java:165)
        at com.jdojo.intruder.TestManifestAttributes.main(TestManifestAttributes.java:10)
```

How do you fix this error if you were to use the class path to run this application? Use the `--add-open` command-line option to fix it:

```
C:\Java9Revealed>java --add-opens java.base/java.lang=ALL-UNNAMED
--class-path com.jdojo.intruder\dist\com.jdojo.intruder.jar com.jdojo.intruder.
TestManifestAttributes
```

```
Long.serialVersionUID=4290774380558885855
```

Summary

One of the main goals of JDK 9 is to encapsulate types and resources in modules and export only those packages whose public types are intended to be accessed by other modules. Sometimes, you may need to break the encapsulation specified by a module to enable white-box testing or use unsupported JDK-internal APIs or libraries. This is possible by using non-standard command-line options at compile-time and runtime. Another reason for having these options is backward compatibility.

JDK 9 provides two command-line options, `--add-exports` and `--add-opens`, that let you break encapsulation defined in a module declaration. The `--add-exports` option lets you export a non-exported package in a module to other modules at compile-time and runtime. The `--add-opens` option lets you open a non-open package in a module to other modules for deep reflection at runtime. The value for these options is of the form `<source-module>/<package>=<target-module-list>`, where `<source-module>` is the module that exports or opens `<package>` to `<target-module-list>`, which is a comma-separated list of target module names. You can use `ALL-UNNAMED` as a special value for the list of target modules that exports or opens those packages to all unnamed modules.

There are two new attributes named `Add-Exports` and `Add-Opens` that can be used in the main section of the manifest file of an executable JAR. Effects of using these attributes is the same as using the similarly named command-line options, except that these attributes export or open the specified packages to all unnamed modules. The value for these attributes is a space-separated list of slash-separated module-name/package-name pairs. For example, an `Add-Opens: java.base/java.lang` entry in the main section of a manifest file of an executable JAR will open the `java.lang` package in the `java.base` module for all unnamed modules.

During testing and debugging, it is sometimes required that a module read another module where the first module does not use a `requires` statement in its declaration to read the second module. This can be achieved using the `--add-reads` command-line option whose value is specified in the form `<source-module>=<target-module-list>`. The `<source-module>` is the module whose definition is updated to read the list of modules specified in the `<target-module-list>`, which is a comma-separated list of target module names. A special value of `ALL-UNNAMED` for the target module list makes the source module read all unnamed modules.

▦ ▦ ▦

## CHAPTER 10

The Module API

In this chapter, you will learn:

- What the Module API is
- How to represent a module and a module descriptor in a program
- How to read a module descriptor in a program
- How to represent a module's version
- How to read a module's properties using the `Module` and `ModuleDescriptor` classes
- How to update a module's definition at runtime using the `Module` class
- How to create annotations that can be used on modules and how to read annotations used on modules
- What module layers and configurations are
- How to create custom module layers and load modules into them

What Is the Module API?

The Module API consists of classes and interfaces that give you programmatic access to modules. Using the API, you can programmatically:

- Read, modify, and build module descriptors
- Load modules
- Read modules' contents
- Search for loaded modules
- Create new layers of modules

The Module API is small. It consists of about 15 classes and interfaces spread across two packages:

- `java.lang`
- `java.lang.module`

© Kishori Sharan 2017
K. Sharan, *Java 9 Revealed*, DOI 10.1007/978-1-4842-2592-9_10

The Module, ModuleLayer, and LayerInstantiationException classes are in the java.lang package and the rest are in the java.lang.module package. Table 10-1 contains the list of classes in the Module API with a brief description of each. The list is not sorted. I list Module and ModuleDescriptor first because application developers use them most frequently. All other classes are typically used by containers and libraries. The list does not contain exceptions classes in the Module API. I discuss these classes in detail in the subsequent sections.

Table 10-1. *Commonly Used Classes and Their Descriptions in the Module API*

Class	Description
Module	Represents a runtime module.
ModuleDescriptor	Represents a module descriptor. It is immutable.
ModuleDescriptor.Builder	A nested builder class used to build module descriptors programmatically.
ModuleDescriptor.Exports	A nested class that represents an exports statement in a module declaration.
ModuleDescriptor.Opens	A nested class that represents an opens statement in a module declaration.
ModuleDescriptor.Provides	A nested class that represents a provides statement in a module declaration.
ModuleDescriptor.Requires	A nested class that represents a requires statement in a module declaration.
ModuleDescriptor.Version	A nested class that represents a module's version string. It contains a parse(String v) factory method that returns its instance from a version string.
ModuleDescriptor.Modifier	An enum whose constants represent modifiers used on a module declaration such as OPEN for an open module.
ModuleDescriptor.Exports. Modifier	An enum whose constants represent modifiers used on an exports statement in a module's declaration.
ModuleDescriptor.Opens. Modifier	An enum whose constants represent modifiers used on an opens statement in a module's declaration.
ModuleDescriptor.Requires. Modifier	An enum whose constants represent modifiers used on a requires statement in a module's declaration.
ModuleReference	A reference to a module's contents. It contains the module's descriptor and its location.
ResolvedModule	Represents a resolved module in a module graph. Contains the module's name, its dependencies, and a reference to its contents. It can be used to walk though all transitive dependencies of a module in a module graph.
ModuleFinder	An interface used to find modules on specified paths or system modules. Found modules are returned as instances of ModuleReference. It contains factory methods to get its instances.
ModuleReader	An interface used to read a module's contents. You can obtain a ModuleReader from a ModuleReference.
Configuration	Represents a module graph of resolved modules.
ModuleLayer	Contains a module graph (a Configuration) and a mapping between modules in the graph and class loaders.
ModuleLayer.Controller	A nested class used to control modules in a ModuleLayer. Methods in the ModuleLayer class return instances of this class.

Representing Modules

An instance of the Module class represents a runtime module. Every type loaded into the JVM belongs to a module. JDK 9 added a method named getModule() in the Class class that returns the module to which the class belongs. The following snippet of code shows how to get the module of a class named BasicInfo:

```
// Get the Class object for of the BasicInfo class
Class<BasicInfo> cls = BasicInfo.class;

// Get the module reference
Module module = cls.getModule();
```

A module can be named or unnamed. The isNamed() method of the Module class returns true for a named module and false for an unnamed module.

Every class loader contains an unnamed module that contains all types loaded by the class loader from the class path. If a class loader loads types from a module path, those types belong to named modules. The getModule() method of the Class class may return a named or unnamed module. JDK 9 added a method named getUnnamedModule() to the ClassLoader class that returns the unnamed module of the class loader. In the following snippet of code, assuming that the BasicInfo class is loaded from the class path, m1 and m2 refer to the same Module:

```
Class<BasicInfo> cls = BasicInfo.class;
Module m1 = cls.getClassLoader().getUnnamedModule();
Module m2 = cls.getModule();
```

The getName() method of the Module class returns the name of the module. For unnamed modules, it returns null.

```
// Get the module name
String moduleName = module.getName();
```

The getPackages() method in the Module class returns a Set<String> containing all packages in the module. The getClassLoader() method returns the class loader for the module.

The getLayer() method returns the ModuleLayer that contains the module; if the module is not in a layer, it returns null. A module layer contains only named modules. So, this method always returns null for unnamed modules.

Describing Modules

An instance of the ModuleDescriptor class represents a module definition, which is created from a module declaration—typically from a module-info.class file. A module descriptor can also be created on the fly using the ModuleDescriptor.Builder class. A module declaration may be augmented using command-line options such as --add-reads, --add-exports, and --add-opens, and using methods in the Module class such as addReads(), addOpens(), and addExports(). A ModuleDescriptor represents a module descriptor added at the time of module declaration, not an augmented module descriptor. The getDescriptor() method of the Module class returns a ModuleDescriptor:

```
Class<BasicInfo> cls = BasicInfo.class;
Module module = cls.getModule();

// Get the module descriptor
ModuleDescriptor desc = module.getDescriptor();
```

■ **Tip** A ModuleDescriptor is immutable. An unnamed module does not have a module descriptor. The getDescriptor() method of the Module class returns null for an unnamed module.

You can also create a ModuleDescriptor object by reading the binary form of the module declaration from a module-info.class file using one of the static read() methods of the ModuleDescriptor class. The following snippet of code reads a module-info.class file from the current directory. Exception handling is excluded for clarity:

```
String moduleInfoPath = "module-info.class";
ModuleDescriptor desc = ModuleDescriptor.read(new FileInputStream(moduleInfoPath));
```

Representing Module Statements

The ModuleDescriptor class contains the following static nested classes whose instances represent a statement with the same name in a module declaration:

- ModuleDescriptor.Exports
- ModuleDescriptor.Opens
- ModuleDescriptor.Provides
- ModuleDescriptor.Requires

Notice that there is no ModuleDescriptor.Uses class to represent a uses statement. This is because a uses statement represents a service interface name that can be represented as a String.

Representing the exports Statement

An instance of the ModuleDescriptor.Exports class represents an exports statement in a module declaration. The following methods in the class return the components of the exports statement:

- boolean isQualified()
- Set<ModuleDescriptor.Exports.Modifier> modifiers()
- String source()
- Set<String> targets()

The isQualified() method returns true for a qualified export and false for a non-qualified export. The source() method returns the name of the exported package. For a qualified export, the targets() method returns an immutable set of module names to which the package is exported and, for a non-qualified export, it returns an empty set. The modifiers() method returns the set of modifiers for the exports statement that are constants of the nested ModuleDescriptor.Exports.Modifier enum, which contains the following two constants:

- MANDATED: The export was implicitly declared in the source module declaration.
- SYNTHETIC: The export was not explicitly or implicitly declared in the source of the module declaration.

Representing the opens Statement

An instance of the ModuleDescriptor.Opens class represents an opens statement in a module declaration. The following methods in the class return the components of the opens statement:

- boolean isQualified()
- Set<ModuleDescriptor.Opens.Modifier> modifiers()
- String source()
- Set<String> targets()

The isQualified() method returns true for a qualified opens and false for a non-qualified opens. The source() method returns the name of the open package. For a qualified opens, the targets() method returns an immutable set of module names to which the package is open and, for a non-qualified opens, it returns an empty set. The modifiers() method returns the set of modifiers for the opens statement that are constants of the nested ModuleDescriptor.Opens.Modifier enum, which contains the following two constants:

- MANDATED: The opens was implicitly declared in the source of the module declaration.
- SYNTHETIC: The opens was not explicitly or implicitly declared in the source of the module declaration.

Representing the provides Statement

An instance of the ModuleDescriptor.Provides class represents one or more provides statements for a specific service type in a module declaration. The following two provides statements specify two implementation classes for the same service type X.Y:

```
provides X.Y with A.B;
provides X.Y with Y.Z;
```

One instance of the ModuleDescriptor.Provides class will represent both of these statements. The following methods in the class return the components of the provides statement:

- List<String> providers()
- String service()

The providers() method returns the list of the fully qualified class names of the provider classes. In the previous example, the returned list will contain A.B and Y.Z. The service() method returns the fully qualified name of the service type. In the previous example, it will return X.Y.

Representing the requires Statement

An instance of the ModuleDescriptor.Requires class represents a requires statement in a module declaration. The following methods in the class return the components of the requires statement:

- Optional<ModuleDescriptor.Version> compiledVersion()
- Optional<String> rawCompiledVersion()
- String name()
- Set<ModuleDescriptor.Requires.Modifier> modifiers()

Suppose a module named M having a `requires` N statement is compiled. If the module version of N is available at the time of compilation, that version is recorded in the module descriptor of M. The `compiledVersion()` method returns that recorded version of N in an `Optional`. If no version for N was available, the method returns an empty `Optional`. The module version of the module specified in the `requires` statement is recorded in the module descriptor only for informative purposes. It is not used at any phase by the module system. However, it can be used by tools and frameworks for diagnostic purposes. For example, a tool may verify that all modules specified as dependence using the `requires` statement must be available with the same or higher version than the one recorded during compilation.

Continuing with the example in the previous paragraph, the `rawCompiledVersion()` method returns the version of module N in an `Optional<String>`. In most cases, the two methods, `compiledVersion()` and `rawCompiledVersion()`, will return the same module version, but in two different formats: one in an `Optional<ModuleDescriptor.Version>` object and another in an `Optional<String>` object. You can have a module with an invalid module version. Such a module may be created and compiled outside the Java module system. You can load such a module with an invalid module version as a Java module. In such a case, the `compiledVersion()` method returns an empty `Optional<ModuleDescriptor.Version>` because the module version cannot be parsed as a valid Java module version, whereas the `rawCompiledVersion()` returns an `Optional<String>` that contains the invalid module version.

■ **Tip**   The `rawCompiledVersion()` method of the `ModuleDescriptor.Requires` class may return an unparseable version of the required module.

The `name()` method returns the name of the module specified in the `requires` statement. The `modifiers()` method returns the set of modifiers for the `requires` statement that are constants of the nested `ModuleDescriptor.Requires.Modifier` enum, which contains the following constants:

- `MANDATED`: The dependency was implicitly declared in the source of the module declaration.

- `STATIC`: The dependency is mandatory at compile-time and optional at runtime.

- `SYNTHETIC`: The dependency was not explicitly or implicitly declared in the source of the module declaration.

- `TRANSITIVE`: The dependency causes any module that depends on the current module to have an implicitly declared dependency on the module named by this `requires` statement.

Representing a Module Version

An instance of the `ModuleDescriptor.Version` class represents a module's version. It contains a static factory method named `parse(String version)` that returns its instance representing a version from the specified version string. Recall that you do not specify a module's version in a module's declaration. You add a module version when you package module's code into a modular JAR, typically using the `jar` tool. The `javac` compiler also lets you specify a module version when you compile module.

A module version string contains three components:

- A mandatory version number

- An optional prerelease version

- An optional build version

A module version is of the following form:

```
vNumToken+ ('-' preToken+)? ('+' buildToken+)?
```

Each component is sequence of tokens; each token is either a non-negative integer or a string. Tokens are separated by the punctuation characters ., -, or +, or by transition from a sequence of digits to a sequence of characters that are neither digits nor punctuation characters, or vice versa. A version string must start with a digit. The version number is a sequence of tokens separated by . characters, terminated by the first - or + character. The prerelease version is a sequence of tokens separated by . or - characters, terminated by the first + character. The build version is a sequence of tokens separated by ., -, or + characters.

The version() method of the ModuleDescriptor class returns an Optional<ModuleDescriptor.Version>.

Other Properties of Modules

There are other module properties that can be set in the module-info.class file while packaging the modular JAR, such as the main class name, OS name, etc. The ModuleDescriptor class contains a method that returns each of such properties. The following methods in the ModuleDescriptor class are of interest:

- Set<ModuleDescriptor.Exports> exports()
- boolean isAutomatic()
- boolean isOpen()
- Optional<String> mainClass()
- String name()
- Set<ModuleDescriptor.Opens> opens()
- Set<String> packages()
- Set<ModuleDescriptor.Provides> provides()
- Optional<String> rawVersion()
- Set<ModuleDescriptor.Requires> requires()
- String toNameAndVersion()
- Set<String> uses()

The method names are intuitive to understand their purposes. I cover two methods that need a little explanation: packages() and provides().

The ModuleDescriptor class contains a method named packages() and the Module class contains a method named getPackages(). Both return a set of package names. Why do you have two methods for the same purpose? In fact, they serve different purposes. In the ModuleDescriptor, the method returns the set of packages defined in the module declaration whether they are exported or not. Recall that you cannot get a ModuleDescriptor for an unnamed module and, in that case, you can get the package names in the unnamed module using the getPackages() method in the Module class. Another difference is that the package names reported by a ModuleDescriptor are static; the package names reported by a Module are dynamic, which reports the packages loaded in the module at the time the getPackages() method is called. A Module reports all packages currently loaded in it at runtime.

The provides() method returns a Set<ModuleDescriptor.Provides>. Consider the following provides statements in a module declaration:

```
provides A.B with X.Y1;
provides A.B with X.Y2;
provides P.Q with S.T1;
```

In this case, the set will contain two elements—one for the service type A.B and one for the service type P.Q. The service() and providers() method of one element will return A.B and a list of X.Y1 and X.Y2, respectively. These methods for another element will return P.Q and a list of one element containing S.T1.

Knowing Module Basic Info

In this section, I show you an example of how to read basic information about a module at runtime. Listing 10-1 contains the module declaration for a module named com.jdojo.module.api. It reads three modules and exports one package. Two of the read modules, com.jdojo.prime and com.jdojo.intro, are from previous chapters. You will need to add these two modules to the module path to compile it and run the code in the com.jdojo.module.api module. The java.sql module is a JDK module.

Listing 10-1. The Declaration of a Module Named com.jdojo.module.api

```
// module-info.java
module com.jdojo.module.api {
    requires com.jdojo.prime;
    requires com.jdojo.intro;
    requires java.sql;
    exports com.jdojo.module.api;
}
```

Listing 10-2 contains the code for a class named ModuleBasicInfo that prints the module details of three modules using the Module and ModuleDescriptor classes.

Listing 10-2. A ModuleBasicInfo Class

```
// ModuleBasicInfo.java
package com.jdojo.module.api;

import com.jdojo.prime.PrimeChecker;
import java.lang.module.ModuleDescriptor;
import java.lang.module.ModuleDescriptor.Exports;
import java.lang.module.ModuleDescriptor.Provides;
import java.lang.module.ModuleDescriptor.Requires;
import java.sql.Driver;
import java.util.Set;

public class ModuleBasicInfo {
    public static void main(String[] args) {
        // Get the module of the current class
        Class<ModuleBasicInfo> cls = ModuleBasicInfo.class;
        Module module = cls.getModule();
```

```java
        // Print module info
        printInfo(module);
        System.out.println("------------------");

        // Print module info
        printInfo(PrimeChecker.class.getModule());
        System.out.println("------------------");

        // Print module info
        printInfo(Driver.class.getModule());
    }

    public static void printInfo(Module m) {
        String moduleName = m.getName();
        boolean isNamed = m.isNamed();

        // Print module type and name
        System.out.printf("Module Name: %s%n", moduleName);
        System.out.printf("Named Module: %b%n", isNamed);

        // Get the module descriptor
        ModuleDescriptor desc = m.getDescriptor();

        // desc will be null for unnamed module
        if (desc == null) {
            Set<String> currentPackages = m.getPackages();
            System.out.printf("Packages: %s%n", currentPackages);
            return;
        }

        Set<Requires> requires = desc.requires();
        Set<Exports> exports = desc.exports();
        Set<String> uses = desc.uses();
        Set<Provides> provides = desc.provides();
        Set<String> packages = desc.packages();

        System.out.printf("Requires: %s%n", requires);
        System.out.printf("Exports: %s%n", exports);
        System.out.printf("Uses: %s%n", uses);
        System.out.printf("Provides: %s%n", provides);
        System.out.printf("Packages: %s%n", packages);
    }
}
```

Let's run the ModuleBasicInfo class in module mode and in legacy mode. The following command will use the module mode:

```
C:\Java9Revealed>java --module-path com.jdojo.module.api\dist;com.jdojo.prime\dist;com.
jdojo.intro\dist
--module com.jdojo.module.api/com.jdojo.module.api.ModuleBasicInfo
```

```
Module Name: com.jdojo.module.api
Named Module: true
Requires: [mandated java.base (@9-ea), com.jdojo.intro, java.sql (@9-ea), com.jdojo.prime]
Exports: [com.jdojo.module.api]
Uses: []
Provides: []
Packages: [com.jdojo.module.api]
------------------
Module Name: com.jdojo.prime
Named Module: true
Requires: [mandated java.base (@9-ea)]
Exports: [com.jdojo.prime]
Uses: [com.jdojo.prime.PrimeChecker]
Provides: []
Packages: [com.jdojo.prime]
------------------
Module Name: java.sql
Named Module: true
Requires: [transitive java.logging, transitive java.xml, mandated java.base]
Exports: [javax.transaction.xa, java.sql, javax.sql]
Uses: [java.sql.Driver]
Provides: []
Packages: [javax.sql, java.sql, javax.transaction.xa]
```

Now let's run the ModuleBasicInfo class in legacy mode by using the class path as follows:

```
C:\Java9Revealed>java -cp com.jdojo.module.api\dist\com.jdojo.module.api.jar;com.jdojo
.prime\dist\com.jdojo.prime.jar com.jdojo.module.api.ModuleBasicInfo
```

```
Module Name: null
Named Module: false
Packages: [com.jdojo.module.api]
------------------
Module Name: null
Named Module: false
Packages: [com.jdojo.module.api, com.jdojo.prime]
------------------
Module Name: java.sql
Named Module: true
Requires: [mandated java.base, transitive java.logging, transitive java.xml]
Exports: [javax.transaction.xa, javax.sql, java.sql]
Uses: [java.sql.Driver]
Provides: []
Packages: [java.sql, javax.transaction.xa, javax.sql]
```

The second time, the `ModuleBasicInfo` and `PrimeChecker` classes are loaded in an unnamed module of the application class loader, which is reflected in the `isNamed()` method returning `false` for both modules. Notice the dynamic nature of the `getPackages()` method of the `Module` class. When it is called the first time, it returns only one package name—`com.jdojo.module.api`. When it is called the second time, it returns two package names—`com.jdojo.module.api` and `com.jdojo.prime`. This is because packages in the unnamed module are added as types from the new packages are loaded into the unnamed module. The outputs for the `java.sql` module remain the same in both cases because platform types are always loaded into the same module irrespective of the mode the `java` launcher is run in.

Querying Modules

Typical queries that you may run against a module include:

- Can a module M read another module N?

- Can a module use a service of a specific type?

- Does a module export a specific package to all or some modules?

- Does a module open a specific package to all or some modules?

- Is this module named or unnamed?

- Is this an automatic module?

- Is this an open module?

You can augment a module descriptor using command-line options and programmatically using the Module API. You can put all queries for module's properties in two categories: ones whose results may change after the module is loaded and ones whose results do not change after the module is loaded. The `Module` class contains methods for queries in the first category and the `ModuleDescriptor` class contains methods for queries in the second category. The `Module` class provides the following methods for queries in the first category:

- `boolean canRead(Module other)`

- `boolean canUse(Class<?> service)`

- `boolean isExported(String packageName)`

- `boolean isExported(String packageName, Module other)`

- `boolean isOpen(String packageName)`

- `boolean isOpen(String packageName, Module other)`

- `boolean isNamed()`

Methods names are intuitive enough to tell you what they do. The `isNamed()` method returns `true` for a named module and `false` for an unnamed module. A module's type, named or unnamed, does not change after the module has been loaded. This method is provided in the `Module` class because you cannot get a `ModuleDescriptor` for an unnamed module.

The ModuleDescriptor contains three methods that tell you about the type of module and how the module descriptor was generated. The isOpen() method returns true if it is an open module and false otherwise. The isAutomatic() method returns true for an automatic module and false otherwise.

Listing 10-3 contains the code for a class named QueryModule, which is a member of the com.jdojo. module.api module. It shows you how to query a module for dependency checks and whether a package is exported or open to all modules or just to a specific module.

Listing 10-3. A QueryModule Class That Demonstrates How to Query a Module at Runtime

```
// QueryModule.java
package com.jdojo.module.api;

import java.sql.Driver;

public class QueryModule {
    public static void main(String[] args) throws Exception {
        Class<QueryModule> cls = QueryModule.class;
        Module m = cls.getModule();

        // Check if this module can read the java.sql module
        Module javaSqlModule = Driver.class.getModule();
        boolean canReadJavaSql = m.canRead(javaSqlModule);

        // Check if this module exports the com.jdojo.module.api package to all modules
        boolean exportsModuleApiPkg =  m.isExported("com.jdojo.module.api");

        // Check if this module exports the com.jdojo.module.api package to java.sql module
        boolean exportsModuleApiPkgToJavaSql =
                m.isExported("com.jdojo.module.api", javaSqlModule);

        // Check if this module opens the com.jdojo.module.api package to java.sql module
        boolean openModuleApiPkgToJavaSql = m.isOpen("com.jdojo.module.api", javaSqlModule);

        // Print module type and name
        System.out.printf("Named Module: %b%n", m.isNamed());
        System.out.printf("Module Name: %s%n", m.getName());
        System.out.printf("Can read java.sql? %b%n", canReadJavaSql);
        System.out.printf("Exports com.jdojo.module.api? %b%n", exportsModuleApiPkg);
        System.out.printf("Exports com.jdojo.module.api to java.sql? %b%n",
                exportsModuleApiPkgToJavaSql);
        System.out.printf("Opens com.jdojo.module.api to java.sql? %b%n",
                openModuleApiPkgToJavaSql);
    }
}
```

```
Named Module: true
Module Name: com.jdojo.module.api
Can read java.sql? true
Exports com.jdojo.module.api? true
Exports com.jdojo.module.api to java.sql? true
Opens com.jdojo.module.api to java.sql? false
```

Updating Modules

In previous chapters, you saw how to add exports and reads to a module using the `--add-exports`, `--add-opens`, and `--add-reads` command-line options. In this section, I show you how to add these statements to a module programmatically. The `Module` class contains the following methods that let you modify a module declaration at runtime:

- `Module addExports(String packageName, Module other)`

- `Module addOpens(String packageName, Module other)`

- `Module addReads(Module other)`

- `Module addUses(Class<?> serviceType)`

There is a significant difference between using command-line options and one of these methods to modify a module's declaration. Using command-line options, you can modify any module's declaration. However, these methods are caller-sensitive. The code that calls these methods must be in the module whose declaration is being modified—except for calling the `addOpens()` method. That is, if you do not have access to the source code of a module, you cannot use these methods to modify that module's declaration. These methods are typically meant to be used by frameworks, which can adapt to runtime needs to interact with other modules.

All of these methods throw an `IllegalCallerException` when dealing with a named module whereby the caller is not allowed to call these modules.

The `addExports()` method updates the module to export the specified package to the specified module. Calling the method has no effect if the specified package is already exported or open to the specified module or if the method is called on an unnamed or open module. An `IllegalArgumentException` is thrown if the specified package is `null` or does not exist in the module. Calling this method has the same effect as adding a qualified export to the module declaration:

```
exports <packageName> to <other>;
```

The `addOpens()` method works the same as the `addExports()` method, except that it updates the module to open the specified package to the specified module. It is similar to adding the following statement in the module:

```
opens <packageName> to <other>;
```

The `addOpens()` method makes an exception to the rule about who can call this method. Other methods can be called from the code of the same module. However, the `addOpens()` method of a module can be called from the code of another module. Suppose module M opens package P to module N using the following declaration:

```
module M {
    opens P to N;
}
```

In this case, module N is allowed to call the `addOpens("P", S)` method on module M, which allowed module N to open package P to module S. This is done when the author of a module may open a package of a module to a known abstract framework module, which discovers and uses another implementation module at runtime. Both the dynamically known modules may need deep reflective access to the module being declared. In this case, the module's author has to know only about the module name of the abstract framework and open the package to it. At runtime, the abstract framework's module can open the same package to the dynamically discovered implementation module. Think about JPA as an abstract framework that defines a `java.persistence` module and discovers other JPA implementation such as Hibernate and EclipseLink at runtime. In this case, the module's author can open a package only to the `java.persistence` module, which can open the same package to Hibernate or EclipseLink modules at runtime.

The `addReads()` method adds a readability edge from this module to the specified module. This method has no effect if the specified module is itself because every module can read itself or if it is called on an unnamed module because an unnamed module can read all modules. Calling this method is the same as adding a `requires` statement to the module declaration:

```
requires <other>;
```

The `addUses()` method updates the module to add a service dependency, so it can use the `ServiceLoader` class to load the service of the specified service type. It has no effect when called on an unnamed or automatic module. Its effect is the same as adding the following `uses` statement in the module's declaration:

```
uses <serviceType>;
```

Listing 10-4 contains the code for an `UpdateModule` class. It is in the `com.jdojo.module.api` module as shown in Listing 10-1. Notice that the module declaration does not contain a `uses` statement. The class contains a `findFirstService()` method, which accepts a service type as an argument. It checks if the module can load the service type. Recall that a module must contain a `uses` statement with a specified service type to load that service type using the `ServiceLoader` class. The method uses the `addUses()` method of the `Module` class to add a `uses` statement for the service type if it was absent. In the end, the method loads and returns the first service provider loaded.

Listing 10-4. An UpdateModule Class Showing How to Add a uses Statement to a Module Declaration at Runtime

```java
// UpdateModule.java
package com.jdojo.module.api;

import java.util.ServiceLoader;

public class UpdateModule {
    public static <T> T findFirstService(Class<T> service) {
        /* Before loading the service providers, check if this module can use (or load) the
           service. If not, update the module to use the service.
        */
        Module m = UpdateModule.class.getModule();
        if (!m.canUse(service)) {
            m.addUses(service);
        }

        return ServiceLoader.load(service)
                        .findFirst()
                        .orElseThrow(
          () -> new RuntimeException("No service provider found for the service: " +
                                service.getName()));
    }
}
```

Now we'll test the `findFirstService()` method of the `UpdateModule` class. Listing 10-5 contains the declaration for a module named `com.jdojo.module.api.test`. It declares a dependency on the `com.jdojo.prime` module, so it can use the `PrimeChecker` service type interface. It declares a dependency on the `com.jdojo.module.api` module, so it can use the `UpdateModule` class to load the service. You will need to add these two modules to the module path of the `com.jdojo.module.api.test` module in NetBeans.

Listing 10-5. The Declaration of a Module Named com.jdojo.module.api.test

```
// module-info.java
module com.jdojo.module.api.test {
    requires com.jdojo.prime;
    requires com.jdojo.module.api;
}
```

Listing 10-6 contains the code for a `Main` class in the `com.jdojo.module.api.test` module.

Listing 10-6. A Main Method in the com.jdojo.module.api.test Module

```
// Main.java
package com.jdojo.module.api.test;

import com.jdojo.module.api.UpdateModule;
import com.jdojo.prime.PrimeChecker;

public class Main {
    public static void main(String[] args) {
        long[] numbers = {3, 10};

        try {
            // Obtain a service provider for the com.jdojo.prime.PrimeChecker service type
            PrimeChecker pc = UpdateModule.findFirstService(PrimeChecker.class);

            // Check a few numbers for prime
            for (long n : numbers) {
                boolean isPrime = pc.isPrime(n);
                System.out.printf("%d is a prime: %b%n", n, isPrime);
            }
        } catch (RuntimeException e) {
            System.out.println(e.getMessage());
        }
    }
}
```

Try running the `Main` class as follows. Make sure to add the `com.jdojo.intro` module to the module path because the `com.jdojo.module.api.test` module reads the `com.jdojo.module.api` module, which reads the `com.jdojo.intro` module.

```
C:\Java9Revealed>java --module-path com.jdojo.prime\dist;com.jdojo.intro\dist;com.jdojo
.module.api\dist;com.jdojo.module.api.test\dist
--module com.jdojo.module.api.test/com.jdojo.module.api.test.Main
```

```
No service provider found for the service: com.jdojo.prime.PrimeChecker
```

The output shows normal execution of this program. It did not find a service provider for the com. jdojo.prime.PrimeChecker service type on the module path, which is indicated in the output. Let's add a service provider, the com.jdojo.prime.generic module, for the com.jdojo.prime.PrimeChecker service type on the module path and re-run the program. If you add a different service provider to the module path, you may get a different output.

```
C:\Java9Revealed>java --module-path com.jdojo.prime\dist;com.jdojo.intro\dist;com.jdojo
.module.api\dist;com.jdojo.module.api.test\dist;com.jdojo.prime.generic\dist
--module com.jdojo.module.api.test/com.jdojo.module.api.test.Main
```

```
3 is a prime: true
10 is a prime: false
```

Accessing Module Resources

A module may contain resources such as images, audio/video clips, property files, and policy files. Class files (.class files) in a module are also considered resources. The Module class contains a getResourceAsStream() method to retrieve a resource using the resource name:

```
InputStream getResourceAsStream(String name) throws IOException
```

Refer to Chapter 8, which covers how to access a module's resources at length.

Annotation on Modules

You can use annotations on module declarations. The java.lang.annotation.ElementType enum has a new value called MODULE. If you use MODULE as a target type on an annotation declaration, it allows the annotation to be used on modules. In Java 9, two annotations—java.lang.Deprecated and java.lang. SuppressWarnings—have been updated to be used on module declarations. They can be used as follows:

```
@Deprecated(since="1.2", forRemoval=true)
@SuppressWarnings("unchecked")
module com.jdojo.myModule {
    // Module statements go here
}
```

When a module is deprecated, the use of that module in requires, but not in exports or opens statements, causes a warning to be issued. This rule is based on the fact that if module M is deprecated, a requires M will be used by the module's users who need to get the deprecation warning. Other statements such as exports and opens are within the module that is being deprecated. A deprecated module does not cause warnings to be issued for uses of types within the module. Similarly, if a warning is suppressed in a module declaration, the suppression applies to elements within the module declaration and not to types contained in that module.

The Module class implements the java.lang.reflect.AnnotatedElement interface, so you can use a variety of annotation related methods to read them. An annotation type to be used on module declarations must include ElementType.MODULE as a target.

> ▓ **Tip** You cannot annotate individual module statements. For example, you cannot annotate an `exports` statement with a `@Deprecated` annotation indicating that the exported package will be removed in a future release. During the early design phase, it was considered and rejected on the ground that this feature will take a considerable amount of time that is not needed at this time. This could be added in the future, if needed. As a result, you will not find any annotation-related methods in the `ModuleDescriptor` class.

Now we'll create a new annotation type and use it on a module declaration. Listing 10-7 contains the module declaration for a module named com.jdojo.module.api.annotation that contains three annotations. The `Version` annotation type has been declared in the same module and its source code is shown in Listing 10-8. The retention policy of the new annotation type is `RUNTIME`.

Listing 10-7. A Module Declaration for a Module Named com.jdojo.module.api.annotation

```
// module-info.java

import com.jdojo.module.api.annotation.Version;

@Deprecated(since="1.2", forRemoval=false)
@SuppressWarnings("unchecked")
@Version(major=1, minor=2)
module com.jdojo.module.api.annotation {
    // No module statements
}
```

Listing 10-8. A Version Annotation Type That Can Be Used on Packages, Modules, and Types

```
// Version.java
package com.jdojo.module.api.annotation;

import static java.lang.annotation.ElementType.MODULE;
import static java.lang.annotation.ElementType.PACKAGE;
import static java.lang.annotation.ElementType.TYPE;
import java.lang.annotation.Retention;
import static java.lang.annotation.RetentionPolicy.RUNTIME;
import java.lang.annotation.Target;

@Retention(RUNTIME)
@Target({PACKAGE, MODULE, TYPE})
public @interface Version {
    int major();
    int minor();
}
```

Listing 10-9 contains the code for an `AnnotationTest` class. It reads the annotations on the com.jdojo. module.api.annotation module. The output does not contain the `@SuppressWarnings` annotation that is present on the module because this annotation uses a retention policy of `RetentionPolicy.RUNTIME`, which means the annotation is not retained at runtime.

Listing 10-9. An AnnotationTest Class to Demonstrate How to Read Annotations on Modules

```java
// AnnotationTest.java
package com.jdojo.module.api.annotation;

import java.lang.annotation.Annotation;

public class AnnotationTest {
    public static void main(String[] args) {
        // Get the module reference of the com.jdojo.module.api.annotation module
        Module m = AnnotationTest.class.getModule();

        // Print all annotations
        Annotation[] a = m.getAnnotations();
        for(Annotation ann : a) {
            System.out.println(ann);
        }

        // Read the Deprecated annotation
        Deprecated d = m.getAnnotation(Deprecated.class);
        if (d != null) {
            System.out.printf("Deprecated: since=%s, forRemoval=%b%n",
                            d.since(), d.forRemoval());
        }

        // Read the Version annotation
        Version v = m.getAnnotation(Version.class);
        if (v != null) {
            System.out.printf("Version: major=%d, minor=%d%n", v.major(), v.minor());
        }
    }
}
```

```
@java.lang.Deprecated(forRemoval=false, since="1.2")
@com.jdojo.module.api.annotation.Version(major=1, minor=2)
Deprecated: since=1.2, forRemoval=false
Version: major=1, minor=2
```

Loading Classes

You can use one of the following static forName() methods of the Class class to load and initialize a class:

- Class<?> forName(String className) throws ClassNotFoundException

- Class<?> forName(String className, boolean initialize, ClassLoader loader) throws ClassNotFoundException

- Class<?> forName(Module module, String className)

In these methods, the className parameter is the fully qualified name of the class or interface to be loaded, such as java.lang.Thread and com.jdojo.intro.Welcome. If the initialize parameter is true, the class will be initialized.

The forName(String className) method initializes the class after loading and uses the current class loader, which is the class loader that loaded the class in which the call to this method appears. The expression

```
Class.forName("P.Q")
```

inside an instance method is equivalent to

```
Class.forName("P.Q", true, this.getClass().getClassLoader())
```

The forName(Module module, String className) was added in JDK 9. It does not initialize the class. Notice that this method does not throw a ClassNotFoundException when the specified class is not found. Rather, it returns null.

None of these methods checks if the caller can access the specified class. That is, you can use these methods to load non-exported classes from a module. Loading a class does not mean that you can instantiate it and access its members. Accessibility checks are performed when you try instantiating the class. For example, you can load a non-exported class, but trying to instantiate it will throw an exception.

Listing 10-10 contains the code for a LoadingClass class that is a member of the com.jdojo.module.api module. The class contains two versions of the loadClass() method. The methods load the specified class and, after successfully loading the class, it tries to instantiate the class using a no-args constructor. Note that the com.jdojo.intro module does not export the com.jdojo.intro package that contains the Welcome class. This example attempts to load and instantiate the Welcome class and two other non-existent classes.

Listing 10-10. A Class Demonstrating How to Load Classes

```java
// LoadingClass.java
package com.jdojo.module.api;

import java.lang.reflect.Constructor;
import java.lang.reflect.InvocationTargetException;
import java.util.Optional;

public class LoadingClass {
    public static void main(String[] args) {
        loadClass("com.jdojo.intro.Welcome");
        loadClass("com.jdojo.intro.XYZ");

        String moduleName = "com.jdojo.intro";
        Optional<Module> m = ModuleLayer.boot().findModule(moduleName);
        if (m.isPresent()) {
            Module introModule = m.get();
            loadClass(introModule, "com.jdojo.intro.Welcome");
            loadClass(introModule, "com.jdojo.intro.ABC");
        } else {
            System.out.println("Module not found: " + moduleName +
              ". Please make sure to add the module to the module path.");
        }
    }
```

```
    public static void loadClass(String className) {
        try {
            Class<?> cls = Class.forName(className);
            System.out.println("Class found: " + cls.getName());
            instantiateClass(cls);
        } catch (ClassNotFoundException e) {
            System.out.println("Class not found: " + className);
        }
    }

    public static void loadClass(Module m, String className) {
        Class<?> cls = Class.forName(m, className);
        if (cls == null) {
            System.out.println("Class not found: " + className);
        } else {
            System.out.println("Class found: " + cls.getName());
            instantiateClass(cls);
        }
    }

    public static void instantiateClass(Class<?> cls) {
        try {
            // Get the no-arg constructor
            Constructor<?> c = cls.getConstructor();
            Object o = c.newInstance();
            System.out.println("Instantiated class: " + cls.getName());
        } catch (InstantiationException | IllegalAccessException |
                    IllegalArgumentException | InvocationTargetException e) {
            System.out.println(e.getMessage());
        } catch (NoSuchMethodException e) {
            System.out.println("No no-args constructor for class: " + cls.getName());
        }
    }
}
```

Try running the LoadingClass class by just adding three required modules to the module path:

```
C:\Java9Revealed>java
--module-path com.jdojo.module.api\dist;com.jdojo.prime\dist;com.jdojo.intro\dist
--module com.jdojo.module.api/com.jdojo.module.api.LoadingClass
```

```
Class found: com.jdojo.intro.Welcome
class com.jdojo.module.api.LoadingClass (in module com.jdojo.module.api) cannot access class
com.jdojo.intro.Welcome (in module com.jdojo.intro) because module com.jdojo.intro does not
export com.jdojo.intro to module com.jdojo.module.api
Class not found: com.jdojo.intro.XYZ
Class found: com.jdojo.intro.Welcome
class com.jdojo.module.api.LoadingClass (in module com.jdojo.module.api) cannot access class
com.jdojo.intro.Welcome (in module com.jdojo.intro) because module com.jdojo.intro does not
export com.jdojo.intro to module com.jdojo.module.api
Class not found: com.jdojo.intro.ABC
```

The output reveals that we can load the com.jdojo.intro.Welcome class. However, we cannot instantiate it as it is not exported in the com.jdojo.intro module. The following command uses an --add-exports option to export the com.jdojo.intro package in the com.jdojo.intro module to the com.jdojo.module.api module. The output shows that we can load as well as instantiate the Welcome class.

```
c:\Java9Revealed>java
--module-path com.jdojo.module.api\dist;com.jdojo.prime\dist;com.jdojo.intro\dist
--add-exports com.jdojo.intro/com.jdojo.intro=com.jdojo.module.api
--module com.jdojo.module.api/com.jdojo.module.api.LoadingClass
```

```
Class found: com.jdojo.intro.Welcome
Instantiated class: com.jdojo.intro.Welcome
Class not found: com.jdojo.intro.XYZ
Class found: com.jdojo.intro.Welcome
Instantiated class: com.jdojo.intro.Welcome
Class not found: com.jdojo.intro.ABC
```

Working with Module Layers

Working with module layers is an advanced topic. A typical Java developer will not need to work with module layers directly. Existing applications will not use module layers. If you migrate your applications to JDK 9 or develop new applications using JDK 9, whether you want it or not, you are using at least one module layer, which is created by the JVM at startup. Typically, applications using plugin or container architecture will use module layers. In this section, I give a brief overview of module layers using a simple example. I will use the terms, module layers and layers interchangeably for the balance of the book.

A *layer* is a set of resolved modules (a module graph) with a function that maps each module to a class loader that is responsible for loading all types in that module. The set of resolved modules is called a *configuration*. You can visualize the relationship between modules, class loaders, configurations, and layers like so:

```
Configuration = A module graph
Module Layer = Configuration + (Module -> Class loader)
```

Modules are arranged into layers. Layers are arranged hierarchically. A layer has at least one parent layer, except the *empty* layer, which, as its name suggests, contains no modules and primarily exists to serve as the parent layer for the *boot* layer. The boot layer is created by the JVM at startup by resolving the application's initial modules (the root modules) against a set of observable modules. Loading types using class loaders has not changed in JDK 9. Class loaders, typically, use the parent-first delegation model in which a request to load a type is delegated to the parent, which in turn delegates to its parent until the bootstrap class loader. If none of the parents loads the type, the class loader that initially received the request loads it. Figure 10-1 shows an example of the way modules, class loaders, and layers are arranged.

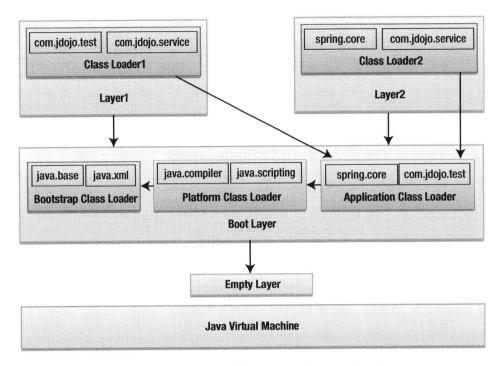

Figure 10-1. *An example of arranging modules into layers in an application*

In the figure, an arrow pointing from X to Y means that X is the parent of Y, where X and Y could be class loaders or layers. Layers are stacked—the empty layer and the boot layer are the lowest two layers. I will ignore referring to the empty layer in our further discussion and will treat the boot layer as the lowest layer in the stack of layers. The boot layer is the parent layer of the two custom layers named Layer1 and Layer2.

Modules in a given layer in the stack can read modules in layers below it. That is, both Layer1 and Layer2 can read modules in the boot layer. However, Layer1 cannot read modules in Layer2 because they are siblings. Neither can the boot layer read modules in Layer1 and Layer2 because the boot layer is the parent layer for them. As shown in Figure 10-1, the class loaders in both user-defined layers have the application class loader as their parent, which most often would be the case. Making the application class loader the parent of the custom class loader ensures that the latter will be able to read all types in modules in the boot layer. The readability property of modules is respected when modules in one layer read modules in layers below it.

Allowing modules to be arranged in layers works for two use cases—override mechanism and extension mechanism—that are often encountered in advanced Java applications like Java EE application/web servers that act as containers for hosted applications. In the override mechanism, a hosted application needs to override the functionalities provided by the container such as using a different version of the same module. In the extension mechanism, a hosted application needs to supplement the functionalities that are already provided by the container such as providing additional service providers. In Figure 10-1, the com.jdojo.test module is in the boot layer as well as Layer1. This is the case of overriding modules. The module version in Layer1 will be used by Layer1, whereas Layer2 will use the version of this module from the boot layer.

It is often required that a container allows hosted applications to provide their own set of modules that may override the modules embedded in the container. This is made possible by loading modules of the hosted applications in a layer on top of the container layer. Modules loaded into the application-specific layers will override the modules in the server-level layers. This way, you can use multiple versions of the same module in the same JVM.

A hosted application may want to use a different service provider than the one provided by the container. This is possible by adding the application-specific service provider modules to a layer on top of the container layer. You can use the load(ModuleLayer layer, Class<S> service) method of the ServiceLoader class to load service providers. The specified layer would be the hosted application specific layer. This method loads service providers from the specified layer and its parent layers.

■ **Tip**   Layers are immutable. Once you create a layer, you cannot add modules to it or remove modules from it. If you need to add modules or substitute a module with another version of it, you must tear down the layer and recreate it.

Creating a layer is a multi-step process. You need to

- Create module finders
- Create a set of root modules
- Create a configuration object
- Create a layer

Once you create a layer, you can use it to load types. I walk you through these steps in detail in the next sections. In the end, I show you how to use multiple versions of a module using layers.

Finding Modules

A module finder is an instance of the ModuleFinder interface. It is used to find ModuleReferences during module resolution and service binding. The interface contains the two factory methods to create module finders:

- static ModuleFinder of(Path... entries)
- static ModuleFinder ofSystem()

The of() method locates modules by searching the specified sequence of paths, which can be paths to directories or packaged modules. The method finds the first occurrence of a module name searching the specified paths in order. The following snippet of code shows how to create a module finder that will search for modules in the C:\Java9Revealed\lib and C:\Java9Revealed\customLib directories:

```
// Create the module paths
Path mp1 = Paths.get("C:\\Java9Revealed\\lib");
Path mp2 = Paths.get("C:\\Java9Revealed\\customLib");

// Create a module finder using two module paths
ModuleFinder finder = ModuleFinder.of(mp1, mp2);
```

Sometimes, you need a reference to a ModuleFinder, for example, to pass to a method, but that module finder need not find any module. You can use the ModuleFinder.of() method without passing any paths as arguments to create, such as a module finder.

The ofSystem() method returns a module finder that finds system modules linked to the runtime. This method always finds the java.base module. Note that you can link a custom set of modules to a runtime image, which means that modules located using this method depend on the runtime image. A custom runtime image contains JDK modules as well as application modules. This method will find both types of modules.

You can also compose a module finder from a sequence of zero of more module finders using the compose() method:

```
static ModuleFinder compose(ModuleFinder... finders)
```

This module finder will use each module finder in the order specified. The second module finder will find all modules not found by the first module finder, the third module finder will find all modules not found by the first and second module finders, and so on.

The ModuleFinder interface contains the following methods to find modules:

- Optional<ModuleReference> find(String name)

- Set<ModuleReference> findAll()

The find() method finds a module with the specified name. The findAll() method finds all modules that the finder can locate.

Listing 10-11 contains the code for a FindingModule class that shows you how to use a ModuleFinder. The code uses paths on Windows such as C:\Java9Revealed\lib, where modules are stored. You may need to change the module paths before you run the class. The class is a member of the com.jdojo.module.api module. You may get a different output.

Listing 10-11. Using a ModuleFinder to Locate Modules

```
// FindingModule.java
package com.jdojo.module.api;

import java.lang.module.ModuleDescriptor;
import java.lang.module.ModuleFinder;
import java.lang.module.ModuleReference;
import java.net.URI;
import java.nio.file.Path;
import java.nio.file.Paths;
import java.util.Optional;
import java.util.Set;

public class FindingModule {
    public static void main(String[] args) {
        // Create module paths
        Path mp1 = Paths.get("C:\\Java9Revealed\\lib");
        Path mp2 = Paths.get("C:\\Java9Revealed\\customLib");

        // Create a module finder
        ModuleFinder finder = ModuleFinder.of(mp1, mp2);

        // Find all modules that this finder can locate
        Set<ModuleReference> moduleRefs = finder.findAll();

        // Print the details of the modules found
        moduleRefs.forEach(FindingModule::printInfo);
    }
```

```
    public static void printInfo(ModuleReference mr) {
        ModuleDescriptor md = mr.descriptor();
        Optional<URI> location = mr.location();
        URI uri = null;
        if(location.isPresent()) {
            uri = location.get();
        }

        System.out.printf("Module: %s, Location: %s%n", md.name(), uri);
    }
}
```

```
Module: com.jdojo.prime.probable, Location: file:///C:/Java9Revealed/lib/com.jdojo.prime.
probable.jar
Module: com.jdojo.person, Location: file:///C:/Java9Revealed/lib/com.jdojo.person.jar
Module: com.jdojo.address, Location: file:///C:/Java9Revealed/lib/com.jdojo.address.jar
...
```

Reading Module Contents

In the previous section, you learned how to use a ModuleFinder to find module references, which are instances of the ModuleReference class. A ModuleReference encapsulates the ModuleDescriptor and the location of a module. You can use the open() method of the ModuleReference class to obtain an instance of the ModuleReader interface. A ModuleReader is used to list, find, and read the contents of a module. The following snippet of code shows how to obtain a ModuleReader for the java.base module:

```
// Create a system module finder
ModuleFinder finder = ModuleFinder.ofSystem();

// The java.base module is guaranteed to exist
Optional<ModuleReference> omr = finder.find("java.base");
ModuleReference moduleRef = omr.get();

// Get a module reader
ModuleReader reader = moduleRef.open();
```

The open() method of the ModuleReference class throws an IOException. I have omitted the exception handling in this snippet of code to keep the code simple.

The following methods in the ModuleReader are used to work with the contents of a module. The method names are intuitive enough to tell you what they do.

- void close() throws IOException

- Optional<URI> find(String resourceName) throws IOException

- Stream<String> list() throws IOException

- default Optional<InputStream> open(String resourceName) throws IOException

- default Optional<ByteBuffer> read(String resourceName) throws IOException

- default void release(ByteBuffer bb)

The resource name passed to these methods is a / separated path string. For example, the resource name for the java.lang.Object class in the java.base module is java/lang/Object.class.

Once you are done working with a ModuleReader, you need to close it using its close() method. If you try to read a module's contents using a closed ModuleReader, an IOException is thrown. The read() method returns an Optional<ByteBuffer>. You need to call the release(ByteBuffer bb) method to release the byte buffer after consuming it to avoid a resource leak.

Listing 10-12 contains a program that shows how to read contents of a module. It reads the contents of the Object class in a ByteBuffer and prints its size in bytes. It also prints the name of five resources in the java.base module. You may get a different output.

Listing 10-12. Using a ModuleReader to Read a Module's Contents

```java
// ReadingModuleContents.java
package com.jdojo.module.api;

import java.io.IOException;
import java.lang.module.ModuleFinder;
import java.lang.module.ModuleReader;
import java.lang.module.ModuleReference;
import java.nio.ByteBuffer;
import java.util.Optional;

public class ReadingModuleContents {
    public static void main(String[] args) {
        // Create a system module finder
        ModuleFinder finder = ModuleFinder.ofSystem();

        // The java.base module is guaranteed to exist
        Optional<ModuleReference> omr = finder.find("java.base");
        ModuleReference moduleRef = omr.get();

        // Get a module reader and use it
        try (ModuleReader reader = moduleRef.open()) {
            // Read the Object class and print its size
            Optional<ByteBuffer> bb = reader.read("java/lang/Object.class");

            bb.ifPresent(buffer -> {
                System.out.println("Object.class Size: " + buffer.limit());

                // Release the byte buffer
                reader.release(buffer);
            });

            System.out.println("\nFive resources in the java.base module:");
            reader.list()
                    .limit(5)
                    .forEach(System.out::println);
        } catch (IOException e) {
            e.printStackTrace();
        }
    }
}
```

```
Object.class Size: 1859

Five resources in the java.base module:
module-info.class
sun/util/BuddhistCalendar.class
sun/util/PreHashedMap$1$1.class
sun/util/PreHashedMap$1.class
sun/util/PreHashedMap$2$1$1.class
```

Creating Configurations

A *configuration* represents a set of resolved modules. A resolved module is a module whose dependencies, specified using the requires statements, have been computed. The module resolution process uses two sets of modules: a set of root modules and a set of observable modules. Each module in the set of root modules is used as an initial module and its requires statements are resolved against the set of observable modules. A root module may require another module, which in turn may require another module, and so on. The resolution process computes the chain of dependencies for all root modules. The resulting graph of modules is called a *dependency* graph.

A dependency graph only takes into account the requires statements. If a module uses a requires transitive statement, modules depending on this module implicitly depend on the module specified in the requires transitive statement. The dependency graph is augmented with additional readability of modules caused by the requires transitive statements resulting in a module graph called a *readability* graph.

The uses and provides statements in modules also form a dependency. If a module M uses a service type S and another module N provides an implementation S with T, the module M depends on module N for using the service type S. The readability graph is augmented with modules computed for such service-use dependencies.

When the configuration for the boot layer is created, it contains modules by resolving the dependencies (requires statements), implied readability (requires transitive), and service-use dependencies (uses and provides statements). When you create a configuration for a user-defined layer, you have an option to include or exclude the service-use dependencies.

An instance of the Configuration class represents a configuration. A configuration has at least one parent, except an empty configuration.

An instance of the ResolvedModule class represents a resolved module in a configuration. Its reads() method returns a Set<ResolvedModule> that a resolved module reads. Its configuration() method returns the Configuration that the resolved module is a member of. Its reference() method returns a ModuleReference that you can use to obtain a ModuleReader to reads the module's contents.

The following methods in the Configuration class create a Configuration object:

- static Configuration empty()

- Configuration resolve(ModuleFinder before, ModuleFinder after, Collection<String> roots)

- Configuration resolveAndBind(ModuleFinder before, ModuleFinder after, Collection<String> roots)

- static Configuration resolve(ModuleFinder before, List<Configuration> parents, ModuleFinder after, Collection<String> roots)

- static Configuration resolveAndBind(ModuleFinder before, List<Configuration> parents, ModuleFinder after, Collection<String> roots)

237

The empty() method returns an empty Configuration. This primarily exists to serve as the parent configuration for the configuration of the boot layer.

There are two versions of the resolve() and resolveAndBind() methods: instance methods and static methods. There is only one difference between them. The instance methods create a new configuration using the current configuration as the parent configuration, whereas the static methods let you pass a list of parent configurations for the new configuration.

The resolve() method creates a new Configuration object by resolving dependencies resulting from requires and requires transitive statements in the module declarations. Modules in the specified roots are used as root modules. During resolution process, modules are searched using the specified before module finder first. If the module is not found, the parent configurations are searched. If the module is still not found, the specified after module finder is used to search for the module. If your configuration is supposed to override a module in the parent configurations, you will place that module in the before module finder path.

The resolveAndBind() method works the same as the resolve() method, except that it also resolves service-use dependencies. The following snippet of code shows how to create a configuration using the boot layer's configuration as its parent configuration:

```
// Define the module finders
String modulePath = "C:\\Java9Revealed\\customLib";
Path path = Paths.get(modulePath);

ModuleFinder beforFinder = ModuleFinder.of(path);

// Our after module finder is empty
ModuleFinder afterFinder = ModuleFinder.of();

// Set up the root modules
Set<String> rootModules = Set.of("com.jdojo.layer");

// Create a configuration using the boot layer's configuration as its parent configuration
Configuration parentConfig = ModuleLayer.boot().configuration();
Configuration config = parentConfig.resolve(beforFinder, afterFinder, rootModules);
```

The following methods in the Configuration class are used to retrieve the details of resolved modules in a configuration:

- Optional<ResolvedModule> findModule(String name)
- Set<ResolvedModule> modules()
- List<Configuration> parents()

These methods' names and signatures are intuitive enough to understand their use. I will not discuss the Configuration class any further in this section. In the next section, I show how to use a Configuration to create a module layer.

Creating Module Layers

A module layer is a configuration and a function that maps each module to a class loader. To create a layer, you must first create a configuration and have one or more class loaders to map modules to them. The class loader for a module is responsible for loading all types in that module. You can map all modules in a configuration to one class loader; you can map each module to a different class loader; or you can have a custom mapping strategy. Typically, class loaders use a delegation strategy that delegates class loading requests to their parent class loaders. You can use this strategy as well when you define class loaders for modules in layers.

An instance of the ModuleLayer class, which is in the java.lang package, represents a layer. The class contains two methods, empty() and boot(), that return an empty layer with an empty configuration and the boot layer, respectively. The following methods in the class are used to create a custom layer:

- ModuleLayer defineModules(Configuration cf, Function<String,ClassLoader> clf)

- static ModuleLayer.Controller defineModules(Configuration cf, List<ModuleLayer> parentLayers, Function<String,ClassLoader> clf)

- ModuleLayer defineModulesWithManyLoaders(Configuration cf, ClassLoader parentClassLoader)

- static ModuleLayer.Controller defineModulesWithManyLoaders(Configuration cf, List<ModuleLayer> parentLayers, ClassLoader parentLoader)

- ModuleLayer defineModulesWithOneLoader(Configuration cf, ClassLoader parentClassLoader)

- static ModuleLayer.Controller defineModulesWithOneLoader(Configuration cf, List<ModuleLayer> parentLayers, ClassLoader parentLoader)

The defineModulesXxx() methods have two variants: one set contain instance methods and another set contain static methods. Instance methods use the layer on which they are called as the parent layer, whereas static methods let you specify a list of parent layers for the new layer. The static methods return a ModuleLayer.Controller object, which you can use to work with modules in the new layer. ModuleLayer.Controller is a nested class in the java.lang package with the following methods:

- ModuleLayer.Controller addOpens(Module source, String packageName, Module target)

- ModuleLayer.Controller addReads(Module source, Module target)

- ModuleLayer layer()

The addOpens and addReads() methods let you open a package in a module in this layer to another module and add a read edge from a module in this layer to another module. The layer() method returns the ModuleLayer that this controller is managing.

The defineModules(Configuration cf, Function<String,ClassLoader> clf) method takes a configuration as its first argument. The second argument is a mapping function that takes a module name in the configuration and returns a class loader for that module. The method call may fail if:

- Multiple modules with the same package are mapped to the same class loader.

- A module is mapped to a class loader that already has a module of the same name defined in it.

- A module is mapped to a class loader that has already defined types in any of the packages in the module.

The defineModulesWithManyLoaders(Configuration cf, ClassLoader parentClassLoader) method creates a layer using the specified configuration. Each module in the configuration is mapped to a different class loader, which is created by this method. The specified parent class loader (the second argument) is set as the parent of the class loaders created by this method. Typically, you would use the application class loader as the parent class loader for all class loaders created by this method. You can use null as the second argument to use the bootstrap class loader as the parent for all the class loaders created by this method. This method will create a new class loader for each module in the configuration.

The defineModulesWithOneLoader(Configuration cf, ClassLoader parentClassLoader) method creates a layer using the specified configuration. It creates one class loader using the specified parent class loader as its parent. It maps all modules in the configuration to that one class loader. You can use null as the second argument to use the bootstrap class loader as the parent for all the class loaders created by this method.

The following snippet of code creates a layer with the boot layer as its parent layer. All modules in the layer will be loaded by one class loader whose parent is the system class loader.

```
Configuration config = /* create a configuration... */
ClassLoader sysClassLoader = ClassLoader.getSystemClassLoader();
ModuleLayer parentLayer = ModuleLayer.boot();
ModuleLayer layer = parentLayer.defineModulesWithOneLoader(config, sysClassLoader);
```

Once you create a layer, you need to load classes from modules in that layer. All types in a module are loaded by the class loader mapped to that module. Note that you may have the same module defined in more than one layer, but those modules will be mapped to different class loaders. The ModuleLayer class contains a findLoader(String moduleName) method that accepts a module name as an argument and returns the ClassLoader for that module. If the module in not defined in the layer, the parent layers are checked. If the module does not exist in this layer or its ancestor layers, an IllegalArgumentException is thrown. Once you get the ClassLoader for the module, you can call its loadClass(String className) method to load a class from that module. The following snippet of code, excluding the exception handling logic, shows how to load a class in a layer:

```
ModuleLayer layer = /* create a layer... */

// Load a class using the layer
String moduleName = "com.jdojo.layer";
String className = "com.jdojo.layer.LayerInfo";
Class<?> cls = layer.findLoader(moduleName)
                    .loadClass(className);
```

Once you get the Class object, you can use it to instantiate its objects and call methods on that object. The following snippet of code creates an object of the loaded class and calls a method named printInfo on that object:

```
// A method name that prints the details of an object
String methodName = "printInfo";

// Instantiate the class using its no-args constructor
Object obj = cls.getConstructor().newInstance();

// Find the method
Method method = cls.getMethod(methodName);

// Call the method that will print the details
method.invoke(obj);
```

The following methods in the ModuleLayer class can be used to obtain information about the layer itself or the modules contained in the layer:

- Optional<Module> findModule(String moduleName)
- Set<Module> modules()
- List<ModuleLayer> parents()

The findModule() method finds a module with the specified name in the layer or its parent layers. The modules() method returns a set of modules in the layer, which may be an empty set if the layer does not contain any modules. The parent() method returns a list of parent layers for this layer, which will be empty for the empty layer.

Next, we walk through a complete example of how to create a custom layer and how to load the two versions of the same module in two layers in the same application.

The module name is com.jdojo.layer and it consists of one package named com.jdojo.layer that contains only one class named LayerInfo. You will have two versions of the same modules, so everything will be repeated. I created two NetBeans projects in the source code with the names com.jdojo.layer.v1 and com.jdojo.layer.v2.

Listing 10-13 and Listing 10-14 contain version 1.0 of the module definition for the com.jdojo.layer module and the class declaration for the LayerInfo class, respectively.

Listing 10-13. Version 1.0 of the com.jdojo.layer Module

```
// module-info.com version 1.0
module com.jdojo.layer {
    exports com.jdojo.layer;
}
```

Listing 10-14. The LayerInfo Class in Version 1.0 of the com.jdojo.layer Module

```
// LayerInfo.java
package com.jdojo.layer;

public class LayerInfo {
    private final static String VERSION = "1.0";

    static {
        System.out.println("Loading LayerInfo version " + VERSION);
    }

    public void printInfo() {
        Class cls = this.getClass();
        ClassLoader loader = cls.getClassLoader();
        Module module = cls.getModule();
        String moduleName = module.getName();
        ModuleLayer layer = module.getLayer();

        System.out.println("Class Version: " + VERSION);
        System.out.println("Class Name: " + cls.getName());
        System.out.println("Class Loader: " + loader);
        System.out.println("Module Name: " + moduleName);
        System.out.println("Layer Name: " + layer);
    }
}
```

The LayerInfo class is very simple. It stores its version information in a static variable named VERSION. It prints a message in a static initializer that includes the version information. This message will help you understand which version of the LayerInfo class is being loaded. The printInfo() method prints the details of the class: the version, class name, class loader, the module name, and the layer.

Listing 10-15 and Listing 10-16 contain version 2.0 of the module definition for the com.jdojo.layer module and the class declaration for the LayerInfo class, respectively. Only one thing has changed from version 1.0 to version 2.0 of this module—the value of the static variable VERSION changed from 1.0 to 2.0.

Listing 10-15. Version 2.0 of the com.jdojo.layer Module

```
// module-info.com version 2.0
module com.jdojo.layer {
    exports com.jdojo.layer;
}
```

Listing 10-16. The LayerInfo Class in Version 2.0 of the com.jdojo.layer Module

```
// LayerInfo.java
package com.jdojo.layer;

public class LayerInfo {
    private final static String VERSION = "2.0";

    static {
        System.out.println("Loading LayerInfo version " + VERSION);
    }

    public void printInfo() {
        Class cls = this.getClass();
        ClassLoader loader = cls.getClassLoader();
        Module module = cls.getModule();
        String moduleName = module.getName();
        ModuleLayer layer = module.getLayer();

        System.out.println("Class Version: " + VERSION);
        System.out.println("Class Name: " + cls.getName());
        System.out.println("Class Loader: " + loader);
        System.out.println("Module Name: " + moduleName);
        System.out.println("Layer Name: " + layer);
    }
}
```

You are ready to test layers and load both versions of the com.jdojo.layer modules in two different layers in the same JVM. Create a modular JAR for version 2.0 of this module, name it com.jdojo.layer. v2.jar or give it any other name you want, and place the modular JAR into a C:\Java9Revealed\customLib directory. If you place your modular JAR in other directory, you need to change the path in the code in Listing 10-18.

The program to test layers is in a module named com.jdojo.layer.test module whose declaration is shown in Listing 10-17. This module declares a dependency on version 1.0 of the com.jdojo.layer module. How can you ensure that version 1.0 of the com.jdojo.layer module is used with the com.jdojo.layer. test module? All you have to do is place the code for version 1.0 of the com.jdojo.layer module on the module path when you run the com.jdojo.layer.test module. To achieve this in NetBeans, add the com.jdojo.layer.v1 project to the module path of the com.jdojo.layer.test module.

Listing 10-18 contains code for a LayerTest class that contains the logic to create a custom layer and load modules into it. A detailed explanation of the logic used in this class follows the output of this class.

Listing 10-17. A Module Declaration for a Module Named com.jdojo.later.test

```
// module-info.java
module com.jdojo.layer.test {
    // This module reads version 1.0 of the com.jdojo.layer module
    requires com.jdojo.layer;
}
```

Listing 10-18. The LayerTest Class

```
// LayerTest.java
package com.jdojo.layer.test;

import java.lang.module.Configuration;
import java.lang.module.ModuleFinder;
import java.lang.reflect.Method;
import java.nio.file.Path;
import java.nio.file.Paths;
import java.util.Set;

public class LayerTest {
    public static void main(String[] args) {
        /* Location for the custom module. You will need to change the
           path to point to a directory on your PC that contains the
           modular JAR for the com.jdojo.layer (version 2.0) module.
         */
        final String CUSTOM_MODULE_LOCATION = "C:\\Java9Revealed\\customLib";

        // Define the set of root modules to be resolved in the custom layer
        Set<String> rootModules = Set.of("com.jdojo.layer");

        // Create a custom layer
        ModuleLayer customLayer = createLayer(CUSTOM_MODULE_LOCATION, rootModules);

        // Test the class in the boot layer
        ModuleLayer bootLayer = ModuleLayer.boot();
        testLayer(bootLayer);
        System.out.println();

        // Test the class in the custom layer
        testLayer(customLayer);
    }

    public static ModuleLayer createLayer(String modulePath, Set<String> rootModules) {
        Path path = Paths.get(modulePath);

        // Define the module finders to be used in creating a
        // configuration for the custom layer
        ModuleFinder beforFinder = ModuleFinder.of(path);
        ModuleFinder afterFinder = ModuleFinder.of();
```

```java
        // Create a configuration for the custom layer
        Configuration parentConfig = ModuleLayer.boot().configuration();
        Configuration config =
                parentConfig.resolve(beforFinder, afterFinder, rootModules);

        /* Create a custom layer with one class loader. The parent for
           the class loader is the system class loader. The boot layer is
           the parent layer of this custom layer.
         */
        ClassLoader sysClassLoader = ClassLoader.getSystemClassLoader();
        ModuleLayer parentLayer = ModuleLayer.boot();
        ModuleLayer layer = parentLayer.defineModulesWithOneLoader(config, sysClassLoader);

        // Check if we loaded the module in this layer
        if (layer.modules().isEmpty()) {
            System.out.println("\nCould not find the module " + rootModules
                    + " at " + modulePath + ". "
                    + "Please make sure that the com.jdojo.layer.v2.jar exists "
                    + "at this location." + "\n");
        }

        return layer;
    }

    public static void testLayer(ModuleLayer layer) {
        final String moduleName = "com.jdojo.layer";
        final String className = "com.jdojo.layer.LayerInfo";
        final String methodName = "printInfo";

        try {
            // Load the class
            Class<?> cls = layer.findLoader(moduleName)
                                .loadClass(className);

            // Instantiate the class using its no-args constructor
            Object obj = cls.getConstructor().newInstance();

            // Find the method
            Method method = cls.getMethod(methodName);

            // Call the method that will print the details
            method.invoke(obj);
        } catch (Exception e) {
            e.printStackTrace();
        }
    }
}
```

I explain the logic in the LayerTest class by methods. The main() method declares a variable named CUSTOM_MODULE_LOCATION, which stores the location of version 2.0 of the com.jdojo.layer module. You must change the path to point to a directory on your computer that contains the compiled module code for version 2.0 of the com.jdojo.layer module.

```
final String CUSTOM_MODULE_LOCATION = "C:\\Java9Revealed\\customLib";
```

The code stores com.jdojo.layer as the sole root module for the custom layer's configuration:

```
Set<String> rootModules = Set.of("com.jdojo.layer");
```

The createLayer() method is called to create a custom layer. The method uses logic to create a custom layer with version 2.0 of the com.jdojo.layer module at CUSTOM_MODULE_LOCATION:

```
ModuleLayer customLayer = createLayer(CUSTOM_MODULE_LOCATION, rootModules);
```

The main() method obtains the reference of the boot layer:

```
ModuleLayer bootLayer = ModuleLayer.boot();
```

Now, the testLayer() method is called—once for boot layer and once for the custom layer. The method finds the class loader for the com.jdojo.layer module in the layer and loads the com.jdojo.layer.LayerInfo class.

```
final String moduleName = "com.jdojo.layer";
final String className = "com.jdojo.layer.LayerInfo";
final String methodName = "printInfo";
Class<?> cls = layer.findLoader(moduleName)
                    .loadClass(className);
```

An object of the LayerInfo class is created using its no-args constructor:

```
Object obj = cls.getConstructor().newInstance();
```

Finally, the reference of the printInfo() method of the LayerInfo class is obtained and the printInfo() method is invoked, which prints the details of the LayerInfo class:

```
Method method = cls.getMethod(methodName);
method.invoke(obj);
```

You can run the LayerTest class in NetBeans or using the following command. You may get a different output. The layer name is the list of all the modules in that layer, which is returned by the toString() method of the ModuleLayer class.

```
C:\Java9Revealed>java --module-path com.jdojo.layer.v1\dist;com.jdojo.layer.test\dist
--module com.jdojo.layer.test/com.jdojo.layer.test.LayerTest
```

```
Loading LayerInfo version 1.0
Class Version: 1.0
Class Name: com.jdojo.layer.LayerInfo
Class Loader: jdk.internal.loader.ClassLoaders$AppClassLoader@6e3c1e69
Module Name: com.jdojo.layer
Layer Name: java.security.jgss, jdk.unsupported, jdk.jlink, jdk.security.jgss, jdk.javadoc,
jdk.crypto.cryptoki, java.naming, jdk.jartool, java.xml.crypto, jdk.deploy, java.logging,
jdk.snmp, jdk.zipfs, jdk.crypto.mscapi, jdk.naming.dns, java.smartcardio, java.base, jdk.
crypto.ec, jdk.dynalink, jdk.compiler, java.compiler, jdk.jdeps, java.rmi, java.xml, com.
jdojo.layer.test, jdk.management, java.datatransfer, jdk.scripting.nashorn, java.desktop,
java.management, jdk.naming.rmi, java.scripting, jdk.localedata, jdk.accessibility,
jdk.charsets, com.jdojo.layer, java.security.sasl, jdk.security.auth, jdk.internal.opt,
java.prefs

Loading LayerInfo version 2.0
Class Version: 2.0
Class Name: com.jdojo.layer.LayerInfo
Class Loader: jdk.internal.loader.Loader@4cb2c100
Module Name: com.jdojo.layer
Layer Name: com.jdojo.layer
```

Summary

The Module API consists of classes and interfaces that give you programmatic access to modules. Using the API, you can programmatically read/modify/build module descriptors, load modules, read module's contents, create layers, etc. The Module API is small, comprising about 15 classes and interfaces spread across two packages: java.lang and java.lang.module. The Module, ModuleLayer, and LayerInstantiationException classes are in the java.lang package and the rest are in the java.lang. module package.

An instance of the Module class represents a runtime module. Every type loaded into the JVM belongs to a module. JDK 9 added a method named getModule() to the Class class that returns the module to which the class belongs.

An instance of the ModuleDescriptor class represents a module definition, which is created from a module declaration—typically from a module-info.class file. A module descriptor can also be created on the fly using the ModuleDescriptor.Builder class. A module declaration may be augmented using command-line options such as --add-reads, --add-exports, and --add-opens, and using methods in the Module class such as addReads(), addOpens(), and addExports(). A ModuleDescriptor represents a module descriptor that exists at the time of module declaration, not an augmented module descriptor. The getDescriptor() method of the Module class returns a ModuleDescriptor. A ModuleDescriptor is immutable. An unnamed module does not have a module descriptor. The getDescriptor() method of the Module class returns null for an unnamed module. The ModuleDescriptor class contains several nested classes, for example, the ModuleDescriptor.Requires nested class; each of them represents a module statement in programs.

You can augment a module descriptor using command-line options and programmatically using the Module API. You can put all queries for a module's properties in two categories: ones that may change after the module is loaded and ones that do not change after the module is loaded. The Module class contains methods for queries in the first category and the ModuleDescriptor class contains methods for queries in the second category.

You can update a module's definition at runtime using one of the methods in the Module class: addExports(), addOpens(), addReads(), and addUses().

You can use annotations on module declarations. The java.lang.annotation.ElementType enum has a new value called MODULE. You can use MODULE as a target type on an annotation declaration, which allows the annotation type to be used on modules. In Java 9, two annotations—java.lang.Deprecated and java. lang.SuppressWarnings—have been updated to be used on module declarations. Using these annotations on a module affects only the module declaration, not the types contained in the module.

Modules are arranged into layers. A layer is a set of resolved modules with a function that maps each module to a class loader that is responsible for loading all types in that module. The set of resolved module is called a *configuration*. Layers are arranged hierarchically. A layer has at least one parent layer, except the *empty* layer, which, as its name suggests, contains no modules and primarily exists to serve as the parent layer for the *boot* layer. The boot layer is created by the JVM at startup by resolving the application's initial modules (the root modules) against a set of observable modules. You can create custom layers. Layers allow multiple versions of the same module to be loaded into different layers and used in the same JVM.

CHAPTER 11

■ ■ ■

The Java Shell

In this chapter, you will learn:

- What the Java shell is
- What the JShell tool and the JShell API are
- How to configure the JShell tool
- How to use the JShell tool to evaluate snippets of Java code
- How to use the JShell API to evaluate snippets of Java code

What Is the Java Shell?

The Java shell, which is called JShell in JDK 9, is a command-line tool that provides an interactive way to access the Java programming language. It lets you evaluate snippets of Java code instead of forcing you to write an entire Java program. It is a REPL (Read-Eval-Print loop) for Java. JShell is also an API that you can use to develop an application to provide the same functionality as the JShell command-line tool.

Read-Eval-Print loop (REPL) is a command-line tool (also known as interactive language shell) that lets users evaluate snippets of code quickly without having to write a complete program. The name REPL comes from the three primitive functions in Lisp—read, eval, and print—used in a loop. The read function reads the user input and parses into a data structure; the eval function evaluates the parsed user input to yield a result; the print function prints the result. After the result is printed, the tool is ready to accept user input again, hence triggering a read-eval-print loop. The term REPL is used for an interactive tool that lets you interact with a programming language. Figure 11-1 shows a conceptual diagram for a REPL. A UNIX shell or a Windows command prompt acts like a REPL that reads an operating system command, executes it, prints the output, and waits to read another command.

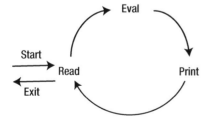

Figure 11-1. *A conceptual diagram for a read-eval-print loop*

© Kishori Sharan 2017
K. Sharan, *Java 9 Revealed*, DOI 10.1007/978-1-4842-2592-9_11

Why was JShell included in JDK 9? One of the main reasons to include it in JDK 9 was the feedback from academia that has a steep learning curve. Other programming languages such as Lisp, Python, Ruby, Groovy, and Clojure have been supporting REPL for a long time. Just to write a "Hello, world!" program in Java, you have to resort to an Edit-Compile-Execute loop (ECEL) that involves writing a full program, compiling it, and execute it. If you need to make a change, you must repeat these steps. Apart from some other housekeeping work such as defining the directory structure, compiling, and executing the program, the following is the minimum you have to write to print a "Hello, world!" message using the modular Java program in JDK 9:

```
// module-info.java
module HelloWorld {
}

// HelloWorld.java
package com.jdojo.intro;

public class HelloWorld {
    public static void main(String[] args) {
        System.out.println("Hello, world!");
    }
}
```

This program, when executed, prints a message on the console: "Hello, world!". Writing a full program to evaluate a simple expression such as this is overkill. This was the main reason academia was moving away from teaching Java as the initial programming language to students. Java designers listened to the feedback from teaching communities and introduced the JShell tool in JDK 9. To achieve the same as this program, you need to write only one line of code on a jshell command prompt:

```
jshell> System.out.println("Hello, world!")
Hello, world!

jshell>
```

The first line is the code you enter on the jshell command prompt; the second line is the output. After printing the output, the jshell prompt returns and you can enter another expression to evaluate.

■ **Tip** JShell is not a new language or a new compiler. It is a tool and an API used to access the Java programming language interactively. For beginners, it provides a way to explore the Java programming language quickly. For experienced developers, it provides a quick way to see results of a code snippet without having to compile and run an entire program. It also provides a way to quickly develop a prototype using an incremental approach. You add a snippet of code, get immediate feedback, and add another snippet code until your prototype is complete.

JDK 9 ships with a JShell command-line tool and the JShell API. All features supported by the tool are also supported by the API. That is, you can run snippets of code using the tool or programmatically using the API. You should be able to distinguish between the two using the context in this discussion. Most of the chapter is devoted to explaining the tool. At the end, I include a section describing the API with an example.

The JShell Architecture

The Java compiler does not recognize snippets such as method declarations or variable declarations by themselves. Only classes and `import` statements can be top-level constructs, which can exist by themselves. Other types of snippets have to be part of a class. JShell lets you execute snippets of Java code and lets you evolve them.

The guiding principle for the current JShell architecture is to use the existing Java language support and other Java technologies in the JDK to keep it compatible with the current and future versions of the language. As the Java language evolves over time, so will its support of JShell with little or no modification to the JShell implementation. Figure 11-2 shows the high-level architecture of JShell.

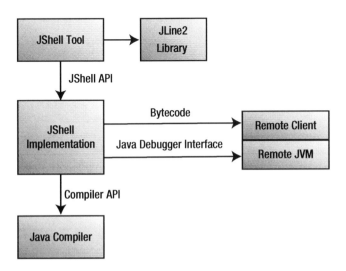

Figure 11-2. *The JShell architecture*

The JShell tool uses version 2 of JLine, which is a Java library for handling console input. The standard JDK compiler does not know how to parse and compile snippets of Java code. Therefore, the JShell implementation has its own parser that parses snippets and determines the type of snippets, for example, a method declaration, a variable declaration, etc. Once the snippet type is determined, the snippet is wrapped in a synthetic class using the following rules:

- Import statements are used "as-is". That is, all `import` statements are placed "as-is" at the top of the synthetic class.

- Variables, methods, and class declarations become static members of a synthetic class.

- Expressions and statements are wrapped in a synthetic method within a synthetic class.

All synthetic classes belong to a package called `REPL`. Once snippets are wrapped, the wrapped source code is analyzed and compiled by standard Java compiler using the Compiler API. The compiler takes the wrapped source code in string format as input and compiles it into bytecode, which is stored in memory. The generated bytecode is sent over a socket to a remote process running a JVM for loading and execution. Sometimes, existing snippets loaded into the remote JVM need to be replaced by the JShell tool, which it accomplishes using the Java Debugger API.

Starting the JShell Tool

JDK 9 ships with a JShell tool, which is located in the JDK_HOME\bin directory. The tool is named jshell. If you installed JDK 9 in the C:\java9 directory on Windows, you will have an executable file named C:\java9\bin\jshell.exe, which is the JShell tool. To start the JShell tool, you need to open a command prompt and enter the jshell command:

```
C:\Java9Revealed>jshell
|  Welcome to JShell -- Version 9-ea
|  For an introduction type: /help intro

jshell>
```

Entering the jshell command on the command prompt may give you an error:

```
C:\Java9Revealed>jshell
'jshell' is not recognized as an internal or external command,
operable program or batch file.

C:\Java9Revealed>
```

This error indicates that the JDK_HOME\bin directory is not included in the PATH environment variable on your computer. I installed JDK 9 in the C:\java9 directory, so the JDK_HOME is C:\java9 for me. To fix this error, you either include the C:\java9\bin directory in the PATH environment variable or use the full path of the jshell command, which would be C:\java9\bin\jshell for me. The following sequence of commands show you how to set the PATH environment variable on Windows and run the JShell tool:

```
C:\Java9Revealed>SET PATH=C:\java9\bin;%PATH%

C:\Java9Revealed>jshell
|  Welcome to JShell -- Version 9-ea
|  For an introduction type: /help intro

jshell>
```

The following command shows you how to use the full path of the jshell command to launch the tool:

```
C:\Java9Revealed>C:\java9\bin\jshell
|  Welcome to JShell -- Version 9-ea
|  For an introduction type: /help intro

jshell>
```

When jshell is launched successfully, it prints a welcome message with its version information. It also prints the command, which is /help intro. You can use this command to print a short introduction to the tool itself:

```
jshell> /help intro
|
|  intro
|
|  The jshell tool allows you to execute Java code, getting immediate results.
```

```
| You can enter a Java definition (variable, method, class, etc), like:  int x = 8
| or a Java expression, like:  x + x
| or a Java statement or import.
| These little chunks of Java code are called 'snippets'.
|
| There are also jshell commands that allow you to understand and
| control what you are doing, like:  /list
|
| For a list of commands: /help

jshell>
```

If you need help on the tool, you can enter the command /help on jshell to print a list of commands with their short descriptions:

```
jshell> /help
<<The output is not shown here.>>

jshell>
```

You can use several command-line options with the jshell command to pass values to the tool itself. For example, you can pass values to the compiler used to parse and compile snippets and to the remote JVM used to execute/evaluate snippet. Run the jshell program with a --help option to see a list of all available standard options. Run it with a --help-extra or -X option to see a list of all available non-standard options. For example, using these options, you can set class path and module path for the JShell tool. I explain these options later in this chapter.

You can also customize the startup scripts for the jshell tool using the command-line --start option. You can use DEFAULT and PRINTING as arguments to this option. The DEFAULT argument starts jshell with several import statements, so you do not need to import commonly used classes while you use jshell. The following two commands launch the jshell the same way:

- jshell
- jshell --start DEFAULT

You can use System.out.println() method to print messages to the standard output. You can launch jshell using the --start option with a PRINTING argument, which will include all versions of the System. out.print(), System.out.println(), and System.out.printf() methods as print(), println(), and printf() top-level methods. This will allow you to use print(), println(), and printf() methods on jshell instead of their longer versions, System.out.print(), System.out.println(), and System.out. printf().

```
C:\Java9Revealed>jshell --start PRINTING
| Welcome to JShell -- Version 9-ea
| For an introduction type: /help intro

jshell> println("hello")
hello

jshell>
```

You can repeat the `--start` option when you launch `jshell` to include the default `import` statements and the printing methods:

```
C:\Java9Revealed>jshell --start DEFAULT --start PRINTING
|  Welcome to JShell -- Version 9-ea
|  For an introduction type: /help intro

jshell>
```

Exiting the JShell Tool

To exit `jshell`, enter `/exit` on the `jshell` prompt and press Enter. The command prints a goodbye message, exits the tool, and returns you to the command prompt:

```
C:\Java9Revealed>jshell
|  Welcome to JShell -- Version 9-ea
|  For an introduction type: /help intro

jshell> /exit
|  Goodbye

C:\Java9Revealed>
```

The JShell tool is forgiving in a number of ways. If you use a keyword in a Java construct that is not supported, it simply ignores it. You can use partial commands. If the partial command you entered can be auto-completed to a unique command name, the tool would work as if you entered the full command. For example, `/edit` and `/exit` are two commands starting with `/e`. If you enter `/ex` instead of `/exit`, `jshell` will interpret it as an `/exit` command for you.

```
jshell> /ex
|  Goodbye

C:\Java9Revealed>
```

If you enter `/e`, you will receive an error because there are two possible commands starting with `/e`:

```
jshell> /e
|  Command: '/e' is ambiguous: /edit, /exit
|  Type /help for help.

jshell>
```

What Are Snippets and Commands?

You can use the JShell tool to:

- Evaluate snippets of Java code, which are simply called *snippets* in JShell terminology.

- Execute commands, which are used to query the JShell state and set the JShell environment.

To distinguish commands from snippets, all commands start with a slash (/). You have already seen a few of them in previous sections such as /exit and /help. Commands are used to interact with the tool itself, such as to customize its output, print help, exit the tool, and print the history of commands and snippets. I explain more commands later. If you are interested in learning all about the available commands, use the /help command.

Using the JShell tool, you write a fragment of Java code at a time and evaluate it. Those fragments of code are known as *snippets*. Snippets must follow the syntax specified in the Java Language Specification. Snippets can be:

- Import declarations

- Class declarations

- Interface declarations

- Method declarations

- Field declarations

- Statements

- Expressions

▨ **Tip**   You can use all Java language constructs in JShell, except for package declarations. All snippets in a JShell occur in an internal package named REPL and inside an internal synthetic class.

The JShell tool knows when you are done entering a snippet. When you press Enter, the tool will either execute the snippet if it is complete or take you to the next line and wait for you to complete the snippet. If a line begins with ...>, it means the snippet is not complete and you need to enter more text to complete the snippet. The default prompt for more input, which is ...>, can be customized. Here are a few examples:

```
C:\Java9Revealed>jshell
|  Welcome to JShell -- Version 9-ea
|  For an introduction type: /help intro

jshell> 2 + 2
$1 ==> 4

jshell> 2 +
   ...> 2
$2 ==> 4

jshell> 2
$3 ==> 2

jshell>
```

When you enter 2 + 2 and press Enter, jshell considers it as a complete snippet (an expression). It evaluates the expression and prints feedback that the expression was evaluated to 4 and the result was assigned to a variable named $1. The variable named $1 was automatically generated by the JShell tool. I explain variables generated by tools in more detail later. When you enter 2 + and press Enter, jshell prompts you to enter more input because 2 + is not a complete snippet in Java. When you enter 2 on the second line, the snippet is complete; jshell evaluates the snippet and prints feedback. When you enter 2 and press Enter, jshell evaluates the snippet because 2 is a complete expression by itself.

Evaluating Expressions

You can execute any valid Java expression in jshell. The following examples evaluate two expressions that add and multiply numbers:

```
jshell> 2 + 2
$1 ==> 4

jshell> 9.0 * 6
$2 ==> 54.0
```

When you evaluate an expression, jshell prints feedback if the expression evaluates to a value. In these cases, 2 + 2 evaluates to 4 and 9.0 * 6 evaluates to 54.0. The value of an expression is assigned to a variable. The feedback contains the name of the variable and the value of the expressions. In the first case, the feedback $1 ==> 4 means that the expression 2 + 2 evaluated to 4 and the result was assigned to a variable named $1. Similarly, the expression 9.0 * 6 was evaluated to 54.0 and the value was assigned to a variable named $2. You can use these variable names in other expressions. You can print their values by simply entering their names:

```
jshell> $1
$1 ==> 4

jshell> $2
$2 ==> 54.0

jshell> System.out.println($1)
4

jshell> System.out.println($2)
54.0
```

■ **Tip**   In jshell, you do not need to terminate a statement with a semicolon as you do in a Java program. The tool will insert the missing semicolons for you.

In Java, every variable has a data type. In these examples, what are the data types of the variables named $1 and $2? In Java, 2 + 2 evaluates to an int and 9.0 * 6 evaluates to a double. Therefore, the data types for the $1 and $2 variables should be int and double, respectively. How do you verify this? Let's first do it the hard way. You can cast $1 and $2 to an Object and invoke the getClass() method on them, which should give you Integer and Double. Note that primitive values of int and double types are boxed to Integer and Double reference types in these examples when you cast them as an Object:

```
jshell> 2 + 2
$1 ==> 4

jshell> 9.0 * 6
$2 ==> 54.0
```

```
jshell> ((Object)$1).getClass()
$3 ==> class java.lang.Integer

jshell> ((Object)$2).getClass()
$4 ==> class java.lang.Double

jshell>
```

There is an easier way to determine the data type of variables created by jshell—you just tell jshell to give you verbose feedback and it will print the data type of the variables it creates and much more! The following commands set the feedback mode to verbose and evaluate the same expressions:

```
jshell> /set feedback verbose
|  Feedback mode: verbose

jshell> 2 + 2
$1 ==> 4
|  created scratch variable $1 : int

jshell> 9.0 * 6
$2 ==> 54.0
|  created scratch variable $2 : double

jshell>
```

Notice that jshell printed the data types of the variables named $1 and $2 as int and double, respectively. It will be helpful for beginners to execute the following command using a -retain option, so the verbose feedback mode *persists* across the jshell sessions:

```
jshell> /set feedback -retain verbose
```

You can also use the /vars command to list all variables defined in jshell:

```
jshell> /vars
|    int $1 = 4
|    double $2 = 54.0

jshell>
```

If you want to use the normal feedback mode again, use the following command:

```
jshell> /set feedback -retain normal
|  Feedback mode: normal

Jshell>
```

You are not limited to evaluating simple expressions such as 2 + 2. You can evaluate any Java expression. The following example evaluates string concatenation expressions and uses methods of the String class. It also shows you how to use for loops:

```
jshell> "Hello " + "world! " + 2016
$1 ==> "Hello world! 2016"

jshell> $1.length()
$2 ==> 17

jshell> $1.toUpperCase()
$3 ==> "HELLO WORLD! 2016"

jshell> $1.split(" ")
$4 ==> String[3] { "Hello", "world!", "2016" }

jshell> for(String s : $4) {
   ...> System.out.println(s);
   ...> }
Hello
world!
2016

jshell>
```

Listing Snippets

Whatever you enter in jshell ends up being part of a snippet. Every snippet is assigned a unique snippet ID, which you can use to refer to the snippet later, for example, to drop the snippet. The /list command lists all snippets. It has the following forms:

- /list
- /list -all
- /list -start
- /list <snippet-name>
- /list <snippet-id>

The /list command without an argument/option prints all user-entered, active snippets, which may also have been opened from a file using the /open command.

Use the -all option to list all snippets—active, inactive, erroneous, and startup.

Use the -start option to list only the startup snippets. The startup snippets are cached and the -start option prints the cached snippets. It prints startup snippets even if you have dropped them in the current session.

Some of the snippet types have a name (e.g., variable/method declarations) and all snippets have an ID. Using the name or ID of a snippet with the /list command prints the snippet identified by that name or ID.

The /list command prints a list of snippets in the following format:

```
<snippet-id> : <snippet-source-code>
<snippet-id> : <snippet-source-code>
<snippet-id> : <snippet-source-code>
...
```

The JShell tool generates unique snippet IDs. They are s1, s2, s3... for startup snippets, 1, 2, 3..., and so on for valid snippets, and e1, e2, e3... for erroneous snippets. The following jshell session shows you how to list snippets using the /list command. The examples use the /drop command to drop snippets using a snippet name as well as a snippet ID.

```
C:\Java9Revealed>jshell
|  Welcome to JShell -- Version 9-ea
|  For an introduction type: /help intro

jshell> /list

jshell> 2 + 2
$1 ==> 4

jshell> /list

   1 : 2 + 2

jshell> int x = 100
x ==> 100

jshell> /list

   1 : 2 + 2
   2 : int x = 100;

jshell> /list -all

  s1 : import java.io.*;
  s2 : import java.math.*;
  s3 : import java.net.*;
  s4 : import java.nio.file.*;
  s5 : import java.util.*;
  s6 : import java.util.concurrent.*;
  s7 : import java.util.function.*;
  s8 : import java.util.prefs.*;
  s9 : import java.util.regex.*;
 s10 : import java.util.stream.*;
   1 : 2 + 2
   2 : int x = 100;
```

```
jshell> /list -start

  s1 : import java.io.*;
  s2 : import java.math.*;
  s3 : import java.net.*;
  s4 : import java.nio.file.*;
  s5 : import java.util.*;
  s6 : import java.util.concurrent.*;
  s7 : import java.util.function.*;
  s8 : import java.util.prefs.*;
  s9 : import java.util.regex.*;
 s10 : import java.util.stream.*;

jshell> string str = "using invalid type string"
|  Error:
|  cannot find symbol
|    symbol:   class string
|  string str = "using invalid type string";
|  ^----^

jshell> /list

   1 : 2 + 2
   2 : int x = 100;

jshell> /list -all

  s1 : import java.io.*;
  s2 : import java.math.*;
  s3 : import java.net.*;
  s4 : import java.nio.file.*;
  s5 : import java.util.*;
  s6 : import java.util.concurrent.*;
  s7 : import java.util.function.*;
  s8 : import java.util.prefs.*;
  s9 : import java.util.regex.*;
 s10 : import java.util.stream.*;
   1 : 2 + 2
   2 : int x = 100;
  e1 : string str = "using invalid type string";

jshell> /drop 1
|  dropped variable $1

jshell> /list

   2 : int x = 100;
```

```
jshell> /drop x
|  dropped variable x

jshell> /list

jshell> /list -all

   s1 : import java.io.*;
   s2 : import java.math.*;
   s3 : import java.net.*;
   s4 : import java.nio.file.*;
   s5 : import java.util.*;
   s6 : import java.util.concurrent.*;
   s7 : import java.util.function.*;
   s8 : import java.util.prefs.*;
   s9 : import java.util.regex.*;
  s10 : import java.util.stream.*;
    1 : 2 + 2
    2 : int x = 100;
   e1 : string str = "using invalid type string";

jshell>
```

The names of variables, methods, and classes become the snippet names. Note that Java allows you to have a variable, a method, and a class with the same name because they occur in their own namespaces. You can use the names of these entities to list them using the /list command:

```
C:\Java9Revealed>jshell
|  Welcome to JShell -- Version 9-ea
|  For an introduction type: /help intro

jshell> /list x
|  No such snippet: x

jshell> int x = 100
x ==> 100

jshell> /list x

   1 : int x = 100;

jshell> void x(){}
|  created method x()

jshell> /list x

   1 : int x = 100;
   2 : void x(){}
```

```
jshell> void x(int n) {}
|  created method x(int)

jshell> /list x

   1 : int x = 100;
   2 : void x(){}
   3 : void x(int n) {}

jshell> class x{}
|  created class x

jshell> /list x

   1 : int x = 100;
   2 : void x(){}
   3 : void x(int n) {}
   4 : class x{}

jshell>
```

Editing Snippets

The JShell tool offers several ways to edit snippets and commands. You can use navigation keys listed in Table 11-1 to navigate on the command line while entering snippets and commands in jshell. You can use keys listed in Table 11-2 to edit text entered on a line in jshell.

Table 11-1. *List of Navigation Keys While Editing in the JShell Tool*

Key	Description
Enter	Enters the current line
Left-Arrow	Moves one character backward
Right-Arrow	Moves one character forward
Ctrl-A	Moves to the beginning of the line
Ctrl-E	Moves to the end of the line
Meta-B (or Alt-B)	Moves a word backward
Meta-F (or Alt-F)	Moves a word forward

Table 11-2. *List of Keys to Modify Text on the JShell Tooll*

Key	Description
Delete	Deletes character under the cursor
Backspace	Deletes character before the cursor
Ctrl-K	Deletes the text from the cursor to the end of the line
Meta-D (or Alt-D)	Deletes the text from the cursor to the end of the word
Ctrl-W	Deletes the text from the cursor to the previous whitespace
Ctrl-Y	Pastes (or yanks) the most recently deleted text into the line
Meta-Y (or Alt-Y)	After Ctrl-Y, this key combination cycles through previously deleted text

It is hard to edit multi-line snippets in the JShell tool, even though you have access to a rich set of edit key combinations. The tool designer realized this problem and provided a built-in snippet editor. You can configure the JShell tool to use the platform-specific snippet editor of your choice. Refer to the section entitled "Setting the Snippet Editor" for more information on how to set up your own editor.

You need to use the /edit command to start editing a snippet. The command takes three forms:

- /edit <snippet-name>
- /edit <snippet-id>
- /edit

You can use the snippet name or snippet ID to edit a specific snippet. The /edit command without an argument opens all active snippets in an editor for editing. By default, the /edit command opens a built-in editor called JShell Edit Pad, and it is shown in Figure 11-3.

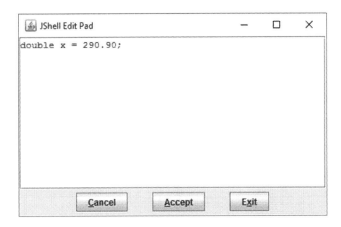

Figure 11-3. *The built-in JShell editor called JShell Edit Pad*

The JShell Edit Pad is written in Swing and it shows a `JFrame` with a `JTextArea` and three `JButtons`. If you edit snippets, make sure to click the Accept button before exiting the window so that the editing takes effect. If you cancel out or exit the editor without accepting the changes, your edits will be lost.

If you know the name of a variable, a method, or a class, you can edit it using its name. The following `jshell` session creates a variable, the methods, and a class with the same name x and uses the `/edit x` command to edit them all at once:

```
C:\Java9Revealed>jshell
|  Welcome to JShell -- Version 9-ea
|  For an introduction type: /help intro

jshell> int x = 100
x ==> 100

jshell> void x(){}
|  created method x()

jshell> void x (int n) {}
|  created method x(int)

jshell> class x{}
|  created class x

jshell> 2 + 2
$5 ==> 4

jshell> /edit x
```

The `/edit x` command opens all snippets with the name x in a JShell Edit Pad, as shown in Figure 11-4. You can edit these snippets, accept the changes, and exit the editing, to continue with the `jshell` session.

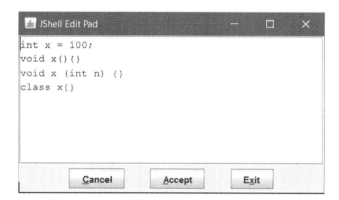

Figure 11-4. *Editing snippets by name*

Rerunning Previous Snippets

In a command-line tool like jshell, you'll often want to rerun previous snippets. You can use the Up/Down arrows to navigate through the snippet/command history and then press the Enter key when you are on a previous snippet/command. You can also use one of the three commands to rerun previous snippets (not commands):

- /!
- /<snippet-id>
- /-<n>

The /! command reruns the last snippet. The /<snippet-id> command reruns the snippet identified by <snippet-id>. The /-<n> command reruns the nth last snippet. For example, /-1 reruns the last snippet, /-2 reruns the second last snippet, and so on. The /! and /-1 commands have the same effect—they both rerun the last snippet.

Declaring Variables

You can declare variables in jshell as you do in Java programs. A variable declaration may occur at the top-level, inside a method, or as a field declaration within a class. The static and final modifiers are not allowed in top-level variable declarations. If use them, they will be ignored with a warning. The static modifier specifies a class context and the final modifier restricts you from changing the variable's value. You are not allowed to use these modifiers because the tool allows you to declare free-standing variables that you would like to experiment with by changing their values over time. The following examples show you how to declare variables:

```
c:\Java9Revealed>jshell
|  Welcome to JShell -- Version 9-ea
|  For an introduction type: /help intro

jshell> int x
x ==> 0

jshell> int y = 90
y ==> 90

jshell> side = 90
|  Error:
|  cannot find symbol
|    symbol:   variable side
|  side = 90
|  ^--^
```

```
jshell> static double radius = 2.67
|   Warning:
|   Modifier 'static'  not permitted in top-level declarations, ignored
|   static double radius = 2.67;
|   ^----^
radius ==> 2.67

jshell> String str = new String("Hello")
str ==> "Hello"

jshell>
```

Using an undeclared variable in top-level expressions generates an error. Notice the use of an undeclared variable named side in the previous example, which generated an error. I show you later that you can use an undeclared variable inside a method's body.

It is also possible to change the data type of a variable. You can declare a variable named x as an int and re-declare it later as a double or a String. The following examples show this feature:

```
jshell> int x = 10;
x ==> 10

jshell> int y = x + 2;
y ==> 12

jshell> double x = 2.71
x ==> 2.71

jshell> y
y ==> 12

jshell> String x = "Hello"
x ==> "Hello"

jshell> y
y ==> 12

jshell>
```

Notice that the value of the variable named y did not change or was not reevaluated when the data type or the value of x changed.

You can also drop a variable using the /drop command, which takes the variable name as an argument. The following command will drop the variable named x:

```
jshell> /drop x
```

You can list all variables in jshell using the /vars command. It will list user-declared variables and the variables automatically declared by jshell, which happens while jshell evaluates result-bearing expressions. The command has the following forms:

- /vars
- /vars <variable-name>
- /vars <variable-snippet-id>
- /vars -start
- /vars -all

The command without an argument lists all active variables in the current session. If you use a snippet name or ID, it lists the variable declaration with that snippet name or ID. If you use it with the -start option, it lists all variables added to the startup script. If you use it with the -all option, it lists all variables including failed, overwritten, dropped, and startup. The following examples show you how to use the /vars command:

```
c:\Java9Revealed>jshell
|  Welcome to JShell -- Version 9-ea
|  For an introduction type: /help intro

jshell> /vars

jshell> 2 + 2
$1 ==> 4

jshell> /vars
|    int $1 = 4

jshell> int x = 20;
x ==> 20

jshell> /vars
|    int $1 = 4
|    int x = 20

jshell> String str = "Hello";
str ==> "Hello"

jshell> /vars
|    int $1 = 4
|    int x = 20
|    String str = "Hello"

jshell> double x = 90.99;
x ==> 90.99
```

```
jshell> /vars
|    int $1 = 4
|    String str = "Hello"
|    double x = 90.99

jshell> /drop x
|    dropped variable x

jshell> /vars
|    int $1 = 4
|    String str = "Hello"

jshell>
```

Import Statements

You can use import statements in jshell. Recall that, in a Java program, all types in the java.lang package are imported by default. To use types from other packages, you need to add appropriate import statements in your compilation unit. We'll start with an example. I will try to create three objects: a String, a List<Integer>, and a ZonedDateTime. Note that the String class is in the java.lang package; the List and Integer classes are in the java.util and java.lang packages, respectively; and the ZonedDateTime class is in the java.time package.

```
jshell> String str = new String("Hello")
str ==> "Hello"

jshell> List<Integer> nums = List.of(1, 2, 3, 4, 5)
nums ==> [1, 2, 3, 4, 5]

jshell> ZonedDateTime now = ZonedDateTime.now()
|    Error:
|    cannot find symbol
|      symbol:   class ZonedDateTime
|    ZonedDateTime now = ZonedDateTime.now();
|    ^-----------^
|    Error:
|    cannot find symbol
|      symbol:   variable ZonedDateTime
|    ZonedDateTime now = ZonedDateTime.now();
|                        ^-----------^

jshell>
```

The examples generate an error if you try to use the ZonedDateTime class from the java.time package. We were also expecting a similar error when we try to create a List because it is in the java.util package, which is not imported in a Java program by default.

The sole purpose of the JShell tool is to make developers' lives easier when evaluating snippets. To achieve this goal, the tool imports all types from a few packages by default. What are those default packages whose types are imported? You can print a list of all active imports in `jshell` using the `/imports` command:

```
jshell> /imports
|    import java.io.*
|    import java.math.*
|    import java.net.*
|    import java.nio.file.*
|    import java.util.*
|    import java.util.concurrent.*
|    import java.util.function.*
|    import java.util.prefs.*
|    import java.util.regex.*
|    import java.util.stream.*

jshell>
```

Notice the default `import` statement that imports all types from the `java.util` package. This is the reason that you can create a list without importing it. You can also add your own imports to `jshell`. The following example shows you how to import the `ZonedDateTime` class and use it. You will get different output when `jshell` prints the value of the current date with the time zone.

```
jshell> /imports
|    import java.util.*
|    import java.io.*
|    import java.math.*
|    import java.net.*
|    import java.util.concurrent.*
|    import java.util.prefs.*
|    import java.util.regex.*

jshell> import java.time.*

jshell> /imports
|    import java.io.*
|    import java.math.*
|    import java.net.*
|    import java.nio.file.*
|    import java.util.*
|    import java.util.concurrent.*
|    import java.util.function.*
|    import java.util.prefs.*
|    import java.util.regex.*
|    import java.util.stream.*
|    import java.time.*

jshell> ZonedDateTime now = ZonedDateTime.now()
now ==> 2016-11-11T10:39:10.497234400-06:00[America/Chicago]

jshell>
```

Note that any imports you add to the jshell session will be lost when you exit the session. You can also drop import statements—the imports and the ones you added. You need to know the snippet ID to drop a snippet. The IDs for startup snippets are s1, s2, s3, etc. and for user-defined snippets, they are 1, 2, 3, etc. The following examples show you how to add and drop import statements in jshell:

```
C:\Java9Revealed>jshell
|  Welcome to JShell -- Version 9-ea
|  For an introduction type: /help intro

jshell> import java.time.*

jshell> List<Integer> list = List.of(1, 2, 3, 4, 5)
list ==> [1, 2, 3, 4, 5]

jshell> ZonedDateTime now = ZonedDateTime.now()
now ==> 2017-02-19T21:08:08.802099-06:00[America/Chicago]

jshell> /list -all

   s1 : import java.io.*;
   s2 : import java.math.*;
   s3 : import java.net.*;
   s4 : import java.nio.file.*;
   s5 : import java.util.*;
   s6 : import java.util.concurrent.*;
   s7 : import java.util.function.*;
   s8 : import java.util.prefs.*;
   s9 : import java.util.regex.*;
  s10 : import java.util.stream.*;
    1 : import java.time.*;
    2 : List<Integer> list = List.of(1, 2, 3, 4, 5);
    3 : ZonedDateTime now = ZonedDateTime.now();

jshell> /drop s5

jshell> /drop 1

jshell> /list -all

   s1 : import java.io.*;
   s2 : import java.math.*;
   s3 : import java.net.*;
   s4 : import java.nio.file.*;
   s5 : import java.util.*;
   s6 : import java.util.concurrent.*;
   s7 : import java.util.function.*;
   s8 : import java.util.prefs.*;
   s9 : import java.util.regex.*;
  s10 : import java.util.stream.*;
    1 : import java.time.*;
    2 : List<Integer> list = List.of(1, 2, 3, 4, 5);
    3 : ZonedDateTime now = ZonedDateTime.now();
```

```
jshell> /imports
|    import java.io.*
|    import java.math.*
|    import java.net.*
|    import java.nio.file.*
|    import java.util.concurrent.*
|    import java.util.function.*
|    import java.util.prefs.*
|    import java.util.regex.*
|    import java.util.stream.*

jshell> List<Integer> list2 = List.of(1, 2, 3, 4, 5)
|  Error:
|  cannot find symbol
|    symbol:   class List
|  List<Integer> list2 = List.of(1, 2, 3, 4, 5);
|  ^--^
|  Error:
|  cannot find symbol
|    symbol:   variable List
|  List<Integer> list2 = List.of(1, 2, 3, 4, 5);
|                        ^--^

jshell> import java.util.*
|    update replaced variable list, reset to null

jshell> List<Integer> list2 = List.of(1, 2, 3, 4, 5)
list2 ==> [1, 2, 3, 4, 5]

jshell> /list -all

   s1 : import java.io.*;
   s2 : import java.math.*;
   s3 : import java.net.*;
   s4 : import java.nio.file.*;
   s5 : import java.util.*;
   s6 : import java.util.concurrent.*;
   s7 : import java.util.function.*;
   s8 : import java.util.prefs.*;
   s9 : import java.util.regex.*;
  s10 : import java.util.stream.*;
    1 : import java.time.*;
    2 : List<Integer> list = List.of(1, 2, 3, 4, 5);
    3 : ZonedDateTime now = ZonedDateTime.now();
   e1 : List<Integer> list2 = List.of(1, 2, 3, 4, 5);
    4 : import java.util.*;
    5 : List<Integer> list2 = List.of(1, 2, 3, 4, 5);
```

```
jshell> /imports
|    import java.io.*
|    import java.math.*
|    import java.net.*
|    import java.nio.file.*
|    import java.util.concurrent.*
|    import java.util.function.*
|    import java.util.prefs.*
|    import java.util.regex.*
|    import java.util.stream.*
|    import java.util.*

jshell>
```

Method Declarations

You can declare and call methods in jshell. You can declare top-level methods, which are methods that are entered in jshell directly and are not inside any class. You can also declare classes (see the next section) with methods. In this section, I show you how to declare and call top-level methods. You can also call methods of existing classes. The following example declares a method named square() and calls it:

```
jshell> long square(int n) {
   ...>    return n * n;
   ...> }
|  created method square(int)

jshell> square(10)
$2 ==> 100

jshell> long n2 = square(37)
n2 ==> 1369

jshell>
```

Forward references are allowed inside a method's body. That is, you can refer to methods or variables, which are not declared yet, inside a method's body. The method being declared cannot be called until all missing referenced methods and variables are defined.

```
jshell> long multiply(int n) {
   ...>    return multiplier * n;
   ...> }
|  created method multiply(int), however, it cannot be invoked until variable multiplier is
declared

jshell> multiply(10)
|  attempted to call method multiply(int) which cannot be invoked until variable multiplier
is declared

jshell> int multiplier = 2
multiplier ==> 2
```

```
jshell> multiply(10)
$6 ==> 20

jshell> void printCube(int n) {
    ...>        System.out.printf("Cube of %d is %d.%n", n, cube(n));
    ...> }
|  created method printCube(int), however, it cannot be invoked until method cube(int) is
declared

jshell> long cube(int n) {
    ...>        return n * n * n;
    ...> }
|  created method cube(int)

jshell> printCube(10)
Cube of 10 is 1000.

jshell>
```

This example declares a method named multiply(int n). It multiplies the argument with a variable named multiplier, which has not been declared yet. Notice the feedback printed after you declare this method. The feedback clearly states that you cannot call the multiply() method until you declare the multiplier variable. Calling the method generates an error. Later, the multiplier variable is declared and the multiply() method is called successfully.

▓ **Tip**   You can also declare a recursive method using a forward reference.

Type Declarations

You can declare all types such as classes, interfaces, enums, and annotations in jshell as you do in Java. The following jshell session creates a class named Counter, creates its object, and calls its methods:

```
jshell> class Counter {
    ...>        private int counter;
    ...>        public synchronized int next() {
    ...>            return ++counter;
    ...>        }
    ...>
    ...>        public int current() {
    ...>            return counter;
    ...>        }
    ...> }
|  created class Counter

jshell> Counter c = new Counter();
c ==> Counter@25bbe1b6
```

```
jshell> c.current()
$3 ==> 0

jshell> c.next()
$4 ==> 1

jshell> c.next()
$5 ==> 2

jshell> c.current()
$6 ==> 2

jshell>
```

You can use the /types command to print a list of all declared types in jshell. The command has the following forms:

- /types
- /types <type-name>
- /types <snippet-id>
- /types -start
- /types -all

The command without an argument lists the current active jshell classes, interfaces, and enums. Commands with a type name and a snippet ID arguments the list types with the specified name and specified snippet ID, respectively. The command with the -start option lists the automatically added startup types. The command with the -all option lists all types, including failed, overwritten, dropped, and startup. The following jshell is a continuation of the previous example session; it shows how to print all active types defined in a jshell session:

```
jshell> /types
|    class Counter

jshell>
```

The Counter class is small. You may quickly realize that it is not easy to enter the source code for bigger classes on a command line. You want to use your favorite Java source code editor such as NetBeans to write the source code and quickly test your classes in jshell. You can open a source code file as a source input in jshell using the /open command. The syntax is as follows:

```
/open <file-path>
```

You can find the source code for the Counter class in the Java9Revealed/com.jdojo.jshell/src/Counter.java file. The following jshell session shows you how to open the saved Counter.java file in jshell. It is assumed that you have saved the source code for this book in C:\ on Windows. If you are using another operating system, just follow the file-path naming convention and your directory structure to use the following example.

```
jshell> /open C:\Java9Revealed\com.jdojo.jshell\src\Counter.java

jshell> Counter c = new Counter()
c ==> Counter@25bbe1b6

jshell> c.current()
$3 ==> 0

jshell> c.next()
$4 ==> 1

jshell> c.next()
$5 ==> 2

jshell> c.current()
$6 ==> 2

jshell>
```

Note that the source code for the Counter class does not contain a package declaration because jshell does not allow you to declare a class (or any type) in a package. All types that you declare in jshell are considered static types of an internal synthetic class. However, you may want to test your own class that is in a package. You can use an already compiled class, which is in a package, in jshell. You will usually need it when you are using libraries to develop your application and you want to experiment with your application logic by writing snippets against library classes. You will need to set the class path using the /env command, so your classes may be found.

A Person class in the com.jdojo.jshell package is included in the book's source code. The class declaration is as shown in Listing 11-1.

Listing 11-1. The Source Code for a Person Class

```java
// Person.java
package com.jdojo.jshell;

public class Person {
    private String name;

    public Person() {
        this.name = "Unknown";
    }

    public Person(String name) {
        this.name = name;
    }

    public String getName() {
        return name;
    }

    public void setName(String name) {
        this.name = name;
    }
}
```

The following jshell command sets the class path on Windows assuming the source code for this book was stored in C:\. Use the syntax for the class path string for your operating system and the source code location on your computer if they are different from the assumed.

```
jshell> /env -class-path C:\Java9Revealed\com.jdojo.jshell\build\classes
|  Setting new options and restoring state.

jshell> Person guy = new Person("Martin Guy Crawford")
|  Error:
|  cannot find symbol
|    symbol:   class Person
|  Person guy = new Person("Martin Guy Crawford");
|  ^----^
|  Error:
|  cannot find symbol
|    symbol:   class Person
|  Person guy = new Person("Martin Guy Crawford");
|                  ^----^
```

Do you know the reason for this error? We used the simple name of the class, Person, without importing it and jshell was not able to locate the class. We need to import the Person class or use its fully qualified name. The following is a continuation of this jshell session that fixes this error:

```
jshell> import com.jdojo.jshell.Person

jshell> Person guy = new Person("Martin Guy Crawford")
guy ==> com.jdojo.jshell.Person@192b07fd

jshell> guy.getName()
$9 ==> "Martin Guy Crawford"

jshell> guy.setName("Forrest Butts")

jshell> guy.getName()
$11 ==> "Forrest Butts"

jshell>
```

Setting Execution Environment

In the previous section, you learned how to set the class path using the /env command. The command can be used to set many other components of the execution context such as the module path. You can also use to resolve modules, so you can use types in modules on jshell. Its complete syntax is as follows:

```
/env [-class-path <path>] [-module-path <path>] [-add-modules <modules>]
[-add-exports <m/p=n>]
```

The /env command without arguments prints values for the current execution context. The -class-path option sets the class path. The -module-path option sets the module path. The -add-modules option adds modules to the default set of root modules, so they can be resolved. You can use special values—ALL-DEFAULT, ALL-SYSTEM, and ALL-MODULE-PATH—with the -add-modules option to resolve the modules. Refer to Chapter 2 for the meanings of these special values. The -add-exports option exports non-exported packages from a module to a set of modules. These options have the same meanings as they have when used with the javac and java commands.

▒ **Tip**   On the command line, these options must start with two dashes, for example, --module-path. In jshell, they can start with one dash or two dashes. For example, both -module-path and --module-path are allowed in jshell.

When you set the execution context, the current session is reset and all previously executed snippets in the current session are replayed in quiet mode. That is, the replayed snippets are not shown. However, errors during the replay will be shown.

You can set the execution context using the /env, /reset, and /reload commands. Each of these command has different effects. The meaning of the context options such as -class-path and -module-path are the same. You can list all options that can be used to set the execution context using the command -/help context.

Let's walk through an example of using the module-related settings using the /env command. You created a com.jdojo.intro module in Chapter 3. The module contains a package named com.jdojo.intro, but it does not export the package. Now, you want to call the static main(String[] args) method of the Welcome class in the non-exported package. Here are the steps you need to perform in jshell:

- Set the module path, so the module will be found.

- Resolve the module by adding it to the default set of root modules. You can do this using the -add-modules option with the /env command.

- Export the package using the -add-exports command. The snippets entered in jshell are executed in an unnamed module, so you will need to export the package to all unnamed modules using the ALL-UNNAMED keyword. If you do not supply target modules in the -add-exports option, ALL-UNNAMED is assumed and the package is exported to all unnamed modules.

- Optionally, import the com.jdojo.intro.Welcome class if you want to use its simple name in snippets.

- Now, you will be able to call the Welcome.main() method from jshell.

The following jshell session shows you how to perform these steps. It is assumed that you are launching the jshell session with C:\Java9Revealed as the current directory and the C:\Java9Revealed\com.jdojo.intro\build\classes directory contains the compiled code for the com.jdojo.intro module. If your directory structure and the current directory are different, substitute the directory paths used in session with yours.

```
C:\Java9Revealed>jshell
|  Welcome to JShell -- Version 9-ea
|  For an introduction type: /help intro

jshell> /env -module-path com.jdojo.intro\build\classes
|  Setting new options and restoring state.

jshell> /env -add-modules com.jdojo.intro
|  Setting new options and restoring state.

jshell> /env -add-exports com.jdojo.intro/com.jdojo.intro=ALL-UNNAMED
|  Setting new options and restoring state.

jshell> import com.jdojo.intro.Welcome

jshell> Welcome.main(null)
Welcome to the Module System.
Module Name: com.jdojo.intro

jshell> /env
|       --module-path com.jdojo.intro\build\classes
|       --add-modules com.jdojo.intro
|       --add-exports com.jdojo.intro/com.jdojo.intro=ALL-UNNAMED

jshell>
```

No Checked Exceptions

In a Java program, if you call a method that throws checked exceptions, you must handle those exceptions using a try-catch block or by adding a throws clause. The JShell tool is supposed to be a quick and easy way to evaluate snippets, so you do not need to handle checked exceptions in your jshell snippets. If a snippet throws a checked exception when it's executed, jshell will print the stack trace and continue.

```
jshell> FileReader fr = new FileReader("secrets.txt")
|  java.io.FileNotFoundException thrown: secrets.txt (The system cannot find the file specified)
|        at FileInputStream.open0 (Native Method)
|        at FileInputStream.open (FileInputStream.java:196)
|        at FileInputStream.<init> (FileInputStream.java:139)
|        at FileInputStream.<init> (FileInputStream.java:94)
|        at FileReader.<init> (FileReader.java:58)
|        at (#1:1)

jshell>
```

This snippet threw a `FileNotFoundException` because a file named `secrets.txt` does not exist in the current directory. If the file existed, you were able to create a `FileReader` without having to use a `try-catch` block. Note that if you try to use this snippet inside a method, the normal Java syntax rule applies and your method declaration will not compile:

```
jshell> void readSecrets() {
   ...> FileReader fr = new FileReader("secrets.txt");
   ...> // More code goes here
   ...> }
|  Error:
|  unreported exception java.io.FileNotFoundException; must be caught or declared to be thrown
|  FileReader fr = new FileReader("secrets.txt");
|                   ^--------------------------^

jshell>
```

Auto-Completion

The `JShell` tool has an auto-completion feature that you can invoke by entering partial text and pressing the Tab key. This feature is available when you are entering a command or a snippet. The tool will detect the context and help you auto-complete the command. When there are multiple possibilities, it shows all possibilities and you will need to enter one of them manually. When it finds a unique possibility, it will complete the text.

▓ **Warning**   At the time of this writing, the auto-completion keys described in this section are being reworked. The proposal is to combine the functionality of the `Tab` and `Tab+Shift` keys into one `Tab` key, and combine the functionality of the `<fix>` key (Alt+Enter or Alt+F1) into the `Tab+Shift` key. The status of these proposed changes is tracked at `https://bugs.openjdk.java.net/browse/JDK-8177076`. You can use the `/help shortcuts` command on the JShell tool to see the currently available auto-completion keys.

The following is an example of the tool finding multiple possibilities. You need to enter /e and press Tab:

```
jshell> /e
/edit    /exit

jshell> /e
```

The tool detected that you were trying to enter a command because your text started with a slash (/). There are two commands (/edit and /exit) that start with /e, and they are printed for you. Now you will need to complete the command yourself by entering the rest of the command. In case of commands, if you enter just enough text to make the command name unique and press Enter, the tool will execute that command. In this case, you can enter /ed or /ex and press Enter to execute the /edit or /exit command, respectively. You can enter a slash (/) and press Tab to see a list of commands:

```
jshell> /
/!           /?           /drop        /edit        /env         /exit        /help
/history     /imports     /list        /methods     /open        /reload      /reset
/save        /set         /types       /vars
```

The following snippet creates a String variable named str with an initial value of "GoodBye":

```
jshell> String str = "GoodBye"
str ==> "GoodBye"
```

Continuing with this jshell session, enter str. and press Tab:

```
jshell> str.
charAt(              chars()              codePointAt(
codePointBefore(     codePointCount(      codePoints()
compareTo(           compareToIgnoreCase( concat(
contains(            contentEquals(       endsWith(
equals(              equalsIgnoreCase(    getBytes(
getChars(            getClass()           hashCode()
indexOf(             intern()             isEmpty()
lastIndexOf(         length()             matches(
notify()             notifyAll()          offsetByCodePoints(
regionMatches(       replace(             replaceAll(
replaceFirst(        split(               startsWith(
subSequence(         substring(           toCharArray()
toLowerCase(         toString()           toUpperCase(
trim()               wait(
```

This snippet printed all method names for the String class that you can invoke on the variable str. Notice that a few method names end with () and others end with only (. This is not a bug. If a method takes no arguments, its name is following with a (). If a method takes arguments, its name is followed with a (.

Continuing with this example, enter str.sub and press Tab:

```
jshell> str.sub
subSequence(   substring(
```

This time, the tool found two methods in the String class that start with sub. You can enter the entire method call, str.substring(0, 4), and press Enter to evaluate the snippet:

```
jshell> str.substring(0, 4)
$2 ==> "Good"
```

Alternatively, you can let the tool auto-complete the method name by entering `str.subs`. When you enter `str.subs` and press Tab, the tool completes the method name, inserts a (, and waits for you to enter the arguments for the method:

```
jshell> str.substring(
substring(

jshell> str.substring(
```

Now you can enter the method's argument and press Enter to evaluate the expression:

```
jshell> str.substring(0, 4)
$3 ==> "Good"

jshell>
```

When a method takes arguments, most likely you would like to see those arguments' types. You can see the method's synopsis by pressing Shift+Tab after you enter the entire method/constructor name and an opening parenthesis. In the previous example, if you enter `str.substring(` and press Shift+Tab, the tool will print the synopsis for the `substring()` method:

```
jshell> str.substring(
String String.substring(int beginIndex)
String String.substring(int beginIndex, int endIndex)
<press shift-tab again to see javadoc>
```

Notice the output. It says if you press Shift+Tab again, it will show you the Javadoc for the `substring()` method. In the following prompt, I pressed Shift+Tab again to print the Javadoc. If more of the Javadoc needs to be displayed, press the spacebar or type Q to return to the `jshell` prompt:

```
jshell> str.substring(
String String.substring(int beginIndex)
Returns a string that is a substring of this string.The substring begins with
the character at the specified index and extends to the end of this string.
Examples:
     "unhappy".substring(2) returns "happy"
     "Harbison".substring(3) returns "bison"
     "emptiness".substring(9) returns "" (an empty string)

Parameters:
beginIndex - the beginning index, inclusive.

Returns:
the specified substring.
String String.substring(int beginIndex, int endIndex)
Returns a string that is a substring of this string.The substring begins at the
specified beginIndex and extends to the character at index endIndex - 1 . Thus
the length of the substring is endIndex-beginIndex .
Examples:
     "hamburger".substring(4, 8) returns "urge"
     "smiles".substring(1, 5) returns "mile"
```

```
Parameters:
beginIndex - the beginning index, inclusive.
endIndex - the ending index, exclusive.

Returns:
the specified substring.

jshell> str.substring(
```

At times, you enter an expression and want to assign the value of the expression to a variable of the appropriate type. Sometimes you know the type and sometimes you don't. The JShell tool will help you auto-complete the assignment part after you enter the complete expression. Enter the complete expression and then press Alt+Enter or Alt+F1 depending on your platform. Now, press Alt+V, which will auto-complete the expression assignment by adding the appropriate variable type and placing the cursor to the position where you can enter the variable name. Let's walk through these steps. Enter the expression 2 + 2 into jshell:

```
jshell> 2 + 2
```

Now, on Windows, press Alt+Enter followed by Alt+V. jshell auto-completes the assignment expression and waits for you to enter the variable name:

```
jshell> int   = 2 + 2
```

The cursor is placed just before the = symbol. Enter x as the variable name and press Enter:

```
jshell> int x = 2 + 2
x ==> 4

jshell>
```

The command prompt in Windows is maximized when you execute these commands. You can press Alt+Enter to return to the normal window.

Snippets and Commands History

JShell maintains a history of all commands and snippets that you enter in all sessions. You can navigate through the history using the Up and Down arrow keys. You can also use the /history command to print the history of all you typed in the current session:

```
jshell> 2 + 2
$1 ==> 4

jshell> System.out.println("Hello")
Hello

jshell> /history

2 + 2
System.out.println("Hello")
/history

jshell>
```

At this point, pressing the Up arrow once shows /history, pressing it twice shows System.out. println("Hello"), and pressing it three times shows 2 + 2. Pressing the Up arrow a fourth time will show you the last entered command/snippet from the previous jshell session. If you want to execute a previously entered snippet/command, use the Up arrow until the desired command/snippet is shown, and then press Enter to execute it. Pressing the Down arrow navigates you to the next command or snippet in the list. Suppose you press the Up arrow five times to navigate to the fifth last snippet/command. Now pressing the Down arrow will navigate you to the fourth last snippet/command. When you are at the first and the last snippet/commands, pressing the Up arrow or the Down arrow does nothing.

Reading JShell Stack Trace

Snippets entered on jshell are part of a synthetic class. For example, Java does not let you declare a top-level method. A method declaration must be part of a type. When an exception is thrown in a Java program, the stack trace prints the type names and the line numbers. In jshell, an exception may be thrown from a snippet. Printing the synthetic class name and line numbers in such cases will be misleading and will make no sense to developers. The format for the location of the code in snippets in the stack trace will be of the form:

```
at <snippet-name> (#<snippet-id>:<line-number-in-snippet>)
```

Note that some snippets may not have a name. For example, entering a snippet 2 + 2 will not give it a name. Some snippets have name such as a snippet declaring a variable is assigned the same name as the variable's name; the same goes with a method and a type declaration. Sometimes, you may have two snippets with the same name, for example, by declaring variable and a method/type with the same name. jshell assigns a unique snippet ID to all snippets. You can find the ID of a snippet using the /list -all command.

The following jshell session declares a divide() method and prints the exception stack trace with a runtime ArithmeticException exception that is thrown when an integer is divided by zero:

```
C:\Java9Revealed>jshell
|  Welcome to JShell -- Version 9-ea
|  For an introduction type: /help intro

jshell> int divide(int x, int y) {
   ...> return x/y;
   ...> }
|  created method divide(int,int)

jshell> divide(10, 2)
$2 ==> 5

jshell> divide(10, 0)
|  java.lang.ArithmeticException thrown: / by zero
|        at divide (#1:2)
|        at (#3:1)
```

```
jshell> /list -all

   s1 : import java.io.*;
   s2 : import java.math.*;
   s3 : import java.net.*;
   s4 : import java.nio.file.*;
   s5 : import java.util.*;
   s6 : import java.util.concurrent.*;
   s7 : import java.util.function.*;
   s8 : import java.util.prefs.*;
   s9 : import java.util.regex.*;
  s10 : import java.util.stream.*;
    1 : int divide(int x, int y) {
         return x/y;
         }
    2 : divide(10, 2)
    3 : divide(10, 0)

jshell>
```

Let's try to read the stack trace. The last line, at (#3:1), is stating that the exception was caused at line 1 of snippet number 3. Notice in the output of the /list -all command that the snippet number 3 is the expression divide(10, 0) that caused the exception. The second line, at divide (#1:2), is indicating that the second level in the stack trace is at line 2 of the snippet with a name divide whose snippet ID 1.

Reusing JShell Sessions

You can enter many snippets and commands in a jshell session and may want to reuse them in other sessions. You can use the /save command to save commands and snippets to a file and use the /open command to load the previously saved commands and snippets. The syntax for the /save command is as follows:

```
/save <option> <file-path>
```

Here, <option> can be one of the options: -all, -history, and -start. <file-path> is the file path where the snippets/commands will be saved.

The /save command with no option saves all active snippets in the current sessions. Note that it does not save any commands or failed snippets.

The /save command with the -all option saves all snippets for the current session to the specified file, including failed and startup snippets. Note that it does not save any commands.

The /save command with the -history option saves everything that you typed in jshell since it was launched.

The /save command with the -start option saves the default startup definitions to the specified file.

You can reload the snippets from a file using the /open command. The command takes the filename as an argument.

The following jshell session declares a class named Counter, creates its object, and invokes methods on the object. Finally, it saves all active snippets to a file named jshell.jsh. Note that the file extension .jsh is customary for jshell files. You can use any other extension you want.

```
C:\Java9Revealed>jshell
|  Welcome to JShell -- Version 9-ea
|  For an introduction type: /help intro

jshell> class Counter {
    ...>     private int count;
    ...>     public synchronized int next() {
    ...>       return ++count;
    ...>     }
    ...>     public int current() {
    ...>       return count;
    ...>     }
    ...> }
|  created class Counter

jshell> Counter counter = new Counter()
counter ==> Counter@25bbe1b6

jshell> counter.current()
$3 ==> 0

jshell> counter.next()
$4 ==> 1

jshell> counter.next()
$5 ==> 2

jshell> counter.current()
$6 ==> 2

jshell> /save jshell.jsh

jshell> /exit
|  Goodbye
```

At this point, you should have a file named jshell.jsh in your current directory with the contents shown in Listing 11-2.

Listing 11-2. Contents of the jshell.jsh File

```
class Counter {
   private int count;
   public synchronized int next() {
     return ++count;
   }
   public int current() {
     return count;
   }
}
Counter counter = new Counter();
counter.current()
counter.next()
counter.next()
counter.current()
```

The following jshell session opens the jshell.jsh file, which will replay all the snippets that were saved in the previous session. After opening the file, you can start calling methods on the counter variable.

```
C:\Java9Revealed>jshell
|  Welcome to JShell -- Version 9-ea
|  For an introduction type: /help intro

jshell> /open jshell.jsh

jshell> counter.current()
$7 ==> 2

jshell> counter.next()
$8 ==> 3

jshell>
```

Resetting the JShell State

You can reset the JShell's execution state using the /reset command. Executing this command has the following effects:

- All snippets you enter in the current session are lost, so be careful before you execute this command.

- The startup snippets are re-executed.

- The execution state of the tool is restarted.

- The jshell configurations that were set using the /set command are retained.

- The execution environment set using the /env command is retained.

The following jshell session declares a variable, resets the session, and attempts to print the variable's value. Note that, on resetting a session, all declared variables are lost, so the variable previously declared is not found:

```
jshell> int x = 987
x ==> 987

jshell> /reset
|  Resetting state.

jshell> x
|  Error:
|  cannot find symbol
|    symbol:   variable x
|  x
|  ^

jshell>
```

Reloading the JShell State

Suppose you played with many snippets in a jshell session and exited the session. Now you want to go back and replay those snippets. One way to do it is to start a new jshell session and re-enter those snippets. Re-entering several snippets in jshell is a hassle. There is an easy way to achieve this—by using the /reload command. The /reload command resets the jshell state and replays all valid snippets and /drop commands in the same sequence they were entered before. You can use the -restore and -quiet options to customize its behavior.

The /reload command without any options resets the jshell state and replays the valid history from one of the following prior actions/events, whichever occurs last:

- Beginning of the current session

- When the last /reset command was executed

- When the last /reload command was executed

You can use the -restore option with the /reload command. It resets and replays the history between the following two actions/events, whichever are the last two:

- The launch of jshell

- Execution of the /reset command

- Execution of the /reload command

The effect of executing the /reload command with the -restore option is a little tricky to understand. Its primary purpose is to restore the previous execution state. If you execute this command in the beginning of every jshell session, starting from the second session, your session will contain all snippets you had ever executed in jshell sessions! This is a powerful feature. That is, you can evaluate snippets, close jshell, restart jshell, and execute the /reload -restore command as your first command, and you never lose any snippets that you previously entered. Sometimes, you will execute the /reset command twice in a session and want to restore the state that existed between those two resets. You can achieve this result by using this command.

The following jshell sessions create a variable in each session and restore the previous session by executing the /reload -restore command in the beginning of each session. The example shows that the fourth session uses the variable named x1 that was declared in the first session.

```
C:\Java9Revealed>jshell
|  Welcome to JShell -- Version 9-ea
|  For an introduction type: /help intro

jshell> int x1 = 10
x1 ==> 10

jshell> /exit
|  Goodbye

C:\Java9Revealed>jshell
|  Welcome to JShell -- Version 9-ea
|  For an introduction type: /help intro

jshell> /reload -restore
|  Restarting and restoring from previous state.
-: int x1 = 10;
```

```
jshell> int x2 = 20
x2 ==> 20

jshell> /exit
|  Goodbye

C:\Java9Revealed>jshell
|  Welcome to JShell -- Version 9-ea
|  For an introduction type: /help intro

jshell> /reload -restore
|  Restarting and restoring from previous state.
-: int x1 = 10;
-: int x2 = 20;

jshell> int x3 = 30
x3 ==> 30

jshell> /exit
|  Goodbye

C:\Java9Revealed>jshell
|  Welcome to JShell -- Version 9-ea
|  For an introduction type: /help intro

jshell> /reload -restore
|  Restarting and restoring from previous state.
-: int x1 = 10;
-: int x2 = 20;
-: int x3 = 30;

jshell> System.out.println("x1 is " + x1)
x1 is 10

jshell>
```

The /reload command displays the history that it replays. You can use the -quiet option to suppress the replay display. You can use this option with or without the -restore option. The -quiet option does not suppress the error messages that may be generated while replaying the history. The following example uses two jshell sessions. The first session declares a variable named x1. The second session uses the -quiet option with the /reload command. Note that, this time, you did not see the replay display that the variable x1 is reloaded in the second session because you used the -quiet option.

```
C:\Java9Revealed>jshell
|  Welcome to JShell -- Version 9-ea
|  For an introduction type: /help intro

jshell> int x1 = 10
x1 ==> 10
```

```
jshell> /exit
|  Goodbye

C:\Java9Revealed>jshell
|  Welcome to JShell -- Version 9-ea
|  For an introduction type: /help intro

jshell> /reload -restore -quiet
|  Restarting and restoring from previous state.

jshell> x1
x1 ==> 10

jshell>
```

Configuring JShell

Using the /set command, you can customize the jshell session, ranging from startup snippets and commands to setting a platform-specific snippet editor. In this section, I explain those customizations in detail.

Setting the Snippet Editor

The JShell tool comes with a default snippet editor. In jshell, you can use the /edit command to edit all snippets or a specific snippet. The /edit command opens the snippet in an editor. The snippet editor is a platform-specific program such as notepad.exe on Windows that will be invoked to edit snippets. You can use the /set command with editor as an argument to set or delete an editor setting. The valid forms of the command are as follows:

- /set editor [-retain] [-wait] <command>
- /set editor [-retain] -default
- /set editor [-retain] -delete

If you use the -retain option, the setting will persist across jshell sessions.

If you specify a command, the command must be platform-specific. That is, you need to specify a Windows command on Windows, a UNIX command on UNIX, and so on. The command may contain flags. The JShell tool will save the snippets to be edited in a temporary file and will append the name of the temporary file to the command. You cannot work with jshell while an editor is open. If your editor exits immediately, you should specify the -wait option, which will make jshell wait until the editor is closed. The following command sets Notepad as an editor on Windows:

```
jshell> /set editor -retain notepad.exe
```

The -default option sets the snippet editor to the default editor. The -delete option deletes the current editor setting. If the -retain option is used with the -delete option, the retained editor setting is deleted:

```
jshell> /set editor -retain -delete
|  Editor set to: -default

jshell>
```

The editor set in one of the following environment variables—JSHELLEDITOR, VISUAL, or EDITOR—takes precedence over the default editor. These environment variables are looked up for an editor in order. If none of these environment variables is set, the default editor is used. The intent behind all these rules is to have an editor all the time and then use the default editor as a fallback. The /set editor command without any arguments and options prints information about the current editor setting.

The following jshell session sets Notepad as an editor on Windows. Note that this example will not work on platforms other than Windows, where you need to specify your platform-specific program as an editor.

```
C:\Java9Revealed>jshell
|  Welcome to JShell -- Version 9-ea
|  For an introduction type: /help intro

jshell> /set editor
|  /set editor -default

jshell> /set editor -retain notepad.exe
|  Editor set to: notepad.exe
|  Editor setting retained: notepad.exe

jshell> /exit
|  Goodbye

C:\Java9Revealed>jshell
|  Welcome to JShell -- Version 9-ea
|  For an introduction type: /help intro

jshell> /set editor
|  /set editor -retain notepad.exe

jshell> 2 + 2
$1 ==> 4

jshell> /edit

jshell> /set editor -retain -delete
|  Editor set to: -default

jshell> /exit
|  Goodbye

C:\Java9Revealed>SET JSHELLEDITOR=notepad.exe

C:\Java9Revealed>jshell
|  Welcome to JShell -- Version 9-ea
|  For an introduction type: /help intro

jshell> /set editor
|  /set editor notepad.exe

jshell>
```

Setting Feedback Mode

When you execute a snippet or a command, jshell prints feedback. The amount and format of the feedback depends on the *feedback mode*. You can use one of the four predefined feedback modes or a custom feedback mode:

- silent
- concise
- normal
- verbose

The silent mode gives you no feedback at all and the verbose mode gives you the most feedback. The concise mode gives you the same feedback as the normal mode, but in a compact format. The command to set the feedback mode is as follows:

```
/set feedback [-retain] <mode>
```

Here, <mode> is one of the four feedback modes. Use the -retain option if you want to persist the feedback mode across the jshell sessions.

You can also launch jshell in a specific feedback mode:

```
jshell --feedback <mode>
```

The following command starts jshell in verbose feedback mode:

```
C:\Java9Revealed>jshell --feedback verbose
```

The following examples show you how to set different feedback modes:

```
C:\Java9Revealed>jshell
|  Welcome to JShell -- Version 9-ea
|  For an introduction type: /help intro

jshell> 2 + 2
$1 ==> 4

jshell> /set feedback verbose
|  Feedback mode: verbose

jshell> 2 + 2
$2 ==> 4
|  created scratch variable $2 : int

jshell> /set feedback concise
jshell> 2 + 2
$3 ==> 4
jshell> /set feedback silent
-> 2 + 2
```

```
-> System.out.println("Hello")
Hello
-> /set feedback verbose
|  Feedback mode: verbose

jshell> 2 + 2
$6 ==> 4
|  created scratch variable $6 : int
```

The feedback mode set in jshell is temporary. It is set only for the current session. To persist the feedback mode across your jshell sessions, use the /set command with feedback as an argument and -retain as an option:

```
jshell> /set feedback -retain
```

This command will persist the current feedback mode. When you start jshell again, it will configure the feedback mode that was set before you executed this command. It is still possible to change the feedback mode temporarily in a session. If you want to set a new feedback mode permanently, you need to use the /set feedback <mode> command and execute the command again to persist the new setting.

It is also possible to set a new feedback mode and, at the same time, persist it for future sessions by using the -retain option. The following command will set the feedback mode to verbose and retain it in future sessions:

```
jshell> /set feedback -retain verbose
```

To determine the current feedback mode, you just execute the /set command with the feedback argument. It prints the command used to set the current feedback mode in the first line followed by all available feedback modes, as shown:

```
jshell> /set feedback
|  /set feedback normal
|
|  Available feedback modes:
|     concise
|     normal
|     silent
|     verbose

jshell>
```

■ **Tip** When learning jshell, it is recommended you start it in verbose feedback mode, so you get a lot of details about the state of execution of your commands and snippets. This will help you learn about the tool faster.

Creating Custom feedback Modes

The four preconfigured feedback modes are good to work with jshell. They provide you different levels of granularity to customize your jshell. You can have your own custom feedback mode. I doubt you will ever need a custom feedback mode, but the feature is there, if you need it. Creating a custom feedback mode is a little more involved. You have to write several customization steps. Most likely, you will want to customize a few items in a predefined feedback mode. You can create a custom feedback mode from scratch or by copying one from an existing feedback mode and customizing it selectively. The syntax to create a custom feedback mode is as follows:

```
/set mode <mode> [<old-mode>] [-command|-quiet|-delete]
```

Here, <mode> is the name of the custom feedback mode; for example, kverbose. <old-mode> is the name of an existing feedback mode whose settings will be copied to the new mode. Using the -command option displays information about the mode when it is set, whereas using the -quiet option does not display any information when the mode is set. The -delete option is used to delete the mode.

The following command creates a new feedback mode called kverbose by copying all settings from the predefined verbose feedback mode:

```
/set mode kverbose verbose -command
```

The following command will persist the new feedback mode named kverbose for future use:

```
/set mode kverbose -retain
```

You need to use the -delete option to delete a custom feedback mode. You cannot delete a predefined feedback mode. If you persisted the custom feedback mode, you can use the -retain option to delete it from current and all future sessions. The following command will delete the kverbose feedback mode:

```
/set mode kverbose -delete -retain
```

At this point, there is no difference between the predefined verbose mode and the custom kverbose mode. After you create a feedback mode, you need to customize three settings:

- Prompts
- Output truncation limits
- Output format

▓ **Tip** Once you are done defining a custom feedback mode, you need to use the /set feedback <new-mode> command to start using it.

You can set two types of prompts for feedback—the main prompt and the continuation prompt. The main prompt is displayed when jshell is ready to read a new snippet/command. The continuation prompt is displayed at the beginning of a line when you are entering a multi-line snippet. The syntax for setting prompts is as follows:

```
/set prompt <mode> "<prompt>" "<continuation-prompt>"
```

Here, `<prompt>` is the main prompt and `<continuation-prompt>` is the continuation prompt. The following command sets the prompts for the kverbose mode:

```
/set prompt kverbose "\njshell-kverbose> " "more... "
```

You can set the maximum number of characters displayed for each type of action/event for a feedback mode using the following command:

```
/set truncation <mode> <length> <selectors>
```

Here, `<mode>` is the feedback mode for which you set the truncation limit; `<length>` is the maximum number of characters displayed for the specified selectors. `<selectors>` is a comma-separated list of selectors that determines the context to which the truncation limit applies. Selectors are predefined keywords that represent specific contexts, for example, vardecl is a selector that represents a variable declaration without initialization. Use the following command for more information about setting the truncation limits and selectors:

```
/help /set truncation
```

The following commands set the truncation limit to 80 characters for everything and to five characters for a variable value or expression:

```
/set truncation kverbose 80
/set truncation kverbose 5 expression,varvalue
```

Note that the most specific selector determines the actual truncation limit to be used. The following settings use two selectors—one for all types of snippets (80 characters) and one for expressions and variable values (5 characters). For an expression, the second setting is the most specific setting. In this case, if you have a variable whose value is more than five characters, it will be truncated to five characters when displayed.

Setting the output format is a complex job. You will need to set the format for all types of output you are expecting based on the actions/events. I do not go through defining all types of output formats. Use the following command for more information about setting the output formats:

```
/help /set format
```

The syntax for setting an output format is as follows:

```
/set format <mode> <field> "<format>" <selectors>
```

Here, `<mode>` is the name of the feedback mode for which you are setting the output format; `<field>` is the context-specific format to define; "`<format>`" is used for displaying the output. `<format>` can contain names of predefined fields in braces—for example, {name}, {type}, {value}, etc.—which will be replaced with actual values based on the context. `<selectors>` are selectors that determine the context in which this format will be used.

The following command sets a display format for feedback when an expression is added, modified, or replaced for entered snippets. The entire command is entered in one line.

```
/set format kverbose display "{result}{pre}created a temporary variable named {name} of type
{type} and initialized it with {value}{post}" expression-added,modified,replaced-primary
```

The following jshell session creates a new feedback mode called kverbose by copying all settings from the predefined verbose feedback mode. It customizes the prompts, truncation limits, and output formats. It uses the verbose and kverbose feedback modes to compare jshell behavior. Note that all commands in the following examples need to be entered in one line even though they sometimes appear on multiple lines in the book.

```
C:\Java9Revealed>jshell
|  Welcome to JShell -- Version 9-ea
|  For an introduction type: /help intro

jshell> /set feedback
|  /set feedback -retain normal
|
|  Available feedback modes:
|     concise
|     normal
|     silent
|     verbose

jshell> /set mode kverbose verbose -command
|  Created new feedback mode: kverbose

jshell> /set mode kverbose -retain

jshell> /set prompt kverbose "\njshell-kverbose> " "more... "

jshell> /set truncation kverbose 5 expression,varvalue

jshell> /set format kverbose display "{result}{pre}created a temporary variable named {name}
of type {type} and initialized it with {value}{post}" expression-added,modified,replaced-
primary

jshell> /set feedback kverbose
|  Feedback mode: kverbose

jshell-kverbose> 2 +
more... 2
$2 ==> 4
|  created a temporary variable named $2 of type int and initialized it with 4

jshell-kverbose> 111111 + 222222
$3 ==> 33333
|  created a temporary variable named $3 of type int and initialized it with 33333

jshell-kverbose> /set feedback verbose
|  Feedback mode: verbose
```

```
jshell> 2 +
   ...> 2
$4 ==> 4
|  created scratch variable $4 : int

jshell> 111111 + 222222
$5 ==> 333333
|  created scratch variable $5 : int

jshell> /exit
|  Goodbye

C:\Java9Revealed>jshell
|  Welcome to JShell -- Version 9-ea
|  For an introduction type: /help intro

jshell> /set feedback
|  /set feedback -retain normal
|
|  Retained feedback modes:
|     kverbose
|  Available feedback modes:
|     concise
|     kverbose
|     normal
|     silent
|     verbose

jshell>
```

In this jshell sessions, you set the truncation limits for expressions and variable values to five characters for the kverbose feedback mode. This is why in the kverbose feedback mode, the value of the expression 111111 + 222222 is printed as 33333, and not as 333333. This not a bug. This was caused by your setting.

Note that the command /set feedback shows the command used to set the current feedback mode and a list of available feedback modes, which lists your new feedback mode named kverbose.

When you are creating a custom feedback mode, it will be helpful to know all the settings for the existing feedback modes. You can print a list of all settings for all the feedback modes using the following command:

```
/set mode
```

You can also print a list of all settings for a specific feedback mode by passing the mode name as an argument to the command. The following command prints a list of all settings for the silent feedback mode. The first line in the output is the command used to create silent mode.

```
jshell> /set mode silent
|  /set mode silent -quiet
|  /set prompt silent "-> " ">> "
|  /set format silent display ""
|  /set format silent err "%6$s"
|  /set format silent errorline "    {err}%n"
```

```
|  /set format silent errorpost "%n"
|  /set format silent errorpre "|   "
|  /set format silent errors "%5$s"
|  /set format silent name "%1$s"
|  /set format silent post "%n"
|  /set format silent pre "|   "
|  /set format silent type "%2$s"
|  /set format silent unresolved "%4$s"
|  /set format silent value "%3$s"
|  /set truncation silent 80
|  /set truncation silent 1000 expression,varvalue

jshell>
```

Setting Up Startup Snippets

You can use the /set command with a start argument to set up your startup snippets and commands. Startup snippets and commands are automatically executed when you launch jshell. You have seen the default startup snippets that import types from a few commonly used packages. Typically, you would set the class path and module path using an /env command and import statements to your startup script.

You can print a list of default startup snippets using the /list -start command. Note that this command prints the default startup snippets, not the current startup snippets. Remember you can also drop startup snippets. Default startup snippets include what you get when you start jshell. Current startup snippets include the default startup snippets minus those you have dropped in the current jshell session.

You can use one of the following forms of the /set command to set startup snippets/commands:

- /set start [-retain] <file>

- /set start [-retain] -default

- /set start [-retain] -none

Using the -retain option is optional. If it is used, the setting persists across jshell sessions.

The first form is used to set startup snippets/commands from a file. When a /reset or a /reload command is executed in the current session, the file's contents will be used as startup snippets/commands. Once you set the startup code from a file, jshell caches the file's contents for future use. Modifying the file's contents does not affect the startup code until you set the startup snippets/commands again.

The second form is used to set the startup snippets/commands to the built-in default.

The third form is used to set an empty startup. That is, there will be no snippets/commands executed at startup.

The /set start command without any options or files shows the current startup setting. If the startup was set from a file, it shows the filename, the startup snippets, and the time at which the startup snippets were set.

Consider the following scenario. The com.jdojo.jshell directory in the book's source code contains a com.jdojo.jshell.Person class. Let's test this class in jshell and use the types from the java.time package. To do this, your startup settings will look like the contents shown in Listing 11-3.

Listing 11-3. Contents of a File Named startup.jsh File

```
/env -class-path C:\Java9Revealed\com.jdojo.jshell\build\classes
import java.io.*
import java.math.*
import java.net.*
import java.nio.file.*
import java.util.*
import java.util.concurrent.*
import java.util.function.*
import java.util.prefs.*
import java.util.regex.*
import java.util.stream.*
import java.time.*;
import com.jdojo.jshell.*;
void printf(String format, Object... args) { System.out.printf(format, args); }
```

Save the settings in a file named `startup.jsh` in your current directory. If you save it in any other directory, you can use an absolute path for this file while working with this example. Note that the first command is a `/env -class-path` command for Windows assuming that you stored the source code in the `C:\` directory. Change the class path value according to your platform and the location of the book's source code on your computer.

Note the last snippet in the `startup.jsh` file. It defines a top-level function named `printf()` that is a wrapper for the `System.out.printf()` method. The `printf()` function was included in the initial builds of the JShell tool by default. Later, it was removed. If you want to use a short method name, such as `printf()`, instead of `System.out.printf()` in order to print messages on the standard output, you can include this snippet in your startup script. If you want to use `println()` and `printf()` top-level methods in `jshell` by default, you need to start `jshell` as following:

```
C:\Java9Revealed>jshell --start DEFAULT --start PRINTING
```

The `DEFAULT` argument will include all default `import` statements and the `PRINTING` argument will include all versions of the `print()`, `println()`, and `printf()` methods. After you launch `jshell` using this command, execute the `/list -start` command to see all startup `imports` and methods added by the two `--start` options used in the command.

The following `jshell` sessions show you how to set the startup settings from a file and its usage in subsequence sessions:

```
C:\Java9Revealed>jshell
|  Welcome to JShell -- Version 9-ea
|  For an introduction type: /help intro

jshell> /set start
|  /set start -default

jshell> /set start -retain startup.jsh

jshell> Person p;
|  created variable p, however, it cannot be referenced until class Person is declared

jshell> /reset
|  Resetting state.
```

```
jshell> Person p;
p ==> null

jshell> /exit
|  Goodbye

C:\Java9Revealed>jshell
|  Welcome to JShell -- Version 9-ea
|  For an introduction type: /help intro

jshell> /set start
|  /set start -retain startup.jsh
|  ---- startup.jsh @ Feb 20, 2017, 10:06:47 AM ----
|  /env -class-path C:\Java9Revealed\com.jdojo.jshell\build\classes
|  import java.io.*
|  import java.math.*
|  import java.net.*
|  import java.nio.file.*
|  import java.util.*
|  import java.util.concurrent.*
|  import java.util.function.*
|  import java.util.prefs.*
|  import java.util.regex.*
|  import java.util.stream.*
|  import java.time.*;
|  import com.jdojo.jshell.*;
|  void printf(String format, Object... args) { System.out.printf(format, args); }

jshell> Person p
p ==> null

jshell> LocalDate.now()
$2 ==> 2016-11-15

jshell>
jshell> printf("2 + 2 = %d%n", 2 + 2)
2 + 2 = 4

jshell>
```

▓ **Tip**   Setting the startup snippets/commands does not take effect until you relaunch `jshell`, execute a
`/reset`, or execute a `/reload` command. Do not include a `/reset` or a `/reload` command in your startup file.
It will cause an infinite loop when your startup file loads.

There are three predefined scripts whose names are as follows:

- DEFAULT
- PRINTING
- JAVASE

The DEFAULT script contains commonly used import statements as you have seen them in the "Import Statements" section. The PRINTING script defines top-level JShell methods that redirect to the `print()`, `println()`, and `printf()` methods in `PrintStream` as shown in this section. The JAVASE script imports all Java SE packages, which is big and takes a few seconds to complete. The following commands show you how to save these scripts as the startup script:

```
C:\Java9Revealed>jshell
|  Welcome to JShell -- Version 9-ea
|  For an introduction type: /help intro

jshell> println("Hello")
|  Error:
|  cannot find symbol
|    symbol:   method println(java.lang.String)
|  println("Hello")
|  ^-----^

jshell> /set start -retain DEFAULT PRINTING

jshell> /exit
|  Goodbye

C:\Java9Revealed>jshell
|  Welcome to JShell -- Version 9-ea
|  For an introduction type: /help intro

jshell> println("Hello")
Hello

jshell>
```

Notice that using the `println()` method for the first time resulted in an error. After saving the PRINTING script as the startup script and restarting the the tool, the method works.

Using JShell Documentation

The `JShell` tool ships with extensive documentation. Because it is a command-line tool, it is little harder to read the documentation on a command line. You can use the `/help` or `/?` command to display a list of commands and their brief descriptions.

```
jshell> /help
|  Type a Java language expression, statement, or declaration.
|  Or type one of the following commands:
```

```
|   /list [<name or id>|-all|-start]  -- list the source you have typed
|   /edit <name or id>  -- edit a source entry referenced by name or id
|   /drop <name or id>  -- delete a source entry referenced by name or id
...
```

You can use a specific command as an argument to the /help command to get information about the command. The following command prints information about the /help command itself:

```
jshell> /help /help
|
|   /help
|
|   Display information about jshell.
|   /help
|       List the jshell commands and help subjects.
|
|   /help <command>
|       Display information about the specified command. The slash must be included.
|       Only the first few letters of the command are needed -- if more than one
|       each will be displayed.  Example:  /help /li
|
|   /help <subject>
|       Display information about the specified help subject. Example: /help intro
```

The following commands will display information about the /list and /set commands. Outputs are not shown because they are long:

```
jshell> /help /list
|...

jshell> /help /set
|...
```

Sometimes, a command is used to work with multiple topics, for example, the /set command can be used to set the feedback mode, a snippet editor, startup scripts, etc. If you want to print information about a specific topic of a command, you can use the /help command in the following format:

```
/help /<command> <topic-name>
```

The following command prints information about setting the feedback mode:

```
jshell> /help /set feedback
```

The following command prints information about creating a custom feedback mode:

```
jshell> /help /set mode
```

Use the `/help` command with a subject as an argument to print information about the subject. Currently, there are three predefined subjects: `intro`, `shortcuts`, and `context`. The following command will print an introduction to the `JShell` tool:

```
jshell> /help intro
```

The following command will print a list of shortcuts and their descriptions that you can use in the `JShell` tool:

```
jshell> /help shortcuts
```

The following command will print a list of options used to set the execution context. These options are used with the `/env`, `/reset`, and `/reload` commands.

```
jshell> /help context
```

The JShell API

The `JShell` API gives you programmatic access to the snippet evaluation engine. As a developer, you may not use this API. It is meant to be used by tools such as the NetBeans IDE that may include a UI equivalent of the `JShell` command-line tool to let developers evaluate snippets of code from inside the IDE instead of opening a command prompt to do the same. In this section, I briefly introduce the `JShell` API and show its use with a simple example.

The `JShell` API is in the `jdk.jshell` module and the `jdk.jshell` package. Note that if you are using the `JShell` API, your module will need to read the `jdk.jshell` module. The `JShell` API is simple. It consists mainly of three abstract classes and one interface:

- `JShell`
- `Snippet`
- `SnippetEvent`
- `SourceCodeAnalysis`

An instance of the `JShell` class represents a snippet evaluation engine. This is the main class in the `JShell` API. A `JShell` instance maintains the state of all snippets as they are executed.

A snippet is represented by an instance of the `Snippet` class. A `JShell` instance generates snippet events as it executes snippets.

A snippet event is represented by an instance of the `SnippetEvent` interface. A snippet event contains the current and previous statuses of snippets, the value of the snippet for a result bearing snippet, the source code of the snippet that caused the event, an `Exception` object if an exception occurred during the snippet execution, etc.

An instance of the `SourceCodeAnalysis` class provides source code analysis and suggestion features for a snippet. It answers questions like the following:

- Is it a complete snippet?
- Can this snippet be completed by appending a semicolon?

A `SourceCodeAnalysis` instance also provides a list of suggestions, for example, for Tab completion and accessing the documentation. This class is meant to be used by a tool providing the `JShell` functionality. I do not discuss it any further. Refer to the Javadoc of this class if you are interested in exploring it further.

Figure 11-5. shows the use-case diagram for the different components of the JShell API. In subsequent sections, I explain these classes and their uses. I show you a complete example in the last section.

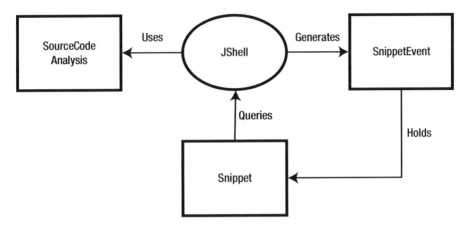

Figure 11-5. *A use-case diagram for the components of the JShell API*

Creating a JShell

The JShell class is abstract. It provides two ways to create its instances:

- Using its static create() method
- Using a static builder class named JShell.Builder

The create() method returns a preconfigured JShell instance. The following snippet of code shows how to create a JShell using the create() method:

```
// Create a JShell instance
JShell shell = JShell.create()
```

The JShell.Builder class lets you configure the JShell instance by letting you specify a snippet ID generator, a temporary variable name generator, a print stream for printing the output, an input stream to read snippets, and an error output stream to log errors. You can obtain an instance of the JShell.Builder class using the builder() static method of the JShell class. The following snippet of code shows how to use the JShell.Builder class to create a JShell, where myXXXStream in the code are references to your stream objects:

```
// Create a JShell instance
JShell shell = JShell.builder()
                    .in(myInputStream)
                    .out(myOutputStream)
                    .err(myErrorStream)
                    .build();
```

Once you have a JShell instance, you can start evaluating snippets using its eval(String snippet) method. You can drop a snippet using its drop(PersistentSnippet snippet) method. You can append a path to the class path using its addToClasspath(String path) method. These three methods change the state of the JShell instance.

■ **Tip** When you are done using a JShell, you need to call its close() method to free resources. The JShell class implements the AutoCloseable interface, and therefore, using a try-with-resources block to work with a JShell is the best way to ensure that it is closed when it is no longer in use. A JShell is mutable and not thread-safe.

You can register snippet event handlers and JShell shutdown event handlers using the onSnippetEvent(Consumer<SnippetEvent> listener) and onShutdown(Consumer<JShell> listener) methods of the JShell class. A snippet event is fired when the status of a snippet changes because it is evaluated the first time or its status is updated because of evaluation of another snippet.

The sourceCodeAnalysis() method in the JShell class returns an instance of the SourceCodeAnalysis class, which you can use for code-assist functionality.

Other methods in the JShell class are used to query the state. For example, the snippets(), types(), methods(), and variables() methods return a list of all snippets, all snippets with active type declarations, snippets with active method declarations, and snippets with active variable declarations, respectively.

The eval() method is the most frequently used method in the JShell class. It evaluates/executes the specified snippet and returns a List<SnippetEvent>. You can query the snippet events in the list for the state of execution. The following is a sample snippet of code that uses the eval() method:

```
String snippet = "int x = 100;";

// Evaluate the snippet
List<SnippetEvent> events = shell.eval(snippet);

// Process the results
events.forEach((SnippetEvent se) -> {
    /* Handle the snippet event here */
});
```

Working with Snippets

An instance of the Snippet class represents a snippet. The class does not provide a way to create its objects. You supply snippets to a JShell as strings and you receive instances of the Snippet class as part of the snippet events. Snippet events also provide you with the previous and current statuses of a snippet. If you have a Snippet object, you can query its current status using the status(Snippet s) method of the JShell class, which returns a Snippet.Staus.

■ **Tip** The Snippet class is immutable and thread-safe.

There are several types of snippets in Java, for example, a variable declaration, a variable declaration with initialization, a method declaration, a type declaration, etc. The `Snippet` class is an abstract class and there is a subclass to represent each specific type of snippet. The following list shows the inheritance hierarchy of classes representing different types of snippets:

- Snippet
    - ErroneousSnippet
    - ExpressionSnippet
    - StatementSnippet
    - PersistentSnippet
        - ImportSnippet
        - DeclarationSnippet
            - MethodSnippet
            - TypeDeclSnippet
            - VarSnippet

The name of the subclasses of the `Snippet` class are intuitive. For example, an instance of the `PersistentSnippet` represents a snippet that is stored in a `JShell` and can be reused such as a class declaration or a method declaration. The `Snippet` class contains the following methods:

- String id()
- String source()
- Snippet.Kind kind()
- Snippet.SubKind subKind()

The id() method returns a unique ID of the snippet and the source() method returns its source code. The kind() and subKind() methods return the type and sub-type of a snippet.

The type of a snippet is one of the constants of the `Snippet.Kind` enum, for example, IMPORT, TYPE_DECL, METHOD, VAR, etc. The sub-type of a snippet provides more specific information about its type, for example, if a snippet is a type declaration, its sub-type will tell you if it is a class, interface, enum, or annotation declaration. The sub-type of a snippet is one of the constants of the `Snippet.SubKind` enum such as CLASS_SUBKIND, ENUM_SUBKIND, etc. The `Snippet.Kind` enum contains an isPersistent property whose value is true if the snippet of this kind is persistent and false otherwise.

Subclasses of the `Snippet` class add more methods to return specific information about the specific type of snippet. For example, the `VarSnippet` class contains a typeName() method, which returns the data type of the variable. The `MethodSnippet` class contains the parameterTypes() and signature() methods, which return parameter types and the full signature of the method as a string.

A snippet does not contain its status. A `JShell` executes and holds the status of a `Snippet`. Note that executing a snippet may affect the status of other snippets. For example, a snippet declaring a variable may change the status of a snippet declaring a method from valid to invalid or vice versa if the method was referencing the variable. If you need the current status of a snippet, use the status(Snippet s) method of the JShell class, which returns one of the following constants of the Snippet.Status enum:

- DROPPED: The snippet is inactive because it was dropped using the drop() method of the JShell class.

- NONEXISTENT: The snippet is inactive because it does not yet exist.

- OVERWRITTEN: The snippet is inactive because it has been replaced by a new snippet.

- RECOVERABLE_DEFINED: The snippet is a declaration snippet containing unresolved references. The declaration has a valid signature and it is visible to other snippets. It can be recovered and used when other snippets change its status to VALID.

- RECOVERABLE_NOT_DEFINED: The snippet is a declaration snippet containing unresolved references. The snippet has an invalid signature and it is not visible to other snippets. It can be used later when its status changes to VALID.

- REJECTED: The snippet is inactive because it failed compilation on initial evaluation and it is not capable of becoming valid with further changes to the JShell state.

- VALID: The snippet is valid in the context of the current JShell state.

Handling Snippet Events

A JShell generates snippet events as part of snippet evaluation or execution. You can handle snippet events by registering event handlers using the onSnippetEvent() method of the JShell class or by using the return value of the eval() method of the JShell class, which is a List<SnippetEvent>. The following snippet code shows you how to process snippet events:

```
try (JShell shell = JShell.create()) {
    // Create a snippet
    String snippet = "int x = 100;";

    shell.eval(snippet)
        .forEach((SnippetEvent se) -> {
            Snippet s = se.snippet();
            System.out.printf("Snippet: %s%n", s.source());
            System.out.printf("Kind: %s%n", s.kind());
            System.out.printf("Sub-Kind: %s%n", s.subKind());
            System.out.printf("Previous Status: %s%n", se.previousStatus());
            System.out.printf("Current Status: %s%n", se.status());
            System.out.printf("Value: %s%n", se.value());
        });
}
```

An Example

Let's look at the JShell API in action. Listing 11-4 contains the module declaration for a module named com.jdojo.jshell.api. Listing 11-5 contains the complete code for a class named JShellApiTest, which is a member of the com.jdojo.jshell.api module.

Listing 11-4. The Module Declaration for the Module Named com.jdojo.jshell.api

```
// module-info.java
module com.jdojo.jshell.api {
    requires jdk.jshell;
}
```

Listing 11-5. A JShellApiTest Class to Test the JShell API

```
// JShellApiTest.java
package com.jdojo.jshell.api;

import jdk.jshell.JShell;
import jdk.jshell.Snippet;
import jdk.jshell.SnippetEvent;

public class JShellApiTest {
    public static void main(String[] args) {
        // Create an array of snippets to evaluate/execute
        // them sequentially
        String[] snippets = { "int x = 100;",
                              "double x = 190.89;",
                              "long multiply(int value) {return value * multiplier;}",
                              "int multiplier = 2;",
                              "multiply(200)",
                              "mul(99)"
                            };

        try (JShell shell = JShell.create()) {
            // Register a snippet event handler
            shell.onSnippetEvent(JShellApiTest::snippetEventHandler);

            // Evaluate all snippets
            for(String snippet : snippets) {
                shell.eval(snippet);
                System.out.println("-----------------------");
            }
        }
    }

    public static void snippetEventHandler(SnippetEvent se) {
        // Print the details of this snippet event
        Snippet snippet = se.snippet();
        System.out.printf("Snippet: %s%n", snippet.source());

        // Print the cause of this snippet event
        Snippet causeSnippet = se.causeSnippet();
        if (causeSnippet != null) {
            System.out.printf("Cause Snippet: %s%n", causeSnippet.source());
        }
```

```
        System.out.printf("Kind: %s%n", snippet.kind());
        System.out.printf("Sub-Kind: %s%n", snippet.subKind());
        System.out.printf("Previous Status: %s%n", se.previousStatus());
        System.out.printf("Current Status: %s%n", se.status());
        System.out.printf("Value: %s%n", se.value());

        Exception e = se.exception();
        if (e != null) {
            System.out.printf("Exception: %s%n", se.exception().getMessage());
        }
    }
}
```

```
Snippet: int x = 100;
Kind: VAR
Sub-Kind: VAR_DECLARATION_WITH_INITIALIZER_SUBKIND
Previous Status: NONEXISTENT
Current Status: VALID
Value: 100
-----------------------
Snippet: double x = 190.89;
Kind: VAR
Sub-Kind: VAR_DECLARATION_WITH_INITIALIZER_SUBKIND
Previous Status: VALID
Current Status: VALID
Value: 190.89
Snippet: int x = 100;
Cause Snippet: double x = 190.89;
Kind: VAR
Sub-Kind: VAR_DECLARATION_WITH_INITIALIZER_SUBKIND
Previous Status: VALID
Current Status: OVERWRITTEN
Value: null
-----------------------
Snippet: long multiply(int value) {return value * multiplier;}
Kind: METHOD
Sub-Kind: METHOD_SUBKIND
Previous Status: NONEXISTENT
Current Status: RECOVERABLE_DEFINED
Value: null
-----------------------
Snippet: int multiplier = 2;
Kind: VAR
Sub-Kind: VAR_DECLARATION_WITH_INITIALIZER_SUBKIND
Previous Status: NONEXISTENT
Current Status: VALID
Value: 2
Snippet: long multiply(int value) {return value * multiplier;}
Cause Snippet: int multiplier = 2;
Kind: METHOD
```

```
Sub-Kind: METHOD_SUBKIND
Previous Status: RECOVERABLE_DEFINED
Current Status: VALID
Value: null
-----------------------
Snippet: multiply(200)
Kind: VAR
Sub-Kind: TEMP_VAR_EXPRESSION_SUBKIND
Previous Status: NONEXISTENT
Current Status: VALID
Value: 400
-----------------------
Snippet: mul(99)
Kind: ERRONEOUS
Sub-Kind: UNKNOWN_SUBKIND
Previous Status: NONEXISTENT
Current Status: REJECTED
Value: null
-----------------------
```

The main() method creates the following six snippets and stores them in a String array:

1. "int x = 100;"

2. "double x = 190.89;"

3. "long multiply(int value) {return value * multiplier;}"

4. "int multiplier = 2;"

5. "multiply(200)"

6. "mul(99)"

A try-with-resources block is used to create a JShell instance. The snippetEventHandler() method is registered as a snippet event handler. The method prints details about the snippets such as its source code, the source code of the snippet that caused the update in the snippet status, the snippet's previous and current status, its value, etc. Finally, a for-each loop is used to iterate through all the snippets and the eval() method is called to execute them.

Let's walk through the state of the JShell engine when each of these snippets is executed:

- When snippet 1 is executed, the snippet did not exist, so it transitions from a NONEXISTENT to a VALID status. It is a variable declaration snippet and it evaluates to 100.

- When snippet 2 is executed, it already existed. Note that it declares the same variable named x with a different data type. Its previous status was VALID and its current status is VALID too. The execution of this snippet changes the status of snippet 1, whose status changes from VALID to OVERWRITTEN, because you cannot have two variables with the same name.

- Snippet 3 declares a method named multiply(), which uses an undeclared variable named multiplier in its body, so its status changes from NONEXISTENT to RECOVERABLE_DEFINED. The method is defined, which means that it can be referenced but cannot be invoked until a variable named multiplier of appropriate type is defined.

- Snippet 4 defines a variable named `multiplier`, which makes snippet 3 valid.

- Snippet 5 evaluates an expression that calls the `multiply()` method. The expression is valid and it evaluates to 400.

- Snippet 6 evaluates an expression that calls a `mul()` method, which you have never defined. The snippet is erroneous and is rejected.

Typically, you will not use JShell API and the JShell tool together. However, let's use them together just for fun. The JShell API is just another API in Java and it can also be used in the JShell tool. The following jshell session instantiates a JShell, registers a snippet event handler, and evaluates two snippets.

```
C:\Java9Revealed>jshell
|  Welcome to JShell -- Version 9-ea
|  For an introduction type: /help intro

jshell> /set feedback silent
-> import jdk.jshell.*
-> JShell shell = JShell.create()
-> shell.onSnippetEvent(se -> {
>>   System.out.printf("Snippet: %s%n", se.snippet().source());
>>   System.out.printf("Previous Status: %s%n", se.previousStatus());
>>   System.out.printf("Current Status: %s%n", se.status());
>>   System.out.printf("Value: %s%n", se.value());
>> });
-> shell.eval("int x = 100;");
Snippet: int x = 100;
Previous Status: NONEXISTENT
Current Status: VALID
Value: 100
-> shell.eval("double x = 100.89;");
Snippet: double x = 100.89;
Previous Status: VALID
Current Status: VALID
Value: 100.89
Snippet: int x = 100;
Previous Status: VALID
Current Status: OVERWRITTEN
Value: null
-> shell.close()
-> /exit

C:\Java9Revealed>
```

Summary

The Java shell, which is called JShell in JDK 9, is a command-line tool that provides an interactive way to access the Java programming language. It lets you evaluate snippets of Java code instead of forcing you to write an entire Java program. It is a REPL for Java. JShell is also an API that provides programmatic access to the REPL functionality for the Java code for other tools such as IDEs.

You can start the JShell command-line tool by running the jshell program that is stored in the JDK_HOME\bin directory. The tool supports executing snippets and commands. Snippets are pieces of Java code. As snippets are evaluated/executed, JShell maintains its state. It also keeps track of the status of all entered snippets. You can use commands to query the JShell state and configure the jshell environment. To distinguish commands from snippets, all the commands start with a slash (/).

JShell contains several features that make developers more productive and provide a better user experience, such as auto-completion of code and displaying the Javadoc inside the tool. JShell attempts to use the already existing functionality in the JDK such as the Compiler API to parse, analyze, and compile snippets, and the Java Debugger API to replace existing snippets with new ones in the JVM. The design of JShell makes it possible to use new constructs in the Java languages without any changes or with few changes to the JShell tool itself.

CHAPTER 12

■ ■ ■

Process API Updates

In this chapter, you will learn:

- What the Process API is
- How to create a native process
- How to get information about a new process
- How to get information about the current process
- How to get information about all system processes
- How to set permissions to create, query, and manage native processes

What Is the Process API?

The Process API consists of classes and interfaces that let you work with native processes. Using the API, you can:

- Create new native processes from Java code
- Get process handles for native processes whether they were created by Java code or by other means
- Destroy running processes
- Query processes for liveness and their other attributes
- Get the list of child processes and the parent process of a process
- Get the process ID (PID) of native processes
- Get the input, output, and error streams of newly created processes
- Wait for a process to terminate
- Execute a task when a process terminates

The Process API consists of the following classes and interfaces in the `java.lang` package:

- `Runtime`
- `ProcessBuilder`
- `ProcessBuilder.Redirect`

© Kishori Sharan 2017

K. Sharan, *Java 9 Revealed*, DOI 10.1007/978-1-4842-2592-9_12

- Process
- ProcessHandle
- ProcessHandle.Info

Support for working with native processes existed since Java 1.0. An instance of the Process class represents a native process created by a Java program. A process is started by calling the exec() method of the Runtime class.

JDK 5.0 added another class named ProcessBuilder and JDK 7.0 added a nested class named ProcessBuilder.Redirect. An instance of the ProcessBuilder class holds a set of attributes for a process. Calling its start() method starts a native process and returns an instance of the Process class that represents the native process. You can call its start() method multiple times; each time, it starts a new process using the attributes held in the ProcessBuilder instance. In Java 5.0, the ProcessBuilder class took over the job of the Runtime.exec() method to start a new process.

There were a few improvements in the Process API in Java 7 and Java 8 in terms of adding a few methods to the Process and ProcessBuilder classes.

Before Java 9, the Process API was still lacking basic support for working with native processes such as getting the PID and owner of a process, the start time of a process, how much CPU time has been used by a process, how many native processes are currently running, etc. Note that before Java 9, you were able to start native processes and work with their input, output, and error streams. However, you were not able to work with native processes that you did not start and were not able to query the details of processes. To work with native processes more closely, Java developers had to resort to writing native code using Java Native Interface (JNI). Java 9 made these much needed features to work with native processes.

Java 9 added an interface named ProcessHandle to the Process API. An instance of the ProcessHandle interface identifies a native process; it lets you query the process state and manage the process.

Compare the Process class and the ProcessHandle interface. An instance of the Process class represents a native process started by the current Java program, whereas an instance of the ProcessHandle interface represents a native process whether it was started by the current Java program or by other means. In Java 9, several methods have been added to the Process class that are also available in the new ProcessHandle interface. The Process class contains a toHandle() method that returns a ProcessHandle.

An instance of the ProcessHandle.Info interface represents a snapshot of attributes of a process. Note that processes are implemented differently by different operating systems, so their attributes vary. The state of a process may change anytime, for example, the CPU time used by the process increases whenever the process gets more CPU time. To get the latest information on a process, you need to use the info() method of the ProcessHandle interface at the time you need it, which will return a new instance of the ProcessHandle.Info interface.

All examples in this chapter were run in Windows 10. You may get a different output when you run these programs on your machine using Windows 10 or a different operating system.

The Current Process

The current() static method of the ProcessHandle interface returns the handle of the current process. Note that the current process returned by this method is always the Java process that is executing the code.

```
// Get the handle of the current process
ProcessHandle current = ProcessHandle.current();
```

Once you get the handle of the current process, you can use methods of the ProcessHandle interface to get details about the process. Refer to the next section for an example on how to get information about the current process.

▓ **Tip** You cannot kill the current process. Attempting to kill the current process by using the `destroy()` or `destroyForcibly()` method of the `ProcessHandle` interface results in an `IllegalStateException`.

Querying Process State

You can use methods in the `ProcessHandle` interface to query the state of a process. Table 12-1 lists this interface's commonly used methods with brief descriptions. Note that many of these methods return the snapshot of the state of a process that was true when the snapshot was taken. There is no guarantee that the process will still be in the same state when you use its attributes later because processes are created, run, and destroyed asynchronously.

Table 12-1. *Methods in the ProcessHandle Interface*

Method	Description
`static Stream<ProcessHandle> allProcesses()`	Returns a snapshot of all processes in the OS that are visible to the current process.
`Stream<ProcessHandle> children()`	Returns a snapshot of the current direct children of the process. Use the `descendants()` method to get a list of children at all levels, for example, child processes, grandchild processes, great grandchild processes, etc.
`static ProcessHandle current()`	Returns a `ProcessHandle` for the current process, which is the Java process executing this method call.
`Stream<ProcessHandle> descendants()`	Returns a snapshot of the descendants of the process. Compare it to the `children()` method, which returns only direct descendants of the process.
`boolean destroy()`	Requests the process to be killed. Returns `true` if termination of the process was successfully requested, `false` otherwise. Whether you can kill a process depends on operating system access control.
`boolean destroyForcibly()`	Requests the process to be killed forcibly. Returns `true` if termination of the process was successfully requested, `false` otherwise. Killing a process forcibly terminates the process immediately, whereas a normal termination allows a process to shut down cleanly. Whether you can kill a process depends on operating system access control.
`long getPid()`	Returns the native process ID (PID) of the process, which is assigned by the operating system. Note that a PID may be reused by operating systems, so two process handles having the same PID may not represent the same process.
`ProcessHandle.Info info()`	Returns a snapshot of information about the process.
`boolean isAlive()`	Returns `true` if the process represented by this `ProcessHandle` has not yet terminated, `false` otherwise. Note that this method may return `true` for some time after you have successfully requested to terminate the process because the process will be terminated asynchronously.
`static Optional<ProcessHandle> of(long pid)`	Returns an `Optional<ProcessHandle>` for an existing native process. Returns an empty `Optional` if a process with the specified `pid` does not exist.

(continued)

Table 12-1. (*continued*)

Method	Description
CompletableFuture <ProcessHandle> onExit()	Returns a CompletableFuture <ProcessHandle> for the termination of the process. You can use the returned object to add a task that will be executed when the process terminates. Calling this method on the current process throws an IllegalStateException.
Optional<ProcessHandle> parent()	Returns an Optional<ProcessHandle> for the parent process.
boolean supportsNormalTermination()	Returns true if the implementation of destroy() normally terminates the process.

Table 12-2 lists the methods and descriptions of the ProcessHandle.Info nested interface. An instance of this interface contains snapshot information about a process. You can obtain a ProcessHandle.Info using the info() method of the ProcessHandle interface or the Process class. All methods in the interface return an Optional.

Table 12-2. *Methods in the ProcessHandle.Info Interface*

Method	Description
Optional<String[]> arguments()	Returns arguments of the process. The process may change the original arguments passed to it after startup. This method returns the changed arguments in that case.
Optional<String> command()	Returns the executable pathname of the process.
Optional<String> commandLine()	It is a convenience method for combining the command and arguments of a process. It returns the command line of the process by combining the values returned from the command() and arguments() methods if both methods return non-empty optionals.
Optional<Instant> startInstant()	Returns the start time of the process. If the operating system does not return a start time, it returns an empty Optional.
Optional<Duration> totalCpuDuration()	Returns the total CPU time used by the process. Note that a process may run for a long time and may use very little CPU time.
Optional<String> user()	Returns the user of the process.

It is time to see the ProcessHandle and ProcessHandle.Info interfaces in action. All classes in this chapter are in the com.jdojo.process.api module, whose declaration is in Listing 12-1.

Listing 12-1. The Module Declaration for a Module Named com.jdojo.process.api

```
// module-info.java
module com.jdojo.process.api {
    exports com.jdojo.process.api;
}
```

Listing 12-2 contains the code for a class named `CurrentProcessInfo`. Its `printInfo()` method takes a `ProcessHandle` as an argument and prints the details of the process. We also use this method in other examples to print the details of a process. The `main()` method gets the handle of the current process running the process, which is a Java process, and prints its details. You may get a different output. The output was generated when the program ran on Windows 10.

Listing 12-2. A CurrentProcessInfo Class That Prints the Details of the Current Process

```java
// CurrentProcessInfo.java
package com.jdojo.process.api;

import java.time.Duration;
import java.time.Instant;
import java.time.ZoneId;
import java.time.ZonedDateTime;
import java.util.Arrays;

public class CurrentProcessInfo {
    public static void main(String[] args) {
        // Get the handle of the current process
        ProcessHandle current = ProcessHandle.current();

        // Print the process details
        printInfo(current);
    }
    public static void printInfo(ProcessHandle handle) {
        // Get the process ID
        long pid = handle.getPid();

        // Is the process still running
        boolean isAlive = handle.isAlive();

        // Get other process info
        ProcessHandle.Info info = handle.info();
        String command = info.command().orElse("");
        String[] args = info.arguments()
                            .orElse(new String[]{});
        String commandLine = info.commandLine().orElse("");
        ZonedDateTime startTime = info.startInstant()
                            .orElse(Instant.now())
                            .atZone(ZoneId.systemDefault());
        Duration duration = info.totalCpuDuration()
                                .orElse(Duration.ZERO);
        String owner = info.user().orElse("Unknown");
        long childrenCount = handle.children().count();

        // Print the process details
        System.out.printf("PID: %d%n", pid);
        System.out.printf("IsAlive: %b%n", isAlive);
        System.out.printf("Command: %s%n", command);
        System.out.printf("Arguments: %s%n", Arrays.toString(args));
        System.out.printf("CommandLine: %s%n", commandLine);
        System.out.printf("Start Time: %s%n", startTime);
        System.out.printf("CPU Time: %s%n", duration);
```

317

```
        System.out.printf("Owner: %s%n", owner);
        System.out.printf("Children Count: %d%n", childrenCount);
    }
}
```

```
PID: 8692
IsAlive: true
Command: C:\java9\bin\java.exe
Arguments: []
CommandLine:
Start Time: 2016-11-27T12:28:20.611-06:00[America/Chicago]
CPU Time: PT0.296875S
Owner: kishori\ksharan
Children Count: 1
```

Comparing Processes

It is tricky to compare two processes for equality or order. You cannot rely on PIDs for equality of processes. Operating systems reuse PIDs after processes terminate. You may check the start time of processes along with the PIDs; if both are same, the two processes may be the same. The equals() method of the default implementation of the ProcessHandle interface checks for the following three pieces of information for two processes to be equal:

- The implementation class of the ProcessHandle interface must be the same for both processes.

- Processes must have the same PIDs.

- Processes must have been started at the same time.

■ **Tip** Using the default implementation of the compareTo() method in the ProcessHandle interface is not very useful for ordering. It compares the PIDs of two processes.

Creating a Process

You need to use an instance of the ProcessBuilder class to start a new process. The class contains several methods to set attributes of the process. Calling the start() method starts a new process. The start() method returns a Process object that you can use to work with the input, output, and error streams of the process. The following snippet of code creates a ProcessBuilder to launch JVM on Windows:

```
ProcessBuilder pb = new ProcessBuilder()
                .command("C:\\java9\\bin\\java.exe",
                        "--module-path",
                        "myModulePath",
                        "--module",
                        "myModule/className")
                .inheritIO();
```

There are two ways to set the command and arguments for this new process:

- You can pass them to the constructor of the ProcessBuilder class.

- You can use the command() method.

The command() method without arguments returns the command set in the ProcessBuilder. Other versions with arguments—one with a var-args of String and one with a List<String>—are used to set the command and arguments. The first argument in the method is the command path and the rest are the arguments to the command.

The new process has its own input, output, and error streams. The inheritIO() method sets the input, output, and error streams of the new process to be the same as the current process. There are several redirectXxx() methods in the ProcessBuilder class to customize the standard I/O for the new process, for example, setting the standard error stream to a file, so all errors are logged to a file. Once you have configured all attributes of the process, you can call start() to start the process:

```
// Start a new process
Process newProcess = pb.start();
```

You can call the start() method of the ProcessBuilder class multiple times to start multiple processes with the same attributes previously stored in it. This has a performance benefit that you can create one ProcessBuilder instance and reuse it to launch the same process multiple times.

You can obtain the process handle of a process using the toHandle() method of the Process class:

```
// Get the process handle
ProcessHandle handle = newProcess.toHandle();
```

You can use the process handle to destroy the process, wait for the process to finish, or query the process for its state and attributes such as its children, descendants, parents, CPU time used, etc. The information you get about a process and the control you have on a process depends on the operating system access controls.

It is tricky to come up with an example to create a process that will run on all operating systems. I came up with an example in which creating a new process launches a new JVM to run a class. If you can run other examples in this book, it means that you have JDK 9 installed on your machine and this example should work on your machine.

Listing 12-3 contains the code for a class named Job. Its main() method expects two arguments: sleep interval and sleep duration in seconds. If they are not passed, the method uses 5 seconds and 60 seconds as the default values. In the first part, the method attempts to extract first and second arguments, if specified. In the second part, it gets the process handle of the current process executing this method using the ProcessHandle.current() method. It reads the PID of the current process and prints a message including the PID, sleep interval, and sleep duration. In the end, it starts a for loop and keeps sleeping for the sleep interval until the sleep duration is reached. In every iteration of the loop, it prints a message.

Listing 12-3. The Declaration of a Class Named Job

```
// Job.java
package com.jdojo.process.api;

import java.io.IOException;
import java.util.ArrayList;
import java.util.List;
import java.util.concurrent.TimeUnit;
import java.util.stream.Collectors;
```

```java
/**
 * An instance of this class is used as a job that sleeps at a
 * regular interval up to a maximum duration. The sleep
 * interval in seconds can be specified as the first argument
 * and the sleep duration as the second argument while running.
 * this class. The default sleep interval and sleep duration
 * are 5 seconds and 60 seconds, respectively. If these values
 * are less than zero, zero is used instead.
 */
public class Job {
    // The job sleep interval
    public static final long DEFAULT_SLEEP_INTERVAL = 5;

    // The job sleep duration
    public static final long DEFAULT_SLEEP_DURATION = 60;

    public static void main(String[] args) {
        long sleepInterval = DEFAULT_SLEEP_INTERVAL;
        long sleepDuration = DEFAULT_SLEEP_DURATION;

        // Get the passed in sleep interval
        if (args.length >= 1) {
            sleepInterval = parseArg(args[0], DEFAULT_SLEEP_INTERVAL);
            if (sleepInterval < 0) {
                sleepInterval = 0;
            }
        }

        // Get the passed in the sleep duration
        if (args.length >= 2) {
            sleepDuration = parseArg(args[1], DEFAULT_SLEEP_DURATION);
            if (sleepDuration < 0) {
                sleepDuration = 0;
            }
        }

        long pid = ProcessHandle.current().getPid();
        System.out.printf("Job (pid=%d) info: Sleep Interval" +
                          "=%d seconds, Sleep Duration=%d " +
                          "seconds.%n",
                          pid, sleepInterval, sleepDuration);

        for (long sleptFor = 0; sleptFor < sleepDuration;
                          sleptFor += sleepInterval) {
            try {
                System.out.printf("Job (pid=%d) is going to" +
                                  " sleep for %d seconds.%n",
                                  pid, sleepInterval);
                // Sleep for the sleep interval
                TimeUnit.SECONDS.sleep(sleepInterval);
```

```
        } catch (InterruptedException ex) {
            System.out.printf("Job (pid=%d) was " +
                                "interrupted.%n", pid);
        }
    }
}

/**
 * Starts a new JVM to run the Job class.
 * @param sleepInterval The sleep interval when the Job
 * class is run. It is passed to the JVM as the first
 * argument.
 * @param sleepDuration The sleep duration for the Job
 * class. It is passed to the JVM as the second argument.
 * @return The new process reference of the newly launched
 * JVM or null if the JVM cannot be launched.
 */
public static Process startProcess(long sleepInterval,
                                    long sleepDuration) {
    // Store the command to launch a new JVM in a
    // List<String>
    List<String> cmd = new ArrayList<>();

    // Add command components in order
    addJvmPath(cmd);
    addModulePath(cmd);
    addClassPath(cmd);
    addMainClass(cmd);

    // Add arguments to run the class
    cmd.add(String.valueOf(sleepInterval));
    cmd.add(String.valueOf(sleepDuration));

    // Build the process attributes
    ProcessBuilder pb = new ProcessBuilder()
                            .command(cmd)
                            .inheritIO();
    String commandLine = pb.command()
                            .stream()
                            .collect(Collectors.joining(" "));
    System.out.println("Command used:\n" + commandLine);

    // Start the process
    Process p = null;
    try {
        p = pb.start();
    } catch (IOException e) {
        e.printStackTrace();
    }
    return p;
}

/**
 * Used to parse the arguments passed to the JVM, which
 * in turn is passed to the main() method.
```

```
 * @param valueStr The string value of the argument
 * @param defaultValue The default value of the argument if
 * the valueStr is not an integer.
 * @return valueStr as a long or the defaultValue if
 * valueStr is not an integer.
 */
private static long parseArg(String valueStr,
                                 long defaultValue) {
    long value = defaultValue;
    if (valueStr != null) {
        try {
            value = Long.parseLong(valueStr);
        } catch (NumberFormatException e) {
            // no action needed
        }
    }
    return value;
}


/**
 * Adds the JVM path to the command list. It first attempts
 * to use the command attribute of the current process;
 * failing that it relies on the java.home system property.
 * @param cmd The command list
 */
private static void addJvmPath(List<String> cmd) {
    // First try getting the command to run the current JVM
    String jvmPath = ProcessHandle.current()
                                .info()
                                .command().orElse("");
    if(jvmPath.length() > 0) {
        cmd.add(jvmPath);
    } else {
        // Try composing the JVM path using the java.home
        // system property
        final String FILE_SEPARATOR =
            System.getProperty("file.separator");

        jvmPath = System.getProperty("java.home") +
                            FILE_SEPARATOR +  "bin" +
                            FILE_SEPARATOR + "java";
        cmd.add(jvmPath);
    }
}

/**
 * Adds a module path to the command list.
 * @param cmd The command list
 */
private static void addModulePath(List<String> cmd) {
    String modulePath =
        System.getProperty("jdk.module.path");
```

```
        if(modulePath != null && modulePath.trim().length() > 0) {
            cmd.add("--module-path");
            cmd.add(modulePath);
        }
    }

    /**
     * Adds class path to the command list.
     * @param cmd The command list
     */
    private static void addClassPath(List<String> cmd) {
        String classPath = System.getProperty("java.class.path");

        if(classPath != null && classPath.trim().length() > 0) {
            cmd.add("--class-path");
            cmd.add(classPath);
        }
    }

    /**
     * Adds a main class to the command list. Adds
     * module/className or just className depending on whether
     * the Job class was loaded in a named module or unnamed
     * module
     * @param cmd The command list
     */
    private static void addMainClass(List<String> cmd) {
        Class<Job> cls = Job.class;
        String className = cls.getName();
        Module module = cls.getModule();
        if(module.isNamed()) {
            String moduleName = module.getName();
            cmd.add("--module");
            cmd.add(moduleName + "/" + className);
        } else {
            cmd.add(className);
        }
    }
}
```

The Job class contains a startProcess(long sleepInterval, long sleepDuration) method that starts a new process. It launches a JVM with the Job class as the main class. It passes the sleep interval and duration to the JVM as arguments. The method attempts to build a command to launch the java command from the JDK_HOME\bin directory. If the Job class were loaded in a named module, it builds a command like this:

```
JDK_HOME\bin\java --module-path <module-path> --module com.jdojo.process.api/com.jdojo.
process.api.Job <sleepInterval> <sleepDuration>
```

If the Job class were loaded in an unnamed module, it attempts to build a command like this:

```
JDK_HOME\bin\java -class-path <class-path> com.jdojo.process.api.Job <sleepInterval>
<sleepDuration>
```

The startProcess() method prints the command used to start a process, attempts to start the process, and returns the process reference.

The addJvmPath() method adds the JVM path to the command list. It attempts to get the command for the current JVM process to use as the JVM path for the new process. If it is not available, it attempts to build it from the java.home system property.

The Job class contains several utility methods that are used to compose parts of commands and parse the arguments passed to the main() method. Refer to their Javadoc for descriptions.

If you want to start a new process that should run for five seconds and wake up every five seconds, you can do so using the startProcess() method of the Job class:

```
// Start a process that runs for 15 seconds
Process p = Job.startProcess(5, 15);
```

You can print the process details using the printInfo() method of the CurrentProcessInfo class that you created in Listing 12-2:

```
// Get the handle of the current process
ProcessHandle handle = p.toHandle();

// Print the process details
CurrentProcessInfo.printInfo(handle);
```

You can use the returned value of the onExit() method of the ProcessHandle to run a task when the process terminates.

```
CompletableFuture<ProcessHandle> future = handle.onExit();

// Print a message when process terminates
future.thenAccept((ProcessHandle ph) -> {
    System.out.printf("Job (pid=%d) terminated.%n", ph.getPid());
});
```

You can wait for the new process to terminate like so:

```
// Wait for the process to terminate
future.get();
```

In this example, future.get() will return the ProcessHandle of the process. I did not use the return value, because I already had it in the handle variable.

Listing 12-4 contains the code for a StartProcessTest class that shows you how to create a new process using the Job class. In its main() method, it creates a new process, prints process details, adds a shutdown task to the process, waits for the process to terminate, and prints the process details again. Note that the process runs for 15 seconds, but it uses only 0.359375 seconds of CPU time because most of the time the main thread of the process was sleeping. You may get a different output. The output was generated when the program ran on Windows 10.

Listing 12-4. A StartProcessTest Class That Creates New Processes

```java
// StartProcessTest.java
package com.jdojo.process.api;

import java.util.concurrent.CompletableFuture;
import java.util.concurrent.ExecutionException;

public class StartProcessTest {
    public static void main(String[] args) {
        // Start a process that runs for 15 seconds
        Process p = Job.startProcess(5, 15);

        if (p == null) {
            System.out.println("Could not create a new process.");
            return;
        }

        // Get the handle of the current process
        ProcessHandle handle = p.toHandle();

        // Print the process details
        CurrentProcessInfo.printInfo(handle);

        CompletableFuture<ProcessHandle> future = handle.onExit();

        // Print a message when process terminates
        future.thenAccept((ProcessHandle ph) -> {
            System.out.printf("Job (pid=%d) terminated.%n", ph.getPid());
        });

        try {
            // Wait for the process to complete
            future.get();
        } catch (InterruptedException | ExecutionException e) {
            e.printStackTrace();
        }

        // Print process details again
        CurrentProcessInfo.printInfo(handle);
    }
}
```

```
Command used:
C:\java9\bin\java.exe --module-path
C:\Java9Revealed\com.jdojo.process.api\build\classes --class-path
C:\Java9Revealed\com.jdojo.process.api\build\classes --module
com.jdojo.process.api/com.jdojo.process.api.Job 5 15
PID: 10928
IsAlive: true
Command: C:\java9\bin\java.exe
```

```
Arguments: []

CommandLine:
Start Time: 2016-11-28T13:43:28.318-06:00[America/Chicago]
CPU Time: PT0S
Owner: kishori\ksharan
Children Count: 1
Job (pid=10928) info: Sleep Interval=5 seconds, Sleep Duration=15 seconds.
Job (pid=10928) is going to sleep for 5 seconds.
Job (pid=10928) is going to sleep for 5 seconds.
Job (pid=10928) is going to sleep for 5 seconds.
Job (pid=10928) terminated.
PID: 10928
IsAlive: false
Command:
Arguments: []
CommandLine:
Start Time: 2016-11-28T13:43:28.318-06:00[America/Chicago]
CPU Time: PT0.359375S
Owner: kishori\ksharan
Children Count: 0
```

Obtaining a Process Handle

There are several ways to get the handle of a native process. For a process created by the Java code, you can get a ProcessHandle using the toHandle() method of the Process class. Native processes can also be created from outside the JVM. The ProcessHandle interface contains the following methods to get the handle of a native process:

- static Optional<ProcessHandle> of(long pid)

- static ProcessHandle current()

- Optional<ProcessHandle> parent()

- Stream<ProcessHandle> children()

- Stream<ProcessHandle> descendants()

- static Stream<ProcessHandle> allProcesses()

The of() static method returns an Optional<ProcessHandle> for the specified pid. If there is no process with this pid, an empty Optional is returned. To use this method, you need to know the PID of the process:

```
// Get the process handle of the process with the pid of 1234
Optional<ProcessHandle> handle = ProcessHandle.of(1234L);
```

The current() static method returns the handle of the current process, which is always the Java process executing the code. You have already seen an example of this in Listing 12-2.

The parent() method returns the handle of the parent process. It returns an empty Optional if the process does not have parent or the parent cannot be retrieved.

The children() method returns a snapshot of all direct child processes of the process. There is no guarantee that a process returned by this method is still alive. Note that a process, which is not alive, does not have children.

The descendants() method returns a snapshot of all child processes of the process direct or indirect.

The allProcesses() method returns a snapshot of all processes that are visible to this process. There is no guarantee that the stream contains all process in the operating system at the time the stream is processed. Processes may have been terminated or created after the snapshot was taken. The following snippet of code prints the PIDs of all processes sorted by their PIDs:

```
System.out.printf("All processes PIDs:%n");
ProcessHandle.allProcesses()
            .map(ph -> ph.getPid())
            .sorted()
            .forEach(System.out::println);
```

You can compute different types of statistics for all running processes. You can also create a task manager in Java that displays a UI showing all running processes and their attributes. Listing 12-5 shows how to get the longest running process details and the process that used the CPU time the most. I compared the start time of the processes to get the longest running process and the total CPU duration to get the process that used the CPU time the most. You may get a different output. I got this output when I ran the program on Windows 10.

Listing 12-5. Computing Process Statistics

```
// ProcessStats.java
package com.jdojo.process.api;

import java.time.Duration;
import java.time.Instant;

public class ProcessStats {
    public static void main(String[] args) {
        System.out.printf("Longest CPU User Process:%n");
        ProcessHandle.allProcesses()
                    .max(ProcessStats::compareCpuTime)
                    .ifPresent(CurrentProcessInfo::printInfo);

        System.out.printf("%nLongest Running Process:%n");
        ProcessHandle.allProcesses()
                    .max(ProcessStats::compareStartTime)
                    .ifPresent(CurrentProcessInfo::printInfo);
    }

    public static int compareCpuTime(ProcessHandle ph1,
                                     ProcessHandle ph2) {
        return ph1.info()
                .totalCpuDuration()
                .orElse(Duration.ZERO)
                .compareTo(ph2.info()
                        .totalCpuDuration()
                        .orElse(Duration.ZERO));
    }
```

```
    public static int compareStartTime(ProcessHandle ph1,
                                       ProcessHandle ph2) {
        return ph1.info()
                .startInstant()
                .orElse(Instant.now())
                .compareTo(ph2.info()
                        .startInstant()
                        .orElse(Instant.now())));
    }
}
```

```
Longest CPU User Process:
PID: 10696
IsAlive: true
Command: C:\Program Files (x86)\Google\Chrome\Application\chrome.exe
Arguments: []
CommandLine:
Start Time: 2016-11-28T10:12:08.537-06:00[America/Chicago]
CPU Time: PT14M26.5S
Owner: kishori\ksharan
Children Count: 0

Longest Running Process:
PID: 0
IsAlive: false
Command:
Arguments: []
CommandLine:
Start Time: 2016-11-29T13:18:22.262776600-06:00[America/Chicago]
CPU Time: PT0S
Owner: Unknown
Children Count: 127
```

Terminating Processes

You can terminate a process using the destroy() or destroyForcibly() method of the ProcessHandle interface and the Process class. Both methods return true if the request to terminate the process was successful, false otherwise. The destroy() method requests a normal termination, whereas the destroyForcibly() method request a forced termination. It is possible for the isAlive() method to return true for a brief period after a request to terminate the process has been made.

■ **Tip** You cannot terminate the current process. Calling the destroy() or the destroyForcibly() method on the current process throws an IllegalStateException. The operating system access controls may prevent a process from being terminated.

A normal termination of a process lets the process terminate cleanly. A forced termination of a process terminates the process immediately. Whether a process is normally terminated is implementation dependent. You can use the `supportsNormalTermination()` method of the `ProcessHandle` interface and the `Process` class to check if a process supports normal termination. The method returns `true` if the process supports normal termination, `false` otherwise.

Calling one of these methods to terminate a process that has already been terminated results in no action. The `CompletableFuture<Process>` returned from `onExit()` of the `Process` class and the `CompletableFuture<ProcessHandle>` returned from `onExit()` of the `ProcessHandle` interface are `completed` when the process terminates.

Managing Process Permissions

When you ran the examples in the previous sections, I assumed that there was no Java security manager installed. If a security manager is installed, appropriate permissions need to be granted to start, manage, and query native processes:

- If you are creating a new process, you need to have `FilePermission(cmd,"execute")` permission, where `cmd` is the absolute path of the command that will create the process. If `cmd` is not an absolute path, you need to have `FilePermission("<<ALL FILES>>","execute")` permission.

- To query the state of native processes and destroy the process using the methods in the `ProcessHandle` interface, the application needs to have `RuntimePermission ("manageProcess")` permission.

Listing 12-6 contains a program that gets a process count and creates a new process. It repeats these two tasks without a security manager and with a security manager.

Listing 12-6. Managing Processes with a Security Manager

```
// ManageProcessPermission.java
package com.jdojo.process.api;

import java.util.concurrent.ExecutionException;

public class ManageProcessPermission {
    public static void main(String[] args) {
        // Get the process count
        long count = ProcessHandle.allProcesses().count();
        System.out.printf("Process Count: %d%n", count);

        // Start a new process
        Process p = Job.startProcess(1, 3);

        try {
            p.toHandle().onExit().get();
        } catch (InterruptedException | ExecutionException e) {
            System.out.println(e.getMessage());
        }

        // Install a security manager
        SecurityManager sm = System.getSecurityManager();
        if(sm == null) {
```

```
            System.setSecurityManager(new SecurityManager());
            System.out.println("A security manager is installed.");
        }

        // Get the process count
        try {
            count = ProcessHandle.allProcesses().count();
            System.out.printf("Process Count: %d%n", count);
        } catch(RuntimeException e) {
            System.out.println("Could not get a " +
                        "process count: " + e.getMessage());
        }

        // Start a new process
        try {
            p = Job.startProcess(1, 3);
            p.toHandle().onExit().get();
        } catch (InterruptedException | ExecutionException |
                RuntimeException e) {
            System.out.println("Could not start a new " +
                            "process: " + e.getMessage());
        }
    }
}
```

Try running the ManageProcessPermission class using the following command assuming that you have not changed any Java policy files:

```
C:\Java9Revealed>java --module-path
C:\Java9Revealed\com.jdojo.process.api\build\classes --module
com.jdojo.process.api/com.jdojo.process.api.ManageProcessPermission
```

```
Process Count: 126
Command used:
C:\java9\bin\java.exe --module-path
C:\Java9Revealed\com.jdojo.process.api\build\classes --module
com.jdojo.process.api/com.jdojo.process.api.Job 1 3
Job (pid=6320) info: Sleep Interval=1 seconds, Sleep Duration=3 seconds.
Job (pid=6320) is going to sleep for 1 seconds.
Job (pid=6320) is going to sleep for 1 seconds.
Job (pid=6320) is going to sleep for 1 seconds.
A security manager is installed.
Could not get a process count: access denied ("java.lang.RuntimePermission" "manageProcess")
Could not start a new process: access denied ("java.lang.RuntimePermission" "manageProcess")
```

You may get a different output. The output indicates that you were able to get the process count and create a new process before a security manager was installed. After the security manager was installed, the Java runtime threw exceptions while requesting the process count and creating a new process. To fix the problem, you need to grant the following four permissions:

- The "manageProcess" RuntimePermission, which will allow the application to query the native process and create a new process.

- The "execute" FilePermission on the Java command path, which will allow launching the JVM.

- The "read" PropertyPermission on the "jdk.module.path" and "java.class.path" system properties, so the Job class can read these properties while building the command line to launch the JVM.

Listing 12-7 contains a script to grant these four permissions to all code. You will need to add this script to the JDK_HOME\conf\security\java.policy file on your machine. The path to the Java launcher is C:\\java9\\bin\\java.exe and it is valid on Windows only if you have installed JDK 9 in the C:\java9 directory. For all other platforms and JDK installations, modify this path to point to the correct Java launcher on your machine.

Listing 12-7. Addendum to the JDK_HOME|conf\security\java.policy File

```
grant {
    permission java.lang.RuntimePermission "manageProcess";
    permission java.io.FilePermission "C:\\java9\\bin\\java.exe", "execute";
    permission java.util.PropertyPermission "jdk.module.path", "read";
    permission java.util.PropertyPermission "java.class.path", "read";
};
```

If you run the ManageProcessPermission class again using the same command, you should get output similar to the following:

```
Process Count: 133
Command used:
C:\java9\bin\java.exe --module-path
C:\Java9Revealed\com.jdojo.process.api\build\classes --module
com.jdojo.process.api/com.jdojo.process.api.Job 1 3
Job (pid=3108) info: Sleep Interval=1 seconds, Sleep Duration=3 seconds.
Job (pid=3108) is going to sleep for 1 seconds.
Job (pid=3108) is going to sleep for 1 seconds.
Job (pid=3108) is going to sleep for 1 seconds.
A security manager is installed.
Process Count: 133
Command used:
C:\java9\bin\java.exe --module-path
C:\Java9Revealed\com.jdojo.process.api\build\classes --module
com.jdojo.process.api/com.jdojo.process.api.Job 1 3
Job (pid=3684) info: Sleep Interval=1 seconds, Sleep Duration=3 seconds.
Job (pid=3684) is going to sleep for 1 seconds.
Job (pid=3684) is going to sleep for 1 seconds.
Job (pid=3684) is going to sleep for 1 seconds.
```

Summary

The Process API consists of classes and interfaces to work with native processes. Java SE has provided the Process API since version 1.0 through the Runtime and Process classes. It allowed you to create new native processes, manage their I/O streams, and destroy them. Later versions of Java SE improved the API. Until Java 9, developers had to resort to writing native code to get basic information such as the ID of a process, the command used to start a processes, etc. Java 9 added an interface named ProcessHandle that represents a process handle. You can use the process handle to query and manage a native process.

The following classes and interfaces comprise the Process API: Runtime, ProcessBuilder, ProcessBuilder.Redirect, Process, ProcessHandle, and ProcessHandle.Info.

The exec() method of the Runtime class is used to start a native process. The start() method of the ProcessBuilder class is a preferred over the exec() method of the Runtime class to start a process. An instance of the ProcessBuilder.Redirect class represents a source of input of a process or a destination output of a process.

An instance of the Process class represents a native process created by a Java program.

An instance of the ProcessHandle interface represents a process created by a Java program or by other means; it was added in Java 9 and provides several methods to query and manage processes. An instance of the ProcessHandle.Info interface represents snapshot information of a process; it can be obtained using the info() method of the Process class or ProcessHandle interface. If you have a Process instance, use its toHandle() method to get a ProcessHandle.

The onExit() method of the ProcessHandle interface returns a CompletableFuture<ProcessHandle> for the termination of the process. You can use the returned object to add a task that will be executed when the process terminates. Note that you cannot use this method on the current process.

If a security manager is installed, the application needs to have a "manageProcess" RuntimePermission to query and manage native processes, and an "execute" FilePermission on the command file of the process that is started from the Java code.

CHAPTER 13

■ ■ ■

Collection API Updates

In this chapter, you will learn:

- How unmodifiable lists, sets, and maps were created before JDK 9 and what were the problems in using them.

- How to create unmodifiable lists using the of() static factory method of the List interface in JDK 9.

- How to create unmodifiable sets using the of() static factory method of the Set interface in JDK 9.

- How to create unmodifiable maps using the of(), ofEntries(), and entry() static factory methods of the Map interface in JDK 9.

The Background

The Collection API consists of classes and interfaces that provide a way to store and manipulate different types of collections of objects such as lists, sets, and maps. It was added to Java SE 1.2. The Java programming language does not support collection literals, which are a simple and easy way to declare and initialize collections. A collection literal would let you create a collection of a specific type by specifying the elements of the collection in an expression in a compact form. An example of a collection literal is a List literal that enables you to create a list of two integers, 100 and 200, as shown:

```
List<Integer> list = [100, 200];
```

A collection literal is compact and simple to use. It can be implemented for efficient use of memory because the number of elements is known at creation time. It can be made immutable to make it thread-safe.

Including collection literals in the Java programming language was considered several times before JDK 9. Java designers decided not to add collection literals to the Java language, at least not in JDK 9. Adding collection literals to Java at this point would require too much effort for too little gain. They decided to achieve the same goal by updating the Collection API by adding static factory methods to the List, Set and Map interfaces, which can be used to create small, unmodifiable collections easily and efficiently.

The existing Collection API creates mutable collections. You can create an immutable (or unmodifiable) collection by wrapping a mutable collection inside another object, which is just a wrapper for the original mutable object. To create an unmodifiable List of two integers in JDK 8 or earlier, you typically used the following snippet of code:

```
// Create an empty, mutable list
List<Integer> list = new ArrayList<>();

// Add two elements to the mutable list
list.add(100);
list.add(200);

// Create an immutable list by wrapping the mutable list
List<Integer> list2 = Collections.unmodifiableList(list);
```

This approach has a serious flaw. The unmodifiable list is just a wrapper for the modifiable list. Intentionally, I kept the variable named list around. You cannot modify the list using the list2 variable; however, you can still use the list variable to modify the list and the modifications will be reflected when you read the list using the list2 variable. Listing 13-1 contains a complete program to create an unmodifiable List and shows you how to change its contents afterward.

Listing 13-1. Creating an Unmodifiable List Before JDK 9

```
// PreJDK9UnmodifiableList.java
package com.jdojo.collection;

import java.util.ArrayList;
import java.util.Collections;
import java.util.List;

public class PreJDK9UnmodifiableList {
    public static void main(String[] args) {
        List<Integer> list = new ArrayList<>();
        list.add(100);
        list.add(200);
        System.out.println("list = " + list);

        // Create an unmodifiable list
        List<Integer> list2 = Collections.unmodifiableList(list);

        System.out.println("list2 = " + list2);

        // Let us add an element using list
        list.add(300);

        // Print the contents of the list using both
        // variables named list and list2
        System.out.println("list = " + list);
        System.out.println("list2 = " + list2);
    }
}
```

```
list = [100, 200]
list2 = [100, 200]
list = [100, 200, 300]
list2 = [100, 200, 300]
```

The output shows that as long as you keep the reference of the original list, you can change its contents and the unmodifiable list is not really unmodifiable! A solution to this problem is to overwrite the original reference variable with a reference to the new unmodifiable list as shown:

```
List<Integer> list = new ArrayList<>();
list.add(100);
list.add(200);

// Create an unmodifiable list and store it in list
list = Collections.unmodifiableList(list);
```

Notice that this example uses multiple statements to create and populate an unmodifiable list. If you need to declare and initialize an unmodifiable list as an instance or static variable in a class, this approach does not work because it involves multiple statements. Such a declaration needs to be simple, compact, and contained in one statement. If you use the previous snippet of code for an instance variable in a class, your code would be similar to the following code:

```
public class Test {
    private List<Integer> list = new ArrayList<>();

    {
        list.add(100);
        list.add(200);
        list = Collections.unmodifiableList(list);
    }
    // ...
}
```

There are other ways to declare and initialize an unmodifiable list such as using an array and converting it to a list. Three of such ways are as follows:

```
public class Test {
    // Using an array and converting it to a list
    private List<Integer> list2 = Collections.unmodifiableList(
            new ArrayList<>( Arrays.asList(100, 200)));

    // Using an anonymous class
    private List<Integer> list3 = Collections.unmodifiableList(
            new ArrayList<>(){{add(100); add(200);}});

    // Using a stream
    private List<Integer> list4 = Collections.unmodifiableList(
            Stream.of(100, 200).collect(Collectors.toList()));

    // More code goes here
}
```

This example proves that you can have an unmodifiable list in one statement. However, the syntax is verbose. These techniques are also inefficient. For example, just to hold two integers in a list, these techniques create multiple objects with a backing array object to hold the values.

JDK 9 solves these problems by providing static factory methods to the List, Set, and Map interfaces. The method is named of() and it is overloaded. In JDK 9, you can declare and initialize an unmodifiable list of two elements as shown:

```
// Create an unmodifiable list of two integers
List<Integer> list = List.of(100, 200);
```

Unmodifiable Lists

JDK 9 added an overloaded of() static factory method to the List interface. It provides a simple and compact way to create unmodifiable lists. Here are all the versions of the of() method:

- static <E> List<E> of()

- static <E> List<E> of(E e1)

- static <E> List<E> of(E e1, E e2)

- static <E> List<E> of(E e1, E e2, E e3)

- static <E> List<E> of(E e1, E e2, E e3, E e4)

- static <E> List<E> of(E e1, E e2, E e3, E e4, E e5)

- static <E> List<E> of(E e1, E e2, E e3, E e4, E e5, E e6)

- static <E> List<E> of(E e1, E e2, E e3, E e4, E e5, E e6, E e7)

- static <E> List<E> of(E e1, E e2, E e3, E e4, E e5, E e6, E e7, E e8)

- static <E> List<E> of(E e1, E e2, E e3, E e4, E e5, E e6, E e7, E e8, E e9)

- static <E> List<E> of(E e1, E e2, E e3, E e4, E e5, E e6, E e7, E e8, E e9, E e10)

- static <E> List<E> of(E... elements)

There are 11 special versions of the of() method to create lists of zero to ten elements. Another version takes a var-args argument to allow creating an unmodifiable list of any number of elements. You might wonder why there are so many versions of the method when the version with the var-args argument can create lists with any number of elements. They exist for performance reason. The API designers wanted lists with small number of elements to be efficient. A var-args argument is implemented using an array. Methods with non-var-args arguments exist to avoid boxing the arguments into an array, which makes them more efficient. These methods use special implementation classes of the List interface for smaller lists.

The returned lists from the of() method have the following characteristics:

- They are structurally immutable. Attempting to add, replace, or delete elements throws an UnsupportedOperationException.

- They do not allow null elements. A NullPointerException is thrown if an element in the list is null.

- They are serializable if all elements are serializable.

- The order of the elements is the same as specified in the of() method or the array used with the var-args version of the of(E… elements) method.

- There is no guarantee about the implementation class of the returned List. That is, do not expect the returned object to be of ArrayList or any other class that implements the List interface. Implementations of these methods are internal and you should make no assumption about their class names. For example, List.of() and List.of("A") may return objects of two different classes.

The Collections class contains a static field named EMPTY_LIST representing an immutable empty list. It also contains a static method named emptyList() to obtain an immutable empty list. Its singletonList (T object) method returns an immutable singleton list with the specified element. The following snippet of code shows pre-JDK 9 and JDK 9 ways of creating immutable empty and singleton lists:

```
// Creating an empty, immutable List before JDK 9
List<Integer> emptyList1 = Collections.EMPTY_LIST;
List<Integer> emptyList2 = Collections.emptyList();

// Creating an empty list in JDK 9
List<Integer> emptyList = List.of();

// Creating a singleton, immutable List before JDK 9
List<Integer> singletonList1 = Collections.singletonList(100);

// Creating a singleton, immutable List in JDK 9
List<Integer> singletonList = List.of(100);
```

How do you use the of() method to create an unmodifiable list from an array? The answer depends on the list you want out of the array. You may want a list whose elements are the same as elements of the array or you may want a list with the array itself as the sole element in the list. Using List.of(array) will invoke the of(E... elements) method and the returned list will have its elements the same as the elements in the array. If you want the array itself to be the sole element in the list, you will need to use List.<array-type>of(array) method, which will invoke the of(E e1) method and the returned list will have one element, which would be the array itself. The following snippet of code demonstrates this with an array of Integer:

```
Integer[] nums = {100, 200};

// Create a list whose elements are the same as the elements
// in the array
List<Integer> list1 = List.of(nums);
System.out.println("list1 = " + list1);
System.out.println("list1.size() = " + list1.size());

// Create a list whose sole element is the array itself
List<Integer[]> list2 = List.<Integer[]>of(nums);
System.out.println("list2 = " + list2);
System.out.println("list2.size() = " + list2.size());
```

```
list1 = [100, 200]
list1.size() = 2
list2 = [[Ljava.lang.Integer;@27efef64]
list2.size() = 1
```

Listing 13-2 contains a complete program that shows you how to use the of() static factory method of the List interface to create unmodifiable lists.

Listing 13-2. Using the List.of() Static Method to Create Unmodifiable Lists

```java
// ListTest.java
package com.jdojo.collection;

import java.util.List;

public class ListTest {
    public static void main(String[] args) {
        // Create few unmodifiable lists
        List<Integer> emptyList = List.of();
        List<Integer> luckyNumber = List.of(19);
        List<String> vowels = List.of("A", "E", "I", "O", "U");

        System.out.println("emptyList = " + emptyList);
        System.out.println("singletonList = " + luckyNumber);
        System.out.println("vowels = " + vowels);

        try {
            // Try using a null element
            List<Integer> list = List.of(1, 2, null, 3);
        } catch(NullPointerException e) {
            System.out.println("Nulls not allowed in List.of().");
        }

        try {
            // Try adding an element
            luckyNumber.add(8);
        } catch(UnsupportedOperationException e) {
            System.out.println("Cannot add an element.");
        }

        try {
            // Try removing an element
            luckyNumber.remove(0);
        } catch(UnsupportedOperationException e) {
            System.out.println("Cannot remove an element.");
        }
    }
}
```

```
emptyList = []
singletonList = [19]
vowels = [A, E, I, O, U]
Nulls not allowed in List.of().
Cannot add an element.
Cannot remove an element.
```

Unmodifiable Sets

JDK 9 added an overloaded of() static factory method to the Set interface. It provides a simple and compact way to create unmodifiable sets. Here are all the versions of the of() method:

- static <E> Set<E> of()

- static <E> Set<E> of(E e1)

- static <E> Set<E> of(E e1, E e2)

- static <E> Set<E> of(E e1, E e2, E e3)

- static <E> Set<E> of(E e1, E e2, E e3, E e4)

- static <E> Set<E> of(E e1, E e2, E e3, E e4, E e5)

- static <E> Set<E> of(E e1, E e2, E e3, E e4, E e5, E e6)

- static <E> Set<E> of(E e1, E e2, E e3, E e4, E e5, E e6, E e7)

- static <E> Set<E> of(E e1, E e2, E e3, E e4, E e5, E e6, E e7, E e8)

- static <E> Set<E> of(E e1, E e2, E e3, E e4, E e5, E e6, E e7, E e8, E e9)

- static <E> Set<E> of(E e1, E e2, E e3, E e4, E e5, E e6, E e7, E e8, E e9, E e10)

- static <E> Set<E> of(E... elements)

All versions of the of() methods are fined-tuned for performance. You can use the first 11 versions to create an unmodifiable set of zero to ten elements. The reason that the first 11 versions of the of() method exist along with a version with a var-args argument is to avoid boxing arguments into an array for sets up to 10 elements. The version with the var-args argument can be used to create an unmodifiable set with any number of elements.

The returned sets from the of() method have the following characteristics:

- They are structurally immutable. Attempting to add, replace, or delete elements throws an UnsupportedOperationException.

- They do not allow null elements. A NullPointerException is thrown if an element in the set is null.

- They are serializable if all elements are serializable.

- They do not allow duplicate elements. Specifying duplicate elements throws an IllegalArgumentException.

- The iteration order of the elements is unspecified.

- There is no guarantee about the implementation class of the returned Set. That is, do not expect the returned object to be of HashSet or any other class that implements the Set interface. Implementations of these methods are internal and you should make no assumption about their class names. For example, Set.of() and Set.of("A") may return objects of two different classes.

The Collections class contains a static field named EMPTY_SET representing an immutable empty set. It also contains a static method named emptySet() to obtain an immutable empty set. Its singleton(T object) method returns an immutable singleton set with the specified element. The following snippet of code shows pre-JDK 9 and JDK 9 ways of creating immutable empty and singleton sets:

```
// Creating an empty, immutable Set before JDK 9
Set<Integer> emptySet1 = Collections.EMPTY_SET;
Set<Integer> emptySet2 = Collections.emptySet();

// Creating an empty Set in JDK 9
Set<Integer> emptySet = Set.of();

// Creating a singleton, immutable Set before JDK 9
Set<Integer> singletonSet1 = Collections.singleton(100);

// Creating a singleton, immutable Set in JDK 9
Set<Integer> singletonSet = Set.of(100);
```

The following snippet of code shows you how to create an unmodifiable Set from an array. You can have a Set whose elements are the same as the elements of the array or you can have a Set with the array as the only element. Note that the array cannot have duplicate elements when you are using array elements as the elements of the Set. Otherwise, the Set.of() method will throw an IllegalArgumentException.

```
Integer[] nums = {100, 200};

// Create a set whose elements are the same as the
// elements of the array
Set<Integer> set1 = Set.of(nums);
System.out.println("set1 = " + set1);
System.out.println("set1.size() = " + set1.size());

// Create a set whose sole element is the array itself
Set<Integer[]> set2 = Set.<Integer[]>of(nums);
System.out.println("set2 = " + set2);
System.out.println("set2.size() = " + set2.size());

// Create an array with duplicate elements
Integer[] nums2 = {101, 201, 101};

// Try creating a set with the array as its sole element
Set<Integer[]> set3 = Set.<Integer[]>of(nums2);
System.out.println("set3 = " + set3);
System.out.println("set3.size() = " + set3.size());

try {
    // Try creating a set whose elements are the elements of
    // the array. It will throw an IllegalArgumentException.
    Set<Integer> set4 = Set.of(nums2);
    System.out.println("set4 = " + set4);
} catch(IllegalArgumentException e) {
    System.out.println(e.getMessage());
}
```

```
set1 = [100, 200]
set1.size() = 2
set2 = [[Ljava.lang.Integer;@47c62251]
set2.size() = 1
set3 = [[Ljava.lang.Integer;@3e6fa38a]
set3.size() = 1
duplicate element: 101
```

Listing 13-3 contains a complete program that shows you how to use the of() static factory method of the Set interface to create unmodifiable sets. Note the output for the set named vowels in the program. Elements of the set may not be output in the same order they were specified when creating the set because a set does not guarantee the order of its elements.

Listing 13-3. Using the Set.of() Static Method to Create Unmodifiable Sets

```java
// SetTest.java
package com.jdojo.collection;

import java.util.Set;

public class SetTest {
    public static void main(String[] args) {
        // Create few unmodifiable sets
        Set<Integer> emptySet = Set.of();
        Set<Integer> luckyNumber = Set.of(19);
        Set<String> vowels = Set.of("A", "E", "I", "O", "U");

        System.out.println("emptySet = " + emptySet);
        System.out.println("singletonSet = " + luckyNumber);
        System.out.println("vowels = " + vowels);

        try {
            // Try using a null element
            Set<Integer> set = Set.of(1, 2, null, 3);
        } catch(NullPointerException e) {
            System.out.println("Nulls not allowed in Set.of().");
        }

        try {
            // Try using duplicate elements
            Set<Integer> set = Set.of(1, 2, 3, 2);
        } catch(IllegalArgumentException e) {
            System.out.println(e.getMessage());
        }

        try {
            // Try adding an element
            luckyNumber.add(8);
        } catch(UnsupportedOperationException e) {
            System.out.println("Cannot add an element.");
        }
```

```
        try {
            // Try removing an element
            luckyNumber.remove(0);
        } catch(UnsupportedOperationException e) {
            System.out.println("Cannot remove an element.");
        }
    }
}
```

```
emptySet = []
singletonSet = [19]
vowels = [E, O, A, U, I]
Nulls not allowed in Set.of().
duplicate element: 2
Cannot add an element.
Cannot remove an element.
```

Unmodifiable Maps

JDK 9 added an overloaded of() static factory method to the Map interface. It provides a simple and compact way to create unmodifiable maps. The methods' implementations are fine-tuned for performance. The following are 11 versions of the of() method that let you create an unmodifiable Map of zero to ten key-value entries:

- static <K,V> Map<K,V> of()

- static <K,V> Map<K,V> of(K k1, V v1)

- static <K,V> Map<K,V> of(K k1, V v1, K k2, V v2)

- static <K,V> Map<K,V> of(K k1, V v1, K k2, V v2, K k3, V v3)

- static <K,V> Map<K,V> of(K k1, V v1, K k2, V v2, K k3, V v3, K k4, V v4)

- static <K,V> Map<K,V> of(K k1, V v1, K k2, V v2, K k3, V v3, K k4, V v4, K k5, V v5)

- static <K,V> Map<K,V> of(K k1, V v1, K k2, V v2, K k3, V v3, K k4, V v4, K k5, V v5, K k6, V v6)

- static <K,V> Map<K,V> of(K k1, V v1, K k2, V v2, K k3, V v3, K k4, V v4, K k5, V v5, K k6, V v6, K k7, V v7)

- static <K,V> Map<K,V> of(K k1, V v1, K k2, V v2, K k3, V v3, K k4, V v4, K k5, V v5, K k6, V v6, K k7, V v7, K k8, V v8)

- static <K,V> Map<K,V> of(K k1, V v1, K k2, V v2, K k3, V v3, K k4, V v4, K k5, V v5, K k6, V v6, K k7, V v7, K k8, V v8, K k9, V v9)

- static <K,V> Map<K,V> of(K k1, V v1, K k2, V v2, K k3, V v3, K k4, V v4, K k5, V v5, K k6, V v6, K k7, V v7, K k8, V v8, K k9, V v9, K k10, V v10)

Note the positions of the arguments in the of() method. The first and the second arguments are the key and the value of the first key-value entry in the map, respectively; the third and the fourth arguments are the key and the value of the second key-value entry in the map, respectively; and so on. Notice that there is no var-args version of the of() method as you have in List and Set. This is because a Map entry contains two values (key and value) and you can have only one var-args argument in a method in Java. The following snippet of code shows you how to create maps using the of() method:

```
// An empty, unmodifiable Map
Map<Integer, String> emptyMap = Map.of();

// A singleton, unmodifiable Map
Map<Integer, String> singletonMap = Map.of(1, "One");

// A unmodifiable Map with two entries
Map<Integer, String> luckyNumbers = Map.of(1, "One", 2, "Two");
```

To create an unmodifiable Map with an arbitrary number of entries, JDK 9 provides a static method named ofEntries() in the Map interface, which has the following signature:

```
<K,V> Map<K,V> ofEntries(Map.Entry<? extends K,? extends V>... entries)
```

To use the ofEntries() method, you need to box each map entry in a Map.Entry instance. JDK 9 provides a convenient entry() static method in the Map interface to create instances of Map.Entry. The signature of the entry() method is as follows:

```
<K,V> Map.Entry<K,V> entry(K k, V v)
```

To keep the expression readable and compact, you need to use a static import for the Map.entry method and use a statement like the following to create an unmodifiable Map with an arbitrary number of entries:

```
import java.util.Map;
import static java.util.Map.entry;

// ...

// Use the Map.ofEntries() and Map.entry() methods to
// create an unmodifiable Map
Map<Integer, String> numberToWord =
        Map.ofEntries(entry(1, "One"),
                      entry(2, "Two"),
                      entry(3, "Three"));
```

The returned maps from the of() and ofEntries() methods of the Map interface have the following characteristics:

- They are structurally immutable. Attempting to add, replace, or delete entries throws an UnsupportedOperationException.

- They do not allow null in keys or values. A NullPointerException is thrown if a key or value in the map is null.

- They are serializable if all keys and values are serializable.

- They do not allow duplicate keys. Specifying duplicate keys throws an
  IllegalArgumentException.

- The iteration order of mappings is unspecified.

- There is no guarantee about the implementation class of the returned Map. That is, do
  not expect the returned object to be of HashMap or any other class that implements the
  Map interface. Implementations of these methods are internal and you should make
  no assumption about their class names. For example, Map.of() and Map.of(1, "One")
  may return objects of two different classes.

The Collections class contains a static field named EMPTY_MAP representing an immutable empty map.
It also contains a static method named emptyMap() to obtain an immutable empty map. Its singletonMap
(K key, V value) method returns an immutable singleton map with the specified key and value. The
following snippet of code shows pre-JDK 9 and JDK 9 ways of creating immutable empty and singleton maps:

```
// Creating an empty, immutable Map before JDK 9
Map<Integer,String> emptyMap1 = Collections.EMPTY_MAP;
Map<Integer,String> emptyMap2 = Collections.emptyMap();

// Creating an empty Map in JDK 9
Map<Integer,String> emptyMap = Map.of();

// Creating a singleton, immutable Map before JDK 9
Map<Integer,String> singletonMap1 =
    Collections.singletonMap(1, "One");

// Creating a singleton, immutable Map in JDK 9
Map<Integer,String> singletonMap = Map.of(1, "One");
```

Listing 13-4 contains a complete program that shows you how to use the of(), ofEntries(), and
entry()static methods of the Map interface to create unmodifiable maps. Notice the order in which days are
specified in the map and the order they are shown in the output. They may not match because a map does
not, like a set, guarantee the retrieval order of its entries.

Listing 13-4. Using the Map.of(), Map.ofEntries() and Map.entry() Static Methods to Create
Unmodifiable Maps

```
// MapTest.java
package com.jdojo.collection;

import java.util.Map;
import static java.util.Map.entry;

public class MapTest {
    public static void main(String[] args) {
        // Create few unmodifiable maps
        Map<Integer,String> emptyMap = Map.of();
        Map<Integer,String> luckyNumber = Map.of(19, "Nineteen");
        Map<Integer,String> numberToWord =
                Map.of(1, "One", 2, "Two", 3, "Three");
```

```java
        Map<String,String> days = Map.ofEntries(
                entry("Mon", "Monday"),
                entry("Tue", "Tuesday"),
                entry("Wed", "Wednesday"),
                entry("Thu", "Thursday"),
                entry("Fri", "Friday"),
                entry("Sat", "Saturday"),
                entry("Sun", "Sunday"));
        System.out.println("emptyMap = " + emptyMap);
        System.out.println("singletonMap = " + luckyNumber);
        System.out.println("numberToWord = " + numberToWord);
        System.out.println("days = " + days);

        try {
            // Try using a null value
            Map<Integer,String> map = Map.of(1, null);
        } catch(NullPointerException e) {
            System.out.println("Nulls not allowed in Map.of().");
        }

        try {
            // Try using duplicate keys
            Map<Integer,String> map = Map.of(1, "One", 1, "On");
        } catch(IllegalArgumentException e) {
            System.out.println(e.getMessage());
        }

        try {
            // Try adding an entry
            luckyNumber.put(8, "Eight");
        } catch(UnsupportedOperationException e) {
            System.out.println("Cannot add an entry.");
        }

         try {
            // Try removing an entry
            luckyNumber.remove(0);
        } catch(UnsupportedOperationException e) {
            System.out.println("Cannot remove an entry.");
        }
    }
}
```

```
emptyMap = {}
singletonMap = {19=Nineteen}
numberToWord = {1=One, 3=Three, 2=Two}
days = {Sat=Saturday, Tue=Tuesday, Thu=Thursday, Sun=Sunday, Wed=Wednesday,
Fri=Friday, Mon=Monday}
Nulls not allowed in Map.of().
duplicate key: 1
Cannot add an entry.
Cannot remove an entry.
```

Summary

Support for collection literals in the Java language has been a much needed feature in Java. Instead of providing support for collection literals, JDK 9 updated the Collection API to add static factory methods in the List, Set, and Map interfaces that return an unmodifiable List, Set, and Map, respectively The method is named of(). The method is overloaded to let you specify zero to ten elements of the collection. The List and Set interface provide a version of the of() method that takes a var-args argument to let you create a List and Set with an arbitrary number of elements. The Map interface provides an ofEntries() static factory method to let you create an unmodifiable Map of an arbitrary number of entries. The Map interface also contains a static entry() method that accepts a key and a value as arguments and returns a Map.Entry instance. The ofEntries() and entry() methods are used together to create an unmodifiable Map of an arbitrary number of entries.

The new static factory methods in these interfaces are fined-tuned for performance. The List.of() and Set.of() methods do not allow null elements. The Set.of() method does not allow duplicate elements. The Map.of() and Map.ofEntries() method do not allow duplicate keys, or null as a key or value.

CHAPTER 14

■ ■ ■

The HTTP/2 Client API

In this chapter, you will learn:

- What the HTTP/2 Client API is
- How to create HTTP clients
- How to make HTTP requests
- How to receive HTTP responses
- How to create WebSocket endpoints
- How to push unsolicited data from server to client

JDK 9 delivered the HTTP/2 Client API as an incubator module named `jdk.incubator.httpclient`. The module exports a `jdk.incubator.http` package that contains all public APIs. An incubator module is not part of the Java SE. In Java SE 10, either it will be standardized and become part of Java SE 10 or it will be removed. Refer to the web page at `http://openjdk.java.net/jeps/11` to learn more about incubator modules in JDK.

An incubator module is not resolved by default at compile-time or runtime, so you will need to add the `jdk.incubator.httpclient` module to the default set of root modules using the `--add-modules` option, like so:

```
<javac|java|jmod...> -add-modules jdk.incubator.httpclient ...
```

An incubator module is resolved if it is read by another module and the second module is resolved. In this chapter, you will create a module that reads the `jdk.incubator.httpclient` module and you will not have to use the `-add-modules` option to resolve it.

Because the API provided by an incubator module is not final yet, a warning is printed on the standard error when you use an incubator module at compile-time or runtime. The warning message looks like this:

```
WARNING: Using incubator modules: jdk.incubator.httpclient
```

The names of an incubator module and packages containing an incubator API start with `jdk.incubator`. Once they are standardized and included in Java SE, their names will be changed to use the standard Java naming convention. For example, the module name `jdk.incubator.httpclient` may become `java.httpclient` in Java SE 10.

Because the jdk.incubator.httpclient module is not in Java SE yet, you will not find Javadoc for this module. I generated the Javadoc for this module and included it with the book's source code. You can access the Javadoc using the Java9Revealed/jdk.incubator.httpclient/dist/javadoc/index.html file in the downloaded source code. I used the JDK 9 early access build 158 to generate the Javadoc. It is likely that the API may change and you may need to regenerate the Javadoc. Here is how you do this:

1. The source code this book contains a jdk.incubator.httpclient NetBeans project in a directory with the same name as the project name.

2. When you install JDK 9, its source code is copied as a src.zip file in the installation directory. Copy everything from the jdk.incubator.httpclient directory in the src.zip file to the Java9revealed\jdk.incubator.httpclient\src directory in the downloaded source code.

3. Open the jdk.incubator.httpclient project in NetBeans.

4. Right-click the project node in NetBeans and select the Generate Javadoc option. You will get errors and a warning that you can ignore. It will generate Javadoc in the Java9Revealed/jdk.incubator.httpclient/dist/javadoc directory. Open the index.html file in this directory to view the Javadoc for the jdk.incubator.httpclient module.

What Is the HTTP/2 Client API?

Java has supported HTTP/1.1 since JDK 1.0. The HTTP API consists of several types in the java.net package. The existing API had the following issues:

*   It was designed to support multiple protocols such as http, ftp, gopher, etc., many of which are not used anymore.

*   It was too abstract and hard to use.

*   It contained many undocumented behaviors.

*   It supported only one mode, blocking mode, which required you to have one thread per request/response.

In May 2015, the Internet Engineering Task Force (IETF) published a specification for HTTP/2. Refer to the web page at https://tools.ietf.org/html/rfc7540 for the complete text of the HTTP/2 specification. HTTP/2 does not modify the application-level semantics. That is, what you know about and have been using about the HTTP protocol in your application have not changed. It has a more efficient way of preparing the data packets and sending then over to the wire between the client and server. All you knew about HTTP before, such as HTTP headers, methods, status codes, URLs, etc., remains the same. HTTP/2 attempts to solve many problems related to performance faced by HTTP/1 connections:

*   HTTP/2 supports binary data exchange instead of textual data supported by HTTP/1.1.

*   HTTP/2 supports multiplexing and concurrency, which means that multiple data exchanges can occur concurrently in both directions of a TCP connection and responses to requests can be received out of order. This eliminates the overhead of having multiple connections between peers, which was typically the case while using HTTP/1.1. In HTTP/1.1, responses must be received in the same order as the requests were sent, which is called *head-of-line* blocking. HTTP/2 has solved the head-of-line blocking problem by enabling multiplexing over the same TCP connection.

- The client can suggest the priority of a request, which may be honored by the server in prioritizing responses.

- HTTP headers are compressed, which reduces the header size significantly, thus lowering latency.

- It allows for unsolicited push of resources from server to clients.

Instead of updating the existing API for HTTP/1.1, JDK 9 provided a new HTTP/2 Client API that supports both HTTP/1.1 and HTTP/2. It is intended that the API will eventually replace the old one. The new API also contains classes and interfaces to develop client applications using the WebSocket protocol. Refer to the web page at https://tools.ietf.org/html/rfc6455 for the complete WebSocket protocol specification. The new HTTP/2 Client API has several benefits over the existing API:

- It is simple and easy to learn and use for most common cases.

- It provides event-based notifications. For example, it generates notifications when headers are received, the body is received, and errors occur.

- It supports server push, which allows the server to push resources to the client without the client making an explicit request. It makes setting up WebSocket communication with servers simple.

- It supports HTTP/2 and HTTPS/TLS protocols.

- It works in both synchronous (blocking mode) and asynchronous (non-blocking mode) modes.

The new API consists of fewer than 20 types, four of which are the main types. Other types are used while you are using one of these four types. The new API also uses a few types from the old API. The new API is in the jdk.incubator.http package in the jdk.incubator.httpclient module. The main types are three abstract classes and one interface:

- The HttpClient class

- The HttpRequest class

- The HttpResponse class

- The WebSocket interface

An instance of the HttpClient class is a container for storing configurations that can be used for multiple HTTP requests instead of setting them separately for each. An instance of the HttpRequest class represents an HTTP request that can be sent to a server. An instance of the HttpResponse class represents an HTTP response. An instance of the WebSocket interface represents a WebSocket client. You can create a WebSocket server using the Java EE 7 WebSocket API. I show you an example of creating WebSocket client and server at the end of this chapter.

Instances of HttpClient, HttpRequest, and WebSocket are created using builders. Each type contains a nested class/interface named Builder that is used to build an instance of that type. Note that you do not create an HttpResponse; it is returned to you as part of an HTTP request that you make. The new HTTP/2 Client API is so simple to use that you can read an HTTP resource in just one statement! The following snippet of code reads the contents at the URL https://www.google.com/ as a string using a GET HTTP request:

```
String responseBody = HttpClient.newHttpClient()
        .send(HttpRequest.newBuilder(new URI("https://www.google.com/"))
            .GET()
            .build(), BodyHandler.asString())
        .body();
```

Typical steps in processing HTTP requests are as follows:

- Create an HTTP client object to store HTTP configuration information.

- Create an HTTP request object and populate it with information to be sent to the server.

- Send the HTTP request to the server.

- Receive an HTTP response object as a response from the server.

- Process the HTTP response.

Setting Up Examples

I use many examples in this chapter that involve interacting with a web server. Instead of using a web application deployed on the Internet, I created a web application project in NetBeans that you can deploy locally. If you prefer using another web application, you need to change the URLs used in the examples.

The NetBeans web application is located in the webapp directory of the book's source code. I tested the examples by deploying the web application on the GlassFish server 4.1.1 and Tomcat 8/9. You can download the NetBeans IDE with the GlassFish server from https://netbeans.org/. I ran the HTTP listener in the GlassFish server at port 8080. If you run it on a different port, you need to change the port number in the example URLs.

All this chapter's HTTP client programs are located in the com.jdojo.http.client directory in the book's source code. They are in the com.jdojo.http.client module whose declaration is shown in Listing 14-1.

Listing 14-1. The Module Declaration for a Module Named com.jdojo.http.client

```
// module-info.java
module com.jdojo.http.client {
    requires jdk.incubator.httpclient;
}
```

Creating HTTP Clients

An HTTP request that is sent to a server needs to be configured so that the server knows which authenticator to use, the SSL configuration details, the cookie manager to be used, proxy information, the redirect policy if the server redirects the request, etc. An instance of the HttpClient class stores these request-specific configurations, and they can be reused for multiple requests. You can override a few of these configurations on a per-request basis. When you send an HTTP request, you need to specify the HttpClient object that will supply the configuration information for the request. An HttpClient holds the following pieces of information that are used for all HTTP requests: an authenticator, a cookie manager, an executor, a redirect policy, a request priority, a proxy selector, an SSL context, SSL parameters, and an HTTP version.

An *authenticator* is an instance of the java.net.Authenticator class. It is used for HTTP authentication. The default is to use no authenticator.

A *cookie manager* is used to manage HTTP cookies. It is an instance of the java.net.CookieManager class. The default is to use no cookie manager.

An *executor* is an instance of the java.util.concurrent.Executor interface, which is used to send and receive asynchronous HTTP requests and responses. A default executor is provided, if it is not specified.

A *redirect policy* is one of the constants of the HttpClient.Redirect enum that specifies how to handle redirects issues by the server. The default is NEVER, which means the redirects issued by the server are never followed.

A *request priority* is the default priority for HTTP/2 requests, which can be between 1 and 256 (inclusive). It is a hint for the server to prioritize the request processing. A higher value means a higher priority.

A *proxy selector* is an instance of the `java.net.ProxySelector` class that selects the proxy server to use. The default is not to use a proxy server.

An *SSL context* is an instance of the `javax.net.ssl.SSLContext` class that provides an implementation for the secure socket protocol. A default `SSLContext` is provided, which works when you do not need to specify protocols or do not need client authentication.

SSL parameters are parameters for SSL/TLS/DTLS connections. They are stored in an instance of the `javax.net.ssl.SSLParameters` class.

An HTTP version is the version of HTTP, which is 1.1 or 2. It is specified as one of the constants of the `HttpClient.Version` enum: `HTTP_1_1` and `HTTP_2`. It requests a specific HTTP protocol version wherever possible. The default is `HTTP_1_1`.

■ **Tip** An `HttpClient` is immutable. A few of the configurations stored in an `HttpClient` may be overridden for HTTP requests when such requests are built.

The `HttpClient` class is abstract and you cannot create its objects directly. There are two ways you can create an `HttpClient` object:

- Using the `newHttpClient()` static method of the `HttpClient` class

- Using the `build()` method of the `HttpClient.Builder` class

The following snippet of code gets a default `HttpClient` object:

```
// Get the default HttpClient
HttpClient defaultClient = HttpClient.newHttpClient();
```

You can also create an `HttpClient` using the `HttpClient.Builder` class. The `HttpClient.newBuilder()` static method returns a new instance of the `HttpClient.Builder` class. The `HttpClient.Builder` class provides a method for setting each configuration value. The value for the configuration is specified as the parameter of the method and the method returns the reference of the builder object itself, so you can chain multiple methods. In the end, call the `build()` method that returns an `HttpClient` object. The following statement creates an `HttpClient` with the redirect policy set to ALWAYS and the HTTP version set to `HTTP_2`:

```
// Create a custom HttpClient
HttpClient httpClient = HttpClient.newBuilder()
                    .followRedirects(HttpClient.Redirect.ALWAYS)
                    .version(HttpClient.Version.HTTP_2)
                    .build();
```

The `HttpClient` class contains a method corresponding to each configuration setting that returns the value for that configuration. Those methods are as follows:

- `Optional<Authenticator> authenticator()`

- `Optional<CookieManager> cookieManager()`

- `Executor executor()`

- `HttpClient.Redirect followRedirects()`

- `Optional<ProxySelector> proxy()`

- `SSLContext sslContext()`

- `Optional<SSLParameters> sslParameters()`

- `HttpClient.Version version()`

Notice that there are no setters in the `HttpClient` class because it is immutable. You cannot use an `HttpClient` object by itself. You need to use an `HttpRequest` object before you use an `HttpClient` object to send a request to a server. I explain the `HttpRequest` class in the next section. The `HttpClient` class contains the following three methods to send a request to a server:

- `<T> HttpResponse<T> send(HttpRequest req, HttpResponse.BodyHandler<T> responseBodyHandler)`

- `<T> CompletableFuture<HttpResponse<T>> sendAsync(HttpRequest req, HttpResponse.BodyHandler<T> responseBodyHandler)`

- `<U,T> CompletableFuture<U> sendAsync(HttpRequest req, HttpResponse.MultiProcessor<U,T> multiProcessor)`

The `send()` method sends the request synchronously, whereas the `sendAsync()` methods send the request asynchronously. I cover these methods in more detail in subsequent sections.

Processing HTTP Requests

A client application communicates with a web server using HTTP requests. It sends a request to the server and the server sends you back an HTTP response. An instance of the `HttpRequest` class represents an HTTP request. The following are the steps you need to perform to process an HTTP request:

- Obtain an HTTP request builder

- Set the parameters for the request

- Create an HTTP request from the builder

- Send the HTTP request to a server synchronously or asynchronously

- Process the response from the server

Obtaining an HTTP Request Builder

You need to use a builder object, which is an instance of the `HttpRequest.Builder` class, to create an `HttpRequest`. You can get an `HttpRequest.Builder` using one of the following static methods of the `HttpRequest` class:

- `HttpRequest.Builder newBuilder()`

- `HttpRequest.Builder newBuilder(URI uri)`

The following snippet of code shows you how to use these methods to get an `HttpRequest.Builder` instance:

```
// A URI to point to google
URI googleUri = new URI("http://www.google.com");

// Get a builder for the google URI
HttpRequest.Builder builder1 = HttpRequest.newBuilder(googleUri);

// Get a builder without specifying a URI at this time
HttpRequest.Builder builder2 = HttpRequest.newBuilder();
```

Setting HTTP Request Parameters

Once you have an HTTP request builder, you can set different parameters for the request using the builder's methods. All methods return the builder itself, so you can chain them. Those methods are as follows:

- `HttpRequest.Builder DELETE(HttpRequest.BodyProcessor body)`
- `HttpRequest.Builder expectContinue(boolean enable)`
- `HttpRequest.Builder GET()`
- `HttpRequest.Builder header(String name, String value)`
- `HttpRequest.Builder headers(String... headers)`
- `HttpRequest.Builder method(String method, HttpRequest.BodyProcessor body)`
- `HttpRequest.Builder POST(HttpRequest.BodyProcessor body)`
- `HttpRequest.Builder PUT(HttpRequest.BodyProcessor body)`
- `HttpRequest.Builder setHeader(String name, String value)`
- `HttpRequest.Builder timeout(Duration duration)`
- `HttpRequest.Builder uri(URI uri)`
- `HttpRequest.Builder version(HttpClient.Version version)`

An `HttpRequest` is sent to a server using an `HttpClient`. When you are building an HTTP request, you can set the HTTP version value through its the `HttpRequest.Builder` object using the `version()` method that will override the HTTP version set in the `HttpClient` when this request is sent. The following snippet of code sets the HTTP version to 2.0 for a request, which overrides the default value of `NEVER` in the default `HttpClient` object:

```
// By default a client uses HTTP 1.1. All requests sent using this
// HttpClient will use HTTP 1.1 unless overridden by the request
HttpClient client = HttpClient.newHttpClient();

// A URI to point to google
URI googleUri = new URI("http://www.google.com");
```

```
// Get an HttpRequest that uses HTTP 2.0
HttpRequest request = HttpRequest.newBuilder(googleUri)
                                 .version(HttpClient.Version.HTTP_2)
                                 .build();

// The client object contains HTTP version as 1.1 and the request
// object contains HTTP version 2.0. The following statement will
// send the request using HTTP 2.0, which is in the request object.
HttpResponse<String> r = client.send(request, BodyHandler.asString());
```

The timeout() method specifies a timeout for the request. If a response is not received within the specified timeout period, an HttpTimeoutException is thrown.

An HTTP request may contain a header named expect with its value "100-Continue". If this header is set, the client sends only headers to the server and the server is expected to send back an error response or a 100-Continue response. Upon receiving this response, the client sends the request body to the server. A client uses this techniques to check if the server can process the request based on the request's headers, before the client sends the actual request body. This header is not set by default. You need to call the expectContinue(true) method of the request builder to enable this. Note that calling the header("expect", "100-Continue") method of the request builder does not enable this feature. You must use the expectContinue(true) method to enable it.

```
// Enable the expect=100-Continue header in the request
HttpRequest.Builder builder = HttpRequest.newBuilder()
                                          .expectContinue(true);
```

The following sections describe how to set the headers, body, and method of an HTTP request.

Setting Request Headers

A header in an HTTP request is a name-value pair. You can have multiple headers. You can use the header(), headers(), and setHeader() methods of the HttpRequest.Builder class to add headers to a request. The header() and headers() methods add headers if they are not already present. If headers were already added, these methods do nothing. The setHeader() method replaces the header if it was present; otherwise, it adds the header.

The header() and setHeader() methods let you add/set one header at a time, whereas the headers() method lets you add multiple headers. The headers() method takes a var-args argument, which should contain name-value pairs in sequence. The following snippet of code shows how to set headers for an HTTP request:

```
// Create a URI
URI calc = new URI("http://localhost:8080/webapp/Calculator");

// Use the header() method
HttpRequest.Builder builder1 = HttpRequest.newBuilder(calc)
    .header("Content-Type", "application/x-www-form-urlencoded")
    .header("Accept", "text/plain");

// Use the headers() method
HttpRequest.Builder builder2 = HttpRequest.newBuilder(calc)
    .headers("Content-Type", "application/x-www-form-urlencoded",
             "Accept", "text/plain");
```

```
// Use the setHeader() method
HttpRequest.Builder builder3 = HttpRequest.newBuilder(calc)
    .setHeader("Content-Type", "application/x-www-form-urlencoded")
    .setHeader("Accept", "text/plain");
```

Setting the Request Body

The body of some HTTP requests contain data such as requests using POST and PUT methods.
The body of an HTTP request is set using a body processor, which is a static nested interface named
HttpRequest.BodyProcessor. The HttpRequest.BodyProcessor interface contains the following static factory
methods that return a body processor for HTTP requests that supply the request body from a specific
type of source such as a String, a byte[], or a File:

- HttpRequest.BodyProcessor fromByteArray(byte[] buf)

- HttpRequest.BodyProcessor fromByteArray(byte[] buf, int offset,
  int length)

- HttpRequest.BodyProcessor fromByteArrays(Iterable<byte[]> iter)

- HttpRequest.BodyProcessor fromFile(Path path)

- HttpRequest.BodyProcessor fromInputStream(Supplier<? extends
  InputStream> streamSupplier)

- HttpRequest.BodyProcessor fromString(String body)

- HttpRequest.BodyProcessor fromString(String s, Charset charset)

The first argument of these methods indicates the source of the data for the request's body. For
example, you use the fromString(String body) method to obtain a body processor if a String object
supplies the request's body.

■ **Tip** The HttpRequest class contains a static noBody() method that returns an HttpRequest.BodyProcessor,
which processes no request body. Typically, you will use this method with the method() method when an HTTP
method does not accept a body, but the method() method requires you to pass a body processor.

Whether a request can have a body depends on the HTTP method used to send the request. The
DELETE, POST, and PUT methods have a body, whereas the GET method does not. The HttpRequest.Builder
class contains a method with the same name as the HTTP method's name to set the method and
the body of the request. For example, to use the POST method with a body, the builder has a
POST(HttpRequest.BodyProcessor body) method.

There are many other HTTP methods such as HEAD and OPTIONS, which do not have a
corresponding method the HttpRequest.Builder class. The class contains a method(String method,
HttpRequest.BodyProcessor body) method that you can use for any HTTP method. When using the
method() method, make sure to specify the method name in all uppercase—for example, GET, POST, HEAD,
etc. The following is a list of those methods:

- HttpRequest.Builder DELETE(HttpRequest.BodyProcessor body)

- HttpRequest.Builder method(String method, HttpRequest.BodyProcessor body)

- HttpRequest.Builder POST(HttpRequest.BodyProcessor body)
- HttpRequest.Builder PUT(HttpRequest.BodyProcessor body)

The following snippet of code sets the body of an HTTP request from a String, which is typically done when you post an HTML form to a URL. The form data consists of three fields named n1, n2, and op.

```
URI calc = new URI("http://localhost:8080/webapp/Calculator");

// Compose the form data with n1 = 10, n2 = 20. And op = +
String formData = "n1=" + URLEncoder.encode("10","UTF-8") +
                  "&n2=" + URLEncoder.encode("20","UTF-8") +
                  "&op=" + URLEncoder.encode("+","UTF-8")  ;

HttpRequest.Builder builder = HttpRequest.newBuilder(calc)
    .header("Content-Type", "application/x-www-form-urlencoded")
    .header("Accept", "text/plain")
    .POST(HttpRequest.BodyProcessor.fromString(formData));
```

Creating HTTP Requests

In previous sections, you learned how to create an HttpRequest.Builder and how to use it to set different properties of an HTTP request. Creating an HTTP request is simply calling the build() method on an HttpRequest.Builder, which returns an HttpRequest object. The following snippet of code creates an HttpRequest that uses the HTTP GET method:

```
HttpRequest request = HttpRequest.newBuilder()
                          .uri(new URI("http://www.google.com"))
                          .GET()
                          .build();
```

The following snippet of code builds an HttpRequest with headers and a body that uses an HTTP POST method:

```
// Build the URI and the form's data
URI calc = new URI("http://localhost:8080/webapp/Calculator");
String formData = "n1=" + URLEncoder.encode("10","UTF-8") +
                  "&n2=" + URLEncoder.encode("20","UTF-8") +
                  "&op=" + URLEncoder.encode("+","UTF-8");

// Build the HttpRequest object
HttpRequest request = HttpRequest.newBuilder(calc)
    .header("Content-Type", "application/x-www-form-urlencoded")
    .header("Accept", "text/plain")
    .POST(HttpRequest.BodyProcessor.fromString(formData))
    .build();
```

Note that creating an HttpRequest object does not send the request to the server. You will need to call the send() or sendAsync() method of the HttpClient class to send the request to the server. In the previous example, the request object is like any other Java object. I explain how to send requests to a server in the next section.

The following snippet of code creates an HttpRequest object with HTTP HEAD request method. Note that it uses the method() method of the HttpRequest.Builder class to specify the HTTP method.

```
HttpRequest request =
    HttpRequest.newBuilder(new URI("http://www.google.com"))
            .method("HEAD", HttpRequest.noBody())
            .build();
```

Processing HTTP Responses

Once you have an HttpRequest object, you can send the request to a server and receive the response synchronously or asynchronously. An instance of the HttpResponse<T> class represents a response received from a server, where the type parameter T indicates the type of the response body such as String, byte[], or Path. You can use one of the following methods of the HttpRequest class to send an HTTP request and receive an HTTP response:

- <T> HttpResponse<T> send(HttpRequest req, HttpResponse.BodyHandler<T> responseBodyHandler)

- <T> CompletableFuture<HttpResponse<T>> sendAsync(HttpRequest req, HttpResponse.BodyHandler<T> responseBodyHandler)

- <U,T> CompletableFuture<U> sendAsync(HttpRequest req, HttpResponse.MultiProcessor<U,T> multiProcessor)

The send() method is synchronous. That is, it blocks until the response is received. The sendAsync() method processes the response asynchronously. It returns immediately with a CompletableFuture<HttpResponse>, which completes when the response is ready to be processed.

Processing Response Status and Headers

An HTTP response contains a status code, headers, and a body. An HttpResponse object is made available to you as soon as the status code and headers are received from the server, but before the body is received. The statusCode() method of the HttpResponse class returns the status code of the response as an int. The headers() method of the HttpResponse class returns the headers of the response as an instance of the HttpHeaders interface. The HttpHeaders interface contains the following methods to conveniently retrieve header's values by name or all headers as a Map<String,List<String>>:

- List<String> allValues(String name)

- Optional<String> firstValue(String name)

- Optional<Long> firstValueAsLong(String name)

- Map<String,List<String>> map()

Listing 14-2 contains a complete program to send a request to the URL, http://www.google.com, with a HEAD request. It prints the received response's status code and headers. You may get different output.

Listing 14-2. Processing an HTTP Response's Status Code and Headers

```java
// GoogleHeadersTest.java
package com.jdojo.http.client;

import java.io.IOException;
import java.net.URI;
import java.net.URISyntaxException;
import jdk.incubator.http.HttpClient;
import jdk.incubator.http.HttpRequest;
import jdk.incubator.http.HttpResponse;

public class GoogleHeadersTest {
    public static void main(String[] args) {
        try {
            URI googleUri = new URI("http://www.google.com");
            HttpClient client = HttpClient.newHttpClient();

            HttpRequest request =
                HttpRequest.newBuilder(googleUri)
                            .method("HEAD", HttpRequest.noBody())
                            .build();

            HttpResponse<?> response =
              client.send(request, HttpResponse.BodyHandler.discard(null));

            // Print the response status code and headers
            System.out.println("Response Status Code:" +
                                response.statusCode());

            System.out.println("Response Headers are:");
            response.headers()
                    .map()
                    .entrySet()
                    .forEach(System.out::println);

        } catch (URISyntaxException | InterruptedException |
                IOException e) {
            e.printStackTrace();
        }
    }
}
```

```
WARNING: Using incubator modules: jdk.incubator.httpclient
Response Status Code:200
Response Headers are:
accept-ranges=[none]
cache-control=[private, max-age=0]
content-type=[text/html; charset=ISO-8859-1]
date=[Sun, 26 Feb 2017 16:39:36 GMT]
expires=[-1]
p3p=[CP="This is not a P3P policy! See https://www.google.com/support/accounts/
answer/151657?hl=en for more info."]
server=[gws]
set-cookie=[NID=97=Kmz52m8Zdf4lsNDsnMyrJomx_2kD7lnWYcNEuwPWsFTFUZ7yli6DbCB98Wv-
SlxOfKAOOoOBIBgysuZw3ALtgJjX67v7-mC5fPv88n8VpwxrNcjVGCfFrxVro6gRNIrye4dAWZvUVfY28eOM;
expires=Mon, 28-Aug-2017 16:39:36 GMT; path=/; domain=.google.com; HttpOnly]
transfer-encoding=[chunked]
vary=[Accept-Encoding]
x-frame-options=[SAMEORIGIN]
x-xss-protection=[1; mode=block]
```

Processing the Response Body

Processing the body of an HTTP response is a two-step process:

- You need to specify a response body handler, which is an instance of the
  HttpResponse.BodyHandler<T> interface, when you send a request using the send()
  or sendAsync() method of the HttpClient class.

- When the response status code and headers are received, the apply() method of the
  response body handler is called. The response status code and headers are passed to
  the apply() method. The apply() method returns an instance of the HttpResponse.
  BodyProcessor<T> interface, which reads the response body and converts the read
  data into the type T.

Don't worry about these details of processing a response body. Several implementations of the
HttpResponse.BodyHandler<T> are provided. You can use one of the following static factory methods of the
HttpResponse.BodyHandler interface to gets its instance for a different type parameter T:

- HttpResponse.BodyHandler<byte[]> asByteArray()

- HttpResponse.BodyHandler<Void> asByteArrayConsumer(Consumer<Optional<by
  te[]>> consumer)

- HttpResponse.BodyHandler<Path> asFile(Path file)

- HttpResponse.BodyHandler<Path> asFile(Path file, OpenOption...
  openOptions)

- HttpResponse.BodyHandler<Path> asFileDownload(Path directory,
  OpenOption... openOptions)

- HttpResponse.BodyHandler<String> asString()

- HttpResponse.BodyHandler<String> asString(Charset charset)

- <U> HttpResponse.BodyHandler<U> discard(U value)

These methods' signatures are intuitive enough to tell you what type of response body they handle. For example, if you want to get the response body as a String, use the asString() method to get a body handler. The discard(U value) method returns a body handler, which will discard the response body and return the specified value as the body.

The body() method of the HttpResponse<T> class returns the response body, which is of type T.

The following snippet of code sends a GET request to the http://google.com URL and retrieves the response body as a String. I ignored the exception handling logic.

```
import java.net.URI;
import jdk.incubator.http.HttpClient;
import jdk.incubator.http.HttpRequest;
import jdk.incubator.http.HttpResponse;
import static jdk.incubator.http.HttpResponse.BodyHandler.asString;
...
// Build the request
HttpRequest request = HttpRequest.newBuilder()
                 .uri(new URI("http://google.com"))
                 .GET()
                 .build();

// Send the request and get a Response
HttpResponse<String> response = HttpClient.newHttpClient()
                                     .send(request, asString());

// Get the response body and print it
String body = response.body();
System.out.println(body);<HTML><HEAD><meta http-equiv="content-type"
```

```
WARNING: Using incubator modules: jdk.incubator.httpclient
<HTML><HEAD><meta http-equiv="content-type" content="text/html;charset=utf-8">
<TITLE>301 Moved</TITLE></HEAD><BODY>
<H1>301 Moved</H1>
The document has moved
<A HREF="http://www.google.com/">here</A>.
</BODY></HTML>
```

The example returns a response body with a status code of 301, which indicates that the URL has moved. The output also contains the moved URL. If we had set the following redirects policy in the HttpClient to ALWAYS, the request would have been resubmitted to the moved URL. The following snippet of code fixes this issue:

```
// The request will follow the redirects issues by the server
HttpResponse<String> response = HttpClient.newBuilder()
    .followRedirects(HttpClient.Redirect.ALWAYS)
    .build()
    .send(request, asString());
```

Listing 14-3 contains a complete program that shows you how to use a POST request with a body and process the response asynchronously. The web application in the source code for this book contains a servlet named Calculator. The source code for the Calculator servlet is not shown here to save space. The servlet accepts three parameters in the request, which are named n1, n2, and op, where n1 and n2 are two numbers and op is an operator (+, -, *, or /). The response is a plain text and summarizes the operator and its result. The URL in the program assumes that you have deployed the servlet locally on your machine and the web server is running on port 8080. If these assumptions are not true, modify the program accordingly. You will get the output shown here if the servlet is called successfully. Otherwise, you will get different output.

Listing 14-3. Processing an HTTP Response's Body Asynchronously

```java
// CalculatorTest.java
package com.jdojo.http.client;

import java.io.IOException;
import java.net.URI;
import java.net.URISyntaxException;
import java.net.URLEncoder;
import jdk.incubator.http.HttpClient;
import jdk.incubator.http.HttpRequest;
import static jdk.incubator.http.HttpRequest.BodyProcessor.fromString;
import jdk.incubator.http.HttpResponse;

public class CalculatorTest {
    public static void main(String[] args) {
        try {
            URI calcUri =
                new URI("http://localhost:8080/webapp/Calculator");

            String formData = "n1=" + URLEncoder.encode("10","UTF-8") +
                              "&n2=" + URLEncoder.encode("20","UTF-8") +
                              "&op=" + URLEncoder.encode("+","UTF-8")  ;

            // Create a request
            HttpRequest request = HttpRequest.newBuilder()
                .uri(calcUri)
                .header("Content-Type", "application/x-www-form-urlencoded")
                .header("Accept", "text/plain")
                .POST(fromString(formData))
                .build();

            // Process the response asynchronously. When the response
            // is ready, the processResponse() method of this class will
            // be called.
            HttpClient.newHttpClient()
                    .sendAsync(request,
                            HttpResponse.BodyHandler.asString())
                    .whenComplete(CalculatorTest::processResponse);

            try {
                // Let the current thread sleep for 5 seconds,
                // so the async response processing is complete
                Thread.sleep(5000);
```

```
            } catch (InterruptedException ex) {
                ex.printStackTrace();
            }
        } catch (URISyntaxException | IOException e) {
            e.printStackTrace();
        }
    }

    private static void processResponse(HttpResponse<String> response,
                                        Throwable t) {

        if (t == null ) {
            System.out.println("Response Status Code: " +
                                    response.statusCode());
            System.out.println("Response Body: " + response.body());
        } else {
            System.out.println("An exception occurred while " +
                "processing the HTTP request. Error: " + t.getMessage());
        }
    }
}
```

```
WARNING: Using incubator modules: jdk.incubator.httpclient
Response Status Code: 200
Response Body: 10 + 20 = 30.0
```

Using the response body handler saves the developer a lot of work. In one statement, you can download and save the contents of a URL in a file. The following snippet of code saves the contents of the URL http://www.google.com as a file named google.html in your current directory. When the download is complete, the path of the downloaded file is printed. If an error occurs, the stack trace of the exception is printed.

```
HttpClient.newBuilder()
        .followRedirects(HttpClient.Redirect.ALWAYS)
        .build()
        .sendAsync(HttpRequest.newBuilder()
                            .uri(new URI("http://www.google.com"))
                            .GET()
                            .build(),
                            asFile(Paths.get("google.html")))
        .whenComplete((HttpResponse<Path> response,
                        Throwable exception) -> {
            if(exception == null) {
                System.out.println("File saved to " +
                                    response.body().toAbsolutePath());
            } else {
                exception.printStackTrace();
            }
        });
```

Processing Response Trailers

HTTP trailers are lists of name-value pairs like HTTP headers that are sent by the server at the end of an HTTP response, after the response body has been sent. HTTP trailers are typically not used by many servers. The HttpResponse class contains a trailers() method that returns response trailers as an instance of the Co mpletableFuture<HttpHeaders>. Notice the name of the returned object type—HttpHeaders. The HTTP/2 Client API does have a type named HttpTrailers. You need to retrieve the response body before you can retrieve the trailers. At the time of this writing, the HTTP/2 Client API does not support processing HTTP trailers. The following snippet of code shows you how to print all response trailers when the API supports it:

```
// Get an HTTP response
HttpResponse<String> response = HttpClient.newBuilder()
                .followRedirects(HttpClient.Redirect.ALWAYS)
                .build()
                .send(HttpRequest.newBuilder()
                            .uri(new URI("http://www.google.com"))
                            .GET()
                            .build(),
                            asString());
// Read the response body
String body = response.body();

// Process trailers
response.trailers()
        .whenComplete((HttpHeaders trailers, Throwable t) -> {
            if(t == null) {
                trailers.map()
                        .entrySet()
                        .forEach(System.out::println);
            } else {
                t.printStackTrace();
            }
        });
```

Setting the Request Redirection Policy

In response to an HTTP request, a web server may return a 3XX response status code, where X is a digit between 0 and 9. This status code indicates that an additional action is required on the client's part to fulfill the request. For example, a status code of 301 indicates that the URL has permanently moved to a new location. The response body contains alternative locations. By default, upon receiving a 3XX status code, the request is not resubmitted to a new location. You can set one of the following constants of the HttpClient.Redirect enum as a policy for your HttpClient to act in case the returned response contains a 3XX response status code:

- ALWAYS

- NEVER

- SAME_PROTOCOL

- SECURE

ALWAYS indicates that the redirects should always be followed. That is, the request should be resubmitted to the new location.

NEVER indicates that the redirects should never be followed. This is the default.

SAME_PROTOCOL indicates that the redirection may occur if the old and new locations use the same protocol—for example, HTTP to HTTP or HTTPS to HTTPS.

SECURE indicates that the redirection should always occur, except when the old location uses HTTPS and the new one uses HTTP.

I covered how to use the follow redirect configuration setting on an HttpClient in previous sections.

Using the WebSocket Protocol

The WebSocket protocol provides a two-way communication between two endpoints—a client endpoint and a server endpoint. The term *endpoint* means any of the two sides of the connection that use the WebSocket protocol. The client endpoint initiates a connection and the server endpoint accepts the connection. The connection is bi-directional, which means the server endpoint can push messages to the client endpoint on its own. You will also come across another term in this context, which is called *a peer*. A peer is simply the other end of the connection. For example, for a client endpoint, the server endpoint is a peer and, for a server endpoint, the client endpoint is a peer. A WebSocket *session* represents a sequence of interactions between an endpoint and a single peer.

The WebSocket protocol can be broken into three parts:

- Opening handshake
- Data exchanges
- Closing handshake

The client initiates an opening handshake with the server. The handshake occurs using HTTP with an upgrade request to the WebSocket protocol. The server responds to the opening handshake with an upgrade response. Once the handshake is successful, the client and the server exchange messages. The message exchanges may be initiated by either the client or the server. In the end, either endpoint can send a closing handshake; the peer responds with the closing handshake. Once the closing handshake is successful, the WebSocket is closed.

The HTTP/2 Client API in JDK 9 supports creating WebSocket client endpoints. To have a complete example of using the WebSocket protocol, you will need to have a server endpoint and a client endpoint. The following sections cover creating both.

Creating a Server Endpoint

Creating a server endpoint requires using Java EE. This book is focused on Java SE 9. I explain briefly how to create a server endpoint to be used in the example in this section. Without covering the details, I use Java EE 7 annotations to create a WebSocket server endpoint.

Listing 14-4 contains the code for a class named TimeServerEndPoint. The class is included in the web application in the webapp directory of the book's source code. When you deploy the web application to a web server, this class will be deployed as a server endpoint.

Listing 14-4. A WebSocket Server Endpoint

```
// TimeServerEndPoint.java
package com.jdojo.ws;

import java.io.IOException;
import java.time.ZonedDateTime;
import java.util.concurrent.TimeUnit;
import javax.websocket.CloseReason;
```

```java
import javax.websocket.OnMessage;
import javax.websocket.OnOpen;
import javax.websocket.OnClose;
import javax.websocket.OnError;
import javax.websocket.Session;
import javax.websocket.server.ServerEndpoint;
import static javax.websocket.CloseReason.CloseCodes.NORMAL_CLOSURE;

@ServerEndpoint("/servertime")
public class TimeServerEndPoint {
    @OnOpen
    public void onOpen(Session session) {
        System.out.println("Client connected. ");
    }

    @OnClose
    public void onClose(Session session) {
        System.out.println("Connection closed.");
    }

    @OnError
    public void onError(Session session, Throwable t) {
        System.out.println("Error occurred:" + t.getMessage());
    }

    @OnMessage
    public void onMessage(String message, Session session) {
        System.out.println("Client: " + message);

        // Send messages to the client
        sendMessages(session);
    }
    private void sendMessages(Session session) {
        /* Start a new thread and send 3 messages to the
           client. Each message contains the current date and
           time with zone.
        */
        new Thread(() -> {
            for(int i = 0; i < 3; i++) {
                String currentTime =
                    ZonedDateTime.now().toString();
                try {
                    session.getBasicRemote()
                            .sendText(currentTime, true);
                    TimeUnit.SECONDS.sleep(5);
                } catch(InterruptedException | IOException e) {
                    e.printStackTrace();
                    break;
                }
            }

            try {
                // Let us close the WebSocket
                session.close(new CloseReason(NORMAL_CLOSURE,
                                              "Done"));
```

```
            } catch (IOException e) {
                e.printStackTrace();
            }
        })
        .start();
    }
}
```

Using the @ServerEndpoint("/servertime") annotation on the TimeServerEndPoint class makes this class a server endpoint when it is deployed to a web server. The value of the value element of the annotation is /servertime, which will make the web server publish this endpoint at this URL.

The class contains four methods, which have been annotated with @onOpen, @onMessage, @onClose, and @onError annotations. I named these methods the same as these annotations. These methods are called at different points in the lifecycle of the server endpoint. They take a Session object as an argument. The Session object represents the interaction of this endpoint with its peer, which would be the client endpoint.

The onOpen() method is called when an opening handshake with a peer is successful. The method prints a message that a client is connected.

The onMessage() is called when a message is received from the peer. The method prints the message it receives and calls a private method named sendMessages(). The sendMessages() method starts a new thread and sends three messages to the peer. The thread sleeps for five seconds after sending each message. The message contains the current date and time with the time zone. You can send messages to peers synchronously or asynchronously. To send a message, you need to get a reference of the RemoteEndpoint interface that represents the conversation with a peer. Use the getBasicRemote() and getAsyncRemote() methods on the Session instance to get a RemoteEndpoint.Basic and RemoteEndpont.Async instances that can send messages synchronously and asynchronously, respectively. Once you get a reference of the peer (the remote endpoint), you can call several of its sendXxx() methods to send different types of data to the peer.

```
// Send a synchronous text message to the peer
session.getBasicRemote()
        .sendText(currentTime, true);
```

The second argument in the sendText() method indicates whether it is the last part of the partial message being sent. If your message is complete, use true.

After all messages are sent to the peer, a close message is sent using the sendClose() method. The method takes an object of the CloseReason class that encapsulates a close code and a close reason. When the peer receives a close message, the peer needs to respond with a close message, and, after that, the WebSocket connection is closed. Note that, after sending a close message, the server endpoint is not supposed to send more messages to its peer.

The onError() method is called when an error occurs that is not handled by the WebSocket protocol.

You cannot use this endpoint by itself. You need create a client endpoint, which I cover in detail in the next section. You will see this endpoint in action in the section entitled "Running the WebSocket Program," later in this chapter.

Creating a Client Endpoint

Developing a WebSocket client endpoint involves using the WebSocket interface, which is part of the HTTP/2 Client API in JDK 9. The WebSocket interface contains the following nested types:

- WebSocket.Builder

- WebSocket.Listener

- WebSocket.MessagePart

An instance of the `WebSocket` interface represents a WebSocket client endpoint. A builder, which is an instance of the `WebSocket.Builder` interface, is used to create a `WebSocket` instance. The `newWebSocketBuilder(URI uri, WebSocket.Listener listener)` method of the `HttpClient` class returns an instance of the `WebSocket.Builder` interface.

When events occur on a client endpoint, for example, the completion of the opening handshake, a message arrival, closing handshake, etc., notifications are sent to a listener, which is an instance of the `WebSocket.Listener` interface. The interface contains a default method for each type of notification. You will need to create a class that implements this interface. You implement only those methods that correspond to the events of which you are interested in receiving notifications. You need to specify a listener when you create a `WebSocket` instance.

When you send a close message to a peer, you may specify a close status code. The `WebSocket` interface contains the following constants of type `int` that can be used as the WebSocket `Close` message status code:

- `CLOSED_ABNORMALLY`: Represents a WebSocket `Close` message status code (1006), which means that the connection was closed abnormally, for example, without sending or receiving a `Close` message.

- `NORMAL_CLOSURE`: Represents a WebSocket `Close` message status code (1000), which means that the connection was closed normally. This means that the purpose for which the connection was established was fulfilled.

The server endpoint may send partial messages. Messages are marked as first, part, last, or whole, which indicates their position. The `WebSocket.MessagePart` enum defines four constants corresponding to a message's position: `FIRST`, `PART`, `LAST`, and `WHOLE`. You will receive these values as part of a message when your listener receives a notification that a message has been received.

The following sections describe each step in setting up a client endpoint in detail.

Creating a Listener

A listener is an instance of the `WebSocket.Listener` interface. Creating a listener involves creating a class that implements this interface. The interface contains the following default methods:

- `CompletionStage<?> onBinary(WebSocket webSocket, ByteBuffer message, WebSocket.MessagePart part)`

- `CompletionStage<?> onClose(WebSocket webSocket, int statusCode, String reason)`

- `void onError(WebSocket webSocket, Throwable error)`

- `void onOpen(WebSocket webSocket)`

- `CompletionStage<?> onPing(WebSocket webSocket, ByteBuffer message)`

- `CompletionStage<?> onPong(WebSocket webSocket, ByteBuffer message)`

- `CompletionStage<?> onText(WebSocket webSocket, CharSequence message, WebSocket.MessagePart part)`

The onOpen() method is called when the client endpoint is connected to the peer whose reference is passed to this method as the first argument. The default implementation requests one message, which means that this listener can receive one more message. The request for messages is made using the request(long n) method of the WebSocket interface:

```
// Allow one more message to be received
webSocket.request(1);
```

■ **Tip**   If a server sends more messages than requested, messages are queued on the TCP connection and may eventually force the sender to stop sending more messages through TCP flow control. It is important that you call the request(long n) method at the appropriate time with an appropriate argument value, so your listener keeps receiving messages from the server. It is a common mistake to override the onOpen() method in your listener and not call the webSocket.request(1) method, which prevents you from receiving messages from the server.

The onClose() method is called when the endpoint receives a close message from the peer. It is the last notification to the listener. An exception thrown from this method is ignored. The default implementation does not do anything. Typically, you need to send a close message to the peer to complete the closing handshake.

The onPing() method is called when this endpoint receives a Ping message from the peer. A Ping message can be sent by both client and server endpoints. The default implementation sends a Pong message with the same message contents to the peer.

The onPong() method is called when the endpoint receives a Pong message from the peer. A Pong message is typically received as a response to a previously sent Ping message. An endpoint may also receive an unsolicited Pong message. The default implementation of the onPong() method requests one more message on the listener and performs no other actions.

The onError() method is called when an I/O or protocol error occurs on the WebSocket. An exception thrown from this method is ignored. The listener receives no more notifications after this method is called. The default implementation does nothing.

The onBinary() and onText() methods are called when a binary message and a text message are received from the peer, respectively. Make sure to check the last argument of these methods, which indicates the position of the message. If you receive partial messages, you will need to assemble them to get the whole message. Returning null from these methods indicates that the message processing is complete. Otherwise, a CompletionStage<?> is returned and it completes when the message processing is complete.

The following snippet of code creates a WebSocket listener that is ready to receive text messages:

```
WebSocket.Listener listener =  new WebSocket.Listener() {
    @Override
    public CompletionStage<?> onText(WebSocket webSocket,
                                     CharSequence message,
                                     WebSocket.MessagePart part) {

        // Allow one message to be received by the listener
        webSocket.request(1);

        // Print the message received from the server
        System.out.println("Server: " + message);

        // Return null indicating that we are done processing this message
        return null;
    }
};
```

Building an Endpoint

You need to build an instance of the WebSocket interface that acts as a client endpoint. The instance is used to connect and exchange messages with the server endpoint. A WebSocket instance is built using a WebSocket.Builder. You can use the following method of the HttpClient class to get a builder:

```
WebSocket.Builder newWebSocketBuilder(URI uri, WebSocket.Listener listener)
```

The HttpClient instance used to obtain the WebSocket builder supplies the connection configuration for the WebSocket. The specified uri is the URI of the server endpoint. The listener is a listener for the endpoint being built, as described in the previous section. Once you have a builder, you can call one of the following methods of the builder to configure the endpoint:

- WebSocket.Builder connectTimeout(Duration timeout)
- WebSocket.Builder header(String name, String value)
- WebSocket.Builder subprotocols(String mostPreferred, String... lesserPreferred)

The connectTimeout() method lets you specify a timeout for the opening handshake. If the opening handshake does not complete within the specified duration, the CompletableFuture returned from the buildAsync() method of the WebSocket.Builder completes exceptionally with an HttpTimeoutException. You can add any custom headers for the opening handshake using the header() method. You can specify a request for given sub-protocols during the opening handshake using the subprotocols() method—only one of them will be selected by the server. The sub-protocols are defined by the application. The client and the server need to agree to work on specific sub-protocols and their details.

Finally, call the buildAsync() method of the WebSocket.Builder interface to build the endpoint. It returns CompletableFuture<WebSocket>, which completes normally when this endpoint is connected to the server endpoint; it completes exceptionally when there was an error. The following snippet of code shows how to build and connect a client endpoint. Notice that the URI for the server starts with ws, which indicates the WebSocket protocol.

```
URI serverUri = new URI("ws://localhost:8080/webapp/servertime");

// Get a listener
WebSocket.Listener listener = ...;

// Build an endpoint using the default HttpClient
HttpClient.newHttpClient()
        .newWebSocketBuilder(serverUri, listener)
        .buildAsync()
        .whenComplete((WebSocket webSocket, Throwable t) -> {
            // More code goes here
        });
```

Sending Messages to a Peer

Once a client endpoint is connected to a peer, both exchange messages. An instance of the WebSocket interface represents a client endpoint and the interface contains the following methods to send messages to a peer:

- CompletableFuture<WebSocket> sendBinary(ByteBuffer message, boolean isLast)

- CompletableFuture<WebSocket> sendClose()

- CompletableFuture<WebSocket> sendClose(int statusCode, String reason)

- CompletableFuture<WebSocket> sendPing(ByteBuffer message)

- CompletableFuture<WebSocket> sendPong(ByteBuffer message)

- CompletableFuture<WebSocket> sendText(CharSequence message)

- CompletableFuture<WebSocket> sendText(CharSequence message, boolean isLast)

The sendText() method is used to send a text message to the peer. If you are sending a partial message, use the version of this method that takes two arguments. If the second argument is false, it indicates part of the partial message. If the second argument is true, it indicates the last part of a partial message. If there were no partial messages sent before, a true in the second argument indicates a whole message. The sendText(CharSequence message) is a convenience method that calls the second version of the method using true as the second argument.

The sendBinary() method sends a binary message to the peer.

The sendPing() and sendPong() methods send a Ping and a Pong message to the peer, respectively.

The sendClose() method sends a Close message to the peer. You can send a Close message as part of a closing handshake initiated by a peer or you can send it to initiate a closing handshake with the peer.

■ **Tip**   If you want to close the WebSocket abruptly, use the abort() method of the WebSocket interface.

Running the WebSocket Program

It is time to see a WebSocket client endpoint and a WebSocket server endpoint exchanging messages. Listing 14-5 contains code for a class named WebSocketClient that encapsulates a client endpoint. Its intended use is as follows:

```
// Create a client WebSocket
WebSocketClient wsClient = new WebSocketClient(new URI("<server-uri>"));

// Connect to the server and exchange messages
wsClient.connect();
```

Listing 14-5. A Class That Encapsulates a Client Endpoint and Its Operations

```
// WebSocketClient.java
package com.jdojo.http.client;

import java.net.URI;
import java.util.concurrent.CompletionStage;
import jdk.incubator.http.HttpClient;
import jdk.incubator.http.WebSocket;
```

```java
public class WebSocketClient {
    private WebSocket webSocket;
    private final URI serverUri;

    private boolean inError = false;

    public WebSocketClient(URI serverUri) {
        this.serverUri = serverUri;
    }

    public boolean isClosed() {
        return (webSocket != null && webSocket.isClosed())
                ||
                this.inError;
    }

    public void connect() {
        HttpClient.newHttpClient()
                .newWebSocketBuilder(serverUri, this.getListener())
                .buildAsync()
                .whenComplete(this::statusChanged);
    }

    private void statusChanged(WebSocket webSocket, Throwable t) {
        this.webSocket = webSocket;

        if (t == null) {
            this.talkToServer();
        } else {
            this.inError = true;
            System.out.println("Could not connect to the server." +
                               " Error: " + t.getMessage());
        }
    }

    private void talkToServer() {
        // Allow one message to be received by the listener
        webSocket.request(1);

        // Send the server a request for time
        webSocket.sendText("Hello");
    }

    private WebSocket.Listener getListener() {
        return new WebSocket.Listener() {
            @Override
            public void onOpen(WebSocket webSocket) {
                // Allow one more message to be received by the listener
                webSocket.request(1);

                // Notify the user that we are connected
                System.out.println("A WebSocket has been opened.");
            }
```

```java
        @Override
        public CompletionStage<?> onClose(WebSocket webSocket,
                        int statusCode, String reason) {
            // Server closed the web socket. Let us respond to
            // the close message from the server
            webSocket.sendClose();

            System.out.println("The WebSocket is closed." +
                        " Close Code: " + statusCode +
                        ", Close Reason: " + reason);

            // Return null indicating that this WebSocket
            // can be closed immediately
            return null;
        }

        @Override
        public void onError(WebSocket webSocket, Throwable t) {
            System.out.println("An error occurred: " + t.getMessage());
        }

        @Override
        public CompletionStage<?> onText(WebSocket WebSocket,
            CharSequence message, WebSocket.MessagePart part) {

            // Allow one more message to be received by the listener
            webSocket.request(1);

            // Print the message received from the server
            System.out.println("Server: " + message);

            // Return null indicating that we are done
            // processing this message
            return null;
        }
    };
    }
}
```

The WebSocketClient class works as follows:

- The webSocket instance variable holds the reference of the client endpoint.

- The serverUri instance variable stores the URI of the server endpoint.

- The isError instance variable stores an indicator whether this endpoint is in error or not.

- The isClosed() method checks whether the endpoint is already closed or is in error.

- The webSocket instance variable will be null until the opening handshake is successful. Its value is updated inside the statusChanged() method.

- The connect() method builds a WebSocket and starts an opening handshake. Note that it calls the statusChanged() method when the opening handshake is complete, irrespective of the connection status.

- The statusChanged() method talks to the server by calling the talkToServer() method when the opening handshake is successful. Otherwise, it prints an error message and sets the isError flag to true.

- The talkToServer() method allows for one more message to be received by the listener and sends a text message to the server endpoint. Note that the server endpoint sends three messages with a five-second interval when it receives a text message from a client endpoint. Sending this message from the talkToServer() method initiates the message exchange between the two endpoints.

- The getListener() method creates and returns a WebSocket.Listener instance. The server endpoint will send three messages followed by a close message. The onClose() method in the listener responds to the close message from the server by sending an empty close message, which will end the client endpoint operations.

Listing 14-6 contains the program to run the client endpoint. If you run the WebSocketClientTest class, make sure that your web application with the server endpoint is running. You will also need to modify the SERVER_URI static variable to match the URI of the server endpoint for your web application. Refer to the next section, "Troubleshooting the WebSocket Application," if you do not get output similar to the one shown. The output prints the current date and time with the time zone, so you may get different output.

Listing 14-6. A Program to Run the Client Endpoint

```
// WebSocketClientTest.java
package com.jdojo.http.client;

import java.net.URI;
import java.net.URISyntaxException;
import java.util.concurrent.TimeUnit;

public class WebSocketClientTest {
    // Please change the URI to point to your server endpoint
    static final String SERVER_URI ="ws://localhost:8080/webapp/servertime";

    public static void main(String[] args)
        throws URISyntaxException, InterruptedException {

        // Create a client WebSocket
        WebSocketClient wsClient = new WebSocketClient(new URI(SERVER_URI));

        // Connect to the Server
        wsClient.connect();

        // Wait until the WebSocket is closed
        while(!wsClient.isClosed()) {
            TimeUnit.SECONDS.sleep(1);
        }

        // Need to exit
        System.exit(0);
    }
}
```

```
A WebSocket has been opened.
Server: 2016-12-15T14:19:53.311-06:00[America/Chicago]
Server: 2016-12-15T14:19:58.312-06:00[America/Chicago]
Server: 2016-12-15T14:20:03.313-06:00[America/Chicago]
The WebSocket is closed.  Close Code: 1000, Close Reason: Done
```

Troubleshooting the WebSocket Application

A number of things can go wrong when you are trying to test the WebSocket application. Table 14-1 lists a few of these problems and their solutions.

Table 14-1. *Possible Errors and Solutions for the WebSocket Application*

Error Message	Solution
Could not connect to the server. Error: java.net.ConnectException: Connection refused: no further information	Indicates that the web server is not running or your server URI is incorrect. Try running the webserver and checking the server URI, which is specified in the WebSocketClientTest class in its SERVER_URI static variable.
Could not connect to the server. Error: java.net.http.WebSocketHandshakeException: 404: RFC 6455 1.3. Unable to complete handshake; HTTP response status code 404	Indicates that the server URI is not pointing to the correct endpoint on the server. Verify that the value of the SERVER_URI static variable in the WebSocketClientTest class is correct.
A WebSocket has been opened. Dec 15, 2016 2:58:03 PM java.net.http.WS$1 onError WARNING: Failing connection java.net.http.WS@162532d6[CONNECTED], reason: 'RFC 6455 7.2.1. Stream ended before a Close frame has been received' An error occurred: null	Indicates that after the opening handshake the server is automatically closing the server endpoint. This is typically done by an antivirus program running on your machine. You need to configure your antivirus program to allow the HTTP connections on the specified port or run the web server with an HTTP listener on another port that is not blocked by your antivirus program.
A WebSocket has been opened. Server: 2016-12-16T07:15:04.586-06:00[America/Chicago]	In this case, the application prints one or two lines of output and waits forever. This happens when you do not have webSocket.request(1) calls in your client endpoint logic. The server is sending messages, which are queued because you have not allowed for more messages. Calling the request(n) method in the onOpen, onText, and other events fixes this problem.

Summary

JDK 9 added an HTTP/2 Client API that lets you work with HTTP requests and responses in Java applications. The API provides classes and interfaces to develop WebSocket client endpoints with authentication and TLS. The API is in the jdk.incubator.http package, which is in the jdk.incubator.httpclient module.

Three abstract classes, HttpClient, HttpRequest, and HttpResponse, and the WebSocket interface are central to the HTTP/2 Client API. Instances of these types are created using builders. The HttpClient class is immutable. An instance of the HttpClient class stores HTTP connection configurations that can be reused for multiple HTTP requests. An instance of the HttpRequest class represents an HTTP request. An instance of the HttpResponse class represents an HTTP response received from a server. You can send and receive HTTP requests and responses synchronously or asynchronously.

An instance of the WebSocket interface represents a WebSocket client endpoint. Communication with the WebSocket server endpoint is accomplished asynchronously. The WebSocket API is event-based. You need to specify a listener, which is an instance of the WebSocket.Listener interface, for a WebSocket client endpoint. The listener is notified—by invoking its appropriate methods—when an event occurs on the endpoint, for example, the listener is notified when the opening handshake with a peer is completed successfully by calling the onOpen() method of the listener. The API supports exchanging text as well as binary messages with peers. Messages can be exchanged in parts.

CHAPTER 15

■ ■ ■

Enhanced Deprecation

In this chapter, you will learn:

- How to deprecate your APIs
- The roles of the @deprecate Javadoc tag and the @Deprecation annotation in deprecating APIs
- The detailed rules that are used to generated deprecation warnings
- Updates to the @Deprecation annotation in JDK 9
- New deprecation warnings in JDK 9
- How to use the @SuppressWarnings annotation to suppress different types of deprecation warnings in JDK 9
- How to use the static analysis tool named jdeprscan to scan your compiled codebase to find the uses of deprecated JDK APIs

What Is Deprecation?

Deprecation in Java is a way to provide information about the lifecycle of the API. You can deprecate modules, packages, types, constructors, methods, fields, parameters, and local variables. When you deprecate an API, you are telling its users:

- Not to use the API because it is dangerous.
- To migrate away from the API because a better replacement for the API exists.
- To migrate away from the API because the API will be removed in a future release.

How to Deprecate an API

The JDK has two constructs that are used to deprecate APIs:

- The @deprecated Javadoc tag
- The @Deprecated annotation

The @deprecated Javadoc tag was added in JDK 1.1 and it lets you specify the details about the deprecation with a rich set of text formatting features of HTML. The java.lang.Deprecated annotation type was added to JDK 5.0 and it can be used on the API element, which is being deprecated. Before JDK 9, the annotation did not contain any elements. It is retained at runtime.

The @deprecated tag and the @Deprecated annotation are supposed to be used together. Both should be present or both absent. The @Deprecation annotation does not let you specify a description of the deprecation, so you must use the @deprecated tag to provide the description.

■ **Tip**   Using a @deprecated tag, but not a @Deprecated annotation, on an API element generates a compiler warning. Prior to JDK 9, you needed to use the -Xlint:dep-ann compiler flag to see such warnings.

Listing 15-1 contains the declaration for class named FileCopier. Suppose this class is shipped as part of a library. The class is deprecated using the @Deprecation annotation. Its Javadoc uses the @deprecated tag to give the deprecation details such as when it was deprecated, its replacement, and its removal notice. Before JDK 9, the @Deprecated annotation type did not contain any elements, so you had to provide all details about the deprecation using the @deprecated tag in the Javadoc for the deprecated API. Note that the @since tag used in the Javadoc indicates that the FileCopier class has existed since version 1.2 of this library, whereas the @deprecated tag indicates that the class has been deprecated since version 1.4 of the library.

Listing 15-1. A FileCopier Utility Class

```
// FileCopier.java
package com.jdojo.deprecation;

import java.io.File;

/**
 * The class consists of static methods that can be used to
 * copy files and directories.
 *
 * @deprecated Deprecated since 1.4. Not safe to use. Use the
 * <code>java.nio.file.Files</code> class instead. This class
 * will be removed in a future release of this library.
 *
 * @since 1.2
 */

@Deprecated
public class FileCopier {
    // No direct instantiation supported.
    private FileCopier() {
    }

    /**
     * Copies the contents of src to dst.
     * @param src The source file
     * @param dst The destination file
     * @return true if the copy is successfully,
     * false otherwise.
     */
```

```
    public static boolean copy(File src, File dst) {
        // More code goes here

        return true;
    }

    // More methods go here
}
```

The Javadoc tool moves the contents of the @deprecated tag to the top in the generated Javadoc to draw the reader's attention. The compiler generates a warning when non-deprecated code *uses* a deprecated API. Note that annotating an API with the @Deprecated annotation does not generate a warning; however, using an API that has been annotated with a @Deprecated annotation does. If you used the FileCopier class outside the class itself, you will receive a compiler warning about using the deprecated class.

Updates to @Deprecated in JDK 9

Suppose you compiled your code and deployed it to production. If you upgraded the JDK version or libraries/frameworks that contain new, deprecated APIs that your old application uses, you do not receive any warnings and you would miss a chance to migrate away from the deprecated APIs. You must recompile your code to receive warnings. There was no tool to scan and analyze the compiled code (e.g., JAR files) and report the use of deprecated APIs. Even worse is the case when a deprecated API is removed from the newer version and your old, compiled code receives unexpected runtime errors. Developers were also confused when they looked at a deprecated element Javadoc—there was no way to express when the API was deprecated and whether the deprecated API will be removed in a future release. All you could do was to specify these pieces of information in text as part of the @deprecated tag. JDK 9 attempted to solve these issues by enhancing the @Deprecated annotation. The annotation has received two new elements in JDK 9: since and forRemoval.

Prior to JDK 9, the annotation declaration was:

```
@Documented
@Retention(RetentionPolicy.RUNTIME)
@Target(value={CONSTRUCTOR, FIELD, LOCAL_VARIABLE, METHOD, PACKAGE, PARAMETER, TYPE})
public @interface Deprecated {
}
```

In JDK 9, the declaration for the Deprecated annotation changed to the following, with changes shown in boldface:

```
@Documented
@Retention(RetentionPolicy.RUNTIME)
@Target(value={CONSTRUCTOR, FIELD, LOCAL_VARIABLE, METHOD, PACKAGE, MODULE, PARAMETER, TYPE})
public @interface Deprecated {
    String since() default "";
    boolean forRemoval() default false;
}
```

Both new elements have default values specified, so the existing uses of the annotation do not break. The since element specifies the version in which the annotated API element became deprecated. It is a string and you are expected to following the same version naming convention as the JDK version scheme, for example "9". It defaults to the empty string. Note that JDK 9 did not add an element to the @Deprecated annotation type to specify a description of the deprecation. This was done for two reasons:

- The annotation is retained at runtime. Adding descriptive text to the annotation would add to the runtime memory.

- The descriptive text cannot be just plain text. For example, it needs to provide a link to the replacement of the deprecated API. The existing @deprecated Javadoc tag already provides this feature.

The forRemoval element indicates that the annotated API element is subject to removal in a future release and you should migrate away from the API. It defaults to false.

■ **Tip** The @since Javadoc tag on an element indicates when the API element was added, whereas the since element of the @Deprecated annotation indicates when the API element was deprecated. In JDK 9, reasonable efforts have been made to backfill these two elements' values in most, if not all, use-sites of the @Deprecated annotations in the Java SE APIs.

Before JDK 9, the deprecation warnings were issues based on the use of the @Deprecated annotation on the API element and its use-site, as shown in Table 15-1. The warnings were issued when a deprecated API element was used at a non-deprecated use-site. If both the declaration and its use-site were deprecated, no warnings were issued. You were able to suppress deprecation warnings by annotating the user-sites with a @SuppressWarnings("deprecation") annotation.

Table 15-1. *Matrix of Deprecation Warnings Issued Before JDK 9*

API Use-Site	API Declaration Site	
	Not Deprecated	Deprecated
Not Deprecated	N	W
Deprecated	N	N

N = No warning, W = Warning

Addition of the forRemoval element in the @Deprecation annotation type has added five more use-cases. When an API is deprecated with forRemoval set to false, such a deprecation is known as *ordinary deprecation* and the warnings issued in such cases are called *ordinary deprecation warnings*. When an API is deprecated with forRemoval set to true, such a deprecation is known as *terminal deprecation* and the warnings issued in such cases are called *terminal deprecation warnings* or *removal warnings*. Table 15-2 shows the matrix of deprecation warnings issued in JDK 9.

Table 15-2. *Matrix of Deprecation Warnings Issued in JDK 9*

API Use-Site	API Declaration Site		
	Not Deprecated	Ordinarily Deprecated	Terminally Deprecated
Not Deprecated	N	OW	RW
Ordinarily Deprecated	N	N	RW
Terminally Deprecated	N	N	RW

N = No warning, OW = Ordinary deprecation warning, RW = Removal deprecation warning

For backward compatibility, four upper-left uses cases in Table 15-2 are the same as in Table 15-1. That is, if your code generated a deprecation warning in JDK 8, it will continue to generate an ordinary deprecation warning in JDK 9. If the API has been terminally deprecated, its use-sites will generate removal warnings irrespective of the deprecated status of the use-site.

In JDK 9, the warning issued in one case, where both the API and its use-site are terminally deprecated, needs a little explanation. Both API and the code that uses it have been deprecated and both will be removed in the future, so what is the point of getting a warning in such a case? This is done to cover cases where the terminally deprecated API and its use-site are in two different codebases and are maintained independently. If the use-site codebase outlives the API codebase, the use-site will get an unexpected runtime error because the API it uses no longer exists. Issuing a warning at the use-site will give its maintainers a chance to plan for alternatives in case the terminally deprecated API goes away before the code at use-sites.

Suppressing Deprecation Warnings

Introduction of removal warnings in JDK 9 has added a new use-case for suppressing deprecation warnings. Before JDK 9, could suppress all deprecation warnings by annotating the use-site with a @SuppressWarnings ("deprecation") annotation. Consider a scenario:

- In JDK 8, an API is deprecated and the use-site suppresses the deprecation warning.

- In JDK 9, the API's deprecation changes from ordinary deprecation to terminal deprecation.

- The use-site compiles fine in JDK 9 because it has suppressed deprecation warnings in JDK 8.

- The API is removed and the use-site receives an unexpected runtime error without receiving any removal warning earlier.

To cover such scenarios, JDK 9 does not suppress removal warnings when you use @SuppressWarnings("deprecation"). It suppresses only ordinary deprecation warnings. To suppress removal warnings, you need to use @SuppressWarnings("removal"). If you want to suppress both ordinary and removal deprecation warnings, you need to use @SuppressWarnings({"deprecation", "removal"}).

A Deprecated API Example

In this section, I show you all use-cases of deprecating APIs, using the deprecated API with and without suppressing warnings with a simple example. In the example, I deprecate only methods and use them to generate compile-time warnings. You are, however, not limited to deprecating only methods. Comments on the methods should help you understand the expected behavior. Listing 15-2 contains the code for a class named Box. The class contains three methods—one in each category of deprecation—not deprecated, ordinarily deprecated, and terminally deprecated. I have kept the class simple, so you can focus on the deprecation being used. Compiling the Box class will not generate any deprecation warnings because the class does not use any deprecated API, rather it contains deprecated APIs.

Listing 15-2. A Box Class with Three Types of Methods: Not Deprecated, Ordinarily Deprecated, and Terminally Deprecated

```
// Box.java
package com.jdojo.deprecation;

/**
 * This class is used to demonstrate how to deprecate APIs.
 */
public class Box {
    /**
     * Not deprecated
     */
    public static void notDeprecated() {
        System.out.println("notDeprecated...");
    }

    /**
     * Deprecated ordinarily.
     * @deprecated  Do not use it.
     */
    @Deprecated(since="2")
    public static void deprecatedOrdinarily() {
        System.out.println("deprecatedOrdinarily...");
    }

    /**
     * Deprecated terminally.
     * @deprecated  It will be removed in a future release.
     *              Migrate your code.
     */
    @Deprecated(since="2", forRemoval=true)
    public static void deprecatedTerminally() {
        System.out.println("deprecatedTerminally...");
    }
}
```

Listing 15-3 contains the code for a BoxTest class. The class uses all methods of the Box class. A few methods in the BoxTest class have been deprecated ordinarily and terminally. The first nine methods correspond to nine use-cases in Table 15-2, which will generate four deprecation warnings—one ordinary warning and three terminal warnings. Methods named like m4X(), where X is a digit, show you how to suppress ordinary and terminal deprecation warnings.

Listing 15-3. A BoxTest Class That Uses Deprecated APIs and Suppresses Deprecation Warnings

```java
// BoxTest.java
package com.jdojo.deprecation;

public class BoxTest {
    /**
     * API: Not deprecated
     * Use-site: Not deprecated
     * Deprecation warning: No warning
     */
    public static void m11() {
        Box.notDeprecated();
    }

    /**
     * API: Ordinarily deprecated
     * Use-site: Not deprecated
     * Deprecation warning: No warning
     */
    public static void m12() {
        Box.deprecatedOrdinarily();
    }

    /**
     * API: Terminally deprecated
     * Use-site: Not deprecated
     * Deprecation warning: Removal warning
     */
    public static void m13() {
        Box.deprecatedTerminally();
    }

    /**
     * API: Not deprecated
     * Use-site: Ordinarily deprecated
     * Deprecation warning: No warning
     * @deprecated Dangerous to use.
     */
    @Deprecated(since="1.1")
    public static void m21() {
        Box.notDeprecated();
    }

    /**
     * API: Ordinarily deprecated
     * Use-site: Ordinarily deprecated
     * Deprecation warning: No warning
     * @deprecated Dangerous to use.
     */
    @Deprecated(since="1.1")
    public static void m22() {
        Box.deprecatedOrdinarily();
    }
```

```
/**
 * API: Terminally deprecated
 * Use-site: Ordinarily deprecated
 * Deprecation warning: Removal warning
 * @deprecated Dangerous to use.
 */
@Deprecated(since="1.1")
public static void m23() {
    Box.deprecatedTerminally();
}

/**
 * API: Not deprecated
 * Use-site: Terminally deprecated
 * Deprecation warning: No warning
 * @deprecated Going away.
 */
@Deprecated(since="1.1", forRemoval=true)
public static void m31() {
    Box.notDeprecated();
}

/**
* API: Ordinarily deprecated
* Use-site: Terminally deprecated
* Deprecation warning: No warning
* @deprecated Going away.
*/
@Deprecated(since="1.1", forRemoval=true)
public static void m32() {
    Box.deprecatedOrdinarily();
}

/**
 * API: Terminally deprecated
 * Use-site: Terminally deprecated
 * Deprecation warning: Removal warning
 * @deprecated Going away.
 */
@Deprecated(since="1.1", forRemoval=true)
public static void m33() {
    Box.deprecatedTerminally();
}

/**
 * API: Ordinarily and Terminally deprecated
 * Use-site: Not deprecated
 * Deprecation warning: Ordinary and removal warnings
 */
public static void m41() {
    Box.deprecatedOrdinarily();
    Box.deprecatedTerminally();
}
```

```
/**
 * API: Ordinarily and Terminally deprecated
 * Use-site: Not deprecated
 * Deprecation warning: Ordinary warnings
 */
@SuppressWarnings("deprecation")
public static void m42() {
    Box.deprecatedOrdinarily();
    Box.deprecatedTerminally();
}

/**
 * API: Ordinarily and Terminally deprecated
 * Use-site: Not deprecated
 * Deprecation warning: Removal warnings
 */
@SuppressWarnings("removal")
public static void m43() {
    Box.deprecatedOrdinarily();
    Box.deprecatedTerminally();
}

/**
 * API: Ordinarily and Terminally deprecated
 * Use-site: Not deprecated
 * Deprecation warning: Removal warnings
 */
@SuppressWarnings({"deprecation", "removal"})
public static void m44() {
    Box.deprecatedOrdinarily();
    Box.deprecatedTerminally();
}
}
```

You need to compile the BoxTest class using the -Xlint:deprecation compiler flag, so the compile emits deprecation warnings. Note that the following command is entered on one line, not two lines.

```
C:\Java9Revealed\com.jdojo.deprecation\src>javac
-Xlint:deprecation
-d ..\build\classes com\jdojo\deprecation\BoxTest.java
```

```
com\jdojo\deprecation\BoxTest.java:20: warning: [deprecation] deprecatedOrdinarily() in
Box has been deprecated
        Box.deprecatedOrdinarily();
            ^
com\jdojo\deprecation\BoxTest.java:29: warning: [removal] deprecatedTerminally() in Box has
been deprecated and marked for removal
        Box.deprecatedTerminally();
            ^
com\jdojo\deprecation\BoxTest.java:62: warning: [removal] deprecatedTerminally() in Box has
been deprecated and marked for removal
        Box.deprecatedTerminally();
```

```
                ^
com\jdojo\deprecation\BoxTest.java:95: warning: [removal] deprecatedTerminally() in Box has
been deprecated and marked for removal
        Box.deprecatedTerminally();
            ^
com\jdojo\deprecation\BoxTest.java:105: warning: [deprecation] deprecatedOrdinarily() in Box
has been deprecated
        Box.deprecatedOrdinarily();
            ^
com\jdojo\deprecation\BoxTest.java:106: warning: [removal] deprecatedTerminally() in Box has
been deprecated and marked for removal
        Box.deprecatedTerminally();
            ^
com\jdojo\deprecation\BoxTest.java:117: warning: [removal] deprecatedTerminally() in Box has
been deprecated and marked for removal
        Box.deprecatedTerminally();
            ^
com\jdojo\deprecation\BoxTest.java:127: warning: [deprecation] deprecatedOrdinarily() in Box
has been deprecated
        Box.deprecatedOrdinarily();
            ^
8 warnings
```

Static Analysis of Deprecated APIs

Recall that deprecation warnings are compile-time warnings. You will not get any warnings if compiled code for your deployed application starts using an ordinarily deprecated API or generates a runtime error because an API that was once valid had been terminally deprecated and removed. Before JDK 9, you had to recompile your source code to see deprecation warnings when you upgraded your JDK or other libraries/ frameworks. JDK 9 improves this situation by providing a *static* analysis tool called jdeprscan that can be used to scan compiled code to see the list of deprecated APIs being used. Currently, the tool reports the use of only deprecated JDK APIs. If your compiled code uses deprecated APIs from other libraries, say, Spring or Hibernate, or your own libraries, this tool will not report those uses.

The jdeprscan tool is located in the JDK_HOME\bin directory. The general syntax to use the tool is as follows:

```
jdeprscan [options] {dir|jar|class}
```

Here, [options] is a list of zero or more options. You can specify a list of space separated directory, JARs, or fully qualified class names as arguments to scan. The available options are as follows:

- -l, --list
- --class-path <CLASSPATH>
- --for-removal
- --release <6|7|8|9>
- -v, --verbose
- --version
- --full-version
- -h, --help

The --list option lists the set of deprecated APIs in Java SE. No arguments specifying the location of compiled classes should be specified when this option is used.

The --class-path specifies the class path to be used to find dependent classes during the scan.

The --for-removal option restricts the scan or list to only those APIs that have been deprecated for removal. It can be used only with a release value of 9 or later because the @Deprecated annotation type did not contain the forRemoval element before JDK 9.

The --release option specifies Java SE release that provides the set of deprecated APIs during scanning. For example, to list all deprecated APIs in JDK 6, you will the tool as follows:

```
jdeprscan --list --release 6
```

The --verbose option prints additional messages during the scanning process.

The --version and --full-version options print the abbreviated and full versions of the jdeprscan tool, respectively.

The --help option prints a detailed help message about the jdeprscan tool.

Listing 15-4 contains the code for a JDeprScanTest class. The code is trivial. It is intended to just compile, not run. Running it will not produce any interesting output. It creates two threads. One thread is stopped using the stop() method of the Thread class and another thread is destroyed using the destroy() method of the Thread class. The stop() and destroy() methods have been ordinarily deprecated since JDK 1.2 and JDK 1.5, respectively. JDK 9 has terminally deprecated the destroy() method, whereas it continued to keep the stop() method ordinarily deprecated. I use this class in the following examples.

Listing 15-4. A JDeprScanTest Class That Uses The Ordinarily Deprecated Method stop() and the Terminally Deprecated Method destroy() of the Thread Class

```
// JDeprScanTest.java
package com.jdojo.deprecation;

public class JDeprScanTest {
    public static void main(String[] args) {
        Thread t = new Thread(() -> System.out.println("Test"));
        t.start();
        t.stop();

        Thread t2 = new Thread(() -> System.out.println("Test"));
        t2.start();
        t2.destroy();
    }
}
```

The following command prints the list of all deprecated APIs in JDK 9. It will print a long list. The command takes a few seconds to start printing the results because it scans the entire JDK.

```
C:\Java9Revealed>jdeprscan --list
```

```
@Deprecated java.lang.ClassLoader
javax.tools.ToolProvider.getSystemToolClassLoader()
...
```

The following command prints all terminally deprecated APIs in JDK 9. That is, it prints all deprecated APIs that have been marked for removal in a future release:

```
C:\Java9Revealed>jdeprscan --list --for-removal
```

```
...
@Deprecated(since="9", forRemoval=true) class java.lang.Compiler
...
```

The following command prints the list of all APIs deprecated in JDK 8:

```
C:\Java9Revealed>jdeprscan --list --release 8
```

```
@Deprecated class javax.swing.text.TableView.TableCell
...
```

The following command prints the list of deprecated APIs used by the java.lang.Thread class.

```
C:\Java9Revealed>jdeprscan java.lang.Thread
```

```
class java/lang/Thread uses deprecated method java/lang/Thread::resume()V
```

Note that the previous command does not print the list of deprecated APIs in the Thread class. Rather, it prints the list of APIs in the Thread class that *uses* deprecated APIs.

The following command lists all uses of deprecated JDK APIs in the chapter's compiled code. The Java9Revealed/com.jdojo.deprecation/build/classes directory in the downloadable code for this book contains the compiled code for this chapter.

```
C:\Java9Revealed>jdeprscan com.jdojo.deprecation\build\classes
```

```
Directory com.jdojo.deprecation\build\classes:
class com/jdojo/deprecation/JDeprScanTest uses deprecated method
java/lang/Thread::stop()V
class com/jdojo/deprecation/JDeprScanTest uses deprecated method
java/lang/Thread::destroy()V (forRemoval=true)
```

```
C:\Java9Revealed>jdeprscan --for-removal com.jdojo.deprecation\build\classes
```

```
Directory com.jdojo.deprecation\build\classes:
class com/jdojo/deprecation/JDeprScanTest uses deprecated method
java/lang/Thread::destroy()V (forRemoval=true)
```

Dynamic Analysis of Deprecated APIs

The jdeprscan tool is a static analysis tool so it will skip dynamic uses of deprecated APIs. For example, you can call a deprecated method using reflection, which this tool will miss during scanning. You can also call deprecated methods in providers loaded by a ServiceLoader, which will be missed by this tool.

In a future release, the JDK may provide a dynamic analysis tool named jdeprdetect that will track the uses of deprecated APIs at runtime. The tool will be useful to find dead code referencing deprecated APIs that are reported by the static analysis tool jdeprscan.

No Deprecation Warnings on Imports

Until JDK 9, the compiler generated a warning if you imported deprecated constructs using import statements, even if you used a @SuppressWarnings annotation on all use-sites of the deprecated, imported constructs. This was an annoyance if you were trying to get rid of all deprecation warnings in your code. You just could not get rid of them because you cannot annotate import statements. JDK 9 improved on this by *omitting* the deprecation warnings on imports.

Consider the class named ImportDeprecationWarning, as shown in Listing 15-5. It used the deprecated class named StringBufferInputStream in three places:

- In an import statement

- In a variable declaration

- In an instance creation expression

Listing 15-5. A ImportDeprecationWarning Class

```
// ImportDeprecationWarning.java
package com.jdojo.deprecation;

import java.io.StringBufferInputStream;

public class ImportDeprecationWarning {
    @SuppressWarnings("deprecation")
    public static void main(String[] args) {
        StringBufferInputStream sbis =
                new StringBufferInputStream("Hello");

        for(int c = sbis.read(); c != -1; c = sbis.read()) {
            System.out.println((char)c);
        }
    }
}
```

Note that the ImportDeprecationWarning class uses a @SuppressWarnings annotation on the main() method to suppress the deprecation warnings. Compiling this class in JDK 8 with a -Xlint:deprecation flag will generate the following warning. Compiling this class in JDK 9 will not generate any deprecation warnings.

```
C:\Java9Revealed\com.jdojo.deprecation\src>javac -Xlint:deprecation -d ..\build\classes com\
jdojo\deprecation\ImportDeprecationWarning.java
```

```
com\jdojo\deprecation\ImportDeprecationWarning.java:4: warning: [deprecation]
StringBufferInputStream in java.io has been deprecated
import java.io.StringBufferInputStream;
               ^
1 warning
```

If you compiled this class in JDK 8, after removing the @SuppressWarnings annotation on the main() method, the compiler would generate three deprecation warnings—one for each use of the StringBufferInputStream deprecated class, whereas JDK 9 will generate only two deprecation warnings—excluding the warning for the import statement.

Summary

Deprecation in Java is a way to provide information about the lifecycle of the API. Deprecating an API tells its users to migrate away because the API is dangerous to use, a better replacement exists, or it will be removed in a future release. Using deprecated APIs generates compile-time deprecation warnings.

The @deprecated Javadoc tag and the @Deprecated annotation are used together to deprecate API elements such as modules, packages, types, constructors, methods, fields, parameters, and local variables. Before JDK 9, the annotation did not contain any elements. It is retained at runtime.

JDK 9 has added two elements to the annotation: since and forRemoval. The since element defaults to an empty string. Its value denotes the version of the API in which the API element was deprecated. The forRemoval element's type is boolean and it defaults to false. Its value of true denotes that the API element will be removed in a future release.

The JDK 9 compiler generates two types of deprecation warnings depending on the value of the forRemoval element of the @Deprecated annotation: *ordinary deprecation warnings* when forRemoval=false and *removal warnings* for forRemoval=true.

Before JDK 9, you could suppress the deprecation warnings by annotating the use-sites of the deprecated APIs with a @SuppressWarnings("deprecation") annotation. In JDK 9, you need to use @SuppressWarnings("deprecation") to suppress ordinary warnings, @SuppressWarnings("deprecation") to suppress removal warnings, and @SuppressWarnings({"deprecation", "removal"}) to suppress both types of warnings.

Before JDK 9, importing a deprecated construct using an import statement generated a compile-time deprecation warning. JDK 9 omits such warnings.

■ ■ ■

## CHAPTER 16

Stack Walking

In this chapter, you will learn:

- What stacks and stack frames are
- How to traverse a thread's stack before JDK 9
- How to traverse a thread's stack in JDK 9 using the StackWalker API
- How to get the caller's class in JDK 9

What Is a Stack?

Each thread in a JVM has a *private* JVM stack that is created at the same time the thread is created. The stack is a List-In-First-Out (LIFO) data structure. A stack stores frames. A new frame is created and pushed to the top of the stack each time a method is invoked. A frame is destroyed (popped out of stack) when the method invocation completes. Each frame on a stack contains its own array of local variables, as well as its own operand stack, return value, and reference to the runtime constant pool of the current method's class. A specific implementation of the JVM may extend a frame to store more pieces of information.

A frame on a JVM stack represents a Java method invocation in a given thread. In a given thread, only one frame is active at any point. The active frame is known as the *current frame* and its method is known as the *current method*. The class that defines the current method is known as the *current class*. A frame is no longer the current frame when its method invokes another method—a new frame is pushed to the stack and the executing method becomes the current method and the new frame becomes the current frame. When the method returns, the old frame becomes the current frame again. For more details on JVM stack and frames, refer to the Java Virtual Machine Specification at https://docs.oracle.com/javase/specs/jvms/se8/html/index.html.

■ **Tip** If a JVM supports native methods, a thread also contains a native method stack that contains a native method frame for each native method invocation.

Figure 16-1 shows two threads and their JVM stacks. The JVM stack for the first thread contains four frames and that of the second thread contains three frames. Frame 4 is the active frame in Thread-1 and Frame 3 is the active frame in Thread-2.

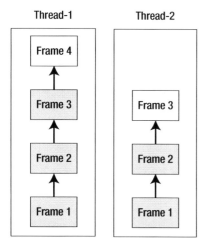

Figure 16-1. *Arrangements of threads and their private JVM stacks in a JVM*

What Is Stack Walking?

Stack walking (or stack traversal) is the process of traversing the stack frames of a thread and inspecting the frames' contents. Starting from Java 1.4, you can get a snapshot of the stack of a thread and get details about each frame such as the class names and method names where the method invocation occurs, the source filename, the line number in the source file, etc. Classes and interfaces used for stack walking are in the Stack-Walking API.

Stack Walking in JDK 8

Before JDK 9, it was possible to traverse all frames in a thread's stack using the following classes in the java.lang package:

- Throwable

- Thread

- StackTraceElement

An instance of the StackTraceElement class represents a stack frame. The getStackTrace() method of the Throwable class returns a StackTraceElement[] that contains the frames of the current thread's stack. The getStackTrace() method of the Thread class returns a StackTraceElement[] that contains the frames of the thread's stack. The first element of the array is the top frame in the stack, which represents the last method invocation in the sequence. Some implementations of JVM may omit some frames in the returned array.

The StackTraceElement class contains the following methods, which return the details of the method invocation represented by the frame:

- String getClassLoaderName()

- String getClassName()

- String getFileName()

- int getLineNumber()

- String getMethodName()

- String getModuleName()

- String getModuleVersion()

- boolean isNativeMethod()

■ **Tip** The getModuleName(), getModuleVersion(), and getClassLoaderName() methods were added to this class in JDK 9.

Most of the methods in the StackTraceElement class have intuitive names, for example, the getMethodName() method returns the name of the method whose invocation is represented by this frame. The getFileName() method returns the name of the source file that contains the method invocation code and the getLineNumber() returns the method invocation code's line number in the source file.

The following snippet of code shows how to inspect the stack of the current thread using the Throwable and Thread classes:

```java
// Using the Throwable class
StackTraceElement[] frames = new Throwable().getStackTrace();

// Using the Thread class
StackTraceElement[] frames2 = Thread.currentThread()
                                    .getStackTrace();
// Process the frames here...
```

All programs in this chapter are part of the com.jdojo.stackwalker module, whose declaration is shown in Listing 16-1.

Listing 16-1. The Declaration of a Module Named com.jdojo.stackwalker

```java
// module-info.java
module com.jdojo.stackwalker {
    exports com.jdojo.stackwalker;
}
```

Listing 16-2 contains the code for a class named LegacyStackWalk. This output was generated when the class ran in JDK 8.

Listing 16-2. Traversing a Thread's Stack Before JDK 9

```java
// LegacyStackWalk.java
package com.jdojo.stackwalker;

import java.lang.reflect.InvocationTargetException;

public class LegacyStackWalk {
    public static void main(String[] args) {
        m1();
    }
```

```
    public static void m1() {
        m2();
    }

    public static void m2() {
        // Call m3() directly
        System.out.println("\nWithout using reflection: ");
        m3();

        // Call m3() using reflection
        try {
            System.out.println("\nUsing reflection: ");
            LegacyStackWalk.class
                        .getMethod("m3")
                        .invoke(null);
        } catch (NoSuchMethodException |
                InvocationTargetException |
                IllegalAccessException |
                SecurityException e) {
            e.printStackTrace();
        }
    }

    public static void m3() {
        // Prints the call stack details
        StackTraceElement[] frames = Thread.currentThread()
                                        .getStackTrace();

        for(StackTraceElement frame : frames) {
            System.out.println(frame.toString());
        }
    }
}
```

```
Without using reflection:
java.lang.Thread.getStackTrace(Thread.java:1552)
com.jdojo.stackwalker.LegacyStackWalk.m3(LegacyStackWalk.java:37)
com.jdojo.stackwalker.LegacyStackWalk.m2(LegacyStackWalk.java:18)
com.jdojo.stackwalker.LegacyStackWalk.m1(LegacyStackWalk.java:12)
com.jdojo.stackwalker.LegacyStackWalk.main(LegacyStackWalk.java:8)

Using reflection:
java.lang.Thread.getStackTrace(Thread.java:1552)
com.jdojo.stackwalker.LegacyStackWalk.m3(LegacyStackWalk.java:37)
sun.reflect.NativeMethodAccessorImpl.invoke0(Native Method)
sun.reflect.NativeMethodAccessorImpl.invoke(NativeMethodAccessorImpl.java:62)
sun.reflect.DelegatingMethodAccessorImpl.invoke(DelegatingMethodAccessorImpl.java:43)
java.lang.reflect.Method.invoke(Method.java:498)
com.jdojo.stackwalker.LegacyStackWalk.m2(LegacyStackWalk.java:25)
com.jdojo.stackwalker.LegacyStackWalk.m1(LegacyStackWalk.java:12)
com.jdojo.stackwalker.LegacyStackWalk.main(LegacyStackWalk.java:8)
```

The main() method of the LegacyStackWalk class calls the m1() method, which calls the m2() method. The m2() method calls the m3() method twice—once directly and once using reflection. The m3() method gets a snapshot of the stack for the current thread using the getStrackTrace() method of the Thread class and prints the frame's details using the toString() method of the StackTraceElement class. You could have used methods of this class to get the same information for each frame. When you run the LegacyStackWalk class in JDK 9, the output includes the module name and module version at the beginning of each line. The JDK 9 output is as follows:

```
Without using reflection:
java.base/java.lang.Thread.getStackTrace(Thread.java:1654)
com.jdojo.stackwalker/com.jdojo.stackwalker.LegacyStackWalk.m3(LegacyStackWalk.java:37)
com.jdojo.stackwalker/com.jdojo.stackwalker.LegacyStackWalk.m2(LegacyStackWalk.java:18)
com.jdojo.stackwalker/com.jdojo.stackwalker.LegacyStackWalk.m1(LegacyStackWalk.java:12)
com.jdojo.stackwalker/com.jdojo.stackwalker.LegacyStackWalk.main(LegacyStackWalk.java:8)

Using reflection:
java.base/java.lang.Thread.getStackTrace(Thread.java:1654)
com.jdojo.stackwalker/com.jdojo.stackwalker.LegacyStackWalk.m3(LegacyStackWalk.java:37)
java.base/jdk.internal.reflect.NativeMethodAccessorImpl.invoke0(Native Method)
java.base/jdk.internal.reflect.NativeMethodAccessorImpl.invoke(NativeMethodAccessorImpl.java:62)
java.base/jdk.internal.reflect.DelegatingMethodAccessorImpl.invoke(DelegatingMethodAccessor
Impl.java:43)
java.base/java.lang.reflect.Method.invoke(Method.java:538)
com.jdojo.stackwalker/com.jdojo.stackwalker.LegacyStackWalk.m2(LegacyStackWalk.java:25)
com.jdojo.stackwalker/com.jdojo.stackwalker.LegacyStackWalk.m1(LegacyStackWalk.java:12)
com.jdojo.stackwalker/com.jdojo.stackwalker.LegacyStackWalk.main(LegacyStackWalk.java:8)
```

Drawbacks to Stack Walking

Prior to JDK 9, the Stack-Walking API had several drawbacks:

- It was not efficient. The getStrackTrace() method of the Throwable class returned a snapshot of the entire stack. There was no way to get just a few top frames in the stack.

- The frames contained method names and class names, not the class references. Class references are instances of the Class<?> class, whereas class names are simply strings.

- The JVM specification allowed a VM implementation to omit some frames in the stack for performance. So, if you were interested in inspecting the entire stack, you could not do so if the VM hid some frames.

- Many APIs—in JDK and other libraries—are caller-sensitive. Their behavior varies based on the caller's class. For example, if you want to call the addExports() method of the Module class, the caller's class must be in the same module. Otherwise, an IllegalCallerException is thrown. In the existing APIs, there was no easy and efficient way to get the caller's class reference. Such APIs depended on using the JDK internal API—the getCallerClass() static method of the sun.reflect.Reflection class.

- There was no easy way to filter out stack frames of specific implementation classes.

Stack Walking in JDK 9

JDK 9 introduced a new Stack-Walking API, which consists of a single class named StackWalker in the java.lang package. The class provides easy and efficient stack walking. It provides a sequential stream of stack frames for the current thread. The stack frames are reported in order, from the top-most frame where the stack was generated to the bottom-most frame. The StackWalker class is very efficient because it evaluates the stack frames lazily. It also contains a convenience method to get the reference of the caller class. The StackWalker class consists of the following members:

- The StackWalker.Option nested enum
- The StackWalker.StackFrame nested interface
- Methods to get an instance of the StackWalker class
- Methods to process stack frames
- A method to get the caller's class

I explain each component of the StackWalker class and their uses in subsequent sections in detail.

Specifying Stack-Walking Options

You can configure a StackWalker by specifying zero or more options. An option is one of the constants of the StackWalker.Option enum. The constants are as follows:

- RETAIN_CLASS_REFERENCE
- SHOW_HIDDEN_FRAMES
- SHOW_REFLECT_FRAMES

If the RETAIN_CLASS_REFERENCE option is specified, the frames returned by the StackWalker will contain the reference of the Class object of the class that declares the method represented by the frame. You also need to specify this option if you want to get the Class object's reference of the caller of a method. By default, this option is absent.

By default, implementation-specific and reflection frames are not included in the stream of frames returned by the StackWalker class. Use the SHOW_HIDDEN_FRAMES option to include all hidden frames.

If the SHOW_REFLECT_FRAMES option is specified, the stream of frames returned by the StackWalker class includes the reflection frames. Using this option may still hide the implementation-specific frames, which you can show using the SHOW_HIDDEN_FRAMES option.

I show you how to use these options and their effects when I explain how to create instances of the StackWalker class in a subsequent section.

Representing a Stack Frame

Prior to JDK 9, an instance of the StackTraceElement class was used to represent a stack frame. The Stack-Walker API in JDK 9 uses an instance of the StackWalker.StackFrame interface to represent a stack frame.

▓ **Tip** There is no concrete implementation class of the StackWalker.StackFrame interface for you to use directly. The Stack-Walking API in JDK provides you with instances of the interface when you retrieve stack frames.

The `StackWalker.StackFrame` interface contains the following methods, most of which are the same as in the `StackTraceElement` class:

- `int getByteCodeIndex()`
- `String getClassName()`
- `Class<?> getDeclaringClass()`
- `String getFileName()`
- `int getLineNumber()`
- `String getMethodName()`
- `boolean isNativeMethod()`
- `StackTraceElement toStackTraceElement()`

In a class file, each method is described using a structure named `method_info`. The `method_info` structure contains an attribute table that holds a variable-length attribute named Code. The Code attribute contains an array named code, which holds the bytecode instructions of the method. The `getByteCodeIndex()` method returns the index to the code array in the Code attribute of the method containing the execution point represented by this frame. It returns -1 for native methods. For more information on the code array and Code attribute, refer to the section 4.7.3 of the Java Virtual Specification at https://docs.oracle.com/javase/specs/jvms/se8/html/.

How do you work with the code array of a method? As an application developer, you will not use the bytecode index for an execution point in a method. JDK does support reading a class file and all its attributes using internal APIs. You can see the bytecode index of each instruction in a method using the javap tool, which is located in the JDK_HOME\bin directory. You will need to use the -c option with javap to print the code array of methods. The following command shows the code array for all methods in the LegacyStackWalk class:

```
C:\Java9Revealed>javap -c com.jdojo.stackwalker\build\classes\com\jdojo\stackwalker\
LegacyStackWalk.class
```

```
Compiled from "LegacyStackWalk.java"
public class com.jdojo.stackwalker.LegacyStackWalk {
  public com.jdojo.stackwalker.LegacyStackWalk();
    Code:
       0: aload_0
       1: invokespecial #1              // Method java/lang/Object."<init>":()V
       4: return

  public static void main(java.lang.String[]);
    Code:
       0: invokestatic  #2              // Method m1:()V
       3: return

  public static void m1();
    Code:
       0: invokestatic  #3              // Method m2:()V
       3: return
```

```
  public static void m2();
    Code:
       0: getstatic      #4           // Field java/lang/System.out:Ljava/io/PrintStream;
       3: ldc            #5           // String \nWithout using reflection:
       5: invokevirtual #6           // Method java/io/PrintStream.println:(Ljava/
lang/String;)V
       8: invokestatic   #7           // Method m3:()V
...
      32: anewarray      #13          // class java/lang/Object
      35: invokevirtual #14          // Method java/lang/reflect/Method.
invoke:(Ljava/lang/Object;[Ljava/lang/Object;)Ljava/lang/Object;
...
  public static void m3();
    Code:
       0: invokestatic   #20          // Method java/lang/Thread.currentThread:()
Ljava/lang/Thread;
       3: invokevirtual #21          // Method java/lang/Thread.getStackTrace:()
[Ljava/lang/StackTraceElement;
...
}
```

When you take a snapshot of the call stack in method m3(), the outputs in the boldface font represent the execution points in each method—main(), m1(), m2() and m3(). Note that the m2() method calls m3() twice. For the first call, the bytecode index is 8 and, for the second time, it is 35.

The getDeclaringClass() method returns the reference of the Class object of the class that declares the method represented by the frame. It throws an UnsupportedOperationException if this StackWalker is not configured with the RETAIN_CLASS_REFERENCE option.

The toStackTraceElement() method returns an instance of the StackTraceElement class representing the same stack frame. This method is handy if you want to use the JDK 9 API to obtain a StackWalker.StackFrame, but keep using your old code that uses the StackTraceElement class to analyze the frame.

Obtaining a StackWalker

The StackWalker class contains the following static factory methods that return a StackWalker instance:

- StackWalker getInstance()

- StackWalker getInstance (StackWalker.Option option)

- StackWalker getInstance (Set<StackWalker.Option> options)

- StackWalker getInstance (Set<StackWalker.Option> options, int
  estimateDepth)

You can configure StackWalker differently using different versions of the getInstance() method. The default configuration is to exclude all hidden frames and not to retain class references. Versions that let you specify StackWalker.Option are configured using those options.

The estimateDepth argument is a hint that indicates the estimated number of stack frames this StackWalker is expected to traverse, so the size of an internal buffer may be optimized.

The following snippet of code creates four instances of the StackWalker class with different configurations:

```
import java.util.Set;
import static java.lang.StackWalker.Option.*;
...

// Get a StackWalker with a default configuration
StackWalker sw1 = StackWalker.getInstance();

// Get a StackWalker that shows reflection frames
StackWalker sw2 = StackWalker.getInstance(SHOW_REFLECT_FRAMES);

// Get a StackWalker that shows all hidden frames
StackWalker sw3 = StackWalker.getInstance(SHOW_HIDDEN_FRAMES);

// Get a StackWalker that shows reflection frames and retains class references
StackWalker sw4 = StackWalker.getInstance(
Set.of(SHOW_REFLECT_FRAMES, RETAIN_CLASS_REFERENCE));
```

▓ **Tip**　A StackWalker is thread-safe and reusable. Multiple threads can use the same instance to traverse their own stacks.

The next section explains how to use a StackWalker to walk through stack frames.

Walking the Stack

It is time to traverse stack frames of a thread. The StackWalker class contains two methods that let you traverse the stack of the *current thread*:

- void forEach(Consumer<? super StackWalker.StackFrame> action)
- <T> T walk(Function<? super Stream<StackWalker.StackFrame>,? extends T> function)

Use the forEach() method if you need to traverse the entire stack. The specified Consumer will be supplied with one frame as a time from the stack, starting with the top most frame. The following snippet of code prints the details of each frame returned by a StackWalker:

```
// Prints the details of all stack frames of the current thread
StackWalker.getInstance()
          .forEach(System.out::println);
```

Use the walk() method if you want to customize the stack traversal such as by using filters and maps. The walk() method takes a Function, which accepts a Stream<StackWalker.StackFrame> as an argument and can return any type of object. The StackWalker will create the stream of stack frames and pass it to your function. When the function completes, the StackWalker will close the stream. The stream passed to the walk() method can be traversed only once. Attempting to traverse the stream a second time throws an IllegalStateException.

The following snippet of code uses the walk() method to traverse the entire stack, printing the details of each frame. This snippet of code does the same as what the previous snippet of code did using the forEach() method.

```
// Prints the details of all stack frames of the current thread
StackWalker.getInstance()
          .walk(s -> {
              s.forEach(System.out::println);
              return null;
          });
```

■ **Tip** The forEach() method of the StackWalker is used to process stack frames one at a time, whereas the walk() method is used to process the entire stack as a stream of frames. You can use the walk() method to simulate the functionality of the forEach() method, but not vice versa.

You might wonder why the walk() method does not return a stream of stack frames instead of passing the stream to your function. Not returning a stream of stack frames from the method is intentional. The elements of the stream are evaluated lazily. Once the stream of stack frames is created, the JVM is free to reorganize the stack and there is no definite way to detect that the stack has changed while you are still holding the reference to its stream. This is the reason that creating and closing the stream of stack frames are controlled by the StackWalker class.

As the Streams API is extensive, so is the use of the walk() method. I show a few of its sample uses before I show you a complete example. The following snippet of code gets a snapshot of the stack frames of the current thread in a List.

```
import java.lang.StackWalker.StackFrame;
import java.util.List;
import static java.util.stream.Collectors.toList;
...
List<StackFrame> frames = StackWalker.getInstance()
                           .walk(s -> s.collect(toList()));
```

The following snippet of code collects the string form of all stack frames of the current thread in a List, excluding frames that represent methods whose names start with m2:

```
import java.util.List;
import static java.util.stream.Collectors.toList;
...
List<String> list = StackWalker.getInstance()
  .walk(s -> s.filter(f -> !f.getMethodName().startsWith("m2"))
            .map(f -> f.toString())
            .collect(toList())
      );
```

The following snippet of code collects the string form of all stack frames of the current thread in a List, excluding frames that represent methods whose declaring class name ends with Test:

```java
import static java.lang.StackWalker.Option.RETAIN_CLASS_REFERENCE;
import java.util.List;
import static java.util.stream.Collectors.toList;
...
List<String> list = StackWalker
    .getInstance(RETAIN_CLASS_REFERENCE)
    .walk(s -> s.filter(f -> !f.getDeclaringClass()
                                .getName().endsWith("Test"))
                .map(f -> f.toString())
                .collect(toList())
        );
```

The following snippet of code collects the entire stack in a string, separating each frame with a platform-specific line separator:

```java
import static java.util.stream.Collectors.joining;
...
String stackStr = StackWalker.getInstance()
 .walk(s -> s.map(f -> f.toString())
                .collect(joining(System.getProperty(
                                "line.separator")
        )));
```

Listing 16-3 contains a complete program to show the use of the StackWalker class and its walk() method. Its main() method calls the m1() method twice, each time passing a different set of options for the StackWalker. The m2() method uses reflection to call the m3() method, which prints the stack frame details. The first time, the reflection frames are hidden and the class references are not available.

Listing 16-3. Using a StackWalker to Traverse Stack Frames of the Current Thread

```java
// StackWalking.java
package com.jdojo.stackwalker;

import java.lang.StackWalker.Option;
import static java.lang.StackWalker.Option.RETAIN_CLASS_REFERENCE;
import static java.lang.StackWalker.Option.SHOW_REFLECT_FRAMES;
import java.lang.StackWalker.StackFrame;
import java.lang.reflect.InvocationTargetException;
import java.util.Set;
import java.util.stream.Stream;

public class StackWalking {
    public static void main(String[] args) {
        m1(Set.of());

        System.out.println();

        // Retain class references and show reflection frames
        m1(Set.of(RETAIN_CLASS_REFERENCE, SHOW_REFLECT_FRAMES));
    }
```

```java
public static void m1(Set<Option> options) {
    m2(options);
}

public static void m2(Set<Option> options) {
    // Call m3() using reflection
    try {
        System.out.println("Using StackWalker Options: " + options);
        StackWalking.class
                .getMethod("m3", Set.class)
                .invoke(null, options);
    } catch (NoSuchMethodException
            | InvocationTargetException
            | IllegalAccessException
            | SecurityException e) {
        e.printStackTrace();
    }
}

public static void m3(Set<Option> options) {
    // Prints the call stack details
    StackWalker.getInstance(options)
                .walk(StackWalking::processStack);
}

public static Void processStack(Stream<StackFrame> stack) {
    stack.forEach(frame -> {
        int bci = frame.getByteCodeIndex();
        String className = frame.getClassName();
        Class<?> classRef = null;
        try {
            classRef = frame.getDeclaringClass();
        } catch (UnsupportedOperationException e) {
            // No action to take
        }

        String fileName = frame.getFileName();
        int lineNumber = frame.getLineNumber();
        String methodName = frame.getMethodName();
        boolean isNative = frame.isNativeMethod();

        StackTraceElement sfe = frame.toStackTraceElement();

        System.out.printf("Native Method=%b", isNative);
        System.out.printf(", Byte Code Index=%d", bci);
        System.out.printf(", Module Name=%s", sfe.getModuleName());
        System.out.printf(", Module Version=%s", sfe.getModuleVersion());
        System.out.printf(", Class Name=%s", className);
        System.out.printf(", Class Reference=%s", classRef);
        System.out.printf(", File Name=%s", fileName);
```

```
            System.out.printf(", Line Number=%d", lineNumber);
            System.out.printf(", Method Name=%s.%n", methodName);
        });

        return null;
    }
}
```

Using StackWalker Options: []
Native Method=false, Byte Code Index=9, Module Name=null, Module Version=null, Class
Name=com.jdojo.stackwalker.StackWalking, Class Reference=null, FileName=StackWalking.java,
Line Number=44, Method Name=m3.
Native Method=false, Byte Code Index=37, Module Name=null, Module Version=null, Class
Name=com.jdojo.stackwalker.StackWalking, Class Reference=null, File Name=StackWalking.java,
Line Number=32, Method Name=m2.
Native Method=false, Byte Code Index=1, Module Name=null, Module Version=null, Class
Name=com.jdojo.stackwalker.StackWalking, Class Reference=null, File Name=StackWalking.java,
Line Number=23, Method Name=m1.
Native Method=false, Byte Code Index=3, Module Name=null, Module Version=null, Class
Name=com.jdojo.stackwalker.StackWalking, Class Reference=null, File Name=StackWalking.java,
Line Number=14, Method Name=main.

Using StackWalker Options: [SHOW_REFLECT_FRAMES, RETAIN_CLASS_REFERENCE]
Native Method=false, Byte Code Index=9, Module Name=null, Module Version=null, Class
Name=com.jdojo.stackwalker.StackWalking, Class Reference=class com.jdojo.stackwalker.
StackWalking, File Name=StackWalking.java, Line Number=44, Method Name=m3.
Native Method=true, Byte Code Index=-1, Module Name=java.base, Module Version=9-ea, Class
Name=jdk.internal.reflect.NativeMethodAccessorImpl, Class Reference=class jdk.internal.
reflect.NativeMethodAccessorImpl, File Name=NativeMethodAccessorImpl.java, Line Number=-2,
Method Name=invoke0.
Native Method=false, Byte Code Index=100, Module Name=java.base, Module Version=9-ea, Class
Name=jdk.internal.reflect.NativeMethodAccessorImpl, Class Reference=class jdk.internal.
reflect.NativeMethodAccessorImpl, File Name=NativeMethodAccessorImpl.java, Line Number=62,
Method Name=invoke.
Native Method=false, Byte Code Index=6, Module Name=java.base, Module Version=9-ea, Class
Name=jdk.internal.reflect.DelegatingMethodAccessorImpl, Class Reference=class jdk.internal.
reflect.DelegatingMethodAccessorImpl, File Name=DelegatingMethodAccessorImpl.java, Line
Number=43, Method Name=invoke.
Native Method=false, Byte Code Index=59, Module Name=java.base, Module Version=9-ea,
Class Name=java.lang.reflect.Method, Class Reference=class java.lang.reflect.Method, File
Name=Method.java, Line Number=538, Method Name=invoke.
Native Method=false, Byte Code Index=37, Module Name=null, Module Version=null, Class
Name=com.jdojo.stackwalker.StackWalking, Class Reference=class com.jdojo.stackwalker.
StackWalking, File Name=StackWalking.java, Line Number=32, Method Name=m2.
Native Method=false, Byte Code Index=1, Module Name=null, Module Version=null, Class
Name=com.jdojo.stackwalker.StackWalking, Class Reference=class com.jdojo.stackwalker.
StackWalking, File Name=StackWalking.java, Line Number=23, Method Name=m1.
Native Method=false, Byte Code Index=21, Module Name=null, Module Version=null, Class
Name=com.jdojo.stackwalker.StackWalking, Class Reference=class com.jdojo.stackwalker.
StackWalking, File Name=StackWalking.java, Line Number=19, Method Name=main.

Knowing the Caller's Class

Before JDK 9, developers depended on the following methods to get caller's calls:

- The getClassContext() method of the SecurityManager class, which required sub-classing because the method is protected.

- The getCallerClass() method of the sun.reflect.Reflection class, which is a JDK internal class.

JDK 9 makes getting the caller class reference easy by adding a method named getCallerClass() in the StackWalker class. The method's return type is Class<?>. Invoking this method throws UnsupportedOperationException if the StackWalker is not configured with the RETAIN_CLASS_REFERENCE option. Invoking this method throws IllegalStateException if there is no caller frame in the stack, for example, running a class whose main() method invokes this method.

Which class is the caller class? You have two callable constructs in Java—methods and constructors. The following discussion uses the term method, however it applies to both methods and constructors. Suppose you invoke the getCallerClass() method inside a method named S, which is called from a method named T. Further suppose that the method named T is in a class named C. In this case, class C is the caller class.

■ **Tip** The getCallerClass() method of the StackWalker class filters out all hidden and reflection frames while finding the caller class, irrespective of the options used to obtain the StackWalker instance.

Listing 16-4 contains a complete program to show how to get the caller's class. Its main() method calls the m1() method, which calls m2() method, which calls the m3() method. The m3() method obtains an instance of the StackWalker class and gets the caller class. Note that the m2() method uses reflection to call the m3() method. In the end, the main() method attempts to get the caller class. When you run the CallerClassTest class, the main() method is called by the JVM and there will be no caller frame on the stack. This will throw an IllegalStateException.

Listing 16-4. Getting the Caller Class Reference Using the StackWalker Class

```java
// CallerClassTest.java
package com.jdojo.stackwalker;

import java.lang.StackWalker.Option;
import static java.lang.StackWalker.Option.RETAIN_CLASS_REFERENCE;
import static java.lang.StackWalker.Option.SHOW_REFLECT_FRAMES;
import java.lang.reflect.InvocationTargetException;
import java.util.Set;

public class CallerClassTest {
    public static void main(String[] args) {
        /* Will not be able to get caller class because because the RETAIN_CLASS_REFERENCE
           option is not specified.
        */
        m1(Set.of());

        // Will print the caller class
        m1(Set.of(RETAIN_CLASS_REFERENCE, SHOW_REFLECT_FRAMES));
```

```
        try {
            /* The following statement will throw an IllegalStateException if this class is run
                because there will be no caller class; JVM will call this method. However,
                if the main() method is called in code, no exception will be thrown.
            */
            Class<?> cls = StackWalker.getInstance(RETAIN_CLASS_REFERENCE)
                                    .getCallerClass();
            System.out.println("In main method, Caller Class: " + cls.getName());
        } catch (IllegalCallerException e) {
            System.out.println("In main method, Exception: " + e.getMessage());
        }
    }

    public static void m1(Set<Option> options) {
        m2(options);
    }

    public static void m2(Set<Option> options) {
        // Call m3() using reflection
        try {
            CallerClassTest.class
                        .getMethod("m3", Set.class)
                        .invoke(null, options);
        } catch (NoSuchMethodException | InvocationTargetException
                | IllegalAccessException | SecurityException e) {
            e.printStackTrace();
        }
    }

    public static void m3(Set<Option> options) {
        try {
            // Print the caller class
            Class<?> cls = StackWalker.getInstance(options)
                                    .getCallerClass();
            System.out.println("Caller Class: " + cls.getName());
        } catch (UnsupportedOperationException e) {
            System.out.println("Inside m3(): " + e.getMessage());
        }
    }
}
```

```
Inside m3(): This stack walker does not have RETAIN_CLASS_REFERENCE access
Caller Class: com.jdojo.stackwalker.CallerClassTest
In main method, Exception: no caller frame
```

In the previous example, the method collecting the stack frames was called from another method of the same class. Let's call this method from a method of another class to see a different result. Listing 16-5 shows the code for a class named CallerClassTest2.

Listing 16-5. Another Example of Getting the Caller Class Using the StackWalker Class

```java
// CallerClassTest2.java
package com.jdojo.stackwalker;

import java.lang.StackWalker.Option;
import java.util.Set;
import static java.lang.StackWalker.Option.RETAIN_CLASS_REFERENCE;

public class CallerClassTest2 {
    public static void main(String[] args) {
        Set<Option> options = Set.of(RETAIN_CLASS_REFERENCE);
        CallerClassTest.m1(options);
        CallerClassTest.m2(options);
        CallerClassTest.m3(options);

        System.out.println("\nCalling the main() method:");
        CallerClassTest.main(null);

        System.out.println("\nUsing an anonymous class:");
        new Object() {
            {
                CallerClassTest.m3(options);
            }
        };

        System.out.println("\nUsing a lambda expression:");
        new Thread(() -> CallerClassTest.m3(options))
            .start();
    }
}
```

```
Caller Class: com.jdojo.stackwalker.CallerClassTest
Caller Class: com.jdojo.stackwalker.CallerClassTest
Caller Class: com.jdojo.stackwalker.CallerClassTest2

Calling the main() method:
Inside m3(): This stack walker does not have RETAIN_CLASS_REFERENCE access
Caller Class: com.jdojo.stackwalker.CallerClassTest
In main method, Caller Class: com.jdojo.stackwalker.CallerClassTest2

Using an anonymous class:
Caller Class: com.jdojo.stackwalker.CallerClassTest2$1

Using a lambda expression:
Caller Class: com.jdojo.stackwalker.CallerClassTest2
```

The main() method of the CallerClassTest2 class calls the four methods of the CallerClassTest class. The caller class is CallerClassTest2 when the CallerClassTest.m3() is called from the CallerClassTest2 class directly. When you call the CallerClassTest.main() method from the CallerClassTest2 class, there is a caller frame and the caller class is the CallerClassTest2 class. Compare this with the output of the previous example when you ran the CallerClassTest class. At that time, the CallerClassTest.main()

method was called from the JVM and you were not able to get a caller class inside the `CallerClassTest.main()` method because there was no caller frame. In the end, `CallerClassTest.m3()` method is called from an anonymous class and a lambda expression. The anonymous class is reported as the caller class. In case of the lambda expression, its enclosing class is reported as the caller class.

Stack-Walking Permissions

When a Java security manager is present and you configure a `StackWalker` with the `RETAIN_CLASS_REFERENCE` option, a permission check is performed to make sure that the codebase is granted a `java.lang.StackFramePermission` with a value of `retainClassReference`. A `SecurityException` is thrown if the permission is not granted. The permission check is performed at the time the `StackWalker` instance is created, not when the stack walking is performed.

Listing 16-6 contains the code for the `StackWalkerPermissionCheck` class. Its `printStackFrames()` method creates a `StackWalker` instance with the `RETAIN_CLASS_REFERENCE` option. The `main()` method calls this method, which prints the stack trace without any problems, assuming that no security manager is present. A security manager is installed and the `printStackFrames()` method is called again. This time, a `SecurityException` is thrown, which is indicated in the output.

Listing 16-6. Creating a StackWalker to Retain Class References When a Java Security Manager Is Present

```
// StackWalkerPermissionCheck.java
package com.jdojo.stackwalker;

import static java.lang.StackWalker.Option.RETAIN_CLASS_REFERENCE;

public class StackWalkerPermissionCheck {
    public static void main(String[] args) {
        System.out.println("Before installing security manager:");
        printStackFrames();

        SecurityManager sm = System.getSecurityManager();
        if (sm == null) {
            sm = new SecurityManager();
            System.setSecurityManager(sm);
        }

        System.out.println(
            "\nAfter installing security manager:");
        printStackFrames();
    }

    public static void printStackFrames() {
        try {
            StackWalker.getInstance(RETAIN_CLASS_REFERENCE)
                    .forEach(System.out::println);
        } catch(SecurityException e){
            System.out.println("Could not create a " +
                "StackWalker. Error: " + e.getMessage());
        }
    }
}
```

```
Before installing security manager:
com.jdojo.stackwalker/com.jdojo.stackwalker.StackWalkerPermissionCheck.printStackFrames(Stac
kWalkerPermissionCheck.java:24)
com.jdojo.stackwalker/com.jdojo.stackwalker.StackWalkerPermissionCheck.
main(StackWalkerPermissionCheck.java:9)

After installing security manager:
Could not create a StackWalker. Error: access denied ("java.lang.StackFramePermission"
"retainClassReference")
```

Listing 16-7 shows you how to grant the required permission to create a StackWalker with the RETAIN_CLASS_REFERENCE option. The permission is granted to all codebases. You need to add this permission block to the end of the java.policy file located in the JAVA_HOME\conf\security directory on your machine.

Listing 16-7. Granting java.lang.StackFramePermission with a "retainClassReference" Value

```
grant {
    permission java.lang.StackFramePermission "retainClassReference";
};
```

When you run the class in Listing 16-6 with the permission granted in Listing 16-7, you should receive the following output:

```
Before installing security manager:
com.jdojo.stackwalker/com.jdojo.stackwalker.StackWalkerPermissionCheck.printStackFrames(Stac
kWalkerPermissionCheck.java:24)
com.jdojo.stackwalker/com.jdojo.stackwalker.StackWalkerPermissionCheck.
main(StackWalkerPermissionCheck.java:9)

After installing security manager:
com.jdojo.stackwalker/com.jdojo.stackwalker.StackWalkerPermissionCheck.printStackFrames(Stac
kWalkerPermissionCheck.java:24)
com.jdojo.stackwalker/com.jdojo.stackwalker.StackWalkerPermissionCheck.
main(StackWalkerPermissionCheck.java:18)
```

Summary

Each thread in a JVM has a *private* JVM stack that is created at the same time the thread is created. A stack stores frames. A frame on a JVM stack represents a Java method invocation in a given thread. A new frame is created and pushed to the top of the stack each time a method is invoked. A frame is destroyed (popped out of stack) when the method invocation completes. In a given thread, only one frame is active at any point. The active frame is known as the *current frame* and its method is known as the *current method*. The class that defines the current method is known as the *current class*.

Before JDK 9, it was possible to walk through all frames in a thread's stack using the following classes: Throwable, Thread, and StackTraceElement. An instance of the StackTraceElement class represents a stack frame. The getStrackTrace() method of the Throwable class returns a StackTraceElement[] that contains the frames of the current thread's stack. The getStrackTrace() method of the Thread class returns a StackTraceElement[] that contains the frames of the thread's stack. The first element of the array is the top frame in the stack, which represents the last method invocation in the sequence. Some implementation of JVM may omit some frames in the returned array.

JDK 9 makes stack traversal easy. It introduced a new class named StackWalker in the java.lang package. You can get an instance of the StackWalker using one of its static factory methods named getInstance(). A StackWalker can be configured using options, which are represented by the constants defined in the enum named StackWalker.Option. An instance of the nested interface named StackWalker.StackFrame represents a stack frame. The StackWalker class works with StackWalker.StackFrame instance. The interface defined a method named toStackTraceElement() that can be used to get an instance of the StackTraceElement class from a StackWalker.StackFrame.

You can use the forEach() and walk() methods of the StackWalker instance to traverse stack frames of the current thread. The getCallerClass() method of the StackWalker instance returns the caller class reference. You must configure a StackWalker instance with the RETAIN_CLASS_REFERENCE if you want the reference of the class representing the stack frame and the reference of the caller's class. By default, all reflection frames and implementation-specific frames are not reported by a StackWalker. Use the SHOW_REFLECT_FRAMES and SHOW_HIDDEN_FRAMES options to configure a StackWalker if you want those frames to be included in stack traversal. Using the SHOW_HIDDEN_FRAMES option also includes reflection frames.

When a Java security manager is present and you configure a StackWalker with the RETAIN_CLASS_REFERENCE option, a permission check is performed to make sure that the codebase is granted a java.lang.StackFramePermission with a value of retainClassReference. A SecurityException is thrown if the permission is not granted. The permission check is performed at the time the StackWalker instance is created, not when the stack walking is performed.

CHAPTER 17

■ ■ ■

Reactive Streams

In this chapter, you will learn:

- What a stream is

- What the Reactive Streams initiative is and its specification and Java API

- The Reactive Streams API in JDK and how to use it

- How to create publishers, subscribers, and processors using the Java API for Reactive Streams in JDK 9

What Is a Stream?

A stream is a sequence of items produced by a producer and consumed by one or more consumers. This producer-consumer model is also known as source/sink model or publisher-subscriber model. I refer to it as a publisher-subscriber model in this chapter. I use the terms *element*, *item*, *data item*, and *data* interchangeably to mean a piece of information that is published by a publisher and received by subscribers.

There are several stream-processing mechanisms, the pull model and push model being the most common. In a push model, the publisher pushes items to the subscriber. In a pull model, the subscriber pulls items from the publisher. These models work great when both the publisher and the subscriber work at the same rate, which is an ideal situation. We will consider a few situations when they do not work at the same rate, the issues involved in such situations, and the possible solutions.

When the publisher is faster than the subscriber, the latter has to have an unbounded buffer to store fast incoming items or it must drop items it cannot handle. Another solution is to use a strategy called *backpressure* in which the subscriber tells the publisher to slow down and hold the items until the subscriber is ready to process more. Using backpressure ensures that a faster publisher doesn't overwhelm a slower subscriber. Using backpressure may require the publisher to have an unbounded buffer if it keeps producing and storing elements. The publisher may implement a bounded buffer to store limited amount of elements and may choose to drop them if its buffer is full. Another strategy may be used in which the publisher retries publishing items to the subscriber, which cannot accept the items when they are published.

What does the subscriber do when it requests items from the publisher and the items are not available? In a synchronous request, the subscriber has to wait, possibly indefinitely, until items are available. If the publisher sends items to the subscriber synchronously and the subscriber processes them synchronously, the publisher has to block until the data processing finishes. The solution is to have an asynchronous processing at both ends, where the subscriber may keep working on other tasks after requesting items from the publisher. When more items are ready, the publisher sends them to the subscriber asynchronously.

© Kishori Sharan 2017
K. Sharan, *Java 9 Revealed*, DOI 10.1007/978-1-4842-2592-9_17

What Is Reactive Streams?

Reactive Streams started in 2013 as an initiative for providing a standard for *asynchronous* stream processing with *non-blocking backpressure*. It is aimed at solving the problems in processing of a stream of items—how to pass a stream of items from a publisher to a subscriber without requiring the publisher to block, or the subscriber to have an unbounded buffer or drop.

The Reactive Streams model is very simple—the subscriber sends an asynchronous request to the publisher for N items. The publisher sends N or fewer items to the subscriber asynchronously.

■ **Tip**   Reactive Streams dynamically switches between the pull model and push model stream-processing mechanisms. It uses the pull model when the subscriber is slower and uses the push model when the subscriber is faster.

In 2015, a specification and Java API for handling Reactive Streams were published. Refer to the web page at `http://www.reactive-streams.org/` for more information on Reactive Streams. The Java API for Reactive Streams consists of only four interfaces:

- `Publisher<T>`
- `Subscriber<T>`
- `Subscription`
- `Processor<T,R>`

A *publisher* is a producer of potentially an unbounded number of *sequenced* items. It publishes (or sends) items to its current subscribers based on the demands received from them.

A *subscriber* subscribes to a publisher to receive items. The publisher sends a subscription token to the subscriber. Using the subscription token, the subscriber requests N number of items from the publisher. When items are ready, the publisher sends N or fewer items to the subscriber. The subscriber can request more items. The publisher may have more than one pending request for items from the subscriber.

A *subscription* represents a token of subscription of a subscriber to a publisher. The publisher passes this to the subscriber when a request to subscribe is successful. The subscriber uses the `Subscription` to interact with the publisher such as to request more items or to cancel the subscription.

Figure 17-1 shows a typical sequence of interactions between a publisher and a subscriber. The subscription is not shown in the diagram. The diagram does not show the error and cancellation events.

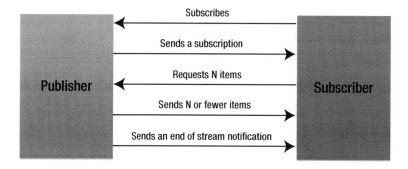

Figure 17-1. *A typical sequence of interactions between a publisher and a subscriber*

A *processor* represents a processing stage that acts as both a subscriber and a publisher. The Processor interface extends both the Publisher and the Subscriber interfaces. It is used to transform items in a publisher-subscriber pipeline. A Processor<T,R> subscribes for data elements of type T, receives and transforms the data to type R, and publishes the transformed data. Figure 17-2 shows the role of a processor as a transformer in a publisher-subscriber pipeline. You can have more than one processor in the pipeline.

Figure 17-2. *Using a processor as a transformer in a publisher-subscriber pipeline*

The Reactive Streams Java API, as provided by the Reactive Streams initiative, is shown in Listing 17-1. Notice that the return type of all methods is void. This is because these methods represent either an asynchronous request or an asynchronous event notification. I explain how this API has been incorporated in JDK 9 and how to use it in the next section.

Listing 17-1. The Reactive Streams Java API

```
public interface Publisher<T> {
    public void subscribe(Subscriber<? super T> s);
}

public interface Subscriber<T> {
    public void onSubscribe(Subscription s);
    public void onNext(T t);
    public void onError(Throwable t);
    public void onComplete();
}

public interface Subscription {
    public void request(long n);
    public void cancel();
}

public interface Processor<T,R> extends Subscriber<T>, Publisher<R> {
}
```

The Java API for Reactive Streams seems very simple to understand. However, it is not simple to implement. The asynchronous nature of all interactions between publishers and subscribers and handling the backpressure make the implementation complex. As application developers, you would find it complex to implement these interfaces. Libraries are supposed to provide implementations to support a broad range of use-cases. JDK 9 provides a simple implementation of the Publisher interface that you can use for simple use-cases or extend to suit your own needs. RxJava (https://github.com/ReactiveX/RxJava) is one of the Java implementations for Reactive Streams.

The Reactive Streams API in JDK 9

JDK 9 provides a Reactive Streams-compliant API in the `java.util.concurrent` package, which is in the `java.base` module. The API consists of two classes:

- `Flow`

- `SubmissionPublisher<T>`

The `Flow` class is final. It encapsulates the Reactive Streams Java API and a static method. The four interfaces specified by the Reactive Streams Java API are included in the `Flow` class as nested static interfaces:

- `Flow.Processor<T,R>`

- `Flow.Publisher<T>`

- `Flow.Subscriber<T>`

- `Flow.Subscription`

These four interfaces contain the same methods as shown in Listing 17-1. The `Flow` class contains a static method named `defaultBufferSize()` that returns the default size for buffers used by publishers and subscribers. Currently, it returns 256.

The `SubmissionPublisher<T>` class is an implementation class for the `Flow.Publisher<T>` interface. The class implements the `AutoCloseable` interface, so you can manage its instances using a `try-with-resources` block. JDK 9 does not provide an implementation class for the `Flow.Subscriber<T>` interface; you will need to implement it yourself. However, the `SubmissionPublisher<T>` class contains a `consume(Consumer<? super T> consumer)` method that you can use to process all items published by this publisher. I explain it in more detail with examples later.

Publisher-Subscriber Interactions

Before you start using the JDK API, it is important to understand the sequence of events that occurs in a typical publisher-subscriber session using Reactive Streams. I include the methods that are used in each event. A publisher can have zero or more subscribers. For the purpose of this discussion, I use only one subscriber.

- You create a publisher and a subscriber and they are instances of the `Flow.Publisher` and `Flow.Subscriber` interfaces, respectively.

- The subscriber attempts to subscribe to the publisher by calling the `subscribe()` method of the publisher. If the subscription is successful, the publisher asynchronously calls the `onSubscribe()` method of the subscriber with a `Flow.Subscription`. If the attempt to subscribe fails, the `onError()` method of the subscriber is called with an `IllegalStateException` and the publisher-subscriber interaction ends.

- The subscriber sends a request to the publisher for N items by calling the `request(N)` method of the `Subscription`. The subscriber can send multiple requests for more items to the publisher without waiting for its earlier requested to be fulfilled.

- The publisher calls the onNext(T item) method of the subscriber up to the number of items requested by the subscriber in all its previous requests—sending an item to the subscriber in each call. If the publisher has no more items to send to the subscriber, the publisher calls the onComplete() method of the subscriber to signal the end of stream, thus ending the publisher-subscriber interaction. If a subscriber requests Long.MAX_VALUE elements, it is effectively an unbounded request and the stream is effectively a push stream.

- If the publisher encounters an error at any time, it calls the onError() method of the subscriber.

- The subscriber can cancel its subscription by calling the cancel() method of its Flow.Subscription. Once a subscription is cancelled, the publisher-subscriber interaction ends. However, it is possible for the subscriber to receive items after canceling its subscription if there were pending requests before requesting the cancellation.

To summarize the previous steps for terminal conditions, once the onComplete() or onError() method is called on the subscriber, the subscriber does not receive any more notifications from the publisher.

After the subscribe() method of the publisher is called, the following sequence of method calls on the subscriber is guaranteed, assuming that the subscriber does not cancel its subscription:

```
onSubscribe onNext* (onError | onComplete)?
```

Here, the symbols, * and ?, are used as keywords in a regular expression—an * meaning zero or more occurrences and a ? meaning zero or one occurrence.

The first method call on the subscriber is the onSubscribe() method, which is a notification for a successful subscription to the publisher. The onNext() method of the subscriber may be called zero of more times, each call indicating publication of an item. One of the onComplete() and onError() methods may be called zero or one times to indicate a terminate state; one of these methods is called as long as the subscriber does not cancel its subscription.

Creating Publishers

Creating a publisher depends on the implementation class of the Flow.Publisher<T> interface. I cover the use of the SubmissionPublisher<T> class that implements this interface. The class contains the following constructors:

- SubmissionPublisher()

- SubmissionPublisher(Executor executor, int maxBufferCapacity)

- SubmissionPublisher(Executor executor, int maxBufferCapacity, BiConsumer<? super Flow.Subscriber<? super T>,? super Throwable> handler)

A SubmissionPublisher uses the supplied Executor to deliver items to its subscribers. If multiple threads are used to generate items to be published and the number of subscribers can be estimated, you use an Executor with a fixed thread pool, which can be obtained using the newFixedThreadPool(int nThread) static method of the Executors class. Otherwise, you use the default Executor, which is obtained using the commonPool() method of the ForkJoinPool class.

The SubmissionPublisher class uses an independent buffer for each subscriber. The buffer size is specified by the maxBufferCapacity argument in the constructor. The default buffer size is the value returned by the defaultBufferSize() static method of the Flow class, which is 256. If the number of published items exceeds the buffer size of a subscriber, the extra elements will be dropped. You can get the current buffer size of each subscriber using the getMaxBufferCapacity() method of the SubmissionPublisher class.

When a subscriber's method throws an exception, its subscription is cancelled. When the onNext() method of a subscriber throws an exception, the handler specified in the constructor is invoked, before its subscription is cancelled. By default, the handler is null.

The following snippet of code creates a SubmissionPublisher that publishes items of the type Long with all attributes set to their default values:

```
// Create a publisher that can publish Long values
SubmissionPublisher<Long> pub = new SubmissionPublisher<>();
```

The SubmissionPublisher class implements the AutoCloseable interface. Calling its close() method invokes the onComplete() method on its current subscribers. Attempting to publish elements after calling the close() method throws an IllegalStateException.

Publishing Items

The SubmissionPublisher<T> class contains the following methods for publishing elements:

- int offer(T item, long timeout, TimeUnit unit, BiPredicate<Flow. Subscriber<? super T>,? super T> onDrop)

- int offer(T item, BiPredicate<Flow.Subscriber <? super T>,? super T> onDrop)

- int submit(T item)

The submit() method blocks until resources for current subscribers are available to publish the item. Consider a case with the buffer capacity of 10 for each subscriber. A subscriber subscribes with the publisher and does not request any items. The publisher publishes 10 items and buffers them all. Attempting to publish another item using the submit() method will block because the subscriber's buffer is full.

The offer() method is non-blocking. The first version of the method lets you specify a timeout, after which the item is dropped. You can specify a drop handler, which is a BiPredicate. The test() method of the drop handler is called before dropping the item for a subscriber. If the test() method returns true, the item is retried one more time. If the test() method returns false, the item is dropped without a retry. A negative integer returned from the offer() method indicates the number of failed attempts to issue the item to a subscriber; a positive integer indicates an estimate of the maximum number of items submitted but not yet consumed among all current subscribers.

Which method should you use to publish an item: submit() or offer()? It depends on your requirement. If each published item must be issued to all subscribers, submit() method is the option. If you want to wait to publish an item for a specific amount of time with a retry, the offer() method is the option.

A Quick Example

Let's look at a quick example of using a SubmissionPublisher as a publisher. A SubmissionPublisher can publish an element using its submit(T item) method. The following snippet of code generates and publishes five integers (1, 2, 3, 4, and 5), assuming pub is a reference to a SubmissionPublisher object:

```
// Generate and publish 10 integers
LongStream.range(1L, 6L)
          .forEach(pub::submit);
```

You need a subscriber to consume items published by a publisher. The SubmissionPublisher class contains a consume(Consumer<? super T> consumer) method that lets you add a subscriber that wants to process all published items and is not interested in any other notifications such as on error and on completion notifications. The method returns a CompletableFuture<Void> that is completed when the publisher calls the onComplete() method of the subscriber. The following snippet of code adds a Consumer, which is internally added as a subscriber, to the publisher:

```
// Add a subscriber that prints the published items
CompletableFuture<Void> subTask = pub.consume(System.out::println);
```

The code in this chapter is part of a module named com.jdojo.stream, whose declaration is shown in Listing 17-2.

Listing 17-2. The Declaration of a Module Named com.jdojo.stream

```
// module-info.java
module com.jdojo.stream {
    exports com.jdojo.stream;
}
```

Listing 17-3 contains the code for a NumberPrinter class, which shows how to use the SubmissionPublisher class to publish integers. A detailed explanation of the example code follows the output of the NumberPrinter class.

Listing 17-3. An Example of a Publisher-Subscriber in Which Five Integers Are Published and Printed

```
// NumberPrinter.java
package com.jdojo.stream;

import java.util.concurrent.CompletableFuture;
import java.util.concurrent.ExecutionException;
import java.util.concurrent.SubmissionPublisher;
import java.util.stream.LongStream;

public class NumberPrinter {
    public static void main(String[] args) {
        CompletableFuture<Void> subTask = null;

        // The publisher is closed when the try block exits
        try (SubmissionPublisher<Long> pub = new SubmissionPublisher<>()) {
            // Print the buffer size used for each subscriber
            System.out.println("Subscriber Buffer Size: " + pub.getMaxBufferCapacity());
```

```
            // Add a subscriber to the publisher. The subscriber prints the published elements
            subTask = pub.consume(System.out::println);

            // Generate and publish five integers
            LongStream.range(1L, 6L)
                      .forEach(pub::submit);
        }

        if (subTask != null) {
            try {
                // Wait until the subscriber is complete
                subTask.get();
            } catch (InterruptedException | ExecutionException e) {
                e.printStackTrace();
            }
        }
    }
}
```

```
Subscriber Buffer Size: 256
1
2
3
4
5
```

The main() method declares a variable named subTask to store the reference of the subscriber's task. The subTask.get() method will block until the subscriber is complete.

```
CompletableFuture<Void> subTask = null;
```

A publisher to publish items of the type Long is created in a try-with-resources block. The publisher is an instance of the SubmissionPublisher<Long> class. The publisher is closed automatically when the try block exits.

```
try (SubmissionPublisher<Long> pub = new SubmissionPublisher<>()) {
  //...
}
```

The program prints the buffer size of each subscriber that will subscribe to the publisher.

```
// Print the buffer size used for each subscriber
System.out.println("Subscriber Buffer Size: " + pub.getMaxBufferCapacity());
```

A subscriber is added to the publisher using the consume() method. Note that the method lets you specify a Consumer, which is converted to a Subscriber internally. The subscriber will be signaled each published item. The subscriber simply prints the item it receives.

```
// Add a subscriber to the publisher. The subscriber prints the published elements
subTask = pub.consume(System.out::println);
```

418

It is time to publish the integers. The program generates five integers, 1 to 5, and publishes them using the submit() method of the publisher.

```
// Generate and publish five integers
LongStream.range(1L, 6L)
        .forEach(pub::submit);
```

Published integers are signaled to the subscriber asynchronously. The publisher is closed when the try block exits. To keep the program running until the subscriber is finished processing all published items, you must call subTask.get(). If you do not call this method, you may not see the five integers in the output.

Creating Subscribers

To have a subscriber, you need to create a class that implements the Flow.Subscriber<T> interface. How you implement the methods of the interface depends on your needs. In this section, you will create a class named SimpleSubscriber that implements the Flow.Subscriber<Long> interface. Listing 17-4 contains the code for this class.

Listing 17-4. A SimpleSubscriber Class That Implements the Flow.Subscriber<Long> Interface

```java
// SimpleSubscriber.java
package com.jdojo.stream;

import java.util.concurrent.Flow;

public class SimpleSubscriber implements Flow.Subscriber<Long> {
    private Flow.Subscription subscription;

    // Subscriber name
    private String name = "Unknown";

    // Maximum number of items to be processed by this subscriber
    private final long maxCount;

    // keep track of number of items processed
    private long counter;

    public SimpleSubscriber(String name, long maxCount) {
        this.name = name;
        this.maxCount = maxCount <= 0 ? 1 : maxCount;
    }

    public String getName() {
        return name;
    }

    @Override
    public void onSubscribe(Flow.Subscription subscription) {
        this.subscription = subscription;
        System.out.printf("%s subscribed with max count %d.%n", name, maxCount);

        // Request all items in one go
        subscription.request(maxCount);
    }
```

```
    @Override
    public void onNext(Long item) {
        counter++;
        System.out.printf("%s received %d.%n", name, item);

        if (counter >= maxCount) {
            System.out.printf("Cancelling %s. Processed item count: %d.%n", name, counter);

            // Cancel the subscription
            subscription.cancel();
        }
    }

    @Override
    public void onError(Throwable t) {
        System.out.printf("An error occurred in %s: %s.%n", name, t.getMessage());
    }

    @Override
    public void onComplete() {
        System.out.printf("%s is complete.%n", name);
    }
}
```

An instance of the SimpleSubscriber class represents a subscriber, which will have a name and the maximum number of items (maxCount) that it wants to process. You need to pass its name and maxCount to its constructor. If maxCount is less than 1, it is set to 1 in the constructor.

In the onSubscribe() method, it stores the subscription passed from the publisher in its instance variable named subscription. It prints a message about the subscription and requests all items it can process in one shot. This subscriber effectively uses a push model because, after this request, no more requests will be sent to the publisher for more items. The publisher will push maxCount or fewer number of items to this subscriber.

In the onNext() method, it increments the counter instance variable by 1. The counter instance variable keeps track of the number of items this subscriber has received. The method prints a message detailing the received item. If it has received the last item it can handle, it cancels the subscription. After cancelling the subscription, it will not receive any more items from the publisher.

In the onError() and onComplete() methods, it prints a message about its status.

The following snippet of code creates a SimpleSubscriber whose name is S1 and that can process maximum 10 items.

```
SimpleSubscriber sub1 = new SimpleSubscriber("S1", 10);
```

It is time to see the SimpleSubscriber in action. Listing 17-5 contains a complete program. It publishes items periodically. After publishing an item, it waits for 1 to 3 seconds. The duration of the wait is random. A detailed explanation follows the output of this program. The program uses asynchronous processing that may result in a different output.

Listing 17-5. A Publisher-Subscriber Example in which a Publisher Publishes Items Periodically and
Instances of the SimpleSubscriber Subscribe to Those Items

```java
// PeriodicPublisher.java
package com.jdojo.stream;

import java.util.Random;
import java.util.concurrent.Flow.Subscriber;
import java.util.concurrent.SubmissionPublisher;
import java.util.concurrent.TimeUnit;

public class PeriodicPublisher {
    final static int MAX_SLEEP_DURATION = 3;

    // Used to generate sleep time
    final static Random sleepTimeGenerator = new Random();

    public static void main(String[] args) {
        SubmissionPublisher<Long> pub = new SubmissionPublisher<>();

        // Create three subscribers
        SimpleSubscriber sub1 = new SimpleSubscriber("S1", 2);
        SimpleSubscriber sub2 = new SimpleSubscriber("S2", 5);
        SimpleSubscriber sub3 = new SimpleSubscriber("S3", 6);
        SimpleSubscriber sub4 = new SimpleSubscriber("S4", 10);

        // Subscriber to the publisher
        pub.subscribe(sub1);
        pub.subscribe(sub2);
        pub.subscribe(sub3);

        // Subscribe the 4th subscriber after 2 seconds
        subscribe(pub, sub4, 2);

        // Start publishing items
        Thread pubThread = publish(pub, 5);

        try {
            // Wait until the publisher is finished
            pubThread.join();
        } catch (InterruptedException e) {
            e.printStackTrace();
        }
    }

    public static Thread publish(SubmissionPublisher<Long> pub, long count) {
        Thread t = new Thread(() -> {
            for (long i = 1; i <= count; i++) {
                pub.submit(i);
                sleep(i);
            }
```

```
                // Close the publisher
                pub.close();
        });

        // Start the thread
        t.start();

        return t;
    }

    private static void sleep(Long item) {
        // Wait for 1 to 3 seconds
        int sleepTime = sleepTimeGenerator.nextInt(MAX_SLEEP_DURATION) + 1;

        try {
            System.out.printf("Published %d. Sleeping for %d sec.%n", item, sleepTime);
            TimeUnit.SECONDS.sleep(sleepTime);
        } catch (InterruptedException e) {
            e.printStackTrace();
        }
    }

    private static void subscribe(SubmissionPublisher<Long> pub, Subscriber<Long> sub,
                                  long delaySeconds) {
        new Thread(() -> {
            try {
                TimeUnit.SECONDS.sleep(delaySeconds);
                pub.subscribe(sub);
            } catch (InterruptedException e) {
                e.printStackTrace();
            }
        }).start();
    }
}
```

```
S2 subscribed with max count 5.
Published 1. Sleeping for 1 sec.
S3 subscribed with max count 6.
S1 subscribed with max count 2.
S1 received 1.
S3 received 1.
S2 received 1.
Published 2. Sleeping for 1 sec.
S1 received 2.
S2 received 2.
S3 received 2.
Cancelling S1. Processed item count: 2.
S4 subscribed with max count 10.
Published 3. Sleeping for 1 sec.
S4 received 3.
S3 received 3.
S2 received 3.
```

```
Published 4. Sleeping for 2 sec.
S4 received 4.
S3 received 4.
S2 received 4.
Published 5. Sleeping for 2 sec.
S2 received 5.
Cancelling S2. Processed item count: 5.
S4 received 5.
S3 received 5.
S3 is complete.
S4 is complete.
```

The PeriodicPublisher class uses two static variables. The MAX_SLEEP_DURATION static variable stores the maximum number of seconds the publisher should wait to publish the next item. It is set to 3. The sleepTimeGenerator static variable stores the reference of a Random object, which is used in the sleep() method to generate the next random duration to wait.

The main() method of the PeriodicPublisher class performs the following actions:

- It creates a publisher that is an instance of the SubmissionPublisher<Long> class.

- It creates four subscribers named S1, S2, S3, and S4. Each subscriber is capable of processing a different number of items.

- Three subscribers are subscribed immediately.

- The subscriber named S4 subscribes in a separate thread after a minimum delay of two seconds. The subscribe() method of the PeriodicPublisher class takes care of this delayed subscription. Notice in the output that S4 subscribes after two items (1, and 2) were already published and it will not receive those two items.

- It calls the publish() method, which starts a new thread to publish five items, which starts the thread and returns the thread reference.

- The main() method calls the join() method of the thread publishing the items, so the program does not terminate before all items are published.

- The publish() method takes care of publishing the five items. It closes the publisher in the end. It calls the sleep() method that makes the current thread sleep for a randomly chosen duration between one and MAX_SLEEP_DURATION seconds.

- Notice in the output that a few subscribers cancel their subscriptions because they receive the specified number of items from the publisher.

Note that this program guarantees that all items will be published before it terminates, but does not guarantee that all subscribers will receive those items. In the output, you see that subscribers received all items published. This happened because the publisher waits for at least one second after publishing the last item, which gives the subscribers enough time, in this small program, to receive and process the last item.

This program did not demonstrate backpressure in action because all subscribers used the push model by requesting items in one shot. You can modify the SimpleSubscriber class as an assignment to see backpressure in action:

- Request for one item in the onSubscribe() method using the subscription.request(1) method.

- In the onNext() method, request more items after a delay. The delay should make the subscriber work at the slower rate at which the publisher publishes items.

- You will need to either publish more than 256 items, which is the default buffer used by the publisher for each subscriber, or use a smaller buffer size using another constructor of the SubmissionPublisher class. This will force the publisher to have more items published than the subscribers can handle.

- Subscribe the subscribers using a drop handler, so you can see when the publisher sees the backpressure.

- Use the offer() method of the SubmissionPublisher class to publish items, so the publisher does not wait indefinitely when the subscribers cannot handle more items.

Using Processors

A processor is a subscriber and a publisher at the same time. To use a processor, you need a class that implements the Flow.Processor<T,R> interface, where T is the subscribed item type and R is the published item type. In this section, I create a simple processor that filters items based on a Predicate<T>. The processor subscribes to a publisher that publishes six integers—1, 2, 3, 4, 5, and 6. A subscriber subscribes to the processor. The processor receives items from its publisher and republishes the same items if they pass the criterion specified by a Predicate<T>. Listing 17-6 contains the code for the FilterProcessor<T> class whose instances act as processors.

Listing 17-6. A Processor that Filters Items Based on a Predicate Before Republishing

```
// FilterProcessor.java
package com.jdojo.stream;

import java.util.concurrent.Flow;
import java.util.concurrent.Flow.Processor;
import java.util.concurrent.SubmissionPublisher;
import java.util.function.Predicate;

public class FilterProcessor<T> extends SubmissionPublisher<T> implements Processor<T,T>{
    private Predicate<? super T> filter;

    public FilterProcessor(Predicate<? super T> filter) {
        this.filter = filter;
    }

    @Override
    public void onSubscribe(Flow.Subscription subscription) {
        // Request an unbounded number of items
        subscription.request(Long.MAX_VALUE);
    }

    @Override
    public void onNext(T item) {
        // If the item passes the filter publish it. Otherwise, no action is needed.
        System.out.println("Filter received: " + item);
        if (filter.test(item)) {
            this.submit(item);
        }
    }
}
```

```
    @Override
    public void onError(Throwable t) {
        // Pass the onError message to all subscribers asynchronously
        this.getExecutor().execute(() -> this.getSubscribers()
                                        .forEach(s -> s.onError(t)));
    }

    @Override
    public void onComplete() {
        System.out.println("Filter is complete.");

        // Close this publisher, so all its subscribers will receive a onComplete message
        this.close();
    }
}
```

The FilterProcessor<T> class inherits from the SubmissionPublisher<T> class and implements the Flow.Processor<T,T> interface. A processor has to be a publisher as well as a subscriber. I inherited the class from the SubmissionPublisher<T> class, so I don't have to write code to make it work as a publisher. The class implements all methods of the Processor<T,T> interface, so it will receive and publish the same type of items.

The constructor accepts a Predicate<? super T> and stores it in an instance variable name filter, which will be used in the onNext() method to filter items.

The onNext() method applies the filter. If the filter returns true, it republishes the item to its subscribers. The class inherits the submit() method, used for republishing items, from its superclass SubmissionPublisher.

The onError() method republishes the error to its subscribers asynchronously. It uses the getExecutor() and getSubscribers() methods of the SubmissionPublisher class, which return the Executor and a list of current subscribers. The Executor is used to publish messages to current subscribers asynchronously.

The onComplete() method closes the publisher part of the processor, which will send a onComplete message to all its subscribers.

Let's see this processor in action. Listing 17-7 contains the code for the ProcessorTest class. You may get a different output because several asynchronous steps are involved in this program. A detailed explanation of the program follows the program's output.

Listing 17-7. Using a Processor in a Publisher-Subscriber Chain

```
// ProcessorTest.java
package com.jdojo.stream;

import java.util.concurrent.CompletableFuture;
import java.util.concurrent.SubmissionPublisher;
import java.util.concurrent.TimeUnit;
import java.util.stream.LongStream;

public class ProcessorTest {
    public static void main(String[] args) {
        CompletableFuture<Void> subTask = null;

        // The publisher is closed when the try block exits
        try (SubmissionPublisher<Long> pub = new SubmissionPublisher<>()) {
            // Create a Subscriber
            SimpleSubscriber sub = new SimpleSubscriber("S1", 10);
```

```
            // Create a processor
            FilterProcessor<Long> filter = new FilterProcessor<>(n -> n % 2 == 0);

            // Subscribe the filter to the publisher and a subscriber to the filter
            pub.subscribe(filter);
            filter.subscribe(sub);

            // Generate and publish 6 integers
            LongStream.range(1L, 7L)
                    .forEach(pub::submit);
        }

        try {
            // Sleep for two seconds to let subscribers finish handling all items
            TimeUnit.SECONDS.sleep(2);
        } catch (InterruptedException e) {
            e.printStackTrace();
        }
    }
}
```

```
S1 subscribed with max count 10.
Filter received: 1
Filter received: 2
Filter received: 3
S1 received 2.
Filter received: 4
S1 received 4.
Filter received: 5
Filter received: 6
Filter is complete.
S1 received 6.
S1 is complete.
```

The main() method of the ProcessorTest class creates a publisher that will publish six integers—1, 2, 3, 4, 5 and 6. The method does a number of things:

- It creates a publisher using a try-with-resources block, so it will be closed automatically when the try block exits.

- It creates a subscriber that's an instance of the SimpleSubscriber class. The subscriber is named S1 and can handle a maximum of 10 items.

- It creates a processor that's an instance of the FilterProcessor<Long> class. A Predicate<Long> is passed that lets the processor republish even integers and discard odd ones.

- The processor is subscribed to the publisher and the simple subscriber is subscribed to the processor. This completes the publisher-subscriber pipeline—publisher-to-filter-to-subscriber.

- At the end of the first `try` block, the code generates the integers from 1 to 6 and publishes them using the publisher.

- At the end of the `main()` method, the program waits for two seconds to make sure that the filter and the subscriber get a chance to process their events. If you remove this logic, your program may not print anything. You had to include this logic because all events are processed asynchronously. The publisher will be done sending all notifications to the filter when the first `try` block exits. However, the filter and the subscriber need some time to receive and process those notifications.

Summary

A *stream* is a sequence of elements produced by a producer and consumed by one or more consumers. This producer-consumer model is also known as source/sink model or publisher-subscriber model.

There are several stream-processing mechanisms, the pull model and push model being the most common. In a push model, the publisher pushes the stream of data to the subscriber. In a pull model, the subscriber pulls the data from the publisher. These models have problems when the two ends do not work at the same rate. The solution is to provide a stream that adapts to the speed of both the publisher and subscriber. A strategy known as *backpressure* is used in which the subscriber notifies the publisher how many items it can handle and the publisher sends only those many items to the subscriber.

Reactive Streams started in 2013 as an initiative for providing a standard for *asynchronous* stream processing with *non-blocking backpressure*. It is aimed at solving the problems with processing a stream of elements—how to pass a stream of elements from a publisher to a subscriber without requiring the publisher to block, or the subscriber to have an unbounded buffer or drop. The Reactive Streams model dynamically switches between the pull model and push model stream-processing mechanisms. It uses the pull model when the subscriber is slower and uses the push model when the subscriber is faster.

In 2015, a specification and Java API for handling Reactive Streams were published. The Java API for Reactive Streams consists of four interfaces: `Publisher<T>`, `Subscriber<T>`, `Subscription`, and `Processor<T,R>`.

A *publisher* publishes items to its subscribers based on the demands received from them. A *subscriber* subscribes to a publisher to receive items. The publisher sends a subscription token to the subscriber. Using the subscription token, the subscriber requests N number of data elements from the publisher. When the data elements are ready, the publisher sends N or fewer data elements to the subscriber. The subscriber can request more data elements.

JDK 9 provides a Reactive Streams-compliant API in the `java.util.concurrent` package, which is in the `java.base` module. The API consists of two classes: `Flow` and `SubmissionPublisher<T>`.

The `Flow` class encapsulates the Reactive Streams Java API. The four interfaces specified by the Reactive Streams Java API are included in the `Flow` class as nested static interfaces: `Flow.Processor<T,R>`, `Flow.Publisher<T>`, `Flow.Subscriber<T>`, and `Flow.Subscription`.

CHAPTER 18

■ ■ ■

Streams API Updates

In this chapter, you will learn:

- New convenience methods added to the Stream interface for stream processing
- New collectors added to the Collectors class

JDK 9 added few convenience methods to the Streams API. I categorize them based on the type they have been added to:

- The Stream interface
- The Collectors class

Methods in the Stream interface define new stream operations, whereas methods in the Collectors class define new collectors. The following sections describe them in detail. The source code for this chapter is in a module named com.jdojo.streams, whose declaration is shown in Listing 18-1.

Listing 18-1. A Module Declaration for a Module Named com.jdojo.streams

```
// module-info.java
module com.jdojo.streams {
    exports com.jdojo.streams;
}
```

New Stream Operations

In JDK 9, the Stream interface has the following new methods:

- default Stream<T> dropWhile(Predicate<? super T> predicate)
- default Stream<T> takeWhile(Predicate<? super T> predicate)
- static <T> Stream<T> ofNullable(T t)
- static <T> Stream<T> iterate(T seed, Predicate<? super T> hasNext, UnaryOperator<T> next)

In JDK 8, the Stream interface had two methods: skip(long count) and limit(long count). The skip() method returns the elements of the stream after skipping the specified count elements from the beginning. The limit() method returns elements from the beginning of the stream that are equal to or less than the specified count. One of these methods drops elements from the beginning and another takes elements from the beginning dropping the remaining. Both work based on the number of elements. The dropWhile() and takeWhile() methods are like skip() and limit() methods, respectively; however, the new methods work on a Predicate rather than number of elements.

© Kishori Sharan 2017

K. Sharan, *Java 9 Revealed*, DOI 10.1007/978-1-4842-2592-9_18

You can think of these methods as similar to the `filter()` method with an exception. The `filter()` method evaluates the predicate on all elements, whereas the `dropWhile()` and `takeWhile()` methods evaluate the predicate on elements from the beginning of the stream until the predicate fails.

For an ordered stream, the `dropWhile()` method returns the elements of the stream, discarding the elements from the beginning for which the specified predicate is `true`. Consider the following ordered stream of integers:

```
1, 2, 3, 4, 5, 6, 7
```

If you use a predicate in the `dropWhile()` method that returns `true` for an integer less than 5, the method will drop the first four elements and return the rest:

```
5, 6, 7
```

For an unordered stream, the behavior of the `dropWhile()` method is non-deterministic. It may choose to drop any subset of elements matching the predicate. The current implementation drops the matching elements from the beginning until it finds a non-matching element.

There are two extreme cases of the `dropWhile()` method. If the first element does not match the predicate, the method returns the original stream. If all elements match the predicate, the method returns an empty stream.

The `takeWhile()` method works the same way as the `dropWhile()` method, except that it returns the matching elements from the beginning of the stream and discards the rest.

▓ **Tip**   Use the `dropWhile()` and `takeWhile()` methods with ordered, parallel streams with great care because you may see a performance hit. In an ordered, parallel stream, elements must be ordered and returned from all threads before these methods can return. These methods perform best with sequential streams.

The `ofNullable(T t)` method returns a stream of a single element containing the specified element if the element is non-`null`. If the specified element is `null`, it returns an empty stream. This method is helpful while using the `flatMap()` method in stream processing. Consider the following map whose values may be `null`:

```
Map<Integer, String> map = new HashMap<>();
map.put(1, "One");
map.put(2, "Two");
map.put(3, null);
map.put(4, "four");
```

How would you obtain a set of values in this map that excludes `null`? That is, how you would get a set that contains "One", "Two", and "Four" from this map? Here is how you get it in JDK 8:

```
// In JDK 8
Set<String> nonNullvalues = map.entrySet()
        .stream()
        .flatMap(e ->  e.getValue() == null ? Stream.empty() : Stream.of(e.getValue()))
        .collect(toSet());
```

Notice the use of a ternary operator inside the lambda expression in the flatMap() method. You can make this expression simpler in JDK 9 using the ofNullable() method:

```
// In JDK 9
Set<String> nonNullvalues = map.entrySet()
        .stream()
        .flatMap(e ->  Stream.ofNullable(e.getValue()))
        .collect(toSet());
```

The new iterate(T seed, Predicate<? super T> hasNext, UnaryOperator<T> next) method lets you create a sequential (possibly an infinite) stream using an initial seed value and iteratively applying the specified next function. The iteration stops when the specified hasNext predicate returns false. Calling this method is the same as using a for loop:

```
for (T n = seed; hasNext.test(n); n = next.apply(n)) {
    // n is the element added to the stream
}
```

The following snippet of code produces a stream that contains all integers between 1 and 10:

```
Stream.iterate(1, n -> n <= 10, n -> n + 1)
```

Listing 18-2 contains a complete program that demonstrates how to use the new methods in the Stream interface.

Listing 18-2. A StreamTest Class That Demonstrates the Use of New Methods in the Stream Interface

```
// StreamTest.java
package com.jdojo.streams;

import java.util.HashMap;
import java.util.List;
import java.util.Map;
import java.util.Set;
import static java.util.stream.Collectors.toList;
import static java.util.stream.Collectors.toSet;
import java.util.stream.Stream;

public class StreamTest {
    public static void main(String[] args) {
        System.out.println("Using Stream.dropWhile() and Stream.takeWhile():");
        testDropWhileAndTakeWhile();

        System.out.println("\nUsing Stream.ofNullable():");
        testOfNullable();

        System.out.println("\nUsing Stream.iterator():");
        testIterator();
    }

    public static void testDropWhileAndTakeWhile() {
        List<Integer> list = List.of(1, 3, 5, 4, 6, 7, 8, 9);
        System.out.println("Original Stream: " + list);
```

```
            List<Integer> list2 = list.stream()
                                    .dropWhile(n -> n % 2 == 1)
                                    .collect(toList());
            System.out.println("After using dropWhile(n -> n % 2 == 1): " + list2);

            List<Integer> list3 = list.stream()
                                    .takeWhile(n -> n % 2 == 1)
                                    .collect(toList());
            System.out.println("After using takeWhile(n -> n % 2 == 1): " + list3);
    }

    public static void testOfNullable() {
        Map<Integer, String> map = new HashMap<>();
        map.put(1, "One");
        map.put(2, "Two");
        map.put(3, null);
        map.put(4, "Four");

        Set<String> nonNullValues = map.entrySet()
                                    .stream()
                                    .flatMap(e ->  Stream.ofNullable(e.getValue()))
                                    .collect(toSet());
        System.out.println("Map: " + map);
        System.out.println("Non-null Values in Map: " + nonNullValues);
    }

    public static void testIterator() {
        List<Integer> list = Stream.iterate(1, n -> n <= 10, n -> n + 1)
                                    .collect(toList());
        System.out.println("Integers from 1 to 10: " + list);
    }
}
```

```
Using Stream.dropWhile() and Stream.takeWhile():
Original Stream: [1, 3, 5, 4, 6, 7, 8, 9]
After using dropWhile(n -> n % 2 == 1): [4, 6, 7, 8, 9]
After using takeWhile(n -> n % 2 == 1): [1, 3, 5]

Using Stream.ofNullable():
Map: {1=One, 2=Two, 3=null, 4=Four}
Non-null Values in Map: [One, Four, Two]

Using Stream.iterator():
Integers from 1 to 10: [1, 2, 3, 4, 5, 6, 7, 8, 9, 10]
```

New Collectors

The Collectors class has the following two new static methods that return a Collector:

- `<T,A,R> Collector<T,?,R> filtering(Predicate<? super T> predicate, Collector<? super T,A,R> downstream)`

- `<T,U,A,R> Collector<T,?,R> flatMapping(Function<? super T,? extends Stream<? extends U>> mapper, Collector<? super U,A,R> downstream)`

The filtering() method returns a Collector that applies a filter before collecting elements. If the specified predicate returns true for an element, the element is collected; otherwise, the element is not collected.

The flatMapping() method returns a Collector that applies a flat mapping function before collecting an element. The specified flat mapping function is applied to each element of the stream and the elements of the stream returned from the flat mapper are accumulated.

Both methods return a Collector that is most useful when used in a multi-level reduction, for example, downstream processing of a groupingBy or partitioningBy. I use an Employee class shown in Listing 18-3 to demonstrate the use of these methods.

Listing 18-3. An Employee Class

```java
// Employee.java
package com.jdojo.streams;

import java.util.List;

public class Employee {
    private String name;
    private String department;
    private double salary;
    private List<String> spokenLanguages;

    public Employee(String name, String department, double salary,
                    List<String> spokenLanguages) {

        this.name = name;
        this.department = department;
        this.salary = salary;
        this.spokenLanguages = spokenLanguages;
    }

    public String getName() {
        return name;
    }

    public void setName(String name) {
        this.name = name;
    }
```

```java
    public String getDepartment() {
        return department;
    }

    public void setDepartment(String department) {
        this.department = department;
    }

    public double getSalary() {
        return salary;
    }

    public void setSalary(double salary) {
        this.salary = salary;
    }

    public List<String> getSpokenLanguages() {
        return spokenLanguages;
    }

    public void setSpokenLanguages(List<String> spokenLanguages) {
        this.spokenLanguages = spokenLanguages;
    }

    @Override
    public String toString() {
        return "[" + name + ", " + department + ", " + salary + ", " + spokenLanguages +
                "]";
    }

    public static List<Employee> employees() {
        return List.of(
                new Employee("John", "Sales", 1000.89, List.of("English", "French")),
                new Employee("Wally", "Sales", 900.89, List.of("Spanish", "Wu")),
                new Employee("Ken", "Sales", 1900.00, List.of("English", "French")),
                new Employee("Li", "HR", 1950.89, List.of("Wu", "Lao")),
                new Employee("Manuel", "IT", 2001.99, List.of("English", "German")),
                new Employee("Tony", "IT", 1700.89, List.of("English"))
        );
    }
}
```

An Employee has a name, a department, a salary, and a list of languages he or she speaks. The toString() method returns a string representing all these properties. The static employees() method returns a list of employees, as shown in Table 18-1.

Table 18-1. *Employees Used in the Example*

Name	Department	Salary	Spoken Languages
John	Sales	1000.89	English, French
Wally	Sales	900.89	Spanish, Wu
Ken	Sales	1900.00	English, French
Li	HR	1950.89	Wu, Lao
Manuel	IT	2001.99	English, German
Tony	IT	1700.89	English

You can get a list of employees grouped by department as follows:

```
Map<String,List<Employee>> empGroupedByDept = Employee.employees()
              .stream()
              .collect(groupingBy(Employee::getDepartment, toList()));
System.out.println(empGroupedByDept);
```

```
{Sales=[[John, Sales, 1000.89, [English, French]], [Wally, Sales, 900.89, [Spanish, Wu]],
[Ken, Sales, 1900.0, [English, French]]], HR=[[Li, HR, 1950.89, [Wu, Lao]]], IT=[[Manuel,
IT, 2001.99, [English, German]], [Tony, IT, 1700.89, [English]]]}
```

This feature has been in the Streams API since JDK 8. Now, suppose you want to get a list of employees grouped by department and employee's salary must be greater than 1900 to be included in the list. Your first attempt would be to use a filter as follows:

```
Map<String, List<Employee>> empSalaryGt1900GroupedByDept = Employee.employees()
              .stream()
              .filter(e -> e.getSalary() > 1900)
              .collect(groupingBy(Employee::getDepartment, toList()));

System.out.println(empSalaryGt1900GroupedByDept);
```

```
{HR=[[Li, HR, 1950.89, [Wu, Lao]]], IT=[[Manuel, IT, 2001.99, [English, German]]]}
```

In one sense, you have achieved the goal. However, your result does not include departments that do not have any employees with a salary greater than 1900. This is because you filtered all such departments before you started collecting the results. You can achieve this by using a collector returned by the new filtering() method. This time, if there are no employees in a department making more than 1900, the department will be included in the final result with an empty list of employees.

```
Map<String, List<Employee>> empGroupedByDeptWithSalaryGt1900 = Employee.employees()
              .stream()
              .collect(groupingBy(Employee::getDepartment,
                           filtering(e -> e.getSalary() > 1900.00, toList())));

System.out.println(empGroupedByDeptWithSalaryGt1900);
```

```
{Sales=[], HR=[[Li, HR, 1950.89, [Wu, Lao]]], IT=[[Manuel, IT, 2001.99, [English,
German]]]}
```

This time, the result contains the Sales department, even though there is no employee in it earning more than 1900.

Let's try to get a set of languages spoken by employees grouped by department. The following snippet of code tries to use a Collector returned by the mapping() method of the Collectors class:

```java
Map<String,Set<List<String>>> langByDept = Employee.employees()
                .stream()
                .collect(groupingBy(Employee::getDepartment,
                        mapping(Employee::getSpokenLanguages, toSet())));

System.out.println(langByDept);
```

```
{Sales=[[English, French], [Spanish, Wu]], HR=[[Wu, Lao]], IT=[[English, German],
[English]]}
```

As the output shows, you received a Set<List<String>> using the mapping() instead of a Set<String>. You need to flatten the List<String> to get a stream of strings before collecting the strings into a set. Using a collector returned by the new flatMapping() method will do the job:

```java
Map<String,Set<String>> langByDept2 = Employee.employees()
                .stream()
                .collect(groupingBy(Employee::getDepartment,
                        flatMapping(e -> e.getSpokenLanguages().stream(), toSet())));

System.out.println(langByDept2);
```

```
{Sales=[English, French, Spanish, Wu], HR=[Lao, Wu], IT=[English, German]}
```

This time, you get the correct result. Listing 18-4 contains a complete program demonstrating how to use filtering and flat mapping while collecting data.

Listing 18-4. A StreamCollectorsTest Class Demonstrating How to Use Filtering and Flat Mapping

```java
// StreamCollectorsTest.java
package com.jdojo. streams;

import java.util.List;
import java.util.Map;
import java.util.Set;
import static java.util.stream.Collectors.filtering;
import static java.util.stream.Collectors.flatMapping;
import static java.util.stream.Collectors.groupingBy;
import static java.util.stream.Collectors.mapping;
import static java.util.stream.Collectors.toList;
import static java.util.stream.Collectors.toSet;
```

```java
public class StreamCollectorsTest {
    public static void main(String[] args) {
        System.out.println("Testing Collectors.filtering():");
        testFiltering();

        System.out.println("\nTesting Collectors.flatMapping():");
        testFlatMapping();
    }

    public static void testFiltering() {
        Map<String, List<Employee>> empGroupedByDept = Employee.employees()
                .stream()
                .collect(groupingBy(Employee::getDepartment, toList()));

        System.out.println("Employees grouped by department:");
        System.out.println(empGroupedByDept);

        // Employees having salary > 1900 grouped by department:
        Map<String, List<Employee>> empSalaryGt1900GroupedByDept = Employee.employees()
                .stream()
                .filter(e -> e.getSalary() > 1900)
                .collect(groupingBy(Employee::getDepartment, toList()));

        System.out.println("\nEmployees having salary > 1900 grouped by department:");
        System.out.println(empSalaryGt1900GroupedByDept);

        // Group employees by department who have salary > 1900
        Map<String, List<Employee>> empGroupedByDeptWithSalaryGt1900 = Employee.employees()
                .stream()
                .collect(groupingBy(Employee::getDepartment,
                        filtering(e -> e.getSalary() > 1900.00, toList())));

        System.out.println("\nEmployees grouped by department having salary > 1900:");
        System.out.println(empGroupedByDeptWithSalaryGt1900);

        // Group employees by department who speak at least 2 languages
        // and 1 of them is English
        Map<String, List<Employee>> empByDeptWith2LangWithEn = Employee.employees()
                .stream()
                .collect(groupingBy(Employee::getDepartment,
                        filtering(e -> e.getSpokenLanguages().size() >= 2
                                    &&
                                    e.getSpokenLanguages().contains("English"),
                                toList())));

        System.out.println("\nEmployees grouped by department speaking min. 2" +
                " languages of which one is English:");
        System.out.println(empByDeptWith2LangWithEn);
    }
```

```java
    public static void testFlatMapping(){
        Map<String,Set<List<String>>> langByDept = Employee.employees()
                .stream()
                .collect(groupingBy(Employee::getDepartment,
                            mapping(Employee::getSpokenLanguages, toSet()))));

        System.out.println("Languages spoken by department using mapping():");
        System.out.println(langByDept);

        Map<String,Set<String>> langByDept2 = Employee.employees()
                .stream()
                .collect(groupingBy(Employee::getDepartment,
                            flatMapping(e -> e.getSpokenLanguages().stream(), toSet()))));

        System.out.println("\nLanguages spoken by department using flapMapping():");
        System.out.println(langByDept2) ;
    }
}
```

```
Testing Collectors.filtering():
Employees grouped by department:
{Sales=[[John, Sales, 1000.89, [English, French]], [Wally, Sales, 900.89, [Spanish, Wu]],
[Ken, Sales, 1900.0, [English, French]]], HR=[[Li, HR, 1950.89, [Wu, Lao]]], IT=[[Manuel,
IT, 2001.99, [English, German]], [Tony, IT, 1700.89, [English]]]}

Employees having salary > 1900 grouped by department:
{HR=[[Li, HR, 1950.89, [Wu, Lao]]], IT=[[Manuel, IT, 2001.99, [English, German]]]}

Employees grouped by department having salary > 1900:
{Sales=[], HR=[[Li, HR, 1950.89, [Wu, Lao]]], IT=[[Manuel, IT, 2001.99, [English,
German]]]}

Employees grouped by department speaking min. 2 languages of which one is English:
{Sales=[[John, Sales, 1000.89, [English, French]], [Ken, Sales, 1900.0, [English, French]]],
HR=[], IT=[[Manuel, IT, 2001.99, [English, German]]]}

Testing Collectors.flatMapping():
Languages spoken by department using mapping():
{Sales=[[English, French], [Spanish, Wu]], HR=[[Wu, Lao]], IT=[[English, German],
[English]]}

Languages spoken by department using flapMapping():
{Sales=[English, French, Spanish, Wu], HR=[Lao, Wu], IT=[English, German]}
```

Summary

JDK 9 added a few convenience methods to the Streams API to make stream processing easier and to write complex queries using collectors.

The Stream interface has four new methods: dropWhile(), takeWhile(), ofNullable(), and iterate(). For an ordered stream, the dropWhile() method returns the elements of the stream, discarding the elements from the beginning for which the specified predicate is true. For an unordered stream, the behavior of the dropWhile() method is non-deterministic. It may choose to drop any subset of elements matching the predicate. The current implementation drops the matching elements from the beginning until it finds a non-matching element. The takeWhile() method works the same way as the dropWhile() method, except that it returns the matching elements from the beginning of the stream and discards the rest. The ofNullable(T t) method returns a stream of a single element containing the specified element if the element is non-null. If the specified element is null, it returns an empty stream. The new iterate(T seed, Predicate<? super T> hasNext, UnaryOperator<T> next) method lets you create a sequential (possibly an infinite) stream using an initial seed value and iteratively applying the specified next function. The iteration stops when the specified hasNext predicate returns false.

The Collectors class has two new methods in JDK 9: filtering() and flatMapping(). The filtering() method returns a Collector that applies a filter before collecting elements. If the specified predicate returns true for an element, the element is collected; otherwise, the element is not collected. The flatMapping() method returns a Collector that applies a flat mapping function before collecting an element. The specified flat mapping function is applied to each element of the stream and the elements of the stream returned from the flat mapper are accumulated.

■ ■ ■

## CHAPTER 19

Platform and JVM Logging

In this chapter, you will learn:

- The new platform logging API

- Command-line options for JVM logging

JDK 9 has overhauled the logging systems for platform classes (JDK classes) and JVM components. There is a new API that lets you specify a logging framework of your choice as logging backend for logging messages from platform classes. There is also a new command-line option that lets you access messages from all JVM components. In this chapter, I describe both logging facilities in detail.

Platform Logging API

Java SE 9 has added a platform logging API that can be used to specify a logger, for example, Log4j, SLF4J, or a custom logger, that can be used by the Java platform classes (classes in the JDK) to log messages. There are a few important points to note about this API. The API is meant to be used by the classes in the JDK, not by application classes. So, you should not be using this API to log your application messages. You need to use your logging framework such as Log4j to log application messages. The API does not let you configure the logger programmatically. The API consists of the following:

- A service interface, java.lang.System.LoggerFinder, which is an abstract static class

- An interface, java.lang.System.Logger, which provides the logging API

- An overloaded method getLogger() in the java.lang.System class, which returns a System.Logger

The details of configuring the platform logger depend on the logger you want to use. For example, if you use Log4j, you will need to configure the Log4j framework separately and configure the platform logger. Configuring the platform logger requires the following steps:

- Create a class that implements the System.Logger interface.

- Create an implementation for the System.LoggerFinder service interface.

- Specify the implementation in a module declaration.

I will configure Log4j 2.0 as a platform logger. Configuring and using Log4j is a vast topic. I cover only the details about Log4i needed to configure the platform logger.

© Kishori Sharan 2017
K. Sharan, *Java 9 Revealed*, DOI 10.1007/978-1-4842-2592-9_19

■ **Tip** If you do not configure a custom platform logger, the JDK uses a default implementation of the `System.LoggerFinder`, which uses `java.util.logging` as the backend framework when the `java.logging` module is present. It returns a logger instance that routes log messages to a `java.util.logging.Logger`. Otherwise, if `java.logging` is not present, the default implementation returns a simple logger instance that routes log messages of `INFO` level and above to the console (`System.err`).

Setting up Log4j Libraries

You will need to download Log4j 2.0 library for the examples in this section to work. The required JARs for Log4j 2.0 framework are in the `Java9Reaveled/extlib` directory in the book's source code. You can also download the Log4J 2.0 library from `https://logging.apache.org/log4j/2.0/download.html`. Unzip the downloaded file and copy the following two JARs to the `C:\Java8Revealed\extlib` directory. If you copy them to another directory, make sure to replace the path in the discussion.

- `log4j-api-2.8.jar`
- `log4j-core-2.8.jar`

The version, which is 2.8 in these JAR filenames, may be different if you download a different version of Log4j. You will use these JARs as automatic modules in this example. The automatic module names will be derived from the JAR filename and they will be `log4j.api` and `log4j.core`. Refer to Chapter 4 for more details on automatic modules.

Setting Up a NetBeans Project

I created a Java project named `com.jdojo.logger` in NetBeans. The two Log4j JARs discussed in the previous section are added to the module path of the project, as shown in Figure 19-1. To add these JARs to the module path in NetBeans, you will need to choose the Add JAR/Folder option from the expanded menu for adding to the module path.

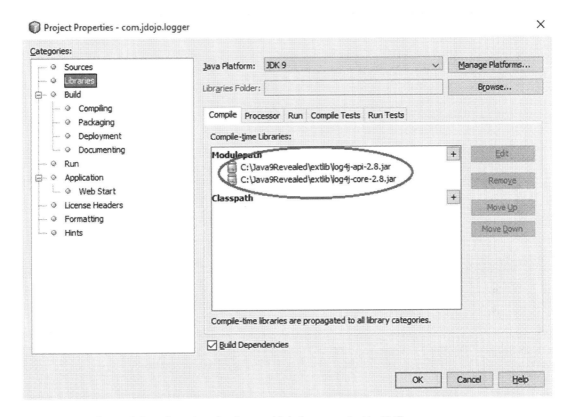

Figure 19-1. *The module path settings for the com.jdojo.logger project in NetBeans*

Defining a Module

All classes and resources for this example will be in a module named com.jdojo.logger, whose declaration is shown in Listing 19-1.

Listing 19-1. A Module Declaration for a Module Named com.jdojo.logger

```
// module-info.java
module com.jdojo.logger {
    requires log4j.api;
    requires log4j.core;

    exports com.jdojo.logger;

    provides java.lang.System.LoggerFinder
        with com.jdojo.logger.Log4jLoggerFinder;
}
```

The first two `requires` statements declare dependency on the Log4j JARs, which are automatic modules in this case. The `exports` statement exports all types in the `com.jdojo.logger` package of this module. The `provides` statement is important for setting up the platform logger. It states that you are providing the `com.jdojo.logger.Log4jLoggerFinder` class as an implementation for the service interface `java.lang.System.LoggerFinder`. You will create this class shortly. Figure 19-2 shows the module graph for the `com.jdojo.logger` module.

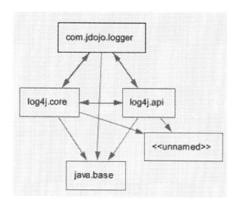

Figure 19-2. *The module graph for the com.jdojo.logger module*

Notice the circular dependencies and the unnamed module in the graph. They are because of automatic modules used in this module declaration. The `com.jdojo.logger` module reads the two automatic modules. Every automatic module reads all other modules, which you see in an arrow going out from the `log4j.code` and `log4j.api` modules to all the other modules. Even if you do not have any unnamed modules in this example, the graph shows it. In this example, the unnamed module will contain no types. The unnamed module appears in the graph because an automatic module reads all other modules including unnamed modules.

Adding a Log4j Configuration File

Listing 19-2 shows the configuration file named `log4j2.xml`, which is placed at the root of the source code of the NetBeans project. In other words, the `log4j2.xml` file is placed in an unnamed package. This configuration will make Log4j to log messages in a file at `logs/platform.log` file under the current directory. Refer to the Log4j documentation for more information on this configuration.

Listing 19-2. A Log4j Configuration File Named log4j2.xml

```
<?xml version="1.0" encoding="UTF-8"?>
<Configuration status="error">
    <Appenders>
        <File name="JdojoLogFile" fileName="logs/platform.log">
            <PatternLayout>
                <Pattern>%d %p %c [%t] %m%n</Pattern>
            </PatternLayout>
        </File>
        <Async name="Async">
            <AppenderRef ref="JdojoLogFile"/>
        </Async>
    </Appenders>
```

```
    <Loggers>
        <Root level="info">
            <AppenderRef ref="Async"/>
        </Root>
    </Loggers>
</Configuration>
```

Creating a System Logger

You need to create a system logger, which is a class that implements the System.Logger interface. The interface contains the following methods:

- String getName()

- boolean isLoggable(System.Logger.Level level)

- default void log(System.Logger.Level level, Object obj)

- default void log(System.Logger.Level level, String msg)

- default void log(System.Logger.Level level, String format, Object... params)

- default void log(System.Logger.Level level, String msg, Throwable thrown)

- default void log(System.Logger.Level level, Supplier<String> msgSupplier)

- default void log(System.Logger.Level level, Supplier<String> msgSupplier, Throwable thrown)

- void log(System.Logger.Level level, ResourceBundle bundle, String format, Object... params)

- void log(System.Logger.Level level, ResourceBundle bundle, String msg, Throwable thrown)

You will need to provide implementation for four abstract methods in the System.Logger interface. The getName() method should return the name of your logger. You can give it any name you want. The isLoggable() method returns true if the logger can log a message of the specified level. The two versions of the log() method are used to log messages, which are called by other default log() methods.

The System.Logger.Level enum defines constants for the level of messages to be logged. A level has a name and severity. Level values are ALL, TRACE, DEBUG, INFO, WARNING, ERROR, OFF, in order of increasing severity. You can get the name and severity of a level using its getName() and getSeverity() methods.

Listing 19-3 contains the code for a class named Log4jLogger, which implements the System.Logger interface.

Listing 19-3. A Log4jLogger Class That Implements the System.Logger Interface

```java
// Log4jLogger.java
package com.jdojo.logger;

import java.util.ResourceBundle;
import org.apache.logging.log4j.LogManager;
import org.apache.logging.log4j.Logger;
```

```
public class Log4jLogger implements System.Logger {
    // The backend logger. Our logger will delegate all loggings
    // to this backend logger, which is Log4j
    private final Logger logger = LogManager.getLogger();

    @Override
    public String getName() {
        return "Log4jLogger";
    }

    @Override
    public boolean isLoggable(Level level) {
        // Get the log4j level from System.Logger.Level
        org.apache.logging.log4j.Level log4jLevel = toLog4jLevel(level);

        // Check if log4j can handle this level of logging and return the result
        return logger.isEnabled(log4jLevel);
    }

    @Override
    public void log(Level level, ResourceBundle bundle, String msg, Throwable thrown) {
        logger.log(toLog4jLevel(level), msg, thrown);
    }

    @Override
    public void log(Level level, ResourceBundle bundle, String format, Object... params) {
        logger.printf(toLog4jLevel(level), format, params);
    }

    private static org.apache.logging.log4j.Level toLog4jLevel(Level level) {
        switch (level) {
            case ALL:
                return org.apache.logging.log4j.Level.ALL;
            case DEBUG:
                return org.apache.logging.log4j.Level.DEBUG;
            case ERROR:
                return org.apache.logging.log4j.Level.ERROR;
            case INFO:
                return org.apache.logging.log4j.Level.INFO;
            case OFF:
                return org.apache.logging.log4j.Level.OFF;
            case TRACE:
                return org.apache.logging.log4j.Level.TRACE;
            case WARNING:
                return org.apache.logging.log4j.Level.WARN;
            default:
                throw new RuntimeException("Unknown Level: " + level);
        }
    }
}
```

An instance of the Log4jLogger will be used as a platform logger to log messages from the platform classes. It delegates all logging work to a backend logger, which is Log4j in this base. The logger instance variable stores a reference to the Log4j Logger instance.

You are dealing with two logging APIs—one defined by System.Logger and one defined by the Log4j. They use different logging levels, which are represented by two different types—System.Logger.Level and org.apache.logging.log4j.Level. To log messages, JDK classes will pass a System.Logger.Level to one of the log() methods of the System.Logger interface, which in turn needs to map the level to the Log4j level. The toLog4jLevel() method does this mapping. It receives a System.Logger.Level and returns a corresponding org.apache.logging.log4j.Level.

The isLoggable() method maps the system level to the Log4j level and queries Log4j if logging is enabled for logging. You can configure Log4j to enable any level of logging using its configuration file shown in Listing 19-2.

I kept the implementation of the two log() methods simple. They just delegate their work to the Log4j. The methods do not use the ResourceBundle argument. You would use it if you want to localize the message before logging.

You have now written the main logic of the platform logger, but it's not ready to test yet. A little more work is needed to see it in action.

Creating a Logger Finder

The Java runtime needs to find your platform logger. It uses a service locator pattern to find it. Recall the following statement in your module declaration in Listing 19-1.

```
provides java.lang.System.LoggerFinder
        with com.jdojo.logger.Log4jLoggerFinder;
```

In this section, you will create an implementation class named Log4jLoggerFinder, which will implement the service interface System.LoggerFinder. Remember that a service interface does not need to be a Java interface. It can be an abstract class. In this case, System.LoggerFinder is an abstract class and your Log4jLoggerFinder class will extend the System.LoggerFinder class. Listing 19-4 contains the code for a Log4jLoggerFinder class that will serve as an implementation for the service interface System.LoggerFinder.

Listing 19-4. A Log4jLoggerFinder Class That Will Be Used as an Implementation for the interface System.LoggerFinder Service

```java
// Log4jLoggerFinder.java
package com.jdojo.logger;

import java.lang.System.LoggerFinder;

public class Log4jLoggerFinder extends LoggerFinder {
    // A logger to be used as a platform logger
    private final Log4jLogger logger = new Log4jLogger();

    @Override
    public System.Logger getLogger(String name, Module module) {
        System.out.printf("Log4jLoggerFinder.getLogger(): " +
                          "[name=%s, module=%s]%n", name, module.getName());

        // Use the same logger for all modules
        return logger;
    }
}
```

The Log4jLoggerFinder class creates an instance of the Log4jLogger class, which was created in Listing 19-3, and stores its reference in an instance variable named logger. The getLogger() method returns the same logger whenever the JDK asks for a logger. The name and module arguments in the getLogger() method are the name of the requested logger and the requestor's module. For example, when the java.util.Currency class needs to log a message, it requests a logger with the name java.util.Currency and the requestor module will be the java.base module. If you want to use separate logger for each module, you can return a different logger based on the module argument. This example returns the same logger for all modules, so all messages are logged to the same place. I left the System.out.println() statement in the getLogger() method, so you can see the name and module arguments' values while running this example.

Testing the Platform Logger

It is time to see everything in action. Listing 19-5 contains the code for a PlatformLoggerTest class, which is used to test the platform logger. You may get different output.

Listing 19-5. A PlatformLoggerTest Class That Tests the Platform Logger

```java
// PlatformLoggerTest.java
package com.jdojo.logger;

import java.lang.System.Logger;
import static java.lang.System.Logger.Level.TRACE;
import static java.lang.System.Logger.Level.ERROR;
import static java.lang.System.Logger.Level.INFO;
import java.util.Currency;
import java.util.Set;

public class PlatformLoggerTest {
    public static void main(final String... args) {
        // Let us load all currencies
        Set<Currency> c = Currency.getAvailableCurrencies();
        System.out.println("# of currencies: " + c.size());

        // Let us test the platform logger by logging a few messages
        Logger logger = System.getLogger("Log4jLogger");
        logger.log(TRACE, "Entering application.");
        logger.log(ERROR, "An unknown error occurred.");
        logger.log(INFO, "FYI");
        logger.log(TRACE, "Exiting application.");
    }
}
```

```
# of currencies: 225
Log4jLoggerFinder.getLogger(): [name=javax.management.mbeanserver, module=java.management]
Log4jLoggerFinder.getLogger(): [name=javax.management.misc, module=java.management]
Log4jLoggerFinder.getLogger(): [name=Log4jLogger, module=com.jdojo.logger]
```

The main() method tries to get a list of available currency symbols and print the number of currency symbols. What is the purpose of doing this? I explain its purpose shortly. For now, it is just a method call in the java.util.Currency class.

Even though you are not supposed to use the logger for logging application messages, you can do so for testing purposes. You can get a reference of the platform logger using the `System.getLogger()` method and start logging messages. The following snippet of code in the `main()` method does this:

```
Logger logger = System.getLogger("Log4jLogger");
logger.log(TRACE, "Entering application.");
logger.log(ERROR, "An unknown error occurred.");
logger.log(INFO, "FYI");
logger.log(TRACE, "Exiting application.");
```

■ **Tip**   In JDK 9, the `System` class contains two static methods that can be used to get a reference of the platform loggers. The methods are `getLogger(String name)` and `getLogger(String name, ResourceBundle bundle)`. Both methods return an instance of the `System.Logger` interface.

The four messages are not shown in the output. Where did they go? Recall that you configured Log4j to log messages to a file called `logs/platform.log` under the current directory. The current directory depends on how you run the `PlatformLoggerTest` class. If you run it from NetBeans, the project's directory, which is `C:\Java9Revealed\com.jdojo.logger`, is the current directory. If you run it from the command prompt, you control the current directory. Assuming that you ran this class from inside NetBeans, you will find a file at `C:\Java9Revealed\com.jdojo.logger\logs\platform.log`. Its contents are shown in Listing 19-6.

Listing 19-6. Contents of the logs/platform.log File

```
2017-02-09 09:58:34,644 ERROR com.jdojo.logger.Log4jLogger [main] An unknown error occurred.
2017-02-09 09:58:34,646 INFO com.jdojo.logger.Log4jLogger [main] FYI
```

■ **Note**   Each time you run the `PlatformLoggerTest` class, Log4j will append messages to the `logs\platform.log` file. The rest of this discussion shows only the output for one run of this program. You can remove the contents of the log file before running the program or simply delete the log file, which will be recreated every time you run the program.

The log file indicates that only two messages, ERROR and INFO, were logged, discarding the TRACE message. This has to do with the logger level setting in the Log4j configuration file, shown in Listing 19-2. You have enabled INFO level logging in the logger:

```
<Loggers>
    <Root level="info">
        <AppenderRef ref="Async"/>
    </Root>
</Loggers>
```

Each logger level has a severity, which is an integer. If you enable a logger with a level x, it will log all messages whose level's severity is greater than or equal to x. Table 19-1 shows the names of all levels defined by the `System.Logger.Level` enum and their associated severity. Note that, in your example, you are using Log4j logger levels, not the levels defined by `System.Logger.Level` enum. However, the relative values of levels defined by Log4j are in the same *order* as shown in this table.

Table 19-1. *Names and Severity Levels Defined by the System.Logger.Level Enum*

Name	Severity
ALL	Integer.MIN_VALUE
TRACE	400
DEBUG	500
INFO	800
WARNING	900
ERROR	1000
OFF	Integer.MAX_VALUE

If you enable your logger for level INFO, the logger will log all messages at the INFO, WARNING, and ERROR levels. If you want to log messages at all levels, you can use trace or all as the level value in the Log4j configuration file shown in Listing 19-2.

Notice in the output that the platform classes requested a logger three times by calling the getLogger() method of the Log4jLoggerFinder class. The first two times, requests were made by the javax.management module. The third request appears in the output because you requested a logger from the main() method of the PlatformLoggerTest class.

You saw your own messages in the log, but not any messages logged from the JDK classes. I am sure you are curious to see messages in the log that come from JDK classes. After all, I started this example to show you that. How do you know the names of JDK classes that log messages to platform logger and how you make them log messages? There is no simple and direct way to know this. Looking at the source code for the JDK and finding the reference of the sun.util.logging.PlatformLogger class, which is used to log platform messages, I found that the javax.management module logs TRACE level messages. To see those messages, you need to set the level of the Log4j logger to trace and rerun the PlatformLoggerTest class. This will log a lot of messages in the log file.

Let's get back to the use of the Currency class in the PlatformLoggerTest class. I used it to show you the messages logged by a JDK class, which is, in this case, the java.util.Currency class. When you request a list of all currencies, the JDK reads its own currency list, which is built into the JDK, and a custom currency. properties file, which is located in the JAVA_HOME\lib directory. In this case, you are running this example using the JDK, so the JAVA_HOME refers to the JDK_HOME. Create a text file with the contents shown in Listing 19-7. The file's path will be JDK_HOME\lib\currency.properties. Note that the file contains only one word, which is ABadCurrencyFile. Using any one word will do.

Listing 19-7. Contents of the JDK_HOME\lib\currency.properties File

```
ABadCurrencyFile
```

The Currency class attempts to load the currency.properties file as a Java property file, which is supposed to contain name=value pairs. This file is not a valid property file. When the Currency class attempts to load it, an exception is thrown and the class logs an error message to the platform logger. Now you know that you created an invalid currency file, so you can see platform logger in action through the JDK class.

Let's run the `PlatformLoggerTest` class again, which gives the following output:

```
Log4jLoggerFinder.getLogger(): [name=javax.management.mbeanserver, module=java.management]
Log4jLoggerFinder.getLogger(): [name=javax.management.misc, module=java.management]
Log4jLoggerFinder.getLogger(): [name=java.util.Currency, module=java.base]
# of currencies: 225
Log4jLoggerFinder.getLogger(): [name=Log4jLogger, module=com.jdojo.logger]
```

The output indicates that the `java.base` module requested a platform logger with a name `java.util.Currency`. This was done because of the invalid currency file you used. Contents of the log file are shown in Listing 19-8, which shows the message logged from the `Currency` class.

Listing 19-8. Contents of the logs/platform.log File

```
2017-02-09 10:45:52,413 INFO com.jdojo.logger.Log4jLogger [main] currency.properties entry
for ABADCURRENCYFILE is ignored because of the invalid country code.
2017-02-09 10:45:52,420 ERROR com.jdojo.logger.Log4jLogger [main] An unknown error occurred.
2017-02-09 10:45:52,420 INFO com.jdojo.logger.Log4jLogger [main] FYI
```

Further Work

I showed you an example of configuring a platform logger using Log4j 2.0 as a backend logger. There is still a lot for work to be done to this example before it can be used in a production environment. One improvement that we could do is log the name of the class that is logging the message. Refer to Listing 19-8 and you will find that all logged messages use the same class name, which is `com.jdojo.logger.Log4jLogger` as the logger's class, which is not correct. You logged two messages from the `com.jdojo.logger.PlatformLoggerTest` class and one message was logged from the `java.util.Currency` class. How can you fix this?

Let's try to understand this issue first. The class name of the logger is determined by Log4j. It simply looks at the caller of its `log()` method and uses that class as the one that's logging the message. In Listing 19-3, the two `log()` methods call the `log()` method of the Log4j to delegate the logging work. Log4j sees the `com.jdojo.logger.Log4jLogger` class as the logger of messages and uses its name as the logger class in the logged message. There are two ways to fix it:

- In the `Log4jLogger` class, format the message yourself using the Stack-Walking API added to JDK 9. The Stack-Walking API will give you the caller's class name and other details. This will make you change the pattern layout in the Log4j configuration file, so Log4j does not determine and include the logger's class name in the message.

- You can wait for the next version of Log4j, which *might* support JDK 9 platform logger out of the box. There is no such announcement from Log4j at the time of this writing.

Unified JVM Logging

JDK 9 added a new command-line option, -Xlog, that gives you a single point of access to all messages logged from all components of the JVM. The usage syntax of this option is a bit complex. I explain the details of the logged messages, before I explain the syntax of the -Xlog option.

▓ **Tip**   You can use the -Xlog:help option with the java command to print the description of the -Xlog option. The description contains the syntax and values for all options with examples.

When the JVM logs a message or when you are looking for a JVM logged message, keep the following points in mind:

- The JVM needs to identify the topic (or the JVM component) to which the message belongs. For example, if a message is related to garbage collection, the messages should be tagged as such. A message may belong to multiple topics. For example, a message may belong to garbage collection and heap management. Therefore, a message may have multiple tags associated with it.

- Like any other logging facility, JVM logging may occur at different levels, such as info, warning, etc.

- You should be able to decorate the logged messages with additional contextual information such as current date and time, thread logging the message, tags used with the message, etc.

- Where should the messages be logged? Should they be logged to stdout, stderr, or one or more files? Should you be able to specify the policies for logging options for log files such as filenames, size, and a file rotation policy.

If you understand these points, it's time to learn the following terms that are used to describe the JVM logging:

- Tags
- Levels
- Decorations
- Output

The following is an example of running the com.jdojo.Welcome class, which you created in Chapter 3, with the -Xlog option. It logs all messages with the gc tag with a severity level of trace or above on standard output with the level, time, and tags decorations.

```
C:\Java9revealed> java -Xlog:gc=trace:stdout:level,time,tags
--module-path com.jdojo.intro\dist
--module com.jdojo.intro/com.jdojo.intro.Welcome
```

```
[2017-02-10T12:50:11.412-0600][trace][gc] MarkStackSize: 4096k   MarkStackSizeMax: 16384k
[2017-02-10T12:50:11.427-0600][debug][gc] ConcGCThreads: 1
[2017-02-10T12:50:11.432-0600][debug][gc] ParallelGCThreads: 4
[2017-02-10T12:50:11.433-0600][debug][gc] Initialize mark stack with 4096 chunks, maximum 16384
[2017-02-10T12:50:11.436-0600][info ][gc] Using G1
Welcome to the Module System.
Module Name: com.jdojo.intro
```

Message Tags

Every logged message is associated with one or more tags called a tag-set. The following is a list of all available tags at the time of this writing. This list may change in the future. To get a list of supported tags, use the -Xlog:help option with the java command.

add, age, alloc, aot, annotation, arguments, attach, barrier, biasedlocking, blocks, bot, breakpoint, census, class, classhisto, cleanup, compaction, constraints, constantpool, coops, cpu, cset, data, defaultmethods, dump, ergo, exceptions, exit, fingerprint, freelist, gc, hashtables, heap, humongous, ihop, iklass, init, itables, jni, jvmti, liveness, load, loader, logging, mark, marking, methodcomparator, metadata, metaspace, mmu, modules, monitorinflation, monitormismatch, nmethod, normalize, objecttagging, obsolete, oopmap, os, pagesize, patch, path, phases, plab, promotion, preorder, protectiondomain, ref, redefine, refine, region, remset, purge, resolve, safepoint, scavenge, scrub, stacktrace, stackwalk, start, startuptime, state, stats, stringdedup, stringtable, stackmap, subclass, survivor, sweep, task, thread, tlab, time, timer, update, unload, verification, verify, vmoperation, vtables, workgang, jfr, system, parser, bytecode, setting, event

If you are interested in logging messages for garbage collection and startup, you use the gc and startuptime tags with the -Xlog option. Most tags in the list have esoteric names and, in fact, they are meant for developers working on the JVM, not for application developers. I could not find descriptions of all these tags. The link https://bugs.openjdk.java.net/browse/JDK-8146948 contains a bug report that requests descriptions for all these tags. The bug is marked as fixed, but I could not see a option that will show the tag descriptions.

▓ **Tip**   You can use a special tag named all with the -Xlog option that tells JVM to log all messages irrespective of the tags associated with them. The default value for tag is all.

Message Levels

Level is the severity level of logging that determines messages to be logged based on severity of messages. Levels have the following values in the increasing order of severity: trace, debug, info, warning, and error. If you enable logging for severity level S, all messages with severity level S and greater will be logged. For example, if you enable logging at the info level, all messages with the info, warning, and error levels will be logged.

■ **Tip**   You can use a special severity level named off with the -Xlog option to disable logging at all levels. The default value for level is info.

Message Decorations

JVM messages can be augmented with additional pieces of information before they are logged. These additional pieces of information are called *decorations*, and they are prepended to the message. Each decoration is enclosed within brackets—[and]. Table 19- contains a list of all decorations with their long and short names. You can use long names or short names with the -Xlog option.

Table 19-2. *Decorations and Their Long and Short Names*

Long Name	Short Name	Description
hostname	hn	Computer name
level	l	Severity level of the message
pid	p	The process identifier
tags	tg	All tags associated with the message
tid	ti	The thread identifier
time	t	Current time and date in ISO-8601 format (e.g., 2017-02-10T18:42:58.418+0000)
timemillis	tm	Current time in milliseconds as a number, which is the same value as generated by System.currentTimeMillis()
timenanos	tn	Current time in nanoseconds as a number, which is the same value as generated by System.nanoTime()
uptime	u	Time since the start of the JVM in seconds and milliseconds (e.g., 9.219s)
uptimemillis	um	Milliseconds since the JVM started
uptimenanos	un	Nanoseconds since the JVM started
utctime	utc	Current time and date in UTC format (e.g., 2017-02-10T12:42:58.418-0600)

■ **Tip**   You can use a special decoration named none with the -Xlog option to turn off decoration. The default value for decoration is uptime,level,tags in this order.

Message Output Destination

You can specify one of three destinations where the JVM log will be sent:

- `stdout`
- `stderr`
- `file=<file-name>`

Use the `stdout` and `stderr` values to print the JVM log on standard output and standard error, respectively. The default output destination is `stdout`.

Use the `file` value to specify a text filename to send the log to a text file. You can use `%p` and `%t` in the filename, which will expand to JVM's PID and startup timestamp, respectively. For example, if you specify `file=jvm%p_%t.log` as an output destination with the `-Xlog` option, for every JVM run, messages will be logged to a file whose name will look like this:

- `jvm2348_2017-02-10_13-26-05.log`
- `jvm7292_2017-02-10_13-26-06.log`

Every time you start the JVM, a log file like the one shown in this list will be created. Here, 2348 and 7292 are JVM's PIDs for two runs.

░ **Tip**   Absence of `stdout` and `stderr` as the output destination indicates that the output destination is a text file. Instead of using `file=jvm.log`, you can simply use `jvm.log` as the output destination.

You can specify additional options for sending output to a text file:

- `filecount=<file-count>`
- `filesize=<file-size>`

These options are used to control the maximum size of each log file and the maximum number of log files. Consider the following option:

`file=jvm.log::filesize=1M,filecount=3`

Note the use of two consecutive colons (`::`). I explain them in the next section. This option uses `jvm.log` as the log file. The maximum size for the log file is 1M (1 MB) and the maximum count for log files is 3. It will create four log files: `jvm.log`, `jvm.log.0`, `jvm.log.1`, and `jvm.log.2`. The current messages are logged to the `jvm.log` file and the other three files are rotated as the logged messages in the current file exceed 1MB. You can specify the file size using `K` for kilobytes and `M` for megabytes. If you specify a file size without including the `K` or `M` suffix, the option assumes it's bytes.

The -Xlog Syntax

The following is the syntax to use the `-Xlog` option:

`-Xlog[:<contents>][:[<output>][:[<decorators>][:<output-options>]]]`

The options used with `-Xlog` are separated by colons (`:`). All options are optional. If a preceding part in `-Xlog` is missing, you must use a colon for that part. For example, `-Xlog::stderr` indicates that all parts are defaulted, except the `<output>` part, which is specified as `stderr`.

The simplest use of -Xlog is as follows, which will log all JVM messages to the standard output:

```
java -Xlog --module-path com.jdojo.intro\dist --module com.jdojo.intro/com.jdojo.intro.
Welcome
```

There are two special -Xlog options: help and disable, which can be used as -Xlog:help to print help on -Xlog and -Xlog:disable to disable all JVM logging. You might think that instead of using -Xlog:disable, you can just not use the -Xlog option at all. You are correct. However, the disable option exists for a different reason. The -Xlog option can be used multiple times with the same command. If multiple occurrences of -Xlog contain the settings of the same kind, the settings in the last -Xlog win. Therefore, you can specify -Xlog:disable as the first option and specify another -Xlog for turning on a specific type of logging. This way, first you turn off all defaults and, then you specify the options you are interested in.

The <contents> part specifies the tags and severity levels for the messages to be logged. Its syntax is as follows:

```
tag1[+tag2...][*][=level][,...]
```

A + in the <contents> part represents a logical AND. For example, gc+exit means log all messages whose tag-set contains exactly two tags—gc and exit. An * in the end of a tag name works as a wildcard, which means "at least". For example, gc* means log all messages whose tag-set contains at least gc, which will log messages with tag-sets [gc], [gc,exit], [gc,remset,exit], etc. If you use gc+exit*, it means log all messages with tag-sets containing at least gc and exit tags, which will log messages with tag-sets [gc,exit], [gc,remset,exit], etc. You can specify the severity level for each tag name to be logged. For example, gc=trace logs all messages with tag-set containing only gc with severity level of trace or higher. You can specify multiple criteria separated by a comma. For example, gc=trace,heap=error will log all messages with gc tag-set at trace or a higher level or with heap tag-set at error level.

I show you commands to log JVM messages using different criteria. The outputs shown are on my computer. You may get different outputs when you run these commands. The following command specifies gc and startuptime as tags, leaving the other settings to the default values:

```
C:\Java9Revealed>java -Xlog:gc,startuptime --module-path com.jdojo.intro\dist
--module com.jdojo.intro/com.jdojo.intro.Welcome
```

```
[0.017s][info][startuptime] StubRoutines generation 1, 0.0002258 secs
[0.022s][info][gc          ] Using G1
[0.022s][info][startuptime] Genesis, 0.0045639 secs
...
```

Using -Xlog is the same as -Xlog:all=info:stdout:uptime,level,tags. It logs all messages at severity level info or higher to stdout with decorators uptime, level, and tags. The following command shows you how to get a JVM log using the default settings. A partial output is shown:

```
C:\Java9Revealed>java -Xlog --module-path com.jdojo.intro\dist
--module com.jdojo.intro/com.jdojo.intro.Welcome
```

```
[0.015s][info][os] SafePoint Polling address: 0x000001195fae0000
[0.015s][info][os] Memory Serialize Page address: 0x000001195fdb0000
[0.018s][info][biasedlocking] Aligned thread 0x000001195fb37f40 to 0x000001195fb38000
[0.019s][info][class,path  ] bootstrap loader class path=C:\java9\lib\modules
[0.019s][info][class,path  ] classpath:
[0.020s][info][class,path  ] opened: C:\java9\lib\modules
[0.020s][info][class,load  ] opened: C:\java9\lib\modules
[0.027s][info][os,thread   ] Thread is alive (tid: 17724).
[0.027s][info][os,thread   ] Thread is alive (tid: 6436).
[0.033s][info][gc          ] Using G1
[0.034s][info][startuptime  ] Genesis, 0.0083975 secs
[0.038s][info][class,load  ] java.lang.Object source: jrt:/java.base
[0.226s][info][os,thread         ] Thread finished (tid: 7584).
[0.226s][info][gc,heap,exit      ] Heap
[0.226s][info][gc,heap,exit      ]  Metaspace       used 6398K, capacity 6510K,
[0.226s][info][safepoint,cleanup ] mark nmethods, 0.0000057 secs
[0.226s][info][os,thread         ] Thread finished (tid: 3660).
...
```

The following command logs all messages tagged with at least gc at severity level debug or higher to a file named gc.log in the current directory with a time decorator. Note that the command will print two lines of messages on the standard output, which come from the main() method of the Welcome class. However, I show a partial output from the gc.log file, not what is printed on the standard output.

```
C:\java9revealed>java -Xlog:gc*=trace:file=gc.log:time --module-path com.jdojo.intro\dist
--module com.jdojo.intro/com.jdojo.intro.Welcome
```

```
[2017-02-11T08:40:23.942-0600]   Maximum heap size 2113804288
[2017-02-11T08:40:23.942-0600]   Initial heap size 132112768
[2017-02-11T08:40:23.942-0600]   Minimum heap size 6815736
[2017-02-11T08:40:23.942-0600] MarkStackSize: 4096k  MarkStackSizeMax: 16384k
[2017-02-11T08:40:23.966-0600] Heap region size: 1M
[2017-02-11T08:40:23.966-0600] WorkerManager::add_workers() : created_workers: 4
[2017-02-11T08:40:23.966-0600] Initialize Card Live Data
[2017-02-11T08:40:23.966-0600] ParallelGCThreads: 4
[2017-02-11T08:40:23.966-0600] WorkerManager::add_workers() : created_workers: 1
...
```

The following command logs the same messages as the previous command does, except it logs messages without any decorations:

```
C:\java9revealed>java -Xlog:gc*=trace:file=gc.log:none --module-path com.jdojo.intro\dist
--module com.jdojo.intro/com.jdojo.intro.Welcome
```

```
    Maximum heap size 2113804288
    Initial heap size 132112768
    Minimum heap size 6815736
MarkStackSize: 4096k  MarkStackSizeMax: 16384k
Heap region size: 1M
WorkerManager::add_workers() : created_workers: 4
Initialize Card Live Data
ParallelGCThreads: 4
WorkerManager::add_workers() : created_workers: 1
...
```

The following command logs the same messages as the previous command does, except it uses a rotating file-set with 10 files with size 5MB with base name gc.log:

```
C:\Java9Revealed>java -Xlog:gc*=trace:file=gc.log:none:filesize=5m,filecount=10
--module-path com.jdojo.intro\dist --module com.jdojo.intro/com.jdojo.intro.Welcome
```

The following command logs all messages that contain a gc tag with severity level of debug or higher. It turns off all messages that contain an exit tag. It will not log messages that contain both gc and exit tags. Messages are logged on stdout with default decorations. A partial output is shown.

```
C:\Java9Revealed>java -Xlog:gc*=debug,exit*=off --module-path com.jdojo.intro\dist
--module com.jdojo.intro/com.jdojo.intro.Welcome
```

```
[0.015s][info][gc,heap] Heap region size: 1M
[0.015s][debug][gc,heap] Minimum heap 8388608  Initial heap 132120576  Maximum heap
2113929216
[0.015s][debug][gc,ergo,refine] Initial Refinement Zones: green: 4, yellow: 12, red: 20, min
yellow size: 8
[0.016s][debug][gc,marking,start] Initialize Card Live Data
[0.016s][debug][gc,marking       ] Initialize Card Live Data 0.024ms
[0.016s][debug][gc               ] ConcGCThreads: 1
[0.018s][debug][gc,ihop          ] Target occupancy update: old: 0B, new: 132120576B
[0.019s][info ][gc               ] Using G1
[0.182s][debug][gc,metaspace,freelist]    space @ 0x000001e7dbeb8260 704K,  99% used
[0x000001e7fe880000, 0x000001e7fedf8400, 0x000001e7fee00000, 0x000001e7ff080000)
[0.191s][debug][gc,refine            ] Stopping 0
...
```

The following command logs messages tagged with startuptime using hostname, uptime, level, and tags as decorations. All other settings are left as the default. It will log messages at info level or higher and they are logged to stdout. Note the use of two consecutive colons (::) in the command. They are needed because we have not specified the output destination.

```
C:\Java9Revealed>java -Xlog:startuptime::hostname,uptime,level,tags
--module-path com.jdojo.intro\dist --module com.jdojo.intro/com.jdojo.intro.Welcome
```

```
[0.015s][kishori][info][startuptime] StubRoutines generation 1, 0.0002574 secs
[0.019s][kishori][info][startuptime] Genesis, 0.0038339 secs
[0.019s][kishori][info][startuptime] TemplateTable initialization, 0.0000081 secs
[0.020s][kishori][info][startuptime] Interpreter generation, 0.0010698 secs
[0.032s][kishori][info][startuptime] StubRoutines generation 2, 0.0001518 secs
[0.032s][kishori][info][startuptime] MethodHandles adapters generation, 0.0000229 secs
[0.033s][kishori][info][startuptime] Start VMThread, 0.0001491 secs
[0.055s][kishori][info][startuptime] Initialize java.lang classes, 0.0224295 secs
[0.058s][kishori][info][startuptime] Initialize java.lang.invoke classes, 0.0015945 secs
[0.162s][kishori][info][startuptime] Create VM, 0.1550707 secs
Welcome to the Module System.
Module Name: com.jdojo.intro
```

Summary

JDK 9 has overhauled the logging systems for platform classes (JDK classes) and JVM components. There is a new API that lets you specify a logging framework of your choice as logging backend for logging messages from platform classes. There is also a new command-line option that lets you access messages from all JVM components.

The platform logging API lets you specify a custom logger that will be used by all platform classes to log their messages. You can use existing logging frameworks such as Log4j as a logger. The API consists of the java.lang.System.LoggerFinder class and the java.lang.System.Logger interface.

An instance of the System.Logger interface represents a platform logger. The System.LogFinder class is a service interface. You will need to provide an implementation for this service interface, which returns an instance of the System.Logger interface. You can use the getLogger() method in the java.lang.System class to get a System.Logger. A module in your application must contain a provides statement indicating the implementation for the System.LogFinder service interface. Otherwise, a default logger will be used.

JDK 9 allows you to log all JVM messages from all components using a single option named -Xlog. The option lets you specify the types of messages, the severity level of messages, log destination, decorations for the logged messages, and the log file properties. A message is identified by a set of tags. Constants of the System.Logger.Level enum specify the severity level of a message. The log destination could be stdout, stderr, or a file.

CHAPTER 20

▥ ▥ ▥

Other Changes in JDK 9

In this chapter, you will learn:

- The underscore as a new keyword
- Improved syntax for using `try-with-resources` blocks
- How to use the diamond operator in anonymous classes
- How to use private methods in interfaces
- How to use the `@SafeVarargs` annotation on private methods
- How to discard outputs of sub-processes
- How to use new methods in the `Math` and `StrictMath` classes
- How to use stream of `Optionals` and other new operations on `Optionals`
- How to use spin-wait hints
- The enhancements to the Time API and the `Matcher` and `Objects` classes
- How to compare arrays and slices of arrays
- The enhancements to the Javadoc and how to use its new search features
- The native desktop supports in JDK 9 and how to use them
- How to use global and local filters during object deserialization
- How to transfer data from an input stream to an output stream and how to duplicate and slice buffers

There are many small and big changes to Java SE 9. The big changes are the introduction of the Module System, HTTP/2 Client API, etc. These big changes warranted a chapter by themselves. This chapter covers all the changes that are important for Java developers, but are not big enough to get a chapter of their own. You do not need to read this chapter sequentially. Each section covers a new topic. If you are interested in learning about a specific topic, you can jump directly to the section on that topic.

© Kishori Sharan 2017
K. Sharan, *Java 9 Revealed*, DOI 10.1007/978-1-4842-2592-9_20

The source for the chapter's examples are in a com.jdojo.misc module whose declaration is shown in Listing 20-1.

Listing 20-1. A Module Declaration for a Module Named com.jdojo.misc

```
// module-info.java
module com.jdojo.misc {
    requires java.desktop;

    exports com.jdojo.misc;
}
```

The module reads the java.desktop module, which you will need in order to implement platform-specific desktop features, which are described in the section entitled "Native Desktop Features".

The Underscore Is a Keyword

In JDK 9, the underscore (_) is a keyword and you cannot use it by itself as a one-character identifier such as a variable name, a method name, a type name, etc. However, you can still use the underscore in a multi-character identifier name. Consider the program in Listing 20-2.

Listing 20-2. A Program That Uses an Underscore as an Identifier

```
// UnderscoreTest.java
package com.jdojo.misc;

public class UnderscoreTest {
    public static void main(String[] args) {
        // Use an underscore as an identifier. It is a compile-time warning in JDK 8 and a
        // compile-time error in JDK 9.
        int _ = 19;
        System.out.println(_);

        // Use an underscore in multi-character identifiers. They are fine in JDK 8 and JDK 9.
        final int FINGER_COUNT = 20;
        final String _prefix = "Sha";
    }
}
```

Compiling the UnderscoreTest class in JDK 8 generates two warnings for using an underscore as an identifier by itself—one for the variable declaration and one for its use in the System.out.println() method call. A warning is generated for every use of the underscore by itself. JDK 8 generates the following two warnings:

```
com.jdojo.misc\src\com\jdojo\misc\UnderscoreTest.java:8: warning: '_' used as an identifier
        int _ = 19;
            ^
  (use of '_' as an identifier might not be supported in releases after Java SE 8)
com.jdojo.misc\src\com\jdojo\misc\UnderscoreTest.java:9: warning: '_' used as an identifier
        System.out.println(_);
                           ^
  (use of '_' as an identifier might not be supported in releases after Java SE 8)
2 warnings
```

Compiling the UnderscoreTest class in JDK 9 generates the following two compile-time errors:

```
com.jdojo.misc\src\com\jdojo\misc\UnderscoreTest.java:8: error: as of release 9, '_' is a
keyword, and may not be used as an identifier
        int _ = 19;
            ^
com.jdojo.misc\src\com\jdojo\misc\UnderscoreTest.java:9: error: as of release 9, '_' is a
keyword, and may not be used as an identifier
        System.out.println(_);
                           ^
2 errors
```

What is the special meaning of an underscore in JDK 9 and where do you use it? In JDK 9, you have been restricted not to use it as an identifier. JDK designers intend to give it a special meaning in a future JDK release. So, wait until JDK 10 or 11 to see it in action as a keyword with a special meaning. Comment these lines in the source code or the entire class code, so you can compile the entire NetBeans project without errors. If the source is commented, you will need to uncomment it to see these errors.

Improved try-with-resources Blocks

JDK 7 added an AutoCloseable interface to the java.lang package:

```
public interface AutoCloseable {
    void close() throws Exception;
}
```

JDK 7 also added a new block called try-with-resources, which can be used to manage AutoCloseable objects (or resources) using the following steps:

- You assign the reference of the resource to a *newly declared* variable at the beginning of the block.
- You work with the resource in the body of the block.
- When the body of the block is exited, the close() method on the variable representing the resource will be called automatically for you.

This avoided boilerplate code written using a finally block before JDK 7. The following snippet of code shows how developers used to manage a closeable resource, assuming that a Resource class exists that implements the AutoCloseable interface:

```
/* Prior to JDK 7*/
Resource res = null;

try{
    // Create the resource
    res = new Resource();

    // Work with res here
```

```
} finally {
    try {
        if(res != null) {
            res.close();
        }
    } catch(Exception e) {
        e.printStackTrace();
    }
}
```

The `try-with-resources` in JDK 7 greatly improved this situation. In JDK 7, you could rewrite the previous snippet of code as follows:

```
try (Resource res = new Resource()) {
    // Work with res here
}
```

This snippet of code will call the `close()` method on `res` when the control exits the `try` block. You can specify more than one resource in the `try` block, each separated by a semicolon:

```
try (Resource res1 = new Resource(); Resource res2 = new Resource()) {
    // Work with res1 and res2 here
}
```

The `close()` method on both resources, `res1` and `res2`, will be called automatically when the `try` block exits. Resources are closed in reverse order in which they are specified. In this example, `res2.close()` and `res1.close()` will be called in order.

JDK 7 and 8 require you to declare the variable referencing the resource in the `try-with-resources` block. If you received a resource reference as an argument in a method, you will not be able to write your logic like this:

```
void useIt(Resource res) {
    // A compile-time error in JDK 7 and 8
    try(res) {
        // Work with res here
    }
}
```

To circumvent this restriction, you had to declare another fresh variable of the resource type and initialize it with your argument value. The following snippet of code shows this approach. It declares a new reference variable called `res1` on which the `close()` method will be called when the `try` block exits:

```
void useIt(Resource res) {
    try(Resource res1 = res) {
        // Work with res1 here
    }
}
```

JDK 9 removed the restriction that you must declare fresh variables for resources that you want to manage using a try-with-resource block. Now, you can use a *final* or *effectively final* variable that references a resource to be managed by a try-with-resources block. A variable is final if it is explicitly declared using the final keyword:

```
// res is explicitly final
final Resource res = new Resource();
```

A variable is effectively final if its value is never changed after it is initialized. In the following snippet of code, the res variable is effectively final even though it is not declared final. It is initialized and is never changed again.

```
void doSomething() {
    // res is effectively final
    Resource res = new Resource();

    res.useMe();
}
```

In JDK 9, you can write something like this:

```
Resource res = new Resource();
try (res) {
    // Work with res here
}
```

If you have multiple resources that you want to manage using a try-with-resources block, you can do it like this:

```
Resource res1 = new Resource();
Resource res2 = new Resource();

try (res1; res2) {
    // Use res1 and res2 here
}
```

You can mix JDK 8 and JDK 9 approaches in the same try-with-resources block. The following snippet of code uses two predeclared effectively final variables and one freshly declared variable in a try-with-resources block:

```
Resource res1 = new Resource();
Resource res2 = new Resource();

try (res1; res2; Resource res3 = new Resource()) {
    // Use res1, res2, and res3 here
}
```

Since JDK 7, variables declared inside a try-with-resource block are implicitly final. The following snippet of code explicitly declares such a variable final:

```
Resource res1 = new Resource();
Resource res2 = new Resource();

// Declare res3 explicitly final
try (res1; res2; final Resource res3 = new Resource()) {
    // Use res1, res2, and res3 here
}
```

Let's look at a complete example. There are several classes in the JDK that are AutoCloseable, such as the InputStream and OutputStream classes in the java.io package. Listing 20-3 contains the code for a Resource class that implements the AutoCloseable interface. Objects of the Resource class can be used as resources to be managed by try-with-resources blocks. The id instance variable is used to track the resources. The constructor and other methods simply print a message when they are called.

Listing 20-3. A Resource Class That Implements the AutoCloseable Interface

```
// Resource.java
package com.jdojo.misc;

public class Resource implements AutoCloseable {
    private final long id;

    public Resource(long id) {
        this.id = id;
        System.out.printf("Created resource %d.%n", this.id);
    }

    public void useIt() {
        System.out.printf("Using resource %d.%n", this.id);
    }

    @Override
    public void close() {
        System.out.printf("Closing resource %d.%n", this.id);
    }
}
```

Listing 20-4 contains the code for a ResourceTest class that shows you how to use the new feature of JDK 9 that lets you manage resources using try-with-resources blocks using final or effectively final variables that reference those resources.

Listing 20-4. A ResourceTest Class to Demonstrate the Use of try-catch Blocks in JDK 9

```java
// ResourceTest.java
package com.jdojo.misc;

public class ResourceTest {
    public static void main(String[] args) {
        Resource r1 = new Resource(1);
        Resource r2 = new Resource(2);

        try(r1; r2) {
            r1.useIt();
            r2.useIt();
            r2.useIt();
        }

        useResource(new Resource(3));
    }

    public static void useResource(Resource res) {
        try(res; Resource res4 = new Resource(4)) {
            res.useIt();
            res4.useIt();
        }
    }
}
```

```
Created resource 1.
Created resource 2.
Using resource 1.
Using resource 2.
Using resource 2.
Closing resource 2.
Closing resource 1.
Created resource 3.
Created resource 4.
Using resource 3.
Using resource 4.
Closing resource 4.
Closing resource 3.
```

Diamond Operator in Anonymous Classes

JDK 7 introduced the diamond operator (<>), which is used in calling the constructor of a generic class as long as the compiler can infer the generic type. The following two statements are the same; the second uses a diamond operator:

```
// Specify the generic type explicitly
List<String> list1 = new ArrayList<String>();

// The compiler infers ArrayList<> as ArrayList<String>
List<String> list2 = new ArrayList<>();
```

JDK 7 did not allow using the diamond operator while creating an anonymous class. The following snippet of code uses an anonymous class with a diamond operator to create an instance of the Callable<V> interface:

```
// A compile-time error in JDK 7 and 8
Callable<Integer> c = new Callable<>() {
    @Override
    public Integer call() {
        return 100;
    }
};
```

The previous statement generates the following error in JDK 7 and 8:

```
error: cannot infer type arguments for Callable<V>
        Callable<Integer> c = new Callable<>() {
                                          ^
  reason: cannot use '<>' with anonymous inner classes
  where V is a type-variable:
    V extends Object declared in interface Callable
1 error
```

You can fix this error by specifying the generic type in place of the diamond operator:

```
// Works in JDK 7 and 8
Callable<Integer> c = new Callable<Integer>() {
    @Override
    public Integer call() {
        return 100;
    }
};
```

JDK 9 added support for the diamond operator in anonymous classes as long as the inferred types are denotable. You cannot use the diamond operator with anonymous classes—even in JDK 9—if the inferred types are non-denotable. The Java compiler uses a many types that cannot be written in Java programs. Types that can be written in Java programs are known as *denotable* types. Types that the compiler knows but cannot be written in Java programs are known as *non-denotable* types. For example, String is a denotable type because you can use it in programs to denote a type; however, Serializable & CharSequence is not a denotable-type, even though it is a valid type for the compiler. It is an intersection type that represents a type that implements both interfaces, Serializable and CharSequence. Intersection types are allowed in generic type definitions, but you cannot declare a variable using this intersection type:

```java
// Not allowed in Java code. Cannot declare a variable of an intersection type.
Serializable & CharSequence var;

// Allowed in Java code
class Magic<T extends Serializable & CharSequence> {
    // More code goes here
}
```

In JDK 9, the following snippet of code, which uses the diamond operator with an anonymous class, is allowed:

```java
// A compile-time error in JDK 7 and 8, but allowed in JDK 9.
Callable<Integer> c = new Callable<>() {
    @Override
    public Integer call() {
        return 100;
    }
};
```

Using this definition of the Magic class, JDK 9 allows you to use an anonymous class like so:

```java
// Allowed in JDK 9. The <> is inferred as <String>.
Magic<String> m1 = new Magic<>(){
    // More code goes here
};
```

The following use of the Magic class does not compile in JDK 9 because the compiler infers the generic type to an intersection type that is a non-denotable type:

```java
// A compile-time error in JDK 9. The <> is inferred as <Serializable & CharSequence>,
// which is non-denotable
Magic<?> m2 = new Magic<>(){
    // More code goes here
};
```

The previous code generates the following compile-time error:

```
error: cannot infer type arguments for Magic<>
        Magic<?> m2 = new Magic<>(){
                          ^
  reason: type argument INT#1 inferred for Magic<> is not allowed in this context
    inferred argument is not expressible in the Signature attribute
  where INT#1 is an intersection type:
    INT#1 extends Object,Serializable,CharSequence
1 error
```

Private Methods in Interfaces

JDK 8 introduced static and default methods to interfaces. If you had to perform the same logic multiple times in these methods, you had no choice but to repeat the logic or move the logic to another class to hide the implementation. Consider the interface named Alphabet, as shown in Listing 20-5.

Listing 20-5. An Interface Named Alphabet Having Two Default Methods Sharing Logic

```java
// Alphabet.java
package com.jdojo.misc;

public interface Alphabet {
    default boolean isAtOddPos(char c) {
        if (!Character.isLetter(c)) {
            throw new RuntimeException("Not a letter: " + c);
        }

        char uc = Character.toUpperCase(c);
        int pos = uc - 64;

        return pos % 2 == 1;
    }

    default boolean isAtEvenPos(char c) {
        if (!Character.isLetter(c)) {
            throw new RuntimeException("Not a letter: " + c);
        }

        char uc = Character.toUpperCase(c);
        int pos = uc - 64;

        return pos % 2 == 0;
    }
}
```

The isAtOddpos() and isAtEvenPos() methods check if the specified character is at odd or even position alphabetically, assuming we are dealing with only English alphabets. The logic assumes that A and a are at position 1, B and b are at position 2, etc. Notice that the logic in two methods differ only in the return statements. The entire body of these methods is identical, except for the last statements. You would agree that you need to refactor this logic. Moving the common logic to another method and calling the new method from both methods would be the ideal case. However, you don't want to do this in JDK 8 because interfaces support only public methods. Doing so will make the third method public, which will expose it to the outside world, which you don't want to do.

JDK 9 is to your rescue. It lets you declare private methods in interfaces. Listing 20-6 shows the refactored version of the Alphabet interface using a private method that contains the common logic used by the two methods. This time, I named the interface AlphabetJdk9 just to make sure I can include both versions in the source code. The two existing methods become one-liners.

Listing 20-6. An Interface Named AlphabetJdk9 That Uses a Private Method

```
// AlphabetJdk9.java
package com.jdojo.misc;

public interface AlphabetJdk9 {
    default boolean isAtOddPos(char c) {
        return getPos(c) % 2 == 1;
    }

    default boolean isAtEvenPos(char c) {
        return getPos(c) % 2 == 0;
    }

    private int getPos(char c) {
        if (!Character.isLetter(c)) {
            throw new RuntimeException("Not a letter: " + c);
        }

        char uc = Character.toUpperCase(c);
        int pos = uc - 64;

        return pos;
    }
}
```

Before JDK 9, all methods in an interface used to be implicitly public. Remember these simple rules that apply to all programs in Java:

- A private method is not inherited and, therefore, cannot be overridden.

- A final method cannot be overridden.

- An abstract method is inherited and is meant to be overridden.

- A default method is an instance method and provides a default implementation. It is meant to be overridden.

With the introduction of private methods in JDK 9, you need to follow a few rules while declaring methods in an interface. All combinations of modifiers—abstract, public, private, static, and final—are not supported because they do not make sense. Table 20-1 lists a combination of modifiers supported and not supported in method declarations of interfaces in JDK 9. Note that the final modifier is not allowed in method declarations for interfaces. According to this list, you can have a private method in an interface that is either a non-abstract, non-default instance method, or a static method.

Table 20-1. *Supported Modifiers in Method Declarations in Interfaces*

Modifiers	Supported?	Description
public static	Yes	Supported since JDK 8.
public abstract	Yes	Supported since JDK 1.
public default	Yes	Supported since JDK 8.
private static	Yes	Supported since JDK 9.
private	Yes	Supported since JDK 9. This is a non-abstract instance method.
private abstract	No	This combination does not make sense. A private method is not inherited, so it cannot be overridden, whereas an abstract method must be overridden to be useful.
private default	No	This combination does not make sense. A private method is not inherited, so it cannot be overridden, whereas a default method is meant to be overridden, if needed.

@SafeVarargs on Private Methods

A *reifiable* type is a type whose information is fully available at runtime such as String, Integer, List, etc. A *non-reifiable* type is a type whose information has been removed by the compiler using type erasure such as List<String>, which becomes List after compilation.

When you use a var-args argument of the non-reifiable type, the type of the argument makes it only to the compiler. The compiler erases the parameterized type and replaces it with an array of an actual type—Object[] for an unbounded types and a specific array whose type is the upper bound for a bounded type. The compiler cannot guarantee the operations performed on such non-reifiable var-args argument inside the method's body is safe. Consider the following definition of a method:

```
<T> void print(T... args) {
    for(T element : args) {
        System.out.println(element);
    }
}
```

The compiler will replace print(T... args) with print(Object[] args). This method's body does not perform any unsafe operation on the args argument. Consider the following method declaration that performs an unsafe operation:

```
public static void unsafe(List<Long>... rolls) {
    Object[] list = rolls;
    list[0] = List.of("One", "Two");

    // Unsafe!!! Will throw a ClassCastException at runtime
    Long roll = rolls[0].get(0);
}
```

The `unsafe()` method assigns the `rolls`, which is an array of `List<String>`, to an `Object[]`, which is fine. It stores a `List<String>` into the first element of the `Object[]`, which is also permitted. The last statement compiles fine because the type of `rolls[0]` is inferred as `List<Long>` and the `get(0)` method is supposed to return a `Long`. However, the runtime throws a `ClassCastException` because the actual type returned by `rolls[0].get(0)` is a `String`, not a `Long`.

When you declare methods like `print()` and `unsafe()` that use a non-reifiable var-args argument type, the Java compiler emits an unchecked warning like this:

```
warning: [unchecked] Possible heap pollution from parameterized vararg type List<Long>
    public static void unsafe(List<Long>... rolls) {
                                            ^
```

The compiler generates a warning for such method declaration and a warning for each call to the method. If the `unsafe()` method is called five times, you will receive six warnings (one for declaration and five for the calls). You can suppress these warnings at method declarations and call sites by using a `@SafeVarargs` annotation on such methods. By adding this annotation to the method declaration, you are assuring the method's users and the compiler that, in the method's body, you are not performing any unsafe operations on the non-reifiable var-args argument. Your assurance is good enough for the compiler not to issue the warning. However, if your assurance proves to be untrue at runtime, the runtime will throw an appropriate type of exception.

Before JDK 9, you could use the `@SafeVarargs` annotation on the following executables (constructors and methods):

- Constructors

- Static methods

- Final methods

Constructors, static methods, and final methods are non-overridable. The idea behind allowing the `@SafeVarargs` annotation only on non-overridable executables was to safeguard against developers using this annotation on an overridden executable that violates the annotation's constraint on the overridden executable. Suppose that you have a class X, which contains a method `m1()`, which contains a `@SafeVarargs`. Further suppose that you have a class Y that inherits from class X. Class Y may override the inherited method `m1()` and may have unsafe operations. This will have runtime surprises because developers may write code in terms of the superclass X and may not expect any unsafe operation as promised by its method `m1()`.

A private method is also non-overridable, so JDK 9 decided to allow the `@SafeVarargs` annotation also on private methods. Listing 20-7 shows a class with a private method using a `@SafeVarargs` annotation. The new list of executables that can have a `@SafeVarargs` annotation in JDK 9 is as follows:

- Constructors

- Static methods

- Final methods

- Private methods

Listing 20-7. Using the @SafeVarargs Annotation on a Private Method in JDK 9

```java
// SafeVarargsTest.java
package com.jdojo.misc;

public class SafeVarargsTest {
    // Allowed in JDK 9
    @SafeVarargs
    private <T> void print(T... args) {
        for(T element : args) {
            System.out.println(element);
        }
    }

    // More code goes here
}
```

Compiling this class in JDK 8 generates the following error, which states that the @SafeVarargs cannot be used on a non-final method, which is a private method in this case. You need to compile the source code using the -Xlint:unchecked option to see the errors.

```
com\jdojo\misc\SafeVarargsTest.java:6: error: Invalid SafeVarargs annotation. Instance
method <T> print(T...) is not final.
    private <T> void print(T... args) {
                     ^
  where T is a type-variable:
    T extends Object declared in method <T>print(T...)
```

Discarding Process Outputs

JDK 9 added a new constant named DISCARD to the ProcessBuilder.Redirect nested class. Its type is ProcessBuilder.Redirect. You can use this as a destination for output and error streams of sub-processes when you want to discard the outputs. Implementation discards the outputs by writing to an operating system specific "null file". Listing 20-8 contains a complete program that shows how to discard a sub-process' outputs.

Listing 20-8. Discarding a Process' Outputs

```java
// DiscardProcessOutput.java
package com.jdojo.misc;

import java.io.IOException;

public class DiscardProcessOutput {
    public static void main(String[] args) {
        System.out.println("Using Redirect.INHERIT:");
        startProcess(ProcessBuilder.Redirect.INHERIT);

        System.out.println("\nUsing Redirect.DISCARD:");
        startProcess(ProcessBuilder.Redirect.DISCARD);
    }
```

```
    public static void startProcess(ProcessBuilder.Redirect outputDest) {
        try {
            ProcessBuilder pb = new ProcessBuilder()
                    .command("java", "-version")
                    .redirectOutput(outputDest)
                    .redirectError(outputDest);

            Process process = pb.start();
            process.waitFor();
        } catch (IOException | InterruptedException e) {
            e.printStackTrace();
        }
    }
}
```

```
Using Redirect.INHERIT:
java version "9-ea"
Java(TM) SE Runtime Environment (build 9-ea+157)
Java HotSpot(TM) 64-Bit Server VM (build 9-ea+157, mixed mode)
Using Redirect.DISCARD:
```

The startProcess() method starts a process by launching the java program with the -version argument. The method is passed an output destination. The first time, the Redirect.INHERIT is passed as the output destination, which allows the sub-process to use the standard output and standard error to print messages. The second time, Redirect.DISCARD is passed as the output destination and there is no output from the sub-process.

New Methods in the StrictMath Class

The JDK contains two classes, Math and StrictMath, in the java.lang package. Both classes consist of only static members and they contain methods to provide basic numeric operations such as square root, absolute, sign, trigonometric functions, and hyperbolic functions. Why do we have two classes to provide similar operations? The Math class is not required to return the same results in all implementations. This allows it to use native implementations of libraries for operations, which may return slightly different results on different platforms. The StrictMath class is required to return the same results in all implementations. Many methods in the Math class call the methods of the StrictMath class. JDK 9 added the following static methods to the Math and StrictMath classes:

- long floorDiv(long x, int y)
- int floorMod(long x, int y)
- double fma(double x, double y, double z)
- float fma(float x, float y, float z)
- long multiplyExact(long x, int y)
- long multiplyFull(int x, int y)
- long multiplyHigh(long x, long y)

The floorDiv() method returns the largest long value that is less than or equal to the algebraic quotient of dividing x by y. When both arguments have the same sign, the division result is rounded toward zero (truncation mode). When they have different signs, the division result is rounded toward negative infinity. When the dividend is the Long.MIN_VALUE and the divisor is -1, the method returns Long.MIN_VALUE. An ArithmeticException is thrown when the divisor is zero.

The floorMod() method returns floor modulus, which is equal to

```
x - (floorDiv(x, y) * y)
```

The sign of the floor modulus is the same sign as the divisor y, and is in the range of

```
-abs(y) < r < +abs(y).
```

The fma() methods correspond to the fusedMultiplyAdd operation defined in IEEE 754-2008. It returns the result of (a * b + c) as if with unlimited range and precision, and rounded once to the nearest double/float value. The rounding is done using the round to nearest even rounding mode. Note that the fma() method returns a more accurate result than the expression (a * b + c) because the latter involves two rounding errors—one for multiplication and one for addition—whereas the former involves only one rounding error.

The multiplyExact() method returns the product of the two arguments throwing an ArithmeticException if the result overflows a long.

The multiplyFull() method returns the exact product of the two arguments as a long.

The multiplyHigh() method returns as a long the most significant 64 bits of the 128-bit product of two 64-bit arguments. When you multiply two 64-bit long values, the result could be a 128-bit value. This method returns the most significant (high) 64 bits as a result. Listing 20-9 contains a complete program to demonstrate the use of these new methods in the StrictMath class.

Listing 20-9. A StrictMathTest Class That Demonstrates the Use of the New Methods in the StrictMath Class

```java
// StrictMathTest.java
package com.jdojo.misc;

import static java.lang.StrictMath.*;

public class StrictMathTest {
    public static void main(String[] args) {
        System.out.println("Using StrictMath.floorDiv(long, int):");
        System.out.printf("floorDiv(20L, 3) = %d%n", floorDiv(20L, 3));
        System.out.printf("floorDiv(-20L, -3) = %d%n", floorDiv(-20L, -3));
        System.out.printf("floorDiv(-20L, 3) = %d%n", floorDiv(-20L, 3));
        System.out.printf("floorDiv(Long.Min_VALUE, -1) = %d%n", floorDiv(Long.MIN_VALUE, -1));

        System.out.println("\nUsing StrictMath.floorMod(long, int):");
        System.out.printf("floorMod(20L, 3) = %d%n", floorMod(20L, 3));
        System.out.printf("floorMod(-20L, -3) = %d%n", floorMod(-20L, -3));
        System.out.printf("floorMod(-20L, 3) = %d%n", floorMod(-20L, 3));

        System.out.println("\nUsing StrictMath.fma(double, double, double):");
        System.out.printf("fma(3.337, 6.397, 2.789) = %f%n", fma(3.337, 6.397, 2.789));
```

```
        System.out.println("\nUsing StrictMath.multiplyExact(long, int):");
        System.out.printf("multiplyExact(29087L, 7897979) = %d%n",
                multiplyExact(29087L, 7897979));
        try {
            System.out.printf("multiplyExact(Long.MAX_VALUE, 5) = %d%n",
                    multiplyExact(Long.MAX_VALUE, 5));
        } catch (ArithmeticException e) {
            System.out.println("multiplyExact(Long.MAX_VALUE, 5) = " + e.getMessage());
        }

        System.out.println("\nUsing StrictMath.multiplyFull(int, int):");
        System.out.printf("multiplyFull(29087, 7897979) = %d%n", multiplyFull(29087, 7897979));

        System.out.println("\nUsing StrictMath.multiplyHigh(long, long):");
        System.out.printf("multiplyHigh(29087L, 7897979L) = %d%n",
                multiplyHigh(29087L, 7897979L));
        System.out.printf("multiplyHigh(Long.MAX_VALUE, 8) = %d%n",
                multiplyHigh(Long.MAX_VALUE, 8));
    }
}
```

```
Using StrictMath.floorDiv(long, int):
floorDiv(20L, 3) = 6
floorDiv(-20L, -3) = 6
floorDiv(-20L, 3) = -7
floorDiv(Long.Min_VALUE, -1) = -9223372036854775808

Using StrictMath.floorMod(long, int):
floorMod(20L, 3) = 2
floorMod(-20L, -3) = -2
floorMod(-20L, 3) = 1

Using StrictMath.fma(double, double, double):
fma(3.337, 6.397, 2.789) = 24.135789

Using StrictMath.multiplyExact(long, int):
multiplyExact(29087L, 7897979) = 229728515173
multiplyExact(Long.MAX_VALUE, 5) = long overflow

Using StrictMath.multiplyFull(int, int):
multiplyFull(29087, 7897979) = 229728515173

Using StrictMath.multiplyHigh(long, long):
multiplyHigh(29087L, 7897979L) = 0
multiplyHigh(Long.MAX_VALUE, 8) = 3
```

Changes to the ClassLoader Class

JDK 9 added the following constructor and methods to the java.lang.ClassLoader class:

- protected ClassLoader(String name, ClassLoader parent)

- public String getName()

- protected Class<?> findClass(String moduleName, String name)

- protected URL findResource(String moduleName, String name) throws IOException

- public Stream<URL> resources(String name)

- public final boolean isRegisteredAsParallelCapable()

- public final Module getUnnamedModule()

- public static ClassLoader getPlatformClassLoader()

- public final Package getDefinedPackage(String name)

- public final Package[] getDefinedPackages()

These methods have intuitive names. I do not discuss all these methods in this section. Refer to the API documentation for the description of these methods. The protected constructor and methods are meant for developers creating new class loaders.

A class loader can have an optional name, which you can get using the getName() method. The method returns null when class loader does not have a name. The Java runtime will include the class loader names, if present, in the stack trace and exception messages. This will be helpful in debugging.

The resources() method returns a stream of URLs of all resources found with the specific resource name.

Every class loader contains an unnamed module that contains all types loaded by this class loader from the class path. The getUnnamedModule() method returns the reference of the unnamed module of the class loader.

The static getPlatformClassLoader() method returns the reference of the platform class loader.

New Methods in the Optional<T> Class

The java.util.Optional<T> class has received three new methods in JDK 9:

- void ifPresentOrElse(Consumer<? super T> action, Runnable emptyAction)

- Optional<T> or(Supplier<? extends Optional<? extends T>> supplier)

- Stream<T> stream()

Before I describe these methods and present a complete program showing their use, consider the following list of Optional<Integer>:

```
List<Optional<Integer>> optionalList = List.of(Optional.of(1),
                                               Optional.empty(),
                                               Optional.of(2),
                                               Optional.empty(),
                                               Optional.of(3));
```

The list contains five elements, two of which are empty Optional and three contain values as 1, 2, and 3. I refer to this list in the subsequent discussion.

The `ifPresentOrElse()` method lets you provide two alternate courses of actions. If a value is present, it performs the specified `action` with the value. Otherwise, it performs the specified `emptyAction`. The following snippet of code iterates all the elements in the list using a stream to print the value if `Optional` contains a value and an "Empty" string if `Optional` is empty:

```
optionalList.stream()
        .forEach(p -> p.ifPresentOrElse(System.out::println,
                                        () -> System.out.println("Empty")));
```

```
1
Empty
2
Empty
3
```

The `or()` method returns the `Optional` itself if it contains the value. Otherwise, it returns the `Optional` returned by the specified `supplier`. The following snippet of code creates a stream from a list of `Optional` and uses the `or()` method to map all empty `Optionals` to an `Optional` with a value of zero.

```
optionalList.stream()
        .map(p -> p.or(() -> Optional.of(0)))
        .forEach(System.out::println);
```

```
Optional[1]
Optional[0]
Optional[2]
Optional[0]
Optional[3]
```

The `stream()` method returns a sequential stream of elements containing the value present in the `Optional`. If the `Optional` is empty, it returns an empty stream. Suppose you have a list of `Optional` and you want to collect all present values in another list. You can achieve this in Java 8 as follows:

```
// list8 will contain 1, 2, and 3
List<Integer> list8 = optionalList.stream()
                            .filter(Optional::isPresent)
                            .map(Optional::get)
                            .collect(toList());
```

You had to use a filter to filter out all empty `Optionals` and map the remaining `Optionals` to their values. With the new `stream()` method in JDK 9, you can combine the `filter()` and `map()` operations into one `flatMap()` operation as shown:

```
// list9 contain 1, 2, and 3
List<Integer> list9 = optionalList.stream()
                            .flatMap(Optional::stream)
                            .collect(toList());
```

Listing 20-10 contains a complete program to demonstrate the use of these methods.

Listing 20-10. Using the New Methods Added to the Optional Class in JDK 9

```java
// OptionalTest.java
package com.jdojo.misc;

import java.util.List;
import java.util.Optional;
import static java.util.stream.Collectors.toList;

public class OptionalTest {
    public static void main(String[] args) {
        // Create a list of Optional<Integer>
        List<Optional<Integer>> optionalList = List.of(
                Optional.of(1),
                Optional.empty(),
                Optional.of(2),
                Optional.empty(),
                Optional.of(3));

        // Print the original list
        System.out.println("Original List: " + optionalList);

        // Using the ifPresentOrElse() method
        optionalList.stream()
                    .forEach(p -> p.ifPresentOrElse(System.out::println,
                                                () -> System.out.println("Empty")));
        // Using the or() method
        optionalList.stream()
                    .map(p -> p.or(() -> Optional.of(0)))
                    .forEach(System.out::println);

        // In Java 8
        List<Integer> list8 = optionalList.stream()
                                    .filter(Optional::isPresent)
                                    .map(Optional::get)
                                    .collect(toList());
        System.out.println("List in Java 8: " + list8);

        // In Java 9
        List<Integer> list9 = optionalList.stream()
                                    .flatMap(Optional::stream)
                                    .collect(toList());
        System.out.println("List in Java 9: " + list9);
    }
}
```

```
Original List: [Optional[1], Optional.empty, Optional[2], Optional.empty, Optional[3]]
1
Empty
2
Empty
3
Optional[1]
Optional[0]
Optional[2]
Optional[0]
Optional[3]
List in Java 8: [1, 2, 3]
List in Java 9: [1, 2, 3]
```

Additions to the CompletableFuture<T> Class

The CompletableFuture<T> class, which is in the java.util.concurrent package, has received the following new methods in JDK 9:

- `<U> CompletableFuture<U> newIncompleteFuture()`

- `Executor defaultExecutor()`

- `CompletableFuture<T> copy()`

- `CompletionStage<T> minimalCompletionStage()`

- `CompletableFuture<T> completeAsync(Supplier<? extends T> supplier, Executor executor)`

- `CompletableFuture<T> completeAsync(Supplier<? extends T> supplier)`

- `CompletableFuture<T> orTimeout(long timeout, TimeUnit unit)`

- `CompletableFuture<T> completeOnTimeout(T value, long timeout, TimeUnit unit)`

- `static Executor delayedExecutor(long delay, TimeUnit unit, Executor executor)`

- `static Executor delayedExecutor(long delay, TimeUnit unit)`

- `static <U> CompletionStage<U> completedStage(U value)`

- `static <U> CompletableFuture<U> failedFuture(Throwable ex)`

- `static <U> CompletionStage<U> failedStage(Throwable ex)`

Consult the Javadoc for the class for more information about these methods.

Spin-Wait Hints

In a multi-threaded program, threads often need to coordinate. One thread may have to wait for another thread to update a volatile variable. When the volatile variable is updated with a certain value, the first thread may proceed. If the wait could be longer, it is suggested that the first thread relinquish the CPU by sleeping or waiting and it be notified when it can resume work. However, making a thread sleep or wait has latency. For a short time wait and to reduce latency, it is common for a thread to wait in a loop by checking for a certain condition to be true. Consider code in a class that uses a loop to wait for a volatile variable named dataReady to be true:

```
volatile boolean dataReady;
...

@Override
public void run() {
    // Wait until data is ready
    while (!dataReady) {
        // No code
    }

    processData();
}

private void processData() {
    // Data processing logic goes here
}
```

The while loop in this code is called a spin-loop, busy-spin, busy-wait, or spin-wait. The while loop keeps looping until the dataReady variable is true.

While spin-wait is discouraged because of its unnecessary use of resources, it is commonly needed. In this example, the advantage is that the thread will start processing data as soon as the dataReady variable becomes true. However, you pay for performance and power consumption because the thread is actively looping.

Certain processors can be hinted that a thread is in a spin-wait and, if possible, can optimize the resource usage. For example, x86 processors support a PAUSE instruction to indicate a spin-wait. The instruction delays the execution of the next instruction for the thread for a finite small amount of time, thus improving resource usage.

JDK 9 added a new static onSpinWait() method to the Thread class. It is a pure hint to the processor that the caller thread is momentarily not able to proceed, so resource usage can be optimized. A possible implementation of this method may be no-op when the underlying platform does not support such hints.

Listing 20-11 contains sample code. Note that your program's semantics do not change by using a spin-wait hint. It may perform better if the underlying hardware supports the hint.

Listing 20-11. Sample Code for Using a Spin-Wait Hint to the Processor Using the Static Thread. onSpinWait() Method

```java
// SpinWaitTest.java
package com.jdojo.misc;

public class SpinWaitTest implements Runnable {
    private volatile boolean dataReady = false;

    @Override
    public void run() {
        // Wait while data is ready
        while (!dataReady) {
            // Hint a spin-wait
            Thread.onSpinWait();
        }

        processData();
    }

    private void processData() {
        // Data processing logic goes here
    }

    public void setDataReady(boolean dataReady) {
        this.dataReady = dataReady;
    }
}
```

Enhancements to the Time API

The Time API has been enhanced in JDK 9 with a lot of new methods in several interfaces and classes. It is not possible to explain all the enhancements. I list the new methods by interfaces and classes with brief descriptions. If the new method is complex, I provide examples. The Time API consists of java.time.* packages, which are in the java.base module.

I use snippets of code for examples in this section. You can find the complete program for this section in the com.jdojo.misc.TimeApiTest class in the com.jdojo.misc module in the book's source code. Many examples print the current date and time. You may get a different output when you run those examples.

The Clock Class

The following method has been added to the Clock class:

```java
static Clock tickMillis(ZoneId zone)
```

The tickMillis() method returns a clock that provides current instant ticking in whole milliseconds. The clock uses the best available system clock. The clock truncates the time value at a precision higher than milliseconds. Calling this method is equivalent to the following:

```java
Clock.tick(Clock.system(zone), Duration.ofMillis(1))
```

The Duration Class

You can divide new methods in the Duration class into three categories based on their use:

- Methods to divide a duration by another duration

- Methods to get a duration in terms of a specific time unit and methods to get a specific part of a duration such as days, hours, seconds, etc.

- Methods to truncate a duration to a specific time unit

I use a duration of 23 days, 3 hours, 45 minutes, and 30 seconds. The following snippet of code creates this as a Duration object and stores its reference in a variable named compTime:

```
// Create a duration of 23 days, 3 hours, 45 minutes, and 30 seconds
Duration compTime = Duration.ofDays(23)
                            .plusHours(3)
                            .plusMinutes(45)
                            .plusSeconds(30);
System.out.println("Duration: " + compTime);
```

```
Duration: PT555H45M30S
```

After the days are converted to hours by multiplying them by 24, as the output shows, this duration represents 555 hours, 45 minutes, and 30 seconds.

Dividing a Duration by Another Duration

There is only one method in this category:

```
long dividedBy(Duration divisor)
```

The dividedBy() method lets you divide a duration by another duration. It returns the number of times the specific divisor occurs within the duration on which the method is called. To know how many whole weeks are in this duration, you call the dividedBy() method using seven days as the duration. The following snippet of code shows you how to compute number of whole days, weeks, and hours in a duration:

```
long wholeDays = compTime.dividedBy(Duration.ofDays(1));
long wholeWeeks = compTime.dividedBy(Duration.ofDays(7));
long wholeHours = compTime.dividedBy(Duration.ofHours(7));

System.out.println("Number of whole days: " + wholeDays);
System.out.println("Number of whole weeks: " + wholeWeeks);
System.out.println("Number of whole hours: " + wholeHours);
```

```
Number of whole days: 23
Number of whole weeks: 3
Number of whole hours: 79
```

Converting and Retrieving Duration Parts

There are several methods added to the Duration class in this category:

- long toDaysPart()

- int toHoursPart()

- int toMillisPart()

- int toMinutesPart()

- int toNanosPart()

- long toSeconds()

- int toSecondsPart()

The Duration class contains two sets of methods. They are named toXxx() and toXxxPart(), where Xxx may be Days, Hours, Minutes, Seconds, Millis, and Nanos. In this list, you may notice that toDaysPart() is included, but toDays() is missing. If you see methods in one set missing for some Xxx, it means those methods already existed in JDK 8. For example, the toDays() method has been in the Duration class since JDK 8.

Methods named toXxx() convert the duration to the Xxx time unit and return the whole part. Methods named toXxxPart() break down the duration in parts as days:hours:minutes:seconds:milils:nanos and return the Xxx part from it. In this example, toDays() will convert the duration to days and return the whole part, which will be 23. The toDaysPart() will break down the duration to 23Days:3Hours:45Minutes:30Seconds:0Millis:0Nanos and return the first part, which is 23. Let's apply the same rules to toHours() and toHoursPart() methods. The toHours() method will convert the duration to hours and return the whole number of hours, which will be 555. The toHoursPart() method will break the duration into parts as it did for the toDaysPart() method and return the hours part, which is 3. The following snippet of code shows you a few examples:

```
System.out.println("toDays(): " + compTime.toDays());
System.out.println("toDaysPart(): " + compTime.toDaysPart());
System.out.println("toHours(): " + compTime.toHours());
System.out.println("toHoursPart(): " + compTime.toHoursPart());
System.out.println("toMinutes(): " + compTime.toMinutes());
System.out.println("toMinutesPart(): " + compTime.toMinutesPart());
```

```
toDays(): 23
toDaysPart(): 23
toHours(): 555
toHoursPart(): 3
toMinutes(): 33345
toMinutesPart(): 45
```

Truncating Duration

There is only one method added to the Duration class in this category:

```
Duration truncatedTo(TemporalUnit unit)
```

The truncatedTo() method returns a copy of the duration with conceptual time units smaller than the specified unit truncated. The temporal unit specified must be DAYS or smaller. Specifying a temporal unit greater than DAYS such as WEEKS and YEARS throws a runtime exception.

▓ **Tip** A truncatedTo(TemporalUnit unit) method already existed in the LocalTime and Instant classes in JDK 8.

The following snippet of code shows you how to use this method:

```
System.out.println("Truncated to DAYS: " + compTime.truncatedTo(ChronoUnit.DAYS));
System.out.println("Truncated to HOURS: " + compTime.truncatedTo(ChronoUnit.HOURS));
System.out.println("Truncated to MINUTES: " + compTime.truncatedTo(ChronoUnit.MINUTES));
```

```
Truncated to DAYS: PT552H
Truncated to HOURS: PT555H
Truncated to MINUTES: PT555H45M
```

The duration is 23Days:3Hours:45Minutes:30Seconds:0Millis:0Nanos. When you truncate this to DAYS, all parts smaller than days are dropped and it returns 23 days, which is the same as 552, hours as shown in the output. When you truncate to HOURS, it drops all parts smaller than hours and returns 555 hours. Truncating it to MINUTES keeps parts up to minutes and drops all smaller parts such as seconds and milliseconds.

The ofInstant() Factory Method

The Time API is all about efficiency and the developer's convenience. There were a few frequently used use-cases where conversion between date and time types forced developers to use more methods calls than necessary. Two such use-cases were:

- Converting a java.util.Date to a LocalDate
- Converting an Instant to LocalDate and LocalTime

JDK 9 added a static factory method, ofInstant(Instant instant, ZoneId zone), to the LocalDate and LocalTime classes to ease these two types of conversions. JDK 8 already had this factory method in the ZonedDateTime, OffsetDateTime, LocalDateTime, and OffsetTime classes. The following snippet of code shows both ways—JDK 8 and JDK 9—to convert a java.util.Date to a LocalDate:

```
// In JDK 8
Date dt = new Date();
LocalDate ld= dt.toInstant()
               .atZone(ZoneId.systemDefault())
               .toLocalDate();
System.out.println("Current Local Date: " + ld);

// In JDK 9
LocalDate ld2 = LocalDate.ofInstant(dt.toInstant(), ZoneId.systemDefault());
System.out.println("Current Local Date: " + ld2);
```

```
Current Local Date: 2017-02-11
Current Local Date: 2017-02-11
```

The following snippet of code shows both ways—JDK 8 and JDK 9—to convert an Instant to a LocalDate and a LocalTime:

```
// In JDK 8
Instant now = Instant.now();
ZoneId zone = ZoneId.systemDefault();
ZonedDateTime zdt = now.atZone(zone);
LocalDate ld3 = zdt.toLocalDate();
LocalTime lt3 = zdt.toLocalTime();
System.out.println("Local Date: " + ld3 + ", Local Time:" + lt3);

// In JDK 9
LocalDate ld4 = LocalDate.ofInstant(now, zone);
LocalTime lt4 = LocalTime.ofInstant(now, zone);
System.out.println("Local Date: " + ld4 + ", Local Time:" + lt4);
```

```
Local Date: 2017-02-11, Local Time:22:13:31.919339400
Local Date: 2017-02-11, Local Time:22:13:31.919339400
```

Obtaining Epoch Seconds

There are times when you want to get the number of seconds since the epoch 1970-01-01T00:00:00Z from a LocalDate, LocalTime, and an OffsetTime. In JDK 8, the OffsetDateTime class contained a toEpochSecond() method for this purpose. If you wanted to get the number of seconds since the epoch from a ZonedDateTime, you had to convert it to an OffsetDateTime using its toOffsetDateTime() method and use the toEpochSecond() method of the OffsetDateTime class. JDK 8 did not contain a toEpochSecond() method for LocalDate, LocalTime, and OffsetTime classes. JDK 9 added these methods:

- LocalDate.toEpochSecond(LocalTime time, ZoneOffset offset)

- LocalTime.toEpochSecond(LocalDate date, ZoneOffset offset)

- OffsetTime.toEpochSecond(LocalDate date)

Why are signatures of the toEpochSecond() method different in these classes? To get a number of seconds from the epoch 1970-01-01T00:00:00Z, you need to define another instant. An instant can be defined with three parts: a date, a time, a zone offset. The LocalDate and LocalTime classes contain only one of the three parts of an instant. The OffsetTime class contains two parts—a time and an offset. The missing parts need to be specified as arguments by these classes. So, these classes contain the toEpochSecond() method whose argument specifies the missing parts to define an instant. The following snippet of code uses the same instant to get the number of seconds from the epoch using three classes:

```
LocalDate ld = LocalDate.of(2017, 2, 12);
LocalTime lt = LocalTime.of(9, 15, 45);

ZoneOffset offset = ZoneOffset.ofHours(6);
OffsetTime ot = OffsetTime.of(lt, offset);

long s1 = ld.toEpochSecond(lt, offset);
long s2 = lt.toEpochSecond(ld, offset);
long s3 = ot.toEpochSecond(ld);
System.out.println("LocalDate.toEpochSecond(): " + s1);
System.out.println("LocalTime.toEpochSecond(): " + s2);
System.out.println("OffsetTime.toEpochSecond(): " + s3);
```

```
LocalDate.toEpochSecond(): 1486869345
LocalTime.toEpochSecond(): 1486869345
OffsetTime.toEpochSecond(): 1486869345
```

Stream of LocalDate

JDK 9 made it easy to step through all dates between two given dates—one day at a time or a given period at a time. The following two methods have been added to the LocalDate class:

- Stream<LocalDate> datesUntil(LocalDate endExclusive)

- Stream<LocalDate> datesUntil(LocalDate endExclusive, Period step)

These methods produce a sequential ordered stream of LocalDates. The first element in the stream is the LocalDate on which the method is called. The datesUntil(LocalDate endExclusive) method increments the elements in the stream one day at a time, whereas the datesUntil(LocalDate endExclusive, Period step) method increments them by the specified step. The specified end date is exclusive. There are several useful computations that you can do on the returned streams. The following snippet of code counts the number of Sundays in 2017. Note that the code uses Jan 1, 2018 as the last date, which is exclusive, and that will make the stream return all dates in 2017.

```
long sundaysIn2017 = LocalDate.of(2017, 1, 1)
                        .datesUntil(LocalDate.of(2018, 1, 1))
                        .filter(ld -> ld.getDayOfWeek() == DayOfWeek.SUNDAY)
                        .count();
System.out.println("Number of Sundays in 2017: " + sundaysIn2017);
```

```
Number of Sundays in 2017: 53
```

The following snippet of code prints all dates between Jan 1, 2017 (inclusive) to Jan 1, 2022 (exclusive) that are Fridays and fall on the 13th of the month:

```
System.out.println("Fridays that fall on 13th of the month between 2017 - 2021: ");
LocalDate.of(2017, 1, 1)
        .datesUntil(LocalDate.of(2022, 1, 1))
        .filter(ld -> ld.getDayOfMonth() == 13 && ld.getDayOfWeek() == DayOfWeek.FRIDAY)
        .forEach(System.out::println);
```

```
Fridays that fall on 13th of the month between 2017 - 2021 (inclusive):
2017-01-13
2017-10-13
2018-04-13
2018-07-13
2019-09-13
2019-12-13
2020-03-13
2020-11-13
2021-08-13
```

The following snippet of code prints the last day of each month in 2017:

```
System.out.println("Last Day of months in 2017:");
LocalDate.of(2017, 1, 31)
        .datesUntil(LocalDate.of(2018, 1, 1), Period.ofMonths(1))
        .map(ld -> ld.format(DateTimeFormatter.ofPattern("EEE MMM dd, yyyy")))
        .forEach(System.out::println);
```

```
Last Day of months in 2017:
Tue Jan 31, 2017
Tue Feb 28, 2017
Fri Mar 31, 2017
Sun Apr 30, 2017
Wed May 31, 2017
Fri Jun 30, 2017
Mon Jul 31, 2017
Thu Aug 31, 2017
Sat Sep 30, 2017
Tue Oct 31, 2017
Thu Nov 30, 2017
Sun Dec 31, 2017
```

New Formatting Options

JDK 9 added a few formatting options to the Time API. The following section describes each of these changes in detail.

Modified Julian Day Formatter

You can use the lowercase letter g in a date time formatter pattern, which formats the date part to a modified Julian day as an integer. You can repeat g multiple times, for example, ggg, which will zero-pad the result if the number of digits in the result is less than the number of g specified. The web page at http://www. unicode.org/reports/tr35/tr35-41/tr35-dates.html#Date_Format_Patterns defines the meaning of the letter g in a formatter as follows:

> *Modified Julian day. This is different from the conventional Julian day number in two regards. First, it demarcates days at local zone midnight, rather than noon GMT. Second, it is a local number; that is, it depends on the local time zone. It can be thought of as a single number that encompasses all the date-related fields.*

▓ **Tip** The uppercase letter G is defined as a date and time formatter symbol in JDK 8, which formats the input as AD, Anno Domini, A, BC, Before Christ, and B.

The following snippet of code shows you how to use the modified Julian day formatting character G to format a ZonedDateTime:

```
ZonedDateTime zdt = ZonedDateTime.now();
System.out.println("Current ZonedDateTime: " + zdt);
System.out.println("Modified Julian Day (g): " +
                zdt.format(DateTimeFormatter.ofPattern("g")));
System.out.println("Modified Julian Day (ggg): " +
                zdt.format(DateTimeFormatter.ofPattern("ggg")));
System.out.println("Modified Julian Day (gggggg): " +
                zdt.format(DateTimeFormatter.ofPattern("gggggg")));
```

```
Current ZonedDateTime: 2017-02-12T11:49:03.364431100-06:00[America/Chicago]
Modified Julian Day (g): 57796
Modified Julian Day (ggg): 57796
Modified Julian Day (gggggg): 057796
```

Generic Time Zone Names

JDK 8 had two letters, V and z, to format the time zone of the date and time. The letter V produces a zone ID such as "America/Los_Angeles; Z; -08:30" and the letter z produces a zone name such as Central Standard Time and CST.

JDK 9 added the lowercase letter v as a formatter symbol that produces generic non-location zone name such as Central Time or CT. The term "non-location" means that it does not identify an offset from UTC. It refers to the wall time—the time shown by the clock on the wall. For example, 8am Central time will have an offset of UTC-06 on March 1, 2017 and an offset of UTC-05 on March 19, 2017. The generic non-location zone name does not specify the time zone offset. You can use it in two formats —v and vvvv—to produce the generic non-location zone name in short form (e.g. CT) and long form (e.g. Central Time), respectively. The following snippet of code shows the difference in formatted results produced by the V, z, and v formatting symbols:

```
ZonedDateTime zdt = ZonedDateTime.now();
System.out.println("Current ZonedDateTime: " + zdt);
System.out.println("Using VV: " +
                zdt.format(DateTimeFormatter.ofPattern("MM/dd/yyyy HH:mm VV")));
System.out.println("Using z: " +
                zdt.format(DateTimeFormatter.ofPattern("MM/dd/yyyy HH:mm z")));
System.out.println("Using zzzz: " +
                zdt.format(DateTimeFormatter.ofPattern("MM/dd/yyyy HH:mm zzzz")));
System.out.println("Using v: " +
                zdt.format(DateTimeFormatter.ofPattern("MM/dd/yyyy HH:mm v")));
System.out.println("Using vvvv: " +
                zdt.format(DateTimeFormatter.ofPattern("MM/dd/yyyy HH:mm vvvv")));
```

```
Current ZonedDateTime: 2017-02-12T12:30:08.975373900-06:00[America/Chicago]
Using VV: 02/12/2017 12:30 America/Chicago
Using z: 02/12/2017 12:30 CST
Using zzzz: 02/12/2017 12:30 Central Standard Time
Using v: 02/12/2017 12:30 CT
Using vvvv: 02/12/2017 12:30 Central Time
```

Stream Operations with Scanner

JDK 9 added the following three methods to the java.util.Scanner. Each method returns a Stream:

- Stream<MatchResult> findAll(String patternString)

- Stream<MatchResult> findAll(Pattern pattern)

- Stream<String> tokens()

The findAll() method returns a stream with all matched results. Calling the findAll(patternString) is equivalent to calling findAll(Pattern.compile(patternString)). The tokens() method returns a stream of tokens from a scanner using the current delimiter. Listing 20-12 contains a program that shows you how to collect only words from a string using the findAll() method.

Listing 20-12. A ScannerTest Class That Prints Words in a String Using the Scanner Class

```
// ScannerTest.java
package com.jdojo.misc;

import java.util.List;
import java.util.Scanner;
import java.util.regex.MatchResult;
import static java.util.stream.Collectors.toList;
```

```java
public class ScannerTest {
    public static void main(String[] args) {
        String patternString = "\\b\\w+\\b";
        String input = "A test string,\n which contains a new line.";
        List<String> words = new Scanner(input)
                .findAll(patternString)
                .map(MatchResult::group)
                .collect(toList());

        System.out.println("Input: " + input);
        System.out.println("Words: " + words);
    }
}
```

```
Input: A test string,
 which contains a new line.
Words: [A, test, string, which, contains, a, new, line]
```

Enhancement to the Matcher Class

The java.util.regex.Matcher class gained a few new methods in JDK 9:

- Matcher appendReplacement(StringBuilder sb, String replacement)

- StringBuilder appendTail(StringBuilder sb)

- String replaceAll(Function<MatchResult,String> replacer)

- String replaceFirst(Function<MatchResult,String> replacer)

- Stream<MatchResult> results()

The Matcher class in JDK 8 already had the first four methods in this list. In JDK 9, they have been overloaded. The appendReplacement() and appendTail() methods used to work with a StringBuffer. Now they also work with a StringBuilder. The replaceAll() and replaceFirst() methods used to take a String as an argument. In JDK 9, they have been overloaded to take a Function<T,R> as an argument.

The results() method returns match results in a stream whose elements are of the MatchResult type. You can query the MatchResult to get the results as strings. It was possible to process the results of a Matcher as a stream in JDK 8. However, the logic was not straightforward. The results() method does not reset the matcher. If you want to reuse the matcher, don't forget to call its reset() method to reset it to a desired position. Listing 20-13 shows a few interesting uses of this method.

Listing 20-13. A MatcherTest Class That Demonstrates the Use of the results() Method in the Matcher Class

```java
// MatcherTest.java
package com.jdojo.misc;

import java.util.List;
import java.util.Set;
import java.util.regex.Matcher;
import java.util.regex.Pattern;
import static java.util.stream.Collectors.toList;
import static java.util.stream.Collectors.toSet;
```

```java
public class MatcherTest {
    public static void main(String[] args) {
        // A regex to match 7-digit or 10-digit phone numbers
        String regex = "\\b(\\d{3})?(\\d{3})(\\d{4})\\b";

        // An input string
        String input = "1, 3342229999, 2330001, 6159996666, 123, 3340909090";

        // Create a matcher
        Matcher matcher = Pattern.compile(regex)
                                 .matcher(input);

        // Collect formatted phone numbers into a list
        List<String> phones = matcher.results()
                    .map(mr -> (mr.group(1) == null ? "" : "(" + mr.group(1) + ") ")
                            + mr.group(2) + "-" + mr.group(3))
                    .collect(toList());
        System.out.println("Phones: " + phones);

        // Reset the matcher, so we can reuse it from start
        matcher.reset();

        // Get distinct area codes
        Set<String> areaCodes = matcher.results()
                                    .filter(mr -> mr.group(1) != null)
                                    .map(mr -> mr.group(1))
                                    .collect(toSet());
        System.out.println("Distinct Area Codes:: " + areaCodes);
    }
}
```

```
Phones: [(334) 222-9999, 233-0001, (615) 999-6666, (334) 090-9090]
Distinct Area Codes:: [334, 615]
```

The main() method declares two local variables named regex and input. The regex variable contains a regular expression to match 7-digit or 10-digit numbers. You will use it to find phone numbers in an input string. The input variable stores text, which has embedded phone numbers.

```java
// A regex to match 7-digit or 10-digit phone numbers
String regex = "\\b(\\d{3})?(\\d{3})(\\d{4})\\b";
```

```java
// An input string
String input = "1, 3342229999, 2330001, 6159996666, 123, 3340909090";
```

Next, you compile the regular expression as a Pattern object and obtain a matcher:

```java
// Create a matcher
Matcher matcher = Pattern.compile(regex)
                         .matcher(input);
```

You want to format a 10-digit phone number as (nnn) nnn-nnnn and a 7-digit phone number as nnn-nnnn. Finally, you want to collect all formatted phone numbers into a List<String>. The following statement performs this:

```
// Collect formatted phone numbers into a list
List<String> phones = matcher.results()
                        .map(mr -> (mr.group(1) == null ? "" : "(" + mr.group(1) + ") ")
                                + mr.group(2) + "-" + mr.group(3))
                        .collect(toList());
```

Note the use of the map() method that takes a MatchResult and returns a formatted phone number as a String. When a match is a 7-digit phone number, the group 1 will be null. Now, you want to reuse the matcher to find distinct area codes in 10-digit phone numbers. You must reset the matcher, so the next match starts at the beginning of the input string:

```
// Reset the matcher, so we can reuse it from start
matcher.reset();
```

The first group in the MatchResult contains the area code. You need to filter out 7-digit phone numbers and collect the value of group 1 in a Set<String> to get a distinct set of area codes. The following statement does this:

```
// Get distinct area codes
Set<String> areaCodes = matcher.results()
                        .filter(mr -> mr.group(1) != null)
                        .map(mr -> mr.group(1))
                        .collect(toSet());
```

Enhancement to the Objects Class

The java.util.Objects class consists of static utility methods that operate on objects. Typically, they are used for verifying method's arguments, for example, to check if a method's argument is a null. JDK 9 added the following static methods to this class:

- <T> T requireNonNullElse(T obj, T defaultObj)

- <T> T requireNonNullElseGet(T obj, Supplier<? extends T> supplier)

- int checkFromIndexSize(int fromIndex, int size, int length)

- int checkFromToIndex(int fromIndex, int toIndex, int length)

- int checkIndex(int index, int length)

JDK 8 already had three versions of the requireNonNull() method. The method is used to check for a value to be non-null. If the value is null, it throws a NullPointerException. JDK 9 added two more versions of this method.

The requireNonNullElse(T obj, T defaultObj) method returns obj if obj is non-null. It returns defaultObj if obj is null and defaultObj is non-null. If both obj and defaultObj are null, it throws a NullPointerException.

The `requireNonNullElseGet(T obj, Supplier<? extends T> supplier)` method works the same way as the `requireNonNullElse(T obj, T defaultObj)` method, except that the former uses a supplier to get the default value. It returns `obj` if it is non-null. If `supplier` is non-null and it returns a non-null value, the value returned from `supplier` is returned. Otherwise, a `NullPointerException` is thrown.

The method named like `checkXxx()` is meant to be used for checking if an index or a sub-range is within a range. They are useful when you are working with arrays and collections, and you need to deal with indexes and sub-ranges. These methods throw an `IndexOutOfBoundsException` if the index or sub-range is out of range.

The `checkFromIndexSize(int fromIndex, int size, int length)` method checks if the specified sub-range, which is `fromIndex` (inclusive) to `fromIndex + size` (exclusive), is within the range, which is 0 (inclusive) to `length` (exclusive). If any of the arguments is a negative integer or the sub-range is out of range, an `IndexOutOfBoundsException` is thrown. If the sub-range is within range, it returns the `fromIndex`. Suppose you have a method that accepts an index and size and returns a sub-range from an array or a list. You can use this method to check if the requested sub-range is within the range of the array or list.

The `checkFromToIndex(int fromIndex, int toIndex, int length)` method checks if the specified sub-range, which is `fromIndex` (inclusive) to `toIndex` (exclusive), is within range, which is 0 (inclusive) to `length` (exclusive). If any arguments is a negative integer or the sub-range is out of range, an `IndexOutOfBoundsException` is thrown. If the sub-range is within range, it returns the `fromIndex`. It is useful to be used for sub-range checking while working with arrays and lists.

The `checkIndex(int index, int length)` method checks if the specified `index` is within range, which is 0 (inclusive) to `length` (exclusive). If any argument is a negative integer or the index is out of range, an `IndexOutOfBoundsException` is thrown. If `index` is within range, it returns the `index`. It is useful when a method receives an index and returns a value in an array or a list at that index.

Comparing Arrays

The `java.util.Arrays` class consists of static utility methods that let you perform various operations on arrays such as sorting, comparing, converting to streams, etc. In JDK 9, this class has gained several methods that let you compare arrays and slices of arrays. The new methods fall into three categories:

- Comparing two arrays or their slices for equality
- Comparing two arrays lexicographically
- Finding the index of the first mismatch in two arrays

The list of methods added to this class is huge. Methods in each category are overloaded for all primitive types and `Object` arrays. To save space, I do not list them here. Refer to the API documentation for the `Arrays` class for a complete list. At the end of this section, I present an example using two `int` arrays.

The `equals()` method lets you compare two arrays for equality. Two arrays are considered equal if the number of elements in the arrays or slices is the same, and all corresponding pairs of elements in the arrays or slices are equal. The following are two versions of the `equals()` method for `int`:

- `boolean equals(int[] a, int[] b)`
- `boolean equals(int[] a, int aFromIndex, int aToIndex, int[] b, int bFromIndex, int bToIndex)`

The first version lets you compare two arrays for equality and it existed before JDK 9. The second version lets you compare slices of two arrays for equality, which has been added in JDK 9. The `fromIndex` (inclusive) and `toIndex` (exclusive) arguments determine the range of the two arrays to be compared. The method returns `true` if two arrays are equal, `false` otherwise. Two arrays are considered equal if both are `null`.

JDK 9 added several methods named `compare()` and `compareUnsigned()`. Both methods compare elements in arrays or arrays' slices lexicographically. The `compareUnsigned()` method treats the integer values as unsigned. A `null` array is lexicographically less than a non-`null` array. Two `null` arrays are equal. The following are two versions of the `compare()` method for `int`:

- `int compare(int[] a, int[] b)`

- `int compare(int[] a, int aFromIndex, int aToIndex, int[] b, int bFromIndex, int bToIndex)`

The `compare()` method returns 0 if the first and second arrays (or slices) are equal and contain the same elements in the same order; returns a value less than 0 if the first array (or slice) is lexicographically less than the second array (or slice); and returns a value greater than 0 if the first array (or slice) is lexicographically greater than the second array (or slice).

The `mismatch()` method compares two arrays or array's slices. The following are two versions of the `mismatch()` method for `int`:

- `int mismatch(int[] a, int[] b)`

- `int mismatch (int[] a, int aFromIndex, int aToIndex, int[] b, int bFromIndex, int bToIndex)`

The `mismatch()` method returns the index of the first mismatch. If there is no mismatch, it returns -1. If either array is null, it throws a `NullPointerException`. Listing 20-14 contains a complete program that compares two arrays and their slices. The program uses two `int` arrays.

Listing 20-14. Comparing Arrays and Array's Slices Using the Arrays Class Methods

```java
// ArrayComparision.java
package com.jdojo.misc;

import java.util.Arrays;

public class ArrayComparison {
    public static void main(String[] args) {
        int[] a1 = {1, 2, 3, 4, 5};
        int[] a2 = {1, 2, 7, 4, 5};
        int[] a3 = {1, 2, 3, 4, 5};

        // Print original arrays
        System.out.println("Three arrays:");
        System.out.println("a1: " + Arrays.toString(a1));
        System.out.println("a2: " + Arrays.toString(a2));
        System.out.println("a3: " + Arrays.toString(a3));

        // Compare arrays for equality
        System.out.println("\nComparing arrays using equals() method:");
        System.out.println("Arrays.equals(a1, a2): " + Arrays.equals(a1, a2));
        System.out.println("Arrays.equals(a1, a3): " + Arrays.equals(a1, a3));
        System.out.println("Arrays.equals(a1, 0, 2, a2, 0, 2): " +
                        Arrays.equals(a1, 0, 2, a2, 0, 2));

        // Compare arrays lexicographically
        System.out.println("\nComparing arrays using compare() method:");
        System.out.println("Arrays.compare(a1, a2): " + Arrays.compare(a1, a2));
```

```
        System.out.println("Arrays.compare(a2, a1): " + Arrays.compare(a2, a1));
        System.out.println("Arrays.compare(a1, a3): " + Arrays.compare(a1, a3));
        System.out.println("Arrays.compare(a1, 0, 2, a2, 0, 2): " +
                            Arrays.compare(a1, 0, 2, a2, 0, 2));

        // Find the mismatched index in arrays
        System.out.println("\nFinding mismatch using the mismatch() method:");
        System.out.println("Arrays.mismatch(a1, a2): " + Arrays.mismatch(a1, a2));
        System.out.println("Arrays.mismatch(a1, a3): " + Arrays.mismatch(a1, a3));
        System.out.println("Arrays.mismatch(a1, 0, 5, a2, 0, 1): " +
                            Arrays.mismatch(a1, 0, 5, a2, 0, 1));
    }
}
```

```
Three arrays:
a1: [1, 2, 3, 4, 5]
a2: [1, 2, 7, 4, 5]
a3: [1, 2, 3, 4, 5]

Comparing arrays using equals() method:
Arrays.equals(a1, a2): false
Arrays.equals(a1, a3): true
Arrays.equals(a1, 0, 2, a2, 0, 2): true

Comparing arrays using compare() method:
Arrays.compare(a1, a2): -1
Arrays.compare(a2, a1): 1
Arrays.compare(a1, a3): 0
Arrays.compare(a1, 0, 2, a2, 0, 2): 0

Finding mismatch using the mismatch() method:
Arrays.mismatch(a1, a2): 2
Arrays.mismatch(a1, a3): -1
Arrays.mismatch(a1, 0, 5, a2, 0, 1): 1
```

The Applet API Is Deprecated

Java applets require the Java browser plugin to work. Many browser vendors have already removed support for the Java browser plugin or will be removing it in the near future. If browsers do not have support for Java plugins, you cannot use applets and hence there will be no reason to use the Applet API. JDK 9 deprecated the Applet API. However, it won't be removed in JDK 10. If it is scheduled to be removed in a future release, developers will get a notice one release in advance. The following classes and interfaces have been deprecated:

- `java.applet.AppletStub`

- `java.applet.Applet`

- `java.applet.AudioClip`

- `java.applet.AppletContext`

- `javax.swing.JApplet`

In JDK 9, all AWT and Swing related classes are packaged in the `java.desktop` module. These deprecated classes and interfaces are also in the same module.

The `appletviewer` tool, which ships with the JDK in its `bin` directory, is used to test applets. The tool is also deprecated in JDK 9. Running the tool in JDK 9 prints a deprecation warning.

Javadoc Enhancements

JDK 9 introduced a few enhancements to the way Javadoc is written, generated, and used. JDK 9 supports HTML5 in Javadoc. By default, the `javadoc` tool still generates output in HTML4. A new option, `-html5`, has been added to the tool to indicate that you want the output in HTML5:

```
javadoc -html5 <other-options>
```

The `javadoc` tool is located in the `JDK_HOME\bin` directory. Running the tool with the `--help` option prints its usage description and all options. A full discussion the `javadoc` tool is beyond the scope of this book.

The NetBeans IDE lets you generate Javadoc for your project. On the Properties dialog box for your project, select Build ➤ Documenting to get the Javadoc properties sheet where you can specify all options for the `javadoc` tool. To generate the Javadoc, select Generate Javadoc from the right-click menu options for your project.

JDK 9 keeps the three-frame or no-frames Javadoc layout. The top-left frame contains three links: ALL CLASSES, ALL PACKAGES, and ALL MODULES. The ALL MODULES link was added in JDK 9, which displays a list of all modules. The ALL CLASSES link lets you view all classes in the bottom-left frame. The other two links let you view all packages, all packages in a module, and all modules. Figure 20-1 shows the changes to the Javadoc page.

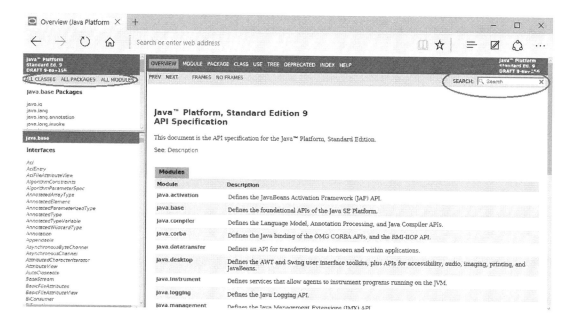

Figure 20-1. *The Javadoc for Java SE 9 in a three-frame layout*

You can also view the Javadoc for a module. Select a module in the upper-left frame, click on the module name link that is shown between the upper and the bottom frames on the left, and you will see module's documentation in the right frame. A module's Javadoc contains a list of all module statements such as requires, exports, etc.

Consider this scenario. You are looking for logic to implement something in Java and find a piece of code on the Internet, which uses a class, but does not show the import statement importing that class. You have access to the Javadoc for Java SE and you want to know little more about the class. How do you get the package name of the class, which is needed to get to the documentation of the class? You search the Internet again. This time, search for the class name, which might get you a link to the Javadoc for the class. Alternatively, you can copy and paste the piece of code in a Java IDE such as NetBeans and Eclipse, and the IDE will help you generate the import statements to give you the package name of the class. Don't worry about this inconvenience of searching for the package name of a class in JDK 9.

There is another addition to the right main frame. All pages in this frame display a Search box on the top-right (see Figure 20-1). The search box lets you search the Javadoc. The javadoc tool prepares an index of terms that can be searched. To know what is searchable, you need to know the terms that are indexed:

- You can search for declared names of modules, packages, types, and members. The type of formal parameters of constructors and methods are indexed, but not the names of those parameters. So, you can search on the type of formal parameter. If you enter "(String, int, int)" in the search box, it will find you the list of constructors and methods that take three formal parameters of String, int, and int. If you enter "util" as a search term, it will show you a list of all packages, types, and members that contain the term "util" in their names.

- JDK 9 introduced a new inline Javadoc tag, @index, which can be used to tell the javadoc tool to index a keyword. It can appear in Javadoc as {@index <keyword> <description>}, where <keyword> is the keyword to be indexed and <description> is the keyword's description. The following Javadoc tag is an example of using the @ index tag with a keyword, jdojo: {@index jdojo Info site (www.jdojo.com) for the Java 9 Revealed book!}.

Everything else that is not listed in this list is not searchable using the Javadoc search box. The search box displays found results as a list when you enter the search term. The results list is divided into categories such as Modules, Packages, Types, Members, and SearchTags. The SearchTags category contains results found from the indexed keywords that are specified using @index tags.

■ **Tip** The Javadoc search does not support regular expressions. The entered search keyword is searched for its occurrence anywhere in the indexed terms.

Figure 20-2 shows you the use of the Javadoc Search box with the list of results. I generated the Javadoc for the com.jdojo.misc module and used it to search for jdojo, as shown on left of the figure. I used the Javadoc for Java SE 9 to search for the term, Module, as shown on the right of the figure.

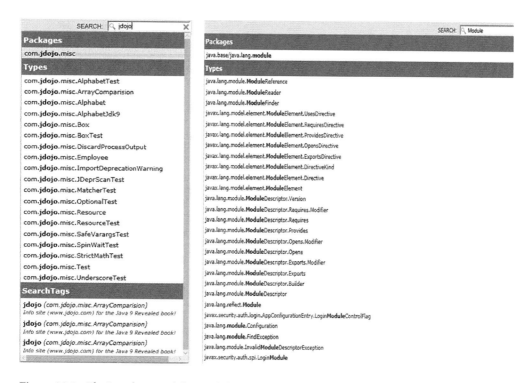

Figure 20-2. *The Javadoc search box with keywords and searched results*

You can use the Up and Down arrow keys to navigate through the search results. You can view the details of the search results in one of the following two ways:

- Click on a search result to open the Javadoc for that topic.

- When a search result is highlighted using the Up/Down arrows, press Enter to open the details on that topic.

■ **Tip**   You can use the -noindex option with the javadoc tool to disable the Javadoc search. No index will be generated and no search box will be available in the generated Javadoc.

A Javadoc search is performed locally using client-side JavaScript. There is no computation or search logic implemented in the server. If you have disabled JavaScript in your browser, you will not be able to use the Javadoc search feature.

Native Desktop Features

Java SE 6 added platform-specific desktop support through the java.awt.Desktop class. The class supported performing the following operations from a Java application:

- Opening a URI in the user-default browser

- Opening a mailto URI in the user-default mail client

- Opening, editing, and printing files using registered applications

Java SE 9 takes the platform-specific desktop support forward and adds public API support for many system and application event notifications, if they are available on the current platform. The `java.awt.Desktop` class is still the central class for working with platform-specific desktop features. To support so many new desktop features, Java SE 9 added a new package, `java.awt.desktop`, to the `java.desktop` module. The `java.awt.Desktop` class has also received many new methods. The new package contains 30 classes and interfaces. In JDK 9, the Desktop API supports 24 platform-specific desktop actions and notifications, which are defined by constants of the `Desktop.Action` enum. To name a few, they are as follows:

- Notifications when the attached displays go into or come out of power save

- Notifications when the system enters sleep or after the system wakes

- Notifications when the user session changes such as locking/unlocking a user session

- Notifications when the application's status changes to be or not to be a foreground application

- Notifications when the application is asked to show its About dialog box

You can use these features to optimize resource usage by your application. For example, if the system goes into sleep mode, you can stop animations and resume them when the system wakes. It is not possible to cover the entire Desktop API in this book. I walk you through a step-by-step example. Refer to the API documentation of the `java.awt.Desktop` class and the classes and interfaces in the `java.awt.desktop` package for more information. The following steps are typical when using a desktop feature:

- Check if the `Desktop` class is supported by the current platform using the static `isDesktopSupported()` method of this class. If the method returns `false`, you cannot use any desktop features.

- If the `Desktop` class is supported, use the static `getDesktop()` method of the `Desktop` class to get a reference of the `Desktop` class.

- Not all desktop features are available on all platforms. Use the `isSupported(Desktop.Action action)` method on the desktop object to check if a specific desktop action is supported. The supported desktop action is represented by constants in the `Desktop.Action` enum.

- If a desktop action is supported, you can call one of the methods of the `Desktop` class to take the action such as opening a file or you can register the event handler using the `addAppEventListener(SystemEventListener listener)` method.

■ **Tip** The `java.awt` and `java.awt.desktop` packages are in the `java.desktop` module. When you are using platform-specific desktop features, make sure that your module reads the `java.desktop` module.

Listing 20-15 contains a complete program to demonstrate a desktop feature. The application registers a user session change listener. When the user session changes, the application is notified and it prints a message on the standard output. You can change a user session by logging in/out remotely, or by locking and unlocking your computer. You can use this desktop notification to pause expensive processing such as animations when a user session is deactivated and restart the process when it is activated. A detailed explanation follows the output of this program. When you run the program, you need to lock and unlock your computer to user session related output. The output shown is when I ran this program on Windows and locked and unlocked my computer once while the program was running. You may get different output. The program quits on its own after two minutes.

501

Listing 20-15. Using Platform-Specific Desktop Features

```java
// DeskTopFrame.java
package com.jdojo.misc;

import java.awt.Desktop;
import java.awt.desktop.UserSessionEvent;
import java.awt.desktop.UserSessionListener;
import java.util.concurrent.TimeUnit;

public class DeskTopFrame {
    public static void main(String[] args) {
        // Check if Desktop class is available
        if (!Desktop.isDesktopSupported()) {
            System.out.println("Current Platform does not support Desktop.");
            return;
        }

        System.out.println("Current platform supports Desktop.");

        // Get the desktop reference
        Desktop desktop = Desktop.getDesktop();

        // Check if user session event notification is supported
        if (!desktop.isSupported(Desktop.Action.APP_EVENT_USER_SESSION)) {
            System.out.println("User session notification is not " +
                               "supported by the current desktop");
            return;
        }

        System.out.println("Lock and unlock your session to see " +
                           "user session change notification in action.");

        // Add an event handler for a change in user session
        desktop.addAppEventListener(new UserSessionListener() {
            @Override
            public void userSessionDeactivated(UserSessionEvent e) {
                System.out.println("User session deactivated. Reason: " + e.getReason());
            }

            @Override
            public void userSessionActivated(UserSessionEvent e) {
                System.out.println("User session activated. Reason: " + e.getReason());
            }
        });

        // Make the current thread sleep for 2 minutes
        try {
            TimeUnit.SECONDS.sleep(120);
        } catch (InterruptedException e) {
            e.printStackTrace();
        }
    }
}
```

```
Current platform supports Desktop.
Lock and unlock your session to see user session change notification in action.
User session deactivated. Reason: LOCK
User session activated. Reason: LOCK
```

The main() method checks whether the Desktop class is available on the current platform. If it is not available, the program quits. If it is available, its reference is obtained.

```
if (!Desktop.isDesktopSupported()) {
    System.out.println("Current Platform does not support Desktop.");
    return;
}
```

```
// Get the desktop reference
Desktop desktop = Desktop.getDesktop();
```

You are interested in getting notifications when the user session changes, so you need to check if this feature is supported. If it is not supported, the program quits.

```
// Check if user session event notification is supported
if (!desktop.isSupported(Desktop.Action.APP_EVENT_USER_SESSION)) {
    System.out.println("User session notification is not " +
                        "supported by the current desktop");
     return;
}
```

If the user session change notification is supported, you need to register an event listener of the UserSessionListener type like so:

```
// Add an event handler for a change in user session
desktop.addAppEventListener(new UserSessionListener() {
    @Override
    public void userSessionActivated(UserSessionEvent e) {
        System.out.println("Use session activated. Reason: " + e.getReason());
    }

    @Override
    public void userSessionDeactivated(UserSessionEvent e) {
        System.out.println("User session deactivated. Reason: " + e.getReason());
    }
});
```

The userSessionActivated() and userSessionDeactivated() methods of the registered UserSessionListener are called when the user session is activated and deactivated, respectively. Both methods get a UserSessionEvent object as an argument. The getReason() method of the UserSessionEvent class returns a UserSessionEvent.Reason, which is an enum whose constants define reasons for the change in user's session. The enum has four constants: CONSOLE, LOCK, REMOTE, and UNSPECIFIED. The CONSOLE and REMOTE constants represent reasons indicating that the user session was connected/disconnected to the console terminal and remote terminal, respectively. The LOCK constant represents a reason indicating that the user session has been locked or unlocked. As the name suggests, the UNSPECIFIED constants represent all other reasons a user session changes. The output in Listing 20-15 shows that I locked and unlocked my user session.

In the end, the main() method makes the current thread sleep for two minutes, so you have a chance to lock and unlock your session to see the program working. If you remove this part of the program, your program will exit without waiting for you to change your user session.

Object Deserialization Filters

Java lets you serialize and deserialize objects. To address the security risk posed by deserialization, JDK 9 introduced the concept of object input filter that can be used to verify the object being deserialized and, if it does not pass a test, the deserialization process can be stopped. The object input filter is an instance of a new interface, java.io.ObjectInputFilter, which was added to JDK 9. A filter can be based on one or more of the following criteria:

- The length of the array being deserialized
- The depth of the nested object being deserialized
- The number of object references being deserialized
- The class of an object being deserialized
- The number of bytes consumed from the input stream

The ObjectInputFilter interface consists of only one method:

```
ObjectInputFilter.Status checkInput(ObjectInputFilter.FilterInfo filterInfo)
```

You can specify a global filter to be used for deserializing all objects. You can override a global filter on a per ObjectInputStream basis by setting a local filter for the object input stream. You can have no global filter and specify a local filter for each object input stream. There are several ways to create and specify filters. I will explain them one by one with examples. This section first introduces the classes and interfaces that were added to JDK 9 that you need to use to work with filters:

- ObjectInputFilter
- ObjectInputFilter.Config
- ObjectInputFilter.FilterInfo
- ObjectInputFilter.Status

ObjectInputFilter is an interface whose instance represent filters. You can create a filter by implementing this interface in a class. Alternatively, you can obtain its instances from a string using the createFilter(String pattern) method of the ObjectInputFilter.Config class, which is discussed next.

`ObjectInputFilter.Config` is a nested static utility class that is used for two purposes:

- To get and set the global filter
- To create filters from patterns specified as strings

The `ObjectInputFilter.Config` class contains the following three static methods:

- `ObjectInputFilter createFilter(String pattern)`
- `ObjectInputFilter getSerialFilter()`
- `void setSerialFilter(ObjectInputFilter filter)`

The `createFilter()` method takes a pattern that describes a filter and returns an instance of the `ObjectInputFilter` interface. The following snippet of code creates a filter that specifies that the length of an array being deserialized should not exceed 4:

```
String pattern = "maxarray=4";
ObjectInputFilter filter = ObjectInputFilter.Config.createFilter(pattern);
```

You can specify multiply patterns in one filter. They are separated by a semicolon (;). The following snippet of code creates a filter from two patterns. The filter will reject the object deserialization if it encounters an array with length greater than 4 or the size of the serialized object is more than 1024 bytes.

```
String pattern = "maxarray=4;maxbytes=1024";
ObjectInputFilter filter = ObjectInputFilter.Config.createFilter(pattern);
```

There are several rules on specifying filter patterns. If you prefer writing the filter logic in Java code, you can do so by creating a class that implements the `ObjectInputFilter` interface and write the logic in its `checkInput()` method. Here are the rules if you want to create a filter from patterns in a string:

There are five filter criteria, four of which are limits. They are `maxarray`, `maxdepth`, `maxrefs`, and `maxbytes`. You can set them using `name=value` pairs in patterns where `name` is one of these keywords and `value` is the limit. If a pattern contains an equals sign (=), the pattern must use one of these four keywords as the name. The fifth filter criterion is used to specify a pattern for a class name of the form:

```
<module-name>/<fully-qualified-class-name>
```

If a class is in unnamed module, the pattern will be matched against the class name. If the object is an array, the class name of the component type of the array is used to match the pattern, not the class name of the array itself. Here are all the rules for a pattern matching a class name:

- If the class name matches the pattern, the object is allowed to be deserialized.
- The ! character at the beginning of a pattern is treated as a logical NOT.
- If the pattern contains a slash (/), the part before the slash is the module name. If the module name matches the module name of the class, the part after the slash is used as a pattern to match the class name. If there is no slash in the pattern, the module name of the class is not considered in matching the pattern.
- A pattern ending with ".**" matches any class in the package and all sub-packages.
- A pattern ending with ".*" matches any class in the package.

- A pattern ending with "*" matches any class with the pattern as a prefix.

- If the pattern is equal to the class name, it matches.

- Otherwise, the pattern is not matched and the object is rejected.

If you set "com.jdojo.**" as a filter pattern, it will allow all classes in the com.jdojo package and its sub-packages to be deserialized and will reject deserializing object of all other classes. If you set "!com.jdojo.**" as a filter pattern, it will reject all classes in the com.jdojo package and its sub-packages to be deserialized and will allow deserializing objects of all other classes.

The getSerialFilter() and setSerialFilter() methods are used to get and set a global filter. You can set a global filter using one of the following three ways:

- By setting a system property named jdk.serialFilter whose value is a series of filter patterns separated by a semicolon.

- By setting a jdk.serialFilter property in the java.security file, which is stored in the JAVA_HOME\conf\security directory. If you are using the JDK to run your program, read JAVA_HOME as JDK_HOME. Otherwise, read it as JRE_HOME.

- By calling the setSerialFilter() static method of the ObjectInputFilter.Config class.

The following command sets the jdk.serialFilter system property as a command-line option when a class is run. Do not worry about the other details of the command at this time.

```
C:\Java9Revealed>java -Djdk.serialFilter=maxarray=100;maxdepth=3;com.jdojo.** --module-path
com.jdojo.misc\build\classes --module com.jdojo.misc/com.jdojo.misc.ObjectFilterTest
```

Listing 20-16 shows the partial contents of the JAVA_HOME\conf\security\java.security configuration file. The file contains a lot more entries. I have shown only one entry that sets a filter, which has the same effect as setting the jdk.serialFilter system property, as shown in the previous command.

Listing 20-16. An Entry in the JAVA_HOME\conf\security\java.security File Showing the jdk.serialFilter property Setting

```
maxarray=100;maxdepth=3;com.jdojo.**
```

■ **Tip** If a filter is set in both the system property and the configuration file, the value in the system property is used.

When you run the java command with a global filter in effect, you will notice messages on stderr similar to the ones shown here:

```
Feb 17, 2017 9:23:45 AM java.io.ObjectInputFilter$Config lambda$static$0
INFO: Creating serialization filter from maxarray=20;maxdepth=3;!com.jdojo.**
```

These messages are logged as platform messages using a logger named java.io.serialization for the java.base module. If you have specified a platform logger (see Chapter 19), these messages will be logged to your logger. One of the messages prints the global filter set in the system property or the configuration file.

You can also set a global filter in code using the static `setSerialFilter()` method of the `ObjectInputFilter.Config` class:

```
// Create a filter
String pattern = "maxarray=100;maxdepth=3;com.jdojo.**";
ObjectInputFilter globalFilter = ObjectInputFilter.Config.createFilter(pattern);

// Set a global filter
ObjectInputFilter.Config.setSerialFilter(globalFilter);
```

▒ **Tip**   You can set the global filter only once. For example, if you set a filter using the `jdk.serialFilter` system property, calling the `Config.setSerialFiter()` in your code will throw an `IllegalStateException`. When you set a global filter using the `Config.setSerialFiter()` method, you must set a non-null filter. These rules exist to make sure that the global filter set using the system property or configuration file cannot be overridden in code.

You can use the static `getSerialFilter()` method of the `ObjectInputFilter.Config` class to get the global filter, irrespective of the way the filter was set. If there is no global filter, this method returns `null`.

`ObjectInputFilter.FilterInfo` is a nested static interface whose instance wraps the current context of deserialization. An instance of `ObjectInputFilter.FilterInfo` is created and passed to the `checkInput()` method of your filter. You will not have to implement this interface and create its instances in your program. The interface contains the following methods that you will use inside the `checkInput()` method of your custom filter to read the current deserialization context:

- `Class<?> serialClass()`
- `long arrayLength()`
- `long depth();`
- `long references();`
- `long streamBytes();`

The `serialClass()` method returns the class of the object being deserialized. For an array, it returns the class of the array, not the class of the array's component type. When a new object is not being created during deserialization, this method returns `null`.

The `arrayLength()` method returns the length of the array being deserialized. It the object being deserialized is not an array, it returns -1.

The `depth()` method returns the depth of the nesting of the object being deserialized. It starts at 1, increments by 1 for each level of nesting, and decrements by 1 when the nested object returns.

The `references()` method returns the current number of object references being deserialized.

The `streamBytes()` method returns the current number of bytes consumed from the object input stream.

An object may pass or fail specified filter criteria. Depending on the test result, you are supposed to return one of the following constants of the `ObjectInputFilter.Status` enum. Typically, you will use these constants as return values in the `checkInput()` method of your custom filter class.

- ALLOWED
- REJECTED
- UNDECIDED

These constants indicate that the deserialization is allowed, rejected, and undecided. Typically, you would return UNDECIDED to mean that some other filter will decide whether the deserialization of the current object continues or not. If you are creating a filter to blacklist classes, you can return REJECTED for a match for the blacklisted classes and UNDECIDED for others. Listing 20-17 contains a simple filter that filters out based on an array's length.

Listing 20-17. An Object Deserialization Filter That Allows Arrays of a Specified Length To Be Deserialized

```java
// ArrayLengthObjectFilter.java
package com.jdojo.misc;

import java.io.ObjectInputFilter;

public class ArrayLengthObjectFilter implements ObjectInputFilter {
    private long maxLenth = -1;

    public ArrayLengthObjectFilter(int maxLength) {
        this.maxLenth = maxLength;
    }

    @Override
    public Status checkInput(FilterInfo info) {
        long arrayLength = info.arrayLength();
        if (arrayLength >= 0 && arrayLength > this.maxLenth) {
            return Status.REJECTED;
        }

        return Status.ALLOWED;
    }
}
```

The following snippet of code uses our custom filter by specifying the maximum length of arrays as 3. If the object input stream contains an array of length greater than 3, the deserialization will fail with a java.io.InvalidClassException. The code does not show the exception handling logic.

```java
ArrayLengthObjectFilter filter = new ArrayLengthObjectFilter(3);
File inputFile = ...
ObjectInputStream in =  new ObjectInputStream(new FileInputStream(inputFile))) {
in.setObjectInputFilter(filter);
Object obj = in.readObject();
```

Listing 20-18 contains the code for a class named Item. I left out getters and setters for this class to keep it short. I use its objects to demonstrate deserialization filters.

Listing 20-18. An Item Class Whose Instances Will Be Used to Demonstrate an Object Input Stream Deserialization Filter

```java
// Item.java
package com.jdojo.misc;

import java.io.Serializable;
import java.util.Arrays;
```

```java
public class Item implements Serializable {
    private int id;
    private String name;
    private int[] points;

    public Item(int id, String name, int[] points) {
        this.id = id;
        this.name = name;
        this.points = points;
    }

    /* Add getters and setters here */

    @Override
    public String toString() {
        return "[id=" + id + ", name=" + name + ", points=" + Arrays.toString(points) + "]";
    }
}
```

Listing 20-19 contains code for a class named ObjectFilterTest to demonstrate the use of filters during object deserialization. A detailed explanation follows the code.

Listing 20-19. An ObjectFilterTest Class That Uses Several Types of Object Deserialization Filters

```java
// ObjectFilterTest.java
package com.jdojo.misc;

import java.io.File;
import java.io.FileInputStream;
import java.io.FileOutputStream;
import java.io.ObjectInputFilter;
import java.io.ObjectInputFilter.Config;
import java.io.ObjectInputStream;
import java.io.ObjectOutputStream;

public class ObjectFilterTest {
    public static void main(String[] args)  {
        // Relative path of the output/input file
        File file = new File("serialized", "item.ser");

        // Make sure directories exist
        ensureParentDirExists(file);

        // Create an Item used in serialization and deserialization
        Item item = new Item(100, "Pen", new int[]{1,2,3,4});

        // Serialize the item
        serialize(file, item);
```

```java
        // Print the global filter
        ObjectInputFilter globalFilter = Config.getSerialFilter();
        System.out.println("Global filter: " + globalFilter);

        // Deserialize the item
        Item item2 = deserialize(file);
        System.out.println("Deserialized using global filter: " + item2);

        // Use a filter to reject array size > 2
        String maxArrayFilterPattern = "maxarray=2";
        ObjectInputFilter maxArrayFilter = Config.createFilter(maxArrayFilterPattern);
        Item item3 = deserialize(file, maxArrayFilter);
        System.out.println("Deserialized with a maxarray=2 filter: " + item3);

        // Create a custom filter
        ArrayLengthObjectFilter customFilter = new ArrayLengthObjectFilter(5);
        Item item4 = deserialize(file, customFilter);
        System.out.println("Deserialized with a custom filter (maxarray=5): " + item4);
    }

    private static void serialize(File file, Item item) {
        try (ObjectOutputStream out =  new ObjectOutputStream(new FileOutputStream(file))) {
            out.writeObject(item);
            System.out.println("Serialized Item: " + item);
        } catch (Exception e) {
            e.printStackTrace();
        }
    }

    private static Item deserialize(File file) {
        try (ObjectInputStream in =  new ObjectInputStream(new FileInputStream(file))) {
            Item item = (Item)in.readObject();
            return item;
        } catch (Exception e) {
            System.out.println("Could not deserialize item. Error: " + e.getMessage());
        }

        return null;
    }

    private static Item deserialize(File file, ObjectInputFilter filter) {
        try (ObjectInputStream in =  new ObjectInputStream(new FileInputStream(file))) {
            // Set the object input filter passed in
            in.setObjectInputFilter(filter);

            Item item = (Item)in.readObject();
            return item;
        } catch (Exception e) {
            System.out.println("Could not deserialize item. Error: " + e.getMessage());
        }
        return null;
    }
```

```
    private static void ensureParentDirExists(File file) {
        File parent = file.getParentFile();
        if(!parent.exists()) {
            parent.mkdirs();
        }
        System.out.println("Input/output file is " + file.getAbsolutePath());
    }
}
```

The ObjectFilterTest serializes an Item class followed by several deserializations of the same Item using different filters. The ensureParentDirExists() method accepts a File and makes sure that its parent directory exists, creating it if needed. The directory also prints the path of the serialized file.

The serialize() method serializes the specified Item object to the specified file. This method is called once from the main() method to serialize an Item object.

The deserialize() method is overloaded. The deserialize(File file) version deserializes the Item object stored at the specified file using the global filter, if any. The deserialize(File file, ObjectInputFilter filter) version deserializes the Item object stored at the specified file using the specified filter. Notice the use of the in.setObjectInputFilter(filter) method call inside this method. It sets the specified filter for the ObjectInputStream. This filter will override a global filter, if any.

The main() method prints the global filter, creates an Item object and serializes it, creates several local filters, and deserializes the same Item object using different filters. The following command runs the ObjectFilterTest class without a global filter. You may get different output.

```
C:\Java9Revealed>java --module-path com.jdojo.misc\build\classes
--module com.jdojo.misc/com.jdojo.misc.ObjectFilterTest
```

```
Input/output file is C:\Java9Revealed\serialized\item.ser
Serialized Item: [id=100, name=Pen, points=[1, 2, 3, 4]]
Global filter: null
Deserialized using global filter: [id=100, name=Pen, points=[1, 2, 3, 4]]
Could not deserialize item. Error: filter status: REJECTED
Deserialized with a maxarray=2 filter: null
Deserialized with a custom filter (maxarray=2): [id=100, name=Pen, points=[1, 2, 3, 4]]
```

The following command runs the ObjectFilterTest class with a global filter, maxarray=1, which will prevent arrays having more than one element from being deserialized. The global filter is set using the jdk. serialFilter system property. Because you are using a global filter, the JDK classes will log messages on stderr. I show those messages in the boldface font in the output.

```
C:\Java9Revealed>java -Djdk.serialFilter=maxarray=1
--module-path com.jdojo.misc\build\classes
--module com.jdojo.misc/com.jdojo.misc.ObjectFilterTest
```

```
Input/output file is C:\Java9Revealed\serialized\item.ser
Serialized Item: [id=100, name=Pen, points=[1, 2, 3, 4]]
Feb 17, 2017 1:09:57 PM java.io.ObjectInputFilter$Config lambda$static$0
INFO: Creating serialization filter from maxarray=1
Global filter: maxarray=1
Could not deserialize item. Error: filter status: REJECTED
Deserialized using global filter: null
Could not deserialize item. Error: filter status: REJECTED
Deserialized with a maxarray=2 filter: null
Deserialized with a custom filter (maxarray=5): [id=100, name=Pen, points=[1, 2, 3, 4]]
```

Notice the output when the global filter was used. Because the Item object contains an array with four elements, the global filter stopped it from being deserialized. However, you were able to deserialize the same object using the ArrayLengthObjectFilter because this filter overrode the global filter and it allowed for a maximum of five elements in an array. This is evident in the last line in the output.

Additions to Java I/O API

JDK 9 added a few convenience methods to the I/O API. The first one is a new method in the InputStream class:

```
long transferTo(OutputStream out) throws IOException
```

You have written code that reads all bytes from an input stream just to write to an output stream. Now, you do not have to write a loop to read bytes from the input stream and write them to the output stream. The transferTo() method reads all the bytes from the input stream and writes those bytes sequentially—as they were read—to the specified output stream. The method returns the number of bytes transferred.

■ **Tip** The transferTo() method does not close either stream. The input stream will be at the end of the stream when this method returns.

Ignoring exception handling and stream closing logic, here is one line of code that copies the contents of the log.txt file to the log_copy.txt file.

```
new FileInputStream("log.txt").transferTo(new FileOutputStream("log_copy.txt"));
```

The java.nio.Buffer class received two new methods in JDK 9:

- abstract Buffer duplicate()
- abstract Buffer slice()

Both methods return a Buffer, which shares the contents of the original buffer. The returned buffer will be direct or read-only only if the original buffer is direct or read-only. The duplicate() method returns a Buffer whose capacity, limit, position, and mark values will be identical to those of the original buffer. The slice() method returns a Buffer whose position will be zero, capacity and limit will be the number of elements remaining in this buffer, and mark will be undefined. The contents of the returned buffer start at the current position of the original buffer. The returned buffers from these methods maintain their position, limit, and mark independent of the original buffer. The following snippet of code shows the characteristics of the duplicated and sliced buffers:

```
IntBuffer b1 = IntBuffer.wrap(new int[]{1, 2, 3, 4});
IntBuffer b2 = b1.duplicate();
IntBuffer b3 = b1.slice();
System.out.println("b1=" + b1);
System.out.println("b2=" + b2);
System.out.println("b2=" + b3);

// Move b1 y 1 pos
b1.get();
IntBuffer b4 = b1.duplicate();
IntBuffer b5 = b1.slice();
System.out.println("b1=" + b1);
System.out.println("b4=" + b4);
System.out.println("b5=" + b5);
```

```
b1=java.nio.HeapIntBuffer[pos=0 lim=4 cap=4]
b2=java.nio.HeapIntBuffer[pos=0 lim=4 cap=4]
b2=java.nio.HeapIntBuffer[pos=0 lim=4 cap=4]
b1=java.nio.HeapIntBuffer[pos=1 lim=4 cap=4]
b4=java.nio.HeapIntBuffer[pos=1 lim=4 cap=4]
b5=java.nio.HeapIntBuffer[pos=0 lim=3 cap=3]
```

Summary

In JDK 9, an underscore (_) is a keyword and you cannot use it by itself as a one-character identifier such as a variable name, a method name, a type name, etc. However, you can still use an underscore in a multi-character identifier name.

JDK 9 removed the restriction that you must declare fresh variables for resources that you want to manage using a try-with-resource block. Now, you can use a *final* or *effectively final* variable that references a resource to be managed by a try-with-resources block.

JDK 9 added support for the diamond operator in anonymous classes as long as the inferred types are denotable.

You can have a private method in an interface that is either a non-abstract non-default instance method or a static method.

JDK 9 allows the @SafeVarargs annotation on private methods. JDK 8 already allowed it on constructors, static methods, and final methods.

JDK 9 added a new constant named DISCARD to the ProcessBuilder.Redirect nested class. Its type is ProcessBuilder.Redirect. You can use it as a destination for output and error streams of sub-processes when you want to discard the output. Implementations discard output by writing to an operating system specific "null file".

JDK 9 added several methods to the Math and StrictMath classes to support more mathematical operations such as floorDiv(long x, int y), floorMod(long x, int y), multiplyExact(long x, int y), multiplyFull(int x, int y), multiplyHigh(long x, long y), etc.

JDK 9 added three methods to the `java.util.Optional` class: `ifPresentOrElse()`, `or()`, and `stream()`. The `ifPresentOrElse()` method lets you provide two alternate courses of actions. If a value is present, it performs one action. Otherwise, it performs another action. The `or()` method returns the `Optional` itself if a value is present. Otherwise, it returns an `Optional` returned by the specified supplier. The `stream()` method returns a sequential stream of elements containing the value present in the `Optional`. If the `Optional` is empty, it returns an empty stream. The `stream()` method is useful in flat maps.

JDK 9 added a new static `onSpinWait()` method to the `Thread` class. It is a pure hint to the processor that the caller thread is momentarily not able to proceed, so resource usage can be optimized. Use it inside a spin-loop.

The Time API received a boost in JDK 9. Several methods were added to the `Duration`, `LocalDate`, `LocalTime`, and `OffsetTime` classes. The `LocalDate` class received a new `datesUntil()` method that returns a stream of dates between two dates by increments of one day or a given period. There are several new formatter symbols in the Time API.

The `Matcher` class received overloaded versions of several existing methods, which used to work with `StringBuffer`, to support working with `StringBuilder`. A new method called `results()` returns a `Stream<MatchResult>`. The `Objects` class received several new utility methods to check the bounds of arrays and collections.

The `java.util.Arrays` gained several methods that let you compare arrays and slices of arrays for equality and mismatch.

Javadoc has been enhanced in JDK 9. It supports HTML5. You can use a new option, `-html5`, with the javadoc tool to generate Javadoc in HTML5 format. Names of all the modules, packages, types, members, and formal parameter types are indexed and can be searched using a new search feature. Javadoc displays a search box on the upper-right corner of the each main page, which can be used to search indexed terms. You can also use a new tag, `@index`, in your Javadoc to make user-defined terms searchable. Searching is performed using the client-side JavaScript and no server communication is made.

Many browser vendors have already removed support for the Java browser plugin or will be removing it in the near future. Keeping this in mind, JDK 9 deprecated the Applet API. All types in the `java.applet` package and the `javax.swing.JApplet` class have been deprecated. The `appletviewer` tool has also been deprecated.

JDK 6 added limited support for platform-specific desktop features through the `java.awt.Desktop` class such as opening a URI in the user-default browser, opening a mailto URI in the user-default mail client, and opening, editing, and printing files using registered applications. Java SE 9 took the platform-specific desktop support forward and added public API support for many system and application event notifications, if they are available on the current platform. To support so many new desktop features, Java SE 9 added a new package, `java.awt.desktop`, to the `java.desktop` module. The `java.awt.Desktop` class also received many new methods. In JDK 9, the Desktop API supports 24 platform-specific desktop actions and notifications such as notifications when the attached displays go into or come out of power save, when the system enters sleep mode, or after the system wakes, etc.

To address the security risk posed by deserialization, JDK 9 introduced the concept of an object input filter that can be used to verify the object being deserialized and, if it does not pass a test, the deserialization process can be stopped. The object input filter is an instance of a new interface, `java.io.ObjectInputFilter`. You can specify a system-wide global filter that can be used while deserializing any object. A global filter can be specified using a new `jdk.serialFilter` system property, using a property named `jdk.serialFilter` in the `JAVA_HOME\conf\security\java.security` file, or using the `setSerialFilter()` method of the `ObjectInputFilter.Config` class. A local filter can be set on an `ObjectInputStream` using its `setObjectInputFilter()` method, which overrides the global filter.

The `java.io.InputStream` class has received a new method, called `transferTo(OutputStream out)`, that can be used to read all bytes from the input stream and write them sequentially to the specified output stream. The method does not close either stream. The `java.nio.Buffer` class received two methods—`duplicate()` and `slice()`—that can be used to duplicate and splice a buffer. The duplicated and sliced buffers share their contents with the original buffer. But they maintain their position, limit, and mark independent of the original buffer.

Index

© Kishori Sharan 2017
K. Sharan, *Java 9 Revealed*, DOI 10.1007/978-1-4842-2592-9

▨ M

▨ N

▨ O

Get the eBook for only $5!

Why limit yourself?

With most of our titles available in both PDF and ePUB format, you can access your content wherever and however you wish—on your PC, phone, tablet, or reader.

Since you've purchased this print book, we are happy to offer you the eBook for just $5.

To learn more, go to http://www.apress.com/companion or contact support@apress.com.

Apress®

62275100R00305

Made in the USA
Middletown, DE
20 January 2018